INTERNATIONAL CAPITAL MARKETS

INTERNATIONAL CAPITAL MARKETS

Law and Institutions

CALLY JORDAN

Consultant Editor
JEFFREY GOLDEN

OXFORD

UNIVERSITY PRESS

Great Clarendon Street, Oxford, OX2 6DP,
United Kingdom

Oxford University Press is a department of the University of Oxford.
It furthers the University's objective of excellence in research, scholarship,
and education by publishing worldwide. Oxford is a registered trade mark of
Oxford University Press in the UK and in certain other countries

© Cally Jordan 2014

The moral rights of the author have been asserted

First Edition published in 2014

Impression: 1

Crown copyright material is reproduced under Class Licence
Number C01P0000148 with the permission of OPSI
and the Queen's Printer for Scotland

Published in the United States of America by Oxford University Press
198 Madison Avenue, New York, NY 10016, United States of America

British Library Cataloguing in Publication Data
Data available

Library of Congress Control Number: 2013956439

ISBN 978–0–19–967111–3 (hbk.)
ISBN 978–0–19–967112–0 (pbk.)

Printed and bound by
CPI Group (UK) Ltd, Croydon, CR0 4YY

PREFACE

This book has had a long gestation. I have followed the development of international capital markets over the last 30 years, from a number of different perspectives: Wall Street practitioner, law professor, international bureaucrat. Each viewpoint has brought its own insights and raised its own questions.

An important caveat though. The book is not a treatise, and is certainly not exhaustive. The aim is more modest, to provide a context in which to better understand the international dynamics of capital markets, their institutions and regulation.

Inevitably, the United States, the United Kingdom, and Europe, together with that venerable market institution, the exchange, absorb the lion's share of attention. The new roles of international financial institutions and organizations, such as the Financial Stability Board, The World Bank, and the International Organization of Securities Commissions, are examined. I have included a chapter on Hong Kong and China and another on niche markets, but a consideration of the fascinating 'rise of the rest', emerging and transition markets more generally, must await another day, and another book. There was neither time nor space to do them justice. A further caveat, as obvious as it may be, bears mentioning. Capital markets, their regulation, and their institutions are changing, fast.

The London School of Economics, the British Institute for International and Comparative Law, and the Netherlands Institute for Advanced Study in the Humanities and Social Sciences, all provided me with visitorships and an intellectual home during the writing of this book. In particular, my thanks to the PRIME Finance Foundation (The Hague) for the inaugural Lord Woolf Fellowship and the Centre for International Finance and Regulation (Sydney, Australia) for its financial support.

Robin Gardner and her team, in particular Cate Read, at the Law Library Research Service, University of Melbourne, were terrific. A book needs time, and Andrew Kenyon, my Deputy Dean at Melbourne Law School, devised a 'write now; pay later' plan. Fittingly enough, the book also benefited from the enthusiasm and unstinting diligence of a very international cohort of research assistants, working from Melbourne, Singapore, Montreal, and parts in between. So my special thanks to Brendan Donohue, Sahil Sondhi, Elizabeth Goodman, and Michael Zhengpeng Chen (Melbourne Law School). At the Faculty of Law at McGill University, John Zelenbaba and his colleagues, Marco Garofalo and Hugo Margoc, provided invaluable support and assistance over the long haul. My thanks also to other McGill law students, Inhong Kim, Nancy Zagbayou, and Katherine Kalinin for their research during the initial phases of the book, and to their Dean, Daniel Jutras, for helping me recruit them. My great thanks to them all.

Thanks too must go to those legions of students over the years who have participated in my courses on international capital markets, at McGill, Osgoode Hall, Georgetown, Duke, Florida, IUC Torino, Melbourne, and the Center for Transnational Legal Studies (London). They brought to the classroom their enthusiasm, ideas, and sharp minds.

A great many people took the time to talk to me, set me straight, and point me in interesting directions: Paul Dudek, Don Langevoort, Eric Pan, and my former colleagues at The World Bank and the IFC (in particular, John Hegarty) in Washington, DC; Jim Cox and Lawrence Baxter in Durham, NC; Pam Hughes in Toronto; Les Silverman in New York City; Brian Cheffins, Len Sealy, Jane Welch, Ruben Lee, Richard Britton, David Kershaw, Stefano Pagliari, Jo Braithwaite, Dan Awrey, Jacek Kubas, David Lawton, and Frédéric Gielen in the United Kingdom; Harold Baum, Walter Doralt and Rüdiger Veil in Hamburg; Doug Arner in Hong Kong; and Greg Tanzer in Madrid and Sydney. My thanks also to Roberto Caranta (University of Torino) and David Luban (Georgetown Law Center) for offering me the opportunity to participate in hosting a workshop, *The Aftermath: Crisis and Legal Change—Future Prospects for Capital Markets, their Regulation and Institutions*, at the Center for Transnational Legal Studies, London, in April 2013. The book gained much from the discussions and all the participants.

My great thanks also to Jeff Golden, my consultant editor, for generously undertaking the task of reading the manuscript, despite heavy prior commitments (and likely against his better judgment). For his efforts, Jeff gets the last word.

The usual disclaimers apply.

Lastly, of course, my gratitude to John and Stephanie, for their patience, understanding, and unwavering support throughout the writing of this book. You are the best.

Cally Jordan
May 2014
Melbourne

CONSULTANT EDITOR'S NOTE

We are very fortunate to have this new work by Professor Cally Jordan and the critical and comprehensive analysis that it contains of the international capital markets, their regulation and their institutions. If the financial turmoil of the past half-dozen years has taught us nothing else, it has been that our prior understanding of all this was woefully inadequate for the challenge when things did not go according to plan. What we have learned the hard way is the lesson of the danger of complacency when contemplating global finance—taking too much for granted or, worse yet, putting our heads in the sand and too much trust in conventional wisdom.

We all know Hans Christian Andersen's tale of *The Emperor's New Clothes*: the vain sovereign who wants desperately to be 'well-covered' and is constantly changing clothes but who gets his real comeuppance when his weavers send him out naked with the false assurance that the Emperor is indeed suited in the height of fashion. The garb that protects him, it is alleged, is in fact beautifully complex and designed for sophisticated needs and tastes. 'Only those unfit for their position, stupid or incompetent would fail to appreciate that.' In the end, sanity is restored only when a young lad looks at the parading sovereign in an unblinkered way and asks, 'Where are your clothes?'.

The story is well known and the message is clear: the facts are important, and even more importantly, don't ignore or turn a blind eye to them when you present yourself as suitably dressed and fit for purpose – or you may do so at your peril! Why should it be any different in the case of today's international capital markets and attempts to regulate or 'dress' them in order to provide protection against the elements?

The moral of *The Emperor's New Clothes* is universally appreciated. However, possibly less well-appreciated or even known is a more modern, arguably ironic, twist in the tale. When Queen Elizabeth II opened a new building at the London School of Economics in 2008, and after having been briefed by academics around her about the origins and effects of the financial crisis, she simply asked that, if all that was so obvious, how come everyone missed it? On this occasion the recent institutional failings and ensuing market turmoil and exposure were very much on everyone's mind. But this time it was the sovereign who knowingly pointed the critical finger.

Well, the fact is not everyone who should have, did 'know all that', and, indeed like the Emperor in the fairy tale, few were prepared to admit their ignorance and preferred to believe that the markets themselves had found new and clever ways of managing risk.

In this book, Professor Jordan gives us an opportunity to study the history, sociology, and policies that shape global finance as well as a chance to learn from the mistakes of the past. That is the first reason why *International Capital Markets: Law and Institutions* is so timely: it tells us more about what we should have known about the international capital markets, key institutional players and how the scheme of things came to be the way it is. All of that is important if we now are to think carefully about where we go from here. And that story is told in an engaging way; those of us who know Professor Jordan and have had the benefit of her lectures and counsel will hear Cally's voice, and delight in her inimitable style, as we read the pages that follow.

The second reason why the book makes a timely entrance is that it arrives at a moment when practitioners in the field, and students trying to come to grips with it, are being overwhelmed by major capital market institutional reform and inundated with relevant new rules and regulations. When the second anniversary of the passage of the Dodd-Frank Act, a key piece of US legislation discussed in the pages that follow, was celebrated this past summer, it was also reported to have generated more than 14,000 pages by then and yet the job of its rule-making was said to be less than 40% complete. With legacy and new legislation and rule-making spread around the world and often in different languages, synthesizing all the relevant text is a challenge. Helpfully, Professor Jordan gives *con*text to text, which makes the challenge more manageable. The author says that providing context is a modest ambition. I say that it is both a relevant and particularly important one at this juncture in time.

I hope that other readers of *International Capital Markets: Law and Institutions* will benefit from Professor Jordan's book as much as I feel that I have. In fact, I am certain that they will!

Jeffrey Golden
London
May 2014

CONTENTS

ABBREVIATIONS

AAOIFI	Accounting and Auditing Organization for Islamic Financial Institutions
ABS	asset backed securities
ADRs	American Depositary Receipts
AIFMD	Directive on Alternative Investment Fund Managers
AIM	Alternative Investment Market
AML	anti-money laundering
ATSs	alternative trading systems
BCBS	Basel Committee on Banking Supervision
BDRs	Brazilian Depositary Receipts
BIS	Bank for International Settlements
BMV	Bolsa Mexicana de Valores
BoE	Bank of England
CA 1985	Companies Act 1985
CDOs	collateralized debt obligations
CESR	Committee of European Securities Regulators
CFA	Chartered Financial Analyst
CFI	Conventional Financial Institutions
CFT	combating financing of terrorism
CFTC	Commodity Futures Trading Commission
CMSD	Capital Markets Supervision Directorate
CSRC	China Securities Regulatory Commission
CUSIP	Committee on Uniform Securities Identification Procedures
DFSA	Dubai Financial Services Authority
DIFC	Dubai International Financial Centre
EBA	European Banking Authority
EBRD	European Bank for Reconstruction and Development
ECBC	European Covered Bond Council
EFSF	European Financial Stability Facility
EIOPA	European Insurance and Occupational Pensions Authority
EMH	efficient market hypothesis
EMIR	European Market Infrastructure Regulation
ESAs	European Supervisory Authorities
ESFS	European System of Financial Supervision
ESMA	European Securities and Markets Authority
ESRB	European Systemic Risk Board
ESRC	European Securities Regulators Committee
ETFs	exchange-traded funds
EU	European Union
EWE	early warning exercise
FCA	Financial Conduct Authority
FIBV	International Federation of Stock Exchanges
FINRA	Financial Industry Regulatory Authority

FPI	foreign private issuer
FSA	Financial Services Authority
FSA 1986	Financial Services Act 1986
FSB	Financial Stability Board
FSAP	Financial Sector Assessment Program
FSMA 2000	Financial Services and Markets Act 2000
FSF	Financial Stability Forum
FSOC	Financial Stability Oversight Council
GAVI	Global Alliance for Vaccines and Immunization
GDRs	Global Depositary Receipts
HFT	high frequency trading
IAIS	International Association of Insurance Supervisors
IASB	International Accounting Standards Board
IBFIM	Islamic Banking and Finance Institute of Malaysia
ICIFB	Institutions Conducting Islamic Financial Business
ICMA	International Capital Markets Association
ICSD	Investor Compensation Schemes Directive
IFI	Islamic Financial Institutions
IFFIm	International Finance Facility for Immunization
IFR	Islamic Finance Rules
IFRS	International Financial Reporting Standards
IFSB	Islamic Financial Services Board
IIFM	International Islamic Financial Market
IIRA	Islamic International Rating Agency
IIROC	Investment Industry Regulatory Organization of Canada
IMF	International Monetary Fund
INCEIF	International Centre for Education in Islamic Finance
IOSCO	International Organization of Securities Commissions
IPMA	International Primary Markets Association
IPOs	initial public offerings
ISD	Investment Services Directive
ISDA	International Swaps and Derivatives Association
ISE	Irish Stock Exchange
ISMA	International Securities Markets Association
JAB	Joint Arab Bourse
JOBS Act	Jumpstart Our Business Startups Act 2012
LCFI	large complex financial institution
LIFFE	London International Financial Futures and Options Exchange
LMC	Liquidity Management Centre
LSE	London Stock Exchange
MAS	Monetary Authority of Singapore
MBS	mortgage backed securities
MiFID	Markets in Financial Instruments Directive
MJDS	Multijurisdictional Disclosure System
MOU	Memorandum of Understanding
MTF	Mutual Trading Facility
NASAA	North American Securities Administrators Association

NASD	National Association of Securities Dealers
ODO	overseas directed offering
OTC	over-the-counter
PF(I)A	Prevention of Fraud (Investments) Acts 1939 and 1958
PRA	Prudential Regulation Authority
QDII	Qualified Domestic Institutional Investor
QFII	Qualified Foreign Institutional Investor
QIB	Qualified Institutional Buyer
REITs	real estate investment trusts
SCNPC	Standing Committee of the National People's Congress
SE	Societas Europaea
SEAQ	Stock Exchange Automated Quotation
SEC	Securities and Exchange Commission
SEFs	Swap Execution Facilities
SEZ	special economic zone
SFC	Securities and Futures Commission
SIB	Securities and Investment Board
SIFIs	Systemically Important Financial Institutions
SFC	Securities and Futures Commission
SNB	Swiss National Bank
SROs	self regulatory organizations
STI	Straits Times Index
SUSMI	substantial US market interest
TIA	Trust Indenture Act 1939
UCIs	Undertakings for Collective Investments
UCITS	Undertakings for Collective Investments in Transferable Securities
US 1933 Act	Securities Act of 1933
US 1934 Act	Securities Exchange Act of 1934
USM	Unlisted Securities Market

TABLE OF CASES

TABLE OF LEGISLATION

PART I

INTERNATIONAL CAPITAL MARKETS IN CONTEXT

1

INTRODUCTION

Money moves, and always has. International capital markets are not a new phenomenon; **1.01** in various forms, they have been around for centuries. Capital has been flowing through empires, across oceans and continents, following trade routes, migration, wars, nation building, and imperial expansion. These markets have largely operated beyond the bounds of local institutions and markets. There have always been rules, express or implied, explicit or implicit, but not necessarily formal regulation as understood in modern times.

The global financial crisis, however, shone a strong light on the workings of international **1.02** capital markets. They had, unmistakably, been purveyors of systemic risk and seemingly attracted little by way of oversight or regulation. There were calls for an international regulatory body[1] and greater coordination among national regulators and institutions. Certain market participants, reckless investment bankers and credit rating agencies, in particular, certain products, such as asset back securities, perhaps unfairly, were singled out for censure, public opprobrium, and regulatory action at various levels.[2] But formal regulation emanates from a national (or perhaps subnational) authority and operates locally. So, how have *international* capital markets been regulated and what lies on the regulatory horizon?

1. Securities Regulation as a Model for the World

Until relatively recently, there has not existed a tidy package of 'securities regulation' in most **1.03** places in the world. 'Securities regulation', the term most often ascribed to a distinct body of formal regulation applicable to primary and secondary markets in financial instruments and their intermediaries, originated in the United States as 1930s depression era legislation, the Securities Act of 1933[3] (the US 1933 Act), and the Securities Exchange Act of 1934[4] (the US 1934 Act). Both Acts continue in force to this day, and in the case of the US 1933 Act, more so than the US 1934 Act, with remarkably few fundamental changes.[5] A vast infrastructure of regulation constructed by the regulator charged with administration of these acts, the

---

[1] See Eric C Chaffee, 'A Moment of Opportunity: Reimagining International Securities Regulation in the Shadow of Financial Crisis' (2010) 15 *Nexus* 29, 40.

[2] China, for example, banned asset backed securities across the board in 2009 and just re-opened the market in late 2012: Simon Rabonovitch, 'China Lifts Bar on Securitisation Sales', *Financial Times* (5 September 2012).

[3] Securities Act of 1933, 15 USC §§ 77a–77mm (2006).

[4] Securities Exchange Act of 1934, 15 USC §§ 78a–77kk (2006).

[5] Arguably, the Jumpstart Our Business Startups Act of 2012 (JOBS Act), Pub L No 112-106, 126 Stat 306 (2012), may be one of the first major shocks to the US 1933 Act. The US 1934 Act, on the other hand, has served as a repository for US federal legislative initiatives over the years and so covers a much broader range of issues.

3

Securities and Exchange Commission (SEC), supports this legislation, hence the terminology, securities regulation.

1.04 But terminology is tricky. Although references to securities regulation (and the legislative framework itself in many cases) now appear all over the world,[6] the term encompasses different aspects of financial markets in different places. In the United States, the focus of securities regulation has been the capital raising process and, to a lesser degree, the intermediaries in the markets, including the big equity exchanges. In the United Kingdom and Europe, the concept of securities regulation is quite new, but generally refers to regulation of the intermediaries and the markets, not the capital raising process or even necessarily investor protection, the traditional regulatory objective in the United States.[7]

1.05 Although securities regulation, as a distinct body of regulation, is rooted in US history and legislation, this does not mean that comparable 'regulation', or at least formal mechanisms designed to achieve similar purposes, did not exist elsewhere. They did, but in a more diffuse fashion. Investor protection, in the form of shareholder protection,[8] found itself embedded in English companies law for the most part; the empire, and then the Commonwealth, followed suit. In fact, unlike US corporation law,[9] modern English companies law had its origins strongly coloured by considerations of investor protection, with the 1844 and following registration statutes in the United Kingdom.[10] It was to this larger body of companies law that the United States turned in fashioning a subset of rules, what is known as 'securities legislation', in the 1930s. It is no coincidence that US securities law refers to 'registration' statements and 'prospectuses', terminology derived from nineteenth-century English companies law.

---

[6] For example, Niamh Moloney in 2002 entitled her text *EC Securities Regulation* (Oxford University Press). The primary international organization in the area is called the International Organization of Securities Commissions, and its first set of international principles, the IOSCO Objectives and Principles of Securities Regulation (1998).

[7] Even in the United States, the terminology is misleading. For historical reasons, the range of financial instruments encompassed by the term 'securities', and thus subject to securities regulation and the jurisdiction of the SEC, is arbitrarily circumscribed. Many types of financial instruments have always fallen outside the ambit of securities regulation in the United States, and with the increase in financial innovation, the list is growing longer. In this text, reference is often made to securities regulation, as it is the regularly used terminology, but increasingly 'capital markets regulation', a less specifically delineated, more broadly understood, term is supplanting 'securities regulation'. Hence, the title of this book.

[8] The original US 1933 Act was enacted very much with the retail equity investor in mind, moms and pops buying shares in the public markets for investment purposes.

[9] American business corporations are descendants of the chartered corporation. After the American revolution, incorporation in the United States involved obtaining a charter from the relevant state legislature. In fact, one of the first 'general' incorporation acts in the common law world was enacted in New York state in 1811. The rejection of monarchial authority to grant charters was taken to imply equality of rights to incorporation. Modern English registered companies, however, are not simply chartered corporations created in another manner. Instead, they are the descendants of the unincorporated joint stock company, an association possessing some of the attributes of a large partnership, but with features from the chartered corporation also added to the joint stock company. On contrasts between British and American corporation law, see LCB Gower, 'Some Contrasts Between British and American Corporation Law' (1956) 69 *Harvard Law Review* 1369.

[10] The Joint Stock Companies Registration and Regulation Act 1844 (UK) is the legislative ancestor of modern corporation law. It took over the deed-of-settlement company and made it a statutory incorporated body. The Limited Liability Act 1855 (UK) gave corporators the option of forming a company on the principle that the liability of the members would be limited to what they agreed to contribute to the company. English company law was later consolidated into the Companies Act 1862 (UK), the descendent of which today is the Companies Act 2006 (UK).

Equally, corporate debt holders found comfort in the provisions of nineteenth-century **1.06**
English companies law requiring the registration of charges and corporate debentures;[11]
these provisions continue to populate older-style Commonwealth legislation around the
world.[12] Together with the deference accorded self-regulation of professionals and the
exchanges, there was little impetus for a stand-alone regulatory apparatus in the United
Kingdom, or continental Europe for that matter (for somewhat different reasons).[13] Until
recently, much of what would be characterized as securities regulation has in Europe taken
the form of companies law directives, inspired primarily by Germany, and forming a regulatory supra-structure on a pan-European basis. For a time, exchanges in many parts of Europe
were treated as regulated utilities, and since there was little interest by retail investors in
equity products, little call for US-style investor protection in the form of a separate body of
securities regulation.

Once the United Kingdom joined what is now the European Union in 1972, a new dynamic **1.07**
emerged. The United Kingdom was forced to embark on the daunting project of conform-
ing its unruly legislative framework to European Commission directives and other legislative instruments. On the other hand, the United Kingdom pushed for implementation of
English approaches to financial markets on a pan-European basis. This dynamic continues
to inform regulatory choices.

However, by distilling rules associated with public capital raising and the regulation of inter- **1.08**
mediaries into an identifiable body of law known as 'securities regulation', the United States
gained a tactical advantage in terms of the regulatory hegemony of its system.[14] An accident
of history (the breakup of the Soviet Union in 1991) unleashed geopolitical forces which
brought US securities regulation to large swathes of Eastern Europe. The aftermath of conflict (ie the War in the Pacific, for example) had already left imprints of US regulation in parts
of Asia. Other accidents of history, the Asian financial crisis, and the rise of capitalism with
Chinese characteristics, also brought US securities regulation (as well as insolvency legislation) to much of modern Asia.

---

[11] Section 43 of the Companies Act 1862 (UK) required a company to keep a register of mortgages and
charges but this register was only open for the inspection of persons who had already become creditors of the
company. Recognizing the inadequacy that this did not allow for inspection by those thinking of providing credit, the UK Parliament amended the Companies Act 1900 in 1908 to provide for a public register at
Somerset House of all mortgages and charges of certain specified classes. A new section in the Companies Act
2006 (section 741) requires companies to register an allotment of debentures with the Registrar of Companies,
so that the existence of debentures is public knowledge. Similar provisions have been implemented through
the Personal Property Securities Acts and have been enacted by all common law provinces and territories of
Canada (beginning in 1976), in New Zealand (1999), and at the Commonwealth level in Australia (effective
only in 2012).

[12] For example, the United States' Trust Indenture Act of 1939, 15 USC §§ 77aaa–bbbb (2006) (TIA). The
TIA governs the public offer and sale of debt securities such as debentures. The SEC administers the TIA which
mandates the appointment of a trustee to take care of the interests of the holders of debt securities or bonds of
the issuer.

[13] There is no substantive body of law which constitutes European company law, however a host of minimum standards are applicable to companies throughout the European Union (EU). Since the formation of the
European Community in 1967, a series of directives have been issued (first by the Council of the European
Communities, now by the European Parliament and the Council of the European Union) to create these
minimum standards. Under the European Company Statute, businesses meeting certain conditions may incorporate as a 'Societas Europaea' (SE).

[14] Edward F Greene, Daniel A Braverman, and Sebastian R Sperber, 'Hegemony or Deference: U.S.
Disclosure Requirements in the International Capital Markets' (1995) 50 *The Business Lawyer* 413.

1.09   At this point, US securities regulation formally transformed itself into international stand-ards, the IOSCO Objectives and Principles of Securities Regulation (1998). By 2001, the Lamfalussy Report (the official title of which was the *Final Report of the Committee of Wise Men on the Regulation of European Securities Markets*[15]) sent up a call to arms; Europe had to have securities regulation, and that meant US-style securities regulation.[16]

1.10   There quickly followed the Prospectus Directive,[17] the Market Abuse Directive,[18] the Transparency Directive,[19] among others: US securities regulation filtered through European regulatory sensibilities. Needless to say, there was some UK consternation at this turn of events. On the other hand, domestic commentators in the United States urged on efforts to propagate US securities regulation around the world through participation in international dialogue and other fora such as IOSCO.[20] The SEC set up training sessions to introduce regulators from around the world to the US model.[21] These were heady days, pre-Enron, pre-Sarbanes-Oxley, pre-global financial crisis, pre-Dodd-Frank.

1.11   And so it came to be that US securities regulation set the standard and became the model. On the part of most US practitioners and regulators, this was all as it should be. At the beginning of this century, there was an unshakeable conviction on their part that the US model was the best.[22] The decade that followed sorely tested this conviction, beginning with the corporate governance failures of Enron and Worldcom and culminating only a few years later with the near collapse of the US, and world, financial system.

1.12   Nevertheless, by then the seeds had been sown, and US-style securities regulation had sprouted around the world. As legal systems demonstrate persistence and path dependency, where US-style securities regulation has taken root, it is unlikely to be replaced, at least not in the near future.

1.13   For this reason, many of the current regulatory techniques that dominate capital markets regulation at the domestic level inevitably derive from US regulation, disclosure based regulation being first among them. For better or worse, the reliance on information, and

---

[15]   No political correctness there.

[16]   For Europe looking to US securities law, see Edward F Greene and Linda C Quinn, 'Building on the International Convergence of the Global Markets: A Model for Securities Reform' (Paper presented at A Major Issues Conference: Securities Regulation in the Global Internet Economy, Washington DC, 14–15 November 2001). For the necessity of action on securities regulation, see European Union, Initial Report of the Committee of the Wise Men on the Regulation of European Securities Markets (9 November 2000) <http://ec.europa.eu/internal_market/securities/docs/lamfalussy/wisemen/initial-report-wise-men_en.pdf> accessed 24 December 2013.

[17]   Directive 2003/71/EC of the European Parliament and of the Council of 4 November, on the Prospectus to be Published When Securities are Offered to the Public or Admitted to Trading and Amending Directive 2001/34/EC, OJ L 345 (2003).

[18]   Directive 2003/6/EC of the European Parliament and of the Council of 28 January 2003, on Insider Dealing and Market Manipulation (Market Abuse), OJ L 96 (2003).

[19]   Directive 2004/109/EC of the European Parliament and of the Council of 15 December 2004, on the Harmonisation of Transparency Requirements in Relation to Information About Issuers Whose Securities are Admitted to Trading on a Regulated Market and Amending Directive 2001/34/EC, OJ L 390 (2004).

[20]   Greene and Quinn (n 16).

[21]   The US Securities and Exchange Commission conducts training of foreign regulators through its International Technical Assistance Program run by the SEC's Office of International Affairs. This International Technical Assistance Program has been operating since 1989. See <http://www.sec.gov/news/press/2010/2010-68-factsheet.htm> accessed 24 December 2013.

[22]   The fact that it was virtually the only model reinforced this conviction.

the process by which it is disclosed, now permeates capital markets regulation everywhere. Originally, at the time the regulatory system was taking shape in the United States of the 1930s, a combination of ideology and pragmatism likely led to disclosure based regulation taking precedence over what was then called 'merit based regulation'.[23] Great faith was placed at the time in the good sense of those stalwart retail investors who formed the majority of participants in US equity markets.[24]

Later though, in a rather circular fashion, the development of the efficient market hypothesis **1.14** (EMH) by Chicago School economists[25] reinforced the legitimacy of disclosure based regulation. US equity markets operated in a disclosure based regulatory environment; US equity markets were efficient in absorbing information which was reflected in the price of publicly traded shares; information produced self-correcting markets; securities regulation should be disclosure based. It is hard to overestimate the influence and importance of the FMH on US regulators and policymakers; it operates implicitly and explicitly in the cornerstone US 1933 Act.[26] Arguably, blind faith in the EMH accounts for the actions of and the near fatal delays by the US administration in addressing the financial meltdown of September 2008. The market had to self-correct; but it didn't.

The failure of Enron and Worldcom, however, prompted new academic thinking in the **1.15** United States in terms of regulation of securities markets. Disclosure based regulation did not detect or deter fraud. The focus shifted to 'gatekeepers', those professionals, the accountants and the lawyers, charged with sifting through the masses of information produced by the disclosure based system.[27] The tensions between a disclosure based model and prescriptive rules (as well as acknowledgement of the role of gatekeepers) appears in the legislative response to Enron and Worldcom, the Sarbanes-Oxley Act of 2002. Much of the statute addresses the accounting and auditing profession, as well as, but to a lesser degree, the legal profession. A strong form of fiduciary duties (which persists in the United Kingdom) having been hollowed out by the courts and state legislatures in the United States, the obligations of corporate executives as gatekeepers had to be explicitly spelled out in Sarbanes-Oxley.

---

[23] Merit-based regulation would ultimately impose on the regulator the onus of making an investment decision with respect to a particular transaction and financial product. A form of merit-based regulation does exist at state level in the United States but is eclipsed by federal legislation.

[24] Other familiar US aphorisms come to mind, such as 'You can fool some of the people some of the time, but not all of the people all of the time'.

[25] Efficient market hypothesis (EMH) was first developed by Professor Eugene Fama, now a Nobel Laureate in Economics, at the University of Chicago in the early 1960s. EMH asserts that financial markets are 'informationally efficient' which therefore results in the inability to consistently achieve returns in excess of average market returns on a risk-adjusted basis. This is due to the information available at the time the investment is made. There are three main variants of EMH: (1) 'Weak' EMH claims that prices on traded assets already reflect all past publicly available information; (2) 'Semi-strong' EMH holds that prices reflect all public available information and that prices also instantly change to reflect new public information; (3) 'Strong' EMH additionally asserts that asset prices instantly reflect even hidden or insider information.

[26] The SEC's introduction of the integrated disclosure system in 1982 coordinated required disclosures under the US 1933 Act and the US 1934 Act, in light of an assumption of EMH that information effectively disseminated to the public will be rapidly reflected in share prices regardless of the source of the data. See Joel Seligman, 'Götterdämmerung for the Securities Act?' (1997) 75 *Washington University Law Quarterly* 887. More explicitly, 'efficiency' was explicitly added to considerations which rule making had to address (§ (b) of US 1933 Act).

[27] John C Coffee, *Gatekeepers: The Role of the Professions in Corporate Governance* (Oxford University Press, 2006).

1.16 Securities regulation in the United States is deeply rooted in the equity culture and public capital markets which dominated much of the twentieth century there. So it is no accident that the innovation so characteristic of the last 25 years has flourished in the unregulated interstices of this regulated world. Securitization or structured finance usually took the form of a less regulated financial product: debt. With the securitized products, the lawyers[28] and accountants were still gatekeepers, at least in theory, but now largely unregulated, private sector, profit driven, credit rating agencies played (or misplayed) the main role.

1.17 Equally, large institutional investors and intermediaries sought the unlit, unregulated corners of the market, the exempt markets. Information was still key, but undisclosed information: no level playing field here. Dark pools, with their sinister connotations, are aptly named and now, estimated conservatively, comprise some 13.3 per cent of the trading market.[29]

1.18 But the seismic shock, and biggest challenge, to disclosure based regulation has been its collision with information technology. Information has run amok; it can no longer be regulated and controlled. The fundamental distinction between public (regulated) and private (unregulated) markets based on the concept of a general solicitation or offer to the public fell victim to election year politics and the JOBS Act of 2012[30] in the United States. Equally, and controversially, the JOBS Act has recognized new, technology driven forms of capital raising through 'crowdfunding', investor protection be damned.[31] It is this same technology that has created modern international capital markets.

1.19 Self-regulation of market participants forms another pillar of the securities regulatory landscape, predating the disclosure based regulation of the 1930s. Self-regulation harkens back centuries, to the medieval guilds, and is inextricably entwined with the history of the City of London, long an autonomous and international financial marketplace.[32] Self-regulation has

---

[28] Although Lee Buchheit maintains that lawyers failed miserably in this respect. See Lee Buchheit, 'Did We Make Things Too Complicated?' (2008) 27(3) *International Financial Law Review* 24, 26: 'Why do some contracts, tantamount to crimes against humanity, not occasion more expressions of outrage from bankers, analysts, rating agencies, investors and regulators? (They do sometimes incur the wrath of the judiciary.) These people often meekly accept a turgid, incestuous, redundant, disorganised and arthritic contract without even a bleat of protest.'

[29] 'Dark pools of liquidity' refers to trading volume or liquidity that is not openly accessible to the public. The majority of these dark pools represent large trades by financial institutions that are offered outside of public exchanges so that such trades are anonymous. According to the US broker Rosenblatt Securities from their regular *Let There Be Light Report*, dark pools accounted for 13.3% of all US equity trading in 2012. See <http://www.tradersmagazine.com/news/dark-pool-volume-down-share-up-2012-110790-1.html> accessed 24 December 2013.

[30] JOBS Act, Pub L No 112-106, 126 Stat 306 (2012). There exists general consensus that the JOBS Act requires the SEC to lift the ban on general solicitation and advertizing of private offerings so long as issuers take reasonable steps to ensure that they sell only to so-called accredited investors. Securities law scholars, state regulators, Democrats in Congress and in the SEC's own Investor Advisory Committee all argue, however, that removing the marketing ban fundamentally alters the nature of private offerings and therefore increases the risk of fraud. They are therefore calling on the SEC to incorporate sensible safeguards when lifting the ban on general solicitation. On the other hand, securities industry representatives and Congressional Republicans are urging the SEC to approve lifting the general solicitation ban without additional investor protections. See <http://www.huffingtonpost.com/barbara-roper/jobs-act-rule-poses-early_b_2389134.html> accessed 24 December 2013.

[31] Steven M Davidoff, 'Trepidation and Restrictions Leave Crowdfunding Rules Weak', *The New York Times* (29 October 2013) <http://dealbook.nytimes.com/2013/10/29/trepidation-and-restrictions-leave-crowdfunding-rules-weak/?_r=0> accessed 24 December 2013.

[32] See Gillian Tett, 'This guilded life', *Financial Times* (3 November 2013) <http://www.ft.com/intl/cms/s/2/41776c74-41bd-11e3-b064-00144feabdc0.html#axzz2jeX5oOyS> accessed 24 December 2013.

much to commend it; it is cheap and can be reasonably effective. However, it usually demands a communality of understanding as to the limits of acceptable behaviour (or alternatively, an elastic view of what is acceptable). As groups of actors become more open and heterogeneous, as with London in the 1980s, self-regulatory mechanisms can break down.

Nevertheless, self-regulation has been remarkably resilient in the United States, in defiance of the institutional difficulties associated with it. Cynics might argue this is a triumph of powerful lobby groups, self-interest and the arcane, closed nature of the trading world. However, in the United States, regulatory oversight to self-regulation provides a counterweight to rampant self-interest. Unlike the United States, self-regulation suffered an abrupt near demise in the United Kingdom in 2000 with the Financial Services and Markets Act and operations of a new regulator, the Financial Services Authority.[33] But with forces as powerful as the denizens of the City of London at work, self-regulation continued to motor away, under the guise of 'light touch' regulation, for another decade. **1.20**

For the United Kingdom, however, 2012 could be known as the year of 'Scandal and the City'. Much criticized financial failures in the banking sector, collateral damage in the disaster of the global financial crisis, were followed by revelations of private sector manipulation of LIBOR and other benchmarks as well as examples of outrageous risk-taking by investment bankers, such as the 'London Whale'.[34] Calls in the United Kingdom went up for 'heads on stakes', very well-coifed heads. The formal regulatory impulses of the European Union appeared, at least in the short term, vindicated. **1.21**

Exchanges, as old institutions, have been naturally self-regulatory. Over time, exchanges experienced growing regulatory encroachment due to recognition of their 'public utility' function, and more recently, their role in the transmission of systemic risk. Demutualization was a major turning point, when the resulting conflicts of interest prompted many exchanges to cede certain aspects of traditional self-regulatory authority. **1.22**

As important as exchanges are in the United States, arguably they have traditionally been a more significant engine of market regulation in Europe and the United Kingdom.[35] Generally

---

[33] The Financial Services Authority was an independent non-government body, which changed its name from the Securities and Investment Board in 1997 and was given statutory powers by the Financial Services and Markets Act 2000 (UK). After a series of financial scandals during the 1990s, culminating in the collapse of Barings Bank, there was a move to end the long-time self-regulation of the financial services industry in the United Kingdom and to consolidate regulation responsibilities which were previously split among multiple financial regulators. As of 1 April 2013, the Financial Services Act 2012 (UK) entered into force, abolishing the Financial Services Authority and replacing it with three successor bodies: (1) the Prudential Regulation Authority (PRA) is responsible for ensuring the stability of financial firms (including banks, investment banks, building societies and insurance companies) and is part of the Bank of England; (2) the Financial Conduct Authority (FCA) is now responsible for the regulation of financial firms providing services to consumers and maintains the integrity of the United Kingdom's financial markets; (3) the Bank of England's powerful Financial Policy Committee has also gained a direct supervisory role for the whole banking system and can instruct both the PRA and FCA.

[34] Further scandals have emerged, for example in currency markets; London is the premier market for currency trading in the world. Scandal is not new to the City, as noted by the 'City of London Corporation Inquiry' [1853] *Law Review & Quarterly Journal of British & Foreign Jurisprudence* 389, 426–7: 'The present members of the Corporation of London ... seem to have imbibed the notion that in order to divert a reform of the present system, and the substitution of one which should really serve the purposes of a Metropolitan municipality, it would suffice to urge that there is no ground for the imputation of "moral turpitude or personal corruption".' This situation was in contradistinction to their predecessors in the eighteenth century where '[h]eavy tavern expenses were allowed, the cause of charity and education was neglected, and publicity avoided'.

[35] The role of Nomads (Nominated Advisors who advise on compliance with financial regulatory rules), for example in the AIM (Alternative Investment Market). There may be any number of factors contributing

speaking, both continental Europe and the United Kingdom focused more on prudential regulation of institutions and their actors, leaving the activities of market professionals among themselves alone. [36] There may be any number of factors contributing to this difference: the relative weakness of the equity culture in Europe making the exchanges themselves less significant sources of regulatory failure and of less interest to governmental authorities; universal banking focusing regulatory attention on the banks; London's determination to position itself as the premier international marketplace justifying 'light touch' regulation.

1.23   In addition to providing wide latitude for unregulated or self-regulated activities in the private or exempt professional markets, in the United Kingdom this approach placed a heavier responsibility on professionals to act in the best interests of their clients and to maintain high standards of professional conduct. Mixed results ensued, and as London had become the centre of the world for international capital markets, the reverberations were worldwide. The global financial crisis also sparked greater regulatory interest in the United States in the activities of the big professional actors. The failure of the New York investment bank, Lehman Brothers, in September 2008 shocked the US administration, the financial community, and regulators alike. This failure too reverberated around the world, nearly taking the US financial system with it. Once largely immune from intensive scrutiny by Congress, US legislators now took a close, and exhaustive, look at their capital market institutions and intermediaries.[37] The resulting Dodd Frank Wall Street Reform and Consumer Protection Act of 2010 adopted aspects of European-style 'institutional' regulation, an approach which had not been characteristic of US securities regulation.

2. The Trajectory of International Capital Markets Regulation

1.24   In the recent past, the story of international capital markets regulation has been a US story; the imprint of US securities regulation is everywhere. On the other hand, markets around the world demonstrated surprising diversity and resistance to formal regulation. Until the global financial crisis, the forces of competition and convergence, transmitted along the Washington-New York-London-Brussels corridor, drove regulatory agendas and absorbed much of the attention. But the jolt of crisis has changed the trajectory of markets and their regulation, or at least perceptions of them. Despite the public face of the traditional stock

---

to this: the relative weakness of the equity culture in Europe making the exchanges themselves less significant sources of regulatory failure and of less interest to governmental authorities; universal banking focused regulatory attention on the banks; London's determination to position itself as the premier international marketplace justified 'light touch' regulation, for example.

[36] For decades, a distinction was made in the regulatory approaches as between the United States and Europe, between transactional or functional regulation in the United States and institutional regulation in Europe.

[37] Dodd-Frank Wall Street Reform and Consumer Protection Act, Pub L No 111-203, 124 Stat 1376 (2010) (Dodd-Frank Act). US securities regulation adopted aspects of European-style 'institutional' regulation, not one of its hallmarks. Together with a greater emphasis on regulatory oversight of systemic risk in the capital markets, 'SIFIs', Systemically Important Financial Institutions, must be identified and subjected to greater scrutiny. The Dodd-Frank Act requires that SIFIs must submit resolution plans annually to the Federal Reserve and the Federal Deposit Insurance Corporation. Each plan (commonly known as a living will) must describe the SIFI's strategy for aid and orderly resolution under the US bankruptcy law in the event of significant financial distress or failure of the company. However, according to the Republican controlled House Financial Services Committee, 'the jury remains very much out on the question of whether Dodd-Frank has created a more stable banking system'—Financial Services Committee, United States House of Representatives, *One Year Later: The Consequences of the Dodd-Frank Act* (2011), 3.

exchange, much of the world of finance has long been a fine and private place.[38] Crisis and scandal now cast a strong regulatory light into the corners of finance.[39] Masses of regulation are being churned out.

New forces are at work. Regulatory convergence appears less likely and more problematic outside the EU, while operating strongly within it.[40] Along the transatlantic corridor, the lines of regulatory communication now are always open; the tangible effects of coordination and cooperation are evident in the broad outlines of new regulatory institutions and initiatives. Yet, look more closely, and there are fundamental differences emerging. Both the United Kingdom and the European Union have new, as yet untested, capital markets regulators, with the regulatory balance of power as yet undetermined. Europe is moving away from the disclosure model, such as it was, exerting regulatory control over retail investment products and previously unregulated market participants such as hedge funds and credit rating agencies, in a decidely unAmerican way. On the other hand, ironically perhaps, the European Union is flexing regulatory muscle in a decidedly American and extraterritorial fashion. **1.25**

The spectre of systemic risk is changing the nature and role of capital markets regulation, which now operates more strongly as a tool of macroeconomic policy. In the process, capital markets regulation has become more politicized, but not necessarily better. There are new forms of capitalism too, populated increasingly by the 'inadvertent' investor: individuals are more and more exposed to market risk through governmental investment activity, mandatory pension schemes, and sovereign wealth funds, which due to their size and appetite are inherently internationally diversified (and interconnected). New trading patterns, new trading platforms, new trading possibilities, new methods of capital raising are racing ahead of regulators. Roaring capitalism with Chinese characteristics is already reshaping the financial world,[41] while it is still an open question as to the impact of Islamic finance.[42] Overenthusiastic, but ultimately artificial, experiments in internationalism, like Dubai, have so far disappointed. **1.26**

And then there are the international institutions, organizations, fora, industry associations, new and old, which have surged to prominence in the new interconnected world of modern finance. So far, the proliferation of many international financial standards has not produced lasting, or even intended, results.[43] Sceptics abound.[44] Nonetheless, to an already complex juxtaposition of regulation, rules, and practices, has been added another layer. **1.27**

---

[38] With apologies to John Donne (1572–1631).

[39] The term 'shadow banking' is not an idle metaphor.

[40] See Stéphane Rottier and Nicolas Véron, 'Not all financial regulation is global', Breugel Policy Brief 2010/07, August 2010 where they discuss the phenomenon of 'multipolarity' and re-regulation. Within the European Union there is now a dominant trend towards regulation (of immediate and direct applicability within member states) and maximum harmonization.

[41] Although the capital market as casino mentality appears to be subsiding, there is no evidence that the interventionist inclinations of the Chinese government regulator are.

[42] Islamic finance, with its potential market of some 1.6 billion adherents, is inherently international and growing rapidly. However, its innate diversity and resistance to commercial standardization, impedes its significance.

[43] For example, despite obtaining an almost perfect score on ratings involving the IOSCO Objectives and Principles of Securities Regulation (compared to very mixed results for the United States when measured against the same benchmarks), the Dubai International Financial Centre has so far failed to deliver. See Ch 9 in this book. See also Cally Jordan, 'How International Finance Really Works' (2013) 7 *Law and Financial Markets Review* 256.

[44] 'Admittedly, the G20 has entrusted the Financial Stability Board with the mission of monitoring the standard-setting activity and has mandated the Basel Committee, IOSCO, and the IAIS (among others) with

1.28 There is no doubt that in a dozen years from now, the regulatory and institutional landscape of international capital markets will have been transformed. Adjustments to the shock of financial crisis are working their way through systems around the world. Demographics and geopolitical forces are shifting, changing with them investment patterns, institutional models, and long-held assumptions about market behaviour. Information technology has profoundly impacted information-based regulatory systems, outpacing regulatory responses. Traditional market institutions, such as exchanges, are scrambling to adapt. The private underbelly of finance is being exposed, at least to a limited extent. Theories of regulatory design are being challenged and rethought. Indeed, a new world of finance is already upon us.

the task of developing new rules. However, this choice seems more a quick-fix than a sustainable strategy. It will neither preserve state unity on the international stage, nor solve the issues of circumvention of national and regional democratic processes.' Régis Bismuth, 'The Independence of Domestic Financial Regulators: An Underestimated Structural Issue in International Financial Governance' (2010) 2 *Goettingen Journal of Internaltional Law* 93, 108–9.

2

MAKING INTERNATIONAL MARKETS WORK—REGULATORY TECHNIQUES

1. Introduction

Regulation, as it is usually understood, emanates from a national (or perhaps sub-national) **2.01** authority and operates locally. Capital markets predate the nation state and have been boundary blind. So, how have modern *inter*national capital markets been regulated? Different approaches have waxed and waned in popularity, but several broad groupings can be discerned: inaction; unilateralism; formal and informal cooperative efforts; and international or supra-national initiatives. In modern capital markets, the powerful geopolitical forces of empire, the emergence of the supra-national state, and hegemony have been determinants.

2. Geopolitical Forces as Determinant of Regulatory Techniques

The different regulatory approaches operating in modern international capital markets are **2.02** not mutually exclusive; they often coexist or interact, in both a positive and negative manner. Over time, states have developed different strategies and approaches to the regulation of cross-border capital markets' activities, borrowing freely from one another and adapting to changing circumstances as well as regulatory and political imperatives. The different regulatory approaches to international capital markets, which ones dominate, which ones wither away, have been shaped by the geopolitical forces of empire, the emergence of the supranational state and hegemony.

2.1 Empire

In terms of forging common rules and harmonization of regulation across borders, empire **2.03** was remarkably successful. In particular, the nineteenth-century British empire spread British financial models, institutions, and legislation around the world, creating an interconnected, international network which persists to this day. This was not convergence as it is understood today; English law was simply imposed and directly applicable in the colonies to varying degrees.[1] Local English-style judiciaries were set up, applying both indigenous and English law, but the ultimate court of final appeal was the Privy Council in London. The result was common rules and harmonization in a strong, and remarkably enduring, form.

---

[1] Depending on the territory, there was a complex interaction of English, colonial, and pre-colonial law.

2.04   Even decades after formal independence, as nation states broke away to form the Commonwealth,[2] former colonies and spheres of influence (including the United States from time to time),[3] continued to look to English models for institutions, legislation, and regulatory techniques.[4] Path dependency was at play, of course, but also more pragmatic considerations associated with continued alignment with British law, institutions, and regulatory ways. There were cost and efficiency savings in compatible commercial concepts operating across borders, easing the flow of trade, services, and capital.

2.05   Empire, and to a lesser extent Commonwealth, produced a generally harmonized system across several continents, with a high level of regulatory convergence within the system. It is no accident that the Nairobi Stock Exchange[5] would be organized along the lines of the London Stock Exchange, that the Johannesburg Stock Exchange would have longstanding cross-listing arrangements with London,[6] that Dubai would adopt English law and import English bankers and judges for its international financial centre,[7] or, for that matter, that the London Stock Exchange would attempt a friendly merger with the Toronto Stock Exchange.[8]

2.06   Over time, growing sentiments of independence, revolution, political, and economic shocks changed the dynamics of the system, resulting in greater divergence and individualization of regulation. The entry of the United Kingdom into what is now the European Union was a final blow, however, imposing a massive regulatory realignment in the United Kingdom. The Commonwealth was orphaned and left to its own devices. Smaller, developing economies became stuck in a time-warp, with old colonial institutions and legislation for which there was no longer a model suitable for emulation. A country such as Canada changed horses quite naturally, looking to the United States for new commercial models while retaining some of the better aspects of the old system. Other jurisdictions with continuing British affinities, such as Hong Kong and Australia, experimented with mix and match, occasionally unwittingly introducing continental European legal concepts which had been grudgingly implemented in the United Kingdom by way of European Commission directive.[9] Elsewhere, the choice of institutional

---

[2] Appeals to the Privy Council from all Australian courts were finally abolished in 1986 with the passing of the Australia Acts. In New Zealand, appeals to the Privy Council were not abolished until 2003 with the passing of the Supreme Court Act 2003 (NZ).

[3] Upon its creation in 1792, the Delaware Court of Chancery adopted the jurisdiction of English Chancery Courts to hear all matters and causes in equity; the persistence of self-regulation in the US market is an example.

[4] For example, major revisions to the English Companies Act, in particular in 1927 and 1948, replicated like a virus, with a few years delay and some local tweaking, in jurisdiction after jurisdiction throughout the Commonwealth.

[5] Established in 1954.

[6] In 2001 an agreement was reached with the London Stock Exchange to enable cross-trading and to replace the Johannesburg Stock Exchange's trading system with that of the London Stock Exchange.

[7] The Dubai International Financial Centre is an autonomous jurisdiction based in Dubai, where the civil and commercial laws of the United Arab Emirates do not apply. The legal system is instead based on common law and the courts are presided over by judges from leading commercial common law jurisdictions such as England, Singapore, and Hong Kong: see further Reza Mohtashami and Sami Tannous, 'Arbitration at the Dubai International Financial Centre: A Common Law Jurisdiction in the Middle East' (2009) 25 *Arbitration International* 173; see also Ch 9 of this book.

[8] Seen off by a consortium of Canadian banks and pension funds called 'Maple' with strong backing from Quebec institutions. Old colonial grudges die hard. See Ian Austen, 'London and Toronto Exchanges Call Off Merger', *New York Times* (New York, 29 June 2011).

[9] For example, the Australian Corporations Act 2001 introduced on 15 July 2001, from the United Kingdom, the concept of large and small proprietary companies. This distinction finds its source in the Fourth Companies Law Directive of the European Council on accounts: see Fourth Council Directive of 25 July 1978 based on Article 54(3)(g) of the Treaty on the annual accounts of certain types of companies (78/660/EEC) [1978] OJ L 222/11. This directive was reluctantly adopted in the United Kingdom. See Paul L Davies, *Gower*

structure and borrowings determined domestic regulation but also provided the link to a greater metropolis.

2.2 The supra-national state—the European Union

In empire, the forces of harmonization and convergence, strong as they were, operated almost unconsciously. The rules were dictated from the centre and radiated outwards to the colonial outposts, like it or not. Time and distance ultimately worked against both harmonization and convergence though; the centre did not hold.

2.07

The European Union, on the other hand, has been a deliberate political construct, created by consent of its members and built on the principles of harmonization and regulatory convergence in furtherance of the creation of a single market in goods, services, and capital. Superimposed on the member states are the supra-national legal institutions created by the 1957 Treaty of Rome.[10] Despite this formal treaty framework, capital markets in the European Union remained obstinately fragmented.

2.08

The European Union is dominated by civil code countries, which prize the systematization and formality of written law; vast resources are deployed in its creation. By its nature, the European Union has had to create formal legislative instruments that operate across national boundaries. Many of the regulatory techniques which have been employed in modern international capital markets ultimately find their origins in those employed by the European Union. These techniques have been extensively documented and put through their paces in the European Union, albeit operating with the support of formal treaty institutions absent elsewhere in the world.

2.09

For much of its history, the European Union has promoted harmonization through the use of directives, legislative instruments which set broad principles and objectives and which must be implemented at the nation state level, state by state. Political expediency drove this approach. Harmonization and regulatory convergence were the ultimate goals, but directives were flexible and less contentious than more coercive forms of legislative instrument. Directives permitted variety and diversity to persist among member states, so the use of directives had to be predicated on the operation of principles of mutual recognition, or passporting. Legislation and regulation implemented in one member state in conformity with EU directives had to be recognized and given effect in other member states, on a reciprocal basis.

2.10

Despite its predilection for multilateralism and mutual recognition, the European Union has been open to the operation of unilateral recognition principles for relations with non-member states, fostering trade and interaction. The European Union is also inherently internationalist in fact and predisposition, so cognizant of international standards and standard setting; international standards are put to regulatory use. At one level, directives could be viewed as international standards (applicable on a regional basis) but deriving a normative force through the operation of treaty.

2.11

---

and Davies Principles of Modern Company Law (9th edn, Sweet & Maxwell, 2012). At a recent presentation by the author to Australian regulators, no one could identify the origins of the distinction, now an established part of Australian law.

[10] Treaty Establishing the European Economic Community (opened for signature 25 March 1957, entered into force 1 January 1958) 298 UNTS 11 (Treaty of Rome).

2.12 For policymakers and legislators, crisis often provides opportunity. Since 2008, there has been a decided shift towards the use of European Commission regulation, a legislative instrument directly applicable in the member states, and producing immediate convergence and harmonization. Most significantly, the European Union has created the first supra-national capital markets regulator, the European Securities and Markets Authority which opened its doors in Paris in 2011. The interaction with national regulatory authorities is the new European dynamic in capital markets.

2.3 Hegemony

2.13 The United Kingdom has had empire and the Commonwealth through which to exert its influences; as a strong form of empire wound down, a weaker form continued in the colonial institutions and legislative frameworks left behind. The amorphous nature of the English common law, infused by commercial practice and custom and shaped by English courts through choice of law and jurisdiction clauses, also suited places where formal legislative institutions were problematic, for one reason or another. The European Union, on the other hand, is piecing together the old Roman Empire in a new supra-national formulation. The process is slow, formal, deliberate, and evolutionary.

2.14 But the United States has been the hegemonic force of the post World War II period. The war in the Pacific and its aftermath, the break-up of the former Soviet Union, the opening up of Latin America, the rise of China, have all provided opportunities to exert influence in terms of exporting ideology as well as institutional and regulatory models.

2.15 With its mass, the powerful gravitational force of its capital markets has pulled issuers and intermediaries alike into the United States. Canadian issuers and regulators clamoured for access by means of a tailor-made regulatory relationship. In the decades leading up to the global financial crisis, Latin American issuers piled onto US exchanges with American Depositary Receipt programmes and the rest of the world ploughed into US private markets. US-style regulation and institutions sprouted around the world. The United States was the benchmark and set the international standards. US financial institutions and institutional investors fanned out across the world, bringing with them their expectations and demands. US stock exchanges though have encountered mixed receptions in their forays outside the United States, caught in the turbulent waters of changing trading patterns and practices.

2.16 Yet, the United States remains resolutely domestically focused in the face of the incontrovertible evidence of the internationalization of capital markets. Lines of communication with Europe and the United Kingdom are kept open. There is coordination and cooperation across borders, up to a point. But influence in Asia and the Gulf remains elusive. Islam, the China factor, the rapid rise of other Asian economies, complex forms of legal plurality in operation, incompatible ideologies, are all factors now pushing against US hegemony in international capital markets regulation.

3. Regulatory Techniques in the International Capital Markets

3.1 Inaction

2.17 Until the global financial crisis exposed once obscure corners of marketplaces, simply doing nothing was an effective, and underappreciated, regulatory technique. In the interstices of national markets and their regulatory structures, marketplaces resistant to formal regulation flourished. Although well known to the participants, the extent of these more or less unregulated markets came as a surprise, and sometimes a particularly nasty surprise, to many. Regulators and policymakers since 2009 have repeated the same mantra, the need to reconsider the 'perimeter of regulation'.[11]

As capital markets and their institutions predate the regulatory inclinations of national authorities, unsurprisingly, significant unregulated markets and institutions have persisted. One legacy of unregulated markets is the tradition of self-regulation, in its stronger and weaker modern manifestations, in the United Kingdom, the United States, and elsewhere in the Commonwealth.   **2.18**

The power and influence of industry associations, such as the International Capital Markets Association (ICMA, and its predecessors) and the International Swaps and Derivatives Association (ISDA),[12] are another example. These industry associations, despite their old-style clubbiness, rulebooks, standard form contracts and exclusionary proceedings, are rising in prominence. For example, ISDA played a crucial role in sorting out the vast morass of unsettled contracts left in the wake of the collapse of Lehman Brothers in 2008. Working in cooperation with regulators, ISDA has assisted in implementation of initiatives to move certain derivatives trading to formal trading platforms.[13] The industry associations are a natural extrapolation, at the international level, of the domestic recognition of self-regulation and in keeping with their distant ancestors, the medieval guilds.[14]   **2.19**

Modern finance does demonstrate continuity with an old body of custom and practice, a subset and continuation of a form of *lex mercatoria*, or more precisely *lex financeria*, supporting modern financial transactions. This *lex financeria*, inherently international, floats free of the regulatory constraints of the nation state.[15]   **2.20**

---

[11] The 'perimeter of regulation' is a phrase, which began to appear in about 2009, in association with exhortations to regulators and policymakers to pay close attention to where the regulated markets ended and the unregulated markets began. This was not a new issue; the International Organization of Securities Commissions (IOSCO) had commissioned its report, 'Unregulated Financial Markets and Products: Final Report' (September 2009), before the true impact of the events of September 2008 was known. In 2010, IOSCO added eight new principles to its keystone 'Objectives and Principles of Securities Regulation', a number of which addressed the issue of 'perimeter of regulation': see eg IOSCO, *Objectives and Principles of Securities Regulation* (June 2010), principles 7, 24–28. The first iteration of the IOSCO *Objectives and Principles of Securities Regulation* was published in 1998.

[12] The acronym remains the same, but the original name of this association was the International Swaps Dealers Association, in simpler times before derivatives exploded onto the market place.

[13] Since the 2008 global financial crisis, world leaders have been keen to reform over-the-counter derivatives trades—contracts transacted beyond the view of regulators—by bringing them onto formal trading platforms. As the industry's trade body, the ISDA has been intimately involved. The derivatives are being transitioned to electronic-trading platforms called Swap Execution Facilities, but their inauguration has been plagued with problems. These stem from uncertainties at the Commodity Futures Trading Commission (CFTC), America's and thus the world's main derivatives regulator, as well as European discomfort about America's 'extraterritorial ambitions' through the CFTC: 'Not With a Bang: A Chaotic Launch for a Set of Electronic-Trading Platforms', *The Economist* (Paris, 5 October 2013).

[14] Cally Jordan and Pamela Hughes, 'Which Way for Market Institutions: The Fundamental Question of Self-Regulation' (2007) 4 *Berkeley Business Law Journal* 205; Gillian Tett, 'Calls for Radical Rethink of Derivatives Body', *Financial Times* (26 August 2010).

[15] See Cally Jordan, 'How International Finance Really Works' (2013) 7 *Law and Financial Markets Review* 256.

2.21 So it is no accident that the use of bilateral contracts, designed to keep the financial products which they create 'private' and out of the regulatory net, is so prevalent in these markets. Most derivatives (so structured) wriggled free of Securities and Exchange Commission (SEC) regulatory oversight in the United States in 2000 legislative reforms.[16] These innovative financial products often originated in the unregulated, international markets. In some cases, they were a response to market needs specific to the international markets (eg currency and interest rate swaps, sovereign debt credit default swaps). In other cases, the international markets served as a laboratory where new products could be tested (without untoward regulatory implications) before being customized for use in a domestic or retail market (eg various index products).

2.22 Regulatory indifference is not necessarily a bad thing. Although not currently a popular view, in the absence of abuse, benign neglect may be good for markets, especially given the alternative of ineffective, unsuitable or clumsy regulatory interference. In some cases, regulators may appear to turn a blind eye to certain markets and practices, either because they truly do not see them or else do not identify them as phenomena to be regulated. Indifference may also be deliberate regulatory deference.

2.23 The traditional Eurobond market is an example. In Europe, the activities of brand name US issuers selling US dollar denominated, long-term debt to the apocryphal 'Belgian dentist' took place in an unregulated space for the most part, and for a very long time.[17] Despite the identity of the issuer and the reputation of US courts and legislators for engaging in the extraterritorial application of US law, US securities regulators looked the other way. For several decades, from a US perspective, this market was unregulated, provided the securities were distributed in a manner resulting in their 'coming to rest abroad', so as not to 'flow into the hands of American investors'.[18] No legislative instrument or judicial interpretation was involved. The SEC simply issued a release stating its position. On the European side, industry associations successfully fended off EU level regulatory attention to this market by beefing up their rulebooks and persuading Brussels to insert a 'eurosecurities' exemption into the 1992 Investment Services Directive.[19]

2.24 By 1990, the diversification and increasingly obvious integration of capital markets[20] had sparked renewed US regulatory interest in the Euromarket. The SEC adopted

---

[16] See Commodity Futures Modernization Act of 2000, Pub L No 106-554, § 1(a)(5), 114 Stat 2763 (2000). Almost all derivatives benefit from a specific exemption in the Securities Act of 1933, see 15 USC § 77d (2006).

[17] In 1964, the SEC stated that the definition of interstate commerce in the US 1933 Act 'might be construed to encompass virtually any offering of securities made by a United States corporation to foreign investors. However, the Commission [SEC] has traditionally taken the position that the registration requirements of Section 5 of the [1933] Act are primarily intended to protect American investors. Accordingly, the Commission has not taken any action for failure to register securities of United States corporations distributed abroad to foreign nationals'. See Securities Act of 1933, Release No 4708; Securities Exchange Act of 1934, Release No 7366 (8 July 1964), 1964 SEC LEXIS 95; 29 Fed Reg 9828.

[18] See (n 17).

[19] Council Directive 93/22/EEC of 10 May 1993 on investment services in the securities field was replaced by Directive 2004/39/EC of the European Parliament and of the Council of 2004 on markets in financial instruments (MiFID).

[20] Integration of capital markets, increasing volatility of markets and trading activity, as well as dematerialization of financial instruments made it much more difficult to assume that a financial instrument had 'come to rest abroad'.

Regulation S,[21] governing offshore offerings, at least from a US perspective. Despite its formal avowals of eschewing an extraterritorial application of certain aspects of US securities laws, Regulation S purports to cast its regulatory net worldwide; it is applicable to both US and non-US issuers in the offshore markets.[22]

With a certain delay, but inevitably, the exemptive definition of 'eurosecurities' vanished **2.25** from EU directives and the Eurobond market succumbed to the EU regulatory reach. The Law Society of England and Wales, the legal profession's self-regulatory body, nevertheless put up a good fight against the regulatory encroachment of the proposed Prospectus Directive.[23]

> In addition, we are very concerned that the proposals would require fundamental changes to procedures for raising capital, which are understood and trusted by investors, and which have worked successfully for many years. The result, we fear, would be more bureaucracy, less accessible, more expensive capital markets and investment being driven away from Europe. In particular, we share concerns expressed by IPMA [International Primary Markets Association[24]] and others that the proposals would destroy the market in specialist securities for sophisticated investors from which Europe has benefited so much. . . . Put more starkly, the [Prospectus] Directive will take what is a currently the only market that can claim to be even vaguely pan-European BACK several steps.[25]

These statements illustrate the alliance of the powerful self-regulatory organization and 'gatekeeper', the UK Law Society, and international industry associations, principal proponents of the unregulated markets. Ultimately, although the European Union prevailed in adopting the Prospectus Directive, in fact, not much changed for the Eurobond market.[26]

Sometimes regulatory deference is a 'better part of valour' strategy by a regulator, for exam- **2.26** ple in the case of American Depositary Receipts (ADRs). ADRs and their variations[27] are a staple financial instrument in the international markets and a striking example of inventive regulatory arbitrage. Purportedly dating back to the 1920s, ADRs could also be considered an early form of derivative product.[28] Issued by a small number of US banks, like the Bank of New York Mellon Corporation,[29] ADRs are marketed to US investors.

---

[21] Regulation S—Rules Governing Offers and Sales Made Outside the United States Without Registration Under the Securities Act of 1933, 17 CFR 230.901—230.905.

[22] Again, from the US perspective.

[23] Ultimately adopted as Directive 2003/71/EC of the European Parliament and of the Council of 4 November 2003 on the prospectus to be published when securities are offered to the public or admitted to trading and amending Directive 2001/34/EC.

[24] IPMA was an industry association, which merged in 2005 with another international industry association, the International Securities Markets Association (ISMA), to form the current International Capital Markets Association (ICMA).

[25] The Law Society (UK), Company Law Committee, Proposal for a Directive on the Prospectus to be Published When Securities Are Offered to the Public or Admitted to Trading, No 422, July 2001, 1–2 (emphasis, capitalization, in the original).

[26] Although Switzerland, which is not a member of the EU, had initially thought to profit from a shift in issuance and trading out of the EU.

[27] For example, GDRs (Global Depositary Receipts) and BDRs (Brazilian Depositary Receipts), financial products structured in a similar manner to ADRs but designed to trade in markets outside the United States.

[28] When the author suggested to an SEC official that ADRs would fall within an accepted definition of derivative products, there was a vehement denial; almost without exception, the SEC does not have jurisdiction over derivative products.

[29] The result of a 2007 merger between the Bank of New York and Mellon Financial Corporation.

2.27 ADRs are structured like a hat check chit, or more technically, a warehouse receipt (hence their name), in an attempt to deflect regulatory attention as 'securities'. ADRs represent the right to claim delivery of a certain number of specified shares of a non-US company, which are being held on deposit, offshore, with the depositary bank in the United States issuing the ADRs. The depositary or issuing bank is the hat check attendant and the holder of the hat check chit gets to claim the hat, or pass it along to someone else who gets to claim the hat. The ADRs, being a negotiable instrument, can be transferred; they can be traded. The issuing bank agrees to pass on to the ADR holder, in US dollars, the economic benefits associated with the underlying shares, such as dividends. The issuing bank takes care of the currency conversion and other services for a fee.

2.28 Originally, depositary banks would obtain the publicly traded shares of non-US companies in their home country markets, pool the shares of a particular company, and then create and sell ADRs, denominated in US dollars, in the United States to US investors.[30] Obviously, the price at which the ADR was issued and traded was determined by the value of the underlying share.[31] The commercial rationale for ADRs has always been that they produce a financial instrument that looks and acts like the share of a US company, while in fact permitting the US holder economic diversification and exposure to foreign markets.

2.29 Unsurprisingly, the US SEC expressed a regulatory interest in a US dollar denominated financial instrument, issued by a US entity to US investors, and which economically mimicked an equity security. However, there was a problem; the banks creating ADRs could invoke section 3(a)(2) of the Securities Act of 1933, which exempts securities issued or guaranteed by a bank. The SEC would not have jurisdiction over the bank. The SEC took the position that the exemption did not apply because the securities being issued did not represent any interest in the bank itself but rather in a third party's obligation.[32] Instead of confrontation or a direct attempt at regulation (which might have resulted in a complete loss of potential oversight), the SEC chose a different route: a negotiated, somewhat conceptually ambivalent, stance in which the main US depositary banks acquiesced.[33]

2.30 An abbreviated regulatory filing called Form F-6 was created in 1983 with respect to the 'Depositary Shares evidenced by American Depositary Receipts' (not to be confused with the underlying deposited securities of the non-US issuer). The issuing/depositary bank would file Form F-6; the issuer of the underlying non-US securities might or might not sign Form F-6, depending on the degree of formal cooperation with the issuing/depositary bank. Although much of Form F-6 is couched in US securities regulatory terminology ('registration statement' and 'prospectus'), it is, in fact, pretty much an empty shell. Buried in the instructions is the statement that: 'the depositary for the issuance of ADRs itself shall not

---

[30] Originally, shares were purchased in the non-US market and pooled without the consent of the non-US company which had issued the shares; these were known as unsponsored ADRs. Over time, there was a decided move (with perhaps a few regulatory nudges) towards programmes structured with the consent of the non-US company.

[31] Thus giving rise to the implication that they are derivative products, deriving their value from the value of some other financial instrument.

[32] See Edward Greene et al, *U.S. Regulation of the International Securities and Derivatives Markets* (6th edn, Aspen Law & Business, 2002), 2–12, fn 28.

[33] Greene et al (n 32): 'As a compromise, the SEC decided to permit Depositaries to register ADRs on behalf of the ADR program itself, which is considered the issuer of the ADRs. As a result, the banks have no liability with respect to the registration statement; the liability is that of the program itself.'

be deemed to be an issuer.' The issuing/depositary bank is thus off the hook for regulatory purposes with respect to the ADRs. 'This altogether laudable demonstration of administrative flexibility means that nobody has the liability of an "issuer"...as far as Form F-6 is concerned.'[34]

The Form F-6 process, however, was a bit of a camel's nose;[35] it encouraged regulatory creep. **2.31** ADR programmes became more formalized, with the SEC encouraging various arrangements and structures. The programmes became stratified, different 'levels' identified, depending on whether the non-US issuer of the underlying securities could be persuaded to formally enter the US market by way of public offering or listing on a US stock exchange— a canny move by the SEC.

With the increasing use of ADRs during the boom years of the US markets in the 1990s, **2.32** the ambiguous status of ADRs raised other complex issues. For example, were ADR holders (usually, but not always, US resident investors) entitled to the protections of US securities law, in particular under the anti-fraud provisions of section 10b-5?[36] This issue arose in the Vivendi case,[37] where all the ordinary shares in Vivendi were listed in France, but its ADRs with respect to such shares were listed and traded on the New York Stock Exchange.

Generally speaking, inaction has likely been the historical norm when it comes to regula- **2.33** tion of international capital markets. The major players[38] and specialized trading hubs aside, regulatory energy is limited and directed to domestic concerns. Changes in the direction of capital flows and shifting geopolitical forces, however, may be provoking unexpected developments begging for a regulatory response. For example, BDRs, an ADR knockoff, have popped up in Brazil as the local investor class diversifies.[39] China, once intensely domestically focused, is opening up an offshore RMB market and positioning Shanghai as an international financial centre.[40] The wide-open spaces of unregulated markets are in the process of being fenced in.

---

[34] L Loss and J Seligman, *Securities Regulation*, vol 2 (3rd edn, Aspen Publishers, 1989), 816, n 74; as quoted in SEC Release No 33-6894 (23 May 1991), usually referred to as the ADR Concept Release.

[35] The expression refers to the cautionary tale about the camel; if you permit the camel to put its nose in the tent so as to come in from the cold, soon there is an entire camel in the tent and it is the former occupant who is out in the cold.

[36] 17 CFR 240 10b-5. SEC 'Rule 10b-5: Employment of Manipulative and Deceptive Practices' prohibits any act or omission resulting in fraud or deceit in connection with the purchase or sale of any security. In order to establish a claim under the rule, plaintiffs must show (i) manipulation or deception (through misrepresentation and/or omission); (ii) materiality; (iii) 'in connection with' the purchase or sale of securities; and (iv) scienter.

[37] *In re Vivendi Universal Securities Litigation (Master File No 02 CV 5571)*. In early 2010, a jury ruled in favour of shareholders who said Vivendi lied to the public about the company's dire financial situation. The company, but not its executives, were found liable and the ruling created the potential of billions of dollars of damages for investors. However, in mid-2010, the US Supreme Court issued its opinion in *Morrison v National Australia Bank*, 130 S Ct 2869 (2010), deciding that section 10(b) of the US 1934 Act does not apply extraterritorially. Thus, in February 2011, the *Vivendi* court held that *Morrison* barred claims brought by purchasers of ordinary shares and instead the company's liability was limited to certain investors who purchased the company's ADRs.

[38] The United States, the United Kingdom, the European Union.

[39] Joe Leahy, 'Brasilagro to issue ADRs in New York', *Financial Times* (Sao Paulo, 7 November 2012) <http://www.ft.com/intl/cms/s/0/39967456-28f4-11e2-86d7-00144feabdc0.html#axzz2puHaavJj> accessed 6 January 2014.

[40] 'Not-so-dim sums?', *The Economist* (2 July 2013) <http://www.economist.com/blogs/graphicdetail/2013/07/focus> accessed 6 January 2014; Josh Noble, 'China bond market emerges from the shadows',

3.2 Unilateralism

2.34 In terms of the most widespread response to internationalization of capital markets, unilateralism probably comes nipping at the heels of inaction. Concerted cross-border coordination on a sustained basis is difficult, and national interests frequently bump it off track. Judicial and legislative action at a purely domestic level is the norm.

2.35 Regulatory and judicial action in the domestic context though may produce significant consequences internationally; sometimes that is the desired effect, but it may also occur quite inadvertently, as a by-product of local action. Additionally, at a time when the desirability of convergence, cooperation and coordination has dominated international discourse, it is important to remember that these goals are not always acknowledged and promoted. Quite the contrary, examples of isolationist sentiments, exclusionary tactics, assertions of sovereignty, and protection of domestic industries and institutions, all abound. Different markets engage in different strategies at different times.

3.2.1 Isolationism and exclusionary regulation

2.36 The closed economies of the 1970s and 1980s saw an opening of massive proportions in the last two decades, but strictures have not completely disappeared. Far from it. China, for example, despite the 'open door' policy[41] of 1978, controls in bound investment in its domestic market (the so-called A-share market) as guardedly, although perhaps not as successfully, as it does participation in overseas markets by Chinese companies seeking capital offshore.

2.37 The transatlantic corridor has also been the scene of long simmering tensions between the European Union and the United States over exclusionary licensing regulation on the US side. US financial intermediaries, aggressive and highly peripatetic while overseas, demonstrate fiercely protectionist instincts at home. One dispute between the European Union and the United States involved unequal access by investors to trading screens permitting direct overseas investment. There were few regulatory impediments to such screens being placed in Europe, permitting European investors to trade directly in the US market. The commodities and futures regulator in the United States, the CFTC, had authorized European screens for use in the US markets the CFTC regulated, but the US securities regulator, the SEC, severely limited access in the United States for European equity trading screens.[42]

2.38 The regulatory culprit was a rather innocuous licensing provision, as seen in Rule 15a-6 under the US 1934 Act,[43] which had first ensnared Canadian-based intermediaries dealing with the Canadian portfolios of their US-based clients. On its face, the rule did not prohibit this activity; however, a conservative interpretation of the rule produced a chilling effect. In order to continue servicing the Canadian portfolios of their (mostly Canadian) clients in the United States, the intermediaries might have had to become fully registered US broker-dealers. For most Canadian financial intermediaries, this was not a financially attractive proposition given the duplicative compliance burdens it imposed. Canadians resident

---

Financial Times (Hong Kong, 23 October 2013) <http://www.ft.com/intl/cms/s/0/4f0950da-3b98-11e3-87fa-00144feab7de.html#axzz2puHaavJj> accessed 6 January 2014.

[41] See Ch 8 of this book.

[42] Howell E Jackson, Andreas M Fleckner, and Mark Gurevich, 'Foreign Trading Screens in the United States' (2006) 1 *Capital Markets Law Journal* 54. The circumstances were narrowly defined and in effect marginalized the possibilities for such trading.

[43] Rule 15a-6—Exemption of Certain Foreign Brokers or Dealers, 17 CFR 15a-6.

in the United States[44] found their trading accounts in Canada frozen and their Canadian brokers refusing to accept orders. On the sidelines, and behind the scenes, US financial intermediaries were the prime beneficiaries.

Ironically, the Canadian intermediaries had been somewhat accidental victims of promotion **2.39** of cross-border cooperation in capital raising, the implementation of the Multijurisdictional Disclosure System, or MJDS, between Canada and the United States.[45] Discussions on facilitation of cross-border offerings raised the profile of the cross-border activities of the Canadian financial intermediaries, and the US industry, not liking the potential competition, effectively lobbied to shut them out.

Leading international practitioners in the United States have repeatedly called for greater **2.40** deference, ie unilateral recognition, by US regulators towards non-US regulatory requirements.[46] This has proven a hard sell in the United States. Nearly 20 years after Rule 15a-6, a staff member at the SEC floated the concept of 'substituted compliance',[47] influenced to a certain degree by principles of unilateral recognition and deference to non-US licensing of market intermediaries. Essentially, the SEC would view compliance with home country licensing as 'substituted' compliance with US rules. However, rather than simple deference and recogntion, the substituted compliance regime proposed a complicated system of cross-border regulatory negotiation premised on alignment of the foreign regime to that of the United States. Ultimately, the proposal did not go far, pre-empted as it was by the global financial crisis.

3.2.2 Extraterritoriality

Isolationist or exclusionary strategies are one side of regulatory unilateralism; **2.41** extraterritoriality[48] is another. The United States suffers from a reputation for notorious extraterritorialism, although the reality is much more nuanced. One factor supporting extraterritorial application of US law has been the invocation of the personality principle; US citizens should have the benefits (and burdens) of US law wherever they are in the world. Empire in operation, without the formalities of empire. Until 1990 and the implementation of Regulation S under the Securities Act of 1933, the SEC took the view that US citizens should benefit from the protections, and strictures, of US securities law, wherever they were in the world. The operation of the personality principle in US securities law has been much attenuated since then, being replaced to a significant degree by the 'sandbox rule'.[49]

---

[44] There are an estimated 900,000 Canadians legally resident in the United States.

[45] See Ch 5 of this book.

[46] Edward F Greene and Linda C Quinn, 'Building on the International Convergence of the Global Markets: A Model for Securities Law Reform' (A Major Issues Conference: Securities Regulation in the Global Internet Economy, Washington DC, 14–15 November 2001); Edward F Greene, 'Beyond Borders: Time to Tear Down the Barriers to Global Investing' (2007) 48 *Harvard International Law Journal* 85.

[47] Ethiopis Tafara and Robert J Peterson, 'A Blueprint for Cross-Border Access to US Investors: A New International Framework' (2007) 48 *Harvard International Law Journal* 31; Edward F (n 46); Susan Wolburgh Jenah, 'Commentary on "A Blueprint for Cross-Border Access to US Investors: A New International Framework"' (2007) 48 *Harvard International Law Journal* 69.

[48] Chris Brummer, 'Territoriality as a Regulatory Technique: Notes from the Financial Crisis' (2010) 79 *University of Cincinnati Law Review* 499.

[49] My rules apply if you are playing in my sandbox, ie territoriality. However, US tax law continues to be a personal law, following US citizens around the world.

2.42 The courts have also played a significant role in furthering the reputation of the United States for extraterritorial action. For many decades, US courts also took an expansive interpretation of the conduct and effects doctrine,[50] permitting them to assert jurisdiction over a broad range of claimants, defendants, and disputes in the capital markets. The litigious environment in the United States had been a serious deterrent to non-US companies entering US markets for purposes of capital raising, but a boon for non-US investor claimants, who flocked to US courts seeking redress. In particular, the availability of class action procedures was a magnet.

2.43 The expansiveness of the US judiciary in asserting its jurisdiction under the conduct and effects doctrine spilled over into administrative action as well. A possibly apocryphal story recounted the adventures of SEC investigators, in pursuit of testimony in a cross-border anti-fraud investigation, being met, as they disembarked in Paris by French authorities challenging their jurisdiction to conduct investigations in France.

2.44 It was during this period that several governments[51] enacted 'blocking' statutes, prohibiting cooperation by their citizens and domestic institutions with the demands for information by US authorities; these demands were viewed as an egregious affront to sovereignty. Even that good neighbour, Canada, enacted blocking legislation.[52]

2.45 Given the hostility engendered by unilateral SEC administrative action (all in the good cause of fighting international financial fraud), the SEC changed tack. It approached overseas regulators one on one and proposed bilateral administrative understandings, regulator to regulator, proposing cooperative arrangements for information sharing. Thus, the MOU, or Memorandum of Understanding, was born. Originally a negotiated bilateral instrument, MOUs have now become standard form, multilateral instruments among regulators under the auspices of IOSCO.

2.46 Even the venerable conduct and effects doctrine, a judicial given in the United States for decades, has been dealt a blow, at least temporarily. In the 2010 decision, *NAB v Morrison*,[53] known colloquially as the 'F-cubed' decision,[54] the US Supreme Court denied non-US plaintiffs access to the US courts as part of a class action involving alleged securities fraud. Although Justice Scalia deliberately targeted the conduct and effects doctrine, invoking the presumption of territoriality, an underlying hostility towards class action litigation per se may be the real motivating factor in the decision. But it may be too early to discount the continued vitality of an expansive conduct and effects doctrine, which opens the doors to US courts. Only a month after the *Morrison* decision, the US financial crisis legislation, the Dodd Frank Act, specifically recognized the authority of the SEC to invoke the conduct and effects doctrine in pursuing international anti-fraud efforts.

---

[50] The conduct and effects doctrine has formed part of US private international law for decades, justifying US courts assuming jurisdiction over matters where either the conduct occurred in the United States or the conduct occurred outside the United States but had effects within the United States: James Armstrong, 'Swiss Exchange Stock Buyers Can't Sue Credit Suisse', *Law360* (28 July 2010) <http://www.law360.com/articles/183833/swiss-exchange-stock-buyers-can-t-sue-credit-suisse> accessed 6 January 2014.

[51] Cally Jordan, 'Canadian Participation in International Capital Markets: A Reassessment', *Meredith Lectures, Crossborder Transactions* (25 November 2009), 5.

[52] See (n 51).

[53] *Morrison v National Australia Bank Ltd*, 130 S Ct 2869 (2010).

[54] F-cubed refers to foreign plaintiff, purchasing securities of a foreign issuer, on a foreign stock exchange: *Morrison v National Australia Bank Ltd* (No 08-1191) 547 F 3d 167 at 172.

Nevertheless, old-fashioned, US-style extraterritorialism of the overt variety has lost a good **2.47** deal of traction; it became counterproductive,[55] as competing regulatory regimes gained in vigour and sophistication. Regulator to regulator cooperation, at least at certain levels, has become the norm. However, extraterritorialism remains hard-wired in the US regulatory psyche and it may have found a less obvious, but quite influential, expression in international financial standards such as the IOSCO Objectives and Principles of Securities Regulation.[56] In fact, some US commentators have urged greater US participation in the formulation of international financial standards, as a means of spreading the influence of US regulation abroad.[57]

Although extraterritoriality is most often associated with US courts and administrative agen- **2.48** cies, the United Kingdom and English law have a long arm as well. English law and the English courts are often chosen by parties to financial contracts, a choice which will be recognized in the United Kingdom despite no commercial relationship of the parties or transaction to the United Kingdom. Until recently, the reach of empire gave the United Kingdom direct jurisdiction over many places in the world and English law exercised hegemony throughout much of the modern Commonwealth and Asia.

Most recently, the global spread of interconnected and related financial institutions inevita- **2.49** bly results in extraterritorial implications, both advertent and inadvertent, by virtue of the application of domestic law in various jurisdictions. Post-crisis EU initiatives with respect to credit rating agencies and hedge funds, for example, have garnered complaints of extraterritoriality from affected institutions having a European presence.

3.2.3 Domestic regulation and international capital markets

Only the most important capital markets can purport to seriously impact the international **2.50** capital markets by means of domestic regulation. Since Japan, despite its size, cannot shake off its traditional insularity (as well as having languished in the economic doldrums for two decades now) that has left the field to the United States and the United Kingdom. The European Union has been concentrating its efforts on integrating its internal markets. However, a surprising number of other places in the world have used tailored domestic law and institutions as a means of luring international financial activity to their shores.

The United Kingdom has had the advantage of empire to exert its influences internationally. **2.51** Its courts, used to deliberating on international matters coming in from the far-flung colonies, liberally recognized 'proper law of the contract' and 'choice of forum' clauses thereby permitting commercial parties anywhere to choose English courts and English law. The world of international commerce has long been used to coming through London.

---

[55] Brummer (n 48).
[56] See Cally Jordan, 'The Dangerous Illusion of International Financial Standards and the Legacy of the Financial Stability Forum' (2011) 12 *San Diego International Law Journal* 333 for a discussion on how US regulation and institutions of the 1990s provide the framework for these IOSCO Objectives.
[57] Greene and Quinn (n 46), 4: 'Historically, the United States has been the most open of all markets. It is critically important both to investors and the continued preeminence of the American capital market that the United States continue to attract issuers from around the world. Widespread foreign issuer participation in the U.S. market: ... exports American investor protection and disclosure principles abroad; and assures the continued preeeminence of the U.S. market, which enhances the SEC's leadership role in developing international disclosure, accounting and auditing and governance standards.'

2.52 In recognition of the diversity of institutions and participants engaging, intermittently or on an ongoing basis, in activity in the City of London, accommodations were made, mostly by tweaking here and there existing domestic legislation, like the companies law or listing rules. But the strong self-regulatory tradition and the preeminence of the London Stock Exchange eclipsed formal regulatory action for the most part. It has scarcely been more than a decade that the United Kingdom has had a regulator, first the Financial Services Authority (FSA), now the Financial Conduct Authority (FCA), comparable to the SEC in Washington. Nonetheless, the FSA was emulated in jurisdiction after jurisdiction, a testament to regulatory leadership.[58]

2.53 However, one secret weapon of London, as the leader among international financial centres, has been its ability to attract talent, the intermediaries that turn the wheels of finance. There have been tax incentives and accommodations with respect to visa applications.[59] As the provision of financial services, especially international financial services, represents such a significant part of the overall UK economy, UK authorities pay close attention to fostering a facilitative environment. This has not been without criticism, as creating a two-tier economy and making London prohibitively expensive for the English middle class. 'Regulation lite' or 'light touch regulation',[60] was also long seen as a competitive advantage to the London market, although much tarnished since the global financial crisis. But the point here is that rather than, or perhaps more accurately, in addition to, exporting regulatory models (the FSA has been a remarkably successful export), the United Kingdom has focused on importing the industry.

2.54 Unlike the United Kingdom, the United States has had a powerful regulator and extensive, perhaps too extensive, body of formal regulation in place since the 1930s. US legislation, like its generator, the US Congress, is intensely domestic in focus.[61] This has produced two interesting phenomena. On the one hand, domestic US legislation may have inadvertent international consequences (because the US Congress does not look beyond the domestic implications to consider possible international ones). On the other, given the powerful centre of gravity which US capital markets exert, a varied assortment of international issues inevitably arise. US regulators have thus, in practice, dealt with the international implications of US capital markets, albeit often in a very quiet way.[62]

2.55 A striking example of US legislation producing unintended consequences in the international markets is the Sarbanes-Oxley Act of 2002. This legislation, a response to two corporate scandals, the collapse of Enron and WorldCom in a splash of fraud and adverse publicity,

---

[58] See Eilis Ferran, 'The Break-Up of the Financial Services Authority' (2011) 31 *Oxford Journal of Legal Studies* 455.

[59] Quality of life may be a factor as well; for wealthy families with school-aged children, London may be more attractive than New York or Hong Kong.

[60] 'Tiner's Tightrope: The City Has Thrived Because of Light Regulation. A Heavier Handed Approach May Be on its Way', *The Economist* (18 September 2003) <http://www.economist.com/node/2071982> accessed 6 January 2014; Patrick Jenkins, Simon Rabinovitch, and Sam Fleming, 'US Bankers Attack London And China's Lovefest', *Financial Times* (15 October 2013) <http://www.ft.com/intl/cms/s/0/1b00d4da-35c5-11e3-b539-00144feab7de.html#axzz2puHaavJj> accessed 6 January 2014.

[61] 'All politics is local', a phrase attributed to one-time Speaker of the US House of Representatives, Tip O'Neill.

[62] Informal guidance, technical rulemaking, no-action letters that do not attract the attention of a protectionist Congress.

was intensely domestically focused.[63] Sarbanes-Oxley created an oversight board for the accounting and auditing profession, which was seen to have lost its independence in these cases by getting too close to their clients. Otherwise, Sarbanes-Oxley is primarily corporate governance legislation, and unlike the disclosure-based regime characteristic of US securities law, replete with mandatory and directive provisions.

Given that corporate law is state law in the United States, the corporate governance provisions **2.56** of Sarbanes-Oxley were cast as securities regulation so as to give them national reach and put them under the jurisdiction of the federal regulator, the SEC. Although the US Congress, technically, has jurisdiction to create federal corporate law, there is a long tradition of deference, called the internal affairs doctrine. Federal legislators defer to state legislation for the governance of the internal affairs of corporations, unless and until inaction or inadequate responses raise issues to the level of national importance.[64] Sarbanes-Oxley was enacted in defiance of the internal affairs doctrine, one source of the controversy surrounding it.[65]

In the past, corporate governance provisions had been recast as securities regulation so as to **2.57** provide one federal set of rules rather than a multitude of state responses. The proxy voting rules of the Securities Exchange Act of 1934 are another example. These older corporate governance rules, tucked into federal securities legislation, differ though in one vital respect; foreign issuers participating in US markets had been, quietly, exempted from their application by later SEC rule-making.[66] It was recognized that US corporate governance provisions, with respect to proxy voting for example, would unnecessarily conflict with the voting and shareholder meeting rules of non-US corporate law under which foreign issuers were organized.

And so it was with Sarbanes-Oxley. Certain of the main corporate governance provisions, **2.58** such as those dealing with audit committees, potentially conflicted (or were unnecessarily duplicative) with European corporate statutes. Additionally, and importantly, there was a generalized distaste for the somewhat clumsy and expensive internal compliance mechanisms imposed by Sarbanes-Oxley. The non-US issuers participating in the public US markets were caught; as federal securities legislation, Sarbanes-Oxley applied indiscriminately to all public issuers and companies listed on US exchanges, irrespective of country of origin. Domestic US issuers intensely disliked Sarbanes-Oxley, but the non-US issuers, in particular the Europeans, had a choice. And that choice was to exit from the US public markets.

Which they did, in a significant and very public way.[67] These companies were the large, **2.59** well-known brand names of Europe, Asia, and Australia. They had been aggressively courted

---

[63] To the point where individual provisions of the legislation could be linked to the names of specific individuals in the scandals, for example section 302, requiring certain senior executives to certify as to the accuracy of financial statements is the Ken Lay provision. Ken Lay was the CEO of Enron and disclaimed personal knowledge of financial impropriety.

[64] See Mark Roe, 'Delaware's Competition' (2003) 117 *Harvard Law Review* 588.

[65] See Roberta Romano, 'The Sarbannes-Oxley Act and the Making of Quack Corporate Governance' (2005) 114 *Yale Law Journal* 1521.

[66] See Greene et al (n 32).

[67] As of July 2007, a long list of European and other major international companies had delisted from US exchanges: Bayer, British Airways, Ducati Motors, Fiat, Genesys, Danone, Merck, PCCW, Telecom Italia, and Telstra: Eric Uhlfelder, 'US Delistings Changing the Landscape for Investors', *Financial Times* (23 July 2007) <http://www.ft.com/intl/cms/s/0/5b1367f8-397e-11dc-ab48-0000779fd2ac.html#axzz2puHaavJj> accessed 6 January 2007; Gerrit Wiesmann and Jeremy Grant, 'German Group Seeks to Delist From NYSE', *Financial Times* (26 March 2007) <http://www.ft.com/intl/cms/s/0/7df64012-dbd0-11db-9233-000b5df10621.html#axzz2puHaavJj> accessed 6 January 2014.

by the New York Stock Exchange, in particular, in the 1990s. Daimler Benz had been first over the fence in 1993; the big German industrials had been resisting on the basis of the compliance with US GAAP then required.[68] But a small goldrush of foreign issuers piled on to US exchanges. And as the tide had come in, with Sarbanes-Oxley, the tide also went out. Non-US companies began to delist from US exchanges in protest over Sarbanes-Oxley.[69]

2.60 But delisting was not enough. In what became colourfully known as the 'cockroach hotel',[70] or 'Hotel California',[71] these non-US issuers were still caught by the reporting and other compliance requirements of the Securities Exchange Act of 1934, the repository of many Sarbanes-Oxley provisions. For technical reasons, they were precluded from taking advantage of the 1960s origin exemptive rule designed to relieve non-US issuers from US reporting and compliance obligations.[72]

2.61 Because the non-US companies at issue were major international corporations, many supported by the lobbying efforts of the European Union, pressure was brought to bear on resolving this anomalous situation. The SEC moved to put in place a new set of rules, Rule 12h-6 in particular, to permit exit from the US regulatory net. Interestingly, the rules created parallel, but slightly different, requirements for US issuers and non-US issuers, a likely attempt to demonstrate a 'level playing field'.

2.62 However, the United States has a long history of accommodating non-US issuers in its domestic markets, in fact creating an entire 'parallel' regime applicable to them, complete with accommodations and exemptions.[73] The SEC soft-pedalled the parallel regime though, as accommodations for non-US companies have always been contentious among domestic issuers, seen as unfairly tilting the level playing field. Although non-US issuers long enjoyed accommodations in the interests of enticing them into US markets, it was a different story for non-US financial intermediaries. The US investment services industry lobbied hard, and successfully, against concessions; it did not want the competition. Consideration of a 'substituted compliance' regime floated in 2007, foundered, in part a victim of the global financial crisis, but also due to its inherent complexity and perhaps lack of industry support.

3.2.4 *Free-riding as a regulatory technique*

2.63 Although their hegemony is being challenged, in modern finance, the United Kingdom and the United States have set the industry, institutional, and regulatory pace. Others have profited by drafting the leaders, free-riding on their efforts. Free-riding can take a number of different forms.[74] Commonwealth countries, already endowed with English-style institutions

---

[68] For non-US issuers interested in US markets, one beneficial consequence of the global financial crisis was that the United States, in a moment of weakness, permitted non-US issuers to drop US GAAP compliance or reconciliation in favour of IFRS, greatly simplifying accounting issues and associated costs for them.

[69] There may also have been other considerations, such as disappointment with the results of an expensive US listing, and SOX provided the pretext for a noisy withdrawal.

[70] After cockroach traps (found in every New York City apartment) which permit cockroaches to enter the trap but not exit.

[71] After the nightmarish 1977 popular song, *Hotel California*, which contains the lines: ' You can check out anytime you like, But you can never leave.'

[72] Rule 12g3-2(b), in particular. See Ch 4 of this book.

[73] See Ch 4 of this book for a detailed description of the 'parallel system' created by the F-series forms.

[74] Cally Jordan, 'Regulation of Canadian Capital Markets in the 1990's: The United States in the Driver's Seat' (1995) 4 *Pacific Rim Law & Policy Journal* 577.

such as the judiciary and stock exchanges, have looked to the United Kingdom for inspiration in legislative and policy matters for well over a century. Smaller countries have looked to their larger neighbours, copying and often improving on regulatory and institutional initiatives. During the last 20 years, with the 'rise of the rest' in Asia, Latin America, and Eastern Europe, international development agencies and financial institutions have jockeyed to provide the best 'model' to be emulated in promoting economic growth, with mixed success.[75]

Small jurisdictions with aspirations to be offshore financial centres will usually import a **2.64** recognized financial and regulatory system. Given the flexibility and informality of the English common law and its ability to sit comfortably among other local systems, this has often been in the English style. Rather than going to the trouble of actually importing and indigenizing foreign models, free-riding sometimes simply involves incorporating foreign law (or international standards, now) by reference. For example, in a bout of overenthusiastic internationalism, Canadian (Ontario) securities regulators once proposed recognizing as acceptable for domestic use prospectuses prepared in accordance with requirements in any G7 country.[76] The EU Prospectus Directive includes a provision recognizing disclosure documents prepared in accordance with international standards, assuming their equivalency to EU requirements.[77] Dubai has dropped the City of London, replete with its bankers, rulebooks, institutions, and judiciary, into the middle of Dubai City. Free-riding is cheap and easy, provided the leader doesn't crash.

3.3 Formal and informal cooperative efforts

Much of the modern history of international capital markets regulation has been marked by **2.65** the dynamic interaction of formal and informal cooperative efforts. Informal regulator to regulator communications have been ongoing for decades and market participants are continuously looking over each other's shoulders. The International Organization of Securities Commissions (IOSCO)[78] has grown from a modest talk shop for North American regulators to the world focal point for international capital markets regulation: a standard setter, think tank, implementer. Other IOSCO-like committees and organizations have sprung up as well, some operating regionally such as those formerly found within the European Union, others associated with Islamic finance. IOSCO, and related fora, also provide the opportunity for interface between the gatekeepers (the professionals), the industry actors and their associations, operators of the market infrastructure, and regulatory and financial authorities.

Agreement among regulators on a formal set of common rules, in the interests of reducing **2.66** compliance costs and increasing market efficiency,[79] has been elusive though. Even in the European Union, which attaches enormous importance to harmonization and convergence,

---

[75] Katharina Pistor, Daniel Berkowitz, and Jean-Francois Richard, 'Economic Development, Legality and the Transplant Effect' (2003) 47 *European Economic Review* 165.

[76] Maxime-Olivier Thibodeau, 'Proposed Federal Securities Regulator', Background Paper, Ottawa, Canada, Library of Parliament (30 April 2013), 2. The proposal was short-lived, as there were questions raised as to the appropriateness of accepting Italian disclosure documents in the highly regulated North American environment.

[77] Pierre-Marie Boury and Jar Panasar, 'The Prospectus Directive: Creating a Single European Passport', Practical Law Company Global Counsel (June 2004), 32.

[78] See Ch 3 of this book.

[79] Hal S Scott, 'Internationalization of Primary Public Securities Markets' (2000) 63 *Duke Journal of Law and Contemporary Problems* 71, 78.

the process is complex and fraught.[80] Mutual recognition techniques,[81] pioneered in the European Union in the face of the difficulties associated with producing a common set of rules, have also had somewhat limited impact. Without formal supra-national institutions (such as exist in the European Union), the process of negotiating mutual recognition regimes, based on home country/host country principles, is a time-consuming exercise in ad hocery. Canada and the United States,[82] to a limited degree, managed to do so with the MJDS, but it took five years of bilateral negotiations and considerable efforts at harmonization on the Canadian side. Australia and New Zealand implemented their own version of the MJDS,[83] but given the small size of the economies involved (when compared to Canada and the United States), this initiative may be more symbolic than anything else.

IOSCO has institutionalized administrative MOUs among regulators. Once negotiated on a bilateral basis, there is now a standard form multilateral agreement, created by IOSCO that is a condition to membership. These understandings are usually restricted to somewhat innocuous matters such as information sharing, more a political gesture of goodwill than anything else.

3.4 International and supra-national initiatives

2.67 Crises and contagion, first in Asia, then globally, revealed the inadequacies associated with regulation operating at a nation state level in an interconnected world. Even the European Union experienced difficulties with coordination among member states in the face of crisis, despite the European Union's long history and formal structure as a supra-national entity. International institutions, such as IOSCO, and international standard setting, such as International Accounting Standards (now International Financial Reporting Standards), predate by a decade or more even the Asian financial crisis. But crises on an international scale have prompted the call for formal international solutions.

2.68 The Asian financial crisis of 1997–98 was the tipping point. A new forum was created in its wake in 1999, the Financial Stability Forum (FSF), which set about selecting sets of international financial standards and devising a way to implement them as both prophylactic and diagnostic tools. The International Monetary Fund and The World Bank, standard setters in their own right, were recruited to the task. So began the fascinating experiment with Financial Sector Assessments (FSAPs); as with all experiments, there are sometimes unintended consequences and untoward developments. The global financial crisis was one of them. This story is told in the next chapter, International Organizations and the Capital Markets.

---

[80] Scott (n 79); Jordan (n 51).
[81] Scott (n 79); Jordan (n 51).
[82] See Ch 5 in this book and the discussion of the MJDS.
[83] *Agreement on the Mutual Recognition of Securities Offerings*, modelled on the Canada/US MJDS.

3

INTERNATIONAL ORGANIZATIONS AND THE CAPITAL MARKETS

1. Introduction

Until recently, formal international institutions have paid capital markets scant atten- **3.01** tion. International capital markets have not been amenable to regulation by treaty or treaty institutions, in large measure because these markets have been resistant to formal regulation of any kind, operating in the interstices of national regulation. Industry associations, such as the International Swaps and Derivatives Association (ISDA) or the International Capital Markets Association (ICMA), in their various iterations, together with exchanges, trading platforms, and the financial intermediaries themselves, have been the front line of oversight and source of market rules. Additionally, international capital markets activities in modern times have been dominated by a handful of jurisdictions, primarily the United States and the United Kingdom, the former providing regulatory accommodations and an extraterritorial framework for cross-border activities, with the latter more reliant on the operation of non-statutory 'rulebooks' and self-regulatory principles.

The International Organization of Securities Commissions (IOSCO) has been excep- **3.02** tional, and quite alone, in this respect. But IOSCO is not a regulator nor a treaty organization, and its origins were not even particularly international. Over the three decades of its existence, however, as its composition and roles have rapidly evolved, and in the absence of any other body, IOSCO has become a focal point with respect to the oversight and operation of international capital markets.

Crises, first the regional Asian financial crisis of 1997–98 and then, barely ten years later, **3.03** the global financial crisis, have dramatically changed IOSCO. Crises have also thrust capital markets from their technical penumbra into the international limelight, and led to the appearance of new international institutions. First, the Financial Stability Forum (FSF) emerged from the aftermath of the Asian financial crisis, to be unceremoniously unseated by its successor a decade later, the Financial Stability Board (FSB), a more formal institution based in Basel, Switzerland with a permanent secretariat. Although not exclusively focused on capital markets, the distinction of both these institutions was to bring capital markets, and not just banking, under the umbrella of international financial institutions.

Unlike IOSCO, both the FSF and its successor, the FSB, were political initiatives (on the **3.04** part of the G7 and G20, respectively). As such, they also drew into their orbit formal treaty organizations such as the IMF and The World Bank, among others.[1] IOSCO, once an obscure association of technically minded national and sub-national regulators, became an instrument of the larger geopolitical universe, enmeshed in agendas not of its own making. Mimicking at the international level a tripartite approach to financial services regulation found in consolidated national regulators like the Financial Services Authority (FSA) in the United Kingdom, IOSCO was soon joined by the well-known Basel Committee on Banking Supervision (BCBS) and a later organization modelled on IOSCO, the International Association of Insurance Supervisors (IAIS), to form the Joint Forum.[2]

2. The Changing Role of IOSCO

2.1 The background of IOSCO

3.05 IOSCO had its beginnings in a regional North American initiative, so it is hardly surprising that the United States has played a leading role in its development. Because of the federal nature of both Canada and the United States, there are over 60 capital markets regulators in the region, in addition to the well-known federal regulator in the United States, the SEC. Since 1919, these regulators have met regularly under the auspices of the North American Securities Administrators Association (NASAA)[3] in an effort to promote a coordinated approach to what, in fact, has become an integrated market.[4] Many years later in 1974, a new regional association of regulators was set up to bring in Latin America as well. It is out of this latter organization that IOSCO emerged; the United Kingdom and France (representing Europe) and Korea and Indonesia (representing Asia) joined and the organization was renamed in 1983.

3.06 Again, the United States was a driving force in the creation of IOSCO, and its first initiatives, bilateral memoranda of understanding (MOUs) with respect to cooperation and information sharing among regulators in different jurisdictions. Although the MOUs formally contemplated bilateral administrative actions, they operated as one way streets. The information sharing and cooperation was usually at the request of the United States. MOUs marked a change in strategy on the part of the Securities and Exchange Commission (SEC) which had encountered push back to its assertive extraterritorial regulatory actions in other parts of the world. Rather than face confrontation in its more vigorous offshore enforcement efforts, the SEC pulled back and looked to more persuasive means to obtain its ends, invoking the intermediation of IOSCO and the MOU initiatives which it had endorsed.

---

[1] On the implications of this interaction of political actors with IOSCO, see Stefano Pagliari, 'The Domestic Foundations of Transnational Regulatory Networks: IOSCO and the Reassertion of National Authority in Global Securities Regulation', SASE Annual Conference 2012, Boston, 28 June 2012.

[2] 'The Joint Forum was established in 1996 under the aegis of the Basel Committee on Banking Supervision (BCBS), the International Organization of Securities Commissions (IOSCO) and the International Association of Insurance Supervisors (IAIS) to deal with issues common to the banking, securities and insurance sectors, including the regulation of financial conglomerates. The Joint Forum is comprised of an equal number of senior bank, insurance, and securities supervisors representing each supervisory constituency': See Bank of International Settlement 'Joint Forum' <http://www.bis.org/bcbs/jointforum.htm> accessed 16 January 2013.

[3] 'North American Securities Administrators Association' (NASAA) <http://www.nasaa.org/> accessed 11 April 2013.

[4] NASAA still exists.

In its early days, IOSCO was very much about the transatlantic dialogue, the United States **3.07** on one side and the United Kingdom, primarily, on the other. A tiny secretariat[5] based in Montreal, Canada, provided administrative support, in particular with respect to annual meetings, which became a gathering point for regulators, exchanges, industry associations, and consultants. Montreal had the virtue of being neither Washington, New York, nor London, in effect, neutral ground.[6] Only securities commissions, ie governmental regulatory agencies in their various guises, are full voting members,[7] there being a triple-tiered membership structure. Since self-regulation has historically been a significant aspect of capital markets regulation, exchanges constitute the second tier of members (associate members) with industry associations and other self-regulatory organizations occupying the third tier (affiliate members). It is into this third tier that the international financial institutions, the International Monetary Fund and The World Bank, made their way a decade ago, creating a new dynamic within the organization.

The work of IOSCO was, and continues to be, executed through its committee structure by **3.08** the member regulatory agencies and market institutions themselves, under the administrative coordination of the Secretariat. This inevitably means that the agenda, and the work product itself, has until recently been determined by those developed economy regulators with the greatest resources. IOSCO's predecessor institutions, NASAA and the Inter-American association of securities regulators, worked to smooth out the technical bumps in the regulatory road through administrative cooperation and other initiatives. IOSCO maintained this focus and thus the Technical Committee has been the powerhouse within IOSCO. For example, over decades of collaborative (and not always easy) efforts, the Technical Committee was a prime mover in the development of international accounting and auditing standards (now embodied in International Financial Reporting Standards (IFRS)).[8]

IOSCO does not provide an open forum.[9] However, for a fairly hefty fee, individuals and **3.09** non-members of IOSCO[10] can attend certain sessions of the annual meeting.[11] Committee meetings, member sessions, and their related social events remain closed-door affairs so as to promote candid discussion and communication among the regulatory authorities[12] not wishing to see their views appear the next day in the financial press.

---

[5] Originally two administrators and some secretarial support.

[6] The Secretariat was later moved to Madrid, allegedly based on complaints about ease of airline access to Montreal, but more likely due to the shocks to the delicate constitutions of committee members attending meetings in January when the temperatures in Montreal can drop to 30°C below.

[7] For historical reasons, the US SEC is the member with voting rights; Canada, with no federal regulator but over a dozen provincial and territorial regulators, somewhat anomalously had two votes (for Ontario and Quebec) although this imbalance in voting power has subsequently been addressed through vote sharing.

[8] Given the preeminent role of the SEC in the Technical Committee, it is somewhat ironic that the SEC has not yet endorsed the use of IFRS for US domestic issuers (although accepting IFRS in 2008 for non-US issuers).

[9] That is not the point of its existence.

[10] Which are comprised of panels and formal presentations. Industry consultants and the occasional academic, for example, are usual non-IOSCO member participants.

[11] As well as some, but not all, of the social events which are often quite memorable. The venue of the annual meeting changes every year and a friendly rivalry on the part of government sponsors has developed in terms of demonstrating national hospitality. In the earlier days of IOSCO, when the world of those interested in international capital markets was small, the annual meetings were much more open to all, members and non-members alike, who participated.

[12] This is, after all, the original mission of IOSCO.

2.2 New roles for IOSCO

3.10 Three interrelated developments have fundamentally changed the role of IOSCO: the changing composition of its membership, the decision to become a standard setter, and the interaction with the wider world of international financial institutions.

2.2.1 Membership composition and the rise of emerging markets

3.11 With now nearly 120 full or ordinary members, 80 of which jurisdictions would be characterized as emerging or transition markets, IOSCO is no longer exclusively about the transatlantic dialogue. Reflecting the changed composition of its membership, in 1994 IOSCO created the Emerging Markets Committee. Initially a large and somewhat unfocused group, the Emerging Markets Committee has come to challenge the Technical Committee in importance and leadership. Early on, IOSCO (and separately, the SEC as well) undertook an educational role, by setting up training sessions for regulators from emerging markets as a means of initiating them into the arcane world of capital markets regulation. The participation in IOSCO by regulators and would be regulators from non-OECD countries has produced several distinct phenomena. For one thing, it has created a common language of securities regulation (as expressed in English) around the world.[13] This does not necessarily constitute regulatory harmonization, but does produce common understandings of market operation and regulatory approaches.

3.12 A less desirable by-product has sometimes been the overenthusiasm demonstrated by emerging market regulators in embracing developed market techniques. By participating in IOSCO meetings and committees, officials from emerging (and some quite emerged) markets pick up the lingo of securities regulation, and from talking the talk, go home to walk the walk. Sometimes with untoward consequences.[14] But as regulatory authorities recognizably modelled on the SEC, or the now defunct UK Financial Services Authority (FSA), have popped up around the world, new regulators have grown in experience, expertise, and the desire for voice.

3.13 This is a new dynamic at IOSCO; there has always been an educational dimension to its activities, with training sessions for fledgling regulators in developing economies being regularly offered. But now the Emerging Markets Committee is coming into its own, with leadership from heavyweight markets such as Malaysia and Turkey. As IOSCO evolves more and more into a policymaking and advisory body, if not an actual quasi-regulator, and market centres disperse beyond the transatlantic corridor, the balance of power at IOSCO could begin to tip. For example, the call for the creation of a separate IOSCO research foundation to undertake research and policymaking has come from the Emerging Markets Committee.[15] The national commissions of emerging market members, where resources and

---

[13] And not just as between OECD and non-OECD members, but across the divide of the English Channel as well.

[14] For example, prospectus disclosure is a fundamental tenet of securities regulation, but mandatory disclosure and prospectus requirements are balanced by various exemptive mechanisms in developed economies. However, the author has seen prospectus level disclosure imposed on issuance of commercial paper in some emerging markets. See World Bank, 'Capital Market Integration in the East African Community' (December 2002) <http://info.worldbank.org/etools/docs/library/83617/capmktsintegration.pdf> accessed 16 April 2013.

[15] OICV-IOSCO, 'IOSCO Emerging Markets Prepare for Bigger Role in the Global Economy' (Media Release IOSCO/MR/30/2012, 20 November 2012), 2 <http://www.iosco.org/news/pdf/IOSCONEWS258.pdf> accessed 15 April 2013.

expertise are scarce, are hampered by the current arrangements where reports are delegated to member commissions to prepare. Because of their resources, a handful of developed economies with large, well-staffed, regulators naturally take the lead and frame the issues. More and more, the demands being placed on IOSCO require it to act as a policymaker or even an OECD-style think tank, but IOSCO has not had the institutional structure to meet these expectations.

2.2.2 IOSCO as standard setter

Related to these issues is the role of IOSCO as a standard setter. IOSCO embarked on **3.14** this new direction in 1998 in the aftermath of the Asian financial crisis. The Technical Committee of IOSCO had for many years participated in the formulation of international accounting and auditing standards (now IFRS), but not as a standard setting body per se. The appearance of the Objectives and Principles of Securities Regulation in 1998 (the 1998 Objectives) was a significant moment in IOSCO's history. This was a new role, and one which was to rapidly transform the institution. The 1998 Objectives appeared in response to the Asian financial crisis of 1997–98 and the Securities and Futures Commission (SFC) in Hong Kong was a prime participant in the committee formulating them. At the time, the Hong Kong regulator was less than 10 years old, having been created in 1989 in the wake of the 1987 market correction (which now looks like a minor, albeit ominous, tremble in comparison to subsequent events). Hong Kong markets had, embarrassingly, closed for four days at that time and the SFC was born.[16]

As the situation in Hong Kong indicates, stand alone capital markets regulators were not an **3.15** established feature in the regulatory landscape around the world in the 1990s, particularly in Commonwealth countries which were using British institutional models. Thus, the 1998 Objectives provided a blueprint for the creation of North American style capital markets regulators. In tandem with the rise in interest in capital markets and their formal regulation in parts of Asia,[17] the break up of the former Soviet Union had created a large cluster of jurisdictions looking to reintroduce, and regulate, capital markets. The 1998 Objectives became the touchstone for these efforts. At the time of applying to IOSCO for membership, these newly minted regulators were required to conduct a self-assessment benchmarked against the 1998 Objectives.

Over time, IOSCO has produced numerous other sets of principles and standards, but the **3.16** 1998 Objectives are likely the best known and most influential.[18] The other sets of principles and standards, however, have been a decidedly mixed assortment of instruments. For example, contemporaneously with the 1998 Objectives (targeting emerging economies), there appeared International Disclosure Standards for Cross-Border Offerings and Initial

---

[16] Paul B McGuinness, *A Guide to the Equity Markets of Hong Kong* (Oxford University Press 1999), 50.

[17] As indicated by the presence of Indonesia and Korea in the creation of IOSCO in 1983, capital markets institutions and their regulators were not completely unknown in Asia, but where they did exist they were often a response to historical and geopolitical forces. For example, Korea's institutions (like Japan's) had been formed in the aftermath of war and defeat at the hands of the United States. Other jurisdictions, Hong Kong, Singapore, Malaysia, for example, had inherited stock exchanges and self-regulatory concepts as part of their British colonial legacy.

[18] For reasons which will be discussed, primarily IOSCO's use in the FSAP assessments. See also Pagliari (n 1), who argues that IOSCO's most significant achievements have been the promulgation of the 1998 Objectives and the establishment of the non-binding Multilateral Memorandum of Understanding Concerning Consultation and Cooperation and the Exchange of Information.

Listings by Foreign Issuers (the International Disclosure Standards). These standards are completely different from the 1998 Objectives; they target large multinational issuers and purport to provide 'a generally accepted body of non-financial statement disclosure standards that could be addressed in a single disclosure document to be used by foreign issuers in cross-border offerings and initial listings, subject to the host country review or approval processes'.[19]

3.17 The International Disclosure Standards attempt to create the bases for mutual or reciprocal recognition arrangements more generally, based on the experiences with bilateral arrangements such as the Multijurisdictional Disclosure System (MJDS) between Canada and the United States dating from 1991.[20] These standards run on for over 65 densely packed, single-spaced pages, full of technical detail. In fact, these standards are a thinly veiled exercise in US hegemony, being based on the Form 20-F,[21] the disclosure required by the US SEC for use by non-US issuers entering the United States. Rather disingenuously, Form 20-F was subsequently 'modified' to bring it into line with IOSCO International Disclosure Standards. Could this have been a public relations exercise on the part of the United States to demonstrate deference to international standards?

3.18 Interestingly enough, five years after their appearance, the IOSCO International Disclosure Standards were rolled into the EU Prospectus Directive, amid trenchant criticism from the Law Society of the United Kingdom. The International Disclosure Standards did not form the basis for relations among member states in the European Union, but EU regulators would recognize compliance with them by non-EU issuers for use in the European Union. English solicitors, generally, were critical of the Prospectus Directive to the extent it posed a threat to lucrative Euromarket activities centred in London, so their criticisms were somewhat self-serving; however, they did correctly identify the underlying assumptions of the International Disclosure Standards: they were based on the operation of US equity markets.[22] The UK solicitors noted the inappropriateness of these standards as applicable to the major international European market, the Eurobond market, and to debt securities. A common prospectus, or at least, a form of mutually recognized offering document, had been on the SEC agenda since at least 1985.[23] IOSCO again obligingly provided the instrumentality for this US policy initiative. In 2007, validating the UK criticisms, IOSCO produced the 'International Disclosure Principles for Cross-Border Offerings and Listings of *Debt* Securities by Foreign Issuers' (emphasis added).[24]

---

[19] International Organization of Securities Commissions, 'International Disclosure Standards for Cross-Border Offerings and Initial Listings by Foreign Issuers' (September 1998), 3 <http://www.sec.gov/about/offices/oia/oia_corpfin/crossborder.pdf> accessed 16 April 2013.

[20] Australia and New Zealand put in place a similar system based on the MJDS.

[21] See Ch 4 of this book for a further explanation of Form 20-F.

[22] The Law Society (UK), Representation and Law Reform, 'Proposal for a Directive on the Prospectus to be Published When Securities are Offered to the Public or Admitted to Trading' (Memorandum, No 422, July 2001).

[23] Securities and Exchange Commission, 'Facilitation of Multinational Securities Offerings' (28 February 1985) Securities Act Release No 6568.

[24] Technical Committee of the International Organization of Securities Commissions, 'International Disclosure Principles for Cross-Border Offerings and Listings of *Debt* Securities by Foreign Issuers', Final Report, March 2007 <http://www.iosco.org/library/pubdocs/pdf/IOSCOPD242.pdf> accessed 11 December 2013 (emphasis added).

IOSCO's role as a standard setter has thus been somewhat ad hoc. Certainly, the standards, **3.19** principles, and guidelines produced vary enormously. With the winds of the global financial crisis and the G20 behind it though, IOSCO went into high gear on standard setting. Since 2009, IOSCO has produced an astonishing array of guidelines and principles, published or in the pipeline: the supervision of financial conglomerates, periodic disclosure by listed entities, point-of-sale disclosure, activities of credit rating agencies, cross-border supervisory cooperation, direct electronic access to markets, financial market infrastructure, supervision of commodities derivatives markets, ongoing disclosure for asset backed securities, valuation of collective investment schemes, exchange traded funds, oil price reporting agencies, the list goes on.[25]

2.2.3 Interaction of IOSCO and International Financial Institutions (IFIs)

Although the IMF and The World Bank did not formally join IOSCO (as affiliate mem- **3.20** bers) until well after the Asian financial crisis, IOSCO's role as a standard setter caught the attention of these international financial institutions during the post-Asian crisis cleanup. In 1999, shortly after the first sets of IOSCO principles had appeared in 1998, the IMF and The World Bank were charged by the newly created FSF with a mandate to promote international financial standards and to act as standards assessors. This set the stage for the collaboration between formal treaty organizations, newly created 'policy networks', and IOSCO; it would set IOSCO on a new course which continues to this day.

The interaction did not begin smoothly. The 1998 Objectives were publicly available, of **3.21** course, but IOSCO felt somewhat proprietary about them. The 1998 Objectives had been developed by IOSCO for its own purposes as a tool for potential members, fellow regulators, and technocrats. The FSF rather arbitrarily plucked the 1998 Objectives out of cyberspace and charged the IMF and The World Bank to engage in country by country financial sector assessments making use of the 1998 Objectives as an assessment tool. To say that capital markets regulatory expertise at these international financial institutions was modest is an understatement; there was concern at the sometimes amateurish and inconsistent results which these assessments were churning out. IOSCO set about reclaiming the 1998 Objectives by producing detailed explanatory methodologies on their use.

IOSCO in this manner became entwined in the activities of the FSF, IMF, and World Bank **3.22** in carrying out their financial sector assessments. IOSCO was pulled into the new international financial policy network and its role as a standard setter affirmed.

3. International Financial Institutions and the Capital Markets

Like IOSCO, the roles of treaty-based international financial institutions have been chang- **3.23** ing over time; some changes have been politically driven (the break-up of the former Soviet Union, for example, or the economic rise of China); others, like the financial sector assessment programme, crises driven.

---

[25] See generally The International Organization of Securities Commissions, 'IOSCO Public Documents' <http://www.iosco.org/library/index.cfm?CurrentPage=1&section=pubdocs&criteria=none&year=none&rows=10> accessed 30 September 2013.

3.24 Treaty organizations such as the IMF, The World Bank and the regional development banks,[26] are pillars of the international financial architecture. But first and foremost, they are banks, engaged in sophisticated international borrowing and lending, in multiple capacities. In keeping with the shift to 'knowledge based' economies and the revolution in information technologies, they have also become 'knowledge banks',[27] collectors, mediators, and purveyors of information and 'technical assistance'. And, in the last decade or so, they have become financial assessors to the world, the creators and custodians of the scorecards on levels of financial development.

3.1 IFIs as International Financial Institutions

3.25 The treaty based international financial institutions (IFIs) have traditionally been structured as classic intermediaries, with a twist. Rather than borrowing low, lending higher and pocketing the difference (which they do), they also borrow low, and lend on a concession basis, with loans being forgiven over time. Their funding sources are contributions from their members and capital raising in the international debt markets, universally on an exempt basis and with the implicit guarantee of governments, big and small, around the world. Their credit ratings are impeccable, their costs of funding rock bottom, their debt securities in high demand, and their clients sovereign states.[28]

3.26 As the IFIs have historically engaged in funding physical infrastructure in borrowing countries, ancillary services such as project guarantees developed along with international project finance expertise. From lending to sovereigns, later activities expanded to include private equity-like investments and joint ventures in industry. As an equity investor, the International Finance Corporation (IFC, the sister organization to The World Bank) has proved to be a canny and profitable enterprise.[29]

3.27 The treasury operations of an international financial institution like The World Bank are sophisticated and innovative; as an issuer, The World Bank is usually on the cutting edge of international finance, well resourced and well advised. The Asian Development Bank was one of the first non-Chinese issuers to offer 'dim sum' bonds, denominated in mainland Chinese currency (RMB), in this nascent Hong Kong market. It was quickly followed a few months later by The World Bank. As treaty organizations, they are not subject to the strictures of national regulation on the one hand, but act in conformity with international practices and

---

[26] European Bank for Reconstruction and Development, Council of Europe Development Bank, Asian Development Bank, African Development Bank, Development Bank of Central African States, and the Inter-American Development Bank, for example.

[27] This concept was introduced in James D Wolfensohn, 'People and Development', Autumn Meeting Address, Washington, 1 October 1996.

[28] Which until the default by Argentina in 2001 were considered no risk borrowers.

[29] Standard and Poor's rating of the IFC notes that it 'recorded net income of US$1.3 billion in fiscal 2012, and US$1.5 billion before net losses on non-trading financial instruments; the latter measure represented a return on equity of more than 5% in each of the past 10 years except fiscal 2009 (in which IFC lost about 3.5%, by this measure)': Nikola G Swann, 'Ratings on International Finance Corporation Affirmed at "AAA/A-1+" on Criteria Revision; Outlook Stable', Standard and Poor's Research Update (27 December 2012), 3 <http://www.ifc.org/wps/wcm/connect/f4c0c6004cb890b58e88cff81ee631cc/S%26P+Dec+2012+Report. pdf?MOD=AJPERES> accessed 16 April 2013. The European Bank for Reconstruction and Development has similarly recorded consistent profits, recording a net profit of €173 million in the 2011 financial year, and an expected net profit of approximately €1 billion in 2012: Anthony Williams, 'EBRD Projects Hit Record High Level in 2012' (European Bank for Reconstruction and Development, 18 January 2013) <http://www.ebrd. com/pages/news/press/2013/130118a.shtml> accessed 16 April 2013.

investor expectations, on the other. For a fee, The World Bank treasury also provides admin-istrative and financial services to programmes in which sovereigns are providing funding. For example, The World Bank acts as a servicer, treasury manager, and swaps counterparty for the International Finance Facility for Immunisation (IFFIm) supporting the Global Alliance for Vaccines and Immunization (GAVI). By adapting innovative structured finance techniques from the private sector, IFFIm has been able to tap international capital markets through Luxembourg (in much the same way as The World Bank does on its own behalf), thereby frontloading funding to immunization programmes, to 70 of the poorest countries in the world. Bondholders in the Euromarket are ultimately repaid by payment streams originating in donor country grants staggered over a 20-year period. It has been estimated that five million child deaths and five million future adult deaths could be averted with the incremental fund-ing which IFFIm provides.[30] Good international finance for the international good.

3.2 IFIs as knowledge banks

Over the last 15 years, as the IFIs have moved away from financing physical infrastructure, **3.28** technical assistance became a more important element in their services. Technical assistance involves the provision of advice and information on a wide range of subjects, directly to gov-ernments or other local institutions. The smaller regional development banks rely primarily on outside consultants to provide advice and conduct studies on a country or regional basis whereas the larger institutions such as The World Bank and the IMF have large teams of in-house experts supported by impressive research departments.

Nevertheless, capital markets expertise was scarce on the ground. For one thing, financial **3.29** regulatory and legal expertise in this area is expensive, and its practitioners outside the main-stream of academic PhD economists and government officials who populate the IFIs. The IMF has traditionally been the realm of central banks and monetary policy experts, so even capital markets have been viewed from that perspective. On The World Bank/International Finance Corporation side, in the years leading up to the global financial crisis, capital markets and regulatory expertise was deliberately trimmed in favour of high profile, low level, data intensive exercises such as the annual Investment Climate Assessments or 'Doing Business' reports. Above all, the activities of the financial sector experts in these institutions have been virtually monopolized by the Financial Sector Assessment Program (FSAP) mandated by the Financial Stability Forum (FSF) and its successor, the FSB.

3.3 IFIs as international financial assessors

The newest, and probably the most problematic, role for the IMF and The World Bank has **3.30** been that of international financial system assessors. Two devastating international finan-cial crises in a decade forced national regulators and international financial institutions to consider how best to respond. It has been impossible to repress the urge for international approaches and solutions, looking to the creation of new international bodies to set and coordinate agendas, opening lines of communication with existing international organiza-tions (such as IOSCO), pulling together international standards to provide benchmarks and

---

[30] 'It is estimated by the World Health Organization that IFFIm's resources could lead to the vaccination of more than 500 million people over the next ten years, with the objective of preventing the deaths of 5 million children and 5 million adults . . .' IFFIm supporting Gavi, Global Debt Issuance Programme Prospectus dated 3 November 2006, 7.

putting in place an assessment system (in the absence of any enforcement mechanisms at the international level). It has certainly been a learning experience for those involved, beginning with the formation of the Financial Stability Forum (FSF) in 1999.

3.3.1 The role of the FSF and the FSAP

3.31 Chaos theory, as applied to financial systems, would suggest that crises, like hurricanes, are predictable. The question then is why so many were caught unawares by the global financial crisis of 2007 onwards. In particular, how and why did international financial institutions and their various initiatives fail to detect or prevent the financial contagion propagated through the international capital markets. Mechanisms to do so had been set in place a decade before with the creation of the FSF and the FSAP conducted by the IMF and The World Bank. The FSF had been created *specifically* to detect 'vulnerabilities' in financial systems and serve as an early warning system. However, the FSF was caught flat-footed.[31] This was despite the mass of information collected by the IMF and The World Bank pursuant to the FSF-mandated Financial Sector Assessment Program, the FSAP.

3.32 **The FSF and soft law**   The FSF was envisaged as a 'grouping of technocratic authorities with relevant expertise and experience'.[32] Representatives of central banks and ministries of finance met on a regular basis with a view to promoting convergence to minimum standards in the form of 'soft law', with compliance by force of example and moral suasion.[33] For the implementation phase, the IMF and The World Bank were recruited to carry out financial sector assessments on a country by country basis. The composition of the FSF is telling, central bankers, treasury officials, used to looking at systemic risk on an institutional basis, and not at the international capital markets as purveyors of that risk.

3.33 The global financial crisis, however, raised serious doubts as to the utility of these exercises and painfully highlighted the ineffectiveness of the FSF. As Arner and Taylor point out, the crisis put into question the international 'soft law' approach and the workings of 'policy networks'.[34] With the FSF, it was 'not at all clear what action will follow . . . or, indeed, who will act'.[35] Eatwell called the FSF a 'think tank with nowhere to go'.[36] Not only did the FSF toil in obscurity, it was 'invisible'.[37] The obscurity of the FSF, its private membership, may have detracted from its perceived legitimacy as well.[38]

---

[31] See Douglas W Arner and Michael W Taylor, 'The Global Financial Crisis and the Financial Stability Board: Hardening the Soft Law of International Financial Regulation' (2009) 32 *UNSW Law Journal* 488.

[32] Arner and Taylor (n 31), 491. See also Enrique R Carrasco, 'Crisis and Opportunity: How the Global Financial Crisis May Give Emerging Economies Greater Voice in International Finance via the Financial Stability Board', University of Iowa Legal Studies Research Paper No 09-43 (December 2009), 8–10 <http://papers.ssrn.com/sol3/papers.cfm?abstract_id=1477975&download=yes> accessed 16 April 2013.

[33] Arner and Taylor (n 31), 489.

[34] Arner and Taylor (n 31), 489.

[35] John Eatwell, 'The Challenges Facing International Financial Regulation', Western Economic Association International Conference, San Francisco, 4–8 July 2001, 14 <http://www.financialpolicy.org/DSCEatwell.pdf> accessed 16 April 2013.

[36] Eatwell (n 35).

[37] See Laura Barton, 'On the Money', *The Guardian* (London, 31 October 2008) <http://www.guardian.co.uk/business/2008/oct/31/creditcrunch-gillian-tett-financial-times> accessed 16 April 2013.

[38] See Regis Bismuth, 'The Independence of Domestic Financial Regulators: An Underestimated Structural Issue in International Financial Governance' (2010) 2 *Goettingen Journal of International Law* 93, 108 (arguing that the FSF and FSB approach amounts to a 'circumvention of national and regional democratic processes').

The invisibility of the FSF was related to its predilection for 'soft law' approaches. Lacking **3.34** the transparency and contestation[39] of the legislative process, soft law is easy. Everything happens behind the scenes, away from the glare of the press and the inconvenience of serious questioning. Consensus ruled and hard questions went unaddressed. The product of the soft law process often has an airy vagueness to it, lacking in the detail and sharp edges of legislation.

But even soft law has shown some arthritic symptoms. In theory, one of the advantages **3.35** of soft law is that it can be easily changed, responsive to fast moving events, given that it bypasses the time-consuming legislative process. But that has not necessarily been the case; path dependency operates on soft law as well as hard law, preserving less than optimal elements. The 1998 Objectives, as discussed in due course, have suffered this fate.[40]

The FSAP experience   Implementation of the FSF agenda focused primarily on the use of **3.36** the FSAP, the Financial Sector Assessments, conducted by the IMF in developed economies, and jointly by the IMF and The World Bank in developing economies. The mandate was to identify 'vulnerabilities' in financial systems, on a country by country basis, with a view to nipping financial crises in the bud. In particular, priority was to be given to systematically important countries. The FSF identified 12 international standards to be used in the process of 'benchmarking' or 'rating' a financial system.[41] The FSAPs produced a veritable gold mine of data over time.[42] Unfortunately, some of the data is of dubious reliability and quality, for a number of reasons. The international standards themselves are not all of the same calibre. Among the 12 international standards chosen by the FSF, there is overlap, duplication, and inconsistency. The methodology of the FSAP process was in a constant state of flux. The teams themselves conducting the FSAPs varied in expertise and sophistication. *Querelles de chapelle*[43] between the IMF and The World Bank teams were not unheard of.

Nevertheless, the data accumulated was impressive, but the difficulty was that it could not **3.37** be used in a narrow, scientific way, given its deficiencies. Rather, it needs a kind of qualitative interpretation which has not always been available. With hindsight though, some of the early FSAP observations appear spot on. Iceland was identified as vulnerable as far back as in 2002. The importance of supervision and risk assessment of large, complex financial institutions was also recognized early on. Difficulties with some of the standards, such as the 1998 Objectives were noted.[44] Given the volume of data and its variable quality, however, important observations may have been lost in the noise.

---

[39] See Arner and Taylor (n 31), 494.

[40] International Organization of Securities Commissions (May 2003) <www.iosco.org/library/pubdocs/pdf/IOSCOPD154.pdf> accessed 16 April 2013.

[41] See Financial Stability Board, 'Key Standards for Sound Financial Systems' <http://www.financialstabilityboard.org/cos/key_standards.htm> accessed 16 April 2013.

[42] This huge volume of data does not seem to find its way readily into the academic literature, although several people at the IMF, in particular, Jennifer Elliott, have laudably been publishing papers making use of the data. See eg Ana Carvajal and Jennifer Elliott, 'The Challenge of Enforcement in Securities Markets: Mission Impossible?', International Monetary Fund Working Paper No 09/168 <http://ssrn.com/abstract=1457591> accessed 16 April 2013.

[43] The expression translated from French as 'petty disputes', refers to pointless internal disputes and rivalries within an organization.

[44] They are not designed to identify systemic risk; rather they focus on investor protection and traditional structures of a securities regulatory regime.

3.38 **Inadequacies of the FSAP experience** Most importantly, the FSAPs were sometimes asking the wrong questions, failing to identify the operative initial conditions and the direction and magnitude of the perturbations to follow. Some international standards failed to differentiate among financial markets in different parts of the world, or to recognize the stratification of any one particular market. Financial markets, even internal domestic ones, are not monolithic. Most ironically, for standards billing themselves as 'international', many of the standards employed completely missed the international and cross-border aspects of financial markets. This was due to the fact that many of the so-called 'international' standards were simply reheated domestic regulation, which did not look to international dimensions of an issue, and the assessments themselves were conducted on a country by country basis.

3.39 **Problems with execution of the FSAP exercises** Both the IMF and The World Bank periodically engage in internal evaluations of their work product; the FSAPs, like other programmes, were subjected to critical internal scrutiny. In 2006, an evaluation of the FSAP program[45] by the IMF noted that there had been an improvement in the quality of execution but that the programme was at a 'critical crossroads'.[46]

3.40 Inconsistencies in execution and results persisted despite the introduction of detailed 'methodologies'. The quality of the data itself was not subject to rigorous enough scrutiny. One continuing problem was the 'parachute' approach; the IMF teams of experts, including The World Bank if involved, parachuted in and out of countries, never spending enough time to absorb country specific circumstances. Some analysis and 'ratings' indicated a 'check the box' mentality,[47] more egregiously manifesting itself in standardized advice being given, irrespective of the country involved.[48] In the words of the 2006 IMF evaluation, 'overly simplistic' messages were being conveyed with respect to the strength of the financial system in any one country. The evaluation called for more subtle interpretation of the results which could form the basis of 'health warnings'.

3.41 A more controversial aspect of the FSAP experience, and one which may account for the inconsistencies and variability of the results, focuses on the level of technical skills within the IMF (and The World Bank) to conduct the exercises. A former member of the executive boards of the IMF and The World Bank groups points to the 'various recent independent evaluations [that] have noticed the persistence of technical and organizational weaknesses that impair the IMF's ability to integrate macroeconomic and financial sector analyses, and to draw credible risk indications from them . . . Notwithstanding follow-up action from the IMF, the opinion remains today widespread that the technical skills of its economists are inadequate to understand the financial markets, and to appreciate how they interact with the real economy'.[49]

---

[45] David Goldsborough et al, *Evaluation Report: Financial Sector Assessment Program* (International Monetary Fund, 2006) <http://www.ieo-imf.org/ieo/files/completedevaluations/FSAP_Main_Report.pdf> accessed 16 April 2013. See also Jose Vinals and Penelope J Brook, 'The Financial Sector Assessment Program after Ten Years: Experiences and Reforms for the Next Decade' (International Monetary Fund and The World Bank, 28 August 2009) <http://www.imf.org/external/np/pp/eng/2009/082809B.pdf> accessed 16 April 2013.

[46] Goldsborough et al (n 45), 1.

[47] Goldsborough et al (n 45), 4 (referring to a ' "checklist" approach').

[48] A possibly apocryphal story circulated at one time that sometimes the same advice was given, country by country, without even a change in the name of the country.

[49] Biagio Bossone, 'The IMF, the US Subprime Crisis, and Global Financial Governance', *VoxEU* (3 Febuary 2009) <http://www.voxeu.org/index.php?q=node/2973> accessed 16 April 2013. Bossone cites several

One obvious difficulty with the technical proficiency of IMF (and World Bank) staff con- **3.42** ducting FSAPs was perhaps too obvious to merit mention in the critiques of the process. Financial regulation is law, and law of a particularly technical kind, strongly influenced by practitioners of the financial arts and massaged by political process.[50] In the area of capital markets regulation in particular, economists, for better or for worse, are conspicuously absent from the law-making processes. The IMF and The World Bank, on the other hand, are institutions bursting at the seams with economists. A few lawyers operate undercover, disguising themselves as financial or private sector specialists, and outside consultants who may incidentally (and, incidentally is the operative word here) have legal training, were brought in to participate in the FSAP exercises.[51]

However, within the IMF and The World Bank, the process and results of the FSAP exercises **3.43** remained dominated by an academic and somewhat 'econocentric' view of the financial world. Internal legal expertise was scarce (most of the financial sector legal expertise being concentrated in internal Treasury and co-financing operations). Despite the reams of advice dispensed as to regulatory reforms in the financial sector, one would be hard pressed to find more than a handful of staff in these institutions who would have actually read, much less fully understood, a comprehensive set of financial sector regulations, such as the US securities regulatory regime (which has served as model to innumerable reforms propagated around the world). There were several implications resulting from this paucity of legal expertise applied to financial sector initiatives at the IMF and The World Bank. Lawyers dominate the operation of many capital markets regulatory regimes around the world—as well as being responsible for creating them. Economists and lawyers often have difficulty communicating with one another, given the assumptions and confines of their intellectual and professional frameworks.

The other implication may be explanatory of the sometimes inept use to which international **3.44** standards have been put and the conclusions drawn from their application (the 'check the box' mentality observed by the independent evaluations of the FSAP process). Remember that the 1998 Objectives were not developed with the FSAP process in mind; they were originally developed by regulators (read lawyers), for use by other regulators (read lawyers) in the creation or critical self-assessment of regulatory regimes (read law). They were not designed for use by non-professionals and pre-date the FSAP exercises. In any event, in 2003, IOSCO created a detailed 'methodology' to accompany the 1998 Objectives, targeted largely to FSAP use.

The number of codes and standards used in the FSAP process has also been a problem. As **3.45** noted previously, the standards varied greatly in their origins and level of sophistication; they demonstrated overlap and inconsistencies. Inadequate integration of the results diminished

---

examples of IMF statements in 2007 which indicate obliviousness to the impending financial disaster: 'in the summer of 2007, the IMF staff indicated that in the United States "[c]ore commercial and investment banks are in a sound financial position, and systemic risks appear low".'

[50] It is notable that during the period leading up to the global financial crisis, The World Bank was winding down its Financial Sector Development Vice-Presidency. Some of the first professionals to go were those with legal training.

[51] World Bank and IMF legal departments are primarily service departments for the internal governance and operational activities of the institutions. In the last decade, efforts have been made to broaden the scope of activities at The World Bank, by the creation of various thematic groups with more specialized expertise, in addition to the groupings of lawyers organized by region.

their relevance. As the 'ratings' of countries on various standards began to circulate publicly, countries began 'gaming' the system, by enacting legislation or adopting measures that would 'tick the boxes' without necessarily being of any effect.[52]

3.46 As well, the voluntary nature of the FSAP process was problematic. Canada, that boy scout of the international world, was the first country to volunteer, some say to its chagrin.[53] However, as of the date of the 2006 IMF evaluation, 'some 20 to 25% of countries that are "systemically important" and/or have vulnerable financial systems—two key criteria endorsed by the IMF and The World Bank Boards—have not been assessed'.[54] As of 2006, four systemically important countries in particular stood out: Turkey, Indonesia, China, and most importantly of all, the United States.[55]

3.47 In reacting to criticism that it did not see the global financial crisis coming, the IMF identified the failure of the United States to volunteer for an FSAP as a major factor.[56] The United States, for its part, had justified its objections to participating in the FSAP, by invoking the heavy burden such an assessment would place 'on the scarce resources of the [IMF]'.[57]

3.48 It may seem curious that the United States, which in fact was a driving force behind many of the international standards (sometimes for ideological and political reasons)[58] and whose regulatory framework defined the content of the standards themselves,[59] for many years stubbornly resisted volunteering for a financial sector assessment. Putting aside tender concerns for the workload of IMF staff, was this hubris, a misguided conviction as to the stability and superiority of the US financial system? Was it a 'we have nothing to learn from anyone else' response? Rather, did it reflect awareness of the problems in the domestic financial regulatory structure, but the view that these problems could be dealt with domestically given the vast resources at the disposal of the United States? Was the US financial system considered too complex to tackle (and too big to fail)? Irrespective of the reasons, it is tragically ironic that the global financial crisis began as a failure in the domestic US regulatory structure, and one which, despite the inadequacies of the various benchmarks and standards at the disposal of the IMF, would undoubtedly have been flagged by an FSAP.[60]

---

[52] See Curtis J Milhaupt and Katharina Pistor, *Law and Capitalism: What Corporate Crises Reveal About Legal Systems and Economic Development Around the World* (Chicago University Press, 2008), 47–173. See also Cally Jordan, 'The Conundrum of Corporate Governance' (2005) 30 *Brooklyn Journal of International Law* 983 (discussing Germany's introduction of a voluntary code of corporate governance).

[53] Canada's financial system, the star of the global financial crisis, was assessed as being somewhat deficient when benchmarked against international standards.

[54] Goldsborough et al (n 45), 10.

[55] Turkey subsequently volunteered and the US finally permitted an FSAP to be conducted in the wake of the global financial crisis. In 2010 and 2011, Indonesia and China respectively also completed the FSAP.

[56] 'The Fund has also deflected criticism of its failure to predict the crisis. Because the United States refuses to be subject to an IMF Financial Sector Assessment Program (FSAP), Managing Director Strauss-Kahn argues, the Fund cannot be responsible for a lack of supervision. The FSAP is one of the IMF's main supervisory instruments, and it was not employed in the United States during the lead-up to the crisis': Laurie Glapa, 'The IMF Faces Post-Crisis Criticism', University of Iowa Center for International Finance and Development, 15 October 2009 <http://uicifd.blogspot.com/2009/10/imf-faces-post-crisis-criticism.html> accessed 16 April 2013.

[57] Bossone (n 49).

[58] Eg anti-money laundering (AML) and combating financing of terrorism (CFT).

[59] See eg International Organization of Securities Commissions, 'Objectives and Principles of Securities Regulation' (May 2003) <http://www.iosco.org/library/pubdocs/pdf/IOSCOPD154.pdf> accessed 13 January 2014.

[60] Arner and Taylor (n 31), 495 (stating that the FSAP process was not designed to deal with US domestic problems in a predictive fashion or otherwise).

The essentially domestic focus of the FSAP process had also been singled out for criticism. **3.49**
Although 'contagion' had been a marked phenomenon in the Asian financial crisis which led
to the creation of the FSF and FSAPs, this was not an issue which was addressed in adequate
manner by the FSAP process which ignored cross-border implications. As the 2006 IMF
evaluation diplomatically put it: 'Greater efforts by the IMF to distill common cross-country
messages from the various FSAP exercises would be welcome.'[61]

Finally, updating FSAPs, especially in view of the constantly evolving methodologies, was **3.50**
problematic. For any country, submitting to the highly intrusive, labour-intensive FSAP
process was a chore and a burden; for smaller countries, or those with limited resources,
handling the logistics involved in meeting the demands of large teams of financial experts,
was a brutally exhausting exercise. And, like Canada perhaps, there were countries which felt
they had been burned by the experience.

Problems with the substance of the FSAP exercise The difficulties associated with execu- **3.51**
tion of the FSAP programme were exacerbated by the substantive nature of some of the
international standards (putting aside for the moment International Financial Reporting
Standards and the BIS Capital Adequacy standards which have a long history behind them).
Some of the standards, unfortunately, swallowed whole the precepts of an influential but
misguided body of literature, usually referred to as the 'law and finance' literature, which was
subsequently widely criticized on both the law and finance sides.[62] As noted earlier, some
'international' standards are not international at all, but rather reheated domestic, often US
domestic, law. The weakness, in this case, is that such standards are riddled with the hidden
assumptions and deficiencies of their country of primary origin. And where that country of
origin is the United States, implementing such standards (as is the ultimate goal of the FSAP
exercise) may mean adopting inappropriate and suboptimal regulatory approaches.

For example, the 1998 Objectives, formulated in the shadow of the Asian financial crisis, **3.52**
are backward looking, taking as their point of departure the institutions and regulatory
framework of the United States, as it existed in the mid-1990s. At the time of their original
formulation, for example, Dick Grasso was still presiding over the New York Stock Exchange
and its open outcry trading floor.[63] The idea of a transatlantic merger of that venerable old
dame with a continental consolidated exchange, Euronext, would have been unthinkable.
Alternative trading systems and online trading were in their infancy and high frequency trading
a glint in the eye.

The 1998 Objectives, because they looked to the US markets and regulation of the 1990s, **3.53**
subsumed the hidden assumptions of the time and place, assumptions which are rarely explicitly acknowledged. First, there is the 1930s' emphasis on retail investors and equity trading.
Derivatives, of course, are not on the radar screen (for the most part, they do not come under the
SEC's authority) and debt markets virtually ignored (derivatives are usually structured as debt
instruments). The 'unregulated' or private placement markets (wherein hedge funds lurk) are

---

[61] Goldsborough et al (n 45), 5.
[62] The 'law and finance' literature is voluminous. See generally Holger Spamann, ' "Law and Finance"
Revisited' (1 February 2008), Harvard Law School John M Olin Center for Law, Economics, and Business
Discussion Paper No 12 <http://ssrn.com/abstract=1095526> accessed 16 April 2013.
[63] Predating his ignominious departure on governance issues which prompted the demutualization of the
venerable institution.

also ignored, having received perfunctory treatment in the 1930s legislative framework which still governs in the United States. Securities were still pieces of paper in the 1930s, and the US regulation continues to play catch up in terms of recognizing the implications of the electronic age. Faith in self-regulatory market institutions remained a deeply entrenched notion in the United States and the efficient market hypothesis (a theory now somewhat battered by the global financial crisis) formally acknowledged in US securities legislation.[64] Finally, US regulation is notoriously focused on domestic issues.

3.54   These features of US securities regulation shine through the 1998 Objectives. They are also the areas of weaknesses, in terms of where the global financial crisis exerted its greatest pressures. Utilising the 1998 Objectives, the FSAP process, even at the best of times, would only have detected these pressure points with difficulty.[65]

3.55   For many years there had been a somewhat puzzling reluctance on the part of IOSCO to seriously revisit the 1998 Objectives.[66] In the years between 1998 and 2010, there had been certainly enough experience with implementation and assessment (through self-assessments under the auspices of IOSCO itself as well as the FSAP process) to make the limitations of the 1998 Objectives obvious. But rather than reconsidering the substance in light of the recognition of new market conditions and regulatory approaches, there was fiddling at the

---

[64] See 15 USC § 77b(b) (2006) (*'Consideration of Promotion of Efficiency, Competition and Capital Formation*—Whenever pursuant to this title the Commission is engaged in rulemaking and is required to consider or determine whether an action is necessary or appropriate in the public interest, the Commission shall also consider, in addition to the protection of investors, whether the action will promote efficiency, competition, and capital formation').

[65] Although there is little doubt that other standards and assessments would have detected some of the greater institutional and regulatory weaknesses in the US banking system.

[66] In June 2010, IOSCO announced a major revision to the IOSCO Objectives and Principles of Securities Regulation, '... to incorporate eight new principles based on the lessons learned from the recent financial crisis and subsequent changes in the regulatory environment, which are designed to strengthen the global regulatory system against future crises. The eight new principles cover specific policy areas such as hedge funds, credit rating agencies and auditor independence and oversight, in addition to broader areas including monitoring, mitigating and managing systemic risk; regularly reviewing the *perimeter* of regulation and requiring that conflicts of interest and misalignment of incentives are avoided, eliminated, disclosed or otherwise managed', OICV-IOSCO, 'Global Securities Regulators Adopt New Principles and Increase Focus on Systemic Risk' (Media Release IOSCO/MR/10/2010, 10 June 2010) <http://www.iosco.org/news/pdf/IOSCONEWS188.pdf> accessed 16 April 2013.
The eight new principles are:

- 'Principle 6: The regulator should have or contribute to a process to monitor, mitigate and manage systemic risk, appropriate to its mandate;
- Principle 7: The regulator should have or contribute to a process to review the perimeter of regulation regularly;
- Principle 8: The regulator should seek to ensure that conflicts of interest and misalignment of incentives are avoided, eliminated, disclosed or otherwise managed;
- Principle 19: Auditors should be subject to adequate levels of oversight;
- Principle 20: Auditors should be independent of the issuing entity that they audit;
- Principle 22: Credit rating agencies should be subject to adequate levels of oversight. The regulatory system should ensure that credit rating agencies whose ratings are used for regulatory purposes are subject to registration and ongoing supervision;
- Principle 23: Other entities that offer investors analytical or evaluative services should be subject to oversight and regulation appropriate to the impact their activities have on the market or the degree to which the regulatory system relies on them; and
- Principle 28: Regulation should ensure that hedge funds and/or hedge funds managers/advisers are subject to appropriate oversight.'

margins, revisions to methodology. Revisions undertaken in 2008, according to IOSCO, were absolutely identical to 2003.[67]

Could it be that the reluctance to thoroughly revisit the 1998 Objectives derived in part from **3.56** the transformation of elements of their 'soft law' principles into hard law regulation, in country after country, in response to FSAP recommendations?[68] It would be somewhat embarrassing for the IMF and The World Bank teams to return to these countries, acknowledging perhaps that the 1998 Objectives were not optimal for these countries' markets.

On 10 June 2010, eight new principles 'based on the lessons learned from the financial **3.57** crisis and subsequent changes in the regulatory environment'[69] were added to the 1998 Objectives to become the 2010 IOSCO Objectives. However, the original 30 principles and their underlying assumptions are not revisited. Importantly, the eight new principles do recognize that the 'financial markets which IOSCO members regulate, *or may be exempt from regulation*, can be the mechanism by which risk is transferred within the financial system' (emphasis added).[70] Unregulated markets finally appear on the radar screen, and the markets themselves—not just institutions—are recognized as systemically important.

Criticism of the 1998 Objectives is not, in any way, to suggest that IOSCO itself has been **3.58** a flawed initiative. Quite to the contrary, IOSCO has been a resounding success. Its significance to international capital markets has been growing by leaps and bounds, and its members increasingly convinced of the importance of its mission.[71] IOSCO saw the crisis coming[72] and continues to produce topical and informed reports on a wide variety of timely issues, such as practices and requirements for asset-backed securities, exchange traded funds, collective investment schemes, and unregulated markets.[73]

Nevertheless, the original 30 principles of the 1998 IOSCO Objectives remain untouched. **3.59** IOSCO has been working around them, addressing significant issues in new initiatives and reports, as well as by the addition of the eight new principles. The assumptions underlying the eight new principles, however, are different; 'regulation' has dethroned both the 'efficient market' and 'self-regulation', thus creating certain internal tensions within the enlarged set of principles.[74] For example, the limitations of self-regulation in particular (one of the

---

[67] IOSCO admits that the Objectives were insufficient and that only rules of conduct were revised. Roberta Karmel, 'IOSCO's Response to the Financial Crisis', Brooklyn Law School, Legal Studies Paper No 268 (March 2012) <http://papers.ssrn.com/sol3/papers.cfm?abstract_id=2025115> accessed 23 January 2014.

[68] This is to say nothing of the 'country rankings' based on the FSAP exercises.

[69] OICV-IOSCO (n 66).

[70] OICV-IOSCO (n 66).

[71] Some academic commentary would disagree with this assertion on the basis that the political actors, eg the G20, now set IOSCO's agenda. See Pagliari (n 1).

[72] In May 2008, the Technical Committee of IOSCO had already published a report on the matter. See Technical Committee of the International Organization of Securities Commissions, 'Report on the Subprime Crisis', Final Report, OICV-IOSCO (May 2008) <http://www.iosco.org/library/pubdocs/pdf/IOSCOPD273.pdf> accessed 13 January 2014.

[73] The full range of current IOSCO initiatives may be consulted on the IOSCO home page: 'International Organization of Securities Commissions' <http://www.iosco.org> accessed 16 April 2013.

[74] See Technical Committee of the International Organization of Securities Commissions, 'Unregulated Financial Markets and Products', Final Report, OICV-IOSCO (2009), 3 <http://www.iosco.org/library/pubdocs/pdf/IOSCOPD301.pdf> accessed 13 January 2014 ('all systemically important financial markets and instruments should be subject to an appropriate degree of regulation and oversight, consistently applied and proportionate to their local and global significance'). The report acknowledges both the existence of the

1998 Objectives), are openly critiqued in the 2009 IOSCO Unregulated Markets study as 'typically voluntary and the standards lack regulatory status and consistent implementation. Moreover, neither the industry initiatives nor market discipline averted the deficiencies that contributed to the global financial crisis'.[75] Such candour is refreshing and bodes well for a more critical look at international standards.

3.60 But the updated 2010 IOSCO Objectives remain at the heart of the FSAP exercise, which brings us back to contagion and predictability. The FSF and the FSAPs did not address contagion issues. Neither did they predict the global financial crisis. They were asking the wrong questions, looking in the wrong directions, and, blinded by the glare of international standards, failed to appreciate the complexity and diversity of financial markets and the problems posed by their regulation.

3.3.2 Prospects for the FSB and FSAPs

3.61 In April 2009, the Group of Twenty (G-20) announced the creation of a successor institution to the FSF, the new FSB, housed at the Bank for International Settlements (BIS) headquarters in Basel, Switzerland. The immediate question is the extent to which the FSB can overcome the legacy of the FSF.

3.62 On the face of it, the FSB is attempting to address certain criticisms directed towards the FSF. Certainly it has made an effort to be visible to the public eye. Membership has been expanded to a larger number of countries so as to include China and Indonesia, two of the three holdouts in the 'systemically important' category of financial economies. The private club will no longer be quite so exclusive, or reclusive. There is a specific mandate to promote financial stability, but there is nothing new there. What is new, however, is that members have agreed to 'peer review' of their financial systems, overcoming the drawbacks to the voluntary FSAP process, at least with respect to members of the FSB.

3.63 It is early yet to judge how the FSB will succeed where the FSF failed. The FSB had a tentative start, working at the margins. Its first review under the new FSB Framework for Strengthening Adherence to International Standards was completed in March 2010, 'Thematic Review on Compensation'.[76] To consider the trivial political football of executive compensation as a priority in supporting financial stability in the midst of a global financial crisis is a bit like the band playing on as the Titanic sinks. The FSB though is a creation of the G20, so exquisitely sensitive to geopolitical winds.

3.64 It is likely, however, that the FSB must be modest in its own initiatives. Staffing is limited, with many being relatively short-term secondees, borrowed from other institutions. Its most important role may be to serve as a clearinghouse for the initiatives of others. Certainly, a document which the FSB prepared in June 2010, 'Ongoing and Recent Work Relevant to Sound Financial Systems',[77] could be an indication of this role. The document, over 90

---

unregulated markets, and their importance particularly to international markets; in fact, that unregulated markets are at the origins of the international capital markets as well as the complexity of the issues involved.

[75] Final Report, OICV-IOSCO (2009) (n 74), 5.

[76] See Financial Stability Board, 'Thematic Review on Compensation', Peer Review Report (30 March 2010) <http://www.financialstabilityboard.org/publications/r_100330a.pdf> accessed 16 April 2013.

[77] See Financial Stability Board, 'Ongoing and Recent Work Relevant to Sound Financial Systems: Cover Note by the Secretariat for the FSB Meeting on 14 June 2010' (10 June 2010) <http://www.financialstability-board.org/publications/on_1006.pdf> accessed 16 April 2013.

pages in length, is a very useful compilation, with contact names and responsible authorities, summarizing dozens of diverse initiatives ongoing around the world. The FSB is, in fact, a minor player in this work, viewed as a whole; the IMF and IOSCO feature prominently as responsible authorities with the heavy lifting left to them. In fact, the recent politicization at IOSCO and the orientation of its recent efforts arise from its new relationship with the FSB.

It would also not be surprising to find a central bank mentality pervading the institutional **3.65** culture of the FSB, given its proximity to BIS and the background of its leadership.[78] Capital markets and their regulation often do not fall within a central banker's purview, yet they propagated systemic risk on a transnational scale, this time round. Transmission of systemic risk through the global capital markets is what has made this financial crisis different.

The most notable legacy of the FSF, however, is the policy of the FSB to put continued faith **3.66** in the use of a particular set of international standards, with all their demonstrated drawbacks. However, developments elsewhere may be producing more nuanced, sophisticated standards, and fostering a more subtle application of them. The Chairman of the FSB, in addressing remarks in March 2010 to the Committee on Economic and Monetary Affairs of the European Parliament qualified the significance of international standards by declaring: 'ultimately [it is] national and regional legislatures, accountable to their voters, that must decide and implement reforms'.[79] Then Chairman Draghi may have been playing to his audience (the European Parliament, after all), but at the least is indicating awareness of the debates surrounding the undemocratic nature of the indiscriminate use of international standards.[80]

Another hopeful sign of a more nuanced approach to markets and standards is the *Review of* **3.67** *the Differentiated Nature and Scope of Financial Regulation—Key Issues and Recommendations*[81] published in January 2010 by yet another international association of international organizations—the Joint Forum composed of BIS, IOSCO, and IAIS. The Joint Forum, unlike the FSB, is an association of regulators—banking, capital markets, and insurance—with real life technical expertise. They understand the nuances of capital markets, institutions, and regulation, domestic and international.

If there can be any conclusions drawn at this point, it may be not to have unrealistic expecta- **3.68** tions of what may be accomplished by the FSB, and on the other hand, not to underestimate the nature and degree of change taking place.

---

[78] Recently the chairman of the FSB, and former Governor of the Bank of Canada, Mark Carney, criticized the Bank of England's Andy Haldane for his critique of the Basel III Rules that Mr Carney has championed: see Philip Aldrick, 'Carney Attack on Haldane Hints at Bank of England Rift', *The Telegraph* (London, 27 November 2012) <http://www.telegraph.co.uk/finance/economics/9705748/Carney-attack-on-Haldane-hints-at-Bank-of-England-rift.html> accessed 16 April 2013.

[79] Mario Draghi, 'Modernisation of the Global Financial Architecture—Global Financial Stability' (Committee on Economic and Monetary Affairs of the European Parliament, Brussels, 17 March 2010) <http://www.bis.org/review/r100318b.pdf> accessed 16 April 2013.

[80] See Bismuth (n 38), 94, 99–102, 105–8, 110 (discussing the bypassing of the democratic process resulting from adoption of international standards).

[81] See generally Basel Committee on Banking Supervision, *Review of the Differentiated Nature and Scope of Financial Regulation: Key Issues and Recommendations* (Bank for International Settlements, January 2010) <http://www.bis.org/publ/joint24.pdf> accessed 16 April 2013.

4. A Natural Experiment: the US FSAP and the 1998 IOSCO Objectives

3.69 The FSAP process, according to then Chairman Mario Draghi in his April 2009 speech announcing the creation of the FSB, would continue apace.[82] A few months later, in September 2009, the IMF and The World Bank, jointly,[83] published a 10-year review of the FSAP process, featuring some 'key' new approaches.[84] In addition, 'Early Warning Exercises' were to be conducted by The World Bank together with the IMF, which was announced at the FSB inaugural meeting in June 2009.[85] 'Procyclicality' is now the watchword of the day, that is, acting with a view to a 'system wide approach to financial stability and embed a macroprudential orientation to regulatory and supervisory frameworks'.[86] The goal is to induce a 'race to the top' in the 'implementation of international supervisory and regulatory standards'.[87] For example, the FSB announced a 'name and shame' programme to publish the names of 'non-cooperative jurisdictions' at the end of 2010.[88]

3.70 In May 2010, the US FSAP was made public. The United States had long resisted agreeing to an FSAP, but in the face of international pressure during the heat of the global financial crisis, did so. The US inspired 1998 IOSCO Objectives were included, as they usually are, in the assessment. Governments do not have to agree to publication of the full FSAP reports, but in this case, a commitment to transparency and ideological imperatives assured that they would be. The US FSAP provides an interesting check on the operation of international financial standards in the context of the FSAPs. How would the United States be graded against standards essentially of its own making?

3.71 First of all, the team (comprised of regulators or former regulators from Canada, the United Kingdom, and Germany) acknowledged that it was holding the United States to a higher standard. The methodology employed in the FSAP uses a five level rating system for each principle: FI (fully implemented); BI (broadly implemented); PI (partially implemented);

---

[82] Mario Draghi, 'Re-establishment of the FSF as the Financial Stability Board' (Summit of the Financial Stability Board, London, 2 April 2009) <http://www.financialstabilityboard.org/publications/r_090402.pdf> accessed on 13 January 2014. The IMF and The World Bank Boards published their latest review of the FSAP in September 2009. The IMF and The World Bank, in reviewing the FSAP process, decided that in order to facilitate the integration of the stability assessment done in the context of FSAPs into IMF surveillance and The World Bank's financial sector work, a key innovation introduced by this review was the option to conduct FSAP updates in smaller, more flexible modules, focused on either stability or development aspects: see Vinals and Brook (n 45), 22.

[83] A joint publication is in itself an indication of greater cooperation and communication between the IMF and The World Bank.

[84] See Vinals and Brook (n 45).

[85] In addition to the joint early warning exercises (EWEs) proposed by the FSB, the IMF is developing its own EWEs for large complex financial institutions (LCFIs). Significantly, the 'methodology builds on and will supplement current LCFI monitoring and analysis that is conducted through *bottom up* analysis of balance sheets' (emphasis in the original): see Financial Stability Board (n 77), 1, 33.

[86] Financial Stability Board, 'Report of the Financial Stability Forum on Addressing Procyclicality in the Financial System' (2 April 2009), 8 <http://www.financialstabilityboard.org/publications/r_0904a.pdf> accessed 16 April 2013.

[87] Financial Stability Board, 'Financial Stability Board Holds Inaugural Meeting in Basel' (Press Release, 27 June 2009) <http://www.financialstabilityboard.org/press/pr_090627.pdf> accessed 16 April 2013.

[88] See Financial Stability Board, 'FSB Launches Initiative to Promote Global Adherence to International Cooperation and Information Exchange Standards' (Press Release, 10 March 2010) <http://www.financialstabilityboard.org/press/pr_100310.pdf> accessed 16 April 2013.

NI (not implemented); and NA (not applicable). How did the United States score? Thirteen out of 29 principles rated were either BI or PI, which might be considered a C+ perhaps, or a low B.

The findings make for a fascinating read. The US capital markets regulatory framework was **3.72** marked by complexity and specialization, but missing the 'big picture'. Due to the complexity and fragmentation of the regulatory apparatus, there were gaps in coverage of a wide range of activities. The power of self-regulation of the industry permitted conflicts of interest, inadequate capitalization and underqualification on the part of the intermediaries to persist. Enforcement problems in certain industries appeared acute and a lack of regulation and transparency in certain sectors troubling.[89]

Authorities participating in the FSAP experience have a right of rebuttal, exercised in this **3.73** case. This too makes for interesting reading. There is no shortage of domestic criticism of US securities regulation,[90] but international criticism is another matter. US authorities provided a pugilistic response to the FSAP findings:

> The overall ratings in the Report, however, do not reflect the CFTC's and SEC's regulatory successes and, in some cases, suggest a misunderstanding of the U.S. regulatory system. Thus the Commissions strongly disagree with many of the ratings in the Report.... Further, the SEC believes that the Report's conclusions are seemingly at odds with those of investors from around the world, both large and small.... Judging by the degree of global investment in the U.S. market and taking into account the cost of capital in the United States, it would appear that those whose money is at stake view the U.S. regulatory system in a different, more positive light—even in light of recent regulatory failings.[91]

Take that, IMF.

5. Conclusion

Exploring international solutions to international problems may appear intuitive, but it is **3.74** not obvious. With crisis has come more suggestions for a formal international regulatory body; some have suggested the IMF take on the role,[92] or IOSCO as a super-supervisor. Another suggestion has been a European-style council of ministers sitting atop the IMF. 'Broader reform could be achieved by creating a ministerial body with decision-making powers not inside but above the [International Monetary] Fund. It would also be responsible for political supervision of the other international institutions, including The World Bank, the Financial Stability Board, and the World Trade Organisation.'[93] Such suggestions are a

---

[89] In particular, the lack of regulation of over-the-counter derivatives and the market share of untransparent trading in dark pools (estimated at 25% of US trading).

[90] See eg Cary Coglianese (ed), *Regulatory Breakdown: The Crisis of Confidence in US Regulation* (University of Pennsylvania Press, 2012).

[91] International Monetary Fund, 'United States: Publication of Financial Sector Assessment Program Documentation—Detailed Assessment of Implementation of the IOSCO Objectives and Principles of Securities Regulation', IMF Country Report No 10/125, May 2010, 26, 28 <http://www.imf.org/external/pubs/ft/scr/2010/cr10125.pdf> accessed 16 April 2013.

[92] See eg Rosa M Lastra, 'The Role of the IMF as a Global Financial Authority' (2011) 2 *European Yearbook of International Economic Law* 121.

[93] Timothy Adams and Arrigo Sadun, 'Global Economic Council Should Oversee All' *Financial Times* (London, 16 August 2009), 9.

variation on the 'World Financial Authority' idea floated several years ago by Eatwell and Taylor,[94] and recently called an 'unrealistic yet notorious—proposal'.[95] It is hard to escape the conclusion that promotion of simplistic, high level, 'solutions' to complex and deep-rooted structural problems in various parts of the global financial system is a futile search for quick fixes.[96]

3.75 The realities of regulatory and institutional response are defying such suggestions. The prospect of convergence of world regulatory regimes to internationally set standards, once considered inevitable, is now subject to serious questioning. Capital markets are crossing through a period of renationalization of regulation. As Karmel notes, national politics and regulatory responses are trumping longstanding efforts at harmonization.[97] 'Where national regulators perceive a strong national interest in a regulatory reaction to a problem in the capital markets, they go their own ways.'[98]

3.76 Consensus-based international standards coming out of IOSCO are too compromised, too ethereal to be of great use in the complex and technical world of capital markets regulation. In a recent speech in London, Greg Medcraft, the head of the Technical Committee and Chair of ASIC, the Australian regulator, downplayed consensus-based action and harmonization in favour of fostering mutual recognition principles, in the face of the diversity of regulatory approaches.

3.77 Karmel considers that IOSCO does not have enough clout to deliver on its agenda (which, in any event, is now politically determined by the G20 acting through the FSB), an observation shared by Pagliari.[99] A decade or two ago, with the US domination of the Technical Committee of IOSCO, US hegemony (and harmonization to its norms) seemed assured. IOSCO, though, has lost its identity as an 'epistemic community', united by similarities of professional training, technical expertise, and like-mindedness.[100] As Karmel notes, issues and initiatives driven by the US domestic agenda are failing to rise to the international level at IOSCO in the same manner as they have in the past; IOSCO members question their relevance. Equally, approaches endorsed by IOSCO are failing to take hold at the national level.[101] 'Will IOSCO, as an international body, be able to generate

---

[94] See John Eatwell and Lance Taylor, 'A World Financial Authority' in John Eatwell and Lance Taylor (eds), *International Capital Markets: Systems in Transition* (Oxford University Press, 2002).

[95] Bismuth (n 38), 108–9.

[96] 'Admittedly, the G20 has entrusted the Financial Stability Board with the mission of monitoring the standard-setting activity and has mandated the Basel Committee, IOSCO and the IAIS (among others) with the task of developing new rules. However, this choice seems more a quick-fix than a sustainable strategy. It will neither preserve state unity on the international stage, nor solve the issues of circumvention of national and regional democratic processes.' Bismuth (n 38), 108.

[97] See Roberta S Karmel, 'IOSCO's Response to the Financial Crisis' (2012) 37 *Journal of Corporation Law* 849.

[98] Karmel (n 97), 883.

[99] Karmel (n 97), 901; See also Pagliari (n 1).

[100] See Pagliari (n 1).

[101] For example, high frequency transactions are a problem that emerged in the United States and are therefore of little current relevance to most IOSCO members. Nonetheless, such transactions are now the subject of IOSCO's Consultation Report on Regulatory Issues Raised by the Impact of Technological Changes on Market Integrity and Efficiency, a report issued at the behest of the G-20: Karmel (n 97), 897. The disparity between international and national policies for securities regulation is evidenced by the divergence between EU and IOSCO policy for the regulation of 'short selling'. Whereas IOSCO's proposed reforms sought to limit political pressure for absolute bans on short-selling, a number of EU states have reinstituted such bans: Karmel (n 97), 880. Similarly, the European Union and the United States have introduced detailed provisions for the

reforms that the SEC, CFTC, and other national regulators are unwilling or unprepared to undertake?'[102]

Some see IOSCO acting as the technical mouthpiece of political actors in the G20, and, despite the quantity of reports and initiatives being undertaken, a body which is no longer setting its own agenda.[103] But this is perhaps too negative a view, and one which assumes the necessity of convergence and international harmonization. If there are different views within IOSCO, if national regulators are not meekly copying international standards or taking on board IOSCO recommendations holus bolus, IOSCO still serves a valuable role. It is a repository of technical expertise (which is in short supply at the international financial institutions such as the IMF or The World Bank) and a public forum of immense importance. **3.78**

In the process, some sacred cows of capital markets are receiving a goring. Efficiency appears to be taking a back seat to regulation: the goal is 'improving the functioning, integrity and oversight' of the markets.[104] 'All systemically important financial markets and instruments should be subject to an appropriate degree of regulation and oversight, consistently applied and proportionate to their local and global significance.'[105] **3.79**

In particular, IOSCO is undergoing a marked transformation, on several fronts. Its members are now convinced of the significance of its role and prepared to devote more resources. There is a new operating structure being put in place, including a research function. Although the resource base of the organization, its national regulators, operate at a national level, there is less emphasis being placed on simply aggregating national experiences and more on developing a global perspective. Rather than focusing on systemic risk in the context of institutions (the Basel approach), IOSCO will be looking at how international markets disperse risk.[106] **3.80**

The financial industry too seems prepared to welcome an approach which is less reliant on top-down, assumption-ridden, one-size-fits-all international standards. Speaking in the *Financial Times*,[107] Jim O'Neill, chief economist at Goldman Sachs stated: **3.81**

> When everyone is suffering from what appears to be the same shock, the desire to implement a co-ordinated response is high, and because of that desire, the ability is stronger. When everyone is starting to recover, the desire to co-ordinate is inevitably lessened, and as a result it will be more difficult. Luckily, this is probably a good thing.... G20 members and their leaders have been very wise in the past 12 months. The G20 creation itself is a fantastic development. But let's not require it always to have its members do the same thing at the same time.

regulation of rating agencies, which extend to such agencies' internal procedures, the number and expertise of their staff and the composition of their supervisory boards. Such reforms diverge significantly from the 'principle-based nature' of IOSCO's Code of Conduct for Rating Agencies (Pagliari (n 1)).

[102] Karmel (n 97), 900.

[103] Pagliari (n 1).

[104] Technical Committee of the International Organization of Securities Commissions, 'Unregulated Financial Markets and Products' (September 2009) Final Report, 5 (n 74).

[105] Technical Committee of the International Organization of Securities Commissions, 'Unregulated Financial Markets and Products' (September 2009) Final Report, 3 (n 74).

[106] See OICV-IOSCO (n 66).

[107] Jim O'Neill, 'No Need for an Orderly Queue to Exit', *Financial Times* (London, 18 September 2009) <www.ft.com/cms/s/0/84ab191e-a3d3-11de-9fed-00144feabdc0.html> accessed 16 April 2013.

PART II

THE TRANSATLANTIC DIALOGUE

4

THE PARALLEL SYSTEM—THE UNITED STATES

1. Introduction

In the 1930s, by creating a regulator—the Securities and Exchange Commission (SEC)[1]—and a **4.01** separate body of regulation applicable to capital market transactions, intermediaries and institutions,[2] the United States can claim to have invented securities regulation. This is not to say that the issues dealt with by the SEC are unknown or unregulated elsewhere (although that may be the case). Neither is the US securities regulatory regime all-encompassing; by the standards of modern finance, there are some startling lacunae.[3] As broadly as the term 'security' is defined by the statutes and interpreted by the courts,[4] it does not include a wide range of financial products which are regulated elsewhere, or not at all.[5]

---

[1] The Securities and Exchange Commission (SEC) is based in Washington, DC. Prior to the 1929 stock market crash, trade in securities had been regulated through various state laws and internal control systems on Wall Street, both of which came to be perceived as inadequate in the wake of the crash: Anne M Khademian, 'The Securities and Exchange Commission: A Small Regulatory Agency with a Gargantuan Challenge' (2003) 62 *Public Administration Review* 515, 516. A package of economic reforms, known as the New Deal, sought to respond to this crisis by centralizing power over fiscal policy in the Federal Government: Michael Walsh, 'The Great Depression, the New Deal and the American Legal Order' (1983) 59 *Washington Law Review* 723. As a component of these reforms, the SEC was symbolically situated in Washington. During World War II, securities regulation was de-prioritized, and, consequently, in 1942 the SEC was moved to Philadelphia. The SEC returned to Washington in 1948, three years after the war had ended. Norman S Poser, 'Why the SEC Failed: Regulators Against Regulation' (2008) 3 *Brooklyn Journal of Corporate Finance and Commercial Law* 292.

[2] As distinct from corporate or companies law.

[3] Most derivative products, for example.

[4] 15 USC § 77b(a)(1) (2006): 'The term "security" means any note, stock, treasury stock, security future, security-based swap, bond, debenture, evidence of indebtedness, certificate of interest or participation in any profit-sharing agreement, collateral-trust certificate, preorganization certificate or subscription, transferable share, investment contract, voting-trust certificate, certificate of deposit for a security, fractional undivided interest in oil, gas, or other mineral rights, any put, call, straddle, option, or privilege on any security, certificate of deposit, or group or index of securities (including any interest therein or based on the value thereof), or any put, call, straddle, option, or privilege entered into on a national securities exchange relating to foreign currency, or, in general, any interest or instrument commonly known as a "security", or any certificate of interest or participation in, temporary or interim certificate for, receipt for, guarantee of, or warrant or right to subscribe to or purchase, any of the foregoing.' See also 15 USC § 78c(a)(1) (2006). The definitions of securities in the US 1933 Act and US 1934 Act are taken to be coextensive: *Reves v Ernst & Young* 494 US 56, 61 (1990). For a discussion of the differences between the definitions adopted in federal legislation and the Uniform Commercial Code, see Lynn A Soukup, 'Securities Law and the UCC: When Godzilla Meets Bambi' (2005) 38 *Uniform Commercial Code Law Journal* 3, 5–12.

[5] Barbara Black, 'Staff Report on MF Global Failure Reopens Debate on SEC-CFTC Merger', Securities Law Prof Blog (15 November 2012) <http://lawprofessors.typepad.com/securities/2012/11/staff-report-on-mf-global-failure-reopens-debate-on-sec-cftc-merger.html> accessed 22 April 2013, citing Randy Neugebauer,

4.02   Nevertheless, by looking at the regulation of capital markets from the perspective of the investor and market institutions and participants (rather than as a matter of companies law), the United States re-characterized the regulation of capital markets. The suite of legislative acts, undertaken in the midst of the Great Depression of the 1930s,[6] has provided the framework on which modern securities regulation has been constructed. Later statutes, responsive to subsequent developments, were bolted on to this 1930s framework and until recently, when the pace of legislative change decidedly accelerated, legislative action was remarkably restrained.[7]

4.03   Securities regulation is aptly named; the law grew by regulatory action through concept releases, no-action letters, administrative rule-making, with somewhat limited judicial intervention (much of dispute resolution now taking place in arbitral fora).

4.04   This is old legislation, creaky and archaic, dating back to the desperate 1930s. A reform initiative begun in 1998, dubbed 'the Aircraft Carrier' for its ambitious scope and comprehensiveness,[8] sank in ignominy a few years later in the face of corporate scandals demanding more immediate attention. Given the decades of accretion and the volume of regulatory action, it is complex and hard to manipulate (reinforcing the entrenched position of those professionals knowledgeable in its ways).

4.05   But unlike other areas of the law, where legislative and regulatory accretion is the source of complexity, the US legislation has been arcane since its very beginnings. One description of the drafters of the key statute, the US Securities Act of 1933 (US 1933 Act), is telling: each 'was brilliant, and from the statute they created it is apparent that they delighted in mental challenges involving interwoven complexities and neatly hidden traps.... The [1933] Act is a masterpiece, an intellectual tour de force.... [W]hen one works with the Securities Act,

---

'Staff Report', 112th Congress, Washington, 15 November 2012 <http://lawprofessors.typepad.com/files/mfglobalstaffreport1115121.pdf> accessed 22 April 2013. 'The staff report prepared for the House Subcommittee on Oversight & Investigations, Committee on Financial Services, investigating the collapse of MF Global was released today. (Download MFGlobalStaffReport111512[1])....In addition, the report reopens the perennial debate over whether the SEC and CFTC should be merged. It finds that "The SEC and the CFTC Failed to Share Critical Information about MF Global with One Another, Leaving Each Regulator with an Incomplete Understanding." It recommends: "The apparent inability of these agencies to coordinate their regulatory oversight efforts or to share vital information with one another, coupled with the reality that futures products, markets and market participants have converged, compel the Subcommittee to recommend that Congress explore whether customers and investors would be better served if the SEC and the CFTC streamline their operations or merge into a single financial regulatory agency that would have oversight of capital markets as a whole."'

   [6]   Those Acts that are still in force are: the Securities Act of 1933, 15 USC §§ 77a–77aa (2006); the Securites Exchange Act of 1934, 15 USC §§ 78a–78pp (2006); the Trust Indenture Act of 1939, 15 USC §§ 77aaa–77bbbb (2006); the Investment Company Act of 1940, 15 USC §§ 80a-1–80a-64 (2006); the Investment Advisers Act of 1940, 15 USC §§ 80b-1–80b-21 (2006); the latter two statutes originally being enacted in 1939.

   [7]   Prior to the enactment of the Sarbanes-Oxley Act of 2002, 15 USC §§ 7201–66 (2006) originally enacted in 2002, the Dodd-Frank Wall Street Reform and Consumer Protection Act, Pub L No 111-203, 124 Stat 1376 (2010) and the Jumpstart Our Business Startups Act, Pub L No 112-106, 126 Stat 306 (2012) (JOBS Act), the major instances of legislative reform were the Williams Act Pub L No 90-439, 82 Stat 455 (1968); Securities Acts Amendments, Pub L No 88-467, 78 Stat 565 (1964); Foreign Corrupt Practices Act, Pub L No 95-213, 91 Stat 1494 (1977); Insider Trading Sanctions Act, Pub L No 98-376, 98 Stat 1264 (1984); Insider Trading and Securities Fraud Enforcement Act, Pub L No 100-704, 102 Stat 4677 (1988); Securities Litigation Uniform Standards Act, Pub L No 105-353, 112 Stat 3227 (1998); Private Securities Litigation Reform Act, Pub L No 104-67, 109 Stat 737 (1995).

   [8]   Keith M Moskowitz, 'Clear the Decks: The SEC's "aircraft carrier" Proposes Sweeping Reforms' (American Bar Association Business Law Section, July/August 1999) <http://apps.americanbar.org/buslaw/blt/8-6clear.html> accessed 29 September 2013.

one plays a complex mental game devised by three exceptional minds, over a weekend, more than half a century ago.'[9] Although 'not conceptually difficult in the way that, say, quantum physics is',[10] the legislation is a 'puzzle',[11] akin to a Houdini illusion.[12]

Oddly perhaps, the challenging nature of the legislation has been a key to its longevity. Any **4.06** tinkering with the trapdoors and hidden mirrors risks producing unintended (and perhaps deadly) consequences for the markets, so legislators tend to leave it alone. But if complexity is a drawback to the legislation, consistency is a virtue. Although there is duplication and overlap, for example in definitional sections,[13] written legislation and regulations demonstrate near Germanic rigour with respect to internal consistency. And concepts, once introduced, are redeployed in new regulatory initiatives, tightening the regulatory web and enriching the body of interpretation.[14] A great deal of effort is put into making the pieces of the puzzle fit and providing, for those with patience and perseverance, answers to potential questions.

US securities law is also highly idiosyncratic, very much a product of its time and its place, **4.07** with an intense domestic focus.[15] Yet, the US regulatory regime has been extremely influential internationally, serving as a model to dozens of countries as well as international standard setters.[16] US regulators and practitioners have been active proselytizers, for a complex set of reasons, ideological and geopolitical, extending well beyond the bounds of US investor protection.[17] International engagement by a US regulator is always a tricky endeavour, given protectionist and other parochial winds blowing at home; however, one argument

---

[9] Larry Soderquist and Theresa Gabaldon, *Securities Law* (4th edn, West Academic Publishing, 2011), 12–13. 'Part of the probably apocryphal lore of securities law is that the Act was drafted not only over a weekend, but over a case of Scotch', 12.

[10] Gabaldon (n 9), 1.

[11] Gabaldon (n 9), 1.

[12] Gabaldon (n 9), 1.

[13] For example, the definitions of 'foreign private issuer' under the rules of the US 1933 Act and US 1934 Act overlap: cf General Rules and Regulations, Securities Exchange Act of 1934, 17 CFR § 240.3b-4(c); General Rules and Regulations, Securities Act of 1933, 17 CFR § 230.405. Similarly, the definition of 'security' adopted in the US 1933 Act and the US 1934 Act overlaps: see discussion (n 4).

[14] For example, the use of the information reporting exemption in 17 CFR § 240.12g3-2(b) satisfies the information requirement of 17 CFR § 230; the concept of primary trading market as constituting 55% of trading is used to prescribe exemptions for registering securities for private issuers (see 17 CFR 240.12g3-2(b)(ii)) and also appears to assist in calculating the percentage of outstanding securities held by US residents (see 17 CFR 230.800(h)).

[15] In teaching the Sarbanes-Oxley legislation, the author shows one of the various documentaries on the collapse of Enron and WorldCom and then has students cross-reference specific statutory provisions to the personalities appearing on the screen; eg the 'Ken Lay provision'—section 302, which requires chief executive officers and chief financial officers to certify the accuracy of corporate financial statements; Ken Lay had said he didn't know Enron was about to collapse.

[16] The International Disclosure Standards for Cross-Border Offerings and Initial Listings by Foreign Issuers, for example is closely modelled on the US Form 20-F: see Technical Committee of the International Organization of Securities Commissions (September 1998) <http://www.iosco.org/library/pubdocs/pdf/IOSCOPD81.pdf> accessed 2 October 2013. This phenomenon also raises the obvious question as to the appropriateness of large economy legislation operating in small economies, for example, and the so-called transplant effect: see eg Daniel Berkowitz, Katharina Pistor, and Jean-Francois Richard, 'The Transplant Effect' (2003) 51 *American Journal of Comparative Law* 163; Katharina Pistor et al, 'Evolution of Corporate Law and the Transplant Effect: Lessons from Six Countries' (2003) 18 *World Bank Research Observations* 89; Daniel Berkowitz, Katharina Pistor, and Jean-Francois Richard, 'Economic Development, Legality and the Transplant Effect' (2003) 47 *European Economic Review* 165.

[17] The SEC runs a 'summer school' for developing economy regulators and has often taken a lead role in IOSCO. See Edward F Greene and Linda C Quinn, 'Building on the International Convergence of the Global Markets: A Model for Securities Law Reform' (A Major Issues Conference: Securities Regulation in the Global Economy, Washington DC, 14–15 November 2001):

supporting such engagement has been its utility in promoting US hegemony and supporting the spread of US regulatory techniques.[18]

4.08 International engagement raises one set of issues; providing accommodations in the United States, on home ground to non-US interests, raises another, especially that of the 'level playing field'. Often argued in the context of trade issues as 'national treatment' (which, in fact, may produce prejudicial and discriminatory effects for non-US parties), the level playing field is also trotted out when reforms to capital markets regulation are under consideration.[19] Nevertheless, there is a long history of domestic US accommodations to non-US interests engaging in international capital markets activities. But before turning to these accommodations, and the major international initiatives of the United States, it is necessary to investigate a few pieces of the puzzle in closer detail.

2. Some Basic Concepts in US Securities Regulation

4.09 Legislative and regulatory instruments provide a framework for the operation of capital markets in the United States, but they are not the whole story. Traditional self-regulatory organizations, such as the Financial Industry Regulatory Authority (FINRA),[20] and the stock exchanges, which predate the formal regulatory regime, continue to play an important role. Both the self-regulatory industry associations and the exchanges have been evolving rapidly in response to enormous pressures exerted by technology, changing market structures, scandal and crises.[21] However, legislation—in particular, the US 1933 Act and the US Securities Exchange Act of 1934 (US 1934 Act)—continue to dominate the regulatory landscape.

2.1 The keystone statutes and their regulations

4.10 Although there is a large body of legislation and regulation which does not directly emanate from the US 1933 Act and the US 1934 Act, these two statutes and the concepts which they introduced remain central to US securities regulation. Generally speaking, the US 1933 Act governs the primary markets; the US 1934 Act, the secondary markets. They differ markedly in scope and substance; the US 1933 Act retains much of its original structure

---

'Widespread foreign issuer participation in the US market:

- offers American investors the broadest scope of investment opportunities without foregoing the protection of US laws, as well as the efficiencies and cost benefits of transacting in their home market; American investors who want to invest in foreign companies' securities should not be relegated to offshore secondary markets;
- enhances the competitiveness of the US exchanges and Nasdaq;
- provides a market platform to support the competitive strength of American industry;
- allows the SEC more direct oversight of onshore transactions involving US investors;
- exports American investor protection and disclosure principles and procedures abroad; and
- assures the continued preeminence of the US market, which enhances the SEC's leadership role in developing international disclosure, accounting, auditing and governance standards.'

[18] Greene and Quinn (n 17).

[19] Eg the registration of broker-dealers and the long dispute with the European Union on the placement of European trading screens in the United States.

[20] The Financial Industry Regulatory Authority (FINRA) was born from the consolidation of the National Association of Securities Dealers and the regulatory arm of the New York Stock Exchange in 2007.

[21] For a discussion of self-regulation and the direction in which market institutions are heading, see Cally Jordan and Pamela Hughes, 'Which Way for Market Institutions: The Fundamental Question of Self-Regulation' (2007) 4 *Berkeley Business Law Journal* 205.

whereas the US 1934 Act has become a repository for a variety of miscellaneous regulatory developments. The two statutes, and the regimes they create, co-exist in a state of dynamic interaction.

The US 1933 Act is narrowly focused on the public offering process, initial and subsequent; **4.11** it established the principle that every offer or sale of securities must be accompanied by registration[22] unless an exemption exists. Therein lies the problem of the US 1933 Act—all is caught unless exempted and it has proven quite difficult to delineate the circumstances in which an exemption is available.[23] Although neatly characterized as exemptions based on the nature of the securities on offer (section 3) and the nature of the transaction (section 4), there is, in fact, overlap and some blurring of this tidy distinction. For purposes of greater certainty, in 1982 some regulatory assistance was provided in the form of Regulation D,[24] compliance with which provides a 'safe harbour' from the untoward consequences of getting it wrong by targeting, but missing, an exemptive provision.

The US 1934 Act, as its title suggests, governs the old-fashioned stock exchange in the **4.12** United States, adding a layer of formal regulation to a very old self-regulatory institution. Regulation under the US 1934 Act addresses as well the new variants that electronic trading has thrown up. But the US 1934 Act covers much more. The intermediaries in the markets (registered broker-dealers), acting in their various capacities, are governed by the US 1934 Act, in addition to their self-regulatory industry association, FINRA. From the perspective of reporting issuers,[25] the US 1934 Act imposes ongoing informational requirements, triggered primarily by a listing of securities on an exchange or a public offering conducted under the US 1933 Act. Originally, the US 1934 Act did not extend much beyond these areas; but, over time, as new legislation appeared and required implementation, many enactments found themselves wedged into the US 1934 Act.

In particular, the US 1934 Act could also be called the source of federal corporate law. In the **4.13** United States, corporate law is usually a state matter and there is no national corporations legislation as such. However, there is no constitutional impediment to Congress enacting

---

[22] Of a package of information documents to be made publicly available (including the primary selling document, the prospectus).

[23] The JOBS Act is designed, in part, to address some of the difficulties associated with the all-encompassing application of the registration requirements of section 5 of the US 1933 Act by making a distinction between offer and sale.

[24] Introduced in 1982 and composed of eight rules which provide a variety of brightline tests designed to ensure compliance with the exemptive provisions of the US 1933 Act, Regulation D contains three substantive exemptions. Rule 504 applies to the offer or sale of securities not exceeding US$1,000,000 by a non-reporting company. Those securities need not be registered if: the sale is made in a state that requires registration of those securities and the public filing and delivery to investors of disclosure documents; if the registration and sale occur in a state that requires disclosure and delivery; or if the sale complies with the applicable state law. Rule 505 establishes an exemption to registration for the offer or sale of securities not exceeding US$5,000,000 by a non-reporting company. Those securities need not be registered for sales up to 35 'unaccredited investors' and an unlimited amount of accredited investors. The exemption to registration provided under Rule 506 applies to the offer or sale of securities of any dollar value. In this case, sales may be made to an unlimited number of accredited investors or up to 35 'sophisticated' unaccredited investors. The JOBS Act introduced a new Rule 506(c), under which issuers can offer securities through means of general solicitation, provided that they satisfy all of the conditions of the exemption; eg the issuer must take reasonable steps to verify that the purchasers of the securities are accredited investors.

[25] TAs noted above, there are also informational requirements imposed on non-reporting issuers in certain circumstances.

federal corporate law.[26] There is simply a convention called 'the internal affairs doctrine' under which the federal Congress usually leaves the 'internal affairs' of corporations, mostly corporate governance issues, to state legislation. However, when lead states, like Delaware, do not appear to respond appropriately to shareholder concerns, or as with Sarbanes-Oxley, political pressures mount in the wake of costly corporate scandals, Congress does act.

4.14 In the absence of a federal corporate law, this essentially 'corporate' legislation is re-characterized as securities law and tucked into the US 1934 Act. Thus the US 1934 Act contains provisions on shareholders voting by proxy at annual meetings, procedures relating to treatment of shareholders during corporate changes of control in the form of tender offers (the US terminology) or takeover bids (as they are known in the Commonwealth), insider reporting and executive compensation. And, with enactment of Sarbanes-Oxley in 2002, many of its corporate governance provisions naturally found a home in the US 1934 Act.

4.15 Registration and a public offering under the US 1933 Act triggers compliance with the US 1934 Act.[27] The issuer registrant, domestic or foreign, becomes a 'reporting issuer', subject to the full brunt of the ongoing informational and other obligations imposed by the US 1934 Act, in particular annual audited financial statements.[28] Certain non-US reporting issuers receive the benefit of a somewhat less onerous regime (see further discussion), and, as a somewhat happy consequence of the global financial crisis, since 2008 may use International Financial Reporting Standards (IFRS) rather than US GAAP or financial statements reconciled to US GAAP.[29]

4.16 The information provided by both reporting and non-reporting issuers[30] under the US 1934 Act then feeds back into the US 1933 Act through the process of 'incorporation by reference', among other things. The introduction of incorporation by reference in 1978, linking the informational requirements of the US 1933 Act and US 1934 Act for purposes of participation in both primary and secondary markets, has been called 'revolutionary' and an 'administrative *trompe l'oeil*'.[31] The idea was to streamline the public offering process so as to permit compliant 'seasoned' reporting issuers, in particular, speedier access to capital raising. However, markets have speeded up beyond the wildest dreams of the original proposers of incorporation by reference, and the shift to private capital raising (aided by subsequent

---

[26] See the discussion in Mark Roe, 'Delaware's Competition' (2003) 117 *Harvard Law Review* 588, 597. According to Roe, federal corporate law has been considered on at least three occasions since 1900.

[27] There are two other triggers to registration under the US 1934 Act (and compliance with periodic information disclosure), both contained in the US 1934 Act itself: listing on a stock exchange in the United States and the number of shareholders exceeding a certain threshold (despite there having been no public offering or listing): 15 USC § 78(l)(a), (g) (2006).

[28] The accommodations for certain non-US issuers are discussed in due course, and are summarized in Tables 4.1 and 4.2.

[29] This was a very significant concession on the part of US regulators and one which European issuers (where the use of IFRS is mandatory) had requested for many years. At the time of granting this concession, the SEC had also announced the move to IFRS for US issuers by 2010 (thereby staving off 'level playing field' objections), but since this time, has backed away from implementation.

[30] As discussed at 3.3, the US 1934 Act attempts to impose informational requirements on companies which have not entered the public markets in the United States, ie have not triggered the registration requirements of the US 1933 Act, based on the number of US shareholders. For certain non-US companies which are not reporting issuers, compliance, to the extent required, with the US 1934 Act may serve other useful purposes under the US 1933 Act, for example with respect to the informational requirement of Rule 144A private placements.

[31] Edward Greene et al, *U.S. Regulation of the International Securities and Derivatives Markets* (6th edn, Aspen Law & Business 2002).

developments such as Rule 144A) at the expense of public markets makes incorporation by reference a less revolutionary concept these days.

In considering these two key statutes, it is important to put them in context. A vast body of **4.17** interpretation and regulation supports them, but the underlying assumptions of their time and place of origin continue to operate below the surface. The first operative assumption is the primacy of the public markets in the United States, an assumption eclipsed in 2006,[32] when for the first time the value of privately placed securities exceeded that of public offerings. The US 1933 Act pays private markets scant attention. Secondly, both statutes were drafted with the retail investor, mom and pop, in mind; institutional investors only began to dominate US markets much later.[33] Also, the focus of each statute was trading, over a formal bricks and mortar stock exchange, in domestic equity securities, in tangible, paper-based form.[34] Electronic trading, as we know it now, much less high frequency trading, obviously did not exist. Neither did the derivative products, usually structured as debt securities, which began to proliferate in the 1980s. Other forms of more complex non-equity financial instruments, originally commodities-based, were traded and regulated under the purview of a competing regulator; they would not fall within the definition of securities. Lastly, in the 1930s the wheels of the public market were greased by a fairly homogenous clutch of professional intermediaries.

There are several implications arising from these observations. The regulatory competition **4.18** between the CFTC and the SEC and fragmentation of oversight along financial product lines persists to this day, a perennial and unresolved source of concern.[35] The underlying assumptions of the US 1933 Act produce 'blind spots' in regulatory oversight; in fact, in these blind spots the financial products, markets, and participants most implicated in the global financial crisis flourished. The use of US legislative models for international standards replicated the same blind spots internationally.

Despite the affection shown by US securities law practitioners for the challenging mental **4.19** game presented by the US 1933 Act, the legislation is highly problematic in modern markets. With its focus on old-fashioned public offerings and simple equity products, it misses the realities of the modern market place. Obviously, the obliqueness of its drafting is not

---

[32] 'Last year, 144A placements raised $162 billion, compared with $154 billion raised through initial and secondary public offerings': Andrew Ross Sorkin and Michael J de la Merced, 'Buyout Firm Said to Seek a Private Market Offering', *The New York Times* (New York, 18 July 2007) <http://www.nytimes.com/2007/07/18/business/18place.html?_r=0> accessed 15 January 2014.

[33] While estimates vary, widely cited sources suggest that retail stock ownership has declined from 90% in the 1950s to as low as 30% in 2007: Brian G Cartwright, 'The Future of Securities Regulation' (University of Pennsylvania School Institute for Law and Economics, Phaildelphia, 24 October 2007) <https://www.sec.gov/news/speech/2007/spch102407bgc.htm> accessed 22 April 2013.

[34] These assumptions, so ingrained as to have become invisible, peek through the surface from time to time. For example, as discussed in Ch 3 of this book, US securities regulation has been the model for some international standards. When the European Union was proposing the 2003 Prospectus Directive, which would incorporate by reference certain international standards, the UK Law Society, ever solicitous of protecting their profession's hold on the Euro *bond* market, pointed out that the international standards under consideration contemplated equity not debt securities. They would thus not be appropriate for a bond market—'The IOSCO Disclosure Standards on which the Directive is based deal with Equity issues only and are not always appropriate to Debt issues'. The Law Society (UK), Company Law Committee, 'Proposal for a Directive on the Prospectus to be Published When Securities are Offered to the Public or Admitted to Trading' (Memorandum, No 422), 3.

[35] See discussion (n 5).

helpful; much is left to surmise and market practice, which in a simpler world where general consensus reigned, may not have been such a bad thing. But the tortured analysis[36] required to distinguish a public offering from a private placement, at a time when the private market is so significant, is not a credit to the legislation. In the early 2000s, the SEC had been urged to address this particular problem;[37] unfortunately, the SEC found itself fire-fighting scandal and crisis, pushing fundamental reform down the agenda.[38]

4.20 The artificiality of re-characterizing corporate governance measures as securities regulation, as with the Sarbanes-Oxley 2002 legislation, has also introduced sub-optimal regulatory methods and unintended consequences. US securities regulation has been dominated by disclosure-based regulatory techniques. Anything goes, so long as everyone knows. Corporate law, on the other hand, is full of rules; they may be default rules much of the time (changeable by contract or constitution), but they are rules. Many of the provisions of Sarbanes-Oxley 2002 demonstrate this tension between the use of disclosure mechanisms, where a clear, mandatory rule might serve the purpose better. But the most significant unintended consequence of Sarbanes-Oxley 2002, and its characterization as securities regulation rather than federal corporate governance law, has been on non-US issuers. In the past, non-US issuers received the benefit of exemptions from the most obvious of corporate governance provisions dropped into the US 1934 Act. These exemptions were not widely heralded (lest the 'level playing field' argument rise up), but soundly grounded in the recognition that the corporate governance—the internal organization—of non-US companies would be governed by home country rules, and usually mandatory home country rules, of corporate law bolstered by stock exchange listing rules, foreign and domestic. Rather than set up needless conflict, non-US issuers in the United States were simply exempted. Not so with Sarbanes-Oxley 2002, which caught a flotilla of large, vociferous, European (and other) companies in its tentacles. Many of these companies had only recently been tempted into a New York Stock Exchange listing.[39] These companies headed for the exits, citing the inappropriateness of the Sarbanes-Oxley measures to their internal governance, or more strenuously, their incompatibility with mandatory provisions of their domestic corporate law. The United States markets were dubbed 'Hotel California', after a popular, nightmarish, 1976 tune.[40]

4.21 In this case, it was the intensely domestic focus of Congress in enacting Sarbanes-Oxley 2002, combined with the re-characterization of corporate governance as securities legislation which produced these untoward consequences. In the rush to produce the Sarbanes-Oxley legislation, Congress did not adequately take into account the effect on non-US companies which had entered the US public markets. The SEC announced administrative accommodations (some of which were somewhat at odds with the literal wording of the statute).[41] An

---

[36] Explained later in this chapter in the context of Rule 144A.

[37] Greene and Quinn (n 17), 14–16.

[38] Both the introduction of Rule 144A and the newly minted JOBS Act target the private market, in particular.

[39] Silvia Ascarelli, 'Citing Sarbanes, Foreign Companies Flee U.S. Exchanges', *The Wall Street Journal* (London, 20 September 2004) <http://online.wsj.com/news/articles/SB109563482817521868> accessed 14 January 2014.

[40] In the Hotel California, you can check out anytime you want, but you can never leave.

[41] US Securities and Exchange Commission, 'SEC Rulemaking and Other Initiatives: Accommodations' (20 October 2006) <http://www.sec.gov/about/offices/oia/oia_rulemaking/accommodations.htm> accessed 24 December 2013.

embarrassing regulatory fix had to be devised to permit these companies to exit the US public markets and terminate their reporting obligations under the US 1934 Act.[42] Again, interestingly enough, a fix was created for domestic US issuers as well; the level playing field yet again the issue. Nevertheless, the US public markets lost companies like Bayer, British Airways, Fiat, Danone, Merck, PCCW, and Telstra.[43] While the lustre of a New York Stock Exchange listing may have already worn off for these companies, Sarbanes-Oxley 2002 was the tipping point.

Not so with the most recent, and perhaps much more revolutionary, Jumpstart Our Business **4.22** Startups Act 2012 (JOBS Act). At a scant 21 pages,[44] for its weight it may be a blockbuster game changer. Fuelled by a powerful combination of US election year politics and the high profile fiasco of a Facebook private placement,[45] this legislation counters those basic concepts of public offering and private placement which reach back to the 1930s. What is significant in this legislation, from an international perspective, is that it makes advertent distinctions between US issuers and non-US issuers (at least some of the time). Some provisions of the JOBS Act do apply to both,[46] some do not.[47] Although one might quibble with where the line is drawn (especially given the underlying goal of US job creation), the recognition of the presence of non-US issuers in the US markets is a sign that Congress, at least to a certain extent, is aware of the implications of their presence and the extent of integration of global markets.

3. The Parallel System

3.1 Background to the parallel system

The participation of non-US companies in US capital markets is not a new phenomenon, **4.23** of course, and the regulatory regime has long recognized and accommodated them. In fact, US securities regulation creates a parallel regime, under both the US 1933 Act and the US 1934 Act, for 'foreign private issuers' (FPIs),[48] a concept first introduced in 1967.[49] The parallel system is built around this concept of FPI which has been put to different uses over the

---

[42] 17 CFR § 240.12h-6.

[43] See Eric Uhlfelder, 'US Delistings Changing the Landscape for Investors: The Exodus of Foreign Companies Directly Affects Schemes That Must Hold Listed Shares', *Financial Times* (London, 23 July 2007), 8.

[44] As compared to the doorstopper Dodd Frank Act 2010 which weighs in at some 1,800 pages.

[45] Goldman Sachs decided to offer Facebook shares only to offshore investors, to avoid any risk the offer could be viewed by the SEC as a 'general solicitation' to the public. In this case, Goldman had strictly complied with the practices for a private offering, but the extensive media coverage could have been viewed as a general solicitation, with the potentially serious consequence of SEC litigation: Steven M Davidoff, 'Why did Goldman Blink?', *The New York Times Dealbook* (New York, 18 January 2011) <http://dealbook.nytimes.com/2011/01/18/why-did-goldman-blink> accessed 24 December 2013.

[46] For example, the increase in the holders of record threshold for reporting requirements, from 500 to 2,000 shareholders: JOBS Act, Pub L No 112-106 § 601, 126 Stat 306 (2012).

[47] The 'crowdfunding' provisions, yet to be implemented by rule-making.

[48] Rules and Regulations, Securities Exchange Act of 1934, 17 CFR § 240.3b-4(c); General Rules and Regulations, Securities Act of 1933, 17 CFR § 230.405. The 'private' in the definition distinguishes them from foreign governments issuing debt securities.

[49] The definition of 'foreign private issuer' was introduced in Securities and Exchange Commission, 'Adoption of Rules relating to Foreign Securities', SEC Release No 8066 (28 April 1967), cited in (1967) 6 *International Legal Materials* 468. The parallel system was introduced through the amendment of Form 20-K to conform to the standards required of domestic issuers: see Securities and Exchange Commission, 'Adoption of Revised Form 20-K and Repeal of Form 21-K', Securities Exchange Act Release No 8068 (28 April 1967). For an overview of the development of this parallel system, see Barbara S Thomas, 'International Accounting and

decades. Interestingly enough, for quite a long time, the existence of the parallel system was not widely known, even among securities practitioners. The usual practitioners handbooks and compilations of statutory and regulatory provisions did not include mention of it.[50] It was not terribly easy, in a pre-electronic age, to even find the applicable provisions, many of which were tucked away in 'instructions' to standard forms used for regulatory filings and not easily accessible. The parallel system was an obscure and little known area of US regulatory practice.

4.24 In hindsight, this may appear odd as the internationalization of capital markets is now such a given. However, it reflects, historically, the intensely domestic nature of US capital markets, especially the equity markets.[51] Unlike London, New York was not an international financial centre. To put this in perspective, in 1990 there were only 96 non-US issuers listed on the New York Stock Exchange, representing 5.6 per cent of 1,704 total listings.[52]

4.25 In fact, the significance of foreign listings on the New York Stock Exchange was even less than appears at first glance, as about half of those issuers were Canadian.[53] At this time, the London Stock Exchange, although a smaller market by capitalization,[54] had 613 non-UK issuers listed, representing 24.6 per cent of total listings.[55] Until the 1990s, the accommodations provided by the parallel system were not attractive enough to offset the regulatory burdens (especially reconciliation to US GAAP) imposed by entering the US public markets.

4.26 All this began to change in the late 1980s. The SEC published a major study in 1987 on internationalization which paved the way for three regulatory initiatives, Regulation S, Rule 144A, and the Multijurisdictional Disclosure System (MJDS, set up with Canada), which changed the regulatory landscape. The MJDS may be viewed as a public relations exercise by

---

Reporting: Developments Leading to the Harmonization of Standards' (1983) 15 *New York University Journal of International Law and Politics* 517, 535–41.

[50] Only the Appeals Handbook contained the provisions of the parallel system when the author was practising in New York City in the 1980s: Andrew J Kohn, Donald J Wall, and Frank J Easterbrook, 'Practitioner's Handbook for Appeals to the United States Court of Appeals for the Seventh Circuit' (United States Court of Appeals 7th Circuit 2012).

[51] Greene and Quinn (n 17). 'As the 1980s drew to a close, the cold war was only just beginning to end and the markets reflected a different political and economic world structure. Equity markets in Europe were local, domestic markets of little consequence to listed companies. A European currency was still only a dream. The eurodollar market was the principal, almost exclusive, cross-border financing market. Latin American and Asian markets were for the most part still closed, controlled economies. Investors also behaved differently. The international private market was a fraction of its current size (mutual funds were a minor player in the international market and the 144A market did not exist), while retail investors outside the United States were primarily debt investors. Finally, technology in general, and the worldwide web in particular, had yet to revolutionize the degree to which information could be disseminated around the world with ease.'

[52] Andrew Karolyi, 'Why Do Companies List Shares Abroad? A Survey of the Evidence and its Managerial Implications' (1998) 7 *Financial Markets, Institutions and Instruments* 1, 9; 'New York Stock Exchange Reports a 39% Rise in Net' *The Wall Street Journal Europe* (New York, 1 July 1991).

[53] Alan Goggins, 'Taking That First Step: The Securities and Exchange Commission's Proposed Multijurisdictional Disclosure System' (1990) 14 *Maryland Journal of International Law* 43, 45.

[54] Christine Pavel and John N McElravey, 'Globalization in the Financial Services Industry' (1990) 14 *Economic Perspectives* 3, 11 (citing data from 1988).

[55] Karolyi (n 52), 9; There were 2,493 listed companies in the United Kingdom in 1990: George Graham, 'Survey of European Finance and Investment—France: Foreign investment doubles; A look at confidence in the capital markets', *Financial Times* (London, 22 October 1990).

US regulators, showcasing their ability to cooperate internationally, but was much written about and heralded in Canada. And, by adding six new instruments[56] to the parallel system, the MJDS brought the parallel system out of the closet. Meanwhile, in an effort to boost revenues, the New York Stock Exchange mounted a campaign to attract non-US issuers. In 1993, Daimler-Benz broke rank with other major German industrials (which had been holding out over reconciliation to US GAAP) and listed on the New York Stock Exchange.[57] A regulatory position on American Depositary Receipts (ADRs) was adopted (and another new instrument added to the parallel system).[58] Latin American issuers, in particular, flocked to the US ADR market. The period between 1990 and 2002 (when Sarbanes-Oxley broke up the party[59]) has been dubbed the golden age of international capital markets, at least from the US perspective.[60]

3.2 The Foreign Private Issuer (FPI) and the parallel system

The key operative concept in the parallel system is the definition of 'foreign private issuer' (FPI), introduced in 1967.[61] The 'private' is used to differentiate private sector business entities from foreign governmental issuers. There are three components to the definition: (i) non-US incorporation or organization; (ii) percentage of shareholders in the United States; and (iii) a 'business presence' in the United States test. **4.27**

---

[56] Forms F-7, F-8, F-9, F-10, F-80, and 40-F. The requirements of these forms are set out in 17 CFR § 239.37–239.40. Form F-7 is used by Canadian companies to register offers made to US shareholders where those companies have a class of securities listed on a Canadian stock exchange. To be registered on this form, US shareholders must be granted rights on terms no less favourable than those granted to other shareholders: Securities and Exchange Commission, 'Registration Statement under the Securities Act of 1933 for Securities of Certain Canadian Issuers Offered for Cash upon the Exercise of Rights Granted to Existing Security Holders', SEC No SEC2289, January 2007 <http://www.sec.gov/about/forms/formf-7.pdf> accessed 30 April 2013. Form F-8 is used by Canadian companies to register securities offered in business combinations or mergers that require a shareholder vote. Again, US shareholders must be granted rights on terms no less favourable than those granted to other shareholders: Securities and Exchange Commission, 'Registration Statement under the Securities Act of 1933 for Securities of Certain Canadian Issuers to be Issued in Exchange Offers or a Business Combination', SEC No SEC2290, January 2007 <http://www.sec.gov/about/forms/formf-8.pdf> accessed 30 April 2013. Form F-9 had been used by Canadian companies to register primarily offers of investment grade debt; Form F-9 was eliminated in 2011. Form F-10 is now used by Canadian companies to register debt and equity.

[57] This coincided with a major marketing campaign for the Mercedes-Benz automobile in the United States, and was soon followed by the announcement of the merger of Daimler Benz and Chrysler.

[58] Form F-6.

[59] Ultimately, resulting in the exit provisions from the US market for those newly listed European companies, in the form of Rule 12h-6 (17 CFR § 240.12h-6), and Form F-15.

[60] See Robert DeLaMater, 'Recent Trends in SEC Regulation of Foreign Issuers: How the U.S. Regulatory Regime is Affecting the United States' Historic Position as the World's Principal Capital Market' (2006) 39 *Cornell International Law Journal* 109.

[61] Rules and Regulations under the Securities Exchange Act of 1934, 17 CFR § 240.3b-4(c): 'The term foreign private issuer means any foreign issuer other than a foreign government except for an issuer meeting the following conditions as of the last business day of its most recently completed second fiscal quarter:

    (1)   More than 50 percent of the issuer's outstanding voting securities are directly or indirectly held of record by residents of the United States; and

    (2)   Any of the following:

        (i)   The majority of the executive officers or directors are United States citizens or residents;

        (ii)   More than 50 percent of the assets of the issuer are located in the United States; or

        (iii)   The business of the issuer is administered principally in the United States.'

This definition was adopted in Securities and Exchange Commission, 'Adoption of Rules relating to Foreign Securities', SEC Release No 8066 (28 April 1967), cited in (1967) 6 *International Legal Materials* 468. In 2000, amendments were made to this definition to allow US ownership to be determined by 'looking through' the record ownership of certain companies to determine the beneficial ownership of those securities: see Securities and Exchange Commission, 'Final Rule: International Disclosure Standards', SEC Release Nos 33-7745, 34-41936 (30 September 2000) <http://www.sec.gov/rules/final/34-41936.htm> accessed 30 April 2013.

4.28 Non-US incorporation or organization combined with 50 per cent or less of shareholders in the United States provides the exemptive benefits of the FPI characterization. Full stop. This is a relatively high threshold, and at the time of its introduction in 1967 may have been designed to exempt (and would have in fact exempted) virtually every non-US corporation with few US connections, with the exception of some Canadian issuers.

4.29 A non-US issuer can still benefit from the exemptive provisions associated with FPI status, even with more than 50 per cent of its shareholders in the United States provided it does not have a significant US business presence. At one level, this could be seen as an anti-avoidance mechanism.[62] Non-US issuers with more than 50 per cent of their shareholders in the United States must 'fail' all three prongs of the fact-based US business presence test in order to retain FPI status: (i) no more than 50 per cent of their directors or executive officers can be US citizens or residents; (ii) no more than 50 per cent of their assets can be in the United States; and (iii) the business cannot be principally administered in the United States (the 'headquarters test').[63]

4.30 For domestic US issuers, the nature of a transaction or reporting requirement is often referred to by the short hand of the 'form', determined by regulation, which sets out in detail the format and itemized content of a particular SEC filing.[64] For example, the documentation associated with an initial public offering by a domestic US corporation must be filed in compliance with and under the cover page of Form S-1[65] and include the itemized business and management discussion outlined in Regulation S-K and the financial information in Regulation S-X.

4.31 The initial public offering triggers periodic reporting under the US 1934 Act, among other things; annual reporting is filed as a Form 10-K, quarterly reporting as a Form 10-Q, material event filings under Form 8-K. Over time, as a compliance record develops and public information circulates in the markets (primarily through the financial press and business analysts), the information made public under the US 1934 Act in the periodic reporting may be 'incorporated by reference' into short-form registration statements for the subsequent issuance of securities by the issuer—under cover of Form S-3.[66] The requirements associated with short-form filings were simplified and an intermediate form of filing, Form S-2, discontinued in 2005.

4.32 'Seasoning' was the term associated with this process of market information infiltration after an initial public offering; in 2005, various categories of issuer were identified on the basis of how well 'seasoned' they had become. In an effort to 'eliminate unnecessary and outmoded restrictions on offerings',[67] the most seasoned issuers, identified by the acronym 'WKSI' (well known

---

[62] For example, deterring US businesses from incorporating offshore so as to take advantage of the exemptive provisions.

[63] As an example, the Seagram Building at 375 Park Avenue in New York City, a Mies van der Rohe 'masterpiece of modernism', was built in 1958 as the headquarters of the Canadian distillers and would lead to loss of FPI status if there were more than 50% US shareholders.

[64] Substantive requirements are often tucked into the instructions in these forms, so that in fact the forms are both highly significant in terms of regulatory compliance and somewhat obscure to non-practitioners.

[65] Form S-1 was introduced in 1982 as part of a tripartite system of registration disclosure forms, encompassing Forms S-1, S-2 (now eliminated), and S-3: see Securities and Exchange Commission, 'Adoption of the Integrated Disclosure System', SEC Release No 33-6383 (3 March 1982).

[66] To be eligible to use Form S-3, a company must have filed reports pursuant to the US 1934 Act for the previous 12 months.

[67] Securities and Exchange Commission, 'Securities Offering Reform', SEC Release Nos 33-8501, 34-50624, IC-26649, 3 November 2004 <http://www.sec.gov/rules/proposed/33-8501.htm> accessed 30 April 2013.

seasoned issuer), had the benefit of the most favourable accommodations. As potential abusive practices subsequently developed,[68] primarily involving Chinese companies,[69] using reverse mergers with a US listed company, so as to achieve a US stock exchange listing, restrictions were subsequently imposed.

The introduction in 1967 of the FPI concept marked the beginning of the parallel system of **4.33** registration and reporting by FPIs, where forms analogous to those under the US 1933 Act and US 1934 Act were created for FPIs, adapted to the regulatory accommodations provided for them. For an initial public offering by an FPI, for example, the registration statement would be in compliance with and filed under cover of Form F-1, analogous to the Form S-1 filing for a domestic issuer. FPIs also got the benefit of incorporation by reference, and subsequent issuances would be under cover of Form F-3, in simplified form.

There were a number of accommodations made for FPIs in the information required of them **4.34** in US 1933 Act filings. Until 2008 when a blanket rule permitted all FPIs to make use of IFRS, financial statements for FPIs had to be in conformity with US GAAP, or, in an accommodation, reconciled to it through extensive notations.[70] In recognition of non-US financial statement preparation, FPIs were excused from 'segment reporting'—breaking out results along operating segment lines which would not be usual outside the United States.

One of the least trivial and most hard fought issues, in terms of accommodations, was execu- **4.35** tive compensation. In the United States, detailed information had long been provided with respect to the compensation packages of the five most highly compensated executive officers, who were personally named in the information filing. The idea of divulging such personal

---

[68] 'Currently, reverse merger companies like other operating companies can pay to be listed on an exchange, where investors can purchase and sell shares of the company. In some cases, regulators and auditors have greater difficulty obtaining reliable information from reverse merger companies, particularly those based overseas. Reverse mergers permit private companies, including those located outside the U.S., to access U.S. investors and markets by merging with an existing public shell company. In summer 2010, the SEC launched an initiative to determine whether certain companies with foreign operations—including those that were the product of reverse mergers—were accurately reporting their financial results, and to assess the quality of the audits being done by the auditors of these companies. The SEC and U.S. exchanges have in recent months suspended or halted trading in more than 35 companies based overseas, citing a lack of current and accurate information about the firms and their finances. These included a number of companies that were formed by reverse mergers... Under [new] rules, Nasdaq, NYSE, and NYSE Amex will impose more stringent listing requirements for companies that become public through a reverse merger': 'SEC Approves New Rules to Toughen Listing Standards for Reverse Merger Companies', Press Release 2011-235, 9 November 2011 <http://www.sec.gov/news/press/2011/2011-235.htm> accessed 30 April 2013.

[69] 'According to published reports, 25% of all securities fraud class action lawsuits filed during the first half of 2011 involved Chinese companies that have gone public through reverse mergers. A 2011 report by Cornerstone Research stated that 12 securities class action complaints were filed in 2010 against Chinese companies listed on US stock exchanges, representing 42.9% of all class action filings against foreign issuers listed in the US. Commentators assert that one factor fuelling this trend is the fact that many Chinese issuers have gone public through reverse mergers with listed US shell companies—a process which, in some cases, results in a significant lack of disclosure associated with the newly public business.' Chris Converse, 'A Net Too Wide: SEC Seasoning Rules and Their Applicability to Newly Public Companies' (*Lexology*, 27 March 2012) <http://www.lexology.com/library/detail.aspx?g=5bfc45eb-a382-481f-9c1b-ae477136d243> accessed 30 April 2013.

[70] For an outline of the standard prior to the 2008 amendments, see Securities and Exchange Commission, 'Acceptance from Foreign Private Issuers of Financial Statements Prepared in Accordance with International Financial Reporting Standards without Reconciliation to US GAAP', SEC Release No 33-8818 (2 July 2007), 8 <http://www.sec.gov/rules/proposed/2007/33-8818.pdf> accessed 30 April 2013. The relevant amendments were introduced pursuant to Securities and Exchange Commission 'Acceptance from Foreign Private Issuers of Financial Statements Prepared in Accordance with International Financial Reporting Standards without Reconciliation to US GAAP', SEC Release Nos 33-8879, 34-57026 (21 December 2007) <http://www.sec.gov/rules/final/2007/33-8879.pdf> accessed 30 April 2013.

Table 4.1 Comparison of forms used for offers by US domestic issuers and foreign private issuers

The Parallel System US 1933 Act Forms used for IPO/Offer by	
US Domestic Issuer	**FPI**
S-1 (IPOs, public offers)	F-1 (IPOs, public offers)
S-2 (discontinued)	F-2 (discontinued)
S-3 (seasoned issuer)	F-3 (seasoned issuer)
S-4 (business combinations)	F-4 (business combinations)
S-K: Business information	
S-X: Financial information	
	F-6 (ADRs)
	F-7, F-8, F-9 (discontinued), F-10 (MJDS—Canadian issuers)
	Accommodations:
	• IFRS (2008)
	• no segment reporting
	• no individual executive compensation

information on an individual basis was an anathema outside the United States. In addition to being culturally offensive, concerns such as potential kidnapping and extortion were raised. Others said European executives were embarassed by their meagre pay packages in comparison to their US peers.

4.36 Once large Canadian issuers had the benefit of the MJDS[71] to use their Canadian prospectuses and information filings in the United States under a reciprocal recognition regime, the Canadian financial press howled. They had long been accustomed to looking to US public filings for Canadian issuers (where they existed) to find information not made publicly available in Canada. In response to the criticisms about the reduction in transparency inadvertently triggered by the MJDS, the Canadian authorities introduced detailed individual compensation reporting similar to the US rules. The accommodation for FPIs was aggregate reporting of executive compensation without naming individuals or breaking out individual compensation packages.

4.37 Under the US 1934 Act, the parallel regime created more extensive accommodations and exemptions from reporting and other requirements, particularly where there were differences in the usual financial reporting cycles outside the United States. Importantly, because the US 1934 Act is also a repository of federal corporate governance provisions, until the arrival of Sarbanes-Oxley 2002, FPIs were exempt from these provisions of the US 1934 Act. This early exercise in deference recognized the validity and equivalency of internal corporate governance requirements outside the United States.

4.38 Form 20-F, the equivalent of the Form 10-K for domestic issuers, was created in 1979 for annual reporting by FPIs; however, there was no equivalent to domestic Form 10-Q, as

---

[71] The MJDS was introduced in 1991.

quarterly reporting of financial information was not usual practice outside North America. Form 20-F is the workhorse of the parallel system, as it is used for stock exchange listings as well as annual reporting by FPIs. Form 6-K—the FPI equivalent of the material event filing, Form 8-K for domestic issuers—was also a precursor of modern international regulatory techniques in that it made use of 'home country' reporting. The FPI makes public in the United States, the information it is required to make public in its home country, or under stock exchange listing rules outside the United States. The information is not considered 'filed' in the United States,[72] but rather 'submitted' to the SEC. This is not simply a semantic distinction without a difference; a filing triggers potential liability in the United States under the US 1934 Act for the content of the information document, whereas a 'submission' does not.

In addition to the accommodations on periodic reporting, the US 1934 Act provides exemptions to FPIs from the proxy rules which detail the processes and information associated with annual general meetings, a clear example of federal corporate governance provisions, where there is a high probability of conflict with mandatory shareholder meeting requirements of other jurisdictions. This includes recent updates, such as 'say-on-pay', introduced by the Dodd-Frank legislation in 2010.[73] Equally, accommodations are made with respect to actions by FPIs which might trigger the Williams Act—the 1967 legislation governing the processes triggered by a tender offer/takeover bid.[74] FPIs are also exempt from insider reporting requirements (where directors and officers must publicly report their personal trading in the securities of their issuer), as well as exclusion from the provisions of Regulation FD, the Fair Disclosure regulation implemented in 2000.[75] The so-called 'short swing profit rule',[76] a kind of deemed insider trading mechanism not usually found in regulation outside the United States, also does not apply to FPIs. **4.39**

---

[72] A similar submission, not filing, distinction used to be made in exemptive Rule 12g3-2(b), see discussion.

[73] Dodd-Frank Wall Street Reform and Consumer Protection Act, Pub L No 111-203, § 951, 124 Stat 1376 (2010).

[74] There is a two-tiered exemption system for foreign private issuers making tender offers: General Rules and Regulations, Securities Exchange Act of 1934, 17 CFR § 240.14d-1(c)-(d). Tier I exemptions apply to tender offers where the shareholder base of the targeted company is comprised of 10% or less US shareholders. Tier II exemptions apply to tender offers where US shareholders own 40% or less of the target company's securities. Where a Tier I exemption applies, the offer will be exempt from the majority of Williams Act provisions governing the offer, including Rules 13e-3, 13e-4, 14e-1, 14e-2 and Regulation 14D, which govern 'disclosure, filing, dissemination, minimum offering period, withdrawal rights and proration requirements': Securities and Exchange Commission, 'Cross-Border Tender and Exchange Offers, Business Combinations and Rights Offerings', Release Nos 33-7759, 34-42054, 39-2378, 22 October 1999 <http://www.sec.gov/rules/final/33-7759.htm> accessed 1 May 2013. Where a Tier II exemption applies, limited exemptions to the Williams Act provisions will apply.

[75] See Rules and Regulations under the Securities Exchange Act of 1934, 17 CFR § 240.3a12-3(b) (which effectively excludes foreign private issuers from insider reporting requirements). See also Regulation FD, 17 CFR § 243.101(b) (which excludes foreign private issuers from the operation of Regulation FD). Regulation FD, controversial at the time of its enactment, was another level playing enactment, this time by promoting equal access to material information by retail as well as institutional investors. 'As discussed in the Proposing Release, we have become increasingly concerned about the selective disclosure of material information by issuers. As reflected in recent publicized reports, many issuers are disclosing important non-public information, such as advance warnings of earnings results, to securities analysts or selected institutional investors or both, before making full disclosure of the same information to the general public. Where this has happened, those who were privy to the information beforehand were able to make a profit or avoid a loss at the expense of those kept in the dark': Securities and Exchange Commission, 'Final Rule: Selective Disclosure and Insider Trading', Release Nos 33-7881, 34-43154, IC-24599, 15 August 2000 <http://www.sec.gov/rules/final/33-7881.htm> accessed 1 May 2013.

[76] 15 USC § 78p(b). Using a somewhat complicated formulation, this rule requires that company insiders return any profits made from any purchases and sales of their shares in the company during a rolling six-month period.

Table 4.2 Comparison of periodic reporting forms used by US domestic issuers and foreign private issuers

The Parallel System US 1934 Act—Periodic and other Reporting Forms

US Domestic Issuer	FPI
10-K (annual reporting)	20-F (annual reporting and stock exchange listing, 1979)
	40-F (Canadian Issuer under MJDS)
15 (deregistration)	15-F (deregistration, 2007)
10-Q (quarterly reporting)	No quarterly reporting
8-K (material event)	6-K (material event—can use home country reporting)
	Accommodations:
	• Rule 12g3-2 (a) and (b): exemption from section 12(g)
	• Exemption from proxy requirements/'say on pay'
	• Do not have to comply with short swing profit rule
	• Do not have to comply with insider reporting requirements
	• Regulation FD exemption

4.40 This is an impressive list of accommodations, stretching back decades, for non-US participants in US markets. Some are straight exemptive provisions, others have strings attached in the form of compliance or eligibility requirements. However, there are the occasional lapses such as Sarbanes-Oxley 2002, which in triggering a massive withdrawal of major European and other corporations from US stock exchanges, produced unexpected and untoward consequences. And, it may be that the most significant accommodation of all, permitting FPIs participating in the public markets in the United States to use IFRS, may have come too grudgingly late to produce short term effects, given that so many large European corporations (which must use IFRS domestically) had already bolted.

3.3 The curious case of Rule 12g3-2(b)

4.41 Strictly speaking, Rule 12g3-2(b) is yet another accommodation to FPIs under the US 1934 Act, relieving them of periodic disclosure and other regulatory burdens imposed on domestic US issuers. However, Rule 12g3-2(b) has been a shape shifter. First introduced in 1967 together with the FPI concept itself, Rule 12g3-2(b) has taken several different forms and serves a number of handy purposes. Unlike many of the other accommodations under the US 1934 Act, Rule 12g3-2(b) operates in the private markets, where there has not been an initial public offering (IPO) or stock exchange listing in the United States, serving as a regulatory trigger. As the private markets have surged in importance, Rule 12g3-2(b) has ridden the tide out of obscurity.

4.42 A listing on a stock exchange or a public offering imposes ongoing informational and other regulatory requirements, in the United States as elsewhere. There is, however, a third trigger which lowers the regulatory net: the number of voting equity securities holders and assets exceeding certain thresholds.[77] The rationale is straightforward. Irrespective as to how it has

---

[77] In the European Union (and Australia which has picked the requirement up through copying UK companies law), there is a somewhat analogous requirement for large private companies (based on turnover, number of employees, etc) to publish annual accounts or financial statements. The impact of this requirement

occurred, once the number of voting shareholders reaches a critical mass, there should be ongoing public information available to them, as well as the other corporate governance protections of the US 1934 Act.

Introduced in 1964, § 12(g)(1) became increasingly problematic over time. Its bright line **4.43** thresholds, 500 voting equity holders and $1 million in assets, were too low for one thing. Despite the $1 million in asset threshold being raised by regulation to $10 million,[78] even this latter threshold became irrelevant. The shareholder threshold (500 voting equity securities holders of any one class[79]), however, remained fixed until 2012 when it finally succumbed to changing times.[80] That this threshold survived as long as it did is somewhat remarkable in and of itself, given corporate growth over that time. However, private equity companies, hedge funds, for example, limited the number of their voting shareholders for other reasons and US companies showed a decided preference for using debt securities, rather than equity, in the private placement market (which was opened up by Rule 144A).[81] Also, the threshold was calculated on a class-by-class basis.

Ultimately, however, the Facebook factor (the use of stock options to reward employees in **4.44** the high tech industry) forced the issue.[82] The JOBS Act raised the threshold to 2,000 voting shareholders for banks and, subject to certain conditions, to non-banks.[83] Employees receiving shares in exempt transactions are not counted towards the 2,000 voting shareholder limit, removing the difficulties surrounding shareholder growth due to the exercise of stock options.

Prior to the enactment of § 12(g)(1) in 1964, it was originally contemplated that non-US **4.45** companies would simply be exempted from the provision, as they are in certain other circumstances.[84] However, a different approach prevailed and no distinction was made in the legislation, although the SEC could make exemptions with respect to FPIs under its rule-making authority. This it did a few years later in 1967, by creating two exemptions from registration requirements under § 12(g)(1) for FPIs which had not 'voluntarily' entered the US public markets by way of a public offering or listing on a US exchange.[85] The first exemption had no-strings attached and applied to FPIs with 300 or fewer voting shareholders in the United States (Rule 12g3-2(a)). FPIs with over 300 voting shareholders in the United

---

on a company is much more limited though than unleashing the full force of the US 1934 Act, as does § 12(g): Fourth Council Directive 78/660/EEC of 25 July 1978 based on Article 54(3)(g) of the Treaty on the Annual Accounts of Certain Types of Companies [1978] OJ L222/11.

[78] General Rules and Regulations, Securities Exchange Act of 1934, 17 CFR § 240.12g-1.

[79] 'Of record': see 15 USC § 78l(g)(1)(A) (West, 2011).

[80] The JOBS Act raised the voting shareholder threshold from 500 to either (1) 2,000 persons, or (2) 500 persons who are not accredited investors (eg high net worth individuals) under Regulation D: see JOBS Act, Pub L No 112-106, § 501, 126 Stat 306 (2012).

[81] Chaplinsky and Ramchand note that 'the total amount of capital raised by debt is nearly eight times the amount of equity raised': Susan Chaplinsky and Latha Ramchand, 'The Impact of SEC Rule 144A on Corporate Debt Issuance by International Firms' (2004) 77 *Journal of Business* 1073, 1074.

[82] Donald C Langevoort and Robert B Thompson, '"Publicness" in Contemporary Securities Regulation after the JOBS Act' (2013) 101 *Georgetown Law Journal* 337, 338.

[83] For non-banks, a distinction is made between accredited investors, a defined term under Regulation D (high net worth individuals assumed to be sophisticated investors, for example), and all other investors. No more than 500 shareholders can be unaccredited investors: JOBS Act, Pub L No 112-106, § 501, 126 Stat 306 (2012).

[84] Cleary Gottlieb Steen and Hamilton LLP, 'Foreign Private Issuer Exemption from SEC Registration: Practical Implications', Client Memorandum (19 September 2008), 2 <http://www.cgsh.com/files/News/a1e91253-608c-40b2-9111-d15b27f4d334/Presentation/NewsAttachment/8a87bd4f-b960-475c-b2ee-d1b7b7c19a0e/CGSH%20Alert%20Memo%20-%20Rule%2012g3-2(b).pdf> accessed 22 April 2013.

[85] 88th United States Congress, 'Congressional Record Volume 29', Senate (24 July 1963).

States could also avoid becoming a US reporting issuer by making certain information public in the United States through the SEC (Rule 12g3-2(b)). At one level, Rule 12g3-2(b) was very modern, an early example of the application of regulatory deference and recognition of home country reporting. To comply with Rule 12g3-2(b), the FPI submitted, in English or English translations, the documents it was obliged to make public or deliver to its shareholders in its home country. This was still the era when huge wads of paper were mailed or hand-delivered to the SEC offices in Washington, DC. As an inducement to compliance, summaries were acceptable, and most importantly, no US liability attached to the documentation submitted.[86]

4.46   As remarkable as these concessions may seem for the time, in fact, they were mostly irrelevant. US investors were not interested in foreign equity in 1967,[87] and few FPIs would actually exceed the 300 shareholder threshold triggering Rule 12g3-2(b).[88] And, of course, from the point of view of the FPI, it had never entered the US public market and would not expect to be caught by regulatory submission requirements. Rule 12g3-2(b) was left to moulder in obscurity.

4.47   Growing permeability of domestic markets; greater US investor appetite, especially among institutional investors, for non-US equity securities; the rise of ADR programmes; North American economic integration; all these factors combined over time to put more and more pressure on Rule 12g3-2(b). Canadian companies, in particular, could easily find themselves inadvertently tripping over Rule 12g3-2(b), which in many cases they would simply ignore even if they knew of its existence. Ignoring Rule 12g3-2(b) had a price though; when the time came for an increasingly popular US stock exchange listing, these issuers would find that they had been in non-compliance with US securities regulations for extended periods.

4.48   Nevertheless, Rule 12g3-2(b) may have been mostly honoured in the breach until the 1990s when two developments gave it greater traction: the regulatory formalization of ADR practices (manifested in Form F-6) and the implementation of Rule 144A.[89] Rule 12g3-2(b) was put to new use; in addition to acting as an exemptive provision, it now became a means to satisfy mandatory informational requirements under Rule 144A and certain ADR programmes.[90] Reporting issuers satisfied these requirements by virtue of their US 1934 Act periodic reporting. Companies which had never entered the US public markets, and FPIs with respect to over-the-counter ADR programmes, could satisfy the informational requirements by complying with Rule 12g3-2(b). Suddenly, it seemed, Rule 12g3-2(b) sprang to life. It was dragged out of obscurity deep in the regulatory hinterlands and dropped straight

---

[86] This was accomplished by way of a fine linguistic distinction between documents which were 'filed' with the SEC (attracting the full force of the liability provisions triggered by material misstatements or omissions) and documents under Rule 12g3-2(b), which were 'submitted', not filed. The latter did not attract the liability provisions of the US 1934 Act. A case of 'shaken not stirred' making a huge difference.

[87] See Cleary Gottlieb Steen and Hamilton LLP (n 84), 2–3.

[88] See Cleary Gottlieb Steen and Hamilton LLP (n 84), 3.

[89] See later discussion.

[90] Cleary Gottlieb Steen and Hamilton (n 84), 3: 'Rule 12g3-2(b) was traditionally used by companies that sought to establish ADR facilities to promote U.S. trading in their shares. The exemption was (and still is) a prerequisite for the establishment of an unrestricted ADR facility by a bank in respect of an unregistered company. To establish the exemption, a company simply sent a letter to the SEC describing the documents it publishes in its home market and furnishing other information, and providing English translations, versions or summaries (depending on the type of document) of the documents published since the end of its most recent fiscal year. To maintain the exemption, it was required to continue to submit the same documents following home country publication.'

into the glare generated by a high profile initiative, Rule 144A. Scarcely an international offering document anywhere would fail to mention it now. The SEC prepared instructions on its usage. Unfortunately, though, compliance with Rule 12g3-2(b) was still an awkward, paper-based process requiring affirmative action by an issuer and constant monitoring. Also, technically, the Rule cast its net wider than it could reasonably expect compliance by non-US issuers. With heightened internationalization and the ease of trading in multiple markets, equity securities could effortlessly slip into the hands of 300 US residents even where a non-US issuer had minimal contacts with the United States.

Finally, in 2008, Rule 12g3-2(b) entered the electronic age. The goal was to modernize and sim- **4.49** plify the operation of the rule, without changing its basic criteria. As before, to take advantage of the exemption, an FPI cannot have listed or publicly offered securities in the United States.[91] Electronic publication of English language information, on a company website or through the facilities of an overseas regulator, replaced the application process[92] required to establish the exemption and the physical delivery of wads of paper to the SEC in Washington, DC.

Although the basic criteria remain, there are significant changes to the operation of the Rule. **4.50** The intent is obviously to permit as many FPIs as possible to meet the new criteria for Rule 12g3-2(b), advertently or inadvertently, but in either case, without affirmative action in the United States. The Rule is thus structured to promote more or less automatic compliance by those companies most likely to have US shareholders—FPIs already listed outside the United States.

The first new requirement is precisely that; the FPI must have its shares listed outside the **4.51** United States. In addition, the 'primary trading market', a defined term that does duty in several other places in the regulatory regime, must be outside the United States.[93] As originally proposed, the new Rule further restricted the eligibility for exemption where the United States constituted more than 20 per cent of worldwide trading volume. This proposition was opposed during the comment period and dropped in the final Rule as adopted.[94] Encouraging FPIs to participate in ADR programmes and permitting greater opportunity for US investors to diversify their non-US holdings proved persuasive. Thirdly, the information to be made available electronically in English, either on the company website or with a regulator, does not permit summaries to substitute for translations (if translation is necessary) of the home country documentation. The information required to be available is material information the FPI makes public in its home country, files with the principal exchange in its primary trading market, or distributes to its security holders.

The new non-US listing requirement may be problematic for unlisted FPIs. This problem **4.52** is particularly acute with the migration of European issuers off exchanges and onto electronic trading platforms. Will they really go through the trouble of listing on a non-US exchange so as to comply with a US rule of marginal interest to them? Likely not, unless they have set their sights on Rule 144A private placement offerings in the United States, where

---

[91] Which would trigger reporting issuer status and full compliance with the US 1934 Act.
[92] See discussion (n 84).
[93] One or two markets that together represent at least 55% of its worldwide trading volume, at least one of which must have greater trading volume than the United States: see 17 CFR § 240.12g3-2(b).
[94] Because of the definition of primary trading market, the United States cannot constitute more than 45% of worldwide trading volume in order for an FPI to be eligible for Rule 12g3-2(b).

compliance with Rule 12g3-2(b) does double duty. The changes introduced in 2008 were designed to adapt Rule 12g3-2(b) to the electronic age, but even just five years later, they have been outpaced by market change.

4.53 There is also the ever-present consideration of US liability for information made available in English outside the United States, advertently or inadvertently. Under the old system, this information was 'submitted' not 'filed' with the SEC and did not trigger US liability for material misstatements or omissions. Is that still the case under new Rule 12g3-2(b)? Lastly, was there a slip with respect to the new thresholds under § 12(g)(1)(A) of the US 1934 Act (up to 2000 shareholders, a maximum of 500 being unaccredited) under the JOBS Act?[95] The general threshold, applicable to both domestic and FPIs, has been raised but 300 remains the number in the exemptive provisions applicable to FPIs under Rule 12g3-2(a) and (b).

4.54 The question arises, of course, that if compliance is designed to be virtually automatic, and indeed inadvertent, why is a rule necessary at all. Is Rule 12g3-2(b), always problematic, simply not worth the effort? Would it be more sensible to revert to the original 1964 proposition of simply exempting FPIs entirely from the operation of § 12(g) of the US 1934 Act?

3.4 The parallel system in a complex world

4.55 For a variety of reasons, domestic US securities regulation has served as a model to the world, either directly or through its influence in international standard setting. The parallel system, though, has not been exported and so remains a somewhat unique aspect of US law, and based on the concept of the FPI, appears firmly entrenched. There are pressures though, such as the rise of competing markets that may draw FPIs away from the United States, or regulatory blunders such as Sarbanes-Oxley 2002 providing the pretext for early exits. Going forward though, it is possible that the domestic and international aspects of US markets may become more integrated, or at least coordinated. Calls for greater EU-style deference to home country regulation for non-US issuers and market participants would certainly simplify, if not undermine, the US parallel system. The acceptance of financial statements prepared in accordance with IFRS by FPIs appears to be a long awaited move in that direction although it may be a crisis-driven aberration not to be repeated.

4.56 There is no doubt as to the decline of US hegemony in regulation of international capital markets. Within the United States, level playing field arguments continue to surface, sometimes in surprising ways. The US market exit provisions of Rule 12h-6, pushed through by persistent EU governmental and corporate lobbying, prompted similar new US rules for domestic issuers, in an interesting reversal of the usual direction in which influence flows. The US Supreme Court, in another surprising development,[96] came out strongly in favour of territorialism but for perhaps the wrong reasons. On the other hand, the global financial crisis, at least temporarily, resulted in concerted transatlantic regulatory action, with similar institutional frameworks created to deal with the crisis. Perhaps, this is an indication of future directions for US regulation of the international aspects of its capital markets, based on externalization and cooperative efforts in creating a new kind of parallel system, this time a transatlantic one.

---

[95] JOBS Act, Pub L No 112-106, §501, 126 Stat 306, 326 (2012).
[96] *Morrison v National Australia Bank Ltd* 130 S Ct 2869 (2010).

5

CULTIVATING THE US OVERSEAS MARKET

1. Introduction

Over 20 years ago, the United States introduced a trio of regulatory initiatives which repre- **5.01**
sented a turning point in international capital markets. The growing significance of international markets could no longer be ignored nor left to the regulatory hinterlands. The first two
initiatives, Regulation S and Rule 144A (under the US 1933 Act),[1] have become standard
features of virtually all international capital raisings. Although very different in conception
and operation, they are fraternal twins, both responses to a 1987 SEC report on internationalization. They were considered and adopted by the SEC on the same day in April 1990.[2]
The third initiative, the creation of a Multijurisdictional Disclosure System (MJDS) between
Canada and the United States, is a younger sibling, conceived in the same flurry of interest
in international markets, but making its appearance a year later.[3]

1.1 The 1987 Report on Internationalization

In 1987, the SEC published a report on internationalization of securities markets (the *1987* **5.02**
Report on Internationalization).[4] The report was not surprising, in that a main competitor
to the US markets, London, had just undergone a major regulatory shift, dubbed 'the Big
Bang', prompting some self-reflection on the other side of the Atlantic. The report was
unusual, though, in at least one respect. Policymakers and regulators in the United States
are sometimes considered self-absorbed by domestic affairs and exceedingly reluctant to
benefit from comparative experiences elsewhere. This report, however, contained a thor-
ough comparative analysis of capital markets regulatory regimes in a significant number of
jurisdictions.[5]

---

[1] Securities Act of 1933, 15 USC §§ 77a–77aa (2006); Securities Exchange Act of 1934, 15 USC §§
78a–78pp; Regulation S, 17 CFR §§ 230.601–230.905; Rule 144A, Private Resales of Securities to Institutions,
17 CFR § 230.144A; United States Securities and Exchange Commission (SEC), 'Internationalization of the
US Securities Markets: Report of the Staff of the US Securities Stock Exchange Commission to the Senate
Committee on Banking, Housing and Urban Affairs and the House Committee on Energy and Commerce',
SEC Report (27 July 1987) <http://www.sechistorical.org/museum/galleries/imp/imp09b.php> accessed 12
December 2013 (1987 Report on Internationalization).
[2] See Robert G DeLaMater, 'Recent Trends in SEC Regulation of Foreign Issuers: How the US Regulatory
Regime is Affecting the United States' Historic Position as the World's Principal Capital Market' (2006) 39
Cornell International Law Journal 109, 111.
[3] See Carol Olson Houston and Roberta Ann Jones, 'The Multijurisdictional Disclosure System: Model
for Future Cooperation?' (1999) 10 *Journal of International Financial Management and Accounting* 227, 229.
[4] See 1987 Report on Internationalization (n 1).
[5] This is notwithstanding the well-known reflection by Karl Llewellyn, one of the most influential legal academics of his time, that to 'identify a proposal as based on foreign law' would be to give it the 'kiss of death' : see

5.03   In addition to laying the groundwork for the formal rulemaking that produced Regulation S, Rule 144A, and the MJDS, the 1987 Report, in hindsight, still appears remarkably prescient.[6] The factors, which the report identified as driving the internationalization of the markets, were dead on:

- deregulation and opening of closed markets;[7]
- financial innovation in the form of derivatives and securitization;[8]
- UK privatizations and the promotion of a retail investor culture in Europe;[9]
- diversification of the traditional Euromarket into equities and innovative products issued by non-US companies;[10]
- integration of North American markets (FTA then NAFTA);[11]
- rise of the institutional investor;[12]
- investor interest in international diversification;[13]
- developments in communications technology;[14]

Stefan Reisenfeld, 'The Impact of German Legal Ideas and Institutions on Legal Thought and Institutions in the United States' in Mathias Reimann (ed), *The Reception of Continental Ideas in the Common Law World: 1820–1920* (Duncker & Humblot, 1993), 91.

[6] It is easy to lose sight of how much markets have changed in 25 years. See eg Edward F Greene and Linda C Quinn, 'Building on the International Convergence of the Global Markets: A Model for Securities Law Reform' (paper presented at A Major Issues Conference: Securities Regulation in the Global Internet Economy, Washington DC, 14–15 November 2001), 2: 'As the 1980s drew to a close, the cold war was only just beginning to end and the markets reflected a different political and economic world structure. Equity markets in Europe were local, domestic markets of little consequence to listed companies. A European currency was still only a dream. The Eurodollar market was the principal, almost exclusive, cross border financing market. Latin American and Asian markets were for the most part still closed, controlled economies. Investors also behaved differently. The international private market was a fraction of its current size (mutual funds were a minor player in the international markets and the 144A market did not exist), while retail investors outside the United States were primarily debt investors. Finally, technology in general, and the world wide web in particular, had yet to revolutionize the degree to which information could be disseminated around the world with ease.'

[7] The United Kingdom and Japan were opening up at this time, although China, Vietnam, and India remain closed; even Canada had been closed to foreign financial intermediaries until 1987.

[8] The report cites interest rate swaps, which now appear, in retrospect, simple and innocuous.

[9] The privatization of UK state-owned enterprises pushed by Prime Minister Margaret Thatcher, because they were too large to be absorbed by the domestic UK market, were structured as international offerings, putting strain on regulatory frameworks which were not designed to accommodate cross-border transactions. For example, despite a high level of interest, US securities regulation interfered with the participation of US investors in these offerings. In addition, a tranche of each offering was deliberately reserved for retail UK investors so as to promote 'mom and pop' share ownership in the United Kingdom (along US lines). The UK privatizations also spurred similar initiatives in other European countries like France and Italy.

[10] Sometimes referred to as the Eurodollar market, a poky, boring market in long-term, fixed rate, US dollar denominated debt instruments issued by big name US companies.

[11] Although the Canada-US Free Trade Agreement (soon replaced by the Canada-US-Mexico North American Free Trade Agreement) did relatively little to change the provision of financial services and the operation of capital markets, by promoting integration of the markets in goods and other services, accelerated integration of the capital markets. Capital flows followed trade flows.

[12] While estimates vary in the exact percentage, direct retail holdings have been steadily dropping in the United States, from more than 90% in the 1950s to 30% in 2007. See eg Brian G Cartwright, 'The Future of Securities Regulation', University of Pennsylvania School Institute for Law and Economics, Philadelphia, 24 October 2007 <https://www.sec.gov/news/speech/2007/spch102407bgc.htm> accessed 22 April 2013. Mutual funds, pension funds, and other collective investment vehicles in the United States were hungrily looking for investment opportunities.

[13] Modern portfolio theory promoted diversification of holdings as a risk reduction strategy, although 'home bias' (overweighting in domestic securities) persistently defied the theory. However, the increase in capitalization of foreign markets, in part due to privatizations, presented enticing opportunities to institutional investors.

[14] In 1987 even the use of mobile phones was rare.

- competition among markets;[15]
- the dominance of Canadian foreign issuers in US markets.[16]

These factors, identified over 25 years ago, look like a blueprint to the future of modern capital markets. Among these factors, the rise of competing markets, in particular the United Kingdom and Japan, was a primary source of concern. One blind spot in the report is the European Union, which at the time, was a fragmented market of little direct consequence to the United States.[17]

The rise of competing markets, together with greater cross-border activity, had tested the US **5.04** regulatory apparatus. US securities regulators had previously found little resistance to their extraterritorial approach to application of US regulation; now, US regulation began to bump up against regulatory regimes in other markets. Ultimately though, the mismatch between the US appetite for non-US investment opportunities and the reluctance of non-US issuers to enter US markets proved to be the greatest concern prompting regulatory action.

At this time, US investors were more or less excluded from many investment opportunities out- **5.05** side the United States by virtue of the operation of the personality principle. It had been a long-standing precept of US securities law that US citizens, wherever they were in the world, had the benefit of the protection of US securities law, whether they wanted it or not. Companies outside the United States offering securities to US citizens (wherever they might be) risked contravention of US law, and the more advertent of them would exclude US citizens.

Equally, non-US companies demonstrated a decided reluctance about entering the US mar- **5.06** ket to offer securities within the United States. Even with the accommodations of the parallel system, the regulatory burden was perceived to be too heavy and the potential for class action litigation in the United States a real and present danger. US retail investors, in particular, were more or less excluded from direct international diversification and the benefits of modern portfolio theory.[18] Investors sophisticated enough to navigate the waterways of international investing faced duplicative costs and multiple intermediaries if they did not have an offshore presence.

1.2 Comparing apples and oranges: Regulation S and Rule 144A

Regulation S and Rule 144A were adopted by the SEC at the same meeting on the same **5.07** day in 1990. They are both directly responsive to the concerns of the *1987 Report on Internationalization*, but there the resemblance stops. They are very different rules.

---

[15] Capitalization of the US markets was growing more slowly than in the past, whereas the growth in markets in the United Kingdom, Japan, and even Italy, was accelerating. In particular, the United States was experiencing a decline in foreign listings, indicating that the domestic US market was not keeping pace with the trend towards internationalization. In 1986 the London Stock Exchange had 512 foreign listings, compared to the New York Stock Exchange with 59 (one third of which were Canadian listings).

[16] One half of all foreign debt and equity offerings in the United States in the decade preceding the 1987 Report on Internationalization had been by Canadian issuers. In reality, North America constituted a regional market in its own right and raised the question as to whether it merited a regulatory system of its own.

[17] The rise of the EU market is a remarkable story, in and of itself. By the time of the de Larosière Report in 2009, the European Union was the largest financial market in the world: see Jacques de Larosière, *Report of the High Level Group on Financial Supervision in the European Union* (Brussels, 25 February 2009), 3.

[18] Collective investment vehicles, mutual funds, did not have the impressive array of international offerings which they do today, charged hefty front end, back end, and management fees as well as having nasty tax consequences.

5.08   Regulation S is a primary market rule (for the most part),[19] replacing simple deference by the SEC to US issuers activities in the traditional Euromarket. It is an offshore rule, applicable to offerings (and some resales) outside the United States. Regulation S attenuates the broad (and extraterritorial) reach of § 5 of the US 1933 Act which requires registration of securities and preparation of a prospectus for offers and sales triggering jurisdictional nexus with the United States. Regulation S offshore offerings are for the most part those that, had they been conducted within the United States, would have been considered a public offering of securities requiring compliance with § 5 of the US 1933 Act.[20]

5.09   Rule 144A, on the other hand, is primarily a secondary market rule for private placements, more specifically, applicable to resales of privately placed securities. Importantly, it is a domestic rule, which is equally available to both US and non-US issuers but with investors restricted to the institutional market. Rule 144A is simply a small adjustment to existing regulatory constructs, but an adjustment of enormous consequence. Although originally framed as a 'resale' rule, it is now usual for large private placements in the United States, international and domestic, to be structured so as to sell directly to an 'initial purchaser' which qualifies as a Rule 144A buyer,[21] and which can resell in accordance with the rule. The 'initial purchaser' will in fact be an intermediary which will be able to structure the transaction using usual distribution practices, associated with a public offering but to a restricted universe of purchasers.

5.10   Regulation S and Rule 144A are very different though. Regulations S, despite its complicated structure, does not actually do very much. As a domestic US rule applicable to 'offshore' offerings, it was necessarily circumscribed in its practical operation. Rule 144A, on the other hand, was market changing.

5.11   Regulation S is a political, big gesture, a statement to the world that the United States respects the international principle of 'comity'.[22] In response to the resistance in the international regulatory community to the extraterritorial application of US law, Regulation S pulls in the regulatory horns and espouses the principle of the territorial application of US securities law. In actual fact, this retrenchment is limited to the operation of only one part of the US 1933 Act, and that is § 5 (registration and prospectus requirements). In part, Regulation S is a face-saving mechanism, making express the accepted status quo.

5.12   Secondly, Regulation S has not aged well; it was on the verge of being outdated virtually upon its adoption. It is backward looking to the markets and practices of the 1980s. As more or less a restatement of the status quo, it adapted existing market practice and a vast body of interpretative pronouncements to a regulatory framework. For example, Rule 902(h)(1)(ii)(B)(1), one arm of the definition of an offshore transaction in Regulation S, refers to a physical trading floor in an overseas market; physical trading floors have vanished for the most part, replaced by electronic trading.[23] The highly detailed drafting of Regulation S reflects the

---

[19]   Regulation S does have a resale rule component, discussed in due course.
[20]   A Regulation S offering may, in fact, not be considered a public offering in its jurisdiction of offering due to the wider ambit and bright line nature of private placement exemptions elsewhere in the world.
[21]   The Qualified Institutional Buyer or 'QIB'.
[22]   US Securities and Exchange Commission, Final Rules: Offshore Offers and Sales, SEC Release Nos 33–6863, 34–27942 (24 April 1990).
[23]   Market practices were shaped by regulatory pronouncements called 'no-action letters'. No-action letters are letters prepared by the SEC staff. They are prepared in response to requests by individuals or entities that

transformation of a body of no-action letters, based on very specific factual circumstances, into a regulatory rule. But more importantly, Regulation S is reworking the practitioners' law which preceded the Regulation, practices which developed in an unregulated space and before technology transformed trading. For example, Regulation S perpetuates reliance on contractual chains of prohibitions on sales to US persons during the distribution process, certifications on residency by purchasers, the use of (paper) 'global' certificates representing the whole issue of debt securities, either permanently or temporarily and 'lockup periods' during which certain operations are restricted. These contractual and procedural practices had developed in the absence of regulatory direction, making use of private law and practice.

These mechanisms, remnants of an earlier age, look increasingly archaic. Certainly they are not adapted to modern technology and trading practices. For one thing, they remain wedded to paper-based securities, which are now exceedingly rare given recourse to book entry processes, if not actually prohibited in some jurisdictions. Equally, requirements based on trading over a physical trading floor are impossible to fulfil as many exchanges have abolished physical trading floors in favour of screen-based trading.[24] Recourse has again had to be had to no action practice or reasoning by analogy to work around these regulatory anachronisms. **5.13**

Moreover, Regulation S is a hard rule. It is detailed and technical. One set of SEC training materials is subtitled 'How to make an offshore offering and not give up and cry'.[25] Detail and technicality often offer certainty and ready answers to a multitude of questions, but with Regulation S, technical compliance is not enough.[26] It is this latter aspect of the Regulation which has added even greater technical complexity by way of highly conservative interpretations by practitioners worried about missing the boat. There is now a body of practitioner interpretation, adding 'prudential Category 2' and 'Category 2 1/2' for example, which loads on requirements that go beyond the letter of the rule in the interests of conservatism.[27] The use of precedents by lawyers and their disinclination to deviate from structures used in past transactions perpetuate this conservative approach and the use of unnecessary paraphernalia.[28] **5.14**

At some levels, Regulation S must be considered a regulatory disappointment. It has simply not been that useful.[29] Its complex, clumsy, and outdated mechanics detract from its utility. **5.15**

---

the SEC not take enforcement action if that individual or entity engages in a particular activity, where the legal status of that activity is unclear. These letters are publicly released and increase the body of knowledge on what is and is not allowed. More importantly, although the interpretation is specifically addressed only to the party requesting the no action letter, in practice, they are relied upon in subsequent transactions by other parties. As interpretive pronouncements, however, while they may be persuasive, they are not binding on the courts.

[24] Practitioners have tried to adapt Regulation S in this respect by reasoning by analogy; now that trading is electronic, it is analogous to trading over a physical trading floor. See Adam Fleisher and Peter Castellon, 'Regulation S Selling and Transfer Restrictions: A Basic Users Guide' (Alert Memoranda, Cleary Gottlieb Steen and Hamilton, 18 July 2012), 5.

[25] In the author's possession.

[26] US Securities and Exchange Commission, Final Rule: Offshore Offers and Sales, SEC Release Nos 33–6863, 34–27942 (24 April 1990), 100.

[27] See Fleisher and Castellon (n 24), 18 and Appendix A.

[28] See Fleisher and Castellon (n 24), 17–18.

[29] There are indications that it may be finding new life with the creation of new products for new markets outside the United States. For example, the Hong Kong dim sum bond market—in which RMB bonds are issued outside of China—falls within the least onerous category of Regulation S, Category 1 (overseas directed offering), even where the issuer is a US corporation such as McDonalds (the first non-Chinese corporate issuer).

Almost immediately after its adoption, abuses, or at least perceived abuses, arose, leading to a narrowing of the categories of offerings and stricter requirements under the Regulation.[30]

5.16 Finally, Regulation S does not entirely embrace the territoriality principle which features so prominently in its implementing release and the high-minded references to comity among nations. This is mostly rhetoric. The territorial approach is narrowly restricted to the application of § 5, and even there its free operation suffers mitigation. Commentators have long criticized the paraphernalia required to invoke the Regulation,[31] the physical trading floor restrictions, waiting periods, selling restrictions, the prohibition on directed selling efforts,[32] and the delays on resales. Although not strictly true, Scott observed in 2001 that no other major investor market except the United States restricted the offshore activities of its domestic investors.[33]

5.17 Rule 144A, on the other hand, has all the virtues which Regulation S lacks: elegance, simplicity, ease of application, and openness to technology. It has had enormous positive market impact and anticipated the rise in importance of both the private markets and the institutional investor. Issuers, investors, and regulators alike love the Rule.

5.18 Rule 144A is not an international rule; it is available to domestic US issuers and foreign private issuers (FPIs) alike for private placements conducted in the United States. It virtually eliminates much of the cumbersome mechanisms associated with privately placed securities, provided the buyers in the secondary market are large institutions or financial intermediaries, at least for a certain period of time.[34]

5.19 Rule 144A is short and sweet, as well as elegant in concept. Making the distinction in the United States between a public offering and a private placement has been an arduous exercise involving the interaction of a general exemptive provision (an offer or sale by an issuer not involving a public offering),[35] an extrapolation from the statutory provision (a resale of privately placed securities not involving a public offering),[36] the definition of underwriter,[37] and

---

[30] In 1998, equity offerings of US issuers were moved from Category 2 to Category 3, imposing almost unworkable procedural requirements; the equity securities themselves becoming 'restricted' securities under Rule 144. See Securities and Exchange Commission, 'Problematic Practices under Regulation S', SEC Interpretative Release No 33-7190 (27 June 1995) <http://www.sec.gov/rules/interp/33-7190.txt> accessed 16 January 2014.

[31] See Hal S Scott, 'Internationalization of Primary Public Securities Markets' (2001) 63 *Law and Contemporary Problems* 71; Edward F Greene, 'Beyond Borders: Time to Tear Down the Barriers to Global Investing' (2007) 48 *Harvard International Law Journal* 85. In 2001 when Scott was writing, the Chinese markets were obviously not on his mind.

[32] These criteria may be affected by the recently enacted Jumpstart Our Business Startups Act, Pub L No 112-106, Stat 306 (2012) (JOBS Act), in terms of the changes to the concept of general solicitation during the private placement process.

[33] He obviously did not consider China in making this remark, but it was still very early days in that market: See Scott (n 31), 100.

[34] Private placement is where a corporation makes an offering on an exempt basis and the securities placed become subject to hold periods and resale restrictions for 6–12 months under Rule 144.

[35] The Securities Act of 1933 Pub L 73-22 § 4(a)(2) 48 Stat 74: 'The provisions of section 5 shall not apply to ... transactions by an issuer not involving any public offering.'

[36] The so-called § 4(1½) exemption (now, technically, 4(a) (1 1/2)), which does not actually exist in the statute, but is an extrapolation from the operation of the § 4(a)(1) exemption (an offer or sale not involving an issuer, underwriter or dealer) and the § 4(a)(2) exemption (an offer or sale by an issuer not involving a public offering). If this all sounds very strained, it is.

[37] The Securities Act of 1933, 15 USC § 77b.(a)(11): 'The term "underwriter" means any person who has purchased from an issuer with a view to, or offers or sells for an issuer in connection with, the distribution of

the concept of a distribution (impliedly, to the public). If a purchaser of securities from an issuer, directly or indirectly, is understood to have done so with a view to distribution, then the purchaser is considered a 'statutory underwriter' and the whole transaction is characterized as a public offering. If it has been structured as a private placement, this recharacterization means that those involved have engaged in an indirect, unregistered, non-exempt public offering, with dire consequences for all concerned. Rule 144A operates by deeming that resales of privately placed securities, effected in accordance with the Rule, are not distributions, thus the buyers and sellers not statutory underwriters and the nature of the transaction as a private placement is preserved.[38]

By this simple deeming mechanism, the Rule provides certainty and a liquid secondary **5.20**
market for large institutional buyers in privately placed securities, thereby lowering the costs to issuers. Although early attempts to create an electronic trading platform (PORTAL) were fraught with difficulties, Rule 144A has, in fact, proved to be very forward looking: it is easily adaptable to the dematerialization of securities and changes in market practices brought about by technology. Rule 144A also fits well with the dominant new profile of investors: they are institutions.

In the early days of its operation, Rule 144A was used primarily for debt securities by US **5.21**
issuers and for equity securities by FPIs.[39] The US issuers, if they were not already reporting issuers, may have preferred to issue debt, rather than equity, in private placements because of the implications of § 12(g), whereby the entire panoply of reporting requirements descended on US issuers which exceeded 500 voting equity shareholders (now increased to 2,000 in most cases by the JOBS Act). FPIs, on the other hand, could benefit from the exemptive provisions of Rule 12g3-2(b) even if they exceeded a 300 shareholder threshold. Privately placed equity, for those who were not already reporting issuers, provided an easy first step into the US markets and, in many cases, led to subsequent public offerings there.[40] All in all, Rule 144A admirably filled the bill in terms of meeting the concerns of the *1987 Report on Internationalization* and is considered a regulatory success.

2. The Euromarket, Release 4708 and Regulation S

In international capital markets, the footprints of Regulation S are ubiquitous. However, its **5.22**
origins are in a narrowly circumscribed pronouncement[41] of the US regulator with respect to an obscure specialty market—the Eurobond or Eurodollar market.

---

any security, or participates or has a direct or indirect participation in any such undertaking, or participates or has a participation in the direct or indirect underwriting of any such undertaking...'

[38] Purchasers reselling under Rule 144A make use of the exemptive provisions of § 4(a)(1), a transaction not involving an issuer, underwriter or dealer.

[39] '[T]he overwhelming majority of capital raised under Rule 144A consists of debt, because Rule 144A's "non-fungibility" condition generally prevents US public companies from undertaking Rule 144A equity offerings. Foreign firms, however, have routinely relied on Rule 144A to issue equity in the US': William K Sjostrom Jr, 'The Birth of Rule 144A Equity Offerings' (2008) 56 *UCLA Law Review* 409, 411.

This may no longer be the case for Canadian issuers, as integration of US and Canadian capital markets has intensified.

[40] By familiarizing themselves with the US markets, non-US issuers would become convinced that the regulatory burdens of the public markets were outweighed by the advantages.

[41] US Securities and Exchange Commission, Registration of Foreign Offerings by Domestic Issuers, SEC Release Nos 33–4708, 34–7366 (9 July 1964) (Release 4708).

2.1 The traditional Euromarket

5.23   The Euromarket has been called the original international capital market of modern times. It linked US corporations to European investors and demonstrated characteristics very different from the domestic US capital markets. Big, brand name US corporations looked to the Euromarket to raise long term (up to 30 years) US dollar denominated fixed rate debt.[42] This was among the simplest of financial products. Despite the fact that the European based investor was often referred to as the 'Belgian dentist',[43] the Euromarket was a professional or institutional market.[44] Capital raising was quick and easy,[45] with obliging stock exchanges, such as Luxembourg, providing listing virtually on demand.

5.24   The market was tax driven, on both sides of the Atlantic. European investors would assume no tax risk; bonds had to be in bearer form, with no withholding tax imposed on interest payments by the US issuer. In the event that there was an adverse development under US tax law, the terms of the financial instruments contained a 'gross-up' clause. Essentially the US issuer would have to increase interest payments to the investor so as to compensate it for any reduction in return arising from changes in US tax law. Sometimes, as protection for the issuer against an unexpected increase in the cost of borrowing, also included was a call provision, which permitted the issuer to buy back the bonds, rather than grossing up interest payments.

5.25   In the early days, many issuances were structured as two separate back-to-back offerings, through jurisdictions such as the Netherlands Antilles, to take advantage of tax treaties producing the desired effects. For some time,[46] taxation also acted as a deterrent to US investors buying or holding these securities. For this reason, the SEC tolerated this offshore market, permitting it to flourish without regulatory intervention; the securities would tend to stay out of the United States and US hands. The transactions had to be structured so as to deflect any implication that they involved an indirect, unregistered, non-exempt, public offering of securities in the United States or to US investors.

2.2 Release 4708

5.26   Until 1990 and the adoption of Regulation S, the only general guidance provided by the US regulator with respect to these transactions was contained in a 1964 release,[47] and a large body of transaction specific 'no-action' letters. The market was essentially, from both a European and a US perspective, unregulated, left to the devices of industry associations and market practitioners.[48]

---

[42] Straight debt would refer to the simplest of debt instruments with no additional features such as convertibility to another financial instrument.

[43] Typifying a conservative investor with large amounts of disposable income.

[44] In fact, US institutional investors were discovered to constitute the vast majority of ultimate holders of the debt when a tax treaty (which had facilitated the structuring of the transactions) lapsed, producing untoward tax consequences for investors, and a lobbying effort on the part of US institutional holders.

[45] Often only ten days or so elapsed from initiation to closing and listing of the issuance.

[46] Until 1974, the Interest Equalization Tax, which had been implemented in 1963, provided a disincentive for US investors to invest in foreign securities. The tax was designed to reduce the balance of payment deficit by reducing capital outflow from the United States.

[47] Release 4708 (n 41).

[48] The Euromarket also represents an example of benign regulatory arbitrage. US securities regulators looked to protect the interests of US investors on the US side; on the European side, issuance of securities was primarily regulated at that time by companies law and stock exchange listing rules. Where you had a non-European company issuing to a non-US investor, the transaction slipped easily between the regulatory cracks.

On the US side, the 1964 SEC Release 4708 provided the foundation for such regulatory   **5.27**
deference. It acknowledged that 'virtually any offering of securities made by a US corporation to foreign investors' would be caught by the broad language of the US 1933 Act and
would require registration with the SEC and preparation of a prospectus. Noting that protection of US, not foreign, investors was the primary purpose of securities regulation, the
SEC said that it would adopt a restrictive interpretation of the application of the registration
provisions (§ 5) of the 1933 Act. The SEC would not take action against US corporations
issuing securities which were distributed abroad to foreign nationals in a manner so as to
'come to rest abroad'. This required procedural precautions to be used so that the offerings
were made 'under circumstances reasonably designed to preclude distribution or redistribution of the securities within, or to nationals of, the United States'.[49]

There are several points to note in Release 4708. It was not a regulatory instrument of any   **5.28**
kind, simply an interpretation by the regulator. It was not an espousal of the principle of
territoriality; US securities law, from the US perspective, would continue to apply to US citizens wherever they were in the world. The main concern was the possibility of 'flowback' into
the US market of securities sold offshore. Since Release 4708 was issued under the aegis of
the 1933 Act, it focused on the 'distribution' process associated with what would otherwise
be considered a public offering in the United States. It did provide, however, some clarity on
concurrent private placements in the United States; there would be no 'integration' of the
offshore offering with the US private placement so as to taint the latter. Yet, as to when and
how resales of securities issued offshore by US issuers could be effected, the SEC remained
silent for decades; that was not within the purview of the 1933 Act.

Because of the cryptic nature of Release 4708 and its focus on the distribution process, legal   **5.29**
practitioners developed a number of fairly crude mechanisms associated with the offering
and distribution process so as to establish compliance with the language of the Release and
have the securities 'come to rest abroad'. Initially, this had not been much of a concern, since
the unpleasant tax consequences for US holders acted as a deterrent. However, with the
repeal of the Interest Equalization Tax, this deterrent disappeared, leaving it to the fertile
imaginations of US securities lawyers to devise mechanisms 'to preclude distribution or
redistribution of the securities in the United States or to US nationals'. Taking this very narrow view, once the distribution process was over, and a reasonable period of time had elapsed,
no further monitoring or restrictive mechanisms were required.

In US securities law, the concept of distribution is important because of the definition   **5.30**
of underwriter: one who purchases, directly or indirectly, from an issuer with a view *to
distribution* of the securities. The term 'distribution' serves as the dividing line between
public offerings, effectuated through a distribution process utilizing underwriters, and
private placements. With Release 4708, the SEC would turn a blind eye to offshore 'public
offerings' making use of customary distribution and redistribution techniques provided
precautions were taken with respect to flowback into the United States or the hands of US
citizens.

In the absence of regulatory backing, the mechanisms devised by legal practitioners to   **5.31**
achieve this result (post-1974) focused on the contractual chains of purchase and sale

---

[49] Release 4708 (n 41), 3–4. The language of 'distribution' implied that the offerings, were they to take place
in the United States, would be considered public offerings subject to registration and prospectus requirements.

among the professional intermediaries, as the securities fanned out, first from the issuer to the underwriter and syndicate, onward to multiple dealers and sub-dealers, and ultimately to the first 'investors'. The underwriters in the syndicate (purchasing from the issuer) would contractually agree never to sell any part of an unsold allotment to a US person (as defined) and to make no offers or sales to US persons or into the United States. The dealers further down the distribution chain would contractually agree not to sell to a US person during the 90-day period following the end of distribution. The confirmation of the trade to the first investor would contain language to the effect that such person was not a US person and would not sell to a US person during the 90-day 'lockup period' following the end of distribution.

5.32 The lockup period (by convention set at an arbitrary 90 days) began once the 'distribution' had been completed and all the securities sold to the first investors. During this period, individual paper certificates were not delivered to investors so as to impede secondary trading (by delivery). Instead, one temporary 'global' paper certificate, representing the entire issue, was physically 'locked up' in a safe in Luxembourg or perhaps Brussels. At the end of the lockup period, 'definitive', ie individual, certificates representing each purchase would be delivered to the investor, who, in order to collect the certificate had to certify that they were not a US person (as defined to include US citizens as well as US residents), nor were they purchasing on behalf of a US person. Since paper-based bearer bonds at this time had physical coupons attached to them, which represented the right to receive periodic interest payments, without a definitive certificate an investor could not collect interest on the bond.

5.33 These procedures, arbitrary and clumsy as they were, became the mark of 'reasonable procedures' designed to preclude distribution or redistribution of the securities in the United States or to US nationals (wherever they might be). Transaction after transaction churned out the same documentation and contractual terms; paper global certificates were couriered from New York to Brussels and Luxembourg, to be locked in a safe or drawer. But once the 90-day lockup expired and the definitive certificates were delivered to investors, the securities could wing their way around the world. The test established in Release 4708 had been met.

2.3 The Euromarket changes

5.34 With time, Release 4708 was overwhelmed by its limitations. The Euromarket started to change dramatically in the 1980s and the operative assumptions of Release 4708 (US name brand issuer, selling US denominated, fixed rate, long-term straight debt to the Belgian dentist) no longer prevailed. The issuers diversified: Canadian and Japanese corporations, sovereign governments, international financial institutions such as The World Bank joined the ranks of US issuers. They were attracted to the ease of issuance, favourable costs of financing, and the investor base offered by the Euromarket.

5.35 The question, of course, was the extent to which the dictates of Release 4708 would apply to these non-US issuers. Would they structure their transactions in the Euromarket so as to adopt the distribution procedures designed to prevent 'flowback' of the securities to the United States? The fact that the issuer was not a US corporation was no guarantee that US investors would not be interested in the securities on offer; quite to the contrary. Because the focus of Release 4708 was on the distribution process, essentially driven by market practice and more or less standardized documentation overseen by international industry associations, these transactions by non-US issuers took on a very similar form to Release 4708 compliant ones.[50]

Not only did the issuers diversify, but, perhaps even more importantly, the financial products **5.36** on offer did as well. In the years leading up to the implementation of Regulation S, there was a burst of innovation in finance. In some cases, due to its more or less unregulated nature, the Euromarket became a laboratory for financial innovation. Complex index products, derivatives of all sorts, products combining plays on currency, interest rate, commodities, and stock exchange movements all rolled together into one package, hybrid debt and equity products, medium-term notes, continuous or tap offerings, were tested in the Euromarket. Some did not go very far; in particular, governments were concerned about plays on their currency. Others became the template for later retail products marketed in the domestic public markets.[51]

Together with product diversity, came currency diversity. For some time the Euromarket had **5.37** been known as the Eurodollar market; that all began to change especially with the arrival of interest rate and currency rate swaps. The Canadian dollar and the Japanese yen were favourites. Prior to the introduction of the euro, there was even a fictitious currency unit used to denominate debt products, the ECU, standing for European Currency Unit and representing a notional, weighted basket of European currencies.

This diversification and innovation happened very quickly, taking governments and regu- **5.38** lators by surprise. The development, which finally caught the attention of US regulators, was the appearance of US equity products in the Euromarket. The view of the SEC was that equity of US issuers offered and sold offshore, unlike debt, would have a strong propensity to flowback into the US market. Equity is designed to trade, unlike debt which, the conventional wisdom went, was held to maturity. The Belgian dentist would place the Euronds under the mattress and clip coupons for 30 years. Moreover, equity tends to flow back to the largest, most liquid trading market; in the case of US issuers (and perhaps others as well, such as Latin Americans and Canadians), this was the United States. This new phenomenon tested the underlying assumptions of the distribution procedures developed for the traditional Euromarket. The 90-day lockup period, through market practice blessed by SEC no-action letters for debt securities, became a gestational nine months for equity of US issuers.

By the late 1980s, Release 4708 had reached the limits of its usefulness. In 1990, it was **5.39** replaced by Regulation S. In the following years, interesting synergies between Regulation S and Rule 144A developed. Offshore offerings under Regulation S often have a concurrent Rule 144A private placement in the United States associated with them. Although the privately placed securities cannot immediately trade in the public markets in the United States (being restricted to resales among qualified institutional investors for a certain period of

---

[50] Most jurisdictions did not have anything comparable to Release 4708 and did not share the concerns of the SEC with respect to flowback into their domestic market. The Ontario (Canada) Securities Commission did prepare a short policy guideline, 'Interpretation Note 1', along the lines of Release 4708 and which is still in effect. See Cally Jordan, 'Regulation of Canadian Capital Markets in the 1990's: The United States in the Driver's Seat' (1995) 4 *Pacific Rim Law & Policy Journal* 577.

[51] Cally Jordan and Giovanni Majinoni, 'Financial Regulatory Harmonization and the Globalization of Finance', Policy Research Working Paper 2919, The World Bank (October 2002).

time), they can be freely resold into European (or other) public or private markets.[52] From a US perspective, these resales, if in compliance with the resale rule imbedded in Regulation S, 'wash off' the private placement restrictions, with one exception; again, US equity.[53]

5.40 Although the Euromarket or Eurodollar market has long been considered the premier international capital market, competitors, modelled on the Euromarket, did emerge: Maple bonds,[54] Samurai bonds,[55] and recently, both the very popular Yankee bonds,[56] and the more specialized Hong Kong 'dim sum bonds'.[57] These alternative markets, inspired by the Euromarket, have been facilitated by the availability of currency and interest rate swaps and regulatory initiatives such as Regulation S and Rule 144A. The result has been the rise of 'multipolarity', the dispersion of the historical concentration of capital raising in the transatlantic corridor.[58]

2.4 Regulation S—how it works

5.41 The story of Regulation S is a long story, reaching back to Release 4708. The regulation has a reputation for difficulty and technicality. It rolls into regulatory form the principles laid down in Release 4708,[59] subsequent market practices focusing on the distribution process and the body of no-action letters which accumulated over the 25 years leading up to 1990. However, Regulation S is not a particularly dynamic rule, and constitutes more a snapshot of market features existing at the time of its enactment. Although it has been redeployed in some interesting ways lately,[60] generally speaking, it looks like a regulatory relic from another

---

[52] A subsequent amendment to Regulation S, precluded US equity taking advantage of resales outside the United States to 'wash off' restrictions on transfer of US privately placed securities. See Securities and Exchange Commission, 'Final Rule: Offshore Offers and Sales (Regulation S)', SEC Release Nos 33-7505, 34-39668 (17 February 1998).

[53] See Securities and Exchange Commission (n 52).

[54] Maple bonds are bonds denominated in Canadian dollars that are sold in Canada by non-Canadian financial institutions and companies. They allow Canadian investors to invest in foreign companies free from uncertainties arising as a result of fluctuations in currency exchange.

[55] Samurai bonds are bonds denominated in Japanese yen that are sold in Japan by non-Japanese financial institutions and companies. They allow Japanese investors to invest in foreign companies free from uncertainties arising as a result of fluctuations in currency exchange.

[56] Low interest rates in the United States and the availability of favourable rates on currency swaps have resulted in a rise of European issuers raising debt capital denominated in US dollars in the United States in the Rule 144A market: see Richard Milne and Anousha Sakoui, 'Europe Leads Way for Yankee Bond Sales', *Financial Times* (22 August 2010) <http://www.ft.com/intl/cms/s/0/f781862a-ae0f-11df-bb55-00144feabdc0. html#axzz2SBUg5UrL> accessed 13 December 2013; Aline Van Duyn, Nicole Bullock and Richard Milne, 'Investors "Snap Up" Yankee Bonds', *Financial Times* (30 January 2011) <http://www.ft.com/intl/cms/s/0/59 123948-2caf-11e0-83bd-00144feab49a.html#axzz2SBUg5UrL> accessed 13 December 2013.

[57] Dim sum bonds are Renminbi denominated bonds issued in Hong Kong (and now elsewhere). The issuers of dim sum bonds are primarily entities based in China or Hong Kong and occasionally foreign companies: see Tanya Powley, 'Keep Dim Sum Bonds Off Menu', *Financial Times* (14 September 2012) <http://www.ft.com/ intl/cms/s/0/76cc67b2-fdc1-11e1-8fc3-00144feabdc0.html#axzz2SBUg5UrL> accessed 13 December 2013; Fiona Law, 'Dim Sum Bonds Issuance Climbs', *Wall Street Journal* (25 March 2013) <http://online.wsj.com/ article/SB10001424127887323466204578382074137672956.html> accessed 13 December 2013.

[58] See Bruegel and Peterson Institute for International Economics, 'Transatlantic Economic Challenge in an Era of Growing Multipolarity', Conference proceedings, European School of Management and Technology, Berlin, 27 September 2011; Cally Jordan, 'The Wider Context: The Future of Capital Market Regulation in the Developed Markets' (2012) 6 *Law and Financial Markets Review* 130, 131.

[59] Avoidance of an offshore transaction constituting an indirect, unregistered, non-exempt, public offering in the United States.

[60] For example, 'dim sum bonds' fall within a specialized subcategory for which they were never intended (overseas directed offering).

age. The concurrent availability and interaction with Rule 144A, however, has amplified its effect in ways which would not otherwise have been possible.[61]

The implementing release for Regulation S justifies the introduction of the rule with some lofty language:[62] comity ('restraint and tolerance by nations in international affairs'), investor expectations ('reasonable expectations of participants in the global markets'), and the sandbox rule (recognizing the primacy of the laws in which a market is located). The stated objective is the adoption of a territorial approach to the application of § 5 of the US 1933 Act (registration and prospectus requirements) to offshore offerings.[63] In action, the rule falls short of fulfilling these aspirations.[64]

5.42

2.4.1 The general conditions of Regulation S

There are two general conditions, both defined terms, which must be met in order for any offering to obtain the benefits, from a US perspective, of Regulation S:[65] the offering must be an offshore transaction,[66] and there must be no directed selling efforts into the United States associated with the offering.[67]

5.43

In the 'offshore transaction' definition, the buyer must be outside the United States or the offering must be made over the physical floor of a non-US stock exchange. The latter requirement is an example of how no-action letters were rolled into the regulatory language of Regulation S; it is based on a 1987 no-action letter granted to a large US-based pension fund, TIAA-Cref, permitting it to participate in the privatization of a French state-owned industry taking place through the facilities of the Paris Bourse.[68] It is also an example of the backward-looking nature of Regulation S. Most major stock exchanges now do not have a physical trading floor, and certainly the London Stock Exchange (LSE) did not at the time of the TIAA-Cref letter.[69] The LSE physical trading floor had been abandoned in 1986, to be

5.44

---

[61] See section 5.39 regarding interaction of Regulation S resale rule with Rule 144A.

[62] US Securities and Exchange Commission, Final Rules: Offshore Offers and Sales, SEC Release Nos 33–6863, 34–27942 (24 April 1990).

[63] Regulation S only applies the territoriality principle to § 5; the notorious anti-fraud provisions of US securities law are unaffected. The US Supreme Court has recently clawed back the reach of these provisions in its decision in *Morrison v National Australia Bank Ltd* 130 S Ct 2869 (2010).

[64] For example, a great deal of US securities law (in particular, the US 1934 Act) were not implicated in Regulation S.

[65] Although it is not clear in all circumstances of its purported application that Regulation S delivers as many benefits as burdens.

[66] For the purposes of Regulation S, the definition of an 'offshore transaction' is provided by General Rules and Regulations, Securities Act of 1933, 17 CFR § 230.902(h)(1): 'an offer or sale of securities is made in an "offshore transaction" if: (i) the offer is not made to a person in the United States; and (ii) either (A) at the time the buy order is originated, the buyer is outside the United States, or the seller and any person acting on its behalf reasonably believe that the buyer is outside the United States; or (B) For purposes of: (1) Section 230.903, the transaction is executed in, on or through a physical trading floor of an established foreign securities exchange that is located outside the United States; or (2) Section 230.904, the transaction is executed in, on or through the facilities of a designated offshore securities market . . . and neither the seller nor any person acting on its behalf knows that the transaction has been pre-arranged with a buyer in the United States; § 230.902'.

[67] For the purposes of Regulation S, the definition of 'directed selling efforts' is provided by General Rules and Regulations, Securities Act of 1933, 17 CFR § 230.902(c)(1): ' "Directed selling efforts" means any activity undertaken for the purpose of, or that could reasonably be expected to have the effect of, conditioning the market in the United States for any of the securities being offered in reliance on this Regulation S. . . . Such activity includes placing an advertisement in a publication "with a general circulation in the United States" that refers to the offering of securities being made in reliance upon this Regulation S.'

[68] No-Action Letter from US Securities and Exchange Commission to College Retirement Equities Fund, 'Participation of US Institutional Investors in French Privatizations' (18 February 1987).

[69] The LSE eliminated the physical trading floor in 1986.

replaced by a quite splendid crystal mobile hanging in the atrium of its new facilities in Canary Wharf. International practitioners have, however, by analogy, extended the 'physical trading' floor language of Regulation S to include electronic trading facilities.[70]

5.45 The first requirement—an offshore transaction cannot be made to persons in the United States—may appear obvious, but there is a twist as Regulation S changes the position adopted in Release 4708. This condition is an example of the narrowing effects of application of a territoriality principle. Release 4708 prohibited offerings to US nationals, wherever they were in the world. This is still the basis of US tax law. In Regulation S, however, the United States took a less imperial approach. A new definition of 'US person' made it clear that offshore transactions would not preclude offers to US nationals *outside* the United States.

5.46 The second general condition, the prohibition on directed selling efforts into the United States, quickly proved more problematic, necessitating additional interpretative rules.[71] The prohibition addressed activities and information flows which might 'condition' the US markets, ie generate interest by US investors in the offshore transaction, leading to a 'pull' on those securities into the United States. As print and paper gave way to electronic communications, it became more and more difficult to insulate the US market from information and marketing efforts associated with offshore transactions.[72] As with Release 4708, rather artificial manoeuvres addressing press conferences, road shows, analyst briefings, newspaper announcements, and then website access,[73] were developed to meet the condition.[74] An unanswered question, for the time being, is how changes to the concept of 'general solicitation' and 'general advertizing' in the JOBS Act[75] may impact the interpretation of no directed selling efforts under Regulation S.

5.47 It is important to remember that Regulation S is based neither on deference to offshore regulation of offshore markets (despite its assertions about the 'sandbox rule' in the implementing release) nor on concepts of mutual recognition. Regulation S still purports to apply to all offerings of securities anywhere in the world. It simply provides, from the US perspective, a wide exemption from US registration and prospectus requirements, for those offshore transactions by (mostly) non-US issuers meeting the two general conditions. Very few US issuers offering securities abroad get a 'pass' on regulatory compliance; for some transactions, the compliance burden has in fact increased over market practices associated with

---

[70] See Fleisher and Castellon (n 24), 5.

[71] For example, Rule 135(e) (now overtaken by the JOBS Act 2012) was introduced to provide a safe harbour from the general requirements of the Securities Act, and allows private issuers to provide both foreign and US journalists with access to press conferences and press releases held or released outside the United States, provided that particular conditions are met: See General Rules and Regulations, Securities Act of 1933, 17 CFR § 230.135(e).

[72] The SEC did, however, attempt to encourage the use of password protected websites and authentication requirements; see US Securities and Exchange Commission, 'Statement of the Commission Regarding use of Internet Web Sites to Offer Securities, Solicit Securities Transactions or Advertise Investment Services Offshore', SEC Release Nos 33-7516, 34-39779 (23 March 1998) <http://www.sec.gov/rules/interp/33-7516.htm> accessed 20 September 2013.

[73] See US Securities and Exchange Commission (n 72). See, especially, Section III on 'Offshore Offers and Solicitations on the Internet', and Section IV on 'Additional Issues under the Securities Act'.

[74] Some commentators were quite critical of restricting the flows of information, arguing that more, not less, information should be available to investors; see, for example, Scott (n 31), 97.

[75] Whereby offers can be made to an unlimited number of potential investors without jeopardizing the exempt nature of a private placement, so long as sales are only made to accredited investors: see US Securities and Exchange Commission, 'Eliminating the Prohibition Against General Solicitation and General Advertising in Rule 506 and Rule 144A Offerings', SEC Release No 33-9354 (29 August 2012).

Release 4708. Additionally, non-US issuers with strong connections to the US market (a defined term, 'substantial US market interest' or 'SUSMI'),[76] also find themselves entangled in the tentacles of Regulation S.

2.4.2 Compliance beyond the general conditions: the four factors

For offerings which do not get the 'pass' on regulatory compliance, there are two formal levels **5.48** of compliance, one more onerous than the other, engaging requirements going beyond the two general conditions. As with market practice under Release 4708, compliance mechanisms focus on the distribution process. In fact, the compliance requirements are taken directly from pre-Regulation S market practices and SEC no-action letters, tweaked in some respects to minimize compliance costs, but, with respect to US equity, increasing the compliance hurdle. So, to a certain extent, the legacy of Release 4708 lives on. In fact, the compliance mechanisms of Regulation S make little sense without an understanding of the pre-Regulation S markets.

The likelihood of 'flowback' into the United States of securities offered and sold offshore **5.49** is still a primary determinant of the precautions to be associated with the distribution process.[77] However, Regulation S interweaves considerations drawn from the much changed nature of the Euromarkets and balances them against the availability of information about the issuer, domestic or not, in the US market. For example, a substantial US market interest in a foreign issuer's securities may be an indicator of the likelihood of 'flowback' of those securities into the United States. However, if there is full-blown, publicly available, information about the issuer in the US market, then the concerns with ultimate flowback of the securities are attenuated.

Regulation S mixes and matches four criteria in determining the nature of distribution pro- **5.50** cedures applicable to a particular offshore transaction. The first is the nature of the issuer, domestic US or non-US. Release 4708 had only considered US (and some Canadian) issuers. However, the Euromarket had attracted a diverse group of issuers, which included sovereigns and large non-US issuers. Although somewhat anomalous, non-US issuers, from a US perspective, had been coming under the purview of Release 4708, and were subsequently rolled into Regulation S.

The second factor is the nature of the security on offer: debt or equity. Again, in response **5.51** to the changing nature of the Euromarket, with product diversification and the appearance of equity securities, the SEC reconsidered the distribution mechanisms created to meet the tests set out in Release 4708. The SEC took the view that equity behaves differently from debt, and is more likely to flowback into the largest, most liquid market for it, which in the case of US issuers would be the United States.

The third factor is the level of US investor interest in the particular securities of an issuer, ie **5.52** whether there is a substantial US market interest (SUSMI). Where there is SUSMI for the particular securities of a non-US issuer, then FPI status does not deflect the necessity to take

---

[76] Substantial US Market Interest, or SUSMI, is defined differently for debt than for equity securities: see General Rules and Regulations, Securities Act of 1933, 17 CFR § 230.902(j).

[77] It is important to remember here that the distribution process begins with the purchase by the underwriter from the issuer, continues through the sales and resales in the chain of distributions (by the professional intermediaries) and ends with the holdings 'coming to rest' with the first ultimate investor.

precautions during the distribution process so as to prevent flowback into the United States. There is a bifurcated, bright-line definition of SUSMI, one branch applicable to debt and the other to equity.[78] To fall within the definition, the issuer's debt or equity, as the case may be, must already be present in the US market. Hot international IPOs are not caught.

5.53 The last factor is the availability of public information about the issuer in the United States. Is the issuer, domestic US or non-US, a reporting issuer subject to periodic disclosure under the US 1934 Act, either domestic US requirements or the parallel regime for FPIs?

2.4.3 The three categories determining compliance level

5.54 Under Regulation S, three categories of transaction are created, each with an increasingly heavy compliance burden, based on the combination of the four factors: identity of the issuer, kind of securities on offer, level of US market interest, and availability of public information in the United States. For transactions falling into Category 1, only the two general conditions need be met (an offshore transaction and no directed selling efforts). Category 2 requires that more attention be paid to the distribution process, as there may be a greater US market interest pulling the securities into the United States. The last category, Category 3, is the most troublesome. Issuers and transactions unfortunate enough to fall into Category 3 must comply with onerous and cumbersome distribution processes, exceeding usual market practices under Release 4708.

5.55 **Category 1—the Status Quo.** Most offerings of securities around the world fall into Category 1 of Regulation S, which is designed to be self-executing; non-US issuers, either advertently or not, tend to comply with the two general conditions. To this extent, Regulation S is a big yawn, simply recognizing, in a formal regulatory way, the status quo. There are several other, quite different kinds of transactions lumped, rather pragmatically, together in Category 1. For the most part, these are transactions to which the United States can lay little by way of legitimate regulatory claim. There is also an odd assortment of transactions, some of which arise from SEC no-action letter practice, where the SEC agrees to exercise deference to non-US markets and regulation.

5.56 In the most all-encompassing subcategory are offerings by non-US issuers (FPIs, as defined) of either debt or equity securities, where there is no SUSMI.[79] The SUSMI test makes no distinction between US and non-US issuers, but the underlying assumption is that there would

---

[78] See General Rules and Regulations, Securities Act of 1933, 17 CFR § 230.902(j):

(1) 'Substantial U.S. market interest' with respect to a class of an issuer's equity securities means:
  (i) The securities exchanges . . . in the United States in the aggregate constituted the single largest market for such class of securities . . .; or
  (ii) 20% or more of all trading in such class of securities took place in, on or through the facilities of securities exchanges . . . in the United States and less than 55% of such trading took place in, on or through the facilities of securities markets of a single foreign country . . .
(2) 'Substantial U.S. market interest' with respect to an issuer's debt securities means:
  (i) Its debt securities, in the aggregate, are held of record . . . by 300 or more U.S. persons;
  (ii) $1 billion or more of . . . [t]he principal amount outstanding of its debt securities . . . in the aggregate, is held of record by U.S. persons; and
  (iii) 20% or more of . . . [t]he principal amount outstanding of its debt securities . . . in the aggregate, is held of record by U.S. persons.

[79] Remember that the two general conditions must be met for Category 1 offerings as well as Category 2 and 3: the offering must be an offshore transaction with no directed selling efforts into the United States.

be US market interest in the securities of US issuers.[80] For debt securities, the test looks at the number of holders in the United States (300 threshold); the outstanding, aggregate, amount of all debt in the United States (US$1 billion threshold); and the percentage of the principal amount of outstanding debt held by US persons (20 per cent threshold). Exceed one of the thresholds and the test deems there to be SUSMI; the transaction then falls into Category 2. Obviously, 20 years later, US$1 billion is not what it used to be and the threshold may now operate to catch more FPIs than originally intended.

For equity securities, SUSMI is determined by looking at the size of the US trading market, **5.57** relative to other trading markets, but just for that class of equity securities. For an FPI to take advantage of Category 1, either (i) the United States does not represent the largest single trading market for that class of equity securities, or (ii) less than 20 per cent of that class of equity securities is trading in the United States and greater than 55 per cent is trading in a single non-US market. Again, at the time of implementation, as with debt securities, SUSMI was intended to exclude from the US regulatory net all but the tiniest percentage of non-US offerings by non-US issuers. It was assumed that even non-US issuers with equity securities listed on a US exchange would not have SUSMI, as their domestic home market would be the major trading market. However, with the rise in cross-listed securities and the influx of Latin American issuers into the United States through the ADR market, over time, more FPIs would be bumped into Category 2.

Category 1 also includes sovereign debt issuances outside the United States. This is a simple **5.58** case of recognition of sovereignty; the United States would have difficulty asserting jurisdiction over the non-US capital markets activities of sovereigns. Sovereigns do raise capital in the Eurobond market, however, so to this extent Category 1 recognizes the diversification of the Euromarket as well as deflecting any implication that the US regulatory net might catch these transactions.

Equally, an issuance by a non-US issuer in one market (assumedly, but not necessarily, its **5.59** domestic market) under local law would elude the US regulatory net as constituting an 'overseas directed offering' (ODO) within the purview of Category 1. Irrespective of the level of US market interest, the SEC would be hard-pressed to dictate the offering conditions applicable to a purely domestic overseas offering of non-US securities (as tempted as they might be in the case of Canadian offerings). Imagine the outrage if the SEC purported to tell the UK regulator in London the requirements to be associated with domestic UK only offerings.

There is one curious twist, however, to the story of ODOs. A second variant of an ODO **5.60** is available to US issuers, not just FPIs. In the circumstances outlined for overseas directed offerings of US issuers, the SEC defers to local law and regulatory oversight. The US issuer can offer only non-convertible debt securities, *not* denominated in US dollars, in one country (obviously not the United States), in accordance with local law. This particular example of regulatory deference originated in accommodations for US issuers listing bonds on Swiss markets.[81] Switzerland, especially in the run up to the implementation of the Prospectus Directive in 2003 and the Market in Financial Instruments Directive in 2007, had ambitions

---

[80] See General Rules and Regulations, Securities Act of 1933 (n 78).
[81] See letter from Union Bank of Switzerland to Jonathan G Katz, Secretary, Securities and Exchange Commission (26 October 1988).

to create an alternative to the traditional Eurobond market which was losing its 'eurosecurities' exemption.[82]

5.61 However, the ODO characterization for offerings of US issuers may have recently proved felicitous in a very different alternative market, the 'dim sum' bond market (a bond offering in Hong Kong, under Hong Kong law, denominated in RMB).[83] The first non-Chinese issuer in the dim sum bond market was McDonalds, followed closely afterwards by the Asian Development Bank and The World Bank, all usual Euromarket issuers. The ODO would not be available for traditional Eurobond offerings by US issuers as these offerings are structured to take place in more than one jurisdiction, given the small size of many European countries.[84]

5.62 Lastly, as an accommodation for US issuers with employees scattered abroad, offerings under employee benefit plans by US issuers are essentially exempt from US regulatory requirements by virtue of their inclusion in Category 1.

5.63 Apart from some of the very narrow circumstances involving US issuers, the SEC would have difficulty in purporting to regulate most of the transactions or issuers in Category 1 except at the margins, so Regulation S is of little practical effect in that respect. With increasing international integration of capital markets though, and during the heyday of the rush by FPIs into the US markets (now somewhat abated), it may be that the broad universe of Category 1 offerings, where the SEC exercised regulatory deference, contracted somewhat.

5.64 **Category 2—the New Euromarket and beyond.** As originally conceived, the primary difference between Category 1 and Category 2 transactions was based on the presence of SUSMI or the identity of a US issuer (which would tend to pull securities issued offshore into the United States). Public availability of information in the US market, however, justified a relaxation in some of the clumsy distribution procedures developed to meet the interpretative statement in Release 4708. Originally, Category 2 did not differentiate between FPIs and domestic US issuers with respect to equity securities, provided they were reporting issuers in the United States; information conquered all. FPIs, for these purposes, were assimilated to US issuers. From the US perspective, SUSMI justified US regulation of offshore transactions by non-US issuers, a somewhat contentious proposition.[85] However, in fact, during the days of Release 4708, US market practices had, to a certain extent at least, been

---

[82] Council Directive 89/298/EEC of 17 April 1989 on Coordinating the Requirements for the Drawing-Up, Scrutiny and Distribution of the Prospectus to be Published when Transferable Securities are Offered to the Public [1989] OJ L 124/8 ('1989 Prospectus Directive') provides that 'eurosecurities which are not the subject of a generalized campaign of advertising or canvassing' be exempted from the general prospectus requirements for securities offerings in the European Union. Under Article 2(1)(f) of the 1989 Prospectus Directive, eurosecurities are 'transferable securities which are to be underwritten and distributed by a syndicate at least two of the members of which have their registered offices in different States, and are offered on a significant scale in one or more States other than that of the issuer's registered office, and may be subscribed for or initially acquired only through a credit institution or other financial institution'.

[83] See Powley (n 57) and Law (n 57).

[84] The 1992 definition of 'eurosecurities' which provided an exempt status for the traditional Eurobond market under the Investment Services Directive, required the offering to take place in more than one jurisdiction.

[85] Likely an extrapolation from the conduct and effects doctrine espoused by the United States to justify the assertion of jurisdiction, here the effects being the likelihood of flowback into the United States. This doctrine, at least as applicable to securities class actions based on Rule 10b-5 has been questioned by the US Supreme Court in *Morrison v National Australia Bank Ltd* 130 S Ct 2869 (2010).

adopted by non-US issuers participating in the Euromarket and the SEC, for its part, over time, had included FPIs within the purview of Release 4708.

The only distinction between FPIs and US issuers in Category 2, as originally formulated, was **5.65** with respect to debt securities; US issuers needed to be reporting issuers in the United States to make use of Category 2 for both debt and equity issuances. FPIs issuing debt securities with SUSMI did not need to be reporting issuers; reporting or not, they had the benefit of Category 2. GAs noted above, given the high thresholds in the SUSMI definition, FPIs falling into Category 2 were originally thought to be the exception and not the rule, an assumption somewhat eroded by inflation and tested by Canadian and Latin Americans issuers.

Perceived abuses by US issuers engaging in offshore equity offerings resulted in a tightening **5.66** of the requirements: all US equity was moved from Category 2 to Category 3 in 1998.[86] This move made issuance of US equities in the Euromarket an unattractive proposition. On the other hand, the profile of US issuers which remained in Category 2 fit very nicely with the profile of the traditional US issuer in the Eurobond market: debt securities of a well-known (at least to the extent indicated by reporting issuer status) US issuer. For these issuers, Regulation S cut through the thicket of distribution procedures associated with the old Release 4708 practices.

Category 2 focuses compliance primarily on the various professional intermediaries par- **5.67** ticipating in the distribution, the assumption being that the intermediaries are knowledgeable and interested in ensuring compliance. The intermediaries must include an assortment of representations, restrictions, notices, and certifications in the chain of contracts linking the issuer to the ultimate first investor. These requirements differ little from prior market practice, but drop the artificiality of temporary global certificates locked in a drawer in Luxembourg or the bother of obtaining investor certifications as in the past.[87] One nod of the head to increasingly fast-paced markets was the change in the length of the now notional 'lockup' period, from the arbitrary 90 days to the equally, but shorter, arbitrary 40 days. In Regulation S, the lockup period becomes known as the 'distribution compliance period',[88] but more or less serves the same purpose as the old lockup period, ie to prevent immediate 'flowback' of the securities into the United States in an indirect, unregistered, non-exempt offering.[89]

Category 3—the catch all and the catch. Category 3 is a catch all category: transactions **5.68** not coming within Category 1 or 2. Of the four factors determining the characterization of transactions for purposes of Regulation S, the lack of publicly available information was originally the determining factor in Category 3. Without publicly available information in the US market, greater precautions needed to be taken to keep the securities offshore. FPIs

---

[86] See discussion of Category 3 at para 5.68.

[87] In addition, the offering materials need to bear a legend indicating that the securities are not being registered in the United States.

[88] See General Rules and Regulations, Securities Act of 1933, 17 CFR § 230.902(f): 'Distribution compliance period' means a period that begins when the securities were first offered to persons other than distributors in reliance upon this Regulation S . . . or the date of closing of the offering, whichever is later, and continues until the end of the period of time specified in the relevant provision of § 230.903'. This general rule is subject to a number of exceptions.

[89] As in the past, an unsold allotment in the hands of the underwriter who has purchased from the issuer remains 'undistributed', and thus never exits the distribution compliance period.

with SUSMI did not need to be reporting issuers in the United States to slip into Category 2 for their debt securities, so for them, Category 3 applied only to equity, where there was SUSMI but the FPI was not a US reporting issuer. It was assumed that this particular combination of factors would occur only rarely, if ever.

5.69 For US issuers, as originally formulated, Category 3 was applicable only to the debt or equity of non-reporting issuers. Although not impossible, few US issuers would fall within these parameters, at least in the traditional Euromarket. Investors there were a discerning bunch and had always preferred brand name US issuers, which would usually be reporting issuers. Moreover, US issuers preferred their home market for equity offerings, by and large. Additionally, prior to the JOBS Act, § 12g of the US 1934 Act would automatically transform non-reporting US issuers into reporting issuers once their voting shareholder base exceeded 500 and their assets US$10 million.[90] Non-reporting US issuers were thus careful about equity offerings generally, and unlikely to look to a specialized market like the Euromarket. But markets were changing rapidly and undermining the regulatory assumptions. With the significant growth in importance of the private market, and technology companies in particular, brand names could emerge very rapidly, yet not be reporting issuers, Facebook prior to its initial public offering in 2012 being one such example.

5.70 In the early days of Regulation S, however, the SEC became concerned about the use of Regulation S by US equity issuers deliberately structuring offshore transactions to avoid the registration provisions of the US 1933 Act. Although offered offshore, seemingly in compliance with Regulation S, the equity securities found their way into the hands of US investors with undue haste. These transactions set off regulatory alarm bells.

5.71 First, in 1996, the SEC required information on the use of Regulation S for US equity to be included in regulatory filings in the US (in the 10-K). Then, in 1998, the ambit of Category 3 was enlarged to catch all offshore US equity offerings, whether the issuer was reporting or not. Also in 1998, US equity issued offshore under Regulation S became 'restricted' securities, subject to the same resale restrictions as if they had been privately placed in the United States. US equity securities which actually sold in a private placement in the United States (often under Rule 144A) and which had thus become restricted securities,[91] could not have the restrictions 'washed off' by being resold outside the United States in conformity with the resale rule of Regulation S.[92] In this way, Category 3, originally contemplated as affecting only the most marginal of transactions, gained much greater significance.

5.72 In Category 3, the old market practice paraphernalia are retained: temporary global (paper-based) certificates and certifications by purchasers that they are not US persons. US issuers of equity securities must additionally put stop transfer restrictions in place, legend their certificates (again

---

[90] Title V and Title VI of the JOBS Act amend § 12(g) and § 15(d) of the US 1934 Act as follows: 'The holders of record threshold for triggering Section 12(g) registration for issuers (other than banks and bank holding companies) has been raised from 500 or more persons to either (1) 2,000 or more persons or (2) 500 or more persons who are not accredited investors' (JOBS Act—Frequently Asked Questions) <http://www.sec.gov/divisions/corpfin/guidance/cfjjobsactfaq-12g.htm> accessed 16 December 2013.

[91] Rule 144, not to be confused with Rule 144A, allows public resale of restricted and control securities if a number of conditions are met, the most important being the hold period and information requirements. The hold periods, as of 2008, are six months for a reporting issuer, and otherwise, one year.

[92] The resale rule of Regulation S requires the two general conditions to be met: see Regulation S: Offshore Resales, 17 CFR § 230.904.

the assumption that securities are paper-based), and the intermediaries refrain from engaging in hedging activities in the United States, which might have the effect of transferring the economic risk there to US investors, breaching in substance if not in form the distribution compliance period.[93] For debt, the distribution compliance period remains 40 days but for equity it is increased to six months or 12 months, depending on whether the issuer is a reporting issuer in the United States. Needless to say, this constitutes a complicated set of compliance rules, some of which are impossible, technically, to meet in the age of book entry securities and modern electronic markets.

2.4.4 *The resale rules*

As Release 4708 was narrowly focused on the circumstances in which the SEC would not insist **5.73** on compliance with § 5 of the US 1933 Act, the registration and the prospectus provisions, nothing was said about resales of securities offered outside the United States. This created a great deal of uncertainty, with issuers and their counsel focusing on what Release 4708 did say about the distribution process. Regulation S rectifies this lacuna by creating a resale rule for securities originally offered in an offshore transaction (but not restricted to them).[94] Both the general conditions are applicable to resales; there must be an offshore transaction and no directed selling efforts into the United States. The resale rule operates for offshore resales of securities offered and sold under Regulation S as well as restricted securities privately placed (by either US issuers or FPIs) in the United States.

Rule 144A is also a resale rule, and easily interacts with Regulation S. International offerings **5.74** are often structured conjointly to take advantage of this interaction. An offshore Regulation S offering (of either a US or non-US issuer) is made contemporaneously with a Rule 144A private placement in the United States. The privately placed securities are 'restricted' in the United States and under Rule 144A may only be sold there to large institutional investors.[95] However, these restricted securities can be freely resold outside the United States under the resale provisions of Regulation S. The restrictions fall away, are 'washed off' and the securities can freely trade in the offshore market. US equity securities are the exception to this rule; restrictions cannot be 'washed off' in this manner.

2.4.5 *The legacy of Regulation S*

Regulation S exemplifies a great deal of regulatory effort for a small amount of gain; it **5.75** changes relatively little. Sovereignty is explicitly acknowledged (in Category 1), distribution practices for US Eurobond offerings are streamlined, and clarification is given on the circumstances in which securities offered and sold outside of the United States can be resold. Canadian and Latin American issuers found themselves potentially worse off, if they fell

---

[93] This latter requirement is a later 1998 amendment to Regulation S: See US Securities and Exchange Commission, Final Rules: Offshore Offers and Sales, SEC Release Nos 33-7505; 34-39668 (17 February 1998).

[94] See Regulation S: Offshore Resales, 17 CFR § 230.904.

[95] Under Rule 144A, as originally implemented, to meet the relevant exemption, securities could only be offered or sold to a 'qualified institutional buyer or to an offeree or purchaser that the seller and any person acting on behalf of the seller reasonably believe is a qualified institutional buyer'. For the purposes of Rule 144A, a Qualified Institutional Buyer (QIB) is an entity which 'in the aggregate owns and invests on a discretionary basis at least $100 million in securities of issuers that are not affiliated with the entity': see Rule 144A, Private Resales of Securities to Institutions, 17 CFR § 230.144A. The JOBS Act 2012 now permits offers to non-QIBs, so long as the sales themselves are made only to QIBs.

into Category 2 because of US market interest. Category 3 is virtually unworkable, and has been subject to regulatory interpretation. Practitioners have added to the complexity of an already complex rule by taking conservative positions in response to ambiguous situations and creating 'prudential' or intermediate categories of distribution compliance procedures. As the transatlantic monopoly on international capital markets breaks down, Regulation S has nevertheless shown its adaptability to new circumstances, aided in large part by the availability of Rule 144A.

3. Rule 144A

5.76 If Regulation S is a long story, Rule 144A is a short one. Rule 144A operates in the private, exempt market. Its purpose is to create a 'liquid and efficient institutional resale market for unregistered securities'.[96]

3.1 US private placements

5.77 Unlike other jurisdictions with bright line rules indicating the dividing line between public and private markets, the cryptic nature of the US 1933 Act creates great uncertainty. The main transaction exemptions are usually referred to as the investor exemption, the dealer exemption and the issuer exemption, all appearing in § 4(a):[97]

> The provisions of section 5 [registration and prospectus requirements] shall not apply to—

(1) transactions by any person other than an issuer, underwriter, or dealer;
(2) transactions by an issuer not involving any public offering;
(3) transactions by a dealer (including an underwriter no longer acting as an underwriter in respect of the security involved in such transaction). . . .

Sections 4(a)(1) and (3) are exemptions for ordinary secondary market trading by investors to other investors and by the dealer intermediaries in the usual course of their business; registration and prospectuses are not required. The private placement exemption, § 4(a)(2), is wedged in between: 'transactions by an issuer not involving any public offering'. Unfortunately, 'public offering' is not defined, and the circumstances in which privately placed securities may be resold, either privately or into the public markets, is not specified.

5.78 The tricky part with these exemptions lies in the possibility that someone purchasing securities, supposedly in reliance on § 4(a)(1), may inadvertently miss the boat by falling within the definition of 'underwriter'.[98] Anyone purchasing securities from an issuer, directly or indirectly, down the chain, 'with a view to distribution',[99] is a statutory underwriter and not

---

[96] US Securities and Exchange Commission, Resale of Restricted Securities; Changes to Method of Determining Holding Period of Restricted Securities Under Rules 144 and 145, SEC Release 33-6806 (23 April 1990).

[97] Note that the numbering of this section changed in 2012 with the enactment of the JOBS Act. Prior to this time it was § 4(2) of the Securities Act of 1933 Pub L No 112-106, 48 Stat 74 that exempted private placements, which were often referred to in short hand as § 4(2) offerings.

[98] In § 2(a)(11) of the US 1933 Act, underwriter is defined as: 'any person who has purchased from an issuer with a view to, or offers or sells for an issuer in connection with, the distribution of any security, or participates or has a direct or indirect participation in any such undertaking, or participates or has a participation in the direct or indirect underwriting of any such undertaking.'

[99] As the definition includes direct and indirect participation in an underwriting, the characterization follows purchasers down the chain of purchases and sales.

eligible for the § 4(a)(1) exemption. Where there is a distribution and an underwriter, there is a public offering.

Some help was put in place in 1982 with the creation of Regulation D, a 'safe harbor' **5.79** designed to inject more certainty into the private placement process. Regulation D, however, is technical and tricky itself; practitioners, in their opinion practice, were leery of it.[100] Market practices, not surprisingly, developed to deflect implications of underwriter involvement in private placements. As with Regulation S procedures, these were primarily contractually based, cumbersome and somewhat artificial. There were investment intent letters from initial purchasers, legends placed on securities providing notice as to their restricted nature, stop transfer instructions with the transfer agent, and legal opinions accompanying all requests to transfer the securities. The securities themselves became 'restricted' and resales within certain time periods after issuance prohibited. Originally, restricted securities had to be held for three years by the initial investor (with a 'dribble out' mechanism permitting a small percentage to be resold after two years). All of this was costly and severely constrained the liquidity in the secondary market; issuers paid more, as investors demanded more, given the risks assumed due to the impediments to trading.

As markets became more volatile, investors were disinclined to commit to holding securities **5.80** for such long time periods. In today's world where securities change hands in milliseconds and prices can drop or jump in the blink of an eye, three years is a lifetime. In recognition of the changing markets, the holding periods were reduced (to two years with dribble out after one, and most recently to six months for reporting issuers and one year for non-reporting issuers).[101] After expiry of the hold periods, the securities can be freely resold into the market, the hold period having demonstrated investment intent and thus refuting any implication that the investor was an underwriter, purchasing from the issuer with a view to distribution.

In addition, inventive practitioners, under pressure from investors to inject more liquidity **5.81** into the secondary market, began to give 'reasoned' opinions with respect to 'private' resales within the hold periods. The reasoning went that although § 4(a)(2), then known as § 4(2), only provided an exemption for the issuer in a transaction not involving a public offering, a 'private' resale by an investor, not involving a public offering, should also be exempt. The private nature of the resales would be indicated by taking the same procedural precautions as had accompanied the initial placement by the issuer. As the reasoning straddled the statutory language of then § 4(1) and (2), it was quickly dubbed the § 4(1½) exemption.

3.2 Background to Rule 144A

Rule 144A is the regulatory embodiment (with a few conditions attached) of the § 4(1½) **5.82** exemption.[102] As originally proposed, Rule 144A would have encompassed a much broader universe of investor and investment product. There would have been three types of investors

---

[100] To address these concerns, Rule 508 was added to Regulation D; insignificant deviations from a term, condition, or requirement of Regulation D do not result in a loss of the exemption provided certain other conditions are met.

[101] See Persons Deemed not to be Engaged in a Distribution and Therefore not Underwriters, 17 CFR § 230.144(d).

[102] The § 4(1½) exemption is still invoked, where, for one reason or another, a particular private placement cannot meet the conditions of Rule 144A (eg if there are investors who do not meet the definition of qualified institutional buyer). Sometimes there are 'side-by-side' placements, using both exemptions, the one based in market practice and the other in regulation.

able to participate in Rule 144A placements, not just the top-tier 'qualified institutional buyers' (QIBs) which now remains; QIBS could also have been smaller (the $100 million threshold would have referred to assets, not assets invested). Any security, even of a class already listed or publicly traded, could have been placed in a Rule 144A transaction.

5.83 As adopted, the ambit of Rule 144A was narrowed. In part, this was in response to criticisms by the professional intermediaries, which saw the potential Rule 144A market as a threat to lucrative underwritings in the public markets. And how right they were. Rule 144A was a blazing success and the private placement market burgeoned, to the point where it had eclipsed issuances in the public markets in the United States by 2008.[103]

5.84 In response to opposition by the intermediaries, the universe of potential participants was restricted to large institutional investors, broker-dealers, and banks. Only securities which were 'not fungible' with securities already listed or trading publicly could form part of a Rule 144A placement. There were continued pressures by investors though to open up the rule, and technical amendments in 1992 broadened somewhat the eligibility requirements. But sometimes, doing nothing is better than nothing. The monetary thresholds in Rule 144A have not been changed since its inception in 1990 and so simple inflation resulted in more and more institutional investors qualifying. As for registered broker-dealers, their 'assets invested' threshold (US$10 million) now appears a pittance. Additionally, with the shortening of the hold periods for privately placed securities, Rule 144A needed only to operate for a more limited period of time before restrictions would drop off and the securities would become freely tradable outside the Rule 144A market.

3.3 How Rule 144A works

5.85 One key to the success of Rule 144A is its elegant simplicity. It deems that persons reselling restricted securities (ie privately placed securities) during the hold periods in compliance with Rule 144A are not engaged in a distribution. They are not underwriters under § 2(a)(11) and are not engaging in an indirect, non-exempt, unregistered public offering. The necessity for many of the costly bells and whistles associated with traditional private placements, designed to deflect the implication of a public offering, drop away. The requirements of Rule 144A are straightforward and easily determinable. Uncertainty is obviated and QIBs can immediately trade among themselves.

5.86 First of all, there must be a valid private placement, a sale by an issuer to an investor (which would benefit from the § 4(a)(2) exemption). Then, that investor, provided Rule 144A conditions are met, may resell in reliance on the § 4(a)(1) exemption, a transaction not involving an issuer, underwriter, or dealer. Even here, Rule 144A has transformed private placement practice, with intermediaries such as registered broker-dealers,[104] wearing their QIB hat, taking the securities from the issuer, as an 'initial purchaser', rather than as an intermediary as such. The initial purchasers can then immediately resell on to other QIBs, in a process which

---

[103] See Alan S Blinder, Andrew W Lo, and Robert M Solow (eds), *Rethinking the Financial Crisis* (Russell Sage Foundation Publications, December 2012), 257. (Rule 144A has tipped the balance in favour of private placements; 2008 is the crucial milestone because of the Oaktree Capital Management LLC sale took place.) See also Sjostrom (n 39); David Weild and Edward Kim, 'Market Structure is Causing the IPO Crisis—and More' (on declining IPOs in the US, GrantThornton, June 2010).

[104] Which need only $10 million in assets invested, as opposed to other institutions which are required to have ten times that amount.

closely resembles a 'distribution' but which, by the sleight of hand of Rule 144A, is deemed not to be one. This structure avoids the sometimes protracted negotiations with multiple investors in a traditional private placement; the initial purchasers do the deal and then resell into the universe of QIBs. In this manner, Rule 144A, originally envisaged as a secondary market resale rule, becomes an instrument for private, primary market offerings.[105]

3.3.1 Who can issue under Rule 144A?

Rule 144A is a domestic private placement rule, but any issuer can structure a Rule 144A private placement, domestic or FPI, no strings attached. Issuers need not meet any size or minimum capitalization requirements (such as those which apply in other rules). Issuers can be big or small, reporting or not reporting. The rulemakers resisted the temptation to cavil or hedge. **5.87**

3.3.2 What can be sold under Rule 144A?

As originally proposed, the same open approach was adopted towards the financial instruments that could be created and sold in a Rule 144A placement; there were no restrictions. Anything that could be traded, could be placed. However, due to pressure from the professional intermediaries, a condition was imposed in the rule as adopted. Securities placed in a Rule 144A transaction cannot be of the same class as those outstanding in a public market; they cannot be 'fungible' with publicly traded securities. Although there were strong suspicions that the professional intermediaries were acting in a self-interested manner in proposing this restriction, the justification was based on the desirability of preventing premature 'leakage' of restricted securities into the public markets before the expiry of regulatory hold periods. **5.88**

Non-fungibility has not proven to be an immense hurdle, in practice. First of all, the hold periods for restricted securities under Rule 144[106] have been shortened considerably, so that the restrictions drop off privately placed securities relatively quickly now. Obtaining a separate CUSIP number[107] for a class of privately placed securities is not an onerous process, and neither is the creation of separate classes of securities sharing similar economic attributes. Moreover, as the market has expanded, the SEC has demonstrated a relaxed approach to the non-fungibility criterion too, as 'leakage' has not been a problem. **5.89**

3.3.3 Who can buy Rule 144A securities?

Rule 144A is a remarkably non-technical rule. The conditions associated with who can buy and resell Rule 144A securities constitute really the only minor technicalities in the entire rule. Rule 144A is available only to institutions; sophisticated individuals who might otherwise qualify under Regulation D, for example, as 'accredited investors', are excluded. **5.90**

---

[105] The term 'distribution' is used advisedly here, as it does imply a public offering is taking place. What Rule 144A has created is an exempt institutional market, but one which bears strong resemblances, in how it operates, to a public market (but restricted to institutions).

[106] The hold periods for all restricted securities, whether or not Rule 144A is used, are specified in Rule 144: Persons Deemed not to be Engaged in a Distribution and Therefore not Underwriters, 17 CFR § 230.144(d).

[107] A Committee on Uniform Securities Identification Procedures (CUSIP) number is a nine character, alphanumeric identifier that is unique to every class of security. The first six digits identify the issuer of the security and the later digits identify the particular type of security issued. Applications for a new identifier can be made online. Applications for a CUSIP number are made to CUSIP Global Services, which is managed on behalf of the American Bankers Association by Standard and Poor's.

5.91 Insurance companies originally comprised the largest class of Rule 144A purchasers, followed by mutual funds (collective investment vehicles), pension funds, registered advisers, registered broker-dealers and commercial banks.[108] QIBs must have at least $100 million in securities invested. Commercial banks must also meet a net worth test of $25 million. Unlike the other QIBs, registered broker-dealers need only $10 million in assets invested, a tribute to their lobbying efforts during the formulation of the rule, as well as the recognition that as sophisticated professional intermediaries, they play an indispensable role in the market. Registered broker-dealers also benefit from characterization as a QIB if they are acting in an agency capacity for a QIB. Time has eroded the significance of these monetary thresholds,[109] expanding the universe of QIBs.

3.3.4 Conditions associated with a Rule 144A placement

5.92 In keeping with the general tenure of Rule 144A, the other conditions associated with its usage are simple. There must be a valid private placement, to start with. This has raised, in the past, the issue of no 'general solicitation',[110] an increasingly problematic requirement in the information age. The difficulties which arose prior to the high profile initial public offering of Facebook shares resulted in this deeply fundamental concept being jettisoned in the JOBS Act.[111]

5.93 Although Rule 144A is technically a resale rule, a Rule 144A placement must be structured properly from the initial sale by the issuer to the first purchaser.[112] A burden is placed on each seller, including the issuer, to ensure that the purchaser is a QIB, based on reasonable belief. In practice, intermediaries maintain proprietary lists of QIBs.[113]

5.94 Notice and availability of basic information are also conditions for using Rule 144A. Each seller in the chain of transactions of purchase and sale under Rule 144A must take reasonable measures

---

[108] US House of Representatives Subcommittee on Investigations of House Energy and Commerce Committee, 'Failed Promises: Insurance Companies Insolvencies', 101st Congress 2nd Session (February 1990).

[109] With the exception of the broadening of the categories of assets that can be included in the calculation of the monetary thresholds.

[110] The JOBS Act lifted the prohibition on general solicitation and general advertizing as applicable to Rule 144A and Rule 506. SEC issuers of securities relying on Rule 144A were prohibited from engaging in conduct that would amount to 'general solicitation' in offering securities pursuant to Rule 144A to persons other than 'qualified institutional buyers'. Similarly, issuers relying on Rule 506 of Regulation D were also prohibited from offering or selling securities through any form of 'general solicitation' or 'general advertising'. Although not defined in the US 1933 Act, examples of a 'general solicitation' include advertisements published in newspapers, magazines or unrestricted websites, communications broadcast over television and radio, and seminars whose attendees have been invited by general solicitation or general advertising: US Securities and Exchange Commission, 'Eliminating the Prohibition Against General Solicitation and General Advertising in Rule 506 and Rule 144A Offerings', SEC Release Nos 33-9415, 34-69959 (10 July 2013) <http://www.sec.gov/News/PressRelease/Detail/PressRelease/1370539707782#.UjwGAndYV8F> accessed 20 September 2013.

[111] Title II of the JOBS Act directs the US SEC to amend Rule 506 of Regulation D and Rule 144A to allow for general solicitation and advertising, provided that certain criteria are met. On 10 July 2013, the SEC adopted a new rule implementing this directive, which permits issuers to use such methods when offering their securities, provided that they take 'reasonable steps' to ensure that investors are accredited, and that such accreditation falls within one of the categories under Rule 501 of Regulation D: SEC Factsheet, 'Eliminating the Prohibition Against General Solicitation and General Advertising in Certain Offerings', SEC Open Meeting (10 July 2013) <http://www.sec.gov/news/press/2013/2013-124-item1.htm> accessed 20 September 2013.

[112] 'Initial purchaser' has become somewhat of a term of art, where a professional intermediary acting as a QIB, takes securities from the issuer in the initial purchase.

[113] The reseller can look at the criteria listed in Rule 144A(d)(1)(i)–(iv) to see whether the potential buyer is a QIB. The list is non-exhaustive and can be trusted. However, there is no official database that lists QIBs. See Securities and Exchange Commission, 'Release of Restricted Securities; Changes to Method of Determining Holding Period of Restricted Securities Under Rules 144 and 145', SEC Release No. 33-6862 (23 April 1990).

to make the buyer aware that the seller is relying on Rule 144A. Breaks in the compliance chain, however, do not climb back up to the issuer, tainting the entire chain of transactions, as is the case with ordinary private placements.[114] Information which is already in the public record in the United States, either by virtue of the issuer being a reporting issuer or, in the case of FPIs, making information available in compliance with Rule 12g3-2(b), satisfies the information requirement of Rule 144A. This is an example of the 'thriftiness' of US securities regulation, putting existing regulatory mechanisms to new use. In the absence of either of these sources of publicly available information, at the time of the placement, the issuer must undertake to make certain basic information available to subsequent purchasers on request;[115] the 'evergreen' provision.

3.4 The significance of Rule 144A

There is no doubt that Rule 144A transformed the US private placement market; incidentally, **5.95** but not coincidentally, it was directly responsive to the *1987 Report on Internationalization*. It served to eliminate costly and cumbersome procedures which had developed in the market place to address the uncertainty created by a very old regulatory regime. It was highly successful in enticing non-US issuers into the US markets. Debt issuances by FPIs quadrupled in value in the years following implementation of the rule.[116] Rule 144A is highly compatible with modern technology and electronic trading.[117] The availability of non-US securities which flooded into US markets satisfied US institutional investors thirsty for diversification, and its interaction with Regulation S permitted immediate resales of privately placed non-US equity securities,[118] in particular, into public markets overseas.[119]

4. Multijurisdictional Disclosure System between the United States and Canada

As regulatory instruments, Regulation S and Rule 144A are as different as chalk and cheese. **5.96** However, to mix metaphors, the MJDS is a completely different kettle of fish. Like Regulation S and Rule 144A, the MJDS is responsive, at least in part, to observations raised in the *1987 Report on Internationalization*. Perhaps the extent of Canadian issuer participation in US capital markets had been underestimated. Canadian issuers tended to obscure their 'Canadian' indicia of origin[120] when entering US markets in order, some have surmised, to

---

[114] Due to the statutory language in the definition of underwriter in § 2(a)(11) of the US 1933 Act.

[115] Under 17 CFR § 230.144A(d)(4)(i), upon request by a holder or prospective purchaser, an issuer must provide 'a very brief statement of the nature of the business of the issuer and the products and services it offers; and the issuer's most recent balance sheet and profit and loss and retained earnings statements, and similar financial statements for such part of the two preceding fiscal years as the issuer has been in operation'.

[116] From $378 million to $12.1 billion between 1991 and 1997. See Susan Chaplinsky and Latha Ramchand, 'The Impact of SEC Rule 144A on Corporate Debt Issuance by International Firms' (2004) 77 *Journal of Business* 1073, 1074.

[117] Despite the disappointing experiences with PORTAL, an early 'closed' trading system.

[118] Under the resale rule of Regulation S: See Regulation S: Offshore Resales, 17 CFR § 230.904.

[119] There have been some perhaps unnecessary inefficiencies associated with Rule 144A. PORTAL did not catch on, primarily because it imposed too many restrictive practices from a prior era (like legending securities). For legal practitioners, old (and lucrative) habits died hard and extensive due diligence, lengthy offering memoranda, and negative disclosure letters, lingered on.

[120] For example, the Royal Bank of Canada becomes RBC and Bank of Montreal becomes BMO: see further Cally Jordan, 'The Chameleon Effect: Beyond the Bonding Hypothesis for Cross-Listed Securities' (2006) 3 *NYU Journal of Law and Business* 37.

take advantage of the 'home bias' effect among US investors.[121] Canadian issuers also did not use ADRs, an immediate indicator of non-US origin. Yet, the statistics which surfaced in the *1987 Report on Internationalization* graphically illustrated the significance of Canadian issuers among the population of FPIs, accounting for nearly 50 per cent in the ten-year period prior to the release of the Report.[122] So the question arose as to whether Canadian issuers merited special treatment within the parallel system. An equally pertinent question was whether they should be assimilated to US issuers. Interestingly, this was a position alluded to in Release 4708 as far back as 1964.

5.97 Unlike Regulation S and Rule 144A, which constituted run-of-the-mill rulemaking in the United States, the MJDS was an exercise in negotiated rulemaking, coordinated with the Canadian authorities to create (without the benefit of an overarching treaty such as existed in the EU), two sets of harmonized, mirror image regulatory regimes, one on each side of that very long border. It took five years to create the MJDS.

5.98 The seeds of the MJDS predated the *1987 Report on Internationalization*, however, and originally did not contemplate Canadian involvement at all. In 1985, the SEC floated a trial balloon, a 'concept release' which looked at ways to facilitate transatlantic offerings using different regulatory techniques, including a common prospectus, harmonized rules, or mutual recognition techniques, that could link the New York and London debt markets.[123] Canada jumped into the debate; big Canadian issuers as well as Canadian governments were active in the Euromarket. The United Kingdom then dropped out,[124] leaving Canada and the United States at the table. What had begun as multijurisdictional negotiations became bilateral. However, somewhat unfounded optimism that a deal banged out with friendly, amenable Canada might be adaptable to markets of then greater interest to the United States resulted in retention of 'multi' in the moniker.[125]

5.99 Even the bilateral aspect of the MJDS, however, is somewhat misleading. The MJDS has been a one way street for Canadian issuers into the US public markets. It created six (now whittled down to five) new forms, specific to Canadian issuers alone, in the F-series parallel system, under both the US 1933 Act and the US 1934 Act. Over time, the SEC has questioned this special treatment of Canadian issuers and threatened to eliminate the MJDS altogether, primarily based on the administrative burdens associated with use of a separate set of filing forms.[126] In particular, a less stringent (from a US perspective) approach to due diligence and disclosure practices in Canada, as well as one or two high profile scandals,[127] put

---

[121] The 'home bias' effect refers to the observed tendency for US investors to overweight domestic stocks in their common stock portfolio: Jordan (n 120), 44.

[122] See *1987 Internationalization Report* (n 1), Chapter II, 84, and Table II-21.

[123] See Cally Jordan, 'Multijurisdictional Disclosure System between Canada and the United States' (1990) 1 *Canada-US Business Law Review* 141.

[124] It was preoccupied with more pressing matters, such as setting off the 'Big Bang' as well as deregulation and reformulating its legislation to comply with EU directives. Additionally, as primary market regulator at that time, the London Stock Exchange was unwilling to list companies without conducting its own review. The Netherlands had been interested in joining the system but decided that it was too much work to set the system up for too few issuers.

[125] Japan was the market the United States had in mind; later, Mexico was considered as a candidate for inclusion, particularly after conclusion of the North America Free Trade Agreement, but quickly rejected.

[126] One F-series form has been eliminated.

[127] In 1997 a Canadian mining company, Bre-X Minerals Ltd, was involved in a major gold-mining fraud, where gold samples were falsified at a mine site in Indonesia, leading to investor losses of an estimated $6 billion.

pressure on the MJDS. Canadian issuers, dealers, and regulators though, have lobbied hard to keep the MJDS operating, as it has with few difficulties for nearly 25 years. The MJDS facilitated cross-listing by Canadian issuers on US exchanges (perhaps to the detriment of the Toronto exchange). The system continues to be extensively used on the Canadian side; Canadian issuers prefer MJDS filings (such as the 40-F) even where they might qualify for US short-form filings. With greater integration of the US and Canadian capital markets, Canadian dealers also profited through their participation in cross-border syndicates.

4.1 How does the MJDS work

In one of the most comprehensive experiments outside the European Union in the application of principles of reciprocal recognition,[128] Canada and the United States implemented the MJDS in 1991.[129] The system is one of mutual recognition, where both countries' regulatory regimes, each the virtual mirror image of the other, recognize and defer to one another. Certain US issuers are permitted, under the Canadian rules, to issue securities in Canada utilizing a US prospectus or other offering document which is in conformity with US requirements.[130] Similarly, certain Canadian issuers are permitted, under US rules, to issue securities in the United States using a Canadian prospectus or other offering document prepared in accordance with Canadian timing and filing requirements.[131]   **5.100**

Inspired by the Euromarket, the MJDS began as a remarkably simple idea: the standardization of the offering documentation for issuances of debt securities in the interests of speeding up the offering process. The SEC at that time took the view that for debt securities an investment decision was much more influenced by an investment grade rating than by prospectus disclosure.[132] Recognition of a foreign prospectus for use in the United States for investment grade debt could thus eliminate the cost and delays associated with regulatory duplication without unduly sacrificing investor protection concerns.   **5.101**

As the idea of reciprocal recognition sprouted, a mighty regulatory oak took shape. Debt and equity offerings, rights and exchange offerings, business combinations, continuous disclosure for both MJDS and other issuers, proxy rules, even recognition of Canada as a sovereign nation, all became part of the system.[133] Needless to say, the increased complexity of the system brought on by these additions had a significant impact on its utilization by Canadian issuers.[134] Despite its name, the MJDS has been US regulation for Canadian issuers (and rarely used by US issuers to go into Canada under the Canadian version of the MJDS rules).   **5.102**

The new system provided Canadian issuers with a wide range of options and choice in terms of entering the US capital markets and broad exemptive relief for all Canadian issuers,   **5.103**

In 1999 YBM Magnex International Inc, a company incorporated in Alberta and listed on the Toronto Stock Exchange, was found to have been set up for the sole purpose of laundering money for Russian organized crime syndicates.

[128] The European Union, of course, has made widespread use of reciprocal recognition techniques.

[129] See Ontario Securities Commission, 'National Policy Statement No 45—Multijurisdictional Disclosure System', 14 *Ontario Securities Commission Bulletin* 2889 (28 June 1991).

[130] See Ontario Securities Commission (n 129).

[131] See Ontario Securities Commission (n 129).

[132] The power, and treachery, of investment grade ratings was exposed in the global financial crisis.

[133] See Ontario Securities Commission (n 129).

[134] The MJDS has proved to be a one-way street, a means of enticing more Canadian issuers into the US public markets.

irrespective of MJDS eligibility, from duplicative regulation in other areas such as proxy solicitation and continuous disclosure. Also, the system delivered more or less what was expected in terms of facilitating US offerings of investment grade debt by Canadian issuers.

5.104 Investment grade debt offerings under the MJDS outnumbered equity offerings two to one in the early days and the principles of mutual recognition appeared to work well.[135] It remains the case, however, that utilization of the regime proved more difficult and complex than originally envisaged, even for investment grade debt offerings. Of the many factors contributing to this, one was the 'capture' of the regime by US lawyers and investment dealers (not known to miss an opportunity to create a demand for their services). The original principle of reciprocal recognition, ie the ability to use a Canadian prospectus to do a public offering in the United States, was distorted by one of the asymmetrical aspects of the regime—the retention of US civil liability by the SEC for the offering document.

5.105 The hook of US civil liability had been used to justify a predictable convergence of Canadian and US disclosure in MJDS documents. US investment dealers promoted such convergence for marketing reasons; in order to sell the securities in the United States, the prospectus should have a US 'look'. US lawyers insist on US-style due diligence and disclosure on the basis of the exposure to US liability.

5.106 Concerns with US civil liability have not materialized in a significant way, a result perhaps of Canadian MJDS documentation having become virtually indistinguishable from US domestic registration statements. It is certainly arguable that this was not the original intent, although given the increasing integration of the North American capital markets, perhaps an inevitable consequence.

5.107 Although not producing the international impact of Regulation S and Rule 144A, the MJDS is interesting in several respects. From the point of view of the SEC, the interest in the MJDS was as a model of future (and in the event, unconsummated) cooperation with bigger fish than Canada. More importantly, again from the US perspective, it was a relatively safe regulatory experiment with a willing and familiar partner, demonstrating that the US regulator, often suffering from a reputation for intransigence, could cooperate internationally.

5.108 The MJDS also showed the extent to which the Canadian regulatory focus was fixed squarely on the United States, largely as a result of the acceleration of integration of North American capital markets. Although of negligible impact from the US perspective, the MJDS does create the infrastructure for an integrated North American capital market. The MJDS tied Canadian regulators to the US regime. They were compelled to take into account, in a very timely fashion, future regulatory developments in the United States, potentially giving rise to hard regulatory choices. The question became to what extent would Canadian regulators set their own agenda in the Canadian market?

5.109 The MJDS heralded the introduction of US-style capital markets regulation in Canada and all the complexity, as well as the benefits, that it entailed. It also demonstrated the interaction between harmonization and mutual recognition as regulatory techniques. Mutual recognition does not require identity or complete convergence of regulation, the reason it has been a fallback

---

[135] According to statistics provided to the author by SEC Staff, debt issues outnumbered equity issues two to one under the MJDS with US$3.5 billion in debt securities being registered with the SEC in 1993 compared to US$6 billion in equity.

position in the European Union for decades. However, the prospects of effecting a mutual recognition regime are poor if there are not strong similarities among systems; in the European Union this is provided by high level principles in the directives. As between Canada and the United States, however, there was no treaty framework within which to work. Nevertheless, as a condition to proceeding with the MJDS, the United States did insist on 'alignment', ie de facto harmonization, of Canadian securities regulation to that of the United States. For example, Canadian authorities had to adopt shelf registration mechanisms, a very welcome development for issuers and their counsel.

Introduction of the MJDS represented a turning point for Canadian securities regulation, **5.110** which, until that point, had been coloured by the more informal 'regulation by persuasion' techniques of the Bank of England.[136] Again, arguably, flexibility and the potential for innovation were compromised on the Canadian side; smaller markets can often adapt and innovate more effectively than the behemoths.[137] On the other hand, a de facto 'twin peaks' structure developed. Banks, insurance, and trust companies were regulated, very much along prudential lines, at the federal level by the Office of the Superintendent of Financial Services,[138] a prototype for the now defunct UK FSA (minus the investment banking component), while securities regulation remained close to the markets in Toronto, invigorated by a more muscular model, the SEC.

The pressures for harmonization associated with the MJDS were decidedly another one way **5.111** street, this time running from Washington to Toronto, but in the process of assessing the Canadian system, the SEC may have learned a few new tricks.[139] Also, some features of the MJDS appear in the 'substituted compliance' system for market intermediaries that had some currency in the United States until it was eclipsed by the global financial crisis.[140]

5. Conclusion

The era that began in 1990 with the introduction of Regulation S and Rule 144A and which **5.112** ended in 2002 with Sarbanes Oxley has been called the 'golden age' of internationalization in the

---

[136] For example, shortly after the introduction of the MJDS and prompted by an influx of US intermediaries permitted by Big Bang style relaxations on foreign ownership in Canada, the main securities regulator, the Ontario Securities Commission, was required to jettison 'policy statements' in favour of delegated rule making (in the SEC style). The normative force of the policy statements had been unchallenged to this point; as in the City of London, in the cosy world of Toronto investment banking, everyone complied. See Cally Jordan, 'Regulation of Canadian Capital Markets in the 1990s: The United States in the Driver's Seat' (1995) 4 *Pacific Rim Law & Policy Journal* 577, 588.

[137] For example, in the private placement rules in Canada which were much simpler and more straightforward than in the United States.

[138] Created as a consolidated regulator in 1987; investment banking and securities regulation could not be rolled into the Office of the Superintendent of Financial Services at that time due to constitutional disputes which persist to this day.

[139] These regulatory initiatives predated the efforts of IOSCO as a standard setter in the capital markets, which debuted in 1998 with the IOSCO Objectives and Principles of Securities Regulation, which have proved influential in disseminating regulatory techniques around the world. With respect to the Canadian regulatory approaches which may have been picked up by US regulators in the course of negotiating the MJDS, there is the 'closed system' for resales of privately placed securities under the then Securities Act, RSO 1990, Chapter S.5. Rule 144A creates a closed system too, and its original three-tiered investor structure (dropped in the final rule) resembled the Ontario closed system even more closely. Also, the changes to Rule 144 in 2008 (distinguishing the hold periods for restricted securities on the basis of whether the issuer is a reporting issuer) has been a feature of the closed system in Ontario since 1978. Ontario Securities Act, RSO 1978, Chapter 426.

[140] Ethiopis Tafara and Robert J Peterson, 'A Blueprint for Cross-Border Access to U.S. Investors: A New International Framework' (2007) 48 *Harvard International Law Journal* 31.

securities markets,[141] at least from the US perspective. Non-US issuers flocked into US private and public markets; the NYSE and NASDAQ welcomed them with open arms.[142] The symbiosis between Regulation S and Rule 144A offerings persists in the international markets, raising awareness of US regulation worldwide.

5.113   The MJDS, although never expanded as originally contemplated by the United States, was picked up in Australia and New Zealand, which implemented a comparable system.[143] This 'golden age' in the United States also galvanized the European Union to action. As stated in the Lamfalussy Report: 'There is no serious alternative available. The status quo would entrench the continuation of European financial market fragmentation. This means lost benefits. Lost opportunities…with European savings diverted to foreign market places'.[144] The gyroscope of competition and coordination between the United States and Europe was set spinning.

5.114   Interest in internationalization generally waxes and wanes in the United States. The golden age came to a thudding end with Sarbanes Oxley, the clumsy extraterritoriality of which grievously offended the Europeans. However, high level coordination was required during the global financial crisis, resulting, not fortuitously, in parallel regulatory structures being put in place on both sides of the Atlantic.[145] The crisis-driven legislative response in the United States (Dodd Frank) has close parallels in EU regulatory initiatives such as the European Market Infrastructure Regulation.[146] This, however, is not convergence, much less harmonization. The responses are different, but the characterization of the issues is the same.

---

[141] DeLaMater (n 2), 113.

[142] More than 300 non-US issuers listed on the NASDAQ and NYSE between 1990 and 2002. See Christopher Woo, 'The Effects of the Sarbanes-Oxley Act on Foreign Private Issuers', International Finance Seminar, Harvard Law School, 2003, 62–75 <http://www.law.harvard.edu/programs/about/pifs/education/llm/2002---2003/sp36.pdf> accessed on 19 January 2014.

[143] The trans-Tasman mutual recognition of securities offerings regime.

[144] Alexandre Lamfalussy, 'Final Report of the Committee of Wise Men on the Regulation of European Securities Markets' (Brussels, 15 February 2001), 8.

[145] The US Financial Stability Oversight Council (within the Treasury Department) and the European Systemic Risk Board.

[146] The Regulation (EU) 648/2012 of the European Parliament and of the Council of 4 July 2012 on OTC derivatives, central counterparties and trade repositories [2012] OJ L201/1. See also Commission Delegated Regulation (EU) 148/2013 to 153/2013 of 19 December 2012 supplementing Regulation (EU) 648/2012 of the Europeans Parliament and of the Council on OTC derivatives, central counterparties and trade repositories [2013] OJ L52/1.

6

THE UNITED KINGDOM—GENTLEMANLY CAPITALISM AND THE INTERNATIONAL MARKETS[*]

1. Introduction

The 'City' is synonymous with finance. The Corporation of the City of London,[1] a geo- **6.01** graphically defined area of some 600 hectares, sits along the River Thames, abutting the once poor and unsavoury East End.[2] Despite ups and downs, international finance has flourished in the City for centuries.

The City has also been the scene of spectacular busts and financial scandals, the most noto- **6.02** rious of which was the infamous South Sea Bubble.[3] Public outrage, ever the initiator of regulatory response, resulted in prohibition of the creation of the popular vehicle for public capital raising, the joint stock company, a ban which lasted over a century.[4] Prohibition of such a useful vehicle for finance in the interests of public investor protection was a blunt instrument indeed, and relatively ineffectual.[5] In 1825, the pressures of a capital hungry

---

[*] The author would like to thank Jane Welch, Brian Cheffins, Len Sealy, David Lawton, and Ruben Lee, in particular, for their assistance with this chapter. The usual disclaimers apply.

[1] 'Established in around AD50, seven years after the Romans invaded Britain, the City, or Square Mile, as it has become known, is the place from which modern-day London grew': See 'City History' (*City of London*, Last modified 26 September 2013) <http://www.cityoflondon.gov.uk/things-to-do/visiting-the-city/archives-and-city-history/city-history/Pages/default.aspx> accessed 9 October 2013.

[2] This juxtaposition has been identified as one of the secrets of the success of the City of London; the 'toffs' graduating from Oxford and Cambridge would work side-by-side with the savvy, street smart traders recruited from the nearby East End. See also the fascinating account of the City of London in David Kynaston, *City of London: The History* (Random House, 2012) and to which the author is partially indebted for the title of this chapter: Kynaston (n 2), 422.

[3] The 'South Sea Bubble', which occurred in 1720, is the name ascribed to arguably the most famous stock market crash in history. Having entered into an arrangement with Queen Anne, the South Sea Company acquired a monopoly on the importation of slaves into America, in exchange for assisting the monarch to restructure England's national debt. Shares traded in the company underwent a sudden boom, followed by a dramatic crash, with the company directors subsequently being accused of fraud. Since 1720, the South Sea Bubble has stood as the benchmark for financial market crashes, such as the 'Dotcom Bubble', and the more recent 'Credit Crunch': Helen J Paul, *The South Sea Bubble: An Economic History of its Origins and Consequences* (Taylor & Francis, 2010), 1.

[4] The prohibition on unchartered companies was effected by the Bubble Act 1720 (6 Geo 1 c 18), which was subsequently repealed by the Bubble Companies, etc Act 1825 (6 Geo 4 c 91). See Margaret Patterson and David Reiffen, 'The Effect of the Bubble Act on the Market for Joint Stock Shares' (1990) 50 *The Journal of Economic History* 163.

[5] Ever ingenious solicitors worked around the prohibition and others simply ignored it. See LCB Gower, 'The English Private Company' (1953) 18 *Law and Contemporary Problems* 535, 535–6, on deed of settlement companies. Between 1825 and 1844, however, companies continued to be associated with fraud. 'Many...were from

industrial age in Britain and an expanding empire led to the repeal of the Bubble Act 1720.[6] Scandals ensued, followed by yet another response, in the form of the Joint Stock Companies Act 1844.[7] This was landmark legislation in the United Kingdom, marking the beginnings of formal companies law. The 1844 statute is rightly known for providing the advantages of legal personality for large unincorporated enterprises, which were then struggling with issues of standing for purposes of litigation and property ownership in their unincorporated form. This monumental achievement overshadows another aspect of the 1844 legislation; it introduced the concepts of a public registration process and public information by way of prospectus; the latter device disappeared and resurfaced in subsequent legislation. But the seed had been sown, and the concepts of public registration and prospectuses, as the bulwarks of investor protection, sound very familiar to modern US securities lawyers.

6.03 Providing investor protection in the United Kingdom, however, has been a fraught and difficult process. Even well into the 1980s, one very popular view in the City, openly espoused, was that it was not the role of government, nor was it necessarily either possible or desirable, to 'protect fools from their own folly'.[8] Rather, the gentlemen of the City, historical evidence to the contrary notwithstanding, insisted that their 'impeccable' behaviour provided all the protections necessary.[9] Professor Gower, in his 1984 report on investor protection, was unimpressed by such protestations; he warned that it would be 'detrimental to the national interest and reputation if regulation is so lax that we become a haven for crooks'.[10]

2. Formative Elements of UK Capital Markets Regulation

6.04 Popular references to the 'Anglo-Saxon' model of finance, lumping together the United States and the United Kingdom, mask the significant differences, historically and conceptually, in the development of financial markets institutions and regulation. Connections and cross-influences there definitely are, stretching across huge chasms of difference. Even the

---

their inception fraudulent shams, particularly the bogus assurance companies such as those pilloried by Dickens in *Martin Chuzzlewit* [fn omitted], and it was primarily the existence of these which led the Board of Trade to secure the appointment in 1841 of a Parliamentary Committee on Joint Stock Companies...The 1844 Act introduced three main principles which have constituted the basis of our company law from that time...[Notably], it provided for full publicity which ever since has been regarded as the most potent safeguard against fraud': Paul L Davies, *Gower's Principles of Modern Company Law* (6th edn, Sweet & Maxwell, 1997), 37–8.

[6] (6 Geo 1 c 18).

[7] (7 & 8 Vict c 110). '[T]he years 1824–1825 witnessed a boom which was compared with that of 1719–1720 and which was followed by a similar slump': LCB Gower, *Gower's Principles of Modern Company Law* (5th edn, Sweet & Maxwell, 1992), 34.

[8] LCB Gower, *Review of Investor Protection Report: Part 1* (Cmd 9125, 1984), para 1.11 (Gower Report Pt 1).

[9] Gower Report Pt 1 (n 8), para 1.14. Gower has an entire paragraph devoted to this 'impeccability' argument, and states at para 1.14: 'That it is necessary, if investors are to be adequately protected, to extend the area of present regulation is generally agreed. But, understandably, some of those at present free from regulation do not agree that it ought to extend to them. Many of them would, no doubt, behave impeccably if it did not—just as many of those at present regulated would have behaved impeccably whether or not they were subject to regulation. But unless it is possible to identify them on acceptable criteria (and no-one who has read the reports of Department of Trade Inspectors over the past 25 years could seriously suggest that there is any definable branch of the investment industry in which all have invariably behaved impeccably) it is impossible to justify failing to extend to them the necessary minimum of regulation.'

[10] Gower Report Pt 1 (n 8), para 1.15, fn 12. Of particular concern was the commodities business.

language of finance, although technically English in both the United States and the United Kingdom, is different: corporation and company; public offering and flotation; investment banker and merchant banker; mutual fund and collective investment scheme; take-over bid and tender offer. It is not only the terminology which differs from one country to the other, but usually the conceptual and legal underpinnings as well as market practices. However, the influx of US investment bankers and securities lawyers into the City since 1986 has been blurring the distinctions.

2.1 Historical and geopolitical factors

The historical and geopolitical differences between the United Kingdom and the United States, and their significance, are perhaps so obvious as to be unexamined. The United Kingdom is a unitary jurisdiction, and has been for a very long time. The United Kingdom lost the 13 colonies to revolution in the eighteenth century but, domestically, resisted the revolutionary flames roaring in France across the Channel. Many of the old ways gave way in the United Kingdom over time, but many did not. The new broom of revolution did not sweep out the cobwebs in the corners nor tidy up the attic.

6.05

The United Kingdom is a parliamentary democracy, with London serving as both a political and financial centre. But within the larger London, the City of London has been a powerful, long autonomous city state and rival to Parliament. The customs and privileges of the City of London were protected by the Magna Carta (1215 CE), and even well into the nineteenth century, a custom of the City could face down a general act of Parliament.[11] Thus, the dynamic which exists between political power in Parliament (sensitive to public outrage) and the financial interests represented by the City, is a particularly complex one.

6.06

Calls for reform can simmer along for decades, perhaps centuries, then, somewhat paradoxically, dramatic change can occur relatively quickly.[12] Over 100 years elapsed between the Bubble Act 1720[13] and its repeal in 1825;[14] the reach of limited liability for companies took nearly half a century to be determined by the courts,[15] despite the existence of legislation to that effect;[16] nearly another century elapsed between the Joint Stock Companies Act 1844[17] and the Prevention of Fraud (Investments) Act 1939.[18] Nearly another 50 years passed before the appearance of the Financial Services Act 1986[19] (which LCB Gower had recommended be called the Investor Protection Act).[20] But given a strong-armed Chancellor of the Exchequer and a parliamentary majority, the legislative and regulatory applecart can be overturned virtually overnight, as occurred with the Financial Services and Markets Act 2000 (FSMA 2000), which introduced the much emulated Financial Services Authority (FSA). A decade or so later, another, but different, new government, dismantled the FSA.[21]

6.07

---

[11] See paras 6.40 et seq.
[12] Some would say a paradigm of path dependency in action.
[13] See (n 6).
[14] Bubble Companies, etc Act 1825 (6 Geo 4 c 91).
[15] *Salomon v A Salomon & Co Ltd* [1897] AC 22.
[16] Limited Liability Act 1855 (18 & 19 Vict c 133).
[17] See (n 7).
[18] (2 & 3 Geo 6 c 16).
[19] (1986 c 60).
[20] Gower Report Part 1 (n 8), para 4.29(a).
[21] (2012 c 21). The reform process leading to the FSMA 2000 actually took a bit longer than implied; 'the civil service and the SIB had been working on reforming the regulatory structure for almost two years before the change of Government in 1997. And the decision to transfer banking supervision to the SIB, renamed the FSA,

Intricate congressional checks and balances, such as exist in the United States, do not operate here; neither does legislative impasse when a government enjoys a majority in Parliament.

2.2 The power of the common law

6.08 The modern common law tradition (found throughout the Commonwealth and, in a different expression, in the United States) finds its source in the United Kingdom. The common law, as a legal tradition, is notoriously untidy and resistant to systematization. Legislation is viewed as a last resort, representing a failure of the common law. Within the formal bounds of the common law, as delineated by judicial decision and acts of Parliament, there is ample space for the coexistence of custom and practices, the common law itself being a customary law *par excellence*. In finance and commerce, this propensity for recognition of custom and practice is buttressed by the special status traditionally accorded to the City of London.

6.09 In finance, much greater reliance has been placed on the usual operation of the common law, in terms of remedies and structural analysis, than on legislative action and the creation of a specialized regulatory regime as found in other jurisdictions. The structural support provided by contract, tort, agency, and fiduciary law have been much more apparent in the United Kingdom where they have only recently begun to be overlaid, if not entirely displaced, by a statutory and regulatory regime. The arcane nature of the common law, accessible only to a select, closed, highly skilled group, appealed to practitioners of the dark financial arts. They were in no hurry to reveal their tricks. Professor Gower,[22] in preparing his reports on investor protection in the United Kingdom in the 1980s,[23] complained of the 'veil of secrecy'[24] which shrouded the financial sector. The sun, apparently, did not shine in the City.[25]

6.10 It is somewhat remarkable that a formal regulatory agency and regime for capital markets (and other financial services) only appeared in the United Kingdom in 2000, after a troubled experiment in 1986 in providing a statutory framework for self-regulation. That such a regime eventually appeared at all, in the form of the FSMA 2000, may owe much to EU directives at the instance of the European Commission, with its predilection for formal written law.[26] Credit must also go to the tenacious Professor Gower and his 1984 Review of Investor Protection reports.

6.11 In the course of preparation of these reports in the 15 years leading up to the FSMA 2000, and his recommendations for greater, and better, regulatory oversight of the financial sector,

---

was taken within weeks, followed by legislation in 1998. FSMA itself had been debated for a couple of years and took another two years to come into force—so the market had plenty of time to get to grips with the shape of the new system': Email from Jane Welch to author (16 October 2013). The actual dismantling of the FSA was effected by the Financial Services Act 2012.

  [22] A monumental figure in English companies law, and no stranger to the arcanities of the common law.

  [23] Gower Report Pt 1 (n 8); LCB Gower, *Review of Investor Protection: Report Part II* (HMSO, 1985) (Gower Report Pt II).

  [24] Gower Report Pt 1 (n 8), para 1.09.

  [25] Probably the most famous quote in the history of US securities regulation, supporting a public disclosure model of regulation, is that of Justice Brandeis: 'Sunlight is said to be the best of disinfectants' (see Louis D Brandeis, *Other People's Money: And How the Bankers Use It* (Frederick A Stoker Co, 1914), 92).

  [26] 'The structure of the listing regime had altered significantly as a result of the domestic implementation of EU directives, which was usually done by statutory instruments, giving legal force to the requirements, but it was as much the desire to separate the Competent Authority function and the market regulatory function, which drove the transfer of responsibilities from the Stock Exchange to the FSA. Such a split was common in continental jurisdictions, which disliked the Stock Exchange having any official regulatory functions': Welch (n 21).

Professor Gower, in his own words, was 'accused . . . of having an excessive passion for logic and tidiness, of wishing to regulate for the sake of regulating, and of thinking that it was both possible and desirable to protect fools from their own folly'.[27] The City appeared contemptuous of the amateurs, the retail investors. At the time of his reports, the only statutory responses to scandal after scandal involving the abuse of public investors had been the Prevention of Frauds (Investments) Act 1939, and then the 1958 amending Act: 'tortuous and complicated',[28] troubled, convoluted, inadequate, and ineffective legislation. Professor Gower didn't mince words: 'A law which is unintelligible or which does not treat like alike, thereby understandably being regarded as capricious by those to whose transactions it does apply, will not be observed and cannot be effectively enforced'.[29]

With its aversion to legislative frameworks and systematization (which smacked much too **6.12** much of European codification), this rudimentary investor protection legislation applied a patchwork of fixes, without tackling the problems. In the common law fashion, the 'law' was an amorphous, inaccessible, writhing mass, impenetrable and inscrutable, full of gaps and conflicts. This was a professional market though and, perhaps in equal measure, the forces of rampant self-interest and self-regulation kept the City in balance. Additionally, in the absence of a formal, dedicated, regulator, and regulatory framework, rivalries among ministries (the then Department of Trade and Industry, the Treasury, the Bank of England) became acute.[30] And the City liked it this way.

That these markets functioned as long as they did without a formal regulatory framework **6.13** or dedicated regulator is a testament to the pragmatism and ingenuity of the common law and the practitioners of finance, legal and otherwise. A number of other factors, discussed in due course, together supported the operation of these markets: the fundamental importance of the Exchange, the dominance of the professional market, the shareholder protections of companies law, and the more beneficial aspects of a strong self-regulatory tradition.

2.3 The company law characterization of investor protection

Investor protection has been the polar star of capital markets regulation, though arguably **6.14** eclipsed by competing objectives in modern times. In the United Kingdom, investor protection finds its origins in companies law, and this characterization continues to colour the regulatory approach. To a certain extent, it is explanatory of some of the inter-ministerial overlap and competition already discussed. The Bubble Act 1720 and the Joint Stock Companies Act 1844 were both, ultimately, investor protection statutes which focused on the vehicle for capital raising, the joint stock company, rather than the activities associated with capital raising.

The early protections included 'requiring companies to disclose numerous facts to investors **6.15** before selling them stock',[31] found in the first codified rule book of the Stock Exchange in

---

[27] Gower Report Pt 1 (n 8), para 1.11.
[28] Gower Report Pt 1 (n 8), para 1.08.
[29] Gower Report Pt 1 (n 8), para 1.12.
[30] The Treasury had responsibility for banking but the Second EU Banking Directive brought in the DTI. The Treasury had ambitions of taking over securities from the DTI in the post-Big Bang era, but the DTI had oversight of companies, where 'securities law' had originated (characterized as companies law) and the DTI resisted giving up jurisdiction. See also Gower (n 7), 72.
[31] Franklin A Gevurtz, 'The Globalization of Corporate Law: The End of History or a Never-Ending Story?' (2011) 86 *Washington Law Review* 475, 491–2.

1812 and section IV of the Joint Stock Companies Act 1844. Section IV of the Joint Stock Companies Act 1844 required 'the registration of a prospectus in relation to each company',[32] and threaded its way, sometimes disappearing, through 150 years of companies law down to 1995.[33]

6.16 Until quite recently,[34] prospectus provisions and the detailed information with respect to accounts or financials[35] were found in the companies legislation in the United Kingdom. Provisions with respect to insider dealing, the first in Europe, appeared initially in the Companies Act 1980.[36]

6.17 There are several implications of this characterization of investor protection as companies law. The United States was able to move rapidly to 'enabling' or 'core' business corporations law in the twentieth century, because the technical and regulatory capital markets issues (and periodically corporate governance issues as well) had migrated to the realm of securities regulation. In the United Kingdom, on the other hand, companies law became a huge and unwieldy compendium of various aspects of commercial law, which included investor protection in the form of shareholder and creditor protections.[37] The most significant implication of this characterization of investor protection as companies law is the focus on equity investors, shareholders, and in particular, existing shareholders.

6.18 Unlike US corporations law, in nineteenth-century UK companies, the balance of power tilted more favourably towards the members, and the law itself, over time, provided a greater array of shareholder protections: the ability to call meetings, the ability to remove directors from the board (as well as to appoint them), preemptive rights and a broad, equitable oppression remedy. Investors, qua shareholders, had better means to protect themselves under companies law.[38] Outside of companies law, this left regulation of the financial intermediaries and the market place as the main domain of non-companies law capital markets regulation, which took on various guises.

---

[32] Alastair Hudson, *Securities Law* (Sweet & Maxwell, 2008), 152, para 4–20.

[33] In 1995 it was finally removed from companies law and placed in the Public Offers of Securities Regulations 1995, SI 1995/1537 ('POS Regulations') in response to EU directive.

[34] The POS Regulations came into force on 19 June 1995: The Public Offers of Securities Regulations 1995, reg 1.

[35] In the United Kingdom, the legislative regulation of company shareholder information commenced in 1908 with the Companies Act 1907 (7 Edw 7 c 50): Brian R Cheffins, 'Does Law Matter? The Separation of Ownership and Control in the United Kingdom' (2001) 30 *The Journal of Legal Studies* 459, 471. Sections 19 and 21 of the 1907 Act outline requirements for, inter alia, company balance sheets to be 'open to inspection by any shareholder' (s 19), and for companies to file an annual statement of affairs 'containing a summary of its capital, its liabilities, and its assets, giving such particulars as will disclose the general nature of such liabilities and assets' (s 21). However, Cheffins notes at 471–2 that this document was 'historically oriented', and did not 'as a general rule, purport to show the trend of profits or the net worth of the undertaking at any particular date'. He adds at 472 that it was not until the Companies Act 1929 that 'Parliament compelled [public companies] to make available to shareholders their annual profit and loss account', although this was in keeping with what had become 'standard practice'.

[36] And were later rolled into separate legislation under the Company Securities (Insider Dealing) Act 1985 (1985 c 8).

[37] The unwinding began in the 1980s under pressures from EU Directives, but the compendium problem persisted until the Companies Act 2006 (UK). The Australian Corporations Act 2001 (Cth), originally UK in origin, has rolled into itself a huge and complex body of financial services regulation.

[38] With some protections also given to bondholders in the registration of debenture and charges provisions of older style UK companies law.

UK companies law statutes, from their mid-nineteenth-century origins, were also designed **6.19** specifically with public companies, and the capital raising process, in mind. Private companies, by definition those with a limited number of members and which did not engage in offering securities to the public, were exempted from the more onerous reporting, accounting, and prospectus provisions of the companies law.[39] This clear distinction between public and private companies facilitated and simplified non-public offerings and private placements. As the modern regulatory framework for capital markets, or securities regulation, emerged with the Financial Services Act 1986 (FSA 1986),[40] the private company was simply dropped out or prohibited from engaging in certain activities (such as issuing an advertisement offering its securities).[41]

Lastly, to the extent issuer focused investor protection was characterized as companies law, **6.20** this counteracted any extraterritorial application of the legislation. The legislation applied to UK registered companies. It also left open to non-UK registered companies a wide variety of activities in the United Kingdom,[42] oversight primarily being provided by the exchange.

2.4 The role of the Bank of England

Often overlooked in the development of capital markets regulation in the United Kingdom **6.21** is the role of the Bank of England (BoE). In the absence of an identifiable regulatory body, the BoE served as a regulator, as well as policymaker and lender of last resort. It was an unlikely role, the BoE having been a private bank until the 1940s and not an institution formally endowed with a public purpose.[43] Nevertheless, all eyes turned to the BoE and the London Stock Exchange (LSE or the Exchange) in times of trouble in the City. At one time the Exchange even shared premises with the BoE.[44]

The BoE was an inadvertent regulator in the capital markets. During the 1980s it played a role **6.22** in both investor protection as well as the oversight of depositaries due to the gaps in the Prevention of Fraud (Investments) Act 1958.[45] Even after the Big Bang of 1986, the BoE and the

---

[39] 'Private companies' first received legislative recognition in the Companies Act 1907, which defined a 'private company' as: 'a company which by its articles—(a) restricts the right to transfer its shares; and (b) limits the number of its members . . . to fifty; and (c) prohibits any invitation to the public to subscribe for any shares or debentures of the company': Companies Act 1907, s 37; Ron Harris, 'The Private Origins of the Private Company: Britain 1862–1907' (2013) 33 *Oxford Journal of Legal Studies* 339, 340. In contrast, the Companies Act 2006 (2006 c 46) defines 'private company' with greater brevity, and simply states that '[a] "private company" is any company that is not a public company': Companies Act 2006, s 4(1).

[40] Gower speaks of the new era of 'Securities Regulation' in this respect. See Gower (n 7), 311.

[41] FSA 1986 (1986 c 60), s 170.

[42] Gower (n 7), 76.

[43] 'Throughout its history the Bank [of England] has always seen itself as a public institution, acting in the national interest. Although privately owned, for much of its life, the activities which it undertook were determined by it governing legislation and by the relationship with government. Nationalisation in 1946 did not greatly affect that; but it meant that the Bank was owned by the Government, rather than by private stockholders, and gave the power to appoint the Governors and Directors to the Crown. The nationalisation Act also gave the Government the power to issue "directions" to the Bank: thus far, the power has not been used': Bank of England, *History, Timeline* 5 <http://www.bankofengland.co.uk/about/Pages/history/timeline.aspx#5> accessed 25 January 2014.

[44] The Exchange occupied the ground floor of the BoE premises until requested to move while renovations took place. The Exchange was never invited back; the story being that the staid bankers were unnerved by the rambunctious goings on of the traders beneath them.

[45] See Gower Report Pt 1 (n 8), para 2.10.

newly created Securities and Investments Board, were required to act in tandem.[46] Unlike the United States at the time with its legislated separation of commercial and investment banking under the Glass-Steagall Act,[47] the universal banking model prevalent in Europe meant that the BoE had an active hand in capital markets regulation.

6.23 Additionally, incipient internationalization of markets and the mobility of financial institutions within and into Europe, provided by the EU Investment Services Directive 1992 (ISD 1992), left regulatory counterparts looking for a contact. The Exchange did not meet the EU definition of 'competent authority'.[48] And neither did the Securities and Investment Board (SIB) created under the FSA 1986. The SIB was not recognized outside the UK as a proper 'regulator' due to its curious hybrid role as oversight panel to a raft of self-regulatory organizations.

6.24 Thus the BoE became the United Kingdom's *de facto* capital markets regulator for international purposes. The BoE spent a great deal of time and effort entering into memoranda of understandings on financial information with overseas supervisors which could not officially interact with the SIB.[49] These cooperative interjurisdictional arrangements had become doubly important with the introduction of 'passporting' of financial institutions within the European Union.[50] The self regulatory organizations (SROs) under SIB could no longer purport to impose self-regulatory requirements, such as fit and proper tests, on the large European universal banks like Deutsche Bank which would now be entirely subject to the supervision of their home regulator under the mutual recognition mechanisms of the ISD 1992. Some of the exchanges, notably LIFFE, were reluctant to drop some of their exchange membership requirements, in effect prudential requirements, for European banks and investment firms.[51] So until 2000, in the absence of a dedicated capital markets regulator, the hand of the BoE was ubiquitous in the City.

---

[46] 'If a bank, whether UK or foreign, wanted to carry on investment business (as defined in the [FSA 1986]) in the UK after 1988 (when it came into force) it had to get separate authorisation to do so, either from the SIB or from an SRO. The Bank remained responsible for the authorisation and prudential supervision of banks [as] deposit-taking institutions, until the implementation of the Second Banking Directive in 1993, when the introduction of the passport for banks meant that the Bank lost any control over the UK branches of EU banks, such as Deutsche Bank. Those branches were, however, still subject to the supervision of the relevant SRO or the SIB in respect of their conduct of investment businesss': Welch (n 21).

[47] Known officially as the Banking Act of 1933, HR 5661, 73rd Cong (48 Stat 162).

[48] Gower (n 7), 65. Subsequently rectified: see Gower (n 7), 312.

[49] 'The Second Banking Directive was the first passporting directive which allowed EEA banks to carry on a wide range of activities including investment business in the UK on the basis of their home state authorisation. This raised the issue of regulatory counterparts for the first time, because EEA banks continued to be subject to conduct of business supervision by the SROs/SIB in the UK if they wanted to carry on investment business. There thus had to be a flow of information between all the relevant authorities. The problem was that overseas banking supervisors were normally prevented by domestic banking secrecy laws from disclosing information other than to other banking supervisors. So from 1988 onwards the SIB (with the approval of the Bank) started negotiations with banking supervisors in every jurisdiction where banks had branched into the UK. The deal was that they would be allowed to branch into the UK (rather than setting up a subsidiary) to carry on investment business, provided that the Home state supervisor entered into an MOU or FISMOU allowing the communication of financial and other prudential information to the SIB/SROs, using the Bank of England as a conduit. In return the SIB/SROs would alert the foreign supervisor if there was any cause for concern in the UK. The Bank became sufficiently attracted to FISMOUS that it started its own series of FISMOUS with other banking supervisors, but these were really redundant after the [Second Banking Directive] because the directive required competent authorities to cooperate and exchange information where necessary': Welch (n 21).

[50] Council Directive 93/22/EEC of 10 May 1993 on investment services in the securities field [1993] OJ L141/27.

[51] Welch (n 21).

2.5 Importance of the exchange

The Exchange has long dominated the world of finance in the United Kingdom and until **6.25** recently remained unchallenged as the premier exchange for international listings.[52] There were other regional exchanges[53] in the United Kingdom, as in the United States, but with the power and advantages of the City of London, others paled in significance. Formally established in 1801, its motto, famously, is *Dictum meum pactum*, or 'my word is my bond'. Despite several hostile takeover bids, as well as an aborted friendly merger (with Deutsche Börse in Frankfurt), the LSE continues to stand (almost) alone.[54]

It would be no exaggeration to say that the LSE was long the United Kingdom's most promi- **6.26** nent capital markets regulator but began losing authority in the years leading up to the crea- tion of the FSA in 2000.[55] Public capital markets revolved around the LSE, unlike the United States where the creation of the Securities and Exchange Commission (SEC) and securities regulation in the 1930s set up a different regulatory dynamic. Waves of exchange demutu- alization then put the regulatory role of exchanges, always resisted in continental Europe, seriously into question.[56] In London, the paucity of formal written law and regulation in this area gave the LSE and its rule books (Yellow, for listed securities and Green, for unlisted)[57] perhaps an even greater authority, which the LSE did not hesitate to exploit.[58]

The focus on the exchange as regulator though produced a distortion in market regulation. **6.27** Exchanges can regulate their members, the intermediaries,[59] and the operation of trading in the secondary markets. But exchanges have little oversight of issuers, especially if they chose not to list on an exchange, nor of the public offering process in the primary market. A tap on the wrist by way of public censure or the draconian delisting of an issuer's securities (likely more harmful to securities holders than the issuer) were the only sanctions available to the exchange.

For much of the history of the LSE, between its regulation of the secondary market and the **6.28** self-regulatory mechanisms applicable to certain of the professional intermediaries, there was a huge regulatory gap. Not all offers to the public (the concept itself being somewhat hazy) fell into the regulatory net. An issuer selling securities directly to retail investors, potentially

---

[52] For example, in 1986 the London Stock Exchange had 512 foreign listings, compared to the New York Stock Exchange with 59 (one-third of which were Canadian listings). See 'Internationalization of the US Securities Markets: Report of the Staff of the US Securities and Exchange Commission to the Senate Committee on Banking, Housing and Urban Affairs and the House Committee on Energy and Commerce', SEC Report (27 July 1987). Felice Barklan, 'The Harmonization of Securities Law: The International Study' in *The Imperial SEC? Foreign Policy and the Internationalization of the Securities Markets, 1934–199* (1 December 2008) <http:// www.sechistorical.org/museum/galleries/imp/imp09b.php> accessed 12 December 2013.

[53] See Gower (n 7), 311–12.

[54] In 2007, the LSE bought shares in the Borsa Italiana based in Milan.

[55] 'The Stock Exchange lost its responsibility for authorising intermediaries with the [FSA 1986]. By then it was already subject to the Listing Directives, as implemented and supervised by the DTI. The exchange's trading rules had to comply with the recognition requirements of the [FSA 1986]. Supervised by the SIB. Througout the 1990s the process of setting up securities commissions, separate from the stock exchanges continued in every member State—a process which was accelerated by the ISD': Welch (n 21).

[56] See Ch 10 of this book.

[57] See Gower (n 7), 321, 336 and 339.

[58] The voluntary 'Cadbury [Report] illustrates the mismatch between the aspirations of the Stock Exchange to be a global market place attracting overseas issuers and the origins of its rules for protecting investors which have many of their roots in UK company law, which can apply only to UK companies. The Stock Exchange took some time to come to terms with limitations on its power to do whatever it thought fit': Welch (n 21).

[59] By denying them trading privileges, and thus disrupting their livelihood.

the most vulnerable of all, was outside the scope of regulation. Neither were all professional intermediaries engaging in transactions involving the public necessarily licensed or subject to any form of regulatory oversight. For example, Gower calls merchant bankers,[60] who benefited from an exempt dealer status, a 'law unto themselves'.[61] They were expected to comply, voluntarily, with the prevailing rules applicable to licensed intermediaries, but in practice this was not always the case.[62]

6.29 Given the fragmented nature of regulatory oversight, and its obvious deficiencies (scathingly critiqued by Gower in his 1992 treatise),[63] compensatory mechanisms appeared, at the instance of the exchange together with market practice. In 1980, faced with a proliferation of off exchange securities,[64] the LSE created the 'Unlisted Securities Market' or USM with its own rule book and set of guidelines (the Green Book), analogous to the rules and guidelines applicable to listed securities (the Yellow Book). Thus, the LSE very successfully began herding issuers and offerings onto the Exchange, either by way of formal listing or inclusion in the USM (ultimately rolled into the later market segment, AIM). Merchant banks (called the issuing house) assisted, profitably, in this process; they subscribed for securities directly from companies and then sold them on; the merchant banks also arranged for the 'introduction' to the Exchange and listing. It became standard practice for initial public offerings to list and off exchange offers dried up.

6.30 Perhaps the most enduring, and certainly most internationally influential, compensatory mechanism developed by the Exchange in the absence of formal regulatory authority was the 'voluntary code' and the principle of 'comply or explain'. Where the Exchange possessed few coercive levers, for example with respect to issuers themselves, a voluntary code could be created. For listed issuers, comply with the code or explain non-compliance, could be made part of the listing rules. The hope was that listed issuers would then lead by example and compliance would spread more generally. There were, and still are, voluntary codes in the City.

6.31 One of the most famous, and certainly most successful in terms of international propagation, is that originating in the 1992 Cadbury Report on corporate governance and its two-page Code of Best Practices.[65] The Exchange was one of the sponsors of the Report which stated:

> The London Stock Exchange intend to require all listed companies registered in the United Kingdom, as a continuing obligation of listing, to state whether they are complying with the Code and to give reasons for any areas of non-compliance... The obligation will be enforced in the same way as all other listing obligations. This may include, in appropriate cases, the publication of a formal statement of censure.[66]

---

[60] For the definition of merchant banker and their status as an exempt dealer, see Gower (n 7), 704.

[61] Gower (n7), 704.

[62] Gower (n7), 704.

[63] See Gower (n 7), 352–3 for his discussion of the inadequacies of primary market regulation.

[64] Gower points out that these off exchange securities did not constitute a US-style over-the-counter market: Gower (n 7), 312 fn 6.

[65] See Cally Jordan, 'Cadbury Twenty Years On' (2013) 58 *Villanova Law Review* 1 for a discussion of the Cadbury Report and its influence internationally.

[66] Committee on the Financial Aspects of Corporate Governance, *The Financial Aspects of Corporate Governance* (Gee, 1 December 1992), para 1.3 <http://www.ecgi.org/codes/documents/cadbury.pdf> accessed 14 October 2013.

The Cadbury Report itself has spawned dozens of voluntary codes of corporate governance **6.32** in countries around the world, some 391 according to the European Corporate Governance Institute.[67] The 'comply or explain' implementation methodology pops up everywhere.[68] Forgotten in this wave of emulation was the fact that the Exchange could do little more than propose a voluntary code,[69] especially with respect to unlisted companies.

Demutualization and the steady encroachment of formal regulation have much diminished **6.33** the significance of the LSE in the regulatory landscape. In 2000, with the creation of the FSA, even control over the listing process migrated to the regulator.

2.6 Importance of the professional market

For much of the twentieth century, the United Kingdom was considered to be primarily **6.34** a professional market, the participants in which could be more or less left to take care of themselves.[70] Thanks to a more shareholder friendly companies law,[71] and a tradition of close communication with company boards, institutional investors had more clout in the United Kingdom than their counterparts in the United States.[72]

As for the intermediaries, they had long benefited from broad exemptions from investor pro- **6.35** tection measures, such as they were, under the Prevention of Fraud (Investments) Acts 1939 and 1958 (PF(I)A) and companies law.[73] The professional exemption of the PF(I)A relieved market participants from licensing requirements if their activities were restricted to professionals; there were no prohibitions on cold calling to flog investment products; and they could freely market securities, circulating expressions of interest and documentation without being caught by restrictions associated with 'circulars' and 'advertising' of securities to the public.[74]

On the other hand, the usual professional exemption of companies law was worded **6.36** somewhat differently: an offer of shares or debentures of a company incorporated outside

---

[67] European Corporate Governance Institute, 'Index of Codes' (*European Corporate Governance Institute*) <http://www.ecgi.org/codes/all_codes.php> accessed 26 September 2013.

[68] There are a number of possible reasons for this. The Cadbury Report was the initiative of the London Stock Exchange, the most international of all exchanges at the time with hundreds of non-UK companies listed and news of the Report would have spread quickly internationally. Secondly, this period marked the beginning of the great re-alignment among exchanges around the world; exchanges were well connected through industry associations (eg the World Federation of Exchanges, the Federation of European Securities Exchanges), and closely monitoring developments in competing markets. In addition, there was the usual, and often underestimated, old colonial network of the Commonwealth. Commonwealth countries span the globe, encompassing economies at all levels of development and remain to this day surprisingly interconnected through the persistence of legislative and judicial legacies. The proposals themselves were also attractive in their simplicity, making them accessible to a broad audience, as well as being championed by an appealing and well-known figure, Sir Adrian Cadbury.

[69] Arguably, the LSE could be more coercive with respect to its listed issuers through its listing rules, but demonstrates reluctance to engage in such prescriptive measures which belong more appropriately in the companies legislation.

[70] In much the same way as retail investors dominated US markets until the mid-1980s.

[71] For example, pre-emptive rights, the ability to call a special meeting and remove directors.

[72] For example, there were no restrictions such as those imposed by Regulation FD (Fair Disclosure) in the United States which attempted to level the playing field with respect to access to issuer information as between retail and institutional investors.

[73] Under the PF(I)A 1958, s 14(5), transactions were exempt if they were with 'persons whose business involves the acquisition and disposal, or the holding of securities (whether as principal or as agent)'; the Companies Act 1948, s.423(2) differed and pertained to an offer of shares or debentures of a company incorporated outside Great Britain to a person whose ordinary business it is to buy or sell shares or debentures (whether as principal or agent) is not be deemed an offer to the public', s 79(1) and (2).

[74] See Gower Report Pt 1 (n 8), para 4.23, quoting the Companies Act 1948, s 423(2).

Great Britain to any person whose ordinary business it is to buy or sell shares or debentures (whether as principal or agent), is not deemed an offer to the public. This exemption eliminated the requirement to prepare a prospectus under companies law, but only applied to non-UK incorporated companies. Essentially, it was a foreign issuer exemption and facilitated offerings in London destined for the Euromarket, particularly by US issuers.

6.37 By the time Professor Gower produced his reports on investor protection in the mid-1980s, scandals[75] had demonstrated the failings of the professional exemption. According to Professor Gower, the 'present exemption has provided a far bigger loophole than could have been intended and has been widely abused'.[76] The potential abuses associated with then current practices raised alarms at this point, not least because of the inchoate state of regulatory checks and balances, but particularly given the political agenda of the Thatcher government to replicate the vibrant retail investor culture of the United States. While it lasted though, the professional exemption made London a freewheeling place to issue securities.[77]

3. Autonomy of the City and the Tradition of Self-Regulation

6.38 Of all these formative elements in the development of UK capital markets, the most significant are two related factors: the fierce autonomy of the City and the long tradition of self-regulation in the financial industry. Both are much diminished; the autonomy of the City has suffered a long, slow decline, particularly over the last century and a half,[78] while self-regulation in the financial industry, in theory, came to an abrupt end with the new millennium and the FSMA 2000.[79]

6.39 However, the City remains a powerful representative of the financial industry in the United Kingdom, both metaphorically and politically.[80] Self-regulation, of course, was not stamped

---

[75] Gower Report Pt 1 (n 8); Gower refers repeatedly to scandals; see eg paras 1.08–1.10.

[76] Gower Report Pt 1 (n 8), para 4.22.

[77] See Gower Report 1 (n 8), para 4.23 for discussion of the professional exemption.

[78] Recent calls for reform and the persistence of the status quo are discussed in James Pickford's article entitled, 'City Ward Hopefuls Face Reform Calls', *Financial Times* (London, 17 March 2013) <http://www.ft.com/intl/cms/s/0/4a0d7ec2-8f35-11e2-be3a-00144feabdc0.html#axzz2hklP1DHM> accessed 26 September 2013. Pickford states that: 'This week's elections to the City of London Corporation will be the most competitive in living memory, underlining the depth of public disquiet over the culture of the Square Mile, the UK's financial hub...But the prospects for a revolution are slim, critics say, because of conventions that help preserve the status quo. The Corporation holds an unusual status as part-local authority, part medieval throwback, with rights and privileges that predate the Norman Conquest...The City Reform Group, launched last year to campaign for change in the Corporation, is asking candidates to back seven pledges ranging from boosting democracy to greater transparency.' See also 'The City of London Corporation Inquiry' (November 1853–February 1854) 19 *Law Review and Quarterly Journal of British and Foreign Jurisprudence* 389.

[79] See Cally Jordan and Pamela Hughes, 'Which Way for Market Institutions: The Fundamental Question for Self-Regulation' (2007) 4 *Berkeley Business Law Journal* 205; Howard Davies, 'What's Left for Self-Regulation?', Roundtable Luncheon, Hong Kong Association of Banks, Hong Kong Securities Institute, Securities and Futures Commission, Hong Kong, 26 March 2004 <http://www.sfc.hk/edistributionWeb/gateway/EN/news-and-announcements/news/other-news/doc?refNo=04PR60> accessed 15 October 2013.

[80] According to Welch, 'with the migration of the large investment banks to Docklands, the City (ie within the remit of the City Corporation) has lost some of its clout. The regulatory balance has been somewhat restored with the transfer of powers to the PRA [Prudential Regulation Authority] but the FCA [Financial Conduct Authority] remains responsible for markets and is still the Listing Authority and keeps its home in Docklands. The fact that the Mayor of London can speak for Docklands while the City Corporation cannot, may help explain why commentators tend increasingly to refer to London's position as an international financial centre, rather than the City': Welch (n 21). 'Wall Street' serves a similar purpose in the United States, but lacks

out in 2000; the FSMA 2000 built upon it and London's once much vaunted 'light-touch' regulation which followed may have subsumed the continued operation of self-regulation. In a speech in Hong Kong, a few years after the FSMA 2000 came into effect, Howard Davies, former Chairman of the FSA, asked: 'What's left for self-regulation?' His 'rapid answer' to this question, he noted, could have been ' "not much…" We could then all have a relaxed lunch and go home. But the answer is a little more complex'.[81] Although self-regulation may have become seriously tarnished in the aftermath of the global financial crisis, it still greases the wheels of finance.

3.1 Autonomy of the City

The financial centre of the United Kingdom and, arguably the world's most important inter-national financial centre, has long been the City of London, usually simply referred to as 'the City'.[82] The City, home to merchants and traders, has been special for centuries, if not mil-lennia. 'The time-honoured City of London, like many other cities which flourished under the auspices of Imperial Rome, seems to have actually constituted, during the lengthened and obscure period of the Middle Ages, a species of independent self-government, contrast-ing by the comparative enlightenment of its municipal institutions, with that dark feudal system, whose iron chains bound down the Nations of Europe to the exclusive service of warfare or the priesthood'.[83] In the City, commerce reigned.   **6.40**

The City predates the Magna Carta (1215 CE). According to The City of London Corporation Inquiry, which was compiled in the 1850s, 'the national importance that was attached to the ancient liberties and franchises of London, may be estimated by the fact that it was made an express provision of Magna Charta itself, that the City of London should have all *its ancient liberties and customs…*'.[84] Not only were the franchises and customs of the City recognized as carrying immunity from the burdens of the feudal system (and the common law gener-ally), but the immunities later extended even to acts of Parliament. The City of London Corporation Inquiry goes on to state that: **6.41**

> Now it must be borne in mind, that when a general statute, silent as to the City of London, passes both Houses of Parliament, for effecting a reform in any branch of the law as to which there happens to exist a peculiar custom of the City of London, it is at least doubtful whether the statute will prevail within the limits of the City. It is laid down in some text-books, that the City customs are of such force that they shall prevail against a general Act of Parliament either using negative or affirmative words. Lord Coke, in numerous passages, lays it down, "that the special customs of the City shall prevail against the general law of the land…".[85]

---

the formal structure (ie the Corporation), concerted clout, and immediate political influence of the 'City'. Traditional forms of self-regulation of the intermediaries and the exchanges in the United States is a direct legacy of the British in the new colonies, but has long been subservient and accountable to Congress.

[81] Davies (n 79), 1.

[82] The City of London is a geographically defined area and a corporation dating back to the twelfth cen-tury. 'The Guildhall body, though nominally the Corporation of London, are restricted both for good and for evil within the small space of 600 acres, and to a population of about one-tenth of the whole Metropolis of London': 'The City of London Corporation Inquiry' (n 78), 424.

[83] 'The City of London Corporation Inquiry' (n 78), 391–2.

[84] 'The City of London Corporation Inquiry' (n 78), 392 (emphasis in the original).

[85] 'The City of London Corporation Inquiry' (n 78), 401–2.

6.42   Customs which can face down acts of Parliament are powerful indeed, so it should not be surprising that vestigial, and perhaps not so vestigial, elements persist in the City. They form a customary law of finance that traces its roots back centuries, and which is inherently international. Perhaps the secret to the success of the City as an international financial centre resides in the unspoken assumptions and operation of this customary law of finance operating within the (now virtual) walls of the City.

3.1.1 Customary law of finance—the case of oral contracts

6.43   Gower's comment, that merchant bankers constitute a 'law unto themselves', represents a more generalized phenomenon arising from the historic autonomy of the City. The City developed its own legal system,[86] distinct from the common law, the traditional jurisdiction of the courts of equity and Parliament. This is a customary law of commerce, a *lex mercatoria*, or perhaps more accurately, a *lex financeria*, of ancient provenance which persists today.

6.44   As an example, the prevalence of oral contracting in the City is one aspect of this *lex financeria*. The use and recognition of oral contracts characterizes the medieval *lex mercatoria*.[87] The *nudum pactum*, i.e. the contract without formalities,[88] did not exist in Roman law but was, in the interests of commercial expediency (and the generalized illiteracy of the age), recognized among merchants and traders across Europe.[89] Napoleon's 1807 *Code de commerce* brought together much of the pre-existing commercial customs and practices found across what is now modern day Europe.[90]

6.45   Historically, oral contracts among merchants were also recognized in the City of London. Given the existence of a recognized commercial practice, the 1677 Statute of Frauds (requiring a writing for the enforceability of certain contracts)[91] did not apply in the City. This was explicitly acknowledged in the case law even as to the transfer of land. According to The City of London Corporation Inquiry, '[e]ver since the Statute of Frauds, the conveyance of estates and interests in land, except by an instrument in writing, has been deemed to be prohibited by law. But here, again, the custom of London conflicts; and the old Guildhall law provides

---

[86]   With its own law enforcement agents and courts.

[87]   Ralf Michaels has recently provided a useful summation of some of the various senses in which the term has been used. He looks at *lex mercatoria* in its linear, chronological manifestations. The 'ancient lex mercatoria' of the Middle Ages was a 'transnational set of norms and procedural principles, established by and for commerce in (relative) autonomy from states': Ralf Michaels, 'The True Lex Mercatoria: Law Beyond the State' (2007) 14 *Indiana Journal of Global Legal Studies* 447, 448.

[88]   Tokens or 'magic words' at various times in Roman law. On *nudum pactum* in general, see WW Buckland, *A Manual of Roman Private Law* (Cambridge University Press, 1925), 307.

[89]   Leon E Trakman, 'The Evolution of the Law Merchant: Our Commercial Heritage' (1980) 12 *Journal of Maritime Law and Commerce* 1, 7–8.

[90]   This would include various aspects of medieval *lex mercatoria*, and the recognition of oral contracts among merchants. To this day, France makes a distinction between 'civil' contracts (among non-merchants, and governed by the *Code civil*), and commercial contracts (among merchants and governed by the *Code de commerce*). Commercial contracts may be proven more simply than ordinary, or 'civil', contracts. Ordinary (civil) contracts for over €1,500 must be made in writing, which now includes electronic forms of writing. Commercial contracts are exempt from this requirement with article L110-3 of the *Code de commerce* providing that commercial agreements may be proven by any means unless otherwise provided by law. By way of contrast, the later German civil code (*Bürgerliches Gestzbuch* or *BGB*) posits a universal principle of consensual contract and the commercial code does not need to make any exceptions for merchants or traders. Oral contracts among merchants are thus enforceable, as are any other contracts.

[91]   Act for the Prevention of Frauds and Perjuries 1677 (26 Car 2 c 3). Now largely repealed in the UK by Law Reform (Enforcements of Contracts) Act 1954 (c 34, s 1).

that *a bargain and sale for valuable consideration of houses or lands in London by word only is sufficient to pass the same*.[92]

So it is no coincidence then that the motto of the LSE is the famous '*Dictum meum pactum*'— **6.46** 'My word is my bond'. Berger maintains that 'the morality and mutual trust' represented by 'my word is my bond' even today is a more generalized characteristic of 'international business [which turns] the contractual promise into a categorical imperative'.[93]

Oral contracts continue to be a hallmark of modern finance in the City, which is home to the **6.47** swaps and derivatives markets. The swaps and derivatives markets developed in the 1980s as a 'telephone market'.[94] Oral, bilateral contracts were entered into over the telephone by specialized traders, relatively few in number. Despite the international reach of these transactions, the traders and much of the trading were geographically concentrated in the City.[95] These contracts were long term (often exceeding ten years in duration) and for very large sums of money, the usual factors militating in favour of written agreements. Despite this, these oral contracts often remained undocumented for months, if not years.

Over time, standardized contracts[96] developed to support the oral contracts and facilitate sub- **6.48** sequent documentation. Radical changes in modern technology did not fundamentally change the nature of the swaps and derivative markets; at least some corners of them remain a telephone market, although regulatory pressures are forcing the contracts onto trading facilities in the interests of promoting greater transparency.

Modern finance is full of such 'closed cells', pockets of professionals repeatedly dealing with each **6.49** other[97] in relative, or perhaps total, obscurity. Even the language of modern finance is metaphorically cloaked in darkness, full of 'dark pools' and 'black boxes'.[98] Although conversations among traders are now recorded as a matter of course, the ephemeral nature and intimacy of the human voice play tricks with the speakers, sometimes resulting in unintended indiscretions (but which only reach the light of day in the event of a major blow-up).

The global financial crisis was obviously a blow-up of major proportions. It exposed the innards **6.50** of the swaps and derivatives markets, among others. But other scandals, such as the burgeoning one over the manipulation of industry determined benchmarks such as the London Interbank Offer Rate, LIBOR,[99] also illuminate market practices which usually operate unknown to the

---

[92] 'The City of London Corporation Inquiry' (n 78), 408 (emphasis in original).
[93] Klaus Peter Berger, 'European Private Law, *Lex Mercatoria* and Globalisation' in AS Hartkamp and EH Hondius (eds), *Towards a European Civil Code* (3rd edn, Kluwer Law International, 2004), 46.
[94] The advanced technology of the day.
[95] Although not exclusively.
[96] Specifically, the ISDA Master Agreements.
[97] 'Many in the industry describe the interdealer market as a cosy club of select banks and brokers, who play by their own rules, fashioned since the early 1970s when the collapse of fixed currencies ushered an era of volatile exchange rates that required a middle man to help banks trade': Michael Mackenzie, 'Libor Probe Shines Light on Voice Brokers', *Financial Times* (16 February 2012) <http://www.ft.com/intl/cms/s/0/51 abc870-57ee-11e1-bf61-00144feabdc0.html#axzz2hvS7fIW6> accessed 17 October 2013.
[98] It is interesting to note that the lack of transparency of dealings in the City of London was one of the concerns of the 1853 report: 'The City of London Corporation Inquiry' (n 78).
[99] Mackenzie reports that: 'Enforcement agencies in the US, Canada, Europe and Japan are investigating whether employees at leading US and European banks colluded to influence where Libor and other key benchmark rates were set, in some cases to profit on interest-rate derivatives linked to the rates': Mackenzie (n 97). On this point, industry insider, James Cawley, notes that: 'When you start trying to collude or price fix a benchmark that affects mortgage rates, and the cost of certain car and school loans, it behoves regulators to take a very hard look': Mackenzie (n 97), quoting James Cawley.

general public. In particular, in the LIBOR scandal, the pivotal role of 'voice brokers' came to light. As Michael Mackenzie writes:

> Computers and Bloomberg terminals dominate trading floors, but the human element remains a crucial feature of transacting across derivatives and other parts of the global financial system. This is no better illustrated than by the presence of so-called 'voice brokers' who act as middle men for banks trading swaps and other fixed income securities in financial centres that link Asia, Europe and the US.[100]

6.51 Working in the interdealer market,[101] voice brokers convey prices to traders by telephone and 'squawk boxes'[102] although they do use computer screens to display certain other information. The voice brokers usually have several clients and a privileged view of where the market may be heading. Unsurprisingly then, according to Mackenzie, 'when a very competitive price enters the market, a voice broker will tell their best account the price before they tell their other accounts'.[103]

6.52 The persistence of oral transactions in finance, and in particular in the City, would seem to defy the logic of modern communications. But perhaps not. The oral contract in the fifteenth century may have been *faute de mieux*, nothing else was available that met the needs of expediency in commerce. But several other aspects of the oral transaction in commercial dealing likely also persist, ensuring its longevity.

6.53 The intimacy and immediacy of the human voice obviously contribute to the building of the mutual trust that is characteristic of specialized industries and which is noted by Berger, among others.[104] This mutual trust develops in the face of rampant self-interest and cutthroat competition. There are self-regulating limits; otherwise the market implodes to everyone's detriment.[105]

6.54 Related to the development of mutual trust, is speed and security. Voice negotiation benefits from quick reaction times and opportunities for repositioning, advantages often cited in the context of the 'open outcry' exchange model before it finally succumbed to technology.[106]

6.55 But perhaps the most intriguing aspect of oral transactions, in addition to their trust-inducing nature, is their security. In modern finance, where trades are negotiated over the telephone and squawk boxes, the human voice is key to identifying your counterparty.

---

[100] Mackenzie (n 97).

[101] That is, 'the private arena where only banks trade with each other as they offset positions they have with clients such as hedge funds, money managers and corporations': Mackenzie (n 97).

[102] Mackenzie (n 97). An indication of how primitive the verbal communications systems were until relatively recently; voices would be distorted and the speakers 'squawk'.

[103] Mackenzie (n 97).

[104] Berger (n 93).

[105] This aspect of the derivatives markets was graphically illustrated in the recent movie *Margin Call* (2011), one of the more authentic renditions of a market panic and collapse. The head trader resists pressures from above to completely liquidate a portfolio of 'toxic assets' on the basis that such an act would destroy the market itself, as well as the firm on the sell side of the transactions. No one would trade with the seller firm's traders again. The depiction of the frenzied selling is also significant; the transactions, in a volatile and rapidly moving market, are voice trades, where seller and buyer know each other.

[106] Again, see *Margin Call* for an example of oral negotiation and repositioning by traders, as the market slides and prices drop rapidly. Algorithmic trading is lightning fast, of course, but predetermined by the algorithm and thus ultimately less flexible than voice trading.

Human beings demonstrate a remarkable capacity for voice recognition, especially 'active' **6.56** voice recognition as opposed to 'passive' voice recognition. The distinction is based on actually participating in a conversation (a negotiation, for example) as opposed to simply overhearing one.[107]

The use of voice recognition as a trading device is explicitly acknowledged in both financial **6.57** industry practices and by their self-regulatory organizations. The interdealer markets are small and clubby so a high degree of voice recognition would be expected among traders and brokers in frequent contact.

The prevalence of oral contracting is just one aspect of a customary law of finance, a *lex* **6.58** *financiera*, with very deep roots in the City. It has grown out of the *lex mercatoria* used by medieval merchants and their bankers, unconstrained by national borders. Its persistence in the City has undoubtedly facilitated the conduct of international finance in the City. This customary law of finance, in its various guises and iterations, also spread along with British bankers, in some cases a very long time ago, beyond the walls of the City to Manhattan, Montreal, Hong Kong, Singapore, Melbourne, and more recently Bahrain, Dubai, and the other Emirates.

3.2 Self-regulation: Success and Failure

It is not an accident that self-regulation of financial institutions found its strongest expres- **6.59** sion, at least until recently, in the United Kingdom.[108] Customary law represents one face of the autonomy of the City; self-regulation of the financial intermediaries is another. Much of the autonomy of the City may have dissipated in the years since 1853.[109] However, up to the financial reforms of the late twentieth century and the creation of the now doomed Financial Services Authority (2000), autonomy and self-regulation defined the financial services industry in the City.

Even the indomitable Professor Gower in his 1980s reports on investor protection bowed to **6.60** the authority of self-regulation. Scandals, he said, had 'sapped confidence in self-regulation and led influential voices to declare that it should be scrapped';[110] Gower considered this 'an exaggerated reaction'.[111] In an ideal world, however, he would have espoused a single capital markets regulator.[112] In deference to the long tradition of self-regulation in the City but acknowledging that self-regulation needed supervision, he recommended a compromise.

---

[107] See, generally, Richard Hammersley and J Don Read, 'The Effect of Participation in a Conversation on Recognition and Identification of the Speakers' Voices' (1985) 9 *Law and Human Behavior* 71.

[108] The United States inherited it from the United Kingdom in pre-revolutionary times, and it persisted through the centuries as it served the interests of finance well.

[109] 'The City of London Corporation Inquiry' recounted perceived abuses associated with the autonomy of the City. It stated that: 'The present members of the Corporation of London . . . seem to have imbibed the notion that in order to divert a reform of the present system, and the substitution of one which should really serve the purpose of a Metropolitan municipality, it would suffice to urge that there is no ground for the imputation of "moral turpitude or personal corruption." ': (n 78), 426. This was in contradistinction to their predecessors in the eighteenth century where '[h]eavy tavern expenses were allowed, the cause of charity and education was neglected, and publicity avoided': (n 78), 427.

[110] Gower Report Pt 1 (n 8), para 1.10.

[111] Gower Report Pt 1 (n 8), para 1.10.

[112] Gower Report Pt II (n 23), para 2.03: 'It is therefore my hope, and, indeed, expectation, that there will be but one top Body.'

Ultimately, the FSA 1986 regrouped and consolidated the disparate self-regulatory organizations in the City under a single coordinating body, the SIB. The justification cited for this deference to self-regulation came from none other than that hardnosed US regulator, the SEC: a government agency should 'provide the grit which enables the oyster to produce the pearl of effective self-regulation'.[113]

6.61 The SIB, and the complicated pyramid of self-regulatory and other bodies it oversaw, suffered the fate of many compromises. By 1992, Professor Gower was desperately repeating his call for reform: 'What we surely need is the nearest possible approach to a single comprehensive code for all public issues, with a single regulatory and rule-making authority; the present overlapping rules and roles of different authorities are a recipe for disaster.'[114] Disaster did finally catch up with the SIB; a number of high profile scandals in the 1990s, particularly those involving pensions, overwhelmed the somewhat makeshift regulatory framework, causing public outrage and political action.[115] The SIB was replaced in 2000 by a single regulatory authority, the much emulated FSA, and none too soon.

6.62 On the other hand, a belief in the beneficial powers of self-regulation was sustained during these times by the 'only remaining relic of pure and unsupervised City self-regulation'. Although 'an anomaly in the post "Big Bang" [1986] era',[116] the Takeover Panel (the product of the 1962 Report of the Company Law Committee)[117] performed 'with conspicuous success'.[118] The Takeover Panel, and its City Code which appeared in 1968, had true autonomy, 'wholly free of any outside surveillance'[119] filling a gap left by the companies law and the Prevention of Fraud (Investments) Act 1958.[120]

6.63 Although not formally even a self-regulatory organization, the Takeovers Panel acted like one, exercising executive, legislative, and judicial powers which over time became recognized and acknowledged, even by the courts. Equally, the City Code was not in any way a legislative instrument,[121] simply industry guidelines. Interestingly, the City Code appeared at the same time (1968) as the Williams Act[122] in the United States, illustrating starkly the different approaches to a similar market problem as between the two countries. The Bank of England,

---

[113] Gower Report Pt 1 (n 8), para 2.02.

[114] Gower (n 7), 353.

[115] In particular, 'The London Stock Exchange, the Financial Reporting Council, and the accountancy profession in the U.K. published their committee report, "*The Financial Aspects of Corporate Governance*", on 1 December 1992, some twenty years ago. The report quickly became known by the name of its chairman, Sir Adrian Cadbury, as the "Cadbury Report"': Jordan (n 65), 1.

[116] Gower (n 7), 705.

[117] See Board of Trade, *Report of the Company Law Committee* (Cmd 1749, June 1962), <http://www.takeovers.gov.au/content/Resources/other_resources/Jenkins_Committee.aspx> accessed 18 October 2013 (also known as the 'Jenkins Committee'). See further, John Armour, Jack B Jacobs, and Curtis J Milhaupt, 'The Evolution of Hostile Takeover Regimes in Developed and Emerging Markets: An Analytical Framework' (2011) 52 *Harvard International Law Journal* 219, 236.

[118] Gower (n 7), 705.

[119] '[W]holly free from any outside surveillance': Gower (n 7), 705.

[120] As Gower explains, the PF(I)A only caught licensed dealers who were not usually involved in takeover activity; merchant bankers did takeovers and they were exempt dealers, and 'a law unto themselves' as Gower put it: see n (61). This distinction between licensed dealers and merchant bankers represented another instance of the compartmentalization of investment professionals in the United Kingdom and the anomalous results which it produced.

[121] To the extent that 'authorised persons', eg, licensed dealers, were involved, they could, in theory, be disciplined for failure to follow the City Code. There existed no sanctions against the companies involved.

[122] Which similarly set down rules for the conduct of tender offers (takeovers).

the Exchange, self-regulatory organizations, all interacted in various ways with the Takeover Panel.[123] However, neither successive Companies Acts nor the FSA 1986 dared impinge on its self-assumed authority. The Panel took its place in the City as a *de facto* public body; such is the way of the common law.

Pure self-regulation though is not the European way and the Takeover Panel collided with the long-awaited and much delayed EU Takeovers Directive.[124] 'The rules implementing the directive had to be given legal force and the Panel had to operate the rules within a statutory framework, as the price for being recognised as a Competent authority.'[125] Preserved in many respects, the Takeover Panel was given statutory backing in the completely revamped Companies Act 2006.[126] **6.64**

Scandals which self-regulation could neither prevent nor address, together with the unrelenting pressures from the European Union for formal legislative structures have forced self-regulation into abeyance in the United Kingdom. But it is difficult to imagine that such a powerful and ancient force in the City has been completely displaced; it may simply be operating silently under the surface. **6.65**

4. Milestones Along the Regulatory Road

In hindsight, the trajectory towards capital markets regulation in the United Kingdom appears inevitable, particularly after 1972 with the momentum provided by the European Union and its proclivity for written legislation. However, the road to regulation has been a long and bumpy one. **6.66**

4.1 The Prevention of Fraud (Investments) Acts 1939 and 1958

The Prevention of Fraud (Investments) Acts of 1939 and 1958 (PF(I)A 1939 and 1958) were, as their titles suggest, of limited reach. Fraudulent 'share pushing' or 'share hawking' by 'outside dealers', ie those not members of an exchange and thus not subject to the exchange's self-regulatory disciplines, were targeted by the legislation. Dealers who were members of an exchange were exempt.[127] **6.67**

---

[123] See Gower (n 7), 704.

[124] Council Directive 2004/25/EC of 21 April 2004 on takeover bids [2004] OJ L142/12.

[125] Welch (n 21).

[126] Companies Act 2006 (UK), Pt 28.

[127] '[T]he Prevention of Frauds (Investments) Act 1939, re-enacted almost without change in 1958, was based on the recommendations of the 1937 Bodkin Committee "appointed to consider...share-pushing and share-hawking and similar activities"': Paul Nelson, *Capital Markets Law and Compliance* (Cambridge University Press, 2008), 12. The report provided as follows: '[T]he victim is persuaded to part with money or valuable securities in exchange for shares which prove to be worthless. In the second...the victim is persuaded to speculate in shares and to deposit cash or his own securities with the dealer on security for the "margin". The victim believes that his deposit...will be returned to him...In fact the dealer...has [not] bought...the shares which he has persuaded the victim to order': Bodkin Report, para 4, quoted in Nelson (n 127), 12. Thus the real necessity to regulate 'outside dealers' prompted the 1939 statute: Harold H Neff, 'Report on the Trading in American Securities on the British Market' (SEC, Washington, 1 March 1940), 2. In the report, Neff states that: 'There has recently been enacted, however, the so-called Share-Pushing Bill, to regulate the business of the "outside dealers", that is, those persons in the securities business who are not members of an exchange. From the compass of this statute, however, are excepted the members of recognized organized exchanges': Neff (n 127), 2. It appears that the 1939 Act was repealed by the 1958 Act to enact provisions for fixed trusts (unit trusts). The 1939 Act did not come into force until 1944 because of the Second World War.

6.68 The PF(I)A 1939 and 1958 did not provide even the modicum of investor protection which their titles promised. Gower considered them unenforceable,[128] and worse,[129] unwieldy, disorganized and ineffective. Since prospectus and financial disclosure requirements appeared in the companies legislation, the PF(I)A focused on the licensing of intermediaries as a means of investor protection, but did so in a piecemeal and ad hoc manner.

6.69 By the early 1980s, with the concerted efforts to create a retail equity investor culture in the United Kingdom under the privatization schemes of the Thatcher government, pressure mounted in some quarters to provide more effective investor protection. Gower argued for regulation: '[T]he fault lies with a system which does not afford the public adequate means of distinguishing between the sheep and the goats except by parting with their money and finding out by happy or bitter experience. What is needed is a system which will help the public to identify the sheep and which will effectively curb the activities of the goats.'[130] But the prospect of greater formal regulation set up howls in the City and had to be approached carefully. '[R]egulation … should be no greater than is necessary to protect reasonable people from being made fools of.'[131] So began an era of 'light touch regulation' in the City.

4.2 The European Union—1972

6.70 The entry of the United Kingdom into what is now known as the European Union[132] undoubtedly marked the beginning of the long march to a regulatory framework. '[G]entlemanly capitalism'[133] could not resist the inexorable rise in the influence of Brussels on financial services and the impetus for formal regulation of the City. In the initial phases, the United Kingdom had to engage in fitting the square peg of its opaque and unruly system into the round hole of pre-existing EU directives. Companies law, which included capital raising and financial disclosure, was the priority; an area which had been dominated by German approaches.[134] On the other hand, this was also an era in which the United States exerted considerable hegemony in terms of providing the standalone model for 'securities regulation', introducing to 'the United Kingdom the clearer distinction between companies' legislation and securities' legislation which more comparable countries have long enjoyed'.[135]

6.71 EU directives forced the LSE to become a 'competent authority', in order to exercise its traditional self-regulatory powers. The Exchange thus lost its autonomy, being reduced to a self-regulatory organization subject to government oversight.[136] Equally, EU directives challenged the status and operation of the Takeover Panel, that paragon of City autonomy.[137]

6.72 At the time of enactment of the FSA 1986, compliance with the main 'securities regulation' directives[138] had been perfunctory. The directives themselves had simply been attached,

---

[128] Gower Report Pt 1 (n 8), para 1.12.
[129] See Gower Report Pt 1 (n 8), para 1.12 for Gower's scathing comments.
[130] Gower Report Pt 1 (n 8), para 1.10.
[131] Gower Report Pt 1 (n 8), para 1.16 (emphasis not included).
[132] Formerly the European Economic Community, or EEC.
[133] Kynaston (n 2), 422.
[134] Culminating, in this first phase with the Companies Act 1985 and Insolvency Act 1986.
[135] Gower Report Pt II (n 23), para 1.04.
[136] See Gower (n 7), 705.
[137] Gower (n 7), 705.
[138] The Listing Particulars Directive, the Public Offer Prospectus Directive and the Insider Dealing Directive.

holus bolus, to a UK regulation. This constituted token compliance with European directives; however, given the inevitable inconsistencies and contradictions with pre-existing legislation, rules, guidelines and practices in the City, the regulations were quite ineffectual. It was left to the Exchange to reconcile the incompatibilities and cobble together responses through Exchange rulemaking in the so-called 'Yellow Book'.[139]

But the influences of EU directives on the United Kingdom are more complex than they   **6.73**
seem at first glance. Early EU directives based on public disclosure and reporting principles actually found their inspiration in US securities regulation and UK exchange rules.[140] The European Commission had sponsored the 1966 Segré Report,[141] on the development of a European capital market, which emphasized 'the link between ongoing disclosure and increased investment in securities',[142] noting the sharp contrast between the US and Member States' disclosure requirements.[143] 'Moreover, in 1975, the International Federation of Stock Exchanges (FIBV) adopted—'[o]bviously under the influence of the United States delegation to FIBV—a proposal on multiple listing... [in which] [m]inimum requirements for admission and disclosure were proposed in order to facilitate multiple listings'.[144] The Admissions Directive[145] and Listing Particulars Directive[146] were the result.

In a curious feedback loop, the European Commission was picking up cues and issues from   **6.74**
both the United States and the United Kingdom, formulating its own particular responses at the EU[147] level by way of directive, which was then fed back into the United Kingdom. For example, the Investor Compensation Schemes Directive (ICSD),[148] after a long delay, was adopted in March 1997. However, for several decades the London Stock Exchange had

---

[139] See Gower (n 7), 321.

[140] There being no governmental regulatory authority and since virtually all public offerings in the United Kingdom were listed.

[141] European Economic Community Commission, *The Development of a European Capital Market* (Brussels, November 1966), <http://ec.europa.eu/economy_finance/emu_history/documentation/chapter1/19661130 en382develeurocapitm_a.pdf> accessed 19 October 2013 ('Segré Report'). Welch notes that this represents the 'normal process of cross-fertilisation which takes place during the process of drafting a proposal for a directive. At this time a Commission working party, consisting of representatives of Member States would normally work on Commission ideas for a directive and the UK was in a strong position with its experience to inject ideas into the process. The Stock Exchange would have sent along an expert to the working party. But I don't think that the Stock Exchange realised that the final product would never replicate the UK regime nor that it would have to be implemented by legally binding requirements': Welch (n 21).

[142] Niamh Moloney, *EC Securities Regulation* (Oxford University Press 2002), 134.

[143] See Moloney (n 142). Also, see Segré Report (n 141), 227: 'Contrary to the practices of other countries, and more especially of the United States, information available on most companies in Member States is still embryonic; but strangely enough, the regular publication of material normally withheld from European shareholders has been readily undertaken by certain companies when they wanted to raise funds on the American or British capital markets.'

[144] Eddy Wymeersch, 'From Harmonization to Integration in the European Securities Markets' (1981) 3 *Journal of Comparative Corporate Law and Securities Regulation* 4.

[145] Council Directive 79/279/EEC of 5 March 1979 coordinating the conditions for the admission of securities to official stock exchange listing [1979] L66/21 ('Admission Directive').

[146] Council Directive 80/390/EEC of 17 March 1980 coordinating the requirements for the drawing up, scrutiny, and distribution of the listing particulars to be published for the admission of securities to official stock exchange listing [1980] OJ L100/1 ('Listing Particulars Directive').

[147] Then known as the European Community.

[148] Council Directive 97/9/EC of 3 March 1997 on investor-compensation schemes [1997] OJ L84/22 ('Investor Compensation Schemes Directive' or 'ICSD').

a compensation fund for investors dealing with its members.[149] On the other hand, new concepts were also introduced, for example, by the UCITS Directive.[150] 'Collective investment schemes, as a particular class of investment schemes so described, have a short history in English law. They were introduced by the Financial Services Act 1986 as a result of the Directive on Undertakings for Collective Investment in Transferable Securities.'[151]

6.75 Where there were differences or inconsistencies with established rules or practices, the United Kingdom balked or pushed back.[152] '[I]n continental Europe offers of unlisted shares were more common, making the need for a public-offers disclosure regime' and the Public Offer Prospectus Directive[153] 'compelling'.[154] In the United Kingdom, public offers were usually of officially listed securities and so subject to the disclosure requirements of the Listing Particulars Directive. Although the public offering of securities and prospectus requirements were included in Part V of the FSA 1986, it is telling that they never came into force.[155] In another example, the LSE succeeded in significantly diluting the impact of the Interim Reports Directive.[156] The Exchange was concerned that 'as a result of the mandatory nature of the obligation to publish half-yearly reports, it would be liable for any failures by companies to report or for incomplete reports by companies. These concerns were ultimately addressed by a drastic reduction in the information requirements...'.[157]

6.76 Some of the most bitter resistance to EU directives arose where their intended purpose was to restrain UK dominance in European trading markets. In the 1990s, the Stock Exchange Automated Quotation (SEAQ) International, based in London, handled '95% of Europe's cross-border equity trading and roughly two thirds of the world's cross-exchange trading...Moreover, it attracts over 50% of all trades in French and Italian equities and a third of the trades in German blue chip companies...[T]he Member States on the continent...targeted the London markets in order to bring the trading in their equity securities back home'.[158] The Investment Services Directive 1993 (ISD 1993)[159] was seen as the means of achieving this objective. Although there was difficult and protracted debate over the ISD

---

[149] The FSA 1986 replaced this scheme by a statutory one. See (n 151).

[150] Council Directive 85/611/EEC of 20 December 1985 on the coordination of laws, regulations, and administrative provisions relating to undertakings for collective investment in transferable securities [1985] OJ L375/3 ('UCITS Directive').

[151] Jonathan Fisher, Jane Bewsey, Malcolm Waters, and Elizabeth Ovey, *The Law of Investor Protection* (2nd edn, Sweet & Maxwell, 2003), 137, para 6-001. The FSA 1986 created a statutory compensation scheme for investment firms, resulting in the winding up of the Stock Exchange compensation scheme. The FSA 1986 also introduced regulation of collective investment schemes implementing UCITS directive and prohibited the promotion of unregulated collective investment schemes to the public; unit trusts, a form of collective investment scheme, had existed in the United Kingdom for a very long time before the UCITS Directive: Welch (n 21).

[152] Usually by way of the London Stock Exchange as primary self-regulator.

[153] Council Directive 89/298/EEC of 17 April 1989 coordinating the requirements for the drawing-up, scrutiny, and distribution of the prospectus to be published when transferable securities are offered to the public [1989] OJ L124/8 ('Public Offer Prospectus Directive').

[154] Moloney (n 142), 177–8.

[155] Public Offer of Securities Regulations 1995, SI 1995/1537 ('POSR 1995'), then Prospectus Regulations 2005, SI 2005/1433 ('PR 2005').

[156] Council Directive 82/121/EEC of 15 February 1982 on information to be published on a regular basis by companies the shares of which have been admitted to official stock-exchange listing [1982] OJ L48/26 ('Interim Reports Directive').

[157] Moloney (n 142), 159–60.

[158] Manning Gilbert Warren III, 'The European Union's Investment Services Directive' (1994) 15 *University of Pennsylvania Journal of International Business Law* 181, 192.

[159] Council Directive 93/22/EEC of 10 May 1993 on investment services in the securities field [1993] OJ L141/27 ('Investment Services Directive or ISD').

1993 prior to its adoption, ultimately the member states agreed that 'the need for liquidity, high-quality prices and a common body of accepted dealing procedures will help some sort of central market to emerge'.[160]

The tensions between London and Brussels continue unabated. Now, however, with the **6.77** creation of a pan-European capital markets regulator in 2011, the European Securities and Markets Authority based in Paris, the stakes have risen. The ESMA has direct rule-making authority, albeit in limited areas and subject to ultimate European Commission veto,[161] but the ESMA can now dictate directly to London in certain circumstances.[162] Even in the historical tussles between London and Brussels, there had been room for manoeuvre; London was famous for 'goldplating' or 'improving' on directive requirements so as to work them more to its liking. Now with the shift to directly applicable regulation (which may emanate from either Brussels or Paris) and the emphasis on maximum harmonization, the City's freewheeling days may be drawing to a close.[163] Some estimate that up to to 75 per cent of regulatory authority has now shifted to the ESMA and away from London.[164] Arguably, because London will not give up without a fight, the EU regulatory agenda for capital markets has eclipsed that of the City and its domestic regulators.[165]

4.3 Financial Services Act 1986 (FSA 1986) and the Big Bang

The FSA 1986[166] coincided with the 'Big Bang', and together they ushered in a new world **6.78** of finance in the City.[167] The FSA 1986 had been preceded by the Companies Act 1985 (CA 1985), the first consolidation of the principles governing prospectuses and allotment of shares that dated back to the nineteenth century. As a consolidation, not a revision, the CA

---

[160] 'One Market or Many?', *The Economist* (London, 16 December 1989), 30, 34.

[161] In certain areas such as credit rating agency regulation.

[162] ESMA is discussed in Ch 7 of this book.

[163] In addition to rule-making authority by way of directly applicable regulation in certain areas, ESMA can make binding technical standards which member states must take into account.

[164] See Ch 7 of this book. According to Welch, the 'more accurate estimate is that 75% of UK financial services regulation derives from EU legislation': Welch (n 21).

[165] See International Monetary Fund, 'United Kingdom: Financial System Stability Assessment' (IMF Country Report No 11/222, July 2011) <http://www.imf.org/external/pubs/ft/scr/2011/cr11222.pdf> accessed 20 October 2013. The IMF has stated that: 'Increasingly, most of the key elements of the UK regulatory regime are effectively EU-determined policy transposed into UK rulebooks. In assessing compliance with the IOSCO Principles, this needs to be taken into account': International Monetary Fund, 'United Kingdom: IOSCO Objectives and Principles of Securities Regulation: Detailed Assessment of Implementation' (IMF Country Report No 11/232, July 2011), 9, para 20 <http://www.imf.org/external/pubs/ft/scr/2011/cr11232.pdf> accessed 20 October 2013.

[166] This is the legislation which Gower suggested be called the Investor Protection Act. Note the shift in emphasis away from investor protection which the title of the legislation suggests.

[167] 'The [FSA 1986] and "Big Bang" were completely separate. [Big] Bang was the result of the Exchange being taken to the Restrictive Practices Court by the Office of Fair Trading [OFT] in 1979. The OFT considered that the then fixed commission system and single capacity trading were anti-competitive. The DTI then introduced legislation to exempt the LSE from the Restrictive Practices Act on condition that the anti-competitive practices were abolished. Hence the end of fixed commissions, non-market member limitations, foreign ownership restrictions and single capacity—thus ending the distinction between stockbrokers and stockjobbers. Trading on the LSE was also later moved off floor and conducted by telephone. Prospectuses moved to the [FSA 1986] in theory but in fact remained with the DTI and the Companies Acts, because Part V was never commenced. Only the provisions on investigation of insider dealing moved to the [FSA 1986]—the substantive criminal provisions stayed in the [CA 1985] until the adoption of the Criminal Justice Act in 1993....[T]he inclusion of any provisions in the [FSA 1986] did not necessarily mean that the SIB/SROs had any power in relation to such matters. Much, like listing and public offer remained with the DTI': Welch (n 21).

1985 made no substantial changes to the pre-existing law relating to the issue of securities. Insider dealing provisions, originally introduced in the Companies Act 1980, were dropped into their own legislation, the Companies Securities (Insider Dealing) Act 1985.[168] A year later, it was all change. The principles governing prospectuses and insider dealing moved to the FSA 1986.[169]

6.79 The FSA 1986 attempted to create a formal regulatory framework within which self-regulation continued to operate. At a more structural level, and independently although coincidentally, the Big Bang had blown open the cosy world of the City: it eliminated the guild-like distinctions which had distinguished and compartmentalized financial intermediaries, with each group following its own particular set of rules. Minimum, fixed commissions which had stifled competition in the interests of easy profits were abolished. More significantly perhaps, with the Big Bang restrictions on outside foreign ownership and the management of intermediaries were lifted. This permitted an influx of competitive, aggressive Wall Street practitioners, unschooled in City ways. Along the way, City firms began to abandon the cohesiveness of partnership form for that of the profit-generating incorporated business.[170]

6.80 The FSA 1986, focusing on the intermediaries, created a unique two-tier regulatory system for the investment business: the SIB overseeing further tiers of SROs. According to Timothy Edmonds, the 'SIB set the overall framework for the detailed standards of regulation, and consulted on and initiated policy objectives'.[171] Below the SIB, SROs such as the Securities and Futures Authority played a significant role: '[i]nvestment firms had to be authorised by an appropriate SRO if they wanted to conduct investment business in the United Kingdom.'[172] The SIB could authorize investment businesses and recognize self-regulating organizations.[173]

6.81 As with the cosmic metaphor, after the Big Bang, chaos reigned. This was a period of frenzied legislative juggling, some of which had to be rethought or unwound shortly thereafter. A major part of the FSA 1986 was never implemented.[174] There were big gaps.[175] Too many different regulatory bodies (DTI, the Exchange, SIB, multiple self-regulatory organizations) resulted in too many rules being triggered, with different and possibly conflicting

---

[168] Companies Securities (Insider Dealing) Act 1985 (UK) (1985 c 8).

[169] Financial Services Act 1986 (UK) (1986 c 60) (FSA 1986).

[170] See Gower (n 23), para 1.08.

[171] Timothy Edmonds, 'Financial Markets: Supervisory and Structural Reform—the Draft Financial Services Bill' (House of Commons Library, 23 December 2011), 5.

[172] Edmonds (n 171), 5.

[173] 'Investment firms had to be authorised to carry on investment business in the UK, but under the Act they could get authorisation either by becoming a member of a recognised SRO or by applying direct to the SIB—the latter route was, however, actively discouraged': Welch (n 21).

[174] Part V of the Financial Services Act 1986 never came into force, although Part IV came into force in 1987. Because of this, Part III of the Companies Act 1985 governed the prospectus requirements for unlisted securities until 1995 when the Public Offers of Securities Regulations 1995 was passed. See Simon Gleeson and Harold S Bloomenthal, 'The Public Offer of Securities in the United Kingdom' (1998–99) 27 *Denver Journal of International Law and Policy* 359, 369–71. The Public Offers of Securities Regulations 1995 was repealed by the Prospectus Regulation 2005 and has been replaced by an extension of the provisions in Part VI of the FSMA 2000. It is the FSMA 2000 that covers the prospectus requirements for both listed and unlisted securities.

[175] For example, unlisted issues which were not on the rather anomalously named Unlisted Securities Market (USM) of the London Stock Exchange fell through the cracks. There was no oversight of such issues except through the definition and involvement of 'authorised persons' and provisions on their use of prospectuses and advertising: ss 160 and 161(4).

outcomes.[176] It was unclear which regulatory body was in charge. In Gower's words, the situation constituted 'a recipe for disaster'.[177] The new regulatory structure, the SIB/SROs, may have somewhat unfairly borne the brunt of the criticism given their somewhat deceptive appearance of a lead regulator (which they were not). In the fragmented state of the regulatory apparatus, the SIB/SROs had limited authority; for example, 'the responsibility of the SIB for public offers of securities was . . . limited to the policing of investment advertisements under s57 of [the FSA 1986]—these were offers which neither required listing particulars nor a prospectus and could therefore be issued lawfully in the UK provided they complied with the requirements of the Act and DTI (later Treasury) regulations made under it'.[178]

4.4 The Financial Services and Markets Act 2000

The FSMA 2000[179] brought about a sea change in UK financial markets regulation. The FSMA 2000 achieved what Gower had proposed, and even what he had not dared hope for, some 20 years earlier. Such is the power of a majority government sweeping into power in 1997 with a mandate for change, and bringing with it a strong armed Chancellor. **6.82**

For the first time, the United Kingdom enjoyed a consolidated and comprehensive legislative regime in financial services, with a regulatory body of the heft and authority of the US SEC (but more so). The SIB had been renamed the Financial Services Authority (FSA) in 1997 and assumed responsibility for the FSMA 2000, in the process becoming a single, statutory, financial services regulator,[180] integrating the two-tier regulatory system of the FSA 1986.[181] The FSMA 2000 eviscerated self-regulation, with the FSA even taking over the role of UK Listing Authority from the LSE. The Bank of England had lost (temporarily as it turned out) its supervisory powers with banking supervision as well as investment services and insurance put under FSA oversight. Moreover, the FSMA 2000[182] reflected 'the movement towards a single market for securities in the EU by means of the single passport regime'.[183] **6.83**

The integrated financial services regulator concept, grouping capital markets, insurance and banking under one supervisory umbrella and pioneered by the FSA,[184] proved very popular; it was rapidly emulated around the world. Arguably, the 20-year gestation period for the FSA was well spent; the FSA quickly established itself as a counterweight, internationally, to the US SEC. **6.84**

However, rather than traipsing in the footsteps of the SEC, the FSA had boldly leapt ahead. In addition to its integrated structure, designed to promote oversight of the financial sector **6.85**

---

[176] See discussion in Gower (n 7), 353.

[177] Gower (n 7), 353.

[178] Welch (n 21). 'They [SIB/SROs] were rightly criticised for overlapping and underlapping regulation of investment business carried on by bank and non bank investment firms and for lax regulation on occasions (though it is worth remembering that the late Lord Bingham in his report on the collapse of BCCI, complimented the securities regulators on their prompt and effective actions, while condemning the Bank of England)': Welch (n 21).

[179] See Kynaston (n 2), 598–9.

[180] Kynaston (n 2), 598–9.

[181] See Kynaston (n 2), 598–9.

[182] Which had made its 'ponderous way' through Parliament: Kynaston (n 2), 598.

[183] Hudson (n 32), 154, 4–23.

[184] The Office of the Superintendent of Financial Institutions (OSFI), created in Canada in 1987 is the original prototype except for the fact that capital markets (in the form of provincial securities regulation) could not be swept in due to entrenched political interests and constitutional difficulties.

as a whole, the FSA, infused by centuries of market practice experience and the operation of self-regulatory principles, adopted quite a different regulatory philosophy to that of the SEC. In popular parlance, this was often referred to as 'light touch' regulation and touted as a comparative advantage for the London markets. And it is true, in the wake of the FSMA 2000, the City and the LSE boomed (until the crash, of course).

6.86 However, 'light touch' regulation was much more nuanced and technically grounded than would at first appear. In July 2011, the IMF conducted a Financial Sector Assessment of the United Kingdom (measuring its capital markets regulation against the IOSCO Objectives and Principles of Securities Regulation 2003)[185] and its report provides a succinct description of the FSA's regulatory approach:

> 11. **The FSA undertakes risk-based supervision and has evolved a structured approach to supervision.** The FSA has in place a 'risk dashboard,' which determines risks against the statutory objectives of the FSA (market confidence, financial stability); these risks are put into various categories: environmental, business, capital, and governance. Particular lines of business or activities are then measured against the risk dashboard to determine a firm's particular risk profile. Every firm is given an impact measure showing the potential harm to the FSA objectives if it fails or if the risks crystallize. This is a proxy for its regulatory footprint or size.
>
> 12. **Once the impact value is calculated, a firm can be classified into one of four categories: Low, Medium-Low, Medium-High, or High.** The impact metrics used to calculate the firm's impact measures differ depending on the sector within which it operates. The risk profile is then used to categorize firms for the type of supervision they will receive. High-impact firms will receive what is called 'close and continuous' supervision, with a dedicated relationship manager and team, including more than one supervisor and a manager. A medium-high impact firm may have a smaller team but still be in close and continuous contact. A medium-low to medium-high firm would be 'relationship managed,' meaning that it is directly supervised on a day-to-day basis, but may be part of a group of firms supervised with a less-intensive cycle of consultations. A low-impact firm will be categorized as a 'small firm' and not 'relationship managed;' it would then be put into a very large pool of (16,000) firms handled by the small-firms group.
>
> 13. **Those firms that are relationship-managed are subject to an Advanced Risk-Responsive Operating Framework (ARROW) assessment.** Medium-low firms are subject to an ARROW light assessment that focuses on core areas. The ARROW determines the risk issues to be monitored by the FSA and includes a review [of] the firm's business model, oversight, and governance structures and operational controls. [Table 2, sets out the number of firms by cateory in each risk category.]
>
> 14. **Small firms are not subject to an ARROW review.** Small firms are, however, profiled—their reporting along with other factors (such as complaints received, type of activity, market intelligence) are used to generate a risk profile that identifies those small firms that require additional supervision. For example, the largest fund manager in the small-firm category has £10.8 billion funds under management, with a market share of 0.043%.
>
> 15. **The FSA supplements this risk-based formula with thematic reviews.** It undertakes special inspections of samples of firms on various topics. For example, the FSA has conducted reviews of 'spread betting' firms to ensure internal controls are sufficient; it has also done a number of reviews looking at handling of client monies. Thematic reviews can apply to any firm.

---

[185] IMF (n 165), 7–8.

Table 2 United Kingdom: Number of firms by risk category

Sector/Impact	Low	Medium Low	Medium High	High
Banking	32	126	45	35
Asset	13	82	45	9
Insurance	12	104	104	17
Capital markets	5	40	33	8
Retail intermediaries	16,000	47	13	1
Total	16,062	399	240	70

Source: Financial Services Authority

Notable in this approach is the focus on the institutions, the financial intermediaries, and across sectors.

Despite the loss of major self-regulatory functions (such as listing), the LSE thrived during this period. The AIM (Alternative Investments Market), which had replaced the Unlisted Securities Market (USM) and the Third Market in 1995, was feted for its innovation and adaptability to new market realities. Like the enthusiasm for 'light touch' regulation, the party did not last however. The LSE, an early adopter[186] and fully demutualized by 2000, became a prime takeover target and merger partner, with multiple potential alliances considered.   **6.87**

When the music stopped and the failures came a few brief years after its creation, the FSA carried on. But the failures which prompted public outcry were on the banking side of the FSA, not the capital markets side (although laxity over insider dealing was criticized). Nevertheless, out went the baby with the bathwater; in June 2010, the FSA was condemned to dismemberment and officially interred 31 March 2013.   **6.88**

4.5 The Financial Services Act 2012 (FSA 2012)

The FSMA 2000 and its integrated regulator, the FSA, were sacrificed to the gods of politics and public opinion, victims of the global financial crisis and a change in government. The FSA had 'palpably failed'.[187] It fell to the incoming UK Chancellor to announce 'the government's intention to replace the FSA as a single financial services regulator with two new successor bodies, and restructure the UK's financial regulatory framework'.[188]   **6.89**

And so, for the second time in scarcely a decade, the United Kingdom   **6.90**

> embarked on a wholesale restructuring of its regulatory arrangements for the financial sector.... [T]he current remit of the FSA will be divided between two separate agencies: the Prudential

---

[186] Although telephone trading had already supplanted the traditional trading floor, the LSE finally eliminated its physical trading floor in 1997 in favour of all-electronic trading. A monumental hanging glass structure in the atrium of its new premises in Canary Wharf symbolizes the trading floor.

[187] In announcing Royal Assent for the FSA 2012, the Secretary to the Treasury stated: 'The Financial Services Act replaces a regulatory structure which palpably failed when tested by crisis. It sets out a comprehensive regulatory framework designed to enhance financial stability in the future and protect consumers.... It is important that the reputation of the UK as a global financial centre is underpinned by a regulatory environment in which the world's investors, as well as British taxpayers, can have confidence': Press release, Financial Services Bill receives Royal Assent, 19 December 2012 <https://www.gov.uk/government/news/financial-services-b ill-receives-royal-assent> accessed 26 October 2013.

[188] 'History' (FSA, 24 February 2011) <http://www.fsa.gov.uk/about/who/history> accessed 27 September 2013.

Regulatory [now Regulation] Authority (PRA) and the Financial Conduct Authority (FCA). It is contemplated that, except for the prudential regulation of the very large investment banks, the full remit of securities regulation will be within the FCA, including prudential regulation of small firms, business and sales conduct regulation of all firms, regulation of secondary markets (issuers and trading systems), and regulation of asset management. The PRA will be responsible for prudential regulation of only the largest firms (generally banks and insurance companies). The current enforcement function, including criminal prosecutions, will go to the FCA. Regulation and supervision of clearing and settlement systems will be carried out by the Bank of England (BoE). A Financial Policy Committee (FPC) will coordinate financial stability across the system—the FPC will be chaired by the BoE and will include representation by the PRA and FCA as well as independent members.[189]

6.91   The IMF team conducting the 2011 FSAP identified the risk and uncertainty associated with these massive regulatory changes as the main vulnerability in the United Kingdom. In their report, they stated that: 'The FSA's supervisory approach relies on the skills and judgment of its experienced supervisors. If there were to be a significant loss of further supervisory skills and experience in the FSA for any reason, this would call in to question the resilience of the current assessment against the IOSCO Principles'. [190]

6.92   The proposed changes struck some as driven more by political opportunism than regulatory necessity. For example, Eilis Ferran argued that: '[T]here was not a clear-cut case for outright abolition of the Financial Services Authority. Fixing it was a solid option in principle and it was politics that dictated a different result.'[191] Arguably, the United Kingdom discarded a sound regulatory model that had not demonstrably fallen into disrepair. The reorganization of regulatory functions, an effort-sapping endeavour, came in the immediate aftermath of a devastating global financial crisis. a time when regulatory energies could have been put to better use elsewhere.[192] The disarray also left the United Kingdom and the City vulnerable to regulatory predation on the part of the European Union. Constitutional quibbles were quickly put aside in Brussels, and the ESMA came into existence on 1 January 2011, more than two full years before the PRA and FCA took up office in London.[193]

---

[189] IMF (n 165), 8, para 17. As enacted, the FSA 2012 creates the Financial Policy Committee (FPC), the Prudential Regulation Authority (PRA) and the Financial Conduct Authority (FCA). The FPC is a macro-prudential authority within the Bank of England, responsible for protecting and enhancing financial stability. The PRA is a new micro-prudential regulator with responsibility for ensuring effective prudential regulation of firms which manage complex risks on their balance sheets, established as a subsidiary of the Bank of England. The FCA has a single strategic objective, to ensure that the relevant markets function well. In addition there are three operational objectives: (i) securing an appropriate degree of protection for consumers; (ii) protecting and enhancing the integrity of the UK financial system; and (iii) promoting effective competition in the interests of consumers. The FCA will take on responsibility for consumer credit regulation from 1 April 2014. To support the FCA in its more proactive, interventionist approach, it has a new product intervention power to ban or impose restrictions on financial products. Additionally, in response to the LIBOR rate setting scandal, the FSA 2012 brings LIBOR activities within the scope of statutory regulation, including the submission and administration of LIBOR and creates a new criminal offence for misleading statements in relation to benchmarks such as LIBOR. See (n 187).

[190] IMF (n 165), 9, para 21.

[191] Eilis Ferran, 'The Break-Up of the Financial Services Authority' (11 October 2010) University of Cambridge Faculty of Law Research Paper Series No 10/04, 1 <http://ssrn.com/abstract=1690523> accessed 20 October 2013.

[192] See Cally Jordan, 'The Wider Context: The Future of Capital Markets Regulation in Developed Markets' (2012) 6 *Law and Financial Markets Review* 130.

[193] In their 2011 report, the IMF commented that: 'The key risk to the system is uncertainty—a risk identified widely by market participants and by the Board and senior management of the FSA. The sheer scale of the

The demise of the FSA is mourned elsewhere. The integrated model had been enthusiasti-   **6.93**
cally embraced around the world. Economies such as France or Germany will make their
own decisions to carry on, but small jurisdictions and emerging markets face a dilemma.
Should they persist with a new, but now defunct model or, yet again, follow the latest UK
path, irrespective of its merits? For example, Belgium, which had adopted an FSA-like integrated regulator for financial services, de-integrated.[194]

However, perhaps in recognition of the successes of the FSA and its muscular post-crisis   **6.94**
responses,[195] earlier proposals to scatter its ashes to the winds were rejected. In fact, the FSA
continued through the transition on 1 April 2013, relatively intact in many respects, albeit
under another name, the Financial Conduct Authority (FCA)[196] and, in some respects, a
somewhat diminished range of action.

5. The New City—The Age of Regulation

Despite the regulatory turmoil of recent years, the City of London remains one of the world's   **6.95**
great financial centres, a 'global hub for financial services ranging (in securities markets) from
the largest global investment and universal banks to very small investment advisers'.[197] Its
strengths are its rich diversity of markets and participants as well as its depth and range of
experience. Scale matters too. The City is a tiny place, but houses a huge, varied, financial
market. Services, practitioners and infrastructure are concentrated within a small radius of
the old BoE, even with the expansion to Docklands or Canary Wharf on the other side of the
Thames from the old City. This small area is home to 'one of the two largest financial sectors
in the world'.[198]

The capital markets, in particular, are out of all proportion to the British economy generally,   **6.96**
due to their European and international significance. The United Kingdom is the leading
equity marketplace in Europe as well as an important listing center for foreign equity issuers.

---

changes creates significant risks: the fundamental revamp in the structure of UK regulation, and the very full
European agenda coming on top of the current demanding internal supervisory enhancement program, which
will inevitably create uncertainty and distraction with potential impact on staff retention and attraction along
with resource pressures. These constitute material downside risks going forward ... [T]he assessors consider
that, while the FSA is taking active steps to manage the transition, there remain considerable risks as a result of
this uncertainty over the next few years': IMF (n 165), 9–10.

[194] The Financial Services and Markets Authority succeeded to the Banking, Finance and Insurance
Commission on 1 April 2011 by Law of 2 August 2002 on the supervision of the financial sector and on financial services as modified by Royal Decree of 3 March 2011.

[195] Enforcement activities were racheted up in the period following the global financial crisis, with the FSA
handing out record fines.

[196] On this point, the IMF's 2011 report notes that: 'An earlier proposal for the regulatory reform included
a recommendation to move the regulation of issuers to a government department and to possibly move the FSA
enforcement function to a public prosecution agency. The decision was made to keep markets intact within
the FCA by keeping the United Kingdom Listing Authority (UK LA) with markets regulation and moving
enforcement into the FCA rather than to split it off into a separate agency. In addition, the regulators' ability
to use criminal sanctions when appropriate is a positive trend. These decisions appear to be widely welcomed
by market participants, given their concerns with the initial proposed arrangements. We generally support
these decisions, as we consider these functions and powers to be an important part of the new FCA': IMF
(n 165), 10, para 24.

[197] IMF (n 165), 4, para 4.
[198] IMF (n 165), 4, para 4.

At end-September 2010, it had 1,101 UK companies and 328 foreign companies listed on its main market, and 1,204 companies (including 224 foreign companies) admitted to its AIM market for small and medium-size enterprises. By September 30, 2010 UK-listed companies had a market value of £1.82 trillion and the AIM companies (United Kingdom and foreign) of £65.6 billion.[199]

6.97 Organized trading markets and platforms proliferate: currency markets, insurance markets, commodities markets, equity markets and bond markets, sovereign debt markets and Euromarkets, derivatives markets of all hues, official markets and over-the-counter markets, domestic markets and foreign markets, markets for Islamic products. Just a listing of the formal, supervised markets in London is astounding in its reach and global diversity. The IMF's 2011 report includes a box (see Box 1) outlining the 'wide range of organized markets . . . for equities, options, corporate bonds, and exchange traded futures'.[200]

6.98 The London Stock Exchange has several listing boards, for large and smaller companies and, unlike the New York Stock Exchange, trades bonds as well as equities. Could it be that the great diversity of financial markets within the hothouse of the City has produced great innovation and cross-pollination, from one market to another? Along with the swirl of money, do ideas and information swirl too?

6.99 And money does swirl, in and out of official markets, propelled by asset managers, hedge funds and other institutional investors and intermediaries. Consider, for example, the IMF's 2011 analysis of the United Kingdom:

> The United Kingdom has a large asset management market, as funds under management (for UK domiciled funds) reached £577.6 billion in December 2010, with total funds under management in the United Kingdom of £3.9 trillion. The United Kingdom is widely recognized as a center for alternative asset management (including hedge funds). There are 450 registered hedge fund managers in the United Kingdom, managing £450 billion in assets (although this does not include the offshore domiciled assets that may also be managed from London).[201]

6.100 The FSA rode herd on an astonishing number of institutions and individuals, which was a justification, or perhaps an imperative, in adopting its selective, risk-based approach to oversight. This is illustrated by figures in the IMF's 2011 report, which show that: 'There are 26,270 regulated firms in the United Kingdom, including 2,059 authorized as investment firms, investment managers, or investment advisors. These range from the largest, global banking groups to independent brokerage houses and investment managers to one- and two-person financial adviser firms.'[202]

---

[199] IMF (n 165), 4–5, para 6.

[200] IMF (n 165), 5, para 6. In their report, the IMF states: 'The over-the-counter fixed income and derivative markets in the United Kingdom are large and global in nature. London is an important center for issuance and trading of international sovereign bonds; 30 percent of the $2.4 trillion in bonds issued in 2009 were issued in London, with 70 percent of total turnover in the international market taking place in London, mainly in the OTC market. The London Exchange is a leading platform for on-exchange bond trading, trading £4.7 trillion in bonds during 2010. London hosts several important on-exchange derivatives markets, including NYSE-LIFFE trading key financial and agricultural futures and options; ICE Futures Europe, which supports the market for several key oil and gas futures as well as clearing for over-the-counter trading in CDS and other derivatives; and the London Metal Exchange, which trades futures and options on metals': IMF (n 165), 5–6, para 7.

[201] IMF (n 165), 6, para 9.

[202] IMF (n 165), 7, para 10.

Box 1 Major infrastructure providers supervised by the FSA*

Equity exchanges:
London Stock Exchange (inc AIM)
PLUS Markets

Derivatives exchanges:
EDX
ICE Futures Europe
LIFFE
London Metal Exchange (LME)

Clearing and settlement providers:
Euroclear UK and Ireland (EUI)
European Central Counterparty
ICE Clear Europe
LCH.Clearnet Ltd

Licensed overseas entities: Trading platforms:
CBOT (US)
CME (US)
Eurex (Swiss)
ICE Futures Inc (US)
NASDAQ (US)
NYMEX (US)
NYSE Liffe US
SIX (Swiss)
Sydney Futures (Aust)

Multilateral trading facilities:
BATS Europe
BrokerTec
Chi-X Europe
EuroMTS
Icap Block Cross
Instinet Block Match
Liquidnet Europe
Pipeline Europe
Smartpool
Tradeweb
Turquoise

Clearinghouses:
Eurex (Germany)
SIS X-Clear (Swiss)
CME (US)
CC & G (Italy)
EMCF (Neth)
ICE Clear US
LCH.Clearnet SA (France)

*Taken from FSA 'Markets Regulatory Agenda', May 2010.

Despite its official demise, the legacy of the guilds and self-regulation may have persisted **6.101** in the United Kingdom, supporting the selective, risk-based approach to regulation by the FSA and noted by the IMF. The FSA, albeit a statutory authority, may have seen its role as one of subsuming the tradition of self regulation, but in a different guise, and with oversight gathered together and placed in the hands of a single regulator. Certainly in the period between the announcement of the break up of the FSA and its reincarnation as the FCA, the FSA demonstrated considerable regulatory muscle. The continued institutional focus of the FSA might have been one aspect of this continuity of traditional oversight. This focus on oversight of the intermediaries, the professionals, may also be a legacy of the involvement of the BoE, in the tradition of banking supervision. Registration of the intermediaries, rather than disclosure of information, is the dominant regulatory principle operating in the United Kingdom, unlike the United States. Hedge funds operating in exempt markets are required to register in the United Kingdom, but not in the United States, for example. This may explain the curious disinterest in the United Kingdom in disclosure-based regulation of the primary markets.[203] The regulator keeps a wary eye on the foxes; and provided the foxes are

---

[203] Noted by Richard Britton, a former FSA official and participant in the US FSAP (May 2010), in an interview with the author, 15 February 2013.

well socialized and aware of their fiduciary duties, the chickens can take care of themselves (and aren't expected to read prospectuses).

6. Conclusion

6.102   Despite the massive changes in the nature of markets and regulatory upheaval in the United Kingdom, the City remains a vibrant, international financial centre. In July 2011, in conducting its FSAP exercise on securities regulation in the United Kingdom, the IMF found that: 'The preconditions for effective supervision (a stable macroeconomic environment, sound legal and accounting framework, and effectiveness of procedures for the efficient resolution of problems in the securities market) appear to be in place in the United Kingdom.'[204]

6.103   The major threat to the City at that point was uncertainty risk, given the sheer scale of regulatory change.[205] In looking to the future, the IMF noted 'three profound forces at play: the post-crisis response of the FSA itself and changes it is introducing in its supervisory philosophy and approach—as the FSA itself has noted, this is very much a work in progress; second, UK regulatory reform; and third, the changes to the regulatory structure in Europe as of January 2011 and the current heavy load of EU regulatory proposals'.[206]

6.104   Since 2011, however, the first two forces (related to regulatory change in the United Kingdom) have subsided dramatically whereas the impact of regulatory change at the EU level has correspondingly increased. Tensions may remain high between Brussels and London, but Paris-based ESMA knows the City and how it works.[207] A loss of UK influence now may be the bigger threat, with the political posturing in the United Kingdom about leaving the European Union. Nevertheless, few doubt that the ESMA has set about constructing a pan-European regulatory regime for securities and markets, and the shift in the balance of power away from the City may be irreversible. In the view of the IMF, this may already have happened.[208]

6.105   For the time being, memoranda of understanding have been put in place to link the new UK regulators and their European counterparts, the ESMA, the European Banking Authority (EBA) and the European Insurance and Occupational Pensions Authority (EIOPA). The division of regulatory responsibility in the United Kingdom, however, does not neatly correspond to that of the three new European regulators. For example, although the FCA represents the United Kingdom at the ESMA table, in the United Kingdom, issues with respect to clearing and settlement now come under the authority of the BoE. Arguably, the United

---

[204] IMF (n 165), 10, para 23.

[205] IMF (n 165), 9–10, paras 19–22.

[206] IMF (n 165), 9, para 21.

[207] Its deputy director, Verena Ross, a German national, worked in the City.

[208] In its report, the IMF states that: 'Regulatory policy initiatives at the European Union (EU) level have become more important than domestic policy initiatives in the securities sphere. There are a large number of directives under review or being implemented, including UCITS IV, to be implemented in July [2011], and the Markets in Financial Instruments Directive (MiFID), which is under review. Further, the new level II European bodies for financial markets regulation have come into place. The ESMA began operations January 1, 2011. While its role continues to evolve, at present it has some direct policymaking responsibilities and will have responsibilities relating to national authorities; it will also be responsible for some direct supervision, beginning with supervision of credit rating agencies in July 2011': IMF (n 165), 9, para 18.

Kingdom has long experience in accommodating and adapting to regulatory dissonance and fragmentation.

An unacknowledged threat to the City though may be the diminution in its international **6.106** significance. The international nature of finance in the City has traditionally been its great comparative advantage, even to New York. The history is longer, of course, buttressed by a far flung Empire, the industrial age and the great interest in building the infrastructure of America, North and South, in the nineteenth century.

The 'professional exemption' and traditional non-public 'placings' practices provided open **6.107** space for non-prospectus offerings, permitting the Euromarket to flourish out of London. The Exchange and the companies legislation assisted, by providing exemptions for the activities of non-UK companies and engaged in unilateral recognition of home country listing standards.[209] The use of guidelines, rather than bright line rules, coupled with 'comply or explain' policies, easily accommodated difference.

The new regulatory age in the City, partially self-imposed, partially imposed by the **6.108** European Union, may affect the flexibility and adaptability of the City, attributes which have made it an attractive international destination. Equally, the 'multipolarity' noted by Rottier and Véron, the shift away from New York and London as financial centres of gravity, to Hong Kong, Sao Paulo, Singapore, Shanghai, Dubai, may also impinge on London as the world's international financial centre. But it is a new age in the City, with yet new scandals, a new regulatory framework, and a new regulatory philosophy; a new chapter has begun.

---

[209] Gower (n 7), 339: If listed overseas and there was 'equivalent' oversight, then there could be 'advertising' in the UK on an exempt basis. Equally, the content of prospectuses for non-UK companies listing on the main board and the then USM board of the London Stock Exchange could be in conformity with foreign rules if equivalent.

Historical Development of Securities Regulation in the United Kingdom

---

Late nineteenth century and early twentieth century

Joint Stock Companies Act 1844, s 4:	The first modern prospectus requirement with compulsory disclosure through the registration of prospectuses inviting subscriptions to corporate shares.[210]
Companies Act 1907	Making prospectus delivery mandatory[211]
Companies Act 1929, s 34	'[R]equirements that any prospectus published by a company be signed by the company's directors and registered'.[212]
Companies Act 1929, s 36(1):	'If the purpose of the prospectus was to "invite persons to subscribe for shares", then any prospectus had to be signed by all of the directors, by any person who had authorised the contents of the prospectus, by any person named in the prospectus as having agreed to become a director, by any promoter of the company, and any person who authorized the issue of the prospectus'.[213]

Pre-1985

Topic	Companies Act 1948	The Prevention of Fraud (Investments) Act 1958	The Panel on Takeovers and Mergers (1968)	Companies Act 1980
Self-regulation/ Registration		Regulating the Business of Dealing in Securities, General Provisions for the Prevention of Fraud		
Prospectus distribution	s 38: Matters to be stated and reports to be set out in prospectus. s 40: Expert's consent to issue of prospectus containing statement by him.			

(Continued)

---

[210] Gevurtz (n 31), 492, note 92, refers to further comment on this point: For example, 'Louis Loss, *Fundamentals of Securities Regulation* (1983) 2–3 (explaining that the English 'Companies Act of 1844 enacted the first modern prospectus requirement' with "compulsory disclosure through the registration of prospectuses inviting subscriptions to corporate shares:"; in the securities acts the United States Congress opted to follow the English compulsory disclosure model)'; and 'Gerard Hertig, Reiner Kraakman, and Edward Rock, *Issuers and Investor Protection*, in The Anatomy of Corporate Law: A Comparative and Functional Approach [(2nd edn, 2009)],... at 275, 282–83 (discussing disclosure regimes in various countries)'.

[211] Brian Cheffins, *Corporate Ownership and Control: British Business Transformed* (Oxford University Press, 2008), 195–6.

[212] Hudson (n 32), 152, para 4–20, quoting Companies Act 1929, s 36(1).

[213] Hudson (n 32), 152, para 4–20, quoting Companies Act 1929, s 36(1).

Pre-1985 (*Continued*)

Topic	Companies Act 1948	The Prevention of Fraud (Investments) Act 1958	The Panel on Takeovers and Mergers (1968)	Companies Act 1980
	s 42: Restriction on alteration of terms mentioned in prospectus or statement in lieu of prospectus			
	s 45: Document containing offer of shares or debentures for sale to be deemed prospectus			
Continuous Disclosure				
Takeover bids			The City Code on Takeovers and Mergers (1968)	
Insider trading				Ch 22, ss 68–73: insider trading – criminal offence[214]
Enforcement, civil liability	s 43: Civil liability for mis-statements in prospectus			
	s 44: Criminal liability			
Civil liability in secondary market		Aimed at controlling traders in securities rather than the issuing of securities		

After 1985 and before 2000

Topic	Companies Act 1985 (and the Company Securities (Insider Dealing) Act 1985)	Financial Services Act 1986	The Public Offers of Securities Regulation 1995 (governing unlisted securities)
Self-regulation/ Registration		Controlling traders: Part I: Regulation of Investment Business	
		Chs III and IV: Authorised persons and Exempted persons	

(*Continued*)

---

[214] Mark A Spitz, 'Recent Developments in Insider Trading Laws and Problems of Enforcement in Great Britain' (1989) 12 *Boston College International and Comparative Law Review* 265, citing B Rider and H Ffrench, *Regulation of Insider Trading* (1979), 167.

After 1985 and before 2000 (*Continued*)

Topic	Companies Act 1985 (and the Company Securities (Insider Dealing) Act 1985)	Financial Services Act 1986	The Public Offers of Securities Regulation 1995 (governing unlisted securities)
Prospectus distribution	Part III, Ch. I: Issues by companies registered in GB, the prospectus, registration of prospectus (s 56) Ch II: Issues by companies incorporated outside GB (s 72) Schedule 3: Mandatory contents of the prospectus	Part IV: Official Listing of Securities (ss 142) Part V: Offers Unlisted Securities (ss 162–4)	Part II: Public Offers of Unlisted Securities, s 8: form and content of prospectus, s 9: general duty of disclosure in prospectus
Continuous Disclosure		s 153: obligations of issuers of listed securities	
Takeover bids	Part XIIIA: Takeover Offers	Part VI and Schedule 12: takeover offers.[215]	
Insider trading	The Company Securities (Insider Dealing) Act 1985: regulation of insider dealing	Part VII: insider trading (ss 177–78)	
Civil liability	ss 66–70: Liabilities and offences in connection with prospectus s 78: consequences of non-compliance with Part III, Ch. II	Part IV: s 150: Compensation for false or misleading particulars s 166: Compensation for false or misleading prospectus	Part II: Public Offers of Unlisted Securities, s 14: compensation for false or misleading prospectus
Civil liability in secondary market			
	All securities regulations were repealed by the Financial Services Act 1986.	Part IV: Official Listing of Securities (sets minimum requirements for the listing rules)	

---

[215] See Andrew Johnston, 'Takeover Regulation: Historical and Theoretical Perspectives on the City Code' (2007) 66 *Cambridge Law Journal* 422, 446–7: 'The City Code has been amended frequently since its introduction in 1968, but its key provisions . . . have not been altered in substance. In response to the requirements of the European Takeover Directive . . . *the Government decided that the Panel should be placed on a statutory footing for the first time and provisions to that effect were included in the Companies Act 2006.* Those statutory provisions . . . are designed to ensure the continuance of the perceived advantages of a self-regulatory approach, while allowing the Panel, for the first time, to impose sanctions directly on wrongdoers.'

After 2000

Topic	Financial Services and Markets Act 2000	Companies Act 2006	Financial Services Act 2012 (1 April 2013)
Self-regulation/ Registration	Part II: Regulated and Prohibited Activities (ss 19–30).		
	Part III: Authorisation and Exemption (ss 31–39A).		
Prospectus distribution	Part VI: Official Listing: Transferable securities: public offers and admission to trading, Approval of prospectus (ss 84–87D)		
	Prohibition of dealing in transferable securities without approved prospectus (s 85)		
	Criteria for approval of prospectus by competent authority (s 87A)		
	Passporting (ss 87H, 87I)		
Continuous Disclosure	ss 96, 96A, B: obligations of issuers of listed securities, disclosure of information requirements		
Takeover bids		Part 28: Takeover etc	
Insider trading	Part VIII: Penalties for Market Abuse: insider trading		
Civil liability	s 90: Compensation for statements in listing particulars or prospectus		
Civil liability in secondary market			

7

THE NEW EUROPEAN CAPITAL MARKETS

1. Introduction

7.01 Finance has prospered in Europe for centuries,[1] but the story of securities or capital markets regulation is remarkably short.[2] Unlike the United States, where the establishment of exchanges and the rise of finance coincided generally with the creation of the new republic,[3] finance in Europe predates the nation state and its regulatory impulses. With the rise of commerce, markets and city states abounded in medieval Europe, each with its own set of rules and expectations for commercial dealing,[4] which over time spread and consolidated among merchants. The importance of trade routes, such as the Silk Road,[5] and the age of exploration, prompted innovation in long distance payment systems and capital raising.[6]

---

[1] For a fascinating, beautifully illustrated, historical perspective on financial instruments, see William N Goetzmann and K Geert Rouwenhorst (eds), *The Origins of Value: The Financial Innovations That Created Modern Capital Markets* (Oxford University Press, 2005).

[2] There are now several texts on European securities or capital markets law: Niamh Moloney, *EC Securities Regulation* (2nd edn, Oxford University Press, 2008); Rüdiger Veil (ed), *European Capital Markets Law* (Hart Publishing, 2013); Raj Panasar and Philip Boeckman (eds), *European Securities Law* (Oxford University Press, 2010). See also Jane Welch and Peter Parker, 'European Financial Services' in George Walker and Robert Purves (eds), *Financial Services Law* (3rd edn, Oxford University Press, forthcoming).

[3] The Declaration of Independence was adopted by Congress on 4 July 1776: Office of the Historian, 'Milestones: 1776–1783', US Department of State <http://history.state.gov/milestones/1776-1783/Declaration> accessed 24 September 2013. On 17 May 1792, an agreement establishing rules for the purchase and sale of bonds and company shares was signed by 24 stockbrokers. Known as the 'Buttonwood Agreement', the signatories subsequently founded the New York Stock and Exchange Board on 8 March 1817: 'New York Stock Exchange', NYSE Euronext <http://www.nyx.com/en/who-we-are/history/new-york> accessed 24 September 2013.

[4] See, for example, HR Hahlo and Ellison Kahn, *The South African Legal System and its Background* (Juta & Co Ltd, 1968), 404–5 and 422–6.

[5] For the history of the Silk Road see the following: Valerie Hansen, *The Silk Road: A New History* (Oxford University Press, 2012); Vadime Elisseeff (ed), *The Silk Roads: Highways of Culture and Commerce* (Berghahn, 2000); and Karen Manchester (ed), *The Silk Road and Beyond: Travel, Trade, and Transformation* (Yale University Press, 2007).

[6] The *commenda* and the 'joint stock company' being examples of financing vehicles supporting the age of exploration. *Commendas* developed in medieval Italy as a response to the strictures imposed upon partnerships by unlimited liability. Associated with the high-risk industry of sea trade, the *commenda* did not completely relax liability, but instead instituted a hybrid form whereby the ship's owner had unlimited liability, whilst investing partners were accorded limited liability only. The *commenda* was seen as an attempt to encourage investment in risky ventures, and was eventually institutionalized in the 1804 Napoleonic code, which facilitated the spread of this financing vehicle throughout continental Europe (Marie-Laure Djelic, 'When Limited Liability was (Still) an Issue: Mobilization and Politics of Signification in 19th-Century England' (2013) 34 *Organization Studies* 595, 602). In the United Kingdom, the Joint Stock Companies Registration and Regulation Act was passed in 1844, which required partnerships of more than 25 members to register as a joint stock company, and imposed reporting obligations upon them. Previously, under the Bubble Act 1720, incorporation had required a royal or parliamentary charter; however, this was widely flouted during the 'speculative boom' of the early nineteenth

Fifteenth-century Italian city states, acting as the gateway for trade between Asia and Europe, are justly famous for their financial innovation: paper cheques, letters of credit, widespread networks of correspondents, and perhaps most infamously, the merchant banker.[7]

Trading venues, accepted practices and dispute resolution mechanisms, developed for and **7.02** among merchants, many of which persist to this day in one form or another.[8] The *lex mercatoria*, the nature and extent of which still gives rise to debate, was a pan European phenomenon.[9] Arguably, the *lex mercatoria* or perhaps more accurately, a *lex financeria*, continues to underpin the regulation of finance in Europe.[10] The public trading market focused on the stock exchange (an institution dating back to the seventeenth century as a venue for merchant traders[11]). Even today, industry associations such as the International Swaps and Derivatives Association continue to play a vital role in European finance.[12] The professional (merchant to merchant) market has always dominated the retail market; Europe is the preserve of the institutional investor.

Non-merchants did not necessarily receive the benefit of this *lex mercatoria* of finance. **7.03** Capital raising from the greater public was punctuated, century after century, by swindles, frauds and bubbles, the most famous being the South Sea Bubble[13] and

---

century, and led to the Act's repeal in 1825. In the interim period, a discernible increase in fraud associated with joint stock companies laid the foundation for the subsequent enactment of the 1844 Act: Djelic (n 6), 600–1.

[7] 'Investment bankers', as understood in the United States, have been known as 'merchant bankers' in London, an indication of the persistence of the institutions and patterns of thought associated with merchant law (the literal translation of *lex mercatoria*). Historically, merchant bankers trace their origins to Jewish bankers specializing in international finance in Italy (bills of exchange, underwriting, financings, futures, grain guarantees, credit, and insurance). They sat among the merchants and used the techniques of the silk route for providing long distance financing. See for example Michael Toch, 'The Jews in Europe, 500–1050' in Paul Fouracre (ed), *The New Cambridge Medieval History vol I* (Cambridge University Press, 2005), 558, 568; Benjamin Ravid, 'An Introduction to the Charters of the Jewish Merchants of Venice' in Elliott Horowitz and Moisés Orfali, *The Mediterranean and the Jews: Society, Culture and Economy in Early Modern Times* (Ramat Gan, 2002), 203–47. Cf Shakespeare's *Merchant of Venice*.

[8] For example, the wholesale diamond markets and 'bourses' in the Netherlands and New York.

[9] On the *lex mercatoria* and the *lex financeria*, see Cally Jordan, 'How International Finance Really Works' (2013) 7 *Law and Financial Markets Review* 256. See further, Ralf Michaels, 'The True Lex Mercatoria: Law Beyond the State' (2007) 14 *Indiana Journal of Global Legal Studies* 447; Emily Kadens, 'The Myth of the Customary Law Merchant' (2012) 90 *Texas Law Review* 1153; Leon E Trakman, 'The Evolution of the Law Merchant: Our Commercial Heritage' (1980) 12 *Journal of Maritime Law and Commerce* 1; and Leon E Trakman, 'The Twenty-First-Century Law Merchant' (2011) 48 *American Business Law Journal* 775. In his analysis of the 'medieval lex mercatoria', Ralf Michaels states: 'Lex mercatoria was a mixture of official laws and established mercantile customs and institutions, of official courts and quasi-private local tribunals: "bundles of public privileges and private practices, public statutes and private customs sheltered under the umbrella concept of merchant law by their association with a particular sort of supra-local trade and the people who carried it out" (citing Emily Kadens, 'Order Within Law, Variety Within Custom: The Character of the Medieval Merchant Law' (2004) 5 *Chicago Journal of International Law* 39, 42). *Lex Mercatoria* was not non-state law—it was an amalgam of state and non-state rules and procedures, kept together by its subject: the merchants': Michaels, (n 9), 454. The French Commercial Code of 1807 was essentially a consolidation of commercial law practices and principles drawn from the age of the *lex mercatoria*, and representing the nationalization of a pan European phenomenon.

[10] Jordan (n 9), 1.

[11] Amsterdam usually lays claim to the oldest formal stock exchange in Europe, the 1602 trading venue created to trade the shares and bonds of the Dutch East India Co (VOC, or Verenigde Oostindische Compagnie).

[12] The acronym originally stood for the 'International Swaps Dealers Association', but evolved with the markets to become the 'International Swaps and Derivatives Association'.

[13] The 'South Sea Bubble', which occurred in 1720, is the name ascribed to arguably the most famous stock market crash in history. Having entered into an arrangement with Queen Anne, the South Sea Co acquired a monopoly on the importation of slaves into America, in exchange for assisting the monarch to restructure

Tulipmania.[14] Somewhat facetiously, it could be suggested that the reluctance of retail investors to enter equity markets in Europe (in comparison to their American counterparts)[15] evidences an atavistic response to past market failures.

2. Characteristics of European Capital Markets

2.1 Difference and similarity

7.04 Europe is a diverse place, and despite the harmonizing influences of the European Union, remains so. Nevertheless, European capital markets have been subject to common influences and, generally speaking, do demonstrate certain identifiable characteristics. The stock exchange, or 'bourse', is the focus for public markets and as an institution, has evolved differently than in the United States. There is a sharp distinction between public and private markets. Professional investors dominate both the public and private markets. Despite greater flutters of interest in the past 20 years, retail investors remain relatively disinterested in equity markets.[16] The perimeter of and tolerance for 'unregulated' markets is significant. A long history of 'universal' banking has blurred sharp distinctions among financial products on offer to retail investors. The regulatory focus has been squarely on the intermediaries, the institutions, rather than on transactions (as in the United States). Regulatory reform, when it happens, can occur rapidly; for example, consolidated financial services regulators, in the style of the now defunct FSA, popped up like mushrooms all over Europe in the course of the last decade: Germany's BaFin was formed in 2002[17] and France's AMF was established in 2003, both within two or three years of the FSA.[18]

2.2 The case of Eastern Europe

7.05 The process of creating capital markets and a regulatory framework in post-Soviet Eastern Europe is a whole story in its own right.[19] Due to the geopolitical sensitivity of the region,

---

England's national debt. Shares traded in the company underwent a sudden boom, followed by a dramatic crash, with the company directors subsequently being accused of fraud. Since 1720, the South Sea Bubble has stood as the benchmark for financial market crashes, such as the 'Dotcom Bubble', and the more recent 'Credit Crunch': Helen Paul, *The South Sea Bubble: An Economic History of its Origins and Consequences* (Taylor & Francis, 2010), 1.

[14] Tulips were so highly prized that they fuelled a speculative bubble. For example, in the rare bulb market—dominated by serious traders and wealthy flower fanciers—a Semper Augustus bulb sold for 2000 guilders in 1625 ('an amount of gold worth about US $16,000 at US $400 an ounce'). By 1739, the prices of most prized bulbs had fallen to 0.1 guilder—'about 1/200 of 1 percent Semper Augustus's peak price': Peter M Garber, 'Famous First Bubbles' (1990) 4 *The Journal of Economic Perspectives* 35, 37–8. The story is perhaps apocryphal and recent studies have cast doubt on its interpretation. The more aptly-labelled locus of rapid price swings and 'mania' was the futures market for common bulbs in which lower classes speculated beginning in November 1636: Garber, (n 14), 38–9.

[15] See Niamh Moloney, *How to Protect Investors. Lessons from the EC and the UK* (Cambridge University Press, 2010), 81–7.

[16] Whereas Margaret Thatcher endeavoured to use the UK privatizations of the 1980s to create a US-style retail equity culture in the United Kingdom.

[17] See <http://www.bafin.de/EN/BaFin/FunctionsHistory/functionshistory_node.html> accessed 20 December 2013.

[18] See <http://www.amf-france.org/en_US/L-AMF/Missions-et-competences/Presentation.html> accessed 20 December 2013.

[19] See John R Lampe (ed), *Creating Capital Markets in Eastern Europe* (Woodrow Wilson Center Press, 1992); Gerhard Pohl, Gregory T Jedrzejczak, and Robert E Anderson, *Creating Capital Markets in Central and Eastern*

huge inflows of funding and technical legal assistance from the United States marked the initial stages of political and market reforms associated with the 'shock therapy' approach adopted. Some 'voucher' privatizations, designed to transform state-owned enterprises into market economy businesses (and the resident population into US-style mom and pop investors), went badly wrong.[20] Old fashioned stock exchanges were resurrected throughout Eastern Europe, sometimes housed in the same pre-Soviet premises, with a handful of bonds or shares trading during an hour or two opening twice a week or so. US-style securities regulation and corporate law were airlifted in, often proving to be ineffectual or worse.[21]

Over time, other influences prevailed. The European Bank for Reconstruction and Development (EBRD) was created in 1992 to facilitate and support the transition of these countries to a market economy. The EBRD was modelled, to a certain extent, on other multilateral international financial institutions,[22] but with a distinctly market economy and private sector orientation.[23] Since a number of the former Soviet republics wished to return to the European mainstream, the European Union and member states, in particular the reunified Germany, began to dominate reforms through the accession process. Twenty years after the breakup of the former Soviet Union,[24] Russia stands alone,[25] but many of the former satellites are firmly aligned with Western Europe, if not already members of the European Union.[26]   **7.06**

2.3 Factors shaping European capital markets

2.3.1 Investment patterns

Some of the factors which differentiate European capital markets from US markets have supported the influential 'law and finance' literature[27] which, mistakenly, views European   **7.07**

Europe (World Bank, 1995); Organisation for Economic Co-operation and Development, *Capital Market Development in Transition Economies: Country Experiences and Policies for the Future* (OECD Publishing, 1998).

[20] The term 'tunnelling' was coined in the context of the mass privatizations in Central and Eastern Europe in the 1990s and refers to a practice in which a majority shareholder or managers diverted assets from a recently privatized enterprise to another entity for their own personal benefit—like a bank robber using a tunnel beneath a vault to make off with the cash.

[21] Bernard Black, Reinier Kraakman, and Anna Tarassova, 'Russian Privatization and Corporate Governance: What Went Wrong?' (2000) 52 *Stanford Law Review* 1731.

[22] Like the IBRD, the International Bank for Reconstruction and Development, more commonly referred to as The World Bank.

[23] Interestingly, as the successful transitions proceeded, there has been less and less need for the EBRD, which has now extended its activities to North Africa in the wake of the Arab spring.

[24] The reunification of Germany is another, different part of this story.

[25] One of the BRICs. An acronym coined by Goldman Sachs in 2001 (see Holly A Bell, 'Status of the "BRIC"s: An Analysis of Growth Factors' (2011) 69 *International Research Journal of Finance and Economics* 19), and standing for the large developing economies of Brazil, Russia, India, and China.

[26] On 1 July 2013, the European Union expanded to 28 member countries with the accession of Croatia. It already includes the following post-Soviet states: Bulgaria, the Czech Republic, Estonia, Hungary, Latvia, Lithuania, Poland, Romania, Slovakia, and Slovenia: European Union, 'Member Countries of the European Union', Europa.eu (1 July 2013) <http://europa.eu/about-eu/countries/member-countries/> accessed 29 September 2013. The countries currently preparing to join the European Union are as follows: Albania, Bosnia and Herzegovina, the former Yugoslav Republic of Macedonia, Iceland, Kosovo, Montenegro, Serbia, and Turkey: European Union, 'Enlargement', Europa.eu <http://ec.europa.eu/enlargement/countries/strategy-and-progress-report/index_en.htm> accessed 29 September 2013.

[27] See Rafael La Porta, Florencio Lopez-de-Silanes, Andrei Shleifer, and Robert W Vishny, 'Legal Determinants of External Finance' (July 1997) 52 *The Journal of Finance* 1131; Rafael La Porta, Florencio Lopez-de-Silanes, Andrei Shleifer, and Robert W Vishny, 'Law and Finance' (1998) 106 *Journal of Political Economy* 1113; Rafael La Porta, Florencio Lopez-de-Silanes, Andrei Shleifer, and Robert W Vishny, 'The

financial markets as 'underdeveloped'[28] when rated against US-derived benchmarks. However, difference does not necessarily constitute deficiency. European markets are simply different. More problematically, the 'law and finance' literature attributes the supposed underdeveloped state of European financial markets to differences in the underlying legal systems (common law versus civil law) and the degree of investor protections on offer.[29] Although much critiqued,[30] this simplistic proposition has entered the realm of conventional wisdom.

7.08　More convincing arguments point to a range of factors that can account for the differences in the markets, investing patterns and regulation in Europe. For example, the relative disinterest in equity investing by European individuals may be a result of a combination of social and economic forces not present in the United States.

7.09　The ownership structure of many European corporations may not make them attractive investments for retail investors. Typically, even large listed companies in Europe may have a majority or controlling shareholder and a smallish public float, characteristics associated with various problems such as market manipulation, insider dealing, illiquidity, and volatility.[31] As a result of either privatizations[32] or advertent industrial policy, the state itself may be

---

Economic Consequences of Legal Origins' (2008) 46 *Journal of Economic Literature* 285. See further, Katharina Pistor, 'Law *in* Finance' (2013) 41 *Journal of Comparative Economics* 311.

[28]　France, in particular, was singled out. For example, La Porta et al—referred to in the 'law and finance' literature as LLSV—examined GDP per capita for 1960–2000, and concluded that growth in 'French legal origin countries' was about 0.6% slower annually, than growth in common law countries: La Porta et al (n 27), 301. See further, Naomi R Lamoreaux and Jean-Laurent Rosenthal, 'Legal Regime and Contractual Flexibility: A Comparison of Business's Organizational Choices in France and the United States during the Era of Industrialization' (2005) 7 *American Law and Economics Review* 28.

[29]　La Porta et al argue that they have established, on the basis of empirical analysis, that 'legal rules protecting investors vary systematically among legal traditions or origins, with the laws of common law countries (originating in English law) being more protective of outside investors than the laws of civil law (originating in Roman law) and particularly French civil law countries', and conclude that '[t]he evidence showed that legal investor protection is a strong predictor of financial development': La Porta et al (n 27), 285–6.

[30]　Raghuram G Rajan and Luigi Zingales, 'The Great Reversals: The Politics of Financial Development in the 20th Century' (National Bureau of Economic Research, Working Paper No 8178, 2001), 7; Mark D West, 'Legal Determinants of World Cup Success' (2002), Michigan Law and Economics Research Paper No 02-009 <http://ssrn.com/abstract=318940> accessed 30 September 2013; Cally Jordan and Mike Lubrano, 'How Effective are Capital Markets in Exerting Governance on Corporations' in Robert E Litan, Michael Pomerleano, and V Sundararajan (eds), *Financial Sector Governance: The Roles of the Public and Private Sectors* (Brookings Institution Press, 2002); Holger Spamann, ' "Law and Finance" Revisited' (1 February 2008), Harvard Law School John M. Olin Center Discussion Paper No 12 <http://ssrn.com/abstract=1095526> accessed 20 December 2013.

[31]　The Porsche affair in 2008 is an example. Porsche denied it was seeking a majority stake in VW in March 2008. In October 2008, it disclosed that it was seeking to acquire a 75% stake through the exercise of options which it already held. There was a surge in the share price as investors holding short positions were forced to buy stock, sending the VW share price to a record high. The panic-buying briefly made VW the biggest company in the world by stock market value, ahead of ExxonMobil. Porsche is now being sued by investors, who claim that it deliberately concealed its intentions and sought to manipulate the markets. On the other hand, some European academics defend the majority shareholder public company prevalent in Europe as providing better corporate governance than the US widely-held model. 'According to this view it is much more easy to prevent majority shareholders from exploiting the minority than to protect minority shareholders in public companies without [a] majority shareholder [from] the abundant exploitation by management. Maybe the US-model is not as succsessful as always claimed and maybe the European one not as bad as commonly perceived?', H. Baum, Max Planck Institute for Comparative and International Private Law, Hamburg, in an email to the author (23 October 2013).

[32]　Popular 30 years ago in Western Europe and more recently in the post-Soviet countries of Eastern Europe.

a shareholder in major European companies. The public participates indirectly, and involuntarily, in this case, in the equity markets. Retail investors may be reluctant to increase their exposure to such politically dominated enterprises.

Relative lack of opportunity to invest in public equity markets may be another factor. Even large European countries are relatively small. The combination of 'home bias'[33] and the prevalence of closely-held, often family controlled, businesses may result in few obvious investment opportunities. Italy, for example, has historically had a tradition of major manufacturers being family held over generations, although that may be changing.[34] A variation on this theme occurs in small countries with a few large, publicly traded corporations (think the Netherlands and Shell); diversification is limited by virtue of the limited number of domestic companies traded and, historically, the prohibitive costs associated with cross-border trading in Europe.[35] **7.10**

The northern European middle class, with the disposable income to invest, may also see better, 'safer', ways in which to deploy discretionary income. For them, investing in the equity markets may be better left to those better able, in theory, to assess the risks. In any event, many Europeans are already invested, indirectly, in domestic and international equity markets through their large public pension funds. The state pension funds may, in fact, be viewed as a form of collective investment vehicle. Generous state pensions (as well as low cost higher education for children and the availability of public healthcare) may also reduce the incentives found in the United States to amass substantial investment wealth through public markets; discretionary income may be put to other uses. **7.11**

---

[33] 'Home bias' refers to investors showing a preference for domestic equities over foreign assets, and has been variously described as a 'puzzle' Joshua D Coval and Tobias J Moscowitz, 'Home Bias at Home: Local Equity Preference in Domestic Portfolios; (1999) 54(6) *The Journal of Finance* 2045, 2045; and as a 'poorly understood' phenomenon: (Michael Fidora, Marcel Fratzscher, and Christian Thimann, 'Home Bias in Global Bond and Equity Markets: The Role of Real Exchange Rate Volatility' (2007) 26 *Journal of International Money and Finance* 631. Different factors have been advanced to explain this behaviour including, inter alia, barriers to, and costs associated with, international investment; geographic proximity to investments; and domestic investor safeguards involving regulation and corporate governance: Coval and Moskowitz (n 33); Fidora, Fratzscher, and Thimann (n 33), 632., Cf Cally Jordan, 'The Chameleon Effect: Beyond the Bonding Hypothesis for Cross-Listed Securities' (2006) 3 *NYU Journal of Law & Business* 37.

[34] In recent years, there has been a spate of Italian initial public offerings (IPOs) by family companies such as Prada and Ferragamo, which both listed in June 2011, but on different stock exchanges: Prada listed in Hong Kong, and Ferragamo listed in Milan: Michel Rose, 'Cucinelli's Stellar Debut Seen Boosting Italy IPO Appeal', *Reuters* (27 April 2012) <http://www.reuters.com/article/2012/04/27/us-cucinelli-idUSBRE83Q0YA20120427> accessed 1 October 2013. Ferragamo's share price has tripled since 2011: 'Brave old world', *The Economist* (14 January, 2014, 47); and in Italy, '[s]mall firms are trotting to the stock exchange's junior market', *The Economist* (14 January 2014), 47. Whilst offerings such as that of Ferragamo do provide opportunities for international investors, they are not a vehicle for obtaining control of such companies, the latter having instituted measures to prevent this from occurring: Lauren Sherman, 'Dissecting Fashion's Deal Frenzy', *The Business of Fashion* (New York, 18 July 2013) <http://www.businessoffashion.com/2013/07/dissecting-fashions-deal-frenzy-2.html> accessed 1 October 2013. IPOs are viewed as a means of raising capital for a company, without relinquishing control: Sherman (n 34). Factors influencing investor interest in such offerings include the rising demand for luxury goods in Asian markets, and the growing perception that Europe's economic problems are easing: Jenny Chan, 'APAC Keeps the Global Luxury Market Flying', *Campaign* (Asia Pacific, 1 November 2012), Factiva Document MEDIAM0020121113e8b10000o accessed 1 October 2013.

[35] Cf Benn Steil, 'Creating Securities Markets in Developing Countries: A New Approach for the Age of Automated Trading' (2001) 4 (2) *International Finance* 257.

7.12 For example, the increased significance of home ownership (with associated, complex financing schemes) may make paying down the mortgage a sensible investment strategy.[36] A higher premium placed on 'safety' may have roots in the turbulent, recent and not so recent, political past. So it may be no accident, that 'safer' debt securities such as 'covered bonds' and even the original mortgage backed security, the eighteenth-century German *Pfandbriefe*,[37] are investments which originated in Europe. Equally, insurance products may also be a more popular form of investment,[38] offering the comfort and assurance of a bulwark against the vicissitudes of an uncertain world. The Dutch, in particular, like insurance products, and their big universal banks oblige by cross-selling to depositors and providing a range of them.

2.3.2 The Stock Exchanges[39]

7.13 Historically, the traditional exchange has been a significant regulatory locus for capital markets, particularly in Europe. Although the concept and trappings of exchanges in Europe may appear similar to those found in the United States, in modern times they demonstrate quite different characteristics. For example, German and other European stock exchanges were from the late nineteenth century regarded as public utilities or state institutions and heavily regulated.[40] Gradual deregulation occurred in the 1990s, and once deregulated, they diversified and innovated in ways which were not possible on the other side of the Atlantic.

7.14 For one thing, the major exchanges in Europe trade a wider variety of financial products than their comparators, such as NYSE or NASDAQ in the United States. Bonds, for example, are exchange traded,[41] whereas in the United States bond trading disappeared from

---

[36] When the author quizzed Dutch academic colleagues at the Netherlands Institute for Advanced Study in Wassenaar, outside The Hague, in June 2013, on their investment strategies, 'investing in the stock exchange' was dismissed out of hand. Stock exchange investments were not seen as 'safe', and why would you risk losing your money. Home ownership as a preferred form of investment, however, does not appeal to Germans, on the other hand, who prefer to rent rather than buy their homes: 'Germany property firms; Safe as houses', *The Economist* (19 October 2013) <http://www.economist.com/news/business/21588074-residential-property-business-growing-and-consolidating-safe-houses> accessed 9 January 2014.

[37] The European Covered Bond Council (ECBC) describes 'covered bonds' as 'debt instruments secured by a cover pool of mortgage loans (property as collateral) or public-sector debt to which investors have a preferential claim in the event of default': 'Introducing Covered Bonds', European Covered Bond Council <http://ecbc.hypo.org/Content/Default.asp?PageID=504> accessed 2 October 2013. Thus, if the issuer becomes insolvent, the investor may look to the segregated pool of assets securing the bond, in order to recoup their loss. Similarly, German *Pfandbriefe*—meaning 'letter of pledge'—are safe, popular bonds issued by German mortgage banks, which are secured by mortgages, and constitute approximately 10% of the global covered bond market. The IMF describes these as 'debt obligations secured by a dedicated reference (or "cover") portfolio of assets, with the issuer being fully liable for all interest and principal payments': International Monetary Fund, 'Germany: Technical Note on the Future of German Mortgage-Backed Covered Bond (PFandBrief) and Securitization Markets' (23 December 2011) IMF Country Report No 11/369, 6, <http://www.imf.org/external/pubs/cat/longres.aspx?sk=25459.0> accessed 2 October 2013. Note that Canadian investors, sharing in some of the social security benefits associated with European life, did not like the early US-style mortgage backed securities products introduced to Canada with the result that 'safer', more obviously collateralized products were created for the Canadian market. See Ankoor Jain and Cally Jordan, 'Diversity and Resilience: Lessons from the Financial Crisis' (2009) 32 *UNSW Law Journal* 416. Covered bonds were also popular in Canada, but covered bond legislation was only introduced in the US House of Representatives in July 2013, although it may struggle to pass the Senate: 'US Covered Bond Legislation Proposed, Again', *Euroweek* (23 July 2013) Factiva Document EURMCM0020130806e97n00031, accessed 2 October 2013.

[38] Dutch colleagues at the Netherlands Institute for Advanced Study in Wassenaar also commented to the author in June 2013 that the Dutch are over-insured. They buy lots of different kinds of insurance products.

[39] Exchanges are discussed in more detail in Ch 10 of this book.

[40] See also Baum (n 31).

[41] In France and Germany and elsewhere. See Panasar and Boeckman (n 2) for further information on EU member state regulations.

the exchanges long ago. Bond trading in North America was captured by the intermediaries, becoming a lucrative over-the-counter market, with intermediaries selling to investors out of inventory. Also, European exchanges were not tied by regulation, as they are in the United States, to trading only certain kinds of financial products.[42] European exchanges could thus freely expand and diversify as financial products changed, for example, moving into derivatives.[43]

As elsewhere, exchanges play several roles, going beyond the mere facilitation of buying and selling of financial instruments. One such role is that of national signifier. Historically, in an age where transactions took place through physical payment and settlement, exchanges proliferated domestically to facilitate commercial transactions; there were lots of exchanges. However, as the physicality of the exchange became less and less important over time, the number of exchanges dropped in favour of more centralized trading with the attendant benefits of greater liquidity and pricing advantages.[44] So throughout Europe, one exchange tended to dominate in every country, becoming in the process, the national symbol of that country's markets: the Paris Bourse, the Frankfurt Exchange, for example. **7.15**

But Europe has a lot of countries, some of which are quite small, and the rationalization and consolidation of exchanges over time, has not been driven by purely market forces.[45] Although regulatory impediments may have been fewer than in the United States recently,[46] national sentiment proved difficult to overcome.[47] Every country wanted its own national symbol. So at the same time as competitive and commercial forces have promoted consolidations and alliances, geopolitical forces cut against these arrangements. The immediate post-Soviet Union era **7.16**

---

[42] For mostly historical reasons, regulators have divided up financial products in the United States and allocated different products to different exchanges, under different regulatory oversight. For example, the NYSE, with very few exceptions, is limited to trading equity securities and cannot venture directly into most derivative products.

[43] EUREX, which operates, inter alia, a major derivatives' exchange, 'Eurex Exchange', is a public company owned by Deutsche Börse AG (DB) (Eurex Group). DB attempted to merge with Euronext in 2006; however, it was overlooked in preference for the NYSE, which officially merged with Euronext in 2007 (BBC; NYSE). In 2012, the European Commission blocked a merger between DB and NYSE Euronext that, if successful, would reportedly have 'created a powerhouse, representing more than 95% of Europe's trading and clearing in benchmark exchange-traded derivatives', with the potential to rival the US-based CME Group (FT). At the time of the merger of NYSE and Euronext in 2007, it was said that one of the motivations for the merger on the New York side was the lucrative derivatives trading business in Europe, from which NYSE was excluded in the United States: Eurex Group, 'Company Overview' (*Eurex Exchange*) <http://www.eurexchange.com/exchange-en/about-us/corporate-overview/> accessed 3 October 2013; 'NYSE and Euronext "Set to Merge"', BBC News (21 May 2006) <http://news.bbc.co.uk/2/hi/business/5002438.stm> accessed 3 October 2013; 'History', NYSE Euronext <http://www.nyx.com/en/who-we-are/history> accessed 3 October 2013; Phillip Stafford, 'Deutsche Börse: Failed NYSE/Euronext Merger Haunts Exchange', FT.com (8 June 2012) <http://www.ft.com/intl/cms/s/0/a2da893c-9f67-11e1-a255-00144feabdc0.html#axzz2gcEgoScD> accessed 3 October 2013.

[44] For a discussion of 'electronic' exchanges, see Graham Bowley, 'The New Speed of Money, Reshaping Markets' (New Jersey, 1 January 2011) <http://www.nytimes.com/2011/01/02/business/02speed.html?pagewanted=all> accessed 3 October 2013. See further, Stijn Claessens, Thomas Glaessner, and Daniela Klingebiel, 'Electronic Finance: Reshaping the Financial Landscape Around the World' (2002) 22 *Journal of Financial Services Research* 29, 36–42.

[45] There are 28 countries, as of 1 July 2013, in the European Union alone.

[46] Although, with the advent of the European Union, competition concerns arise, as illustrated by the failed merger between Deutsche Börse AG and NYSE Euronext: see Stafford (n 43).

[47] Arguably, the recent refusal of the Australian government to agree to a friendly merger of the Singapore and Sydney exchanges was influenced by a desire to maintain a national symbol (perhaps not comparable, as a national symbol, to the Sydney Opera House, but significant enough in the world of finance).

spawned new countries, each looking to create an exchange, irrespective of how viable it might be. Rather simplistic technical assistance from donor agencies supported their creation, more as symbols of the move to a market economy as anything else.[48] By early 2000, according to a World Bank study, '20 of 26 transition economies ha[d] established formal stock markets in the past 10 years. Yet many of these markets are underdeveloped or dormant'.[49] Europe has also been a fractious place over the centuries, with geopolitical tensions and rivalries simmering below the surface, a fact which has also worked against the formation of regional alliances. Exchanges in small economies, such as the Balkans, also suffer liquidity problems, being squeezed by their larger rivals such as the Borsa Istanbul, Vienna, and Warsaw (which incidentally offer better prospects in the ongoing mating game among exchanges).[50]

7.17 The creation of Euronext in 2000,[51] originally a consolidation of the exchanges in Paris, Amsterdam, and Brussels, was a triumph of rationalism over nationalism, at least in theory. The motivations were clearly competitive, with these smaller exchanges caught in the crossfire of the European heavyweights, London and Frankfurt. Yet even then, each individual exchange maintained its own identity, with a careful balancing and weighting of responsibilities.

7.18 Euronext was not alone. The same competitive and commercial forces have operated to create other regional exchange arrangements in Europe. In 1998, Norex created a common trading system for the Copenhagen and Stockholm stock exchanges, subsequently enlarged to include Oslo and Iceland. A joint venture between the Vienna Stock Exchange and the Deutsche Börse in 2000 created Newex, a regional exchange for Eastern Europe. The London Stock Exchange and Borsa Italiana entered into an agreement in 2007.[52] The London Stock Exchange has had several unwanted or unconsummated advances, one of the first being in 2000, from Sweden's OM Group, now known as 'OMX' and part of the NASDAQ OMX Group.[53] A few years later, in 2009, a friendly merger between the LSE and Deutsche Börse in Frankfurt was scuppered by 'locusts'.[54] 'Locusts' entered the financial lexicon after being

---

[48] Stijn Claessens, Simeon Djankov, and Daniela Klingebiel, 'Stock Markets in Transition Economies' (The World Bank, September 2000), Financial Sector Discussion Paper No 5, v.

[49] Claessens, Djankov, and Klingebiel (n 48), v.

[50] Bitter historical rivalries cut against othewise sensible regional consolidations. Would Cyprus really form an alliance with Istanbul? Would Macedonia join with Athens? The EBRD is leading a project on integration of stock exchanges in the Balkans by creation of order routing systems and straight through processing rather than formal mergers; email from Jacek Kubas (EBRD) to the author, 30 October 2013.

[51] Euronext NV was formed by the merger of the Amsterdam, Brussels, and Paris stock exchanges in 2000. In 2002, Euronext expanded with the January purchase of the LIFFE (London International Financial Futures and Options Exchange), and the September acquisition of shares in BVLP (Bolsa de Valores de Lisboa e Porto), which secured the Lisbon-based exchanges. Finally, in 2007, Euronext merged with the NYSE Group to create NYSE Euronext: See, generally, 'History', NYSE Euronext <http://www.nyx.com/en/who-we-are/history/amsterdam> accessed 3 October 2013. See further, Ulf Nielsson, 'Stock Exchange Merger and Liquidity: The Case of Euronext' (2009) 12 *Journal of Financial Markets* 229.

[52] Thomas J Chemmanur, Jie He, and Paolo Fulghieri, 'Competition and Cooperation Among Exchanges: Effects on Corporate Cross-Listing Decisions and Listing Standards' (2008) 20 *Journal of Applied Corporate Finance* 76, 78–9.

[53] The prospect of which stirred nationalistic sentiments, in equal measure of outrage and derision, in the City of London. At the time, the LSE and DB had been in friendly talks. See 'London Stock Exchange's tumultuous history of bids', *The Telegraph* (2 September 2011) <http://www.telegraph.co.uk/finance/newsbysector/banksandfinance/8311679/London-Stock-Exchanges-tumultuous-history-of-bids.html> accessed 19 March 2014.

[54] 'Flight of the Locusts', *The Economist* (8 April 2009) <http://www.economist.com/node/13446602> accessed 3 October 2013. A hostile takeover attempt had been rebuffed by the LSE in 2004, but left open the possibility of further talks: 'LSE Rejects German Takeover Bid', BBC News (13 December 2004) <http://news.bbc.co.uk/2/hi/business/4091065.stm. accessed 19 March 2014.

coined in Germany by Franz Müntefering, then chairman of the Social Democratic Party, who used it to describe 'investor activists'[55] insisting on shareholder wealth maximization. London and Frankfurt continue an on again, off again courtship, pushed together by competitive forces emanating from outside Europe.[56]

Nevertheless, exchanges and trading generally in Europe have demonstrated nimbleness and a flair for technology driven innovation.[57] Dematerialization of securities occurred rapidly and physical trading floors disappeared in Europe long before the open outcry system suffered its final blows in the United States.[58] The Amsterdam Exchange may have declined in significance precipitously from the heady days of the Golden Age and the Dutch East India Company, but Amsterdam has become a venue for technology driven high frequency traders.[59] European exchanges, and the European Union, have pushed for years for unimpeded transatlantic trading;[60] the technology exists but the US securities industry, in a protectionist mood, was successful in having regulatory barricades erected.   **7.19**

Given the diversity of the investment and regulatory landscape in Europe, exchanges also   **7.20**
fill niche markets; they can be turned to purposes going beyond their role as trading venues. Luxembourg, for example, concentrates on the listing of Eurobonds which do not necessarily trade on the exchange; the listing meets investment criteria for institutional investors. The Swiss exchange, at the heart of Europe but unfettered by EU membership and the regulatory compliance which that entails, can act opportunistically, tailoring its rules to attract business.

---

[55] Bertrand Benoit, 'German Deputy Still Targets "Locusts"', FT.com (14 February 2007) <http://www.ft.com/intl/cms/s/0/55437712-bc4e-11db-9cbc-0000779e2340.html#axzz2gcEgoScD> accessed 3 October 2013.

[56] NYSE-Euronext created a more serious rival to either London or Frankfurt individually than had previously been the case, and the US exchange, NASDAQ, had been an unwanted suitor knocking at the doors of the London Stock Exchange for some time.

[57] Not all experiments were successful. For example, the German Neuer Markt, designed to specialize in high technology financial products, went down when the high tech bubble burst. 'Germany's market for technology shares and other supposedly high-growth stocks, the Neuer Markt, is to close after losing nearly all of its value over the past two years. The demise of the Neuer Markt, often described as the European equivalent of the Nasdaq in the US, signals that investors' love affair with technology stocks is finally over. The exchange enjoyed its heyday during the technology-led boom of the late 1990s, when German investors piled into Neuer Markt-listed firms. But the combined market value of the 264 firms listed on the exchange has fallen by about 96% since early 2000, when the internet stock bubble began to deflate. [...]'
The closure of the Neuer Markt forms part of a wider plan to split German-listed stocks into an A-list of firms hoping to attract international investors, and a second tier of companies focused more on the domestic market': 'Germany's Neuer Markt to Close', BBC News (26 September 2002) <http://news.bbc.co.uk/2/hi/business/2283068.stm> accessed 3 October 2013.

[58] This created some dilemmas for US regulators, in association with the extraterritorial application of US securities laws which are often firmly rooted in the past. For example, aspects of Regulation S (1990) which applies to offerings outside the United States (and in Europe, in particular) assumed the existence of physical securities and physical trading floors, which had disappeared in much of Europe: BBC News (26 September 2002) (n 57).

[59] See Jeremy Grant and Michael Mackenzie, 'Ghost in the Machine', *Financial Times* (18 February 2010), Factiva Document FTFT000020100218e62i00006; Jeremy Grant, 'Dutch Lift Lid on a High Frequency Universe', *Financial Times* (26 August 2010), Factiva Document FTFT000020100826e68q0003l.

[60] This is the 'trading screens' dispute between the United States and the European Union which raged a few years ago. Europe permitted US trading screens in Europe but the SEC, egged on by US securities industry lobbyists, restricted reciprocal initiatives in the United States to insignificance: see Howell E Jackson, Andreas M Fleckner, and Mark Gurevich, 'Foreign Trading Screens in the United States' (2006) 1 *Capital Markets Law Journal* 54. The CFTC in Chicago was much more open to facilitating the cross-border trading which technology could support; it permitted European trading screens for the financial products under its jurisdiction: see, for example, Michael S Sackheim, 'US to Allow Access to Global Electronic Futures Trading' (1999) 18 *International Financial Law Review* 17.

7.21 European exchanges can also experiment, creating a variety of listing boards or segments, due to the EU-wide definition of 'regulated markets'[61] which leaves much room for the structuring of unregulated trading venues, not subject to EU directives and regulation. Specialized listing boards, tailored to specific market segments, such as cross-listed securities,[62] non-domestic issuers, professional investors,[63] small and medium-sized businesses (of which the Alternative Investment Market, or AIM, in London is a much emulated[64] example) abound. These include listing boards, such as NYSE Euronext Paris' Professional Compartment, for securities which do not trade publicly;[65] an attractive option for issuers wishing to avoid the more onerous requirements applied to primary listings.[66] Listing on an exchange does not necessarily trigger external regulatory mechanisms and the creation of 'side by side' regulated and non-regulated markets raises few eyebrows.

7.22 In the mass privatizations associated with the move to a market economy in Eastern Europe in the 1990s, everything, willy nilly, was put on the newly resurrected exchanges, with their tiered structures accommodating trading and non-trading enterprises. The majority of enterprises which found their way onto some of the early Eastern European exchanges were never designed to trade; nor would they comply with listing and transparency rules of the exchanges. They formed a vast inert mass, clogging the exchange machinery. In these circumstances, the exchanges served a role as companies registrar rather than trading venue.

7.23 Given the birthing pains associated with these Central and Eastern European markets, in 2000, Frankfurt and Vienna set up a new, regional exchange, NEWEX, which specialized in listing, in different segments, the most viable of the new enterprises.[67] 'For the market

---

[61] The European Commission defines 'regulated markets' as 'a multilateral system, defined by MiFID (article 4), which brings together or facilitates the bringing together of multiple third-party buying and selling interests in financial instruments in a way that results in a contract. Examples: the traditional stock exchanges such as the Frankfurt and London Stock Exchanges': European Commission, 'Investment Services Directive— Markets in Financial Instruments Directive (MiFID)' (20 October 2011), Glossary, <http://ec.europa.eu/internal_market/securities/isd/mifid/index_en.htm> accessed 4 October 2013.

[62] In Germany, for example, 'Prime Standard' listings (a market segment of the DB) are prestigious, and must comply with rigorous transparency standards. Deutsche Börse describes Prime Standard as 'an admission portal for companies that also wish to address international investors': 'Prime Standard', Deutsche Börse_<http://www.boerse-frankfurt.de/en/basics+overview/market+segments/prime+standard> accessed 4 October 2013. See further, Panasar and Boeckman (n 2), 835–6.

[63] For example, in December 2007, NYSE Euronext Paris created the 'Professional Compartment', which enables listings without a public offer of securities. Panasar and Boeckman (n 2), 770–1.

[64] For example, the GEM (Growth Enterprise Market) in Hong Kong. Within Europe, there is now a decided trend to push small and medium-sized businesses into the capital markets: 'In April 2012 the Borsa Italiana, part of the London Stock Exchange (LSE) Group, set up the Elite programme to work with growing export-oriented small firms...In March [2013] the LSE introduced a new High Growth segment to its main market—in addition to its existing Alternative Investment Market for small firms—relaxing the listing requirements for fast growing, mainly high-tech businesses. And in May NYSE Euronext...launched EnterNext, a marketing initiative to raise the profile of the mid-cap and small-cap segments of the main market...along with Alternext, the traditional market for smaller firms.' See 'Capital remedy', *The Economist* (26 October 2013), 79.

[65] Perhaps reflecting the two separate vehicles in European companies law based on the distinction as to whether shares or participations can trade publicly.

[66] Panasar and Boeckman (n 2), 771.

[67] Prior to the launch of NEWEX, Deutsche Börse posted the following statement: 'NEWEX, the special exchange for Central and East European companies, wants to start trading on 3 November [2000]. The announcement was made by the joint venture of Deutsche Börse and Wiener Börse on 7 August. The exchange reports that it has now applied for the exchange-operating license and has thus taken a further step towards the establishment of a quality market for equities from Central and Eastern Europe. "The NEWEX trading and financing platform will close a gap in demand: The considerable need for financing for start-ups and restructuring by companies in Central and Eastern Europe can only be covered through access to international capital.

participants, NEWEX will be creating simple, low-cost access to the most attractive companies from Europe's growth region.'[68] The countries targeted, Poland, the Czech Republic,
Hungary and Russia, were seen at the time as the rising stars, attractive to international
investors.[69] Unfortunately, NEWEX failed to attract sufficient company listings and was
transferred to Frankfurt in 2001, where it became a special segment for Central and Eastern
European equities on the Frankfurt Stock Exchange. [70] In its website glossary, Deutsche
Börse describes the current status of NEWEX as a '[f]ormer trading segment for central and
eastern European securities in free float on [the] Frankfurt Stock Exchange'.[71]

Much of this market dynamism emanates from Frankfurt and the Deutsche Börse.   **7.24**
Frankfurt has also provided a vertically integrated institutional model for a modern stock
exchange, called the 'silo', emulated by demutualizing exchanges.[72] The silo internalizes
within the exchange structure multiple services, such as clearing and settlement, associated
with trading over the exchange. In other models, these services may be handled by outside
providers, not the exchange itself. Silos can be lucrative for exchanges when trading patterns
and business models shift profit-making activities away from listing and trading fees, as has
been the case as alternative trading platforms proliferate. Silos are also criticized as being
anti-competitive and creating barriers to entry, as the exchange controls access by competitors to the services provided within the silo. Silos may also act as a brake on merger and consolidation among exchanges with different institutional structures.[73]

Finally, as elsewhere, the traditional exchange is under siege in Europe. Given the rela-   **7.25**
tively large number of exchanges,[74] realignments, mergers, regional and international alliances, are being forged.[75] All is not smooth sailing on this front; the blockbuster proposed

---

That is what NEWEX offers", as NEWEX Management Board members Dr. Michael Radtke and Dr. Erich
Obersteiner explained in Vienna [...] As things now stand, 20 banks and securities trading firms from Germany,
Austria and the UK will trade on NEWEX when the market is launched; together they make up the bulk of
the current trading volume in Central and East European securities. [...] The exchange will be set up under
Austrian law': 'NEWEX Starts on 3 November', Deutsche Börse (7 August 2000) <http://deutsche-boerse.
com/INTERNET/MR/mr_presse.nsf/maincontent/195BD91DA27853E9C12573D5004E437A?Opendoc
ument&lang=en&location=press&newstitle=newexstartson3november&> accessed 4 October 2013.

[68] See (n 67).

[69] See (n 67).

[70] Stijn Claessens, Ruben Lee, and Josef Zechner, 'The Future of Stock Exchanges in European Union
Accession Countries' (Corporation of London, May 2003), 10; 'WSE Privatisation: Bourse Has to Consider
What It Can Offer Its Potential Partners', *Polish News Bulletin* (13 August 2004), Factiva Document
PNBBAE0020040813e08d00001.

[71] 'Glossary', Deutsche Börse <http://www.boerse-frankfurt.de/en/glossary/n/newex+907> accessed 4
October 2013.

[72] For example, by the recently demutualized Bolsa Mexicana, presented in the case study in Ch 10 of this
book. See also Steffen Juranek and Uwe Walz, 'Vertical Integration, Competition, and Financial Exchanges: Is
there Grain in the Silo?', Goethe University Frankfurt, CFS Working Paper No 2010/22 (December
2011) <http://ssrn.com/abstract=1730152> accessed 4 October 2013.

[73] As may have been the case in the doomed mega-merger proposed in 2011 between NYSE-Euronext and
Deutsche Börse. See (n 72). Reform efforts do appear to be encouraging a trend away from vertical silos. '[I]t
is happening now in Ukraine for example; from the investor side, silo model is very convenient but it increases
systemic risks in my view': Kubas (n 50).

[74] Juranek and Walz compare the number of European and US exchanges, and state that there is 'a much
more fragmented structure in Europe with roughly 20 exchanges and CSDs [security exchanges and central
securities depositories]...as compared to the US market with only a dozen exchanges and only two CSDs': see
(n 72), 2.

[75] Recent examples include Hong Kong Exchanges and Clearing's 2012 purchase of the London Metal
Exchange, and the August 2013 announcement of the BATS-Direct Edge merger, which will challenge the

merger of NYSE-Euronext and Deutsche Börse failed on anti-trust grounds. The European Commission felt that the combined effect of the derivatives components would dominate the EU markets, and 'shut out' rival operators. [76] London still stands alone,[77] as does Frankfurt, and the NYSE-Euronext merger itself appears in difficulty.

3. The European Union

7.26 Although it may go without saying that European capital markets are impacted by the European Union, surprisingly, the influence of Brussels had been somewhat muted. The interaction of national level legislation and EU-level instruments is both complex and dynamic. In addition to the direct interaction of EU legislative instruments with those of the member states, non-EU countries in Europe also act and react in the shadow of Brussels.

7.27 Until fairly recently, capital raising and capital markets per se, received scant attention at the EU level. Companies law directives, dating back to the early days of the European Union (and influenced significantly by Germany) have dealt with various aspects of capital structure and capital raising, but more from a corporate governance perspective. As the European Union has had as its mandate the promotion of the free movement of people, goods, and services (with capital being somewhat overlooked), the means by which financial services are provided and the intermediaries delivering the services dominated the EU agenda.

7.28 Nothing is easy in the European Union, given its political structure and expanding membership, but financial services have proved particularly problematic. The regulation of financial services is technical and sometimes obscure. In finance, powerful interest groups operate close to the heart of political power in member states. Different member states have different stakes and levels of interest in the development of financial markets.

7.29 Brussels has vacillated over time with respect to its priorities and dominant regulatory impetuses. According to Moloney, 'EU financial market regulation has moved from detailed hamonisation in the 1970s, to minimum harmonisation and mutual recognition in the 1980s/early 1990s, to a period of intensive regulation over the Financial Services Action Plan/Lamfalussy era (1999–2004), linked to major institutional reform, and, finally, into a 'dynamic consolidation phase', and 'related "legislative pause" between 2005 and 2007'.[78] Notable here, as much as the waves of action and retrenchment, is the increasingly shortened periodicity.

7.30 Tensions between London and Brussels have been formative. For decades, the City of London has been pitted against Brussels on the regulatory front in connection with financial services. Most obvious have been the difficulties associated with integration of the notoriously

---

NYSE-Nasdaq dominance of the market data business: Francesca Freeman, 'London Metal Exchange Gets New CEO', *Wall Street Journal* (Asia edition, 27 August 2013) <http://online.wsj.com/article/SB1000142412 7887324591204579038413618908886.html> accessed 4 October 2013; Maureen Farrell, 'Merger to Create Second Biggest Stock Exchange', CNN Money (26 August 2013) <http://money.cnn.com/2013/08/26/investing/exchange-merger/index.html> accessed 4 October 2013.

[76] Jeremy Grant, 'D Börse to Sue Brussels Over NYSE Block', FT.com (20 March 2012) <http://www.ft.com/intl/cms/s/0/8f219466-71fa-11e1-90b5-00144feab49a.html#axzz2gjz5fUgM> accessed 4 October 2013.

[77] Apart from its relationship with Milan.

[78] Niamh Moloney, 'The European Securities and Markets Authority and Institutional Design for the EU Financial Market—A Tale of Two Competencies: Part (1) Rule-Making' (2011) 12 *European Business Organization Law Review* 41, 51–2.

idiosyncratic English common law and its long history of self-regulation of financial services in the United Kingdom. As the world's leading international financial centre, the City of London has been, on the one hand, convinced of its superiority in terms of experience and expertise and, on the other, deeply troubled by the prospect of losing competitive advantage through the process of regulatory change and harmonization.

Historically, the EU approached capital markets regulation only tangentially through its **7.31** companies law directives. Upon entry to the European Union in 1972, the United Kingdom was required to beat its unwieldy body of companies law into the EU mould.[79] At the same time, UK influences in the form of early capital markets initiatives began to appear in Brussels: the Listing Particulars Directive (1978), the Public Offering Directive (1985), and the Insider Dealing Directive (1989). By 1992, the first attempt at EU 'passporting' of financial intermediaries, opening up trade in financial services across Europe, had appeared in the form of the Investment Services Directive. EU level financial legislative instruments also operated very much at the surface of the markets, providing leeway for unregulated markets or tailor-made regulatory responses at the member state level. For example, as a result of heavy industry lobbying, the 1992 Investment Services Directive sidestepped the cross-border Eurobond market entirely, by virtue of a bespoke exemption for 'eurosecurities'.[80] EU efforts at harmonization stalled in face of the diversity of the markets in member states; the United Kingdom, in particular, took pride in 'goldplating' EU initiatives, going beyond requirements to maintain the uniqueness and competitiveness of its markets. Enforcement and supervision remained a checkerboard, within the purview of individual member states.[81] Regulatory diversity and competition, championed by the United Kingdom, were 'tolerated rather than welcomed'[82] in the European Union.

By 1999, however, a turning point had been reached and the alarm bells sounded across **7.32** Europe. The roaring 1990s in US capital markets and the impact of increasing internationalization could not be ignored. Daimler Benz, breaking ranks with other German industrials, had listed on the New York Stock Exchange. The US investment banks had poured into London after 1986 and were solidly entrenched, shaking up the industry. Derivative products were proliferating. European investors, particularly in Germany, were developing a taste for the equity markets; direct ownership of shares had been climbing there by 30 per cent a year to 1999.[83] The Financial Services Action Plan (1999) set Belgian Baron Lamfalussy to work on his 'Wisemen's Report'.[84]

---

[79] Gower says to good effect. See LCB Gower, *Gower's Principles of Modern Company Law* (5th edn, Sweet & Maxwell, 1992). This was not an easy task, resulting in the weighty Companies Acts 1985 and 1989, as well as the spinning out of insolvency. The results were not satisfactory, and 20 years later completely new legislation finally appeared; the Companies Act 2006 (UK). The latter was a rethinking of companies law, not a consolidation and dissection as was the case with the earlier statutes.

[80] Giovanni Nardulli and Antonio Segni describe 'euro-securities' as 'units for which an underwriting agreement has been entered into among the offeror and a pool of underwriters which includes participants from at least two Member States. Euro-securities must be initially acquired only by banks or financial institutions': Giovanni Nardulli and Antonio Segni, 'EU Cross-Border Securities Offerings: An Overview' (1996) 19 *Fordham International Law Journal* 887, 895–6.

[81] See more generally, stinging critiques in the Lamfalussy Report: The Committee of Wise Men, 'Final Report of the Committee of Wise Men on the Regulation of European Securities Markets' (Brussels, 15 February 2001) (the Lamfalussy Report), 40<http://ec.europa.eu/internal_market/securities/docs/lamfalussy/wisemen/final-report-wise-men_en.pdf> accessed 5 October 2013.

[82] Moloney (n 78), 53.

[83] Lamfalussy Report (n 81), 78.

[84] This was Europe; no political correctness there.

3.1 From Lamfalussy to de Larosière

7.33 The Lamfalussy Report changed the face of European financial markets regulation, dramatically and in short order, such was the perceived urgency of the situation. The powerful attractions of the US markets (for issuer and investor alike), were the catalysts for change. 'There is no serious alternative available. The status quo would entrench the continuation of European financial market fragmentation. This means lost benefits. Lost opportunities…with European savings diverted to foreign market places.'[85] The Report contained long lists of problems with European markets, primarily associated with the high level of fragmentation in the markets and regulation which had stubbornly resisted pressures towards harmonization and convergence. This latter problem became acute as EU membership rapidly expanded.

7.34 European markets were too old-fashioned, too fragmented, too slow to change,[86] too complex.[87] There were too many exchanges;[88] electronic clearing networks were a reality, but one without a regulatory response; 'passporting' of financial intermediaries[89] had proven easier said than done; the structural impediments and high costs associated with cross-border clearing and settlement undermined pan-European trading; the new market realities created by privatization of public pension funds and state-owned enterprises remained unaddressed; and most significantly, inconsistent transposition and implementation in member countries of existing EU instruments rendered them ineffective.[90] The list went on.[91]

7.35 Implicit in these long lists of problems was the solution: a European-style Securities and Exchange Commission (SEC) along US lines. However, such a proposal had been dismissed at the outset: the view then was that a pan-European regulator, a European-style SEC, could not be created without an amendment to the 1957 Treaty of Rome, a task too lengthy and arduous to even contemplate, much less propose. Instead, the Lamfalussy Report identified several substantive areas to pursue, including the adoption of International Accounting Standards (now known as International Financial Reporting Standards, IFRS), as well as a new procedural framework within the European Union, in an attempt to enhance internal market policy making, coordination and cooperation on a timely basis.

---

[85] Lamfalussy Report (n 81), 8.

[86] It had taken over 12 years to enact the Takeover Directive and the European Company Law Directive took what must have been a record 31 years, 3 months and 8 days.

[87] The Lamfalussy Report documented over 40 different public bodies involved in regulating capital markets in Europe. See Lamfalussy Report (n 81), 14–15 for specific criticisms of the regulatory system.

[88] Although market forces were taking care of that problem.

[89] Under the 1992 Investment Services Directive.

[90] See Lamfalussy Report (n 81), 10–14.

[91] Including: '[L]ack of commonly agreed guiding principles covering all financial services legislation; failure to make the mutual recognition principle work for the wholesale market business in the context of the Investment Services Directive (ISD); for regulated markets themselves; for the retail sector; or for a single passport prospectus working for cross-border capital raising; outdated rules on listing requirements, no distinction between admission to listing and to trading, and lack of a definition of a public offer; ambiguity over the scope and application of conduct of business rules (Article 11 of ISD) as well as on the definition of who is a professional investor; no appropriate rules to deal with alternative trading systems; potential inconsistencies between the E-commerce Directive and financial services directives; no comprehensive market abuse regime; no cross-border collateral arrangements; no set of common European-wide accepted international accounting standards; outdated investment rules for UCITS and pension funds; unresolved public policy issues for clearing and settlement activities; no agreed takeover rules; no high and equivalent levels of consumer protection and no efficient methods for resolving cross-border consumer disputes. And there are more': Lamfalussy Report (n 81), 12.

3.2 Procedural and substantive reforms

The procedural recommendations of the Lamfalussy Report created a complex multi-tiered **7.36** decision making and advisory structure, in the European fashion.[92] However, the substantive reforms,[93] in process but which followed remarkably quickly on the heels of the Wisemen's Report, took a different tack. They keyed off US securities regulation,[94] directly in terms of importing the terminology and conceptual underpinnings as well as indirectly through incorporation of US-inspired international principles.[95] For example, at one level, the Prospectus Directive 2003 represents a principled and systematized updating of the US 1933 Act, creating a new and improved version addressing two of the major drawbacks of the old US legislation; its abstruse approach to private placements and its failure to define the key concept of a 'public offering'.[96]

3.2.1 Substantive reforms

As was usual at the time, the substantive initiatives flowing from the Lamfalussy Report took **7.37** the form of directives, high level principles to be implemented at the member state level (thereby perpetuating the potential for discrepancy and delay). IFRS[97] was an exception to

---

[92] In the Lamfalussy recommendations, the Committee outlined a four-tier structure to support regulatory reform, which included the following: Levels 1 and 2 provided for framework and implementing principles that would be applied against future securities' legislation; Level 2 would be supported through the creation of two committees—the ESC (European Securities Committee), and the ESRC (European Securities Regulators Committee, the acronym soon becoming the more evocative CESR); Level 3 would focus on strengthened cooperation between the regulators, member states, and the European Commission, with reference to, inter alia, 'consistent guidelines for administrative regulations', 'common standards', and the review of regulatory practices; and Level 4 concerned enforcement: Lamfalussy Report (n 81), 4.

[93] That is, the 2003 Market Abuse Directive, the 2003 Prospectus Directive, and the 2004 Transparency Directive: see European Commission, 'Securities Markets: Commission Welcomes Council's adoption of Market Abuse Directive' (IP/02/1789, 3 December 2002) <http://europa.eu/rapid/press-release_IP-02-1789_en.htm?locale=en> accessed 5 October 2013; European Commission, 'Financial Services: Commission Welcomes Council's Adoption of Prospectuses Directive' (IP/03/1018, 15 July 2003) <http://europa.eu/rapid/press-release_IP-02-1789_en.htm?locale=en> accessed 5 October 2013; European Commission, 'Financial Services: Final Adoption of Transparency Directive Will Help Investors and Boost Trust in Markets' (IP/04/1508, 17 December 2004) <http://europa.eu/rapid/press-release_IP-04-1508_en.htm?locale=en> accessed 5 October 2013. The Investment Services Directive (1992) was replaced by the 2007 MiFID (Markets in Financial Instruments Directive). IFRS was adopted by Regulation in the EU in 2002.

[94] And Canadian as well; for example, the 'closed system' of exemptions from registration of intermediaries and prospectus requirements of the Ontario Securities Act.

[95] In particular, the International Organization of Securities Commissions, 'International Disclosure Standards for Cross-Border Offerings and Initial Listings by Foreign Issuers' (September 1998), <https://www.google.com.au/url?sa=t&rct=j&q=&esrc=s&source=web&cd=5&cad=rja&ved=0CEUQFjAE&url=http%3A%2F%2Fwww.sec.gov%2Fabout%2Foffices%2Foia%2Foia_corpfin%2Fcrossborder.pdf&ei=PfZPUvPaKaeziQeTqIDgBg&usg=AFQjCNH8uPrsvDtdjLiA9bYH6Rq3LicElA&bvm=bv.53537100,d.aGc> accessed 5 October 2013, which was modelled on the US registration form for foreign private issuers in the United States, Form 20-F.

[96] In their analysis of the Proposed EU Prospectus Directive, Edward Greene and Linda Quinn note that 'it is interesting to see how the framework principles . . . are designed to achieve in a different fashion the best characteristics of the US market, and indeed, with certain exceptions, how they build on and improve on the US experience': Edward F Greene and Linda C Quinn, 'Building on the International Convergence of the Global Markets: A Model for Securities Law Reform', A Major Issues Conference: Securities Regulation in the Global Internet Economy, Washington DC, 14–15 November 2001, 12.

[97] Regulation 1606/2002 of the European Parliament required that 'all publicly traded Community companies prepare their consolidated financial statements in accordance with one single set of accounting standards, namely International Accounting Standards (IAS) [now known as the International Financial Reporting Standards, or IFRS], at the latest by 2005': Council Regulation (EC) 1606/2002 of 19 July 2002 on the application of international accounting standards [2002] L 243/1, para 12.

the rule, and a precursor of things to come; consistency of interpretation and application was vital to its operation and so it took the form of a regulation, directly applicable in all member states.

7.38 The speed at which the new initiatives were put in place was truly remarkable (although they had been under consideration for some time);[98] much of the substance reflected well-known models and IOSCO initiatives. The results, not surprisingly, were mixed, ranging from the rather well-developed Prospectus Directive to a very much 'first crack' Market Abuse Directive.[99] As in the past, the regulation of market intermediaries, proved complex and difficult. To the extent the objective of the Lamfalussy reforms was to put in place quickly a comprehensive framework for pan-European capital markets regulation, which could be further refined in the future, the exercise was successful. In the event, within half a dozen years or so, all the post-Lamfalussy directives have been amended or are in the process of being completely recast.[100]

7.39 Not that there were not serious critiques at the time of proposal of the new directives. As might be expected, critical voices in the United Kingdom were raised. A fundamental complaint was that the directives were not taking into account the realities of the marketplace (which London had long dominated). Some of the concerns coming out of London were addressed in the directives as adopted; others have been picked up in the subsequent amendments.

7.40 For example, in July 2001, the UK Law Society made blistering comments about the proposed Prospectus Directive: '... [W]e are surprised to see that some of the Commission's proposals would operate against the spirit of the European Union by entrenching national interests and depriving European issuers of choice... Put more starkly the Directive will take what is currently the only market that can claim to be even vaguely pan-European *back* several steps' (emphasis in the original).[101]

7.41 As Lamfalussy had recommended, the principle of mutual recognition of home country regulation threaded its way through all the directives. The UK solicitors, eyeing a potential migration of business out of London in the wake of the rules, were particularly critical of the application of 'pure' mutual recognition of home country regulation. EU issuers, they argued, should not be tied to their 'home country' regulatory regime but be free to choose which member state in which to offer (read the United Kingdom); any of those states should be eligible for mutual recognition.[102] The arguments mustered to support self-interest were not without merit. The home country of an EU issuer might not have the expertise

---

[98] Shortly after publication of the final Lamfalussy Report in 2001, the 2003 Market Abuse Directive appeared, quickly followed by the 2003 Prospectus Directive, and the 2004 Transparency Directive: European Commission (n 93).

[99] A main critique of the Market Abuse Directive has been the discrepancies in enforcement which is left to home states. Other criticisms are now being addressed in the Market Abuse Regulation.

[100] For example, reforms to the Market Abuse Directive have recently been endorsed by the European Parliament in the form of the Market Abuse Regulation: European Commission, 'Statement by Commissioner Michel Barnier on the Endorsement by the European Parliament of the Political Agreement on New European Rules for Market Abuse', MEMO/13/773 (10 September 2013), <http://europa.eu/rapid/press-release_MEMO-13-773_en.htm?locale=en> accessed 5 October 2013.

[101] See Company Law Committee, The Law Society (UK), Memorandum No 422, 'Proposal for a Directive on the Prospectus to be Published When Securities are Offered to the Public or Admitted to Trading', July 2001.

[102] Company Law Committee, The Law Society (UK), Memorandum No 422 (n 101).

to regulate, especially complex structured products such as derivatives.[103] Most Eurobonds listed in London or Luxembourg, where listing rules and market practices provided a consistency which would be lost. A member state (read the United Kingdom) should be able to intervene directly for breach of offering and other ongoing obligations, essentially preempting home country oversight. Leaving sanctions in the hands of home country regulators could produce very different outcomes in terms of liability. Some of these arguments were persuasive, to a limited extent, and resulted in modification of a 'pure' home country mutual recognition principle operating across the board in the Prospectus Directive.

The perspicacity of the London solicitors was borne out by later amendments to the Prospectus **7.42** Directive, and even in development of a new set of IOSCO principles. The Prospectus Directive was casting the regulatory net wider than in the past, catching transactions which had previously operated in a non-regulated space. The UK solicitors presciently noted the burden which one size fits all prospectus provisions imposed on small and medium-sized businesses and start-ups,[104] and the lack of simplified disclosure for sophisticated investors.

The UK solicitors also pointed out that the underlying problem with the IOSCO International **7.43** Disclosure Standards for Cross-Border Offerings and Initial Listings by Foreign Issuers (1998), which in a bout of enthusiastic internationalism, had been incorporated by reference into parts of the Prospectus Directive. Being drawn from US Form 20-F rules, these IOSCO Principles implicitly (although not explicitly) pertained to equity securities; they were not always suited to bonds and products structured as debt, which were much more common in the European markets. IOSCO responded in March 2007 with new principles specifically for cross-border debt offerings; namely, the International Disclosure Principles for Cross-Border Offerings and Listings of Debt Securities by Foreign Issuers.[105]

This particular example demonstrates one of the more beneficial, if somewhat fraught, **7.44** dynamics operating in the EU regulatory world. Brussels constructs theoretical frameworks with the systematizing zeal for which continental European jurists are famous, while London practitioners bring to bear their great technical expertise and a pragmatic approach to the realities of the marketplace. Despite obvious exasperation on both sides, it has been a good combination although certainly not without its critics.[106]

---

[103] Company Law Committee, The Law Society (UK), Memorandum No 422 (n 101). Greece, rather uncharitably, was singled out as an example.

[104] Addressed in the 2010 amendments to the Prospectus Directive, and predating by some two years the US JOBS Act.

[105] IOSCO, 'International Disclosure Principles for Cross-Border Offerings and Listings of Debt Securities by Foreign Issuers' (March 2007) <https://www.google.com.au/url?sa=t&rct=j&q=&esrc=s&source=web&cd =1&cad=rja&ved=0CCwQFjAA&url=http%3A%2F%2Fwww.iosco.org%2Flibrary%2Fpubdocs%2Fpdf% 2FIOSCOPD242.pdf&ei=PfZPUvPaKaeziQeTqIDgBg&usg=AFQjCNHU0NNlUo-a3NFimBnyoWkk-B kAig&bvm=bv.53537100,d.aGc> accessed 5 October 2013.

[106] See Moloney (n 78), 56–7, in which she states that: 'EU rules have suffered from, for example, unclear objectives and unintended consequences (aside altogether from the obvious deficiencies with respect to prudential and systemic risk management...). The Prospectus Directive remains something of a muddle, notwithstanding the 2010 reforms. Its importance to wholesale pan-EU capital raising lies in its carving out of the offers which are not subject to its rules. In terms of the retail markets, it was designed to support a pan-EU market for retail offers which has not emerged, with strong retail investor preference for packaged investment products'. In particular, Moloney notes the distance separating the Prospectus Directive from market reality (n 78), 61. However, Welch and Parker note favourably the cross-fertilization between the European Union and the United Kingdom, with the United Kingdom injecting practical experience. See Welch and Parker (n 2), para 4.24: 'The relationship between EU law and UK law, particularly in the area of securities law is very much

7.45 Several welcome and enduring regulatory concepts emerged from the Lamfalussy process. As Moloney notes: '[The] importance to wholesale pan-EU capital raising lies in [the Prospectus Directive's] carving out of the offers which are not subject to its rules.'[107] This is an enormous improvement on the US 1933 Act, where making the distinction between public offerings and private placements requires adroit sleight of hand. Although there were momentary enthusiasms in the 1990s among retail investors, a vibrant US-style equity market for individuals has not materialized.[108] However, the global financial crisis has dampened retail investors' enthusiasm everywhere, and the 1950s US-style retail market model may be well and truly dead, and not just in Europe.

7.46 The EU insistence on one 'competent authority' per member state,[109] essentially one-stop shopping, has also resulted in greater speed and certainty in negotiating regulatory hurdles. It has also brought regulatory focus, accountability, and reduced possibilities for unwelcome regulatory arbitrage. The consolidated financial services regulator, along now defunct FSA lines, appears throughout Europe, marking an improvement to the regulatory fragmentation of which Baron Lamfalussy complained.[110]

7.47 The key concept of 'regulated market' is also important. Although it serves different functions, depending on the circumstances, its primary purpose is to delineate 'perimeter control'.[111] The area within the perimeter can be expanded or contracted through the regulated market mechanism.

3.2.2 *Procedural reforms—all hail CESR*

7.48 The procedural reforms introduced by the Lamfalussy process were shortlived, supplanted in January 2011 by the new pan-European regulator, ESMA. In 2001, however, the constitutional and very real political difficulties[112] associated with the creation of a pan-European capital markets regulator, meant that the four-tiered procedural structure[113] created by the Lamfalussy process, was a complex and shifting affair. One body, originally called the European Securities Regulators Committee (ESRC) emerged as the focus of activity. Over time ESRC took on aspects of a *de facto* regulator, although such was not its original mandate.[114] Operating at Level 3 in the four-tier structure, the acronym 'ESRC' quickly morphed into a snappier 'CESR'.

---

one of cross-fertilisation. The UK was one of the few Member States to have established a sophisticated system of securties regulation and had a thriving international financial market by the time the EC launched its programme on investment services. Consequently, the UK was in a position to inject ideas based on practical experience into the Community process.'

[107] See Moloney (n 78), 56.

[108] See Moloney (n 78), 56–7.

[109] Where in the past there may have been multiple regulators and ministries involved in any particular issue.

[110] Moloney notes that this regulatory consolidation also increases the risk of systemic regulatory error: See Moloney (n 78), 70–1. With the breakup of the model, the FSA in the United Kingdom, some jurisdictions have followed suit, Belgium for example.

[111] See Moloney (n 78), 57.

[112] The 1957 Treaty of Rome was the perceived constitutional difficulty; the then FSA in London, established in 2000, was the real political difficulty.

[113] See description of the four tiers (n 92).

[114] CESR was established in 2001 to improve coordination among European securities regulators, to act as an advisory group to assist the EU Commission in the 'preparation of draft implementing measures of EU framework directives, and to work to ensure more consistent implementation of Community legislation in the Member States. Over the years, CESR's role has evolved considerably and it has taken up an important role in supervisory convergence and supervision in the EU': Dorothee Fischer-Appelt, 'The European Securities and Markets Authority: The Beginnings of a Powerful European Securities Authority?' (2011) 5 *Law and Financial Markets Review* 21, 22.

In retrospect, it was not surprising that CESR emerged as the leader; it was formed as a   **7.49**
cooperative network of national regulators to promote consistent implementation of initiatives produced by the Lamfalussy process by developing guidelines and joint interpretations. However, as a grouping of regulators, CESR possessed both the technical expertise
and market experience that the more political levels lacked, in addition to the synergies
produced by providing national regulators with a formalized structure in which to meet
and act.[115] CESR too was the model for the creation in 2003 of two other, parallel, financial
bodies; one for banking (CEBS), and the other for insurance and occupational pensions
(CEIOPS). Together, CESR, CEBS, and CEIOPS, came to be known as the 3L3 (three
Level 3) committees.

CESR was originally tasked to assist the European Commission in the field of capital mar-   **7.50**
kets. On its own initiative or at the request of the European Commission, CESR could
produce opinions. As a monitoring body, CESR tried to ensure the uniform application
of EU legislative instruments and was responsible for conducting evaluations, promoting
good practices and publishing guidelines or recommendations. CESR was responsible for
organizing broad consultations with the players in the market, consumers and end-users,
serving as a liaison between the European Commission and the national authorities.
Specifically, the European Commission gave CESR a mandate regarding the implementation of standards.[116]

But CESR had stepped into a pan-European regulatory void, which it began to fill. CESR   **7.51**
used a voluntary 'soft "supervisory convergence" model' including '[p]eer review, mediation,
support of delegation, best practice sharing, institutional support of cross-border cooperation concerning market abuse…and the enforcement of financial reporting'.[117] While CESR's
powers were limited to providing technical advice, gathering information, and suggesting industry standards, the expectation of compliance by national authorities with CESR's recommendations grew. There were two main drawbacks to CESR's evolving role: its recommendations could
be ignored with impunity and there were no private rights of action available.

Had the global financial crisis not intervened in 2008, CESR may have continued along   **7.52**
this trajectory of increasing regulation by persuasion or consensus, a familiar technique in
the United Kingdom and one the FSA would have been quite comfortable with. Some commentators have remarked on the failure of CESR to prevent the financial crisis leading 'to
a push for greater centralization with the creation of the European Securities and Markets
Authority'.[118] To view CESR as a failure though is quite unfair, given the institutional limitations which had been placed upon it. Rather, CESR was the seed from which the new
pan-European capital markets regulator sprouted; all that was needed was the not-so-gentle

---

[115] See Thomas M J Möllers, 'Sources of Law in European Securities Regulation: Effective Regulation, Soft Law and Legal Taxonomy from Lamfalussy to de Larosière' (2010) 11 *European Business Organization Law Review* 379.

[116] Anne-Dominique Merville, 'Autorités Européennes de Supervision Financière' (March 2012) *Répertoire de Droit des Sociétés*, Editions Dalloz, 2013.

[117] Niamh Moloney, 'The European Securities and Markets Authority and Institutional Design for the EU Financial Market—A Tale of Two Competences: Part (2) Rules in Action' (2011) 12 *European Business Organization Law Review* 177, 181.

[118] Eric C Chaffee, 'Contemplating the Endgame: An Evolutionary Model for the Harmonization and Centralization of International Securities Regulation' (2010) 79 *University of Cincinnati Law Review* 587, 614.

rain of crisis driven opportunity. All of CESR's operations were automatically transferred to ESMA at its inception.[119]

7.53　The Lamfalussy epoch lasted less than a decade, a remarkably short period of time. More than the regulatory structures it created (now superseded), or the legislative instruments which its recommendations prompted (now, also in the process of being superseded or amended), it marked a sea change. European securities regulation rose from the waters.[120] The nose of the great ship Brussels was pointed in a new direction and set out to chart new seas.

3.3 De Larosière and crisis driven change

7.54　The UK may have been comfortable with voluntary, consensus-driven regulation by persuasion at the EU level (which incidentally left a measure of autonomy, and a veto, to its own powerful regulator). The European Union, however, was not about to miss the crisis-driven opportunity to act where Baron Lamfalussy had not dared. In 2009, the de Larosière Report picked up where the Lamfalussy Report had left off in 2001.[121] The de Larosière Report, like its predecessor, didn't pull any punches. It was time to create a pan-European financial supervisory structure.

7.55　The Lamfalussy structures had been designed to speed up the regulatory process and lead to convergence in supervisory practices, but had been hamstrung by their lack of legal power and consensus requirements for decision-making.[122] The use of directives[123] to implement the reforms had stymied true convergence; national authorities indulged in optionality and gold plating, interpreting and implementing the directives to suit themselves.

7.56　National authorities bore the brunt of the harshest criticisms in the de Larosière Report. They had subverted the goal of regulatory convergence by their failure to collaborate sufficiently in the cooperative structures created by the Lamfalussy process.[124] National interests continued to run rampant, at the expense of European cohesion. National authorities continued to protect national champions.[125] Competition continued to be throttled. National practices viewed as producing a competitive advantage were preserved.[126] Change was held hostage to bureaucratic inertia.[127]

---

[119] Fischer-Appelt (n 114), 22.

[120] In short order, a number of new texts on 'European Securities Regulation' appeared, Moloney (n 2), Panasar and Broeckman (n 2), although the latest, Veil (n 2), shifts the terminology to 'capital markets'. The Lamfalussy process was keying off US experience and regulation, thus the terminology of 'securities regulation' which is somewhat deceptive as in the United States 'securities' exclude a great many financial products, such as most derivatives, which are included in the purview of capital markets regulation outside the United States.

[121] Demonstrating what Moloney calls 'the evolutionary dynamic which tends to characterise EU institutional reform': Moloney (n 78), 47.

[122] In the absence of qualified majority voting power, any member could veto action.

[123] Directives are not directly applicable in member states of the European Union, but must be implemented by national authorities which may interpret them in their own way.

[124] Moloney has a more nuanced view, noting better national coordination and supervisory convergence in the pre-crisis period (although this may have broken down quickly during the crisis), as well as a 'gradual hardening of the soft convergence powers of the 3L3 committees': Moloney (n 78), 48.

[125] Volkswagen comes to mind.

[126] Those of the City of London, for example.

[127] Since directives were implemented at the member state level, some member states, the United Kingdom among them, were accused of foot dragging with respect to directives not to their liking.

4. The New European Supervisory Authorities

Constitutional impediments to a panoply of pan-European financial markets regulators **7.57** melted away in the face of pragmatic action.[128] The '3L3' committees[129] were transformed into a troika of real authorities, albeit with limited rulemaking powers: the ESMA based in Paris, the European Banking Authority (EBA) based in London, and the European Insurance and Occupational Pensions Authority (EIOPA) based in Frankfurt. The new bodies, known collectively as European Supervisory Authorities (ESAs) have assumed and continued the roles, primarily of policy advisers, of their predecessors to the European Commission.

This is an experiment, but one which is likely to prove enduring. Every three years the new **7.58** regulatory structure must be reconsidered. The European Commission must report on the continued appropriateness of the troika of ESAs and the separate supervision of banking, insurance, and occupational pensions and securities and financial markets. More controversially, the European Commission must also consider whether the ESAs should all be headquartered in the same place (rather than scattered among London, Frankfurt, and Paris) and whether the ESAs should be given further supervisory powers.[130]

Together with the ESAs, a new body was also created, the European Systemic Risk Board **7.59** (ESRB), based in Frankfurt. The European Central Bank is at the helm with the chairs of the three new authorities sitting at the table together with the European Commission.[131] In its task of monitoring and assessing systemic risk, ESMA takes its cues from the ESRB. ESMA responds to warnings and recommendations from the ESRB, and in collaboration with the ESRB, participates in developing mechanisms for addressing systemic risk, with an eye to convergence. ESMA 'may also draw up additional guidelines and recommendations for key financial market participants to take account of' the specific systemic risks they pose.[132]

A second new body, a College of Supervisors for the largest cross-border institutions, was **7.60** also set up.[133] Both of these new bodies mirrored similar initiatives being taken on the other side of the Atlantic, in the United States, in an example of concerted EU/US regulatory coordination. See Figure 7.1.

Day-to-day rulemaking was to remain at the national level but there was no mistaking the **7.61** hollowing out of the autonomy of national authorities. Mutual recognition principles would also continue to operate based on host country deference to home country regulation and supervision. But in the event of disagreement between regulators, binding mediation would produce a decision directly applicable in the member states.

The new authorities would no longer be hobbled by consensus decision making; quali- **7.62** fied majority voting would be adopted. The existing peer reviews by national regulators, a CESR initiative based on similar exercises conducted by IOSCO, would continue, but

---

[128] A delegation mechanism was employed to empower the new ESAs.
[129] 'Unstable', according to Moloney (n 78), 43, and advisory in nature.
[130] Fischer-Appelt (n 114), 21.
[131] The Financial Stability Oversight Council (FSOC) is the US counterpart, established by Title I of the Dodd–Frank Wall Street Reform and Consumer Protection Act, signed into law by President Barack Obama on 21 July 2010.
[132] Fischer-Appelt (n 114), 29.
[133] The Supervisor for Systemically Important Financial Institutions and their Subsidiaries falls under the Federal Reserve.

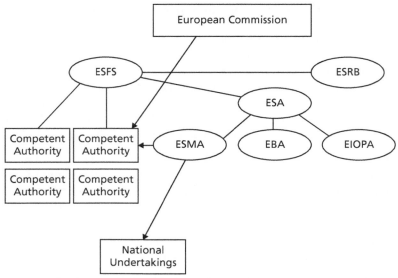

Figure 7.1 ESMA's Place in the European Financial System[134]

ESA = European Supervisory Authority
EBA = European Banking Authority
EIOPA = European Insurance and Occupational Pension Authority
ESMA = European Securities and Markets Authority
ESFS = European System of Financial Supervisors
ESRB = European Systemic Risk Board

with a difference; the European Commission would add muscle to the enforcement of the outcomes. Rulemaking would be by way of 'Guidelines' taken at the initiative of the new authorities, to be adopted and declared binding in all 27 (now 28) member states. The European Commission could reject the guidelines, but only in exceptional circumstances; otherwise, the Commission would give guidelines the force of EC regulation. Numerous new powers and mandates were to be conferred on the new authorities.

5. ESMA and the New European Market

7.63 The creation of ESMA on 1 January 2011 was 'an epochal date for EU financial market regulation'.[135] According to Moloney, there is 'little point in indulging in prescriptions for pulling back the EU's dominance over the Member States in financial market regulation; that

---

[134] See Möllers (n 115).

[135] Moloney (n 78), 43. A large body of commentary and interpretation is now appearing: eg Andrew Shrimpton and Nick Inman, 'ESMA's Guidelines on Automated Trading',*Compliance Monitor*, May 2012, 27–8; Caroline Bradley, 'Transparency and Financial Regulation in the European Union: Crisis and Complexity' (2012) 35 *Fordham International Law Journal* 1171; Didier Martin, 'Proceedings before ESMA: The Necessary Combination of Fairness and Efficiency' (2012) 27 *Butterworths Journal of International Banking and Financial Law* 263–4.

ship has sailed'.[136] By way of consolation to her colleagues in the City of London mourning a loss of autonomy, Moloney suggests that the European Union can now 'act more forcefully as a block' in an increasingly internationalized market.[137] Officially, ESMA was created to 'strengthen financial-market oversight at the European Union level ... [treading] a fine line between still powerful national regulators and the need for a consistent application of market rules across the 27-nation [now 28] member bloc'.[138]

Established on 1 January 2011, ESMA is 'an independent EU authority that contributes to **7.64** safeguarding the stability of the European Union's financial system by ensuring the integrity, transparency, efficiency and orderly functioning of securities markets, as well as enhancing investor protection',[139] with a broad remit.[140]

ESMA, in line with IOSCO Objectives and Principles of Securities Regulation, has been cre- **7.65** ated as an independent agency[141] *vis-à-vis* the European Commission and national authorities. Its accountability is to the European Parliament and the Council to which it must present an annual activity report and a multi-year programme of work. The Chairman of ESMA may also be invited to appear before the European Parliament and ESMA must respond to questions by members of the European Parliament and to report on its activities.[142]

For this reason, individuals and legal entities have been given a personal right of action **7.66** against ESMA decisions. Any physical or legal person can appeal a decision taken by ESMA to a specially constituted Board of Appeal. [143] In addition, proceedings may also be brought before the European Court of Justice either contesting a decision taken by the Board of Appeal or contesting a decision taken by ESMA.[144]

ESMA was created by regulation (the ESMA Regulation),[145] making it directly applicable **7.67** in the member states. It is the umbrella for a large number of other legislative instruments[146]

---

[136] Moloney (n 78), 60.

[137] Moloney (n 78), 60.

[138] Riva Froymovich, 'ESMA to be Strongly "Independent"', *The Wall Street Journal* (2 March 2011) <http://online.wsj.com/article/SB10001424052748703559604576176234286298302.html> accessed 6 October 2013.

[139] ESMA website <http://www.esma.europa.eu/page/esma-short> accessed 6 October 2013.

[140] For an overview of ESMA's internal structure, see <http://www.esma.europa.eu/content/ESMA-Organigramme> accessed 6 October 2013. The ESMA's Board of Supervisors is composed of the Chairperson (non-voting), the head of each member state's competent authority for the supervision of financial market participants, and one representative of each of the Commission, the ESRB and the other two ESAs (all non-voting). Decisions of the Board of Supervisors are taken by a simple majority of its voting members, except for measures that have to be adopted by qualified majority vote.

[141] As an independent legal entity, the ESMA acts in the sole interest of the European Union as a whole, taking instructions from no other Union institutions, bodies, member states government, or any other public or private body: Fischer-Appelt (n 114), 25.

[142] Fischer-Appelt (n 114), 25.

[143] Fischer-Appelt (n 114), 25.

[144] Fischer-Appelt (n 114), 30.

[145] Council Regulation (EU) 1095/2010 of 24 November 2010 establishing a European Supervisory Authority (European Securities and Markets Authority), amending Decision No 716/2009/EC and repealing Commission Decision 2009/77/EC [2010] L331/84 (the ESMA Regulation).

[146] Directive 97/9/EC (investment compensation schemes); Directive 98/26/EC (payment and securities settlement); Directive 2001/34/EC (admission to stock exchange listings); Directive 2002/47/EC (financial collateral arrangements); Directive 2003/6/EC (market abuse); Directive 2003/71/EC (Prospectus Directive); Directive 2004/39/EC (markets in financial instruments) (Directive (MiFID)); Directive 2004/109/EC (Transparency Directive); Directive 2009/65/EC (UCITS investment funds); Directive 2006/49/EC (capital

and their amendments; some specifically mentioned in Article 1(2), as well as any future legally binding acts which confer tasks on ESMA.

7.68 The Omnibus Directive[147] 'sets out amendments to several of these directives, as well as directives that are within the remit of the other two ESAs, specifying their respective powers within these directives'. The specific provisions refer to the ESMA Regulation for the appropriate procedures to be followed. Many of the changes delegate to ESMA the power to develop draft regulatory and implementing technical standards, to be adopted by the Commission, where previously the directives delegated such powers in their entirety to the Commission. In addition, the ESMA Regulation provides that ESMA is not limited to issues covered in the legislative instruments specifically referred to, but can go further to consider matters of corporate governance, auditing and financial reporting, provided action is necessary to ensure the effective and consistent application of those acts.[148]

7.69 ESMA's coordination role is not restricted to riding herd on national authorities. Monitoring and assessing systemic risk has now officially become part of a capital markets regulator's role.[149] The Joint Committee of the ESAs serves as a forum in which ESMA cooperates with other ESAs in order to promote cross-sectoral consistency and coherence in the application of EU law amongst supervisors.[150] In particular, ESMA must cooperate closely with the European System of Financial Supervisors (ESFS) in matters relating to financial conglomerates, accounting and the auditing of accounts, prudential matters, retail financial products, measures to combat money-laundering, and the exchange of information.[151]

7.70 Exceptionally, ESMA has been given direct supervisory oversight of credit rating agencies and the new 'trade repositories'. Of the main rating agencies (S&P, Moody's, Fitch, and DBRS), three are US and one Canadian; once registered in the European Union they fall under ESMA's authority. Needless to say, this potential extraterritorial reach, unusual in the EU context, has raised eyebrows. US rating agencies, however, operate internationally and the sector is often accused of oligopoly,[152] controlling 90 per cent of the world market, so it is not surprising they are tripping regulatory triggers where they operate.

7.71 The regulatory dilemmas of credit rating agencies have not garnered much sympathy. They have been the very public scapegoats of the global financial crisis and so political expediency has dictated a high profile response to past failings. The Credit Rating Agency Regulation

---

adequacy of investment firms and credit institutions) (subject to the prudential supervision of the European Banking Authority); recently adopted Directive on Alternative Investment Fund Managers (AIFM); Regulation (EC) No 1060/2009 (credit rating agencies).

[147] Council Directive (EU) 2010/78/EU of 24 November 2010 amending Directives 98/26/EC, 2002/87/EC, 2003/6/EC, 2003/41/EC, 2003/71/EC, 2004/39/EC, 2004/109/EC, 2005/60/EC, 2006/48/EC, 2006/49/EC, and 2009/65/EC in respect of the powers of the European Supervisory Authority (European Banking Authority), the European Supervisory Authority (European Insurance and Occupational Pensions Authority) and the European Supervisory Authority (European Securities and Markets Authority) [2010] L331/120 (the 'Omnibus Directive').

[148] Fischer-Appelt (n 114), 22.

[149] Having been added to the IOSCO Objectives and Principles of Securities Regulation by the 2010 amendments.

[150] Fischer-Appelt (n 114), 24.

[151] Möllers (n 115).

[152] David Gow, 'EU Steps up Attack on Major Credit Ratings Agencies', *The Guardian* (11 November 2011) <http://www.theguardian.com/business/2011/nov/11/eu-prepares-to-regulate-credit-ratings-agencies>.

462/2013[153] attempts to deter 'agency capture' by requiring businesses to rotate their credit rating agencies at least every five years, a technique inspired by experiences with 'auditor capture'[154] and Sarbanes-Oxley in the United States. ESMA can also suspend sovereign ratings in exceptional circumstances, especially where the European Union and the IMF are involved in providing assistance to the country.[155] The direct regulation of credit rating agencies by ESMA is just the beginning, an indication of ESMA's future ambitions to be the SEC of Europe.[156]

More controversially, and again based on experiences during the global financial crisis, **7.72** ESMA can temporarily prohibit or restrict certain financial products or services activities for up to three months. These are crisis powers; there must be a threat to the proper functioning of markets or the stability of the whole or a part of financial system in Europe. The power may only be exercised where specifically contemplated in a particular legislative instrument, for example, that dealing with short selling.

Even in emergency situations, the first objective of ESMA is to facilitate and coordinate **7.73** actions by national authorities, not to intervene directly using coercive powers. Information is essential to the coordination function of ESMA, so national authorities must report to ESMA on developments and invite ESMA to participate as an observer in any relevant meetings. Given the nature of financial crises and the speed at which they may develop, there are fast track procedures, particularly where concerns are shared among the member states. ESMA can act confidentially, providing a recommendation and assessment of the situation to the political arm of the European Union, the Council, which evaluates the situation and decides as appropriate to call a meeting. If the competent authority does not comply, 'ESMA can adopt decisions addressed directly to a financial institution and requiring it to take the necessary action in urgent cases and cases of manifest breach'.[157] To counterbalance this emergency power, the European Council (not the member states) '[may] block ESMA's actions, but only in cases of a significant or material fiscal impact'.[158]

6. A New Regulatory Paradigm in Europe

There may also be the opportunity for the European Union to forge a new regulatory para- **7.74** digm, given the increased focus and the technical expertise which ESMA brings to bear on capital markets issues. The European Parliament has 'emerged as a formidable, and increasingly expert, voice on financial market matters'.[159] Expert and advisory groups abound and the advisory functions supporting European Commission rulemaking and various soft law activities, once the domain of CESR, are intensifying.[160] In theory, the European Union will no longer be beholden to US or international models for its regulatory initiatives. This may lead to the somewhat anomalous situation where the internal EU market succumbs to

---

[153] Council Regulation (EU) 462/2013 of 21 May 2013 amending Regulation (EC) No 1060/2009 on credit rating agencies [2013] L146/1.

[154] Most famously exemplified in the sorry saga of Enron and Arthur Andersen.

[155] After the experiences with S&P and the downgrading of France.

[156] The direct regulation of credit rating agencies by the ESMA may be the prototype of regulation to come.

[157] Fischer-Appelt (n 114), 22.

[158] Fischer-Appelt (n 114), 22.

[159] Fischer-Appelt (n 114), 47.

[160] Fischer-Appelt (n 114), 47.

strong forces of convergence (with less regulatory arbitrage possible), while internationally the European Union forges its own independent path.[161] In any event, the rulemaking will be less vulnerable to blatant political pressures and more 'nuanced'.[162]

7.75 But there is no doubt that within the European Union, the forces of convergence have been unleashed. 'Maximum harmonization' (which precludes member states from imposing additional rules domestically) is the watchword of the day. Directives are being replaced by directly applicable regulations (eg with respect to credit rating agencies, short selling, OTC derivatives, market abuse). The following chart graphically illustrates this trend towards directly applicable regulations, as opposed to directives. Directives too will permit little wiggle room to national authorities, invoking as they will maximum harmonization.[163]

European Union Current Legislative Process

2003–2007	*2012–2013*
MAD (2003) (Market Abuse Directive)	MAR + CRIM-MAD (2014/2015) (Market Abuse Regulation and Criminal Sanctions Market Abuse Directive)
TD (2004) (Transparency Directive)	TD (2013) (Transparency Directive)
MiFID (2007) (Market in Financial Instruments Directive)	MiFIR-II + MiFID-II (2014/2015) (Market in Financial Instruments Regulation and Market in Financial Instruments Directive II)
	CRA-I (2009), CRA-II (2011), CRA-III (2013) (Credit Rating Agency Regulations)
	SSR (2012) (Short Selling Regulation)[164]

7.76 In addition to the impact of the legislative instruments, the new powers of ESMA itself will grind inexorably toward convergence. In the past, supervision and enforcement issues have been left squarely to the member states; supervisory powers at the EU level were the 'Cinderellas',[165] neglected and marginal. No more. ESMA has direct supervisory powers and can overrule national regulators in a number of circumstances.[166] ESMA may prohibit particular products and services across the European Union and supervises cross-border actors where there are systemic risk implications, in addition to its quasi rule-making power with respect to 'binding technical standards'. [167]

7.77 Because of the continuity and speed with which change has been effected,[168] among some European commentators, there is little doubt that ESMA represents the tipping point. More

---

[161] See Posner and Véron, in relation to how Europe is already diverging, not converging: Elliot Posner and Nicolas Véron, 'The EU and Financial Regulation: Power Without Purpose?' (2010) 17 *Journal of European Public Policy* 400, 402.

[162] Moloney (n 78), 61.

[163] After Professor Dr Rüdiger Veil, 'Enforcement Strategies in European Capital Markets', presentation to the London School of Economics, 20 March 2013. In the author's possession.

[164] For a discussion of directly applicable regulations, see Anne-Dominique Merville, (n 116).

[165] Moloney (n 78), 47.

[166] Including breaches of EU law, emergency situations, and where supervisors disagree: Moloney (n 78), 45.

[167] Moloney (n 78), 45.

[168] Due to crisis driven, and perhaps transitory, political consensus.

centralized rulemaking will inevitably follow, at the expense of national authorities whose significance will fade away.[169]

7. Conclusion

ESMA is the first supra-national capital markets regulator, albeit with restricted powers and operating in a well-established institutional framework. The European Union has pioneered regulatory techniques, emulated elsewhere, which balance national sovereignty against the interests of the greater whole. ESMA, as it matures (as it inevitably will), will serve as a model for other supra-national regulatory initiatives. **7.78**

There are dangers though. Maximum harmonization, in the interests of convergence and consistency, can have a 'paralysing effect on the ability of EU legislation to keep up with developments in the financial markets'.[170] Internationally, too, the European Union is also setting up a new dynamic. Third country issuers and intermediaries have benefited from considerable tolerance and deferential treatment in the European Union.[171] However, increasingly the European Union, in rather the fashion of the United States, is purporting to exercise greater extraterritorial reach, for example, with respect to credit rating agencies under the various credit rating regulations and hedge funds under the Alternative Investment Fund Managers Directive.[172] Nevertheless, truly, 'something new is afoot' here.[173] **7.79**

---

[169] Veil (n 163).

[170] Welch and Parker (n 2), para. 4.52: '...[T]here is a high risk that the lack of any rigorous economic analysis of the likely effect of the rules on market participants, coupled with the absence of any post hoc evaluation, will result in a regulatory environment characterized by high costs of compliance, barriers to entry and market and regulatory failures.'

[171] For example, the ability of third country issuers in the 2003 Prospectus Directive to choose which member state in which to be treated as an EU national.

[172] See Welch and Parker (n 2), para 4.55.

[173] Moloney (n 78), 48.

Part III

BEYOND THE TRANSATLANTIC CORRIDOR

8

CHINA AND HONG KONG—COMPETITION AND SYMBIOSIS[*]

1. Introduction

The concept of Chinese capitalism is 'no longer an irony',[1] and the story of Chinese capital markets, the story of the century. The emphasis, of course, is on 'Chinese'; despite the resemblances, these are not markets like any others. Nor are capitalism and capital markets new to China; between 1860 and 1920, encounters between China and European colonial powers introduced that familiar market institution, the stock exchange, to Beijing and Shanghai. During this period, China, like Japan, rolled European institutions and legal frameworks into their traditional cultures as a defensive measure to counter unwarranted European dominance and to permit trade relations. When the communist party prevailed in the civil war, after 1949 these foreign source institutions were suspended. **8.01**

The starting point of modern Chinese capital markets can be identified as 1978,[2] but momentum only gradually developed in the 1990s with the reintroduction of stock exchanges (in Shenzhen on the border with Hong Kong and in Shanghai) and the adoption of, first, companies legislation and then a securities act.[3] As capital markets institutions and practices appeared in China, regulatory frameworks, imported primarily from the United States, the **8.02**

[*] The author would like to thank Lin Yang, Priyanka Nair and Michael Chen (Melbourne Law School), in particular, for their contribution to this chapter.

[1] Chrystia Freeland, 'Chinese Capitalism: Irony Is Gone', *International Herald Tribune* (New York, 29 April 2011) <http://www.nytimes.com/2011/04/29/us/29iht-letter29.html?_r=0> accessed 2 October 2013.

[2] Deng Xiaoping's 'Open Door' Policy announced in December 1978 embarked China on the transformation of its economy. Prior to this, China's major trading partners were the Soviet Union and its satellite states. Deng re-orientated the Chinese economy towards Western technology and investment, opening the door to foreign businesses that wished to establish operations in China. The first stage of this was the creation of four special economic zones in southern China where tax incentives attracted foreign capital and business. Deng also undertook a series of meetings with foreign heads, meeting with US President Jimmy Carter, British Prime Minister Margaret Thatcher, and Singaporean Prime Minister Lee Kuan Yew.

[3] «中华人民共和国公司法» [The Company Law of the People's Republic of China] (People's Republic of China) National People's Congress Standing Committee, 29 December 1993; «中华人民共和国公司法(2005修订)» [The Company Law of the People's Republic of China (2005 Revision)] (People's Republic of China) National People's Congress Standing Committee, Order No 42, 27 October 2005.

«中华人民共和国证券法» [The Securities Law of the People's Republic of China] (People's Republic of China) National People's Congress Standing Committee, 29 December 1998; «中华人民共和国证券法(2005修订)» [The Securities Law of the People's Republic of China (2005 Revision)] (People's Republic of China) National People's Congress Standing Committee, Order No 43, 27 October 2005.

United Kingdom, and Hong Kong,[4] arose around them. Although many of the formal goals and objectives of these regulatory structures sound reassuringly familiar to international ears, it is clear that the economic and legal assumptions underlying this regulation are quite divorced from the reality of Chinese markets.

8.03 One of the secret ingredients to the dynamism of Chinese capital markets has been Hong Kong. This was not a given in 1997 at the time of the handover of Hong Kong to mainland China. Pessimists pointed to the inevitable decline of Hong Kong as a financial powerhouse in face of the inexorable rise of Shanghai. This was to underestimate the astuteness and resilience of Hong Kong.[5]

8.04 By the end of 2012, HKEx was, by some measures, one of the largest exchange groups in the world, riding on the back of flotations by massive Chinese state-owned enterprises.[6] Rather than an all-out competitive model, symbiosis marks the relationship between the mainland Chinese exchanges and HKEx. Shenzhen lies immediately across the border from Hong Kong, seamlessly integrated by rail transportation; it is easy to discern the outlines of a huge metropolis[7] in the making. Equally, the potential for future integration of the Shenzhen Exchange and HKEx is also discernible.[8] Furthering integration, listings of Chinese state-owned enterprises in Hong Kong since 2006[9] are usually accompanied by a listing of domestic only shares[10] in Shenzhen or Shanghai.[11] Hong Kong has been acting as

---

[4] Historically, Chinese company law was strongly influenced by the German legal system. Comparatively modern Chinese company law was introduced by the Guomindang Government in 1929, with strong influences from the German Commercial Code. This is why China has a two-tier board system, with an executive board of directors ('董事会') and the supervisory board ('监事会'). This German inspired company law of China is still in operation in Taiwan today. See Gu Minkang, *Understanding Chinese Company Law* (2nd edn, Hong Kong University Press, 2010); Lawrence J Trautman, 'American Entrepreneur in China: Potholes and Roadblocks on the Silk Road to Prosperity' (2012) 12 *Wake Forest Journal of Business and Intellectual Property Law* 425, 485–6.

[5] And the astuteness of the Chinese government, as well.

[6] As at 14 December 2012, there were 1,543 companies listed on HKEx's securities market with a total market capitalization (Main Board and Growth Enterprise Market) of $21.7 trillion [HKD]. See <http://www.hkex.com.hk/eng/newsconsul/hkexnews/2012/121220news.htm> accessed 6 October 2013.

[7] Hong Kong has a population of over 7 million and Shenzhen over 10 million already in 2012.

[8] In April 2009 the Shenzhen and Hong Kong stock exchanges signed a cooperation agreement, which mirrors that signed in January of the same year between the Hong Kong and Shanghai stock exchanges. Both agreements aim to improve how China's three stock exchanges share information, develop products and train personnel. See Jonathan Cheng, 'Exchanges in Hong Kong, Shenzhen Tighten Links' *Wall Street Journal* (Asia, 9 April 2009) <http://online.wsj.com/article/SB123919232103900981.html> accessed 25 July 2013.

[9] Shares of mainland Chinese enterprises listed in Hong Kong are referred to as 'H-shares' in mainland China. Their issuance and listing must be approved under Chinese law, but they are denominated in Hong Kong dollars and trade the same as other equities on the Hong Kong stock exchange. In 2007, the Chinese government allowed mainland investors for the first time to invest in H-shares.

[10] So-called 'A-shares', discussed in due course. 'A-shares' are specialized shares in the *yuan* currency (*renminbi*) that are traded on the Shanghai and Shenzhen stock exchanges. Chinese government restrictions initially allowed only mainland Chinese to purchase A-shares.

[11] 'China's securities watchdog has relaxed rules for mainland companies seeking overseas listings to help them obtain the financing they need in the face of a large backlog of applications for domestic share sales.... The new guidelines "better accommodate" the financing needs of smaller companies and will take effect next year, the CSRC said.... There are more than 800 companies jammed up waiting for approval for initial public offerings in the [domestic] A-share market, while only 200-odd companies made their debut in China's stock markets this year—compared to the usual 300 or 400 in previous years', said Zhang Qi of Haitong Securities'. 'So there is still huge yet to be satisfied financing demand among Chinese companies', Mr Zhang said. Patti Waldmeir, 'China relaxes rules for overseas IPOs', *Financial Times* (21 December 2012) <http://www.ft.com/intl/cms/s/0/0ec4aa3a-4b55-11e2-887b-00144feab49a.html#axzz2go7n13Xv> accessed 6 October 2013.

the portal for the world, into and out of China; Shanghai will be China's New York, the domestic centre for a mammoth internal market.

2. Chinese Capital Markets

2.1 Overview

Capital markets are not new to China. From the 1860s until the Japanese invasion of China in 1941, Shanghai's stock market listed not only domestic companies but also foreign firms, such as those now known as HSBC and Standard Chartered Bank.[12] In June 1918, the Beijing Stock Exchange opened and became the first stock exchange established by the Chinese.[13] The introduction and development of the Beijing and Shanghai exchanges, however, were very much driven by foreign imperial powers, unlike the case today. An overlapping period, 1912 (the end of the Qing dynasty) and 1949 (the birth of the People's Republic of China, PRC in the aftermath of civil war), saw experimentation with various Europeanized legal systems, both direct imports from abroad as well as indirectly brought in through Japan. Much of this formal legislation was German in origin, and German law continues to this day to be influential in certain substantive areas. However, between 1949 and 1978, these foreign influences were obliterated and the formal, imported, legal system suspended.[14]   **8.05**

By 1978, China was desperate for capital, and with the introduction of the 'open door' policy,[15] as with the opening to trade in the nineteenth century, the desirability of a formal, internationally compatible, legal system was recognized. This was not at all uncontroversial however. Fierce ideological battles raged, for example, over introduction of that powerful symbol of modern capitalism, the company form.[16] A confluence of circumstances finally overcame the resistance and the PRC Company Act appeared in 1994,[17] followed in 1998 by a Securities Act.[18]   **8.06**

Of note, the creation of the Shenzhen and Shanghai Stock Exchanges in 1990 and 1991, preceded both the Company Act and the Securities Act, to say nothing of the regulator-to-be, the China Securities Regulatory Commission (CSRC).[19] This was possible due to the vehicle for economic experimentation created after 1978, the special economic zone (SEZ). Designated as SEZs in 1980 and 1984 respectively,[20] both Shanghai   **8.07**

---

[12] 'The Shanghai Stock Exchange: Re-enter the Dragon', *The Economist* (Hong Kong, 14 August 2008) <http://www.economist.com/node/11921712> accessed 2 October 2013.

[13] China Securities Regulatory Commission, 'China Capital Markets Development Report' (2008).

[14] It continued, however, intact and uninterrupted, in Taiwan.

[15] China's 'Open Door' policy was introduced following Deng Xiaoping's rise to paramount leader status in China at the Third Plenary Session of the 11th Communist Party of China's Central Committee held from 18 December to 22 December 1978.

[16] See discussion in Andrew Xuefeng Qian, 'Riding Two Horses: Corporatizing Enterprises and the Emerging Securities Regulatory Scheme in China' (1993–94) 12 *UCLA Pacific Basin Law Journal* 62.

[17] «中华人民共和国公司法» [The Company Law of the People's Republic of China] (People's Republic of China) National People's Congress Standing Committee, 29 December 1993 (n 3).

[18] «中华人民共和国证券法» [The Securities Law of the People's Republic of China] (People's Republic of China) National People's Congress Standing Committee, 29 December 1998 (n 3).

[19] China Securities Regulatory Commission is the regulator's current name. Prior institutions were the State Council Securities Commission and, before that, the Securities Supervision Office of PBC: 'China Capital Markets Development Report' (n 13), 164.

[20] Yue-man Yeung, Joanna Lee, and Gordon Kee, 'China's Special Economic Zones at 30' (2009) 50 *Eurasian Geography and Economics* 222, 1980 (223); 1984 (225, n 6).

and Shenzhen became laboratories for experimentation in the socialist market economy. Market activities and institutions, such as trading and stock exchanges, could operate under local regulations in controlled conditions within a geographically defined area.[21] If an experiment did not produce the desired results, it could be shut down before it spread to contaminate the rest of the economy. When successful, the local regulations served as the basis for national 'framework laws' applicable throughout China; the local regulations then withered away.[22]

8.08 In early 1992, Deng Xiaoping had set the stage in a speech in Shenzhen in which he stated: 'Securities, stock markets, are they good or evil? Are they dangerous or safe? Are they unique to capitalism or also applicable to socialism? Let's try and see. Let's try for one or two years; if it goes well, we can relax controls; if it goes badly, we can correct or close it. Even if we have to close it, we may do it quickly, or slowly, or partly. What are we afraid of? If we maintain this attitude, then we will not make big mistakes'.[23] Various provisional rules and regulations on different aspects of the capital markets were operating by 1992; a prototype of the current regulator, the CSRC,[24] set up; a 'quota system' controlling access to capital raising put in place; and 'B-shares'[25] introduced. At this time, there were three national securities firms in existence.[26]

8.09 B-shares permitted non-Chinese to participate in the Chinese markets in China, without disrupting the domestic market (where A-shares, in the same enterprises, were traded among Chinese nationals only).[27] B-shares were a 'foreign investor only' class of shares, traded domestically in China on the Shenzhen and Shanghai Stock Exchanges, denominated in RMB but traded in HK or US dollars. In bifurcating the capital structure of many Chinese enterprises and the domestic trading in their shares based on the nationality of the investor, China introduced serious market distortions. The B-share market remained small, illiquid and unattractive to foreign investors. The A-share market, on the other hand, soared, driven by a huge imbalance in supply (artificially constrained by the state) and demand by domestic Chinese investors (suffering from a severe case of 'get rich quickitis').[28] The huge disparities

---

[21] See eg Qian (n 16), and Wei Ge, 'Special Economic Zones and the Opening of the Chinese Economy: Some Lessons for Economic Liberalization' (1999) 27 *World Development* 1267.

[22] The Company Law and the Securities Law were produced by this process.

[23] 'China Capital Markets Development Report' (n 13), 161.

[24] But with much more limited authority than the CSRC.

[25] B-shares were introduced in 1991: 'China Capital Markets Development Report' (n 13), 170.

[26] 'China Capital Markets Development Report' (n 13), 169.

[27] These distinctions between nationals and non-nationals, sometimes referred to as a 'dual economy', are often found in developing economies.

[28] The 'August 10 incident', also known as the '810 incident' illustrated the downside of constraints imposed upon the A-share market, and the degree to which de-centralized regulation effectively enabled behaviour detrimental to the legitimacy of the markets. On 10 August 1992, the Shenzhen Stock Exchange was the setting for violent riots, which occurred as a result of an IPO subscription form shortage. Potential investors had queued for days, but came away empty-handed, due to the irregular handling of subscription forms by PBC officials. In the wake of the riots, the State Council took steps to centralize market regulation, and created the SCSPC and the CSRC, whilst also relieving the PBC of its regulatory function. See Yuwa Wei, 'The Development of the Securities Market and Regulation in China' (2005) 27 *Loyola of Los Angeles International and Comparative Law Review* 479, 489; Benjamin R Tarbutton, 'China: A National Regulatory Framework for the PRC's Stock Markets Begins to Emerge' (1994–95) 24 *Georgia Journal of International and Comparative Law* 411, 420; 'China Capital Markets Development Report' (n 13), 160; Yi-Chen Zhang and Da Yu, 'China's Emerging Securities Market' (1994) *The Columbia Journal of World Business* 112, 119; Carl E Walter and Fraser JT Howie, *Privatising China: The Stock Markets and their Role in Corporate Reform* (John Wiley & Sons, 2003), 30.

in price as between A-shares and B-shares in the same entities further depressed the B-share market, leading to greater illiquidity and a vicious cycle.

Nevertheless, by 1998 a total of US$7.4 billion had been raised in the B-share market from foreign investors.[29] There were 90 securities firms, with 2412 branches. Shares of Chinese companies had been listed in Hong Kong (H-shares), New York (N-shares), London (L-shares) and Singapore (S-shares). The CSRC had broken away from the orbit of the Bank of China, joined IOSCO and consolidated supervisory authority over capital markets. Outside the confines of the SEZs though, so-called 'spontaneous markets' had sprung up in the hinterlands.[30] Everything and anything was trading in these financial souks, in storefronts and back alleys. The markets were running amok and the central government moved to shut them down. The hasty enactment of the Securities Act in 1998 was one measure designed to impose order and oversight on these unruly markets.

8.10

Despite the caution and incrementalism on the part of the Chinese authorities, by the beginning of 2000 the structures of Chinese capital markets were starting to look, from an international perspective at least, a lot like the developed economies; they have continued relentlessly along this trajectory. China joined the WTO and started to adopt international financial standards, such as the OECD Principles of Corporate Governance.[31] The China Securities Depository and Clearing Corporation Ltd had been created, a special securities crime investigation bureau opened, and a Securities Investment Funds Law[32] enacted. Some of this was window-dressing for the international community; the 2002 Code of Corporate Governance, for example, bore close reading despite its assertions of being in conformity with international standards. Other initiatives, however, served to put in place the basic infrastructure (hard and soft) of modern, very modern, capital markets. There was no longer any question of shutting down the experiment. The State Council issued 'Some Opinions on Promoting the Reform, Opening and Steady Growth of Capital Markets' in 2004, and in 2005, both the Securities Act and the Company Act underwent extensive revisions. The Shenzhen Exchange created a small and medium size listing segment, along the lines of AIM in the United Kingdom or GEM in Hong Kong. By 2009 a third board was added to Shenzhen, ChiNext, a Nasdaq-style trading venue for high growth tech companies. Both these boards represent a shift away from the dominance of state-owned enterprises in the public capital markets.

8.11

During this period, attempts were also made to address the inefficiencies resulting from the fragmentation of investor base; in particular, the distortions produced by the bifurcation of traded shares into A-shares and B-shares. In late February 2001, the B-share market was opened up to domestic investors[33] and, in December 2002, to a limited extent, the A-share

8.12

---

[29] 'China Capital Markets Development Report' (n 13), 170.
[30] William T Allen and Han Shen, 'Assessing China's Top-Down Securities Markets' (2011) NBER Working Paper 16713 <http://www.nber.org/papers/w16713> accessed 2 October 2013.
[31] In 2002, the CSRC adopted a Code of Corporate Governance which it stated was in accordance with international standards.
[32] In November 1997, the Provisional Administrative Procedures on Securities Investment Funds was issued: 'China Capital Markets Development Report' (n 13), 165.
[33] The CSRC opened up the B-share market to 'domestic investors with foreign currency' following 19 February 2001: China Securities Regulatory Commission (see Question and Answer section on the CSRC website <http://www.csrc.gov.cn/pub/csrc_en/about/contact/> accessed 22 December 2013). See also 'China Capital Markets Development Report' (n 13), 170; *Privatising China: The Stock Markets and their Role in*

market opened up to foreign institutional investors, or Qualified Foreign Institutional Investors (QFIIs).[34] QFIIs had to be licensed and quotas imposed on their investments, in the aggregate, in the Chinese market.[35] The number of QFIIs had risen to 52 in 2007 and nearly doubled two years later to 94.[36] To put the number of QFIIs, and international institutional investor participation in Chinese markets into perspective, there were 138.9 million securities accounts in existence in China in 2007.[37] The open door was swinging both ways though, with pressure mounting to officially permit mainland Chinese investors to invest outside China. In April 2007,[38] again subject to caps and limitations, certain domestic institutional investors, or Qualified Domestic Institutional Investors (QDIIs), were permitted to trade in Hong Kong, the QDII programme having been launched in May 2006.[39]

8.13 Another factor, however, acted to produce serious market distortions, 'non-tradeable shares'. These were shares held by legal persons and the state; they were not part of the public float, and as their name suggests, did not trade in the public markets. However, the magnitude of the holdings of non-tradeable shares produced an 'overhang' depressing the market value of shares actually trading in the market. At the point where the non-tradeable shares became tradeable, as they eventually did, they would massively dilute existing holders of tradeable shares.[40]

8.14 If integration of investor types was occurring, at the same time, the kind of financial products which could be traded on the public markets was diversifying. Until the reforms to the Company Act, only the most basic of nineteenth-century financial instruments could be created by Chinese entities—essentially common shares, preferred shares and debentures. Such a limited number of financial instruments acted as a severe brake on development of modern diversified financial markets. In 2006, a range of new financial products was authorized: convertible bonds, asset and mortgage backed securities (ABS and MBS), collective investment schemes and warrants. By the standards of modern finance, with the exception

---

Corporate Reform (n 28), 85; Lin Tan et al, 'Herding Behavior in Chinese Stock Markets: An Examination of A and B Shares' (2008) 16 *Pacific-Basin Finance Journal* 61, 62.

[34] 'China Capital Markets Development Report' (n 13), 185. US influences are discernible in this terminology, in its similarity to the Qualified Institutional Buyers (QIBs) under US Rule 144A introduced in 1990.

[35] 'China Capital Markets Development Report' (n 13), 185. See also Samar Maziad and Joong Shik Kang, 'RMB Internationalization: Onshore/Offshore Links' (May 2012) IMF Working Paper No 12/133, Monetary and Capital Markets Department, 14 <http://www.imf.org/external/pubs/cat/longres.aspx?sk=25941.0> accessed 7 August 2013.

[36] CSRC, Chinese Statistical Yearbooks Database (December 2009): the Statistical Table of QFII.

[37] 'China Capital Markets Development Report' (n 13), 180 (2007 figure).

[38] Hong Kong's status as an approved QDII destination dates from 10 April 2007, according to 'Market Snapshot—China: Qualified Domestic Institutional Investors (QDII)' (Austrade, Australian Government, November 2010), <http://www.austrade.gov.au/Invest/Investor-Updates/2010/101223-China-investment-market-snapshots> accessed 8 August 2013.

[39] 'China Capital Markets Development Report' (n 13), 185. The RMB is a non-convertible currency which constitutes a significant barrier to internationalization of Chinese capital markets and participation by mainland Chinese in overseas markets. However, the Chinese authorities began to permit offshore deposits (in Hong Kong at first) of RMB in January 2004, as a step to internationalization of the currency and greater convertibility. See Samar Maziad and Joong Shik Kang, 'RMB Internationalization: Onshore/Offshore Links', IMF Working Paper No 12/133, Monetary and Capital Markets Department (May 2012), 15 <http://www.imf.org/external/pubs/cat/longres.aspx?sk=25941.0> accessed 7 August 2013. See also Paola Subacchi, ' "One Currency, Two Systems": China's Renminbi Strategy', Chatham House Briefing Paper (October 2010) <http://www.chathamhouse.org/publications/papers/view/109498> accessed 7 August 2013.

[40] In the event, this problem was overcome by shareholder approval and compensation, at least from the point of view of the existing shareholders.

of ABS and MBS, these instruments are not at all new and still quite basic. On the other hand, the simplicity of the financial instruments available (as well as non-convertibility of the currency) insulated the Chinese economy from the effects of the global financial crisis.

However, all was not well with Chinese capital markets. They suffered a period of 'market adjustment' between 2001 and 2005.[41] The markets earned, and still carry,[42] the nickname 'Casino China'; a place to put your money and take your chances. Volatile, corrupt, scandal-ridden, rife with insider trading and market manipulation.[43] It was estimated that a shocking 80 to 90 per cent of companies engaging in initial public offerings before 2005 immediately used the proceeds for purposes of market manipulation.[44] The state remained the largest shareholder in corporate China, and the biggest market manipulator of them all.[45] When markets would decline, investors would petition authorities to take action to stop or reverse losses.[46] The state's ability to manipulate the market was also reflected in the CSRC's

8.15

---

[41] Following the 1998 Securities Law, China's capital markets experienced rapid growth; however, problems embedded within the markets, became more serious as they evolved. Exacerbated by systemic and structural limitations, these problems led to a four-year 'period of adjustment' from 2001–05, in which companies encountered problems with re-financing and securing IPOs, securities' firms struggled to remain afloat, and stock indices underwent a sudden decline. It was a period characterized by successive year-end losses across the industry: 'China Capital Markets Development Report' (n 13), 176–7.

[42] Commenting on recent market drops, the *Financial Times* noted that '[f]oreign investors and analysts say that a big part of the problem is that China's stock market operates like a rigged casino, with rampant insider trading and weak corporate governance'. Simon Rabinovitch and Paul J Davies, 'China hits the road to sell its stock market to foreign investors', *Financial Times* (Asia edn, 20 September 2012), 13.

[43] The following examples are indicative of the insider trading and market manipulation characteristic of this period. Although China's criminal law was amended to capture insider trading activities in 1997, for reasons relating to the complicated nature of such cases and a lack of relevant guidelines, the first case was not prosecuted until March 2003; this was the *Shenshen Fang Case*. In this case, Ye Huanbao, chairman of the Shenshen Fang Joint Stock Company (Shenshen Fang), lent CNY 10 million to Gu Jian, director of Saige Shuma Guangchang Co Ltd (Saige Shuma), so that the latter could purchase shares in Shenshen Fang in May 2000. Shortly thereafter, Shenshen Fang publicly disclosed that it had concluded a substantial investment in Saige Shuma, after which Saige Shuma's director, Gu Jian, sold his shares at a considerable profit. Without providing reasons, the Luo Hu District People's Court rejected defence arguments that inside information was not exchanged and that, in any event, the information was in the public domain. Both individuals were sentenced to prison terms and instructed to pay large fines: Hui Huang, *International Securities Markets: Insider Trading Law in China* (Kluwer Law International, 2006), 33–5. In relation to market manipulation, the Yinchuan Intermediate People's Court ordered, in May 2005, that Yin Guangxia pay compensation to its minority shareholders for loss suffered as a result of the company's inflated profit announcements. When it became apparent that the 1999–2000 profit figure of US$89.6 million had been grossly inflated by, inter alia, the fabrication of commercial documents, the company's stock plummeted and its market capitalization suffered accordingly. Minority shareholders were similarly affected by an earlier scheme involving Zhongke Venture (formerly known as Kondarl), in which a majority shareholder and its various accomplices conducted share trades designed to manipulate the company's share price over the period from November 1998 to January 2001. Although the share price rose to a 1,000 per cent high of US$10.15 per share, it fell sharply when the conspirators—who reportedly controlled up to 1,500 securities' accounts at this point—ran out of funds: 'China Capital Markets Development Report' (n 13), 176.

[44] Maria Trombly, 'Chinese IPOs to Return from Yearlong Break', Securities Industry News (5 June 2006), 24.

[45] The Chinese securities' market has been described as a 'policy market', or *Zhengce Shi*, as it is subject to direct intervention by the Government through its administrative policies. Unsurprisingly then, Government policies are often at the centre of market fluctuations. An example of such intervention is illustrated by the Government's use of official newspaper editorials to influence market activities. Hui Huang cites two examples from the *People's Daily* (*Renmin Ribao*): one, a 1996 editorial, in which concern was expressed about the overheated nature of the market, and thereby triggered a dramatic three-day slump in trading; and the other, in 1999, which followed a two-year bear market period, and was directed at stimulating the market: Huang (n 43), 60–1.

[46] In effect, holding the government accountable for market risk.

power to suspend, and then resume, activities on the IPO market; a power repeatedly utilised since the Chinese capital markets were established. Between 1994 and 2008, IPO applications were suspended on seven separate occasions,[47] with the longest suspension occurring over a year in 2005. According to Fang, Shi, and Xu, practice suggests that IPO applications were suspended during periods of recession, and then opened up again when the market became more prosperous.[48]

8.16 Gradual development and reform of the futures market occurred during this time, including periodic attempts to 'clean up' the brokerage profession. In 1993, the futures market was awash with over forty exchanges, and subject to the reckless trading and underhand activities of badly managed brokerage firms. In an attempt to rectify this situation, the State Council endowed the SCSC and CSRC with the responsibility of supervising the markets, and embarked on a process of decreasing and consolidating the various exchanges. This process included punishments meted out to brokerage firms, trading suspensions on various commodities, and the imposition of rigorous controls over the trading activities of state-owned enterprises.[49] Over the course of the next few years, additional reform efforts were made to further improve legal and regulatory frameworks, including the 1999 regulations on brokerage firms, which were accompanied by the suspension or closure of unqualified or illegal firms. In 2000, a national self-regulatory body was established; and from 2003 onwards, the CSRC took further steps to improve risk management and supervision within the futures market. In the following year, guidelines for corporate governance in futures companies were developed (Provisional Regulations on the Administration of Futures Trading); and, in 2006, the China Futures Margin Monitoring Center and the China Financial Futures Exchange were both established.[50] More recently, the tide that lifted all boats has been ebbing. Chinese markets have been falling: 'The Shanghai Composite Index, the country's main stock index, dropped 14 per cent in 2010 and 23 per cent in 2011. It has retreated a further 6 per cent this year'.[51] In part this drop has been attributed to foreign investors shunning Chinese markets. In September 2012, the Shanghai and Shenzhen Exchanges took the unusual step of conducting a 'roadshow' for institutional investors in Japan and the United States 'to drum up interest'.[52]

8.17 Nevertheless, the creation, from scratch, of a sophisticated, ultramodern capital market infrastructure in less than 25 years is astounding. The exchanges are 'state-of-the-art, with fully electronic trading platforms, efficient settlement and clearing systems and all the obvious metrics such as indices, disclosure, real-time price dissemination and corporate notices. The range of information provided on exchange websites is also impressive and completely accurate'.[53] Some of the biggest IPOs in history are now Chinese.[54] When the Bank of China listed a 10.5 per cent stake in Hong Kong, it raised US$9.7 billion; the offering was

---

[47] November 1994, April 1995, June 1995, September 2001, September 2004, June 2005, and September 2008: Junxiong Fang, Haina Shi, and Haoping Xu, 'The Determinants and Consequences of IPOs in a Regulated Economy: Evidence from China' (2012) 22 *Journal of Multinational Financial Management* 131, 149.

[48] Fang, Shi, and Xu (n 47), 135.

[49] 'China Capital Markets Development Report' (n 13), 172–3.

[50] 'China Capital Markets Development Report' (n 13), 183–4.

[51] Davies and Rabinovitch (n 42), 13.

[52] Davies and Rabinovitch (n 42), 13.

[53] Carl E Walter and Fraser J Howie, *Red Capitalism: The Fragile Financial Foundation of China's Extraordinary Rise* (John Wiley & Sons, 2011), 146.

[54] Agricultural Bank of China listed in August 2010 on HKEx and SHSE raising US$22 billion.

oversubscribed 80 times by retail and 20 times by institutional investors.[55] There are 2,490 listed companies on the Shanghai and Shenzhen Stock Exchanges, representing a total market capitalization of RMB24.5 trillion.[56] Including the Hong Kong market (where mainland Chinese entities represent 47 per cent of listed companies, and approximately 57 per cent of market capitalization),[57] by various measures, China now has the second largest equity capital market in the world after New York.[58]

3. Essential Characteristics of Chinese Capital Markets and Their Regulation

3.1 Legal system and regulatory framework

A formal, written, legal system has been gradually reintroduced in China over the last **8.18** 35 years as a means of facilitating international trade and investment. However, for much of this period, commercial activity was fraught by the uncertainty and opacity of the legal consequences. Little formal law and regulation existed, cryptic regional or local pronouncements had to be deciphered, the exercise of administrative discretion was unpredictable and, what in many societies would be considered corruption and conflicts of interest, endemic. International transactions proceeded on the basis of opinions issued by a tiny coterie of local law firms (and a hope and a prayer). There were few legally trained professionals and legal education was in its infancy.

On all fronts, there has been impressive change since the early decades of the 'open door'. **8.19** A great deal of effort has been invested in creating a formal, written, legal system. The national 'basic' or 'framework' laws, of which the Company Law and the Securities Law are examples, reflect astute choices and eclectic adaptation from existing legal systems.[59] German models, both directly and through Japan, had dominated prior to 1949, and although German law continues to exert strong influences on the framework laws, common law concepts and influences are readily apparent, especially in business law areas.[60]

---

[55] David Lague, 'A Hit IPO for Bank of China $9.7 Billion Raised as Investors Ignore Graft and Bad Loans', *International Herald Tribune* (25 May 2006), 1. Bank of China H-shares were listed on 1 June 2006, whilst the A-shares were listed on 5 July 2006: 'Bank of China was Successfully Listed in Hong Kong and Opened a New Chapter in its One-Hundred-Year History', Bank of China <http://www.boc.cn/en/aboutboc/ab7/200809/t20080926_1601843.html> accessed 12 August 2013.

[56] 'Market Overview', *Shanghai Stock Exchange* <http://english.sse.com.cn/> accessed 12 August 2013; 'Market Overview' *Shenzhen Stock Exchange* <http://www.szse.cn/main/en/> accessed 12 August 2013.

[57] Sophie He, 'IPO's Second Wind' *China Daily* (Asia, 21 June 2013) <http://www.chinadailyasia.com/business/2013-06/21/content_15076385.html> accessed 13 August 2013; 'East & Southeast Asia: Hong Kong', *CIA World Factbook* <https://www.cia.gov/library/publications/the-world-factbook/geos/hk.html> accessed 13 August 2013.

[58] Jessie Wong, Len Jui, and Amir Ghandar, 'Accountancy in China: Young Profession, Ancient Civilisation', *In the Black* (2 May 2013) <http://www.itbdigital.com/opinion/2013/05/02/accountancy-in-china-young-profession-ancient-civilisation/> accessed 13 August 2013.

[59] Cally Jordan, 'Comparative Law and International Organisations: Cooperation, Competition and Connections—Lessons from Hong Kong, China and Viet Nam', University of Melbourne Legal Studies Research Paper (20 February 2011), 7–13 <http://ssrn.com/abstract=1755118> accessed 13 August 2013. To appear in L Heckendorf, C Picker, and D Solenik (eds), *Comparative Law and International Organizations: Competition, Cooperation and Connections* (Schulthess, 2013).

[60] Jordan (n 59), 8–9, 11–13.

8.20 During the 1990s, the United States provided virtually the exclusive model for securities legislation to emerging economies, and assiduously cultivated its hegemony. So it is no accident that Chinese securities law and regulation, on the surface, presents a very familiar face to the world. In terms of regulatory philosophy and administrative action, of course, it is very different. Common law influences from the United Kingdom (many via Hong Kong) also appear, primarily in stock exchange structures and concepts of fiduciary duties and corporate governance in the companies law (despite its German structure, demonstrated by dual boards and codetermination principles). The dominance of Anglo-American models in the creation of international financial standards over the last 15 years reinforces these common law influences. Nevertheless, concepts drawn from differing legal systems often rub uneasily together.[61]

8.21 The Securities Law and the Company Law operate at one of five levels in the legal hierarchy, coming under the Constitution. Two other levels are extremely important, administrative regulation issued by the State Council (for example, in the form of 'opinions'). Despite their appellation as opinions, they have very strong normative force and are ignored at your peril. Regulatory agencies such as the CSRC come under the authority of the State Council; CSRC regulations are thus subject to opinions of the State Council.[62] Interestingly, at the bottom of the hierarchy is something quaintly translated as 'self-discipline',[63] of which stock exchange listing rules are given as an example. Obviously, self-discipline refers to the concept of 'self-regulation', a characteristic of traditional stock exchanges which predate formal regulatory structures. It is a tribute to the power and persistence of this characteristic of traditional stock exchanges, now much attenuated in many places in the world, that it has survived in the Chinese climate.

3.1.1 The Company Law 1994—the basic building block of corporate finance

8.22 The first companies law, the Companies Law 1994[64] is a fascinating read, with familiar structures and concepts drawn from both German and English law and, at first glance, some perplexing omissions. The dominant influence is the German public company model, the Aktiengesellschaft or AG, a corporation limited by shares designed for listing and trading. There is the hallmark dual board structure of the German corporation and European-style workers councils. The complex, judicially-created, fiduciary duties of directors, characteristic of English companies law, have been simplified, reduced to their most basic and essential elements.[65] Capital structure is rudimentary but immediately recognisable to any nineteenth-century investor: shares and debentures. On the other hand, there is a very forward-looking statement of corporate social responsibility. Shareholder rights and remedies are virtually nonexistent, out-delawaring Delaware. All is packaged in a European codal format, simple language, statements of general principle, and systematically organized.

---

[61] Jordan (n 59), 10–11.

[62] See eg 'China Capital Markets Development Report' (n 13) for an account of the regulatory roles of the State Council and the CSRC.

[63] See 'China Capital Markets Development Report' (n 13).

[64] Amended in 2005, but retaining the structure and many of the elements of the original statute.

[65] For example, managers were specifically prohibited from accepting bribes and putting company funds in their personal bank accounts.

This legislation is a deliberate construct. As radical as it may have been within China, it is **8.23** meant to look innocuous and comfortingly familiar to non-Chinese eyes. The tipping point leading to its enactment had been the Chinese need to raise capital outside China. To do so, China created a vehicle for listing shares in New York, Hong Kong, and Europe.[66] It is, however, a bit of a wolf in sheep's clothing, with the potential to snap at unwary foreign investors.

Despite its familiar contours, the Chinese Company Law 1994 was designed to play a **8.24** more specialized and quite different role from its German, English or US counterparts. The Company Law 1994 created the vehicle for 'corporatization' of Chinese state-owned enterprises, permitting them to raise capital more easily, especially overseas. A minority shareholding interest would be floated, with an eye to foreign investors if done overseas, with the majority interest remaining safely behind with the state (which explains why minority shareholder protections were conspicuously absent). Management remained more or less in the same hands, so directors duties were relatively undeveloped; it was expected to be business much as usual. The innocuous statement of corporate social responsibility makes reference to promotion of the national interest, which in China, is not empty rhetoric.

The Company Law 1994 indicated a shift in the direction of the ideological winds in China, **8.25** as much as the creation of a new form of business vehicle. At the outset, it was viewed as an interim measure, designed to operate for ten years, no more; the first stage in a longer range strategy.

The Company Law 1994 was also symptomatic of a more deeply rooted dilemma in China. **8.26** With the measured introduction of national framework laws, an unsettled question was the direction in which China should look in terms of inspiration. The German codes of 1900 had long been influential in Asia;[67] China had looked to them early in the twentieth century (through Japan) and a German-style legal tradition had continued uninterrupted in Taiwan after a formal Western-style legal tradition had been abandoned in mainland China in 1949. At the time of enactment of the Company Act 1994, there were still German-speaking academics in China, whose training pre-dated the Revolution. Their numbers, however, were dwindling and the younger generation of scholars was being trained in the English-speaking, common law world, setting up an inevitable tension as to potential influences and models.

The language of legal sources is not a trivial matter. There is no doubt that the enduring **8.27** influence of Roman law throughout the world is linked to the use of Latin as the language of intellectual endeavour for so many centuries in Europe. An argument can certainly be made for English as the new Latin, especially in Asia where it has remarkably rapidly become a *lingua franca*. However, the use of English as a language of legal expression almost inevitably imbues any discourse with the arcanities and assumptions of the common law, consciously or not. And what may start as, effectively, a transliteration may, in fact, result in the infiltration of substantive legal concepts.[68]

---

[66] Qian (n 16), 89–91, 95. Corporatization also involved the sale of shares, in strictly controlled amounts, to domestic Chinese investors.

[67] Japan, Korea, and Taiwan being prime examples.

[68] The author experienced an enlightening example of transliteration implying a shift in legal meaning at a 2004 Sino-Vietnamese workshop on legal reforms. Simultaneous translation of the proceedings, which were conducted in Chinese and Vietnamese, was in English. At one point, a Chinese commentator was discussing the issues involved in preparing a property law for China. Concepts of legal ownership drawn from European civil codes (and ultimately Roman law), had been codified in the General Principles of Civil Law, Articles 72 et seq (1987) in China. The Chinese commentator began by explaining some basic concepts of property

8.28 The scarcity of English language, non-common law source materials was particularly acute in China at the time of enactment of the Company Law 1994. In the intervening years, with the proliferation of online resources and English language commentary by non-common law scholars, this problem is receding. At the same time there is evidence that common law thinking is exerting more direct influences on the legislative process.

3.1.2 The Securities Law 1998—Into the breach of the spontaneous markets

8.29 The Securities Law 1998[69] followed closely on the heels of the Company Law 1994. Like the Company Law 1994, the Securities Law 1998 was national framework legislation, building on the experiments in the SEZs. Unlike the Company Law 1994, however, the Securities Law 1998 was patently modelled on US legislation, primarily the US 1933 Act.[70] This was not surprising; Europe at that time had not developed a comprehensive regulatory approach to capital markets which could be easily emulated.[71] The United States, on the other hand, was an active exporter of its capital markets regulatory regime which it viewed as supporting the hegemony of US interests.[72] For want of an off-the-shelf alternative, US-style securities legislation was popping up all over the world at this time.

8.30 The Securities Law 1998 was enacted in a hurry. Chinese authorities, always haunted by the prospect of losing control of their vast, sprawling economy, were concerned by the explosive rise of the 'spontaneous markets', off exchange trading markets operating in the nether regions of the informal economy. If it could be reduced to writing and potentially represented value, it would trade. Driven by a sense of urgency to bring these markets under formal control, the Chinese authorities enacted the Securities Law 1998.

8.31 The problem was that the US-style Securities Law 1998 was conceptually incompatible with the German-inspired Company Law 1994. However, the urgency of the situation overrode conceptual quibbles and, in a last-minute reconciliation, interpretation of the Securities Law 1998 was made subject to the Company Law 1994 in the case of conflict or ambiguity. In other words, the Germanists prevailed over the Americanists, at least in the short term.

3.1.3 Rethinking corporate and securities law—the amendments of 2005

8.32 Right on schedule, ten years later in 2004, China proposed amendments to the Company Law 1994. This time, though, changes to both the Company Law 1994 and the Securities Law 1998 were considered at the same time, in an effort to produce a more coordinated result.

---

law, the English translation of which was rendered as property rights being like a 'bouquet of flowers', a more poetic expression of the 'bundle of sticks' familiar to any first year common law property student. This use of metaphor, and the transliteration into English, indicates a shift in conceptual thinking, from the civil code to the common law.

   [69] «中华人民共和国证券法» [The Securities Law of the People's Republic of China] (People's Republic of China) National People's Congress Standing Committee, 29 December 1998 (effective 1 July 1999).

   [70] 15 USC §§ 77a et seq (1933).

   [71] The beginnings of that process in Europe would await the Lamfalussy Report of 2001. See the Committee of Wise Men, 'Final Report of the Committee of Wise Men on the Regulation of European Securities Markets' (Brussels, 15 February 2001) ('the Lamfalussy Report') <http://ec.europa.eu/internal_market/securities/docs/lamfalussy/wisemen/final-report-wise-men_en.pdf> accessed 1 August 2013.

   [72] See Edward F Greene and Linda C Quinn, 'Building on the International Convergence of the Global Markets: A Model for Securities Law Reform', SEC Historical Society/US SEC, A Major Issues Conference: Securities Regulation in the Global Internet Economy, Washington DC, 14–15 November 2001. See also Edward F Greene et al, 'Hegemony or Deference: US Disclosure Requirements in the International Capital Markets' (1994–95) 50 *The Business Lawyer* 413.

As for the Company Law 1994, much of the original legislation remained intact, and the underlying German corporate structure was retained. Shareholder rights, largely ignored in the original legislation (the state, after all, was the majority shareholder), made an appearance; the role of the supervisory board was expanded and the board itself given more teeth; attention was paid to related party transactions and the conflicts of interest arising from them; some of the more cumbersome procedural aspects of the 1994 legislation were streamlined and greater attention was paid to limited liability companies, the greenfielding vehicle of choice for private sector initiatives; a new section on the corporate governance of listed companies was added; and greater flexibility worked into the capital structure and some of the older-fashioned mandatory provisions.   **8.33**

The nature of the proposals reflected not only the changing dynamics of the Chinese economy, but also the influences of the international discourse on corporate governance, then as now, heavily dominated by Anglo-American concepts. The resulting legislation is much more obviously 'hybrid' legislation, expressing itself with a decided American accent, for better and for worse.   **8.34**

On its face, the 'Americanization' of the resulting Chinese Company Law 2006[73] may seem no more than what might be expected, demonstrating the proliferation of US corporate law concepts of the time. It might be assumed that China was just a little slow off the mark in assimilating these concepts in 1994, either through unfamiliarity with them or reservations as to their appropriateness at that time.   **8.35**

In any event, some US commentators lauded their inclusion in the revised legislation,[74] as advancing the cause of better corporate governance in particular. A closer look though tells a somewhat different story. On the one hand, some quite potentially effective improvements were made to the operation of the German-style supervisory board, and shareholders, at least formally, were provided with a greater arsenal of rights and protections, all consistent with the overall structure of the legislation and the characteristic Chinese adaption and tweaking of well-known mechanisms.   **8.36**

However, a new, stand-alone 'corporate governance' section[75] was also dropped into the legislation, drawn from the Anglo-American corporate governance discourse and the then recently enacted, and now much maligned, Sarbanes-Oxley Act of 2002 in the United States. This section is more puzzling and problematic. Some of these provisions were simply unnecessary, given the existence of alternative mechanisms of German-style corporate law; others, more perniciously, could conflict with existing provisions or produce confusion; and yet others, while innocuous, were inevitably destined to be ineffective.[76] The 'corporate governance' section of the   **8.37**

---

[73] 《中华人民共和国公司法(2005修订)》 [The Company Law of the People's Republic of China (2005 Revision)] (n 3).

[74] James V Feinerman, 'New Hope for Corporate Governance in China?' (2007) 191 *The China Quarterly* 590. Also available at <http://scholarship.law.georgetown.edu/cgi/viewcontent.cgi?article=1582&context=facpub>.

[75] The Company Law of the People's Republic of China (2005 Revision) (n 3), Ch 4.

[76] For example, 'independent' directors in a two-tier board structure are somewhat anomalous; the role of 'independent' directors is assumed by the supervisory board itself, which by definition is independent from the management board. In fact, the supervisory board has more extensive powers than Anglo-American independent directors. Secondly, the proposal to use independent directors to give opinions on issues such as nomination and remuneration of the board of directors, etc, may appear innocuous. But unlike US corporate law, in the continental European-style company, the shareholders meeting has extensive management control and is the source of all residual power; including the determination of remuneration of directors and supervisors. Equally, the function of a 'company secretary' (of English origin and also found in Hong Kong and Australia, for

revised Company Law 2006 sticks out like a sore thumb. Is it an indication that the Chinese had lost their deft touch in using comparative legal methods, that they were no longer as adept or discerning in their adaptation of foreign legal concepts to domestic purposes?[77] Unlikely. It would appear that the new corporate governance section was deliberately designed to stand out, as a means of signalling to the international community that China had taken into account the burgeoning international discourse on corporate governance. The conventional wisdom of the time was that better corporate governance would increase the attractiveness of capital markets which would exert pressures on entities to improve corporate governance, a tautology that proved very persuasive.[78] That such a discourse, at the time, was framed very much in Anglo-American terms was a bonus; it provided the illusion of the comforts of home to US institutional investors and regulators. But illusion it was.

8.38 The appearance of the corporate governance section in the Chinese Company Law 2006 indicated somewhat cynical, but perfectly rational, gaming on the part of Chinese legislators. In the decade leading up to its enactment, a raft of corporate governance standards and indicia had appeared. Some indicators, such as those appearing in the influential law and finance literature,[79] rapidly became ubiquitous despite their fundamental misunderstanding of the basics of corporate law.[80] These indicia from the law and finance literature, in particular, were picked up by international financial institutions such as The World Bank and the International Finance Corporation which used them as rather blunt instruments to 'rate' countries' corporate governance. The message was unmistakable: introduce misguided investor protection concepts such as cumulative voting into corporate legislation and score higher in the world-wide ratings game.[81] Score higher and attract more foreign investors.

8.39 International standards have propagated much legislative nonsense around the world.[82] In the case of small economies, or those in severe financial distress, inappropriate legislative approaches have been foisted on governments by bilateral and multilateral development agencies pursuing a variety of political and policy objectives. This is not the case with China,

---

example) is usually performed by an internal auditor in European-style corporations; the internal auditor has even more extensive responsibilities than a company secretary. In the 'dead wrong' category, was the introduction of US-style cumulative voting. Cumulative voting is an outdated, cumbersome concept, not extensively used for publicly traded corporations (if they can avoid it), even though it continues to appear in US corporate law statutes. Other more effective mechanisms have been developed in the United States to provide shareholder representation on management bodies; in European model legislation, cumulative voting is simply confusing and inappropriate.

[77] The author, at the request of The World Bank Beijing Office, provided detailed comments, including these, to the drafters of the Company Law 2006.

[78] See Cally Jordan and Mike Lubrano, 'How Effective are Capital Markets in Exerting Governance on Corporations' in Robert E Litan, Michael Pomerleano, and V Sundararajan (eds), *Financial Sector Governance: The Roles of the Public and Private Sectors* (Brookings Institution Press, 2002).

[79] See eg Rafael La Porta et al, 'Law and Finance' (December 1998) 106 *Journal of Political Economy* 1113.

[80] Holger Spamann, '"Law and Finance" Revisited', Harvard Law School John M Olin Center Discussion Paper No 12 (2008) <http://ssrn.com/abstract=1095526> accessed 1 August 2013.

[81] See Curtis J Mihaupt and Katharina Pistor, *Law and Capitalism: What Corporate Crises Reveal About Legal Systems and Economic Development Around the World* (University of Chicago Press, 2008), 248 (note 18) for the authors' reference to a workshop presentation given by a Chinese scholar who stated that, following recent changes, China's new company law had achieved a greatly improved rating on La Porta et al's investor protection index, than the previous law. The authors sensed a slight wistfulness to the scholar's comment that recent updates to the index would result in a ratings downgrade for China's company law.

[82] See Cally Jordan, 'The Dangerous Illusion of International Financial Standards and the Legacy of the Financial Stability Forum' (2011) 12 *San Diego International Law Journal* 333.

which is neither small nor in severe financial distress. Nevertheless, in the Company Law 2006, China chose, to a certain limited extent, to eschew tailored legislative approaches in favour of implementing ineffective international standards. This was a considered decision, and in typically Chinese fashion, taken for particular Chinese reasons. One unfortunate consequence though is validation of inappropriate legislative concepts, as China inevitably serves as a model to other countries in the region.

As for the Securities Law 2006, there is no shift to the American model; that was in fact the **8.40** starting point in 1998. The legislation rolls together, in the simplified, principle-based codal style typical of Chinese framework laws, the corpus of US securities law, institutions and self-regulatory practices, developed over decades. Sometimes it seems that the best US securities legislation exists outside the United States, where the principles have been distilled and systematized. In the Securities Law 2006 are found the rules on issuance of securities, listing, continuous disclosure, prohibited securities issuance, acquisition of listed companies, regulation of exchanges and securities firms, registration of securities and clearing and settlement institutions, securities trading services, securities industry associations, and securities industry regulatory codes. Not all influences are US, of course; as with many legislative efforts, a potpourri of influences can be detected.

The familiarity of the Securities Law 2006 is treacherously deceptive. US securities law is **8.41** responsive to US markets, supported by industry structures and economic theories alien to China. The realities of the Chinese market, its economic and political underpinnings, will inevitably strain and work against the surface of US-style securities legislation. The efficient market hypothesis, so fundamental to modern financial theory and regulation, does not live in China. Sunlight is not considered the best disinfectant.[83] An informed investment decision is one based on inside information.

4. Capital Markets with Chinese Characteristics

4.1 State control

State control, not the efficient market hypothesis, is the fundamental tenet of Chinese securi- **8.42** ties markets.[84] The CSRC, on its very slick website, prominently displays a banner: 'Investor protection is our top priority'. In contradistinction to the United States, the regulatory approach of the CSRC is sometimes referred to as 'merit based' rather than 'disclosure based', a reference to the US regulatory debates of the 1930s. Such a characterization, however, misconstrues the underlying regulatory philosophy in China, where capital markets regulation is viewed as yet another tool of macroeconomic policy in a controlled economy.

---

[83] Justice Louis Brandeis (1856–1941), of the US Supreme Court, writing extra-judicially in a 1913 *Harper's Weekly* article stated: 'Sunlight is said to be the best of disinfectants'. See Louis D Brandeis, 'What Publicity Can Do' *Harper's Weekly* (20 December 1913), 10. The article was subsequently published in a collection of essays as Chapter V, Louis Dembitz Brandeis, *Other People's Money: And How the Bankers Use It* (Frederick A Stokes Co, 1914), 92.

[84] Control from the centre, of a sprawling territory, has been a centuries old preoccupation of Chinese rulers and one of the motivating factors in imposing a uniform written language in China (as well as one time zone). The complexity of the written language also served as a convenient barrier against undesirable foreign infiltration (the teaching of the Chinese language to foreigners having at one time been prohibited).

8.43   Despite, or perhaps because of, the wild and unruly nature of Chinese capital markets, state control is everywhere. There are quotas and caps on both capital raising and investment activity. Companies have always needed approval both as to the timing and amount of capital to be raised, permitting the state to shut down the pipeline of capital raising at a moment's notice (as it did in 2005). The market slows and the state tightens investment supply. In theory,[85] approval is also required for overseas listings by mainland enterprises although dual listings are now encouraged.

8.44   The state can also determine which sectors of the real economy will prosper and when. For example, in 2010 new IPOs in China were dominated by state-owned enterprises in the financial sector, utilities and infrastructure.

8.45   Investor activity is also controlled; quotas apply to the holdings of select QFIIs participating in mainland markets as well as select QDIIs investing overseas. The state, of course, is the biggest investor in China and abroad. The Chinese sovereign wealth fund, the China Investment Corporation, exports Chinese state capitalism abroad, often to a mixed reception. State control continues to operate through the state's majority shareholding in state-owned enterprises. The 'corporatization' of state-owned enterprises rarely involves the sale of a majority stake. Even now, state-owned enterprises dominate listed companies[86] in China; outsiders cannot gain control.[87] So significant are state-owned enterprises in the Chinese capital markets that the OECD, shortly after revising its ubiquitous and influential *Principles of Corporate Governance*,[88] felt compelled to prepare a separate set of *Guidelines on Corporate Governance of State Owned Enterprises*.[89] Chinese markets are not unique in this respect, but state-owned enterprises manifest themselves on the grandest scale in China.

8.46   There are several implications arising from endemic state control. A longstanding complaint among Chinese entrepreneurs is the favouritism exercised to the benefit of large state-owned enterprises in permitting access to capital markets. There has never been a level playing field[90] between the state sector and the private sector. Since the state has been a majority shareholder in the very largest enterprises, minority shareholder protections have been given short shrift. On the other hand, regulatory action can be seen to be majority shareholder (the state) friendly to the point that it would be considered grossly inappropriate market manipulation.[91] While some investors, especially domestic investors, may take comfort in the 'dirigiste' form of market regulation, the unpredictability and speed of regulatory interventions is most off-putting to international investors.

---

[85]   Because there are ways around the permission requirement, such as backdoor listings.

[86]   Organisation for Economic Co-operation and Development, *OECD Economic Surveys: China* (Vol 2010/6, February 2010), 85–6.

[87]   Thus the 'market for control' is inoperative and exercises no disciplinary effect on management as it is purported to do in the United States.

[88]   *OECD Principles of Corporate Governance* (rev edn, 2004).

[89]   *OECD Guidelines on Corporate Governance of State-Owned Enterprises* (2005).

[90]   This is despite a constitutional amendment in 1988 specifically recognizing the legitimacy of private entrepreneurial activity. See Chen Jianfu, 'The Revision of the Constitution in the PRC' (May–June 2004) 53 *China Perspectives* 6–7; see also Kellee S Tsai, 'Adaptive Informal Institutions and Endogenous Institutional Change in China' (2006) 59 *World Politics* 131.

[91]   The prime example being the closure of the IPO market in 2005–06 in an effort to support the market.

4.2 Defining characteristics of the Chinese markets

4.2.1 Volatility, fraud, and market manipulation

Volatility, often attributed to technological advances and high frequency trading, is one of **8.47** the most worrisome concerns in modern capital markets, especially since the 'flash crash' of May 2010.[92] Many of the unsettling incidents long remained unexplained; some are attributed to deliberate market manipulation but others occur in the context of legitimate trading activity and have their origins in a 'fat finger' event.[93] China, though, has decidedly led the pack when it comes to experiences in market volatility but the reasons differ in significance. Some of the factors described are at play in China too. But other factors are significant: the imbalance between supply and demand for investment securities in the domestic market (which led to riots involving thousands of people in 1992); the unpredictability and extent of regulatory interventions; the casino mentality of retail investors who contribute to a large part of market activity. But rampant market manipulation, insider trading and fraud head the list.[94] 'Rat trading'[95] and 'black mouths'[96] are commonly disparaged.

In China, volatility, fraud, and market manipulation go hand in hand. 'Mismanagement' **8.48** (which may be a euphemism) at the intermediaries resulted in the securities firms reforms of 2004 where they were restructured and recapitalized. In addition to the endemic insider trading, listed companies are milked by majority shareholders and related parties as a matter of course.

---

[92] On 6 May 2010, an historical precedent was set when the Dow Jones Industrial Average (DOW) experienced a sudden drop in stock prices over a period lasting almost 30 minutes, which resulted in a decline of 998.5 points, and the coining of a new term—'the Flash Crash'—by the popular media. Although the DOW recovered sufficiently to recoup most of its loss, the event triggered concerns regarding the structural integrity of the US financial markets. In the subsequent hearing convened by the Commodity Futures Trading Commission (CFTC), and the Securities and Exchange Commission (SEC), various stakeholders expressed fears that such an event could easily recur against the backdrop of a marketplace heavily dependent upon computer technology. This concern was not misplaced, particularly in light of the CFTC-SEC report finding that the crash was precipitated by the 'automated execution of a large sell order: David Easley, Marcos M López de Prado, and Maureen O'Hara, 'The Microstructure of the "Flash Crash": Flow Toxicity, Liquidity Crashes, and the Probability of Informed Trading' (Winter 2011) *The Journal of Portfolio Management* 118; Thomas McInish, James Upson, and Robert Wood, 'The Flash Crash: Trading Aggressiveness, Liquidity Supply, and the Impact of Intermarket Sweep Orders' (23 May 2012) <http://ssrn.com/abstract=1629402> accessed 18 August 2013; Andrei Kirilenko et al, 'The Flash Crash: The Impact of High Frequency Trading on an Electronic Market' (26 May 2011) <http://ssrn.com/abstract=1686004> accessed 18 August 2013.

[93] In other words, a simple keyboarding error. One of the biggest occurred on the Shanghai Exchange in August 2013; see 'China Watchdog Embraces Risk After Everbright Fat Finger', *Bloomberg News* (1 October 2013); accessed 5 October 2013.

[94] 'Qiong Min Yuan, or the Hainan Min Yuan Modern Agriculture Development Company Limited, was once the dark horse of China's stock market in 1996, when its share price rocketed 1,059% that year. The company was investigated on charges of false accounting and its shares were suspended from trading on March 1, 1997. The investigation found that US$79 million of its capital surplus, as well as US$68.1 million out of the US$68.7 million in profits as stated in its 1996 annual report, were fictitious': 'China Capital Markets Development Report' (n 13), 175.

[95] Front running.

[96] A form of ramping by commentators who manipulate the markets by talking up companies in which they have taken a stake. The most famous is Wang Jianzhong who between January 2007 and May 2008 'bought shares in 38 companies, wrote reports on them, and then unloaded the stocks after his recommendations helped lift their share prices...In 55 separate transactions during that time, Wang earned 125 million *yuan* ($19.5 million), according to regulators': Jason Subler, 'Special Report: "Rats" and "Black Mouths" Gnaw at China Stocks', *Reuters* (Shanghai, 29 September 2011) <http://www.reuters.com/article/2011/09/29/us-china-stocks-fraud-idUSTRE78S0Z520110929> accessed 2 August 2013.

4.2.2 Products and investors: fragmentation and differentiation

8.49   The course of development of Chinese capital markets has necessarily followed quite a different trajectory from Western markets, although sharing some similarities with other developing economies of the late twentieth and early twenty-first century. The market began with
the introduction of government bonds in 1986; government and central bank bonds continue to dominate the market. The state is a privileged borrower. Unlike in North America,
where bond trading migrated away from formal exchanges to a less transparent, and more
lucrative, over-the-counter market, in China bonds are traded on the exchanges. Despite
the size and appetite of the retail investor market, bonds trade among banks, as a form of
financial institution currency. Despite the conventional wisdom, and urging of international
development agencies, that development of a government bond market is an essential first
step to the development of financial markets, a buy and hold strategy to bond investing,
common to other developing economies, results in a lack of liquidity and the inability of
government bonds to serve as benchmarks.

8.50   Chinese retail investors are notorious savers, partly because there has been nowhere much to
go.[97] Unlike other developing economies though, there is a huge un-slaked appetite among
retail investors for equity investments. The sheer number of retail investors, as opposed to
institutional investors, has produced a dynamic in the market, which combined with the
restrictions on supply and, at least formally, the inability to participate in markets outside
China, unlike any other market. There is no doubt that this dynamic is also an underlying
source of volatility, as uninformed retail investors scramble to position themselves in the
market. Collective investment schemes were introduced in 2006 as a means of addressing
this imbalance, as well as providing a more diverse assortment of investment products.[98]

8.51   The state-imposed fragmentation of capital structure for Chinese companies, based on the
nature of the shareholder or market in which the shares were trading has also been characteristic of Chinese markets, and much criticized for producing severe market distortions.
There have been A-shares and B-shares, H-shares, N-shares, L-shares, S-shares, red chips,
tradeable and non-tradeable, legal person shares (C-shares) and state-owned shares.[99] Some

---

[97]   The property market in China has in recent years absorbed disposable income, leading to concerns about
the creation of a bubble, but without the subprime lending: John Plender, 'Enter the Untethered Chinese Bull',
Financial Times (London, 8 July 2013).

[98]   However, during the global financial crisis, the issuance of recently introduced asset backed securities was
suspended, perhaps out of an excess of caution and fear of contamination.

[99]   A-shares are issued by companies incorporated in mainland China, and are traded on the Shanghai or
Shenzhen stock exchanges (HKEx Equities, 3). Quoted in *renminbi* (RMB), A-shares were initially available
to domestic investors only; however, this condition was relaxed in 2002, and foreign investors (QFII, or 'qualified foreign institutional investors') were permitted to trade in these shares through a quota system (*Financial
Times*). Whilst B-shares are also issued by companies incorporated in mainland China and traded on the mainland stock exchanges, they are traded in foreign currencies, and were originally available to foreign investors
only (HKEx Equities, 3). In 2001, this latter condition was relaxed, and mainland Chinese investors were
permitted to trade in B-shares, on the proviso that they did so through legal foreign currency accounts (HKEx
Equities, 3). In contrast to B-shares, A-shares generally trade in higher volumes, and at higher prices, even when
they are issued by the same company. Despite the limited nature of the B-share market, they are considered an
important avenue for the entry of foreign capital into China's stock market (Huang (n 43), 11–12). The strict definition of shareholder groups in China is also reflected in the sub-classification of A-shares into three subsets: state
shares, legal person shares, and public individual shares. The latter group are tradeable on the stock market, whilst
the remaining categories are classified as 'non-tradeable shares', which means that they can only be transferred
through private takeover agreements (Huang (n 43), 13). Legal person shares and state shares are both issued by
restructured state-owned entities, and differ in the nature of the receiving entity: legal person shares are issued to

of these markets, the shares of Chinese companies listed in New York or N-shares, faded away as Hong Kong (and H-shares) dominated the Chinese market. The tide may be turning though, as the management of Alibaba, one of the hottest new mainland Chinese IPOs, has chafed at Hong Kong's corporate governance requirements. Alibaba has threatened to list in the United States, which has been more accommodating to high technology companies, such as Google and Facebook, whose founders wish to list yet retain control.[100] In other cases (A- and B-shares, tradeable and non-tradeable shares, for example), the distinctions have been eroded in an effort to integrate the share market and increase its efficiency (in the economic sense).

Chinese capital markets may be following their own unique path, but their trajectory will impact markets everywhere.   **8.52**

5. Hong Kong—The Gateway To and From China

5.1 Colonial backwater to commercial powerhouse

There are hardly two more different places, or markets, than Hong Kong and mainland China.   **8.53**
Hong Kong is small and compact, one of the most densely populated territories in the world; however, with a total population of some 7.1 million people,[101] it would barely qualify as a mid-sized city in the immense sprawl of China. Nearly a century-and-a-half of fairly benign British colonial rule left the city and its institutions with a strong English accent. The influx of mainland Chinese refugees, many of them Shanghainese entrepreneurs, after 1949[102]

---

companies, or 'social entities with independent legal status', who are unable to list on a stock exchange (Green (n 72), 229); state shares are issued to 'administrative bureaus' that are also unable to list on a stock exchange (Green (n 72), 236). Hui Huang suggests that the reasons behind this unusual feature of the Chinese system—namely, the division of shares into tradeable and non-tradeable categories—are both political and economic. On the one hand, there is a concern to prevent state assets from 'falling into the hands of individuals'; and, on the other hand, there is a need to protect these assets from 'depreciation and misappropriation' (Huang (n 43), 14). In any event, Huang believes that the distinction between tradeable and non-tradeable shares will gradually disappear (Huang (n 43), 16). Shares are also classified based on the location at which they were listed (Huang (n 43), 16–17). The companies issuing such shares were either incorporated in mainland China, or incorporated outside the mainland, but still subject to control by mainland entities (also known as China-controlled or 'red chip' companies) (HKEx Equities, 3; HKEx Glossary, 1). Examples of these location-based shares include the following: H-shares (listed on the Hong Kong stock exchange, or HKEx); N-shares (listed on the New York Stock Exchange); L-shares (listed on the London Stock Exchange); S-shares (listed on the Singapore stock exchange, or SGX, by companies known as 'S-chips'); and T-shares (listed on the Tokyo Stock Exchange) (Huang (n 43), 16–17; Minkang (n 4), 260; Greene (n 72), 228). Whilst the market capitalization of such shares pales in comparison to the mainland Chinese market, their value lies in, inter alia, the utilization of foreign capital, and the international exposure of Chinese companies (Huang (n 43), 17). See Hong Kong Exchanges and Clearing Limited, 'Equities', HKEx (July 2004) <http://www.hkex.com.hk/eng/prod/secprod/eqty/eqty.htm> accessed 30 August 2013 ('HKEx Equities'); Hong Kong Exchanges and Clearing Ltd, 'Glossary', HKEx <http://www.hkex.com.hk/eng/csm/include/en_glossary.html> accessed 30 August 2013 ('HKEx Glossary'); Financial Times, 'A-Share Definition', *Financial Times Lexicon* (Undated) <http://lexicon.ft.com/Term?term=A_share> accessed 31 August 2013; Stephen Green, 'China's Stockmarket: A Guide to its Progress, Players and Prospects', *The Economist* (2003); Huang (n 43); Minkang (n 4).

[100] Andrew Hill, 'Alibaba's obsession with control will backfire', *Financial Times Business Blog* (25 September 2013) <http://blogs.ft.com/businessblog/2013/09/alibabas-obsession-with-control-will-backfire/> accessed 3 October 2013.

[101] Central Intelligence Agency, 'East & Southeast Asia: Hong Kong', *The World Factbook* (July 2013) <https://www.cia.gov/library/publications/the-world-factbook/geos/hk.html> accessed 10 September 2013.

[102] End of the civil war in China and creation of the People's Republic of China.

dramatically changed Hong Kong. On the one hand, a vast network of public social services was put into place to accommodate the influx; on the other, a very pure flame of nineteenth-century *laissez-faire* liberal economic policy burned brightly. A nimble, somewhat paternalistic, form of entrepreneurialism bubbled everywhere, simmering along in times of economic downturn and raging to a boil during upswings in the economy.

8.54 The relation between colonizer and colonial proved to be a pragmatic, fruitful one in Hong Kong. The British overseas administrators, some of whom were themselves excluded from the inner sanctums of British power by virtue of ethnicity (those able Scots, Welsh, and Irish),[103] worked easily and well with the Hong Kong Chinese. The elites among the Chinese population of Hong Kong sent their children to British universities and professional training where they absorbed British ways, thus reinforcing the basis for productive cross-cultural collaboration.

5.1.1 Legislative framework

8.55 Until the handover in 1997, Hong Kong had been British territory since 1866. Its legislative assembly was not democratically elected and operated under delegated authority, enacting subsidiary legislative instruments called 'ordinances'. British law continued to apply directly in Hong Kong, to the extent necessary to supplement local ordinances, and English 'silks'[104] could step off the boat (or plane) and proceed directly to court. British magistrates administered either local customary law or British/Hong Kong formal law, at the choice of the parties.[105]

8.56 In the interstices, more or less unfettered, commerce thrived. Chinese custom and customary law (in its widest sense) interacted well with British pragmatism and English common law, suffused with commercial customs and practices of its own and well adapted to international spaces.

8.57 With the handover to mainland China in 1997, came the Basic Law, a mainland Chinese statute which serves as the constitution of Hong Kong, based on a division of powers between Hong Kong and Beijing. An operative concept of the Basic Law, sometimes known as the 'through train,'[106] is that the common law legal system, broadly interpreted and as informed by other common law jurisdictions,[107] would continue for 50 years after the handover. There were a few nuances, conveniently put aside in 1997, to the 'through train' concept. The first is that law is dynamic and responsive to changing circumstances; what emerges from the 'through train' in 2047 will, inevitably, look decidedly different from what went on board in 1997. The

---

[103] See generally, Niall Ferguson, *Empire: How Britain Made the Modern World* (Allen Lane, 2003).

[104] Senior barristers who have been conferred with the title of 'Queen's (or King's) counsel' are called 'silks', as by custom, they are entitled to wear silk, rather than wool, robes to court.

[105] For a most informative, and entertaining, description of this dual system, see Austin Coates, *Myself A Mandarin* (Frederick Muller, 1968); in particular, the story of 'The Errant Cow' (Chapter Two).

[106] The metaphor refers to putting the Hong Kong way of life as it existed on 1 July 1997 in a sealed box car that would chug through to 2047, at which time it would be all change.

[107] Article 8. 'The laws previously in force in Hong Kong, that is, the common law, rules of equity, ordinances, subordinate legislation and customary law shall be maintained, except for any that contravene this Law, and subject to any amendment by the legislature of the Hong Kong Special Administrative Region': The Basic Law of the Hong Kong Special Administrative Region of the People's Republic of China 1990, s 1(8) ('Basic Law').

second is that the ultimate interpretation of the Basic Law lies in the hands of the State Council in Beijing, not the Court of Final Appeal in Hong Kong.[108] And, thirdly, integration is the ultimate goal; sooner rather than later might suit Hong Kong better than originally thought.

5.2 The markets and the exchange

Capital markets in Hong Kong date back to the beginning of British colonial rule in 1866. **8.58**
Several exchanges appeared in and following 1891. However, a market crash in 1973 prompted unification of these small exchanges to form one exchange, the precursor to the consolidated group which now includes trading in equities, futures, commodities, and derivatives. Along the lines of the Deutsche Börse and many other exchanges,[109] the business model adopted by HKEx creates a vertical silo which provides clearing and settlement services as well as a trading venue.[110]

As in the United Kingdom, the exchanges predated formal regulation and regulators. The **8.59**
exchanges and their listing rules were central to capital markets activities. For decades, outside the exchanges lay the land of UK professional rule books, market custom and private transactions. There was no regulator[111] until 1 May 1989, when the Securities and Futures Commission (SFC) was established, following a turbulent period that included a four-day suspension of trading (20–23 October 1987) in the wake of the Black Monday global equities' market crash.[112] The call had gone up for reform and oversight.

With its compactness, to say nothing of its 'clubbiness',[113] and the strong presence of British **8.60**
bankers of various sorts,[114] it was easy in the Central District of Hong Kong to envisage a 'City'[115] in the semi-tropics. And so it was. English-style market practices, custom and old school tie relationships meshed very well with the Chinese aversion to formal written legislation and the importance in business of *guanxi*[116] or personal relationships and connections.

---

[108] As was graphically demonstrated in the right of abode case, *Ng Ka Ling*. After 1997, when sovereignty over Hong Kong reverted to the Chinese Government (to become HKSAR), a test case (*Ng Ka Ling*) challenging HKSAR immigration legislation was sent to the HKSAR Court of Final Appeal. The appeals concerned 'natural' children born in mainland China, with HKSAR-resident parents, who were asserting their right of abode in HKSAR under Article 24 of the Basic Law. The *Ng Ka Ling* case represented the Court's first opportunity to exercise its judicial review power under the Basic Law following the 1997 handover. In its ruling, the Court invalidated two of the three limitations upon the right of abode that were contained in the legislation being challenged. Though the Court was careful to emphasise the consistency between its reasoning and the Basic Law, the SCNPC (Standing Committee of the National People's Congress) issued an interpretation of the relevant Basic Law articles that differed from the Court's interpretation, and effectively overturned the Court's decision. The SCNPC's position was that the Court should have sought an interpretation from the SCNPC. Karmen Kam, 'Right of Abode Cases: The Judicial Independence of the Hong Kong Special Administrative Region v. The Sovereignty Interests of China' (2001–02) 27 *Brooklyn Journal of International Law* 611, 618–31.
[109] Bolsa Mexicana, for example. See Ch 10 in this book.
[110] This model is popular with exchanges, for its cost-effectiveness, control, and fee-generating possibilities. On the other hand, it is criticized as being anti-competitive, creating a barrier to entry and high fees to users.
[111] Other than the Companies Registry.
[112] Hong Kong Exchanges and Clearing Ltd, 'A Glimpse of the Past', HKEx (May 2011) <http://www.hkex.com.hk/eng/exchange/corpinfo/history/documents/hkex-01e.pdf> accessed 13 September 2013, 4–5.
[113] The private club has been essential to conducting business in Hong Kong.
[114] 'Failed in London, Try Hong Kong' (or 'FILTH') was the rather disparaging terminology applied to British bankers in Hong Kong.
[115] The 'City' is shorthand for the circumscribed area (the square mile, formerly with walls) of the ancient City of London, known as a trading and financial centre for centuries.
[116] Although English has no equivalent word for *guanxi*, its many translations include 'back-door connection', which refers to the forming of ties for personal gain: Oxford Dictionaries, '关系'(guānxì), *Pocket*

8.61   The creation of a capital markets regulator in 1989, the SFC, introduced a different dynamic into the mix. There was no artificial distinction among financial instruments as in the United States (as between securities and futures) but otherwise the SFC was organized very much along US (or Canadian and Australian)[117] lines. However, it took nearly 15 years to pull together ten disparate legislative instruments into a consolidated Securities and Futures Commission Ordinance of 2003. The SFC has been very internationally focused since its beginnings, bringing in former regulators from around the world. It remains acutely attuned to international trends and initiatives, as an active member of IOSCO, amending its regulatory framework expeditiously to catch the latest wave.[118]

8.62   At least until somewhat discredited in the wake of the global financial crisis, the UK 'regulation lite' approach suited Hong Kong well. The regulatory goal was not to treat Hong Kong markets like a 'Swedish dairy, but simply keep the alligators in the swamp'.[119] Hong Kong was a small, intensely personal, place and the market was local, despite the veneer of internationalism.[120] Prior to the handover, alligator-like tendencies would come to the surface, and public attention, fairly quickly. The feisty Hong Kong press would see to that.

8.63   The exchange then was dominated by a handful of large, Hong Kong family businesses, with well-known scions such as Li Ka-shing at the helm. The mandatory public float for listed companies, at 25 per cent, permitted founding families to retain 75 per cent voting control.[121] Control of publicly traded companies also ultimately remained in a small number of hands through pyramid holdings. Retail investors traded actively, investment decisions driven by the public reputations of the personalities behind the companies.[122] In egregious circumstances, the regulator could step in, using a remedy based on the statutory shareholder oppression remedy of English companies law, to act on behalf of investors.

Oxford Chinese Dictionary (4th edn, Oxford Language Dictionaries Online, 2009) <http://oxfordlanguagedictionaries.com/view/EntryPage.html?sp=/oldo/b-zh-en/csec18654> accessed 13 September 2013. In a business context, Frederik Balfour states that it is 'loosely translated' to mean 'connections', and is essential to business—and personal—transactions conducted in China. He notes that: 'Guanxi goes back thousands of years and is based on traditional values of loyalty, accountability, and obligation—the notion that if somebody does you a favor, you will be expected to repay it one day': Frederik Balfour, 'You Say Guanxi, I Say Schmoozing', *Bloomberg Businessweek Magazine* (18 November 2007) <http://www.businessweek.com/stories/2007-11-18/you-say-guanxi-i-say-schmoozing> accessed 13 September 2013.

[117]   Senior executives were recruited from both Australia and Canada.

[118]   Such as quickly adding systemic risk and financial stability to regulatory goals in the wake of the global financial crisis and the 2010 amendments to the IOSCO Objectives and Principles of Securities Regulation.

[119]   Anecdote recounted to the author in 1995 by Ermanno Pascutto, former SFC executive director.

[120]   Most publicly traded Hong Kong businesses, as well as many private companies, were incorporated offshore, for a variety of reasons. Bermuda was a favourite jurisdiction of incorporation for publicly listed Hong Kong businesses. These offshore incorporations of essentially local businesses (accounting for nearly 80 per cent of listings) gave the Hong Kong Stock Exchange a deceptively international look: Cally Jordan, 'Review of Hong Kong Companies Ordinance', Consultancy Report commissioned by the Legislative Council of the Hong Kong (March 1997) paras 29 and 42, <http://www.legco.gov.hk/database/english/data_fa/fa-review-of-companies-ordinance.htm> accessed 13 September 2013.

[121]   Required to pass special resolutions under Hong Kong companies law (as inherited from UK companies law), essentially overcoming any veto power by minority shareholders for major decision making.

[122]   In a discussion in 1996 on the introduction of more robust protections for minority shareholders in Hong Kong, the author was told by a member of the listing committee of the Hong Kong Stock Exchange and member of a prominent Hong Kong business family, that Hong Kong shareholders didn't require greater minority shareholder protections, because of the nature of their investment decisions. Retail investors in Hong

At the time of the handover, there were several concerns about the future of Hong Kong **8.64** capital markets: interference by Beijing in the functioning of the markets and the rise of Shanghai at the expense of Hong Kong being prime among them. At the time, few would have predicted that the revamped, and revitalized, HKEx would be among the largest exchange groups in the world 15 years later.[123] Beijing was ultimately responsible for this development by funnelling huge state-owned enterprise flotations through the HKEx. In 2010, over 20 per cent of IPO funding in the world was raised in Hong Kong; Hong Kong topped the leagues for the second year in a row (Shenzhen came second and Shanghai fourth).[124]

Dual listings—A-shares for domestic retail investors in China and H-shares for institutional **8.65** investors in the Hong Kong market—are now the norm.[125] Regulatory approvals, in Hong Kong and on the mainland, are coordinated for these dual listings although there is little by way of formal mutual recognition operating in the areas of overlap. As with A- and B-shares, pricing differs, with H-shares usually selling for less and the costs associated with the capital raising in Hong Kong higher. However, since 70 per cent of H-shares are purchased by institutional investors, these are considered the costs of market access. Thus Hong Kong serves as the professional market for China.

The dual listing, A- and H-shares, although addressed to very different investor groups, **8.66** also promotes the integration of the Hong Kong market and mainland markets, in particular Shenzhen (which is only a few subway stops away from Central District in Hong Kong). In 2009, HKEx signed formal agreements for closer cooperation with the SSE and the SZSE, which included a commitment 'towards the common goals of meeting the domestic and international fund-raising needs of Chinese enterprises, and contributing to the greater development of China's economy'.[126] Management of the SZSE and HKEx meet regularly to promote these goals, and trading in cross-border products should not be far behind.

So from a primarily domestic Hong Kong market in the early 1990s, the burgeoning H-share **8.67** market transformed Hong Kong into the capital formation centre for the mainland. But that was just the first step. Then came the offshore RMB market. China is positioning its currency, long locked within mainland pockets, to become a world currency. The barrier to the RMB seeping into the rest of the world is becoming more permeable and Hong Kong is an exit point. Since RMB deposits have been permitted (selectively) in Hong Kong, demand for RMB denominated financial products has skyrocketed. In addition to the dim sum

---

Kong invested in his family's businesses because they trusted the family to run the business well; they would leave decision-making to the family.

[123] As at 14 December 2012, there were 1,543 companies listed on HKEx's securities market with a total market capitalization (Main Board and Growth Enterprise Market) of $21.7 trillion [HKD], <http://www.hkex.com.hk/eng/newsconsul/hkexnews/2012/121220news.htm> accessed 6 October 2013.

[124] Shenzhen came in second at a little over 15 per cent, New York third at over 12 per cent, and Shanghai fourth at under 10 per cent: Ernst & Young, *Global IPO Trends 2011*, 4. In the following year, Hong Kong slipped to third at just under 15 per cent, whilst New York came first with 18 per cent; Shanghai maintained its position at fourth with just under 9 per cent, as did Shenzhen, which came in second at just over 16 per cent: Ernst & Young, *Global IPO Trends 2012*, 5.

[125] See (n 11).

[126] 'A Glimpse of the Past' (n 112), 14.

bond[127] market, HKEx is preparing for the launch of RMB denominated equity and other products.[128]

8.68 Going forward, HKEx plans to be China's full service, one stop, international financial centre by acting as the interface between mainland Chinese markets and participants and international markets and participants.[129] The listing rules are already very adaptable to international issuers, accommodating 'bespoke' issuance. Listing documents must be in English (what the European Union refers to euphemistically in the Prospectus Directive as a language customary in the sphere of international finance).[130] Financials can be prepared in accordance with HK GAAP, IFRS, or US GAAP, for example. The development of Chinese capital markets and their relationship with Hong Kong is an ongoing story, and, no doubt about it, a story of the century.

---

[127] 'Dim sum bonds'—named after the popular Hong Kong cuisine—are issued outside of China, and denominated in the Chinese *yuan*, or *renminbi* (RMB) (*Washington Post*). First sold in 2007 by the China Development Bank, initial sales in dim sum bonds were limited to Chinese and Hong Kong banks; however, they have since been issued by non-Chinese banks and international companies, including McDonald's and Tesco, although these sales comprise a fraction of the market only (*Washington Post; Financial Times*). The entry of dim sum bonds into the international bond market is believed to reflect 'China's interest in promoting its currency in global trade and investment' (*Washington Post*). Demand for dim sum bonds has slowed recently, in part, due to new regulations permitting foreign investors to use the QFII scheme as a vehicle for investment in China's domestic bond market (*South China Morning Post*): Fion Li, '"Dim Sum Bonds" are Fueling China's Currency Rise', *Washington Post* (20 November 2011) <http://www.washingtonpost.com/dim-sum-bonds-are-fueling-chinas-currency-rise/2011/11/15/gIQAML23cN_story.html> accessed 13 September 2013; Michael Stothard, 'Investors Feast on High Yield Dim Sum Bonds', *Financial Times* (1 July 2013) <http://www.cnbc.com/id/100858450> accessed 13 September 2013; Jeanny Yu, 'Dim Sum Bonds Falter as Money Heads Onshore', *South China Morning Post* (8 July 2013) <http://www.scmp.com/business/money/markets-investing/article/1277582/dim-sum-bonds-falter-money-heads-onshore> accessed 13 September 2013.

[128] Yang Qiu Mei, 'RMB Internationalisation and HKEx RMB Strategies', HKEx (28 July 2011) <http://www.hkex.com.hk/eng/newsconsul/speech/2011/Documents/sp110728.pdf> accessed 13 September 2013.

[129] Yang Qiu Mei, (n 128), 11.

[130] Directive 2003/71/EC of the European Parliament and of the Council of 4 November 2003 on the prospectus to be published when securities are offered to the public or admitted to trading and amending Directive 2001/34/EC [2003], Article 19(2)–(4).

9

NICHE MARKETS AND THEIR LESSONS*

1. Introduction

Markets are full of nooks and crannies. Out of the glare of the big economies and their pub- **9.01**
lic exchanges, markets specializing by financial product, activity, or industry thrive, often
attracting little by way of formal regulatory oversight.[1] Industry associations, such as ISDA,[2]
or even membership in a particular social group,[3] have provided the rules of engagement.

These markets may be primarily domestic, centred in the big economies, but are often inher- **9.02**
ently international, operating in blissful (or wilful) oblivion to national regulatory strictures.
These specialized markets are quite resistant to formal regulatory oversight.[4] As interde-
pendence of financial markets, products, and participants grows, though, the operation of
these specialized markets becomes increasingly significant. Until the global financial crisis,
for example, credit default swaps attracted little attention among the general public and

---

* The author would like to thank Sahil Sondhi (Melbourne Law School), in particular, for his assistance
with this chapter.

[1] The specialized weather derivatives market, which allows firms to hedge against variable weather conditions, is one prominent example. Enron was a party to the first weather derivative trade in 1997, and energy
companies continue to be the biggest users of these instruments. Unmindful of the post-financial crisis regulatory imperatives of standardization and exchange-trading, demand for sophisticated, bespoke over-the-counter
weather derivatives is growing 'far more quickly' than in the standardized contract market: 'Weather derivatives: Come rain or shine', *The Economist* (4 February 2012) <http://www.economist.com/node/21546019>.
A specialized 'niche' market is not one that is necessarily systemically trivial: the notional value of the now
infamously-underregulated global credit default swaps (CDS) market reached US$67 trillion in 2008—more
than four times the value of its underlying assets: Lynn A Stout, Jean Helwege, Peter J Walison and Craig
Pirrong 'Regulate OTC Derivatives by Deregulating Them' (2009) 32(3) *Regulation* 30, 33.
[2] ISDA began as the International Swap Dealers Association in 1985 at the time of development of interest
rate and currency swaps, quite revolutionary financial products at the time but which now appear very simple
instruments in hindsight. With the burgeoning markets in derivative products of increasing complexity, ISDA
kept its acronym but changed its name to the International Swaps and Derivatives Association.
[3] For example, the Hassidic Jewish community and the diamond merchant trade in New York City, with its
close ties to diamond markets and merchants in Antwerp.
[4] For example, the industry associations for participants in the Euromarket successfully evaded the regulatory net of the Investment Services Directive in 1992 by beefing up the industry association rulebooks and
arguing persuasively for the 'eurosecurities' exemption tailored to their particular market. They were not so
successful the second time around with the Prospectus Directive in 2003. Equally, the swaps markets in the
United States escaped regulation in the Commodity Futures Modernization Act of 2000. Similarly, a 2008
report by the English and Scottish Law Commissions determined that the centuries-old concept of 'insurable
interest' was inapplicable to CDS. Instead, the regulation of CDS—which in substance essentially resemble
insurance contracts—was deemed better left to the marketplace. See English and Scottish Law Commission,
Insurable Interest, Insurance Contract Law Issues Paper 4, 2008. See also Cally Jordan, 'The Dangerous Illusion
of International Financial Standards and the Legacy of the Financial Stability Forum' (2011) 12 *San Diego
International Law Journal* 333, 337–40.

few people had heard of, much less were concerned with, the way in which LIBOR[5] was calculated.

9.03 But there is another kind of specialized market, one which is geographically and politically determined albeit internationally focused. The jurisdictions in which these markets are situated become known as international financial marketplaces in their own right: Luxembourg, Ireland, Dubai, Bahrain, Malaysia, Singapore, Switzerland, among others. These are some of the world's niche markets.

2. Characteristics of Niche Markets

9.04 With the exception of Malaysia, which may be the outlier in this group, these niche markets are all small,[6] geographically challenged and independently minded countries which, for various geopolitical reasons, have never reaped the economic benefits of expansion and empire.[7] They have had to be resourceful and self-sufficient, and yet at the same time make the most of relationships with a larger hinterland or a former colonial power.

2.1 Advantages in diversity

9.05 Niche markets demonstrate linguistic advantages in their diversity, openness to English, and in the case of Singapore and Malaysia, proficiency in Chinese. Switzerland has four official languages, not including an unofficial fifth, English, and Luxembourg three, again with English as an unofficial fourth. Ireland has two official languages, English being one of them. Singaporeans are educated in English, but the majority of the population is Mandarin-speaking. Equally, Malaysia's national languages are English, Mandarin, and standard Malay. Dubai may only have Arabic as a national language, but English is spoken widely due to the large expatriate communities where it is a first or second language.[8]

9.06 Although possibly resource poor, niche markets are people rich, even if some of the people have been imported. The diversity of languages, official and otherwise, in these niche markets is a proxy for their complexity and adaptability. At the economic and societal level,

---

[5] LIBOR is a collection of interest rates providing a measure of the cost of borrowing between banks. It is based on the rates at which banks lend each other unsecured funds on the London interbank market, and is given daily. LIBOR is determined by excluding the highest and lowest 25% of submissions, and then averaging the middle of the data. It is considered the most important global benchmark for short-term interest rates. In July 2012, regulators revealed that the rate had been manipulated by banks, allowing them to pass on higher borrowing costs, welfare losses and general distortions onto customers and the real economy. The manipulators' motives were varied, and included seeking profits on derivatives trades pegged to base rates as well as artificially lowering their cost of borrowing to appear less risky during the crisis. See Christopher Alessi and Mohammed Aly Sergie, 'Understanding the Libor Scandal', Council on Foreign Relations (5 December 2013) <http://www.cfr.org/united-kingdom/understanding-libor-scandal/p28729#p2>.

[6] As of 2013, Malaysia had a population of approximately 30 million people, followed by Switzerland with 8 million, Singapore with 5 million, Ireland with 4.5 million, Dubai with 2.1 million, and Luxembourg with 0.5 million.

[7] Although, arguably, some may have reaped the benefits of colonization. See eg Niall Ferguson, *Empire: How Britain Made the Modern World* (Penguin Group, 2004).

[8] There are an estimated 100,000 British expatriates in Dubai, the largest group among the non-Asian expatriates many of whom have English as a second language in addition to Urdu, Hindi, Persian, Bengali, Punjabi, Pashto, Malayang, Tamil, etc.

the local community, as diverse as it may be, provides stability,[9] but is also accommodating (if not exactly friendly) to the influx of non-locals who serve local purposes. Immigration, although temporary in many cases, flourishes, resulting in communities demonstrating a functional and almost medieval stratification. Dual, and triple, and more, economies operate. Education is valued, although not necessarily accessible to all, and technology embraced.

In addition to diversity of language and nationality, niche markets show high tolerance for legal pluralism, permitting the co-existence of quite different forms of law and a multiplicity of legal systems. The civil law jostles with the common law, international practices and a modern law merchant thrive;[10] local law and custom persist over centuries, sometimes peeking through colonial overlays. Switzerland excels at comparative law, putting legal concepts from multiple sources to work.[11] Islam and a very traditional form of imported common law can co-exist in Malaysia. A new legal system, providing international services, can be dropped in like a space station (complete with its denizens, the bankers, legal practitioners, and judges), as in Dubai. **9.07**

Niche markets can also engage in legal free-riding. Ireland and Luxembourg draw heavily on the dominant legal systems, common law and civil law, of their larger neighbours. Let London and Berlin do the heavy lifting in terms of developing codes and legislative frameworks, establishing law reform bodies and commissioning reports; the niche markets will continue with or appropriate the best of it and direct their energies to areas of specialization and value-added. They can focus and innovate. **9.08**

Nimbleness and opportunism are hallmarks of niche markets. They must innovate or perish. Tiny Luxembourg, for example, pioneered the first currency swap in 1981 for The World Bank and IBM, paving the way to the new world of derivative products. The Swiss Exchange was the first fully automated exchange in the world. The Stockholm exchange, now part of Nasdaq OMX, was the first exchange in the world to demutualize in 1993.[12] LuxSE had fully internationalized clearing and settlement in the 1960s and is still the leading European supplier of post-trading services in some 96 currencies in 54 markets worldwide. **9.09**

2.2 Niche markets and state capitalism

Niche markets appear in jurisdictions where governments nurture various forms of state capitalism. Macroeconomic policy and public funds support the creation of an international financial infrastructure in niche markets. The markets may be vibrant and dynamic, some if not all of the time, but market forces are subservient to the directing hand of the political masters (or, at the least, government and the market are holding hands). Government is the market's friend. The LuxSE notes the 'close collaboration between government, banks and corporations' in Luxembourg which results in 'efficient' decision-making; transactions will not be slowed down by bureaucracy.[13] **9.10**

---

[9] Bahrain would be a notable recent exception.

[10] See Cally Jordan, 'How International Finance Really Works' (2013) 7 *Law and Financial Markets Review* 256.

[11] For example, the Swiss Civil Code is a masterly combination of legal thinking from various sources and itself a model for other jurisdictions (such as Turkey).

[12] As a point of comparison, the NYSE did not demutualize until 2007.

[13] Luxembourg Stock Exchange, 'The Luxembourg Stock Exchange' <https://www.bourse.lu/luxembourg-stock-exchange> accessed 7 September 2013.

9.11   State-owned enterprises in various guises, advertent and accidental,[14] dot the financial services landscape in niche markets. In a country such as Switzerland, with two,[15] but only two, major international banks, these banks will not fail. In 2011, as the Swiss franc rose to levels threatening the balance and stability of Switzerland's economy, the Swiss National Bank (SNB) capped the currency. Niche market governments intervene. Relatively small local populations controlling the political process[16] facilitate the nimbleness. Despite sometimes large expatriate communities,[17] political decision-making resides in local hands. Political consensus can be achieved, albeit for different reasons in different places.[18]

9.12   Niche market governments are also international investors in their own right. Many, if not all, have sovereign wealth funds of various sorts.[19] Singapore has two, Temasek and GIC, the portfolio value of the former being some S$215 billion in 2013.[20] Malaysia has the Khazanah Nasional Berhad. The Investment Corporation of Dubai is a high profile international investor, sometimes too high profile for its own good.[21] Ireland has its National Pensions Reserve Fund. Even Switzerland may have a *de facto* sovereign wealth fund by virtue of the sizeable foreign reserve funds of the Swiss National Bank.[22] Tiny Luxembourg has no sovereign wealth fund per se, but provides branch office facilities for the others.[23]

---

[14]   During the global financial crisis, governments found themselves in the position of becoming shareholders in their financial institutions. In some jurisdictions the government will have a 'golden share' of some sort providing it with a lever to intervene in decision making. Often used in European economies during privatizations, Singapore and Indonesia, for example, have also created golden shares. On the other hand, it is a point of pride that golden shares have not been used in Switzerland.

[15]   Credit Suisse and UBS.

[16]   Again, Malaysia, with a population of approximately 30 million, is an outlier here.

[17]   In Dubai, approximately 17% of the population is local, with the remainder being expatriates.

[18]   In the case of Ireland, the rising tide of prosperity followed by the bitter consequences of economic failure, has produced political consensus whereas in Singapore and Dubai it is the result of authoritarian political regimes.

[19]   The IMF defines sovereign wealth fund as: 'government owned investment funds set up for a variety of macroeconomic purposes. They are commonly funded by the transfer of foreign exchange assets that are invested long term overseas'. Robert Jenkins, 'Markets Insight: Swiss example questions need for QE unwinding', *Financial Times* (29 May 2013) <http://www.ft.com/intl/cms/s/0/d60a55ea-c774-11e2-be27-00144feab7de. html#axzz2eAm8D1cp> accessed 7 September 2013.

[20]   Its initial value at its formation in 1974 was S$354 million. Temasek, 'Portfolio' <http://www.temasek. com.sg/portfolio/portfolio_highlights> accessed 7 September 2013.

[21]   In 2006, the acquisition by one of its tiered subsidiaries of a British company owning significant portions of American port facilities was scuppered by American legislators. Although the subsidiary, Dubai Ports World, had complied with the appropriate processes and regulatory requirements, the House of Representatives cited national security concerns in voting to block the deal. Twenty-four hours after the vote, the firm decided to sell off its American port holdings. See Kevin W Lu, Gero Verheyen, and Srilal Mohan Perera, *Investing with Confidence: Understanding Political Risk Management in the 21st Century* (World Bank Publications, 2009), 75.

[22]   Jenkins (n 19): 'Viewed as FX reserves, the SNB ranks fifth in the world. Viewed as a sovereign wealth fund, the holdings approximate those of China Investment Corporation. The Financial Times' front page recently reported Beijing's search for a new head of that wealth fund. Will a future edition announce the search for a chief investment officer of a newly created Swiss SWF?', *Financial Times* (29 May 2013).

[23]   Indeed, it is marketed as the 'domicile of choice for the international investment structures of a number of sovereign wealth funds' (Ernst and Young, 'Luxembourg—the gateway for Islamic finance and the Middle East' (February 2013) <http://www.ey.com/Publication/vwLUAssets/Luxembourg_the_gateway_for_Islamic_ finance_and_the_Middle_East/$FILE/Luxembourg-the-gateway-for-Islamic-finance-and-the-Middle-East. pdf>, 4, accessed 15 January 2014. Luxembourg may host sovereign wealth funds, but does not have one itself.

2.3 Niche markets and exchanges

Exchanges are the public face of niche markets; all the niche markets have them, sometimes **9.13**
several. The exchanges have been on the front line of the adaptive process.[24] Technology has
been friendly to niche markets in this respect, creating new opportunities and overcoming,
at least to a certain extent, isolation and the tyranny of distance.

Niche market exchanges have targeted, or been created to serve, international markets; for **9.14**
the most part, their domestic markets are too small to sustain them.[25] The LuxSE, founded
in 1928, is 'resolutely international in outlook',[26] calling itself the 'European exchange for
international securities'. LuxSE hosts issuers from more than 100 countries.[27] The SIX
Swiss Exchange advertizes itself as an 'internationally oriented and potent capital market',
one which is 'more than a trading venue. Our appeal extends far beyond the borders of
Switzerland'.[28] Singapore is the 'Gateway to Asia'. Dubai has created its own international
exchange, 'Nasdaq Dubai', recycling the wealth that is awash in the Gulf region. Malaysia
has positioned itself as the leading jurisdiction for Islamic finance, which potentially appeals
to over a billion adherents around the world.

In terms of financial products, issuers and investors, the niche market exchanges have adopted **9.15**
different strategies. The LuxSE has specialized in Eurobonds and Malaysia in Islamic financial products. Dubai has created an exchange with ambitions of international reach, recyling
wealth from the Gulf region. Ireland has the LuxSE and Luxembourg's fund management
business in its sights. The SIX Swiss Exchange, on the other hand, is a full service exchange,
trading the whole gamut of financial products, either directly or through its subsidiaries
and joint ventures; it is an independent 'reference market' for 'over 40,000 Swiss securities'. [29] The self-identified selling points of SIX Swiss Exchange are its depth (liquidity) and
multi-asset platforms. SIX Swiss Exchange is also known, perhaps somewhat controversially,
as a friendly place for high frequency trading.[30] Trading occurs on the SIX Swiss Exchange
'in a blink', with thousands of orders per blink.[31]

Some niche market exchanges have not been swept up in the current waves of exchange **9.16**
mergers and consolidations.[32] Luxembourg had no interest in joining Euronext when it was

---

[24] Malaysia being the exception to this.
[25] Again, Malaysia may be the outlier here, but given that it is a developing economy, population size alone
may not be sufficient to sustain a vibrant domestic market.
[26] Bourse de Luxembourg, 'A guide to 50 years of Eurobonds in Luxembourg' (12 May 2013), 11.
[27] 'Bourse de Luxembourg' <https://www.bourse.lu/home> accessed 16 January 2014.
[28] SIX Swiss Exchange, 'Welcome at SIX Swiss Exchange' <http://www.six-swiss-exchange.com/profile/
profil_en.html> accessed 7 September 2013.
[29] SIX Swiss Exchange (n 28).
[30] SIX Swiss Exchange sometimes plays down its attractiveness to high frequency traders.
[31] SIX Swiss Exchange, '10,000 orders in 1 blink—on the world's fastest exchange' <http://www.
six-swiss-exchange.com/news/overview_en.html?id=inet_colo> accessed 15 January 2014.
[32] Singapore failed in its attempt to merge with (or takeover, in the eyes of some Australian commentators) the Sydney exchange, the ASX. The Australian government refused to approve the transaction, dealing
Singapore the 'national interest' card; Singapore had to fold its hand. The Australian Treasurer made his decision to block the merger and described it as a 'no-brainer': 'How the ASX-SGX merger failed', *Sydney Morning
Herald* (21 April 2011) <http://www.smh.com.au/business/how-the-asxsgx-merger-failed-20110421-1dqb2.
html> accessed 7 September 2013, saying that ASX 'operates infrastructure that is critically important for the
orderly and stable operation of Australia's capital markets': Chris V Nicholson 'Australia Rejects Exchange
Deal', *The New York Times* (8 April 2011) especially since it is the country's primary equities and derivatives
exchange, as well as its sole clearing house for equities, derivatives, and bonds. He said that 'not having full

formed as a consolidation of the Paris, Brussels, Amsterdam bourses in 2000; this would simply have diluted its brand.[33] SIX Swiss Exchange (formerly SWX) in Zurich and Deutsche Börse in Frankfurt are very friendly, but no formal merger of the two exchanges is contemplated.[34] SIX Swiss Exchange advertizes itself as 'the most important *independent* exchange in Europe' (emphasis added).[35] Other niche market exchanges have looked to consolidations and mergers to survive and reposition themselves in a highly competitive exchange environment. Singapore took a run at Sydney. Bahrain's exchanges (as there are several, in a tiny country) are likely on the hunt for regional partners. Dubai's experiment in creating an international financial centre and an exchange to match, has been fraught; unable to survive on its own, the DIFX was annexed by NASDAQ and there may be further consolidation on the way.

9.17 Even without formal consolidations however, under the surface, alliances and interconnections exist. Until 1 January 2012, the SIX Swiss Exchange and the Deutsche Börse Group each held 50 per cent of EUREX, the world's largest futures and derivatives exchange. They are also partners in a new joint venture, 'Scoach', to provide a trading platform for derivatives products.[36] SIX Swiss Exchange boasts that its trading platform for equities is the fastest in the world;[37] it was developed by the US-Baltic exchange, NASDAQ OMX.[38] Although not formally a part of Euronext, in 2009 Luxembourg entered into a partnership with a Euronext subsidiary to develop trading platforms.[39] The Irish Stock Exchange (ISE) has an alliance

---

regulatory sovereignty over the ASX-SGX holding company would present material risks and supervisory issues impacting on the effective regulation of the ASX's operations, particularly its clearing and settlement functions': Nicholson (n 32). Some sources suggested, however, that one of the Australian Treasurer's primary concerns was the indirect 23% non-voting stake in SGX held by the Singapore government, although this was never stated publicly. See 'How the ASX-SGX merger failed', *Brisbane Times* (11 April 2011).

[33] LuxSE CEO has said that the exchange wishes to remain independent because, '[m]ergers between exchanges will not always bring more efficiency. An exchange facilitates capital formation and this comes from the ground up—from small and medium-sized enterprises—and the best interests of these companies may not always be served in a mega-merger. We believe that we can deliver better as an independent exchange': Bourse de Luxembourg (n 26), 12.

[34] Amongst other arrangements, on 25 October 2006, Deutsche Börse AG and SIX Group AG agreed in a cooperation agreement to combine their business operations in the area of structured products in a European exchange organization under a joint name and trademark (Scoach). This cooperation agreement was adopted by SIX Swiss Exchange AG in place of SIX Group AG on 24 March 2009: Deutsche Borse Group, 'Annual Report 2010' <http://deutsche-boerse.com/dbg/dispatch/en/binary/gdb_content_pool/imported_files/public_files/10_downloads/12_db_annual_reports/2010/10_complete_version/Annual_Report_2010.pdf> accessed 7 September 2013. However, the partnership unravelled in 2013, and SIX Swiss Exchange now operates the SIX Structured Products Exchange, formerly known as Scoach Switzerland.

[35] SIX Swiss Exchange, 'Regulation of short selling as part of self-regulation', Media Release (10 October 2013), 2, emphasis added <http://www.six-group.com/dam/about/downloads/media/media-releases/2013/1010-e-Short-Selling.pdf>.

[36] A response to crisis driven calls to improve transparency and security by moving derivatives trading to exchanges: SIX Swiss Exchange, 'Scoach: Five Eventful Years' <http://www.six-group.com/about/en/shared/news/2012/scoach.html> accessed 7 September 2013. DB, having acquired SIX Swiss Exchange's 50% share, is now the sole owner of Eurex. See Eurex, 'Corporate Structure' <http://www.eurexchange.com/exchange-en/about-us/corporate-overview/organizational-structure/139878/> accessed 7 September 2013.

[37] Matching trades in 37 microseconds: SIX Swiss Exchange, 'From 800 to 37 Microseconds' <http://www.six-group.com/about/en/shared/news/2012/from-800-to-37-microseconds.html> accessed on 7 September 2013.

[38] The second largest US equities exchange, itself a consolidated international exchange, OMX being a consolidation of Nordic exchanges.

[39] The Luxembourg Stock Exchange, 'NYSE Euronext Cooperation' <https://www.bourse.lu/luxembourg-stock-exchange-nyse-euronext> accessed 7 September 2013.

with the Deutsche Börse for trading ISE's equities on the German exchange's Xetra trading platform. Obviously, compatibility of electronic trading platforms permits cooperation and integration of operations across exchanges, irrespective of physical location or the formalities (and political bother) associated with merger or consolidation. One of the selling points for the (failed) merger of Singapore's SGX and Sydney's ASX was the compatibility of their trading platforms, provided by Nasdaq OMX.

Electronic trading is eclipsing traditional exchanges the world over, leaving the exchanges **9.18** scrambling to find new relevancy, new product and service lines and new fee generation opportunities. Niche market exchanges have been at the forefront of these developments, given their proclivity for innovation and adaptability,[40] as well as their scramble to survive in some cases. SIX Swiss Exchange has an integrated vertical silo providing, through subsidiaries, the lucrative ancillary services of clearing and settlement, custody, share registry, payment systems, etc. LuxSE boasts that it has listed the first sukuk in Europe as well as the first French dim sum bond,[41] in addition to being the leading European supplier of post-trading services. LuxSE can settle in 53 currencies in 70 countries around the world.[42]

2.4 Problems associated with niche markets

It is not hard to imagine the problems associated with niche markets. They can be vulner- **9.19** able to change, as well as profiting from it. One misstep, one hesitation to adapt, and the combination of their small size and possible overspecialization can lead to near extinction.[43] Generalized market malaise may manifest itself in an acute form in niche markets. Niche markets tend to prize their reputations, yet small places are susceptible to cronyism and corruption, as Ireland has recently demonstrated.[44]

Niche markets are fiercely competitive, but competitive pressures may also drive such **9.20** markets under.[45] Their tax friendly environments may be attacked by the big economies intent on capturing tax revenues.[46] The tailored regulation and attentiveness to specialized

---

[40] For example, the SIX Swiss Exchange's high-frequency trading services (see n 37) or the former Scoach's platform for securitized OTC derivatives: SIX Swiss Exchange, 'SIX Swiss Exchange message no 17/2013' (15 March 2013) <http://www.six-swiss-exchange.com/swx_messages/online/swx_message_201305151012_en.pdf> accessed 15 January 2014.

[41] The first sukuk on a European exchange, issued by Malaysia Global Sukuk Inc (which is wholly owned by the Malaysian Ministry of Finance) and the first French dim sum bond were issued on 23 August 2002 and 19 September 2011, respectively. See Luxembourge Stock Exchange, 'History' <https://www.bourse.lu/luxembourg-stock-exchange-history> accessed 7 September 2013.

[42] PwC, 'The Luxembourg Stock Exchange—A prime location for Sukuk Listing' (2013), 2; Association of the Luxembourg Fund Industry, 'UCITS' (17 July 2013) <http://www.alfi.lu/setting-luxembourg/ucits> accessed 23 December 2013.

[43] Iceland is a prime example, as is Ireland. Dubai has also struggled in recent years, with a property bubble and potential collapse of Dubai World.

[44] Ireland, again, suffered the humiliation of a banking scandal as it was pulling out of its global financial crisis quagmire. In July 2012, three former Anglo Irish Bank executives were charged with unlawfully aiding a group of investors in buying its shares in 2008, thereby falsely inflating its share price before nationalization. Its CEO, Sean Fitzpatrick, was well known for his political connections, famously playing a round of golf with Ireland's then prime minister Brian Cowen a few months prior to the nationalization. See Linda Saigol and Jamie Smyth, 'The men behind the Anglo Irish Scandal', *Financial Times* (London and Dublin, 25 June 2013).

[45] Singapore and Ireland are two markets which are struggling.

[46] The tax friendliness of Ireland has been a political football in the United States for Google, for example.

market demands may spark allegations of 'race to the bottom' tactics.[47] Niche markets may create opportunities for regulatory arbitrage, frowned upon by other regulatory authorities.[48]

3. Distinctive Features of the Niche Markets

3.1 European niche markets—Luxembourg, Switzerland, and Ireland

9.21 Luxembourg and Switzerland, each for different reasons, are long-established international financial centres.[49] Each is centrally located within Europe, and giving the lie to the law and finance literature,[50] each is firmly within the European civil law tradition. Luxembourg, a country of barely half a million people, benefits from membership in the larger world of the European Union and, as a founding member, is home to EU institutions, the European Court of Justice and the European Investment Bank.[51] See Figure 9.1 (source: Bourse de Luxembourg (n 26), 4).

9.22 Switzerland, too, benefits from the European Union, albeit in a different way: it is not an EU member state, and so not constrained by the EU agenda set in Brussels. It is a careful line which the SIX Swiss Exchange treads, in affirming its commitment to harmonization with its EU neighbours, yet exploiting its differences as a competitive advantage.[52] Switzerland's prized neutrality has made it the home, not to EU institutions, but to international ones.[53]

9.23 Ireland is a latecomer to the European niche markets club, and one with a more troubled recent past. Still, having missed the first mover advantage captured by Luxembourg in the collective investment fund sector, Ireland has made a dramatic comeback and is now the world's fastest growing domicile for this market.

9.24 Tax incentives in all three countries, as in other international financial centres, act as a money magnet, attracting wealth generating industries and their service providers. A high level of creature comforts and good living assist. Luxembourg, Switzerland, and Ireland all provide an accommodating environment to high income asset managers and the clients they serve.

3.1.1 Switzerland

9.25 One of Switzerland's advantages, and one not shared by many niche markets, is its balanced economy, combining manufacturing and services. It has, of course, adroitly exploited its

---

[47] Chris Newlands, '"Lax" Luxembourg defends regulatory regime', *Financial Times* (26 May 2013) <http://www.ft.com/intl/cms/s/0/e0a51ce4-c47f-11e2-9ac0-00144feab7de.html#axzz2eAm8D1cp> accessed 7 September 2013.

[48] The mandate of the new European Securities and Markets authority specifically refers to deterring regulatory arbitrage (ESMA, 'ESMA in Short' <http://www.esma.europa.eu/page/esma-short> accessed 7 September 2013).

[49] Switzerland is the largest, with a population of nearly 9 million people to Luxembourg's 0.5 million.

[50] Which posits that common law systems produce more highly developed financial markets. See Rafael La Porta, Florencio Lopez-de-Silanes, Andrei Shleifer, and Robert W Vishny, 'Law and Finance' (1998) 106 *Journal of Political Economy* 1113.

[51] The European Investment Bank is the leading issuer listing on the Luxembourg exchange. See Figure 9.1.

[52] SIX Swiss Exchange openly avows its interest in harmonization.

[53] A large number of international organizations have based themselves in Switzerland, including a plethora of UN agencies and, most significantly, the Basel Committee on Banking Supervision as well as the more recently created Financial Stability Board.

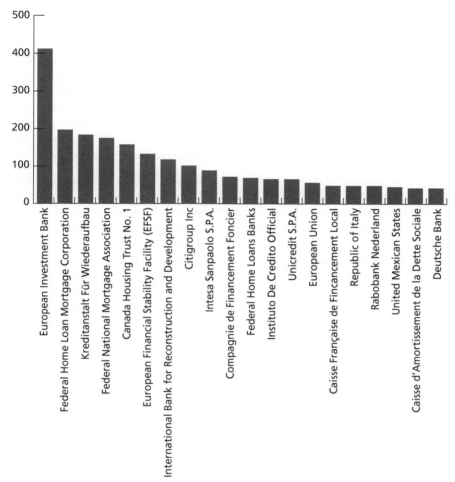

Figure 9.1 Top 20 Issuers by Outstanding Issue Amount in Luxembourg

political neutrality and, over decades, burnished its reputation for financial impeccability and discretion, a task which has lately proved challenging. Switzerland definitely looks outward to the larger international world, but maintains its domestic centre of gravity. Bern is the domestic exchange for Switzerland, whereas SIX Swiss Exchange is the international venue. Unlike LuxSE, which has pursued a successful strategy of specialization, SIX Swiss Exchange is a full service exchange, touting its depth, liquidity, and international outlook. Switzerland has the resources to indulge in the latest technology and has attracted high frequency trading for that reason. But Switzerland treads another fine line here. Providing opportunities for regulatory arbitrage with the European Union, mobilizing technology to attract trading, highlighting its attractive tax regime, all are tempting competitive strategies for Switzerland. The United Kingdom tightens its taxation of high income expatriates, and investment bankers pack their bags for Geneva and Zug. Publicly, though, these possibilities are downplayed. For the Swiss, reputation is all, a lesson which has not been lost on other niche markets.

3.1.2 Luxembourg and Ireland—the great rivalry

9.26 Tiny Luxembourg is home to one of the world's major capital markets, with the LuxSE as the leading European exchange for international bond listing with a market share of 42.1%,[54] and operating in 53 currencies.[55] Also, Luxembourg is a leader in cross-border investment fund activity, the world's second largest investment fund centre after the United States and the world's largest distribution centre for such funds.[56] The LuxSE is home to almost 4,000 collective investment funds, known as UCIs (Undertakings for Collective Investments), collectively managing €2.6 trillion.[57] Luxembourg's UCI industry is home to three-quarters of UCI funds distributed internationally and serves 70 countries.[58]

9.27 The global investment fund industry has traditionally grappled with a complex and fragmented regulatory environment.[59] While the UCITS regime was originally intended to serve the European Union as a single market, it has become the only true global standard in cross-border funds.[60] An increasing number of asset managers are establishing UCITS funds with a strategy for global distribution and Luxembourg is at the forefront of these trends. Luxembourg has been intimately involved in the growth of UCITS as a global brand and owes much of its success as a financial centre to this initiative. Luxembourg benefited from a first mover advantage as the first market to launch a UCITS fund in 1988.[61] Luxembourg was also the first country to implement the UCITS Directive into national law.[62] Moreover, there have been relatively frequent and substantial revisions to the UCITS vehicle and Luxembourg has stayed at the forefront, both by contributing to these changes and by implementing them quickly and efficiently.[63] Today, the country's UCITS funds alone represent 31.2 per cent of European UCI assets,[64] and three-quarters of all UCITS funds distributed internationally.[65]

9.28 The international funds business is the niche Ireland has targeted. The Luxembourg industry association takes pains to downplay the rivalry by saying that Luxembourg's strategy is not aimed at competing with Ireland. In particular, given that currently the unregulated alternative investment funds business must transition to a regulated industry under the Alternative Investment Fund Management Directive (AIFMD) in the European Union, Luxembourg argues that enough new business will be generated for both countries to share.[66] One factor is that AIFMD will force foreign fund houses to establish offices in Europe as it will be easier to comply with the regime from closer proxmity.[67]

---

[54] PwC, 'The Luxembourg Stock Exchange—A prime location for listing' (2012), 3.

[55] PwC (n 54), 2.

[56] Association of the Luxembourg Fund Industry, 'Luxembourg: The Global Fund Centre' (2012–13), 3 <http://www.alfi.lu/sites/alfi.lu/files/Luxembourg-the-global-fund-centre.pdf> accessed 15 January 2014.

[57] Ernst & Young, 'Investment Funds in Luxembourg—A technical guide' (September 2013), 5.

[58] Association of the Luxembourg Fund Industry (n 42).

[59] 'Investment Funds in Luxembourg' (n 57), 8.

[60] Spence Johnson, 'Trends in Cross Border Distribution' (September 2012), 6.

[61] Johnson (n 60), 6.

[62] Association of the Luxembourg Fund Industry (n 56) 11.

[63] Association of the Luxembourg Fund Industry (n 56), 13.

[64] Association of the Luxembourg Fund Industry, 'An Overview of the Luxembourg Fund Industry', PowerPoint Presentation (2012), 2.

[65] Association of the Luxembourg Fund Industry (n 56), 2, 11.

[66] Ellen Kelleher, 'Luxembourg could strike fund gold again', *Financial Times* (3 February 2013).

[67] Kelleher (n 66).

Compared to Luxembourg and Switzerland, Ireland is an upstart as an international finan- **9.29** cial centre. Despite Luxembourg's first mover advantage on UCITS, Ireland was quick off the mark. As a result, between 2000 and 2010 total fund assets domiciled in Ireland grew at an average annual rate of 17 per cent compared with Luxembourg's 10 per cent.[68] Today, Dublin is the world's largest administration centre for hedge fund and alternative managers, with more than 40 per cent of global hedge fund assets being serviced there.[69] And Ireland continues to be the fastest growing UCITS domicile in the world.[70]

In fact, Ireland has been so successful in establishing itself in the financial services industry, **9.30** that it has proven a stabilizing force during turbulent economic times for Ireland. The Irish markets experienced serious and well-publicized difficulties. In part, Ireland was touched by the generalized instability and uncertainty of the Eurozone debt as well as economic difficulties of its own making. But financial services have continued to shine. 'Ireland has been through a very tough period in the past few years; we have grounds to be optimistic now on a number of fronts but in financial services the one constant has been the funds industry. The industry continues to create employment, to showcase our talents and to enhance Ireland's reputation as a place to do business.'[71]

Unlike the United Kingdom, Ireland enthusiastically embraced the European Union, and **9.31** has profited mightily by the relationship. Despite Ireland's choice of investment funds management as its niche putting it on a collision course with Luxembourg, Ireland was remarkably successful in a short period in positioning itself as a fund destination. It created a developed fund infrastructure, enticing participants with low taxes. For example, Ireland's capital gains tax rate fell from 60 per cent in 1985 to 20 per cent in 2001 and its corporate tax rate fell from 50 per cent to 16 per cent in the same years.[72]

The MiFID structure for financial services provided Irish funds with easy access to the rest **9.32** of Europe. However, the crucial EU instruments for Irish purposes have been the UCITS Directives which created a European passport for certain types of securities. Ireland implemented the UCITS Directive early on and has paid close attention to its updating. Finally, Ireland invested in its people, turning an educated and English-speaking population into legions of professionals such as accountants, listing brokers, and lawyers, all of whom form the infrastructure of a financial niche.[73] The result was that funds flocked to set up shop in Ireland; as of 2013, over 12,000 funds are domiciled in Ireland.[74]

Implementing EU directives is one thing; maintaining the regulatory domestic underpin- **9.33** nings is another. EU directives float on top of the domestic legal system, exerting their

---

[68] Marie Lindsay, 'Luxembourg and Ireland remain competitive jurisdictions for UCITS hedge funds', *Hedge Funds Review* (30 September 2011).

[69] David Ricketts, 'Luxembourg's bid for the alternatives', *Financial Times* (2 May 2010).

[70] Matheson, 'Ireland and Luxembourg—a comparison' (30 April 2013) <http://www.matheson.com/images/uploads/publications/Ireland_and_Luxembourg_WEB_May_13.pdf> accessed 15 January 2014.

[71] Mr Michael Noonan, Irish Minister for Finance, 12 June 2013 <http://www.irishfunds.ie/fs/doc/publications/ifia-presentation-tokyo-english.pdf> accessed 23 December 2013.

[72] Marc C Duff, 'Ireland's Economic Progress: on the verge of bankruptcy to economic star of Europe in 5 years' (October 2003), Tax Payers Network, <http://www.taxpayersnetwork.org/_Rainbow/Documents/Irelands%20Economic%20Progress.pdf> accessed 23 December 2013.

[73] Irish Funds Industry Association, 'Why Ireland?' <http://www.irishfunds.ie/why-ireland/> accessed 23 December 2013.

[74] Irish Funds Industry Association (n 73).

harmonizing influences. Ireland, like the United Kingdom and unlike the rest of the European Union, is a common law jurisdiction. For historical and other pragmatic reasons, Irish legislation and institutions very much follow the UK lead. Of late, the United Kingdom has been undergoing great regulatory and institutional change in financial services. Repeated reglatory and institutional overhauls are costly, and potentially disastrous, even in large markets such as the United Kingdom.[75] They are particularly worrisome in small markets such as Ireland, where resources are fewer and the financial system less resilient. In the case of Ireland, it has been the price to pay for dancing to the United Kingdom's legislative and regulatory tune.

3.2 Singapore and Malaysia

9.34 The modern city state of Singapore was born in 1965 when Malaysia and Singapore parted company after a shortlived relationship. The Chinese population, a minority in Malaysia as a whole, formed a majority in the new Singapore. The shared colonial history of Singapore and Malaysia, however, has left behind the legacy of the common law. Although both countries have followed different paths in the ensuing years, both have been able to look to London (although not exclusively to London) to continue to provide the conceptual bases of their financial and legal systems. Within that context, they have forged their own way. A strong form of British colonial law and institutions has persisted in Malaysia, adapted by and adapting to, its Islamic majority population.[76] English law and institutions are also still readily discernible in Singapore, but much influenced by uniquely Singaporean initiatives and idiosyncrasies. Unlike Malaysia, Singapore is more interested in China[77] and Hong Kong, rather than Islam.

3.2.1. Malaysia

9.35 Malaysia is somewhat of an outlier in this discussion of niche markets. It has a relatively large population of 28 million people and a fairly diversified, resource rich economy including a vibrant oil and natural gas industry. Additionally, Malaysia, unlike some of the other niche markets under consideration, would still be considered an emerging economy, although this concept itself is somewhat outdated. Malaysia's particular niche, Islamic finance, also fits somewhat uneasily in the 'niche' category; it is geographically widespread and growing rapidly in importance.

9.36 Nevertheless, Malaysia has adopted, and further developed, niche market strategies. It has recognized the potential which internationalization presents for its domestic economy. The Malaysians are not shy about state capitalism either and the government is an active initiator of economic activity. There is a special offshore financial centre with its own regulator,

---

[75] There were concerns that the regulatory overhauls of the 2008–13 period in London in response to the global financial crises would sow disarray in the markets and permit serious regulatory lapses. However, the dismemberment of the Financial Services Authority into two regulatory bodies, the FCA and the PRA, proceeded fairly smoothly once the direction of regulatory reform had been settled. The cynical might say that was because not much changed, with the FCA picking up, albeit with a more limited jurisdiction, where the FSA left off. Personnel stayed in their offices, the email address may have changed from 'FSA' to 'FCA', but otherwise, everyone carried on.

[76] The process of British colonization usually did not displace local law and custom; the English common law, as introduced, floated on top of it.

[77] Because it is such a direct comparator and traditional rival.

LOFSA, the Labuan Offshore Financial Services Authority. As in other niche markets, Malaysia has created specialized market segments and parallel regulation, similar in general structure, differentiated at the margins, interlinked and generally compatible. Keeping a keen eye on international developments in capital markets, Malaysia has been an early adopter of international financial standards and has assumed a leading role in IOSCO. But the big story in Malaysia, the niche where it has had the greatest impact, is Islamic finance.

Islamic finance   Islamic finance holds about a 1 per cent share of the global market.   **9.37**
However, that represents an industry worth up to US$1.3 trillion and growing nearly 20 per cent annually, sukuk, bonds, being the driving force. Islamic financial institutions are now a global presence, with offices in the major world capitals. Certain characteristics of Islamic finance permitted it to weather well the recent global financial crisis (not to mention the Asian crisis of 1998).[78]

Islamic finance, like Islam itself, is characterized by its diversity, its internal divisions and   **9.38**
disputation centring around its various schools of thought. Nevertheless, two main streams of Islamic finance are usually identified, that of the Middle East (represented by Saudi Arabia, Bahrain, Qatar, and Dubai), and that of Southeast Asia (primarily Malaysia and Indonesia).[79] The conventional view, although somewhat controversial, is that the Southeast Asian version is more flexible when it comes to Sharia compliance, something Malaysia is eager to play down.[80]

Malaysia has taken the lead in Islamic finance in Southeast Asia, although neighbouring   **9.39**
Indonesia, with the largest Islamic population in the world, has positioned itself as a contender.[81] Malaysia though is still the undisputed leader, having one of the most developed Islamic financial systems in the world, as well as the largest trading market in Islamic bonds, the sukuk.[82] Malaysia dominates the global sukuk market, having issued three-quarters of global issuance in 2012 after having issued the world's first sovereign sukuk in 2002.[83] These are remarkable achievements for a country of less than 30 million people, 60 per cent of whom are Muslim. Neighbouring Indonesia, with the world's largest Muslim society—80 per cent of a population of 240 million people—only has 4 per cent of its banking assets in Sharia compliance.[84]

Islamic capital markets are 'ideally characterized by the absence of interest based transac-   **9.40**
tion, doubtful transactions and stocks of companies dealing in unlawful activities or items'. Capital markets are 'one of the [most] important and growing segments in Islamic Finance'.[85] The future is bright for Malaysia and Islamic finance; projections for financial sector growth

---

[78] Jon Gorvett, 'Which Way Forward for Islamic Finance?' (July 2012) *Middle East* 35.
[79] Gorvett (n 78).
[80] Gorvett, (n 78).
[81] Kevin Brown, 'Malaysia: Ahead of the game in local contest', *Financial Times* (12 May 2010).
[82] 'Banking on the ummah: Malaysia leads the charge in Islamic finance', *The Economist* (5 January 2013).
[83] 'Banking on the ummah' (n 82).
[84] 'Banking on the ummah' (n 82).
[85] Wan Razazila Wan Abdullah, Jamal Roudaki, and Murray Clark, 'The Evolution of the Malaysian Islamic Capital Market: Towards a Global Hub', from the AFAANZ Global Conference (2010) <http://www.victoria. ac.nz/sacl/about/events/past-events2/past-conferences/6ahic/publications/6AHIC-75_FINAL_paper.pdf> accessed 4 February 2013, 1, citing SO Alhabshi, 'Development of Capital Market Under Islamic Principles', Paper presented at the Conference on Managing and Implementing Interest Free Banking/Islamic Financial System (1994).

run at 'a buoyant pace by 8–11% per annum', expanding its share of Malaysia's GDP, 'from 2.4 times to 3 times by 2020'.[86]

9.41 **Malaysian capital markets and their preeminence in Islamic finance** The preeminence of Malaysian capital markets in Islamic finance has largely been attributed to 'state nurturing'.[87] Through state leadership and backing, Islamic finance in Malaysia increased to 22 per cent of the country's banking sector in 2011, up from 6 per cent in 2001.[88] Impressive government policy making and planning appear in the *Financial Sector Blueprint of 2011–2020* and the *Economic Transformation Programme*.[89] Malaysia is now beginning to open up its Islamic finance sector to large Islamic banking conglomerates, as well as to multi-national, and even western, Sharia-compliant, banking institutions.

9.42 Currently, the conventional (ie non-Islamic) and Islamic components of capital markets in Malaysia function side by side, with similar regulatory schemes for each. Additional sets of requirements are layered over the conventional finance infrastructure 'to ensure the Islamic products and services are Sharia-compliant'.[90] The Shariah Advisory Council, made up of both financial and Sharia experts, makes the call on compliance, centralizing the process and obviating the need for institution by institution review processes as exist elsewhere. Islamic financial and banking products now dominate the domestic Malaysian market. 'Sharia-compliant securities amounted to RM1.16 trillion at the end of 2011, accounting for 54.4 per cent of the entire capital market. Of the securities listed on Bursa Malaysia Securities, 89 per cent are deemed to be Sharia-compliant. Malaysia is the biggest sukuk market in the world, with RM349.0 billion in outstanding ringgit-denominated sukuk as at the end of 2011, accounting for approximately two-thirds of global sukuk outstanding.'[91]

9.43 In fact, the conventional and Islamic markets are so linked, and have worked so well in parallel, that the International Monetary Fund (IMF) 'does not distinguish between conventional and Islamic markets with respect to expectations or standards'[92] in its assessment methodology. The IMF has also found that, although there are 'some areas where enhancements are advisable', the Securities Commission of Malaysia, 'as the supervisor of the capital markets, has developed a robust supervisory framework that exhibits high levels of implementation of the…IOSCO Principles…in most areas. The regimes governing the regulation of issuers, auditors, collective investment schemes, market intermediaries and secondary markets, and with respect to enforcement, co-operation and information sharing, are extensive'.[93] The IMF's assessment reaffirms the maturity and extensiveness of Malaysia's Islamic capital market at the policy level, concluding that Malaysia is now a leader both in the Islamic financial sector and in the global securities market as a whole.

---

[86] PwC, 'Getting the Picture: Malaysia's Financial Sector Blueprint, Strengthening our Future 2011–2020' (February 2012) <http://www.pwc.com/en_MY/my/assets/publications/fsb-msia_1march2012.pdf> accessed 12 September 2013.

[87] Gorvett (n 78).

[88] Gorvett (n 78).

[89] PwC (n 86).

[90] International Monetary Fund, 'Malaysia: Publication of Financial Sector Assessment Program Documentation—Detailed Assessment of Implementation of IOSCO Objectives and Principles of Securities Regulation' (IMF Country Report No 13/59/, 2013), 15.

[91] International Monetary Fund (n 90).

[92] International Monetary Fund (n 90).

[93] International Monetary Fund (n 90), 6.

Promoting Islamic finance as its niche has proved to be a brilliant strategy for Malaysia. **9.44** Tapping into a neglected but truly international market has invigorated Malaysia's domestic markets, as well as bringing it recognition as a leader internationally. Malaysia identified the factors impeding the growth of Islamic finance such as the lack of standardized products, the costly procedures associated with structuring them, the absence of Islamic specific regulatory and accounting frameworks. Malaysia then proceeded to draw upon techniques developed in the conventional international capital markets to address these problems.

There is an increasingly robust international institutional framework for standard-setting **9.45** which serves to address the problems stemming from lack of standardization. Inspired by the International Accounting Standards Board (IASB), the Accounting and Auditing Organization for Islamic Financial Institutions (AAOIFI) was established in Bahrain by Islamic financial institutions in 1991.[94] AAOIFI regularly issues accounting, auditing, and governance standards for Islamic financial institutions as well as Sharia standards. Thus the AAOIFI aims to achieve harmonization and convergence in the concepts and application among the Sharia supervisory boards of individual Islamic financial institutions so as to avoid contradiction or inconsistency between the *fatwas* and applications by these institutions.[95] Malaysia is a prime proponent of AAOIFI; 'the universe of Islamic finance contracts applied in the Malaysian Islamic finance sector embraces all opinions of the AAOIFI'.[96]

Another international body, the Islamic Financial Services Board (IFSB), somewhat analo- **9.46** gous to IOSCO, is an 'international standard setting body of regulatory and supervisory agencies'[97] and its objective is to promote the 'development of a prudent and transparent Islamic financial services industry through introducing new, or adapting existing, international standards consistent with Sharia principles'.[98] Malaysia established the IFSB, situated in Kuala Lumpur, by national legislation, the Islamic Financial Services Board Act 2002. The IFSB has nearly 200 members, in 39 jurisdictions,[99] including central banks, international multilateral institutions such as the IMF, The World Bank and Bank for International Settlements, and financial institutions.[100]

Malaysia was also one of the founding members of the International Islamic Financial **9.47** Market (IIFM), another international Islamic finance standard setter, a 'standard setting organization focused on the Islamic capital and money market segment of the industry'.[101] IIFM, in a manner similar to that of ISDA (the industry association for the international swaps and derivatives markets), focuses on standardizing Islamic financial products, documentation and related processes.

---

[94] Nicholas HD Foster, 'Islamic Finance Law as an Emergent Legal System' (2007) 21 *Arab Law Quaterly* 170, 179
[95] Foster (n 94), 179.
[96] Kabir Hassan and Michael Mahlknecht, *Islamic Capital Markets: Products and Strategies* (Wiley Finance Series, 2011), 325.
[97] See the IFSB website: <http://www.ifsb.org/background.php> accessed 23 December 2013.
[98] See the IFSB website (n 97).
[99] Oxford Analytica comment, 'Islamic Finance Moves Towards Common Standards', *Forbes* (9 March 2010) <http://www.forbes.com/2010/03/08/islam-finance-sharia-business-oxford-analytica.html> accessed 23 December 2013.
[100] Foster (n 94), 179.
[101] See IIFM website <http://www.iifm.net> accessed 23 December 2013.

9.48 Finally, the Shariah Advisory Council (SAC) of Bank Negara Malaysia, the country's central bank, acts as the highest Sharia authority for Islamic finance in Malaysia and is responsible for both determining Islamic law for the purposes of Islamic finance and for validating all Islamic finance products to ensure their compatibility with Sharia principles.[102] Indeed, 'the Shariah standards of the Shariah Advisory Council of Malaysia incorporate all the Shariah interpretations of the AAOIFI'.[103] Thus, Malaysia's intimate role in the international standard-setting of Islamic finance has been pivotal to its success in becoming the world's centre for Islamic finance. Other initiatives by the Malaysian government have helped the country to carve out this niche. Two institutions set up by Bank Negara Malaysia are of particular importance. First, the International Centre for Education in Islamic Finance (INCEIF), established in 2005, is the world's leading university for Islamic finance drawing its students from 80 countries. Within the INCEIF is the International Sharia Research Academy where scholars formulate an international rule-book for Islamic finance.[104] Secondly, the Islamic Banking and Finance Institute of Malaysia (IBFIM) assists financial institutions in becoming Sharia-compliant through consulting services and certification in Islamic finance.[105]

9.49 Social and political factors, prompted by economic disparities along ethnic lines, played a role in government-led initiatives to establish Islamic finance in Malaysia.[106] IOSCO has identified other triggers: 'two main reasons that have been identified to support the emergence of the Malaysian Islamic Capital Market are the 1997 Asian Financial Crisis and the liquidity problem resulting from surplus funds from the Islamic finance industry'.[107] The Malaysian government acted to deter future financial upheavals.[108] Malaysia began to pay close attention to its regulatory framework and its markets. Incentives promoted the development of both the Islamic financial sector and the regulators.[109] This was state capitalism, but one well attuned to the markets and supported by a strong form of common law and institutions. Building on conventional finance, tweaking and adapting it to Islamic principles and the characteristics of the market were fundamental. In particular, Malaysia recognized the international nature of Islamic finance and drew on international experience. And, importantly, there was a nascent market; it just needed a little watering.

---

[102] See SAC website <http://www.bnm.gov.my/index.php?ch=7&pg=715&ac=802> accessed 23 December 2013.

[103] Hassan and Mahlknecht (n 96), 325.

[104] 'Banking on the ummah' (n 82).

[105] 'Banking on the ummah' (n 82).

[106] Wan Abdullah, Roudaki, and Clark (n 85), 27. 'Initiatives taken by the Malaysian government towards a global hub are substantial. Every perspective, such as product innovation, infrastructure facilities, policy incentives, human capital development, liberalisation and regulatory framework are being well focused. All parties either the regulatory bodies or the market players are involved to ensure the achievement of an international hub for an Islamic Capital Market.'

[107] Wan Abdullah, Roudaki, and Clark (n 85), 1.

[108] Although strongly criticized at the time of the Asian financial crisis for imposing exchange controls, Malaysia's intervention in the market was subsequently vindicated.

[109] '[T]he scope of jurisdiction for these regulating bodies encompasses both Islamic and conventional finance matters. Malaysia's banking and insurance sectors come under the jurisdiction of the Central Bank, Bank Negara Malaysia (BNM) while the capital market is regulated by the Securities Commission Malaysia (SC). Matters related to offshore finance industry are regulated by the Labuan Offshore Financial Services Authority (LOFSA)': Wan Abdullah, Roudaki, and Clark (n 85), 2

3.2.2 Singapore

Singapore, the Lion City, fits the niche market profile in terms of size, geographic location **9.50** (a hinterland rich in opportunity), openness to trade and commerce, richness of human resources, and ease of implementing government-led market and regulatory initiatives. For Singapore, the problem has been finding the niche. Granted, Singapore is Asia's largest overseas market for Asian equity futures (focusing on China, India, and Japan). With the advent of real estate investment trusts (REITs) in 2002 and business trust structures in 2004, the Singapore exchange, SGX, has also established itself as the Asia-Pacific region's largest exchange for REITs.[110] But Malaysia has outmanoeuvered Singapore by commandeering Islamic finance. And despite the recent appearance in Singapore of Rmb-denominated 'lion bonds'[111] and 'S-chips',[112] Hong Kong has secured its own position as the gateway to China.

Looking to London, Singapore sees itself as a primarily international trading venue with a **9.51** focus on foreign listings. Already, 40 per cent of the approximately 800 listed companies in Singapore are non-domestic, more than half of which are from outside China. However, this may disguise a more fundamental problem with the market. Singaporeans themselves are not particularly interested in equity investing; they prefer to punt on property. In looking for growth, Singapore has targeted the regional Asian markets with the ambition of becoming the 'gateway to Asia' (ex-China and ex-Japan) for Europe. However, other Asian markets, in countries like Indonesia or Vietnam, are becoming feisty in their own right. And Singapore recently suffered an embarassing setback in a growth by acquisition strategy, when the Australian government scuppered a friendly merger with the ASX in Sydney.

Singapore has many niche market advantages nevertheless: its strategic geographic posi- **9.52** tion between Asia and Europe (coupled with an orchid-filled airport); a strong tradition of common law and English-style financial institutions; an English educated, majority Mandarin-speaking population; a plethora of financial and legal advisers; tax incentives for both individuals and businesses; a political system which can respond quickly and directly to change; and an intolerance for corruption.

Increasingly, Singapore has become a playground for the rich, the Switzerland of Asia.[113] Let **9.53** Hong Kong handle the massive flotations for the Chinese state-owned enterprises; when it comes time to stash away the profits, Singapore is eager and waiting. Singapore strives to be a hub; economic, legal, scientific, artistic. It is a player and, consequently, for anyone looking to do business in Asia, Singapore is a serious contender. With a top tax bracket of 15 per cent, the wealth managers have poured in together with the wealthy, the hedge funds and the multinationals. Singapore therefore strives to remain as stable, low-cost and efficient as possible.[114]

---

[110] Shirlene Tsui, 'SGX—A prescription for growth', *Wall Street Journal* (New York, 14 March 2011) <http://blogs.wsj.com/exchange/2011/03/14/sgx-a-prescription-for-growth/> accessed 12 September 2013.

[111] Bonds denominated in renminbi, mainland Chinese currency.

[112] S-chips are mainland Chinese companies with securities listed on the Singapore Stock Exchange (SGX). The problem with S-chip companies has been their inferior quality, leading to delisting or being placed on a watch list by the SGX.

[113] The attractions are secure property rights, political stability, independence, and centrality in ASEAN, the region set to become the world's largest economic region.

[114] However, fostering a dual economy always runs the risk of local backlash against the expatriate community. In 2012, the *Straits Times*, Singapore's main newspaper, ran a few articles questioning the need for so many expatriates, lamenting the lack of high paying and quality jobs for Singaporeans and the increasing cost

9.54 **Development of Singapore's capital market** The story of capital markets regulation in Singapore begins in 1973 with the passage of the Securities Industry Act[115] which created the Stock Exchange of Singapore (SES, a predecessor to the current SGX) and the Securities Industry Council (SIC). In the English tradition, at that time, the SES was largely self-regulatory.[116]

9.55 In 1985, the 'Pan-El Crisis' profoundly shook both the Singaporean and Malaysian markets. Pan-Electric was a Singapore-listed company with 71 subsidiaries and a market capitalization of approximately $200 million. When Pan-Electric unexpectedly went into receivership both the Singapore and Malaysian stock markets had to shut down. Singapore responded with a new Securities Industry Act in 1986 and progressively adjusted its financial regulatory framework in the period leading up to the Asian financial crisis of 1997.[117] The calibration continued apace as the Asian financial crisis subsided, culminating in the current Securities and Futures Act of 2002 (the SFA).[118]

9.56 The regulatory framework and institutions in Singapore demonstrate a strong British imprint, of the older variety. The central bank, the Monetary Authority of Singapore (MAS), has ultimate oversight of financial markets while the exchange, the SGX, does the heavy lifting, operating as a self-regulatory organization.

> Under the present regulatory scheme, the Monetary Authority of Singapore ('MAS') supervises the securities industry.[119] It has less oversight of an exchange's disciplinary procedures and rule changes. The day to day supervision of the market is still left with the SGX. The internal management of the SGX is regulated by its Memorandum and Articles of Association. Trading in securities is regulated by the SGX Rules. The criteria for listing and the obligations of listed companies are found in the SGX Listing Manual.[120]

9.57 MAS is a powerful, centralized regulator,[121] specifically charged with maintaining Singapore as a sound and reputable financial centre. A separate, and equally important, mandate is to promote Signapore as an international financial centre.[122] In addition to administering financial legislation and creating a supporting regulatory framework, MAS has a number of other instruments in its regulatory arsenal, both coercive and persuasive. Directions, which 'detail specific instructions to financial institutions or other specified persons to ensure

---

of living. Additionally, there was a public outcry when a mainland Chinese ran his Ferrari through a taxi, killing all involved.

[115] Securities Industry Act 1973 (No 17 of 1973).

[116] Walter Woon, 'Regulation of the Securities Industry in Singapore' (1994) 4 *Pacific Rim Law and Policy Journal* 731.

[117] Professor Hans Tjio and Rachel Eng, *Corporate Finance and Securities Regulation* (Singapore Academy of Law Ed, 2012), para 17.1.2.

[118] Securities and Futures Act 2002 (Ch 289) (2002).

[119] Within the MAS, the Financial Supervision Department looks after capital markets regulation as one of its three units, the two others being Banking and Insurance and Policy, Risk and Surveillance. The Capital Markets unit handles enforcement, markets and infrastructure supervision as well as policy matters. The Policy, Risk and Surveillance unit conducts economic surveillance and develops 'prudential policy'. MAS thus operates as an integrated financial services regulator. Monetary Authority Singapore, 'Monetary Authority Singapore Organizational Chart' (2013), <http://www.mas.gov.sg/about-mas/overview-of-mas/organisation-chart.aspx> accessed 12 September 2013.

[120] Tijo and Eng (n 117), para 17.1.2.

[121] Monetary Authority of Singapore Act (Ch 186) (1999).

[122] Monetary Authority of Singapore Act (Ch 186) (1999), s 4(2)(d).

compliance', permit MAS to attach criminal sanctions. MAS also sets out 'principles or "best practice standards" that govern the conduct of specified institutions or persons' which do not create civil or criminal liability but which assist MAS in its risk assessments. Very much in keeping with English tradition, Singapore also makes use of 'voluntary codes', the Takeover Code,[123] a Code on Collective Investment Schemes,[124] and a Code of Conduct for Credit Rating Agencies.[125] Because they are non-statutory, these codes rely on reputational forces for their traction.[126] A breach of a code obligation may result in a private tap on the wrist by MAS or public naming and shaming. In addition, there are also an assortment of practice notes, circulars and policy statements, none with coercive effect, but useful for informational purposes given the cryptic nature of the legislative instruments. Again, in the English tradition, the Securities Industry Council (SIC), first created in 1973 and composed of bankers, legal experts, MAS staff and other industry experts, advises the Minister for Finance. In addition, the SIC administers the Takeovers Code.

The Singapore Exchange (SGX)   Singapore is best known in world capital markets for its **9.58** exchange. The Singapore Exchange (SGX) was established in December 1999 as an investment holding company after consolidating former exchange companies, namely the Stock Exchange of Singapore, the Singapore International Monetary Exchange and Securities Clearing and Computer Services. SGX offers securities, fixed income, derivatives, and commodities products as well as a suite of services including clearance, settlement and depository, and over-the-counter clearing for oil swaps and forward freight agreements. These are supported by a robust technical infrastructure for market data and access.

As in London prior to the creation of the Financial Services Authority (FSA) in 2000, the **9.59** stock exchange is a front line regulator in Singapore, albeit under the watchful eye of the MAS. As with other modern, demutualized exchanges, SGX is a company limited by shares and has adopted a variety of regulatory approaches,[127] combining the disclosure based regulation of the United States with the risk based targeting pioneered by the FSA in London. With its ambitions to be an international trading venue, the SGX pays attention to international standards and best practices, but always tailored to idiosyncratic Singaporean ways.

Exchanges worldwide are an endangered species, looking for new ways to survive; SGX is no **9.60** exception. On 1 May 2013, SGX began a restructuring process.[128] The proposed merger of the SGX with the ASX in Sydney was another high profile survival strategy, but one which met with failure. SGX, in headlong competition with Hong Kong, was looking for growth potential. Singapore and Hong Kong—two of the region's financial hubs—have been trying to

---

[123] Code on Take-Overs and Mergers (Monetary Authority of Singapore Ed, 2012).
[124] Code on Collective Investment Schemes (Monetary Authority of Singapore Ed, 2011).
[125] Code of Conduct for Credit Rating Agencies (Monetary Authority of Singapore Ed, 2012).
[126] Reputational forces can be quite powerful in a small place.
[127] Singapore Exchange, SGX, 'Regulatory Approach, Philosophy and Guiding Principles' (2013).
[128] Its operations were divided into five business units: Derivatives, Listings, Market Data and Access, Post-Trade, and Securities. SGX said in a statement that these units, 'with the support of the sales and client unit, will collectively drive the expansion of the products and services suite, the attraction of more and larger listings, the growth of retail and professional participation, and the building of the post-trade business'. Jakes Thomases, 'SGX faces a resignation and a restructuring', *Waters Technology* (28 March 2012) <http://www.waterstechnology.com/sell-side-technology/news/2164385/sgx-resignation-restructuring> accessed 12 Septermber 2013.

'outmaneuver one another in pursuit of new listings and investor cash'.[129] The two economies are competitive, open, and approximately the same size. And yet, SGX is a fraction of the size of its Hong Kong counterpart, raising only one-ninth the amount of capital, offering one-third the amount of liquidity and trading less than one-fifth on average per day.[130] This competitive state of affairs propelled SGX to seek growth via the mergers and acquisitions route.

9.61 It is within this context that SGX's proposed US$8.3 billion cash-and-shares offer for ASX was announced in October 2010,[131] under the slogan 'Asia Pacific—the heart of global growth'.[132] ASX-SGX Ltd, to be listed on both the Australian and Singaporean exchanges, would have been the fifth largest exchange group in the world, offering access to 2,700 listed companies from 20 countries—including over 900 resource firms and the largest number of real estate investment trusts and exchange-trade funds[133]—and boasting a combined market capitalization of US$12.3 billion.[134] It would also have been the second-largest in the Asia-Pacific region by market value (after Hong Kong) and second in the Asia-Pacific by number of listings (after India).[135]

9.62 From the Singaporean perspective, this was a tempting prospect. For numerous reasons, SGX and the ASX were widely regarded as highly compatible exchanges for the purposes of a merger. Economically, the Asia-Pacific region is growing and there is increasing competition to provide the most liquid portfolio of financial products.[136] Both exchanges are powered by Nasdaq OMX's Genium INET trading technology permitting creation of a single, multi-asset platform with a single access point in the region, reducing trading costs and increasing technical efficiencies.[137] Despite these persuasive arguments, the Australian Treasurer rejected the merger proposal; SGX and ASX mutually terminated the agreement and SGX stated that it would 'continue to pursue organic as well as other strategic growth opportunities, including further dialogue with ASX on other forms of cooperation'.[138] Putting on a brave face, SGX CEO Magnus Bocker said of his merger attempt, 'it put SGX on the map, it made people sit up and take notice of us and it opened many new doors'.[139] Organic growth and strategic cooperation continued to be possibilities.[140]

---

[129] Chris V Nicholson, 'Regulators Set to Reject Merger of Singapore and Australia Exchanges', *The New York Times* (5 April 2011) <http://dealbook.nytimes.com/2011/04/05/australia-says-its-set-to-reject-sgx-asx-merger/?_r=0> accessed 12 September 2013.

[130] Nicholson (n 129).

[131] Chris V Nicholson, 'Australia Rejects Exchange Deal', *The New York Times* (8 April 2011) <http://dealbook.nytimes.com/2011/04/08/australia-rejects-exchange-deal/> accessed 12 September 2013.

[132] 'Exchange Mergers: Back for More', *The Economist* (London, 11 February 2011) <http://www.economist.com/node/18114593> accessed 12 September 2013.

[133] Michael Richardson, 'ASX Deal Could Bring New Foreign Capital Flows' (10 December 2010) *Australian Financial Review* 67.

[134] Robert Laible, 'ASX/SGX merger presents synergies and hurdles', *The Trade News* (27 October 2010) <http://www.thetradenews.com/newsarticle.aspx?id=5184> accessed 23 December 2013.

[135] Bettina Wassener, 'Singapore Exchange to Buy Australia Counterpart', *The New York Times* (25 October 2010) <http://www.nytimes.com/2010/10/26/business/global/26exchange.html> accessed 12 September 2013.

[136] Robert Laible, 'ASX/SGX merger presents synergies and hurdles', *The Trade News* (27 October 2010) <http://www.thetradenews.com/newsarticle.aspx?id=5184> accessed 23 December 2013.

[137] Robert Laible, 'ASX/SGX merger presents synergies and hurdles', *The Trade News* 27 October 2010 <http://www.thetradenews.com/newsarticle.aspx?id=5184> accessed 23 December 2013.

[138] Nicholson (n 131).

[139] R Sivanithy, 'Failed ASX bid put SGX on the map: Bocker', *The Business Times Singapore* (15 March 2012).

[140] Kevin Brown 'SGX chief plays down failed offer', *Financial Times* (19 April 2011) <http://www.ft.com/cms/s/0/10581860-6aa0-11e0-80a1-00144feab49a.html#axzz2eeAmwUYw> accessed 12 September 2013.

Becoming a global stock exchange   Historically, SGX has focused on listing companies in **9.63**
the Southeast Asia region. More recently, however, Singapore has begun promoting itself as
the 'Asian Gateway'. With Singapore having established itself as a prominent hub for international trade, the city-state is hoping for similar traction in international finance. SGX's
ambitions are to establish itself as a global stock exchange.[141]

SGX established the 'S-chip' market which targets mainland Chinese companies, espe- **9.64**
cially ones that have been unable to list in Hong Kong due to crowding out by the bigger,
state-owned Chinese companies. Generally speaking, SGX regards the S-chip market as
successful.[142] However, this success has come at some reputational cost; SGX is known as an
exchange for sub-par Chinese companies. In 2010, for example, over 20 companies were on
a watch list or were in the process of being delisted because of poor performance. Eight of
these companies were from mainland China, of which one was noted for its 'founders [hav-
ing] fled while owing millions'.[143]

SGX is also expanding product range into derivatives and currency.[144] Noting that **9.65**
Singapore is the world's fourth-largest foreign exchange trading hub, Mr Bocker said that
the addition of Asian foreign-exchange futures would capitalize on Singapore's foothold
in trading in Asian currencies. At the outset, SGX is expected to offer the four currency
pairs of AUD/USD, AUD/Yen, INR/USD and USD/SGD and the contracts 'aim to
make managing currency risk more efficient by allowing investors to rely on some of the
same collateral posted against trades in derivatives ilnked to key Asian stock indexes'.[145]
Derivatives may seem like good news for SGX. In the second quarter of 2013, SGX's
derivatives business grew 21 per cent to $45.7 million. Average month-end open interest
on derivatives also rose 83 per cent to 2.5 million contracts while SGX's OTC clearing
service, saw volumes increase by 56 per cent to 88,650 contracts on the back of a 90 per
cent increase in iron ore swaps. In addition, SGX enjoyed record high volumes for its
China A50 futures and Japan Nikkei 225 options. These contributed to increases of 9.5
per cent in total revenue to $162 million and 16.9 per cent in profit to $76 million for
that quarter.[146]

Yet, these numbers are markedly lower than those of the pre-global financial crisis era. In **9.66**
2008, when SGX's derivatives business was 30 per cent smaller, SGX reported profits of
$444.3 million thanks in large part to daily securities trading that was 75 per cent higher
than it is today. These figures represent a bigger problem in Singaporean capital markets;
trading volume is falling. Notwithstanding that the Straits Times Index (STI) has rebounded
strongly after the global financial crisis, trading volumes have not recovered and share turnover velocity—a measure of trading volume relative to the size of the market—in the second

---

[141] Jeffrey Friedland, 'Singapore Stock Exchange's "Asian Gateway" policy attracts listings by foreign
companies', *Friedland Capital News* (15 March 2011) <http://friedlandcapital.wordpress.com/2011/03/15/
singapore-stock-exchange%E2%80%99s-%E2%80%9Casian-gateway%E2%80%9D-policy-attracts-listing
s-by-foreign-companies/> accessed 12 September 2013.
[142] Friedland (n 141).
[143] Tsui (n 110).
[144] Matthew Walter, Katy Burne, and Jacob Bunge, 'SGX cool on talk of another tilt at ASX', *The
Australian* (14 March 2013) <http://www.theaustralian.com.au/business/wall-street-journal/sgx-cool-on-
talk-of-another-tilt-at-asx/story-fnay3vxj-1226596741407> accessed 12 September 2013.
[145] Walter, Burne, and Bunge (n 144).
[146] Joan Ng, 'Riding the Bull', *The Edge Singapore* (28 January 2013).

quarter of 2013 was 44 per cent, compared to 72 per cent in 2008.[147] Regardless of the reasons for this, as one market analyst wrote, 'while we continue to view the SGX's solid longer-term growth prospects as a regional hub as strong, led by regional derivatives trading where it is gaining good momentum, we highlight that the nearer-term fortunes of the stock are driven by current securities market volumes'.[148]

9.67 The local market in Singapore is problematic. Unlike Hong Kong, Singaporean investors have appeared relatively uninterested in the equity markets; they like real estate. Singapore practices state capitalism, and government has taken several steps since 2009 to cool down the property sector, increasing stamp duties on property transfers and curtailing the availability of mortgages. Some analysts have seen decreases in residential property transaction volumes by 50 per cent and prices by 7 per cent.[149]

9.68 The SGX has also set out to woo the local retail investor, publishing analysis showing that the STI has outperformed property prices over the past decade, with good prospects ahead. On this front, 'to increase trading volumes as well as velocity, [Mr] Bocker has led a concerted push into developing the retail market by working more closely with the local remisier community and stepping up education initiatives'.[150] In 2012, SGX launched My Gateway, an investment education portal that facilitates Singaporean retail investor access to SGX. Through resources such as explanatory videos and notes, the portal informs retail investors about the merits of investing in the stock market and educates them on topics ranging from the business models and risks of telecoms companies to exchange-traded funds (ETFs). Furthermore, SGX has imposed higher standards for companies seeking to list their securities on the Mainboard, sought regulatory approval to require a larger proportion of initial public offerings of shares for the retail market, introduced dual-currency stocks and ETFs, and even run a share-investing contest that drew more than 13,000 participants online.[151] And the SGX Academy, which runs professional training courses and seminars, is rapidly expanding its outreach.

9.69 Growing its domestic market is one strategy for Singapore, but it has not given up on looking outwards, despite the Australian bruising. In the aftermath of the failed SGX-ASX merger, in mid-2012, SGX and ASX established a new trading link for derivatives. Under the arrangement, each exchange sets up a hub in the other's co-location data centre, allowing customers at one exchange's co-location center trade directly on the other's derivatives segments.[152] ASX is set to connect its Australian Liquidity Centre members directly to SGX's derivatives arm, the only international platform offering Chinese and Indonesian futures.[153]

9.70 SGX has been intimately involved in similar cooperation agreements in the Asean region. Forecasted to grow at 5 per cent in 2013, the region is comprised of ten countries with a

---

[147] Ng (n 146).
[148] Ng (n 146).
[149] Ng (n 146).
[150] Ng (n 146).
[151] Ng (n 146).
[152] Anish Puaar, 'ASX and SGX forge derivatives trading link', *The Trade News* (1 July 2012) <http://www.thetradenews.com/news/Asset_Classes/Derivatives/ASX_and_SGX_forge_derivatives_trading_link.aspx> accessed 12 September 2013.
[153] Puaar (n 152).

cumulative GDP of $2 trillion, a rapidly growing middle class and a high savings rate.[154] SGX is an integral member of Asean Exchanges, which is a collaboration of seven stock exchanges from Singapore, Malaysia, Vietnam, Indonesia, Philippines, and Thailand aimed at promoting Asean securities as an asset class. In 2012, Asean Exchanges launched Asean Link, a platform that facilitates cheaper and quicker access to equities listed on the connected exchanges by having brokers in different member countries pick up orders from each other via the Link. This is in stark contrast to previously technically complicated and expensive direct connections that brokers in the various countries had to establish with each other.[155] Asean Link is similar to a three-way South American link established in 2011 between Chile, Peru, and Colombia.[156] In order to drum up activity on the Link, shares in Singapore, Thailand, and Malaysia are exempt from capital gains taxes if purchased over the Link.[157]

Despite the hype, a year after the launch of Asean Link, cross-border volumes using the Link **9.71** remained low. Home bias is keeping Asean investors in their local markets with which they are familiar and where they are not subject to rapid currency fluctuations.[158] The regulatory framework for cross-border trading may also be lagging (advertently or inadvertently), resulting in a regulatory tangle investors are unwilling to negotiate.[159] In a face-saving statement, Asean Exchanges called the Link a 'long-term initiative'.[160] The Link is also targeting the low end of the market, the smaller brokers, since large traders already have existing infrastructure and relationships in place to conduct cross-border equities trading.

In continuous pursuit of outreach, SGX has also established hubs in Chicago and London, **9.72** opened an access point in Frankfurt and tied NYSE Euronext's global trading network into its home market centre.[161] This makes SGX the first Asian-based exchange to have hubs in both Europe and the United States, which SGX promotes as access to the world's largest offshore market for Asian equity futures.[162] Similarly, SGX and Eurex have linked up their data centres.[163] SGX has also entered into a licensing agreement with MSCI, an index provider, to list futures linked to more equity indexes in Asian markets. Also, SGX has entered into an agreement with Korea Exchange (KRX) for over-the-counter derivatives clearing services, enabling clients to transfer positions between their clearinghouses.[164]

Singapore is a speck in the Asia Pacific. Despite its vast hinterland, Singapore's challenge **9.73** is growth; Malaysia and Hong Kong have each established themselves as leaders in niches

---

[154] Jason Ng, 'Slow Start for Southeast Asian Stock-Trade Link', *The Wall Street Journal* (New York, 20 March 2013) <http://online.wsj.com/article/SB10001424127887323419104578372130557048370.html> accessed 12 September 2013.

[155] Ng (n 154).

[156] 'Bursa, SGX in Asean link soon', *New Straits Times* (Malaysia, 4 September 2012).

[157] Ng (n 154).

[158] Ng (n 154).

[159] Ng (n 154).

[160] Ng (n 154).

[161] Tommy Fernandez, 'Singapore Merges Technology, Operations Units', *Securities Technology Monitor* (28 March 2012) <http://www.securitiestechnologymonitor.com/news/Singapore-Reorganizes-Operations-30 265-1.html> accessed 23 December 2013.

[162] 'SGX chooses BT for Chicago and London hubs', *FOWeek* (1 June 2012) <http://www.fointelligence. com/Article/3046336/SGX-chooses-BT-for-Chicago-and-London-hubs.html> accessed 23 December 2013.

[163] Kenneth Lim, 'Singapore Exchange, Eurex complete data centre link-up', *The Business Times Singapore* (13 December 2012) <http://www.businesstimes.com.sg/premium/companies/others/singapore-exchange-eu rex-complete-data-centre-link-20121213 > accessed 23 December 2013.

[164] Walter, Burne, and Bunge (n 144).

which Singapore might have filled. Although Singapore's focus is resolutely international and its ambitions those of a full-service financial centre, the state of its domestic markets is a concern. Additionally, the rise of domestic markets in its much larger, close[165] neighbours hems Singapore in. Nevertheless, the dynamism and relentless opportunism of the SGX keep Singapore on the map, as does Singapore's own variety of state capitalism. As in Malaysia, in Singapore the government and the markets work unabashedly hand in hand.

3.3 Bahrain and Dubai

9.74 Despite their close proximity in the Persian Gulf and membership in the Gulf Cooperation Council (GCC), Bahrain and Dubai are very different places. Bahrain, a constitutional monarchy, is a small archipelago with its main island[166] tethered to Saudi Arabia via a 20km-long causeway.[167] As an ancient centre of human civilization—7,500 years-old by some estimates[168]—Bahrain was an important fresh water oasis along age-old trading routes. Despite recent desertification, perhaps the millennia of traders help explain Bahrain's reputation for openness towards foreigners and large expatriate population.[169]

9.75 Dubai, meanwhile, is a glittering new city studded with spectacular skyscrapers, only made possible through a potent combination of oil wealth and modern technology. Unlike Singapore, Dubai is not a city-state but is one of two major cities within the United Arab Emirates (UAE). From its oil industry origins, the ambitions of Dubai are to transform itself into a major financial hub for the Middle East and Gulf region by diversifying away from oil and into financial services.

3.3.1 Bahrain

9.76 With little by the way of oil resources in comparison to its neighbors, from early on Bahrain looked to different ways of growing its economy. Offshore banking became its vehicle of choice. In building an offshore banking industry, Bahrain brought in British bankers and British banking; the latter arrived, not by way of formal legislation, but the more practical 'rule books' of the banking business.

9.77 As in other places in the Gulf and the Middle East, the legal system in Bahrain is a complicated mix of systems and influences, formal and informal. Bahrain, like similarly situated jurisdictions, demonstrates a high tolerance for what might be called 'applied legal pluralism'. Civil code influences (as adapted by and emanating from Egypt and Lebanon, for example) operate in the region in a formal way, but tend to be somewhat marginalized. Islamic law is pervasive, manifesting itself in multiple guises, to a greater or lesser extent, depending on the circumstances. The legal framework for finance, on the other hand, often finds its inspiration in the City of London and the English common law for a variety of

---

[165] Relatively close, this being the vast expanse of the Asia Pacific.

[166] A tiny 55km by 18km.

[167] And it is soon to be tethered to Qatar by another, longer causeway.

[168] The earliest civilization in modern day Bahrain was the Dilmun civilization, which has also been claimed by some to be the location of the biblical Garden of Eden, <http://www.theregister.co.uk/2010/12/09/ancient_dilmun_garden_eden_gulf_lost_civilisation/> accessed 23 December 2013.

[169] In line with its tolerance and openness, Bahrain also hosts expatriate compounds for foreign workers who are employed in a conservative Saudi Arabia but who return home to Bahrain across the causeway for a gin and tonic after work.

political and historical reasons. More recently, with the internationalization of finance, an overlay of international financial standards adds concepts drawn from the US regulatory system to this already heady mix.

For Bahrain, importing British banking was relatively straightforward; they imported the **9.78** British bankers who knew the rules of the City (and who would bring the rulebooks with them).[170] Being an offshore financial centre though is a competitive business. Growth and diversification are often a part of the adaptive process. In small centres, such as Bahrain, the direction of this growth and diversification is usually a matter of macroeconomic policy (driven by ultimate concerns of basic survival), and not necessarily commercial or market considerations.

Bahrain as a niche market   Bahrain's economy sits as an anomaly among regional econo-   **9.79** mies heavily reliant upon extractive industries. Its finance industry stands out among its regional counterparts as the most mature and developed, providing a conduit to the rest of the world for the region's vast reserve of petrodollars. At the same time, international investors have for long channelled capital into the Gulf region through Bahrain. Most notable, perhaps, is the gateway status that Bahrain has for financial flows to Saudi Arabia, conveniently linked by causeway. Dubai and Doha, though, have begun to encroach on Bahrain's turf,[171] although Bahrain continues to be competitive in terms of a lower cost of living. Incentives always play a role in niche markets; Bahrain offers low tax rates and attractive free-trade agreements.[172] In the 2013 Index of Economic Freedom, Bahrain is ranked first in the MENA (Middle East North Africa) region and twelfth globally.[173]

Most importantly, Bahrain has a longstanding reputation as one of the most efficient and   **9.80** stable finance industries in the Gulf region.[174] Offshore banking is one thing though; capital markets are another. Bahrain's stock exchange lost out to investors seeking quick gains from the volatility elsewhere in the region, despite the country's reputation for efficient regulation and a long-term base of investors.[175] With two new exchanges, Bahrain is over exchanged.

---

[170] The capital (and other markets) are still governed by 'rulebooks'. Decree No 64 of 2006 implemented the Central Bank of Bahrain and Financial Institutions Law (CBB Law 2006) and is the umbrella legislation for the country's financial markets. CBB Law 2006 established the Central Bank of Bahrain (CBB) to replace the BMA as the country's monetary authority and financial markets regulator, which includes oversight of banking, insurance, investment business licensees, and other financial services providers. The CBB also regulates Bahrain's licensed exchanges and clearing houses. The CBB Law also included the development of a new set of capital markets regulations. In addition, laws and regulations were compiled into a Rulebook, in which distinct volumes cover different areas, such as conventional banking, capital markets, collective investment undertakings, and Islamic banking. The regulatory framework for capital markets is comprised of the CBB Law 2006, Volume 6 of the CBB Rulebook and CBB Capital Markets Regulations (collectively, 'Capital Markets Regime'). See OECD, *Global Forum on Transparency and Exchange of Information for Tax Purposes Peer Reviews: Bahrain in 2011: Phase 1: Legal and Regulatory Framework* (OECD Publishing, August 2011), 12.
[171] Simeon Kerr, 'Bahrain: Hopes pinned on niche role', *Financial Times* (12 October 2012).
[172] Rob Denman, 'Bahrain? Bank on it', *Site Selection—The Middle East*, June 2013. In Bahrain, incentives are not restricted to 'zones', but available throughout the country. They include 100% foreign ownership of 95% of business activities, the freedom to repatriate capital, profits, and dividends, and, very attractively, 0% personal and corporate income tax.
[173] Bertelsmann Transformation Index, Bahrain Country Report, 'Organization of the Market and Competition' (2012) <http://www.bti-project.org/laendergutachten/mena/bhr/2012/#economic> accessed 23 December 2013.
[174] Kerr (n 171).
[175] Oxford Business Group, The Report: Bahrain 2008, 'Finding a niche market—building from an established base', 69.

Regulatory reputation matters, though and the Central Bank of Bahrain (CBB), through its capital markets arm, the Capital Markets Supervision Directorate (CMSD), is seen as the most efficient regulator in the Gulf region. It is a consolidated regulator (in the UK FSA style) and noted for robust policymaking.[176] Stability is also supported by a currency pegged to the US dollar.[177]

9.81 Contributing close to 25 per cent of Bahrain's GDP, the finance sector is larger than the energy sector.[178] Bahain hosts a large expatriate community, but Bahrainis represent over 70 per cent of employment in the finance industry,[179] although only 25 per cent of the overall labour force. State 'nurturing' is extensive, prompting rapid growth in the finance industry in recent years; total assets in the industry were close to 22 times larger than the country's GDP.[180] However, the main Bahrain exchange, the BHB, is one of the smallest and least liquid in the region, with an average turnover of less than 4 per cent of overall capitalization. Lack of liquidity is often fatal to an exchange, yet in this case, long term institutional investors like pension funds which do not profit from volatility are cited as the support for this market. Stability, it is said, has sustained the BHB internationally. In 2006, while other regional markets showed sharp losses, Bahrain's primary stock exchange continued to make small gains. Additionally, the BHB's relatively lower levels of trading and volatility also provide for relatively attractive price-to-earnings (P/E) ratios: the average P/E ratio by early 2008 was 15.1, compared with 21.9 for Tadawul in Saudi Arabia and 21.7 for Dubai Financial Market.[181]

9.82 Bahrain has also encouraged the development of a regional hub for mutual funds; in 2007 the CBB refreshed its categories for registration of mutual funds, each with its own set of regulatory requirements, insulating smaller investors from the risks larger institutional investors could take on. By early 2008, there were almost 2,500 mutual funds registered in Bahrain, most foreign-managed,[182] with a net asset value of close to $16 billion, representing an increase of 73 per cent in the preceding 18 months.[183]

9.83 Situated as it is, Bahrain naturally looks to Islamic finance and the market in sukuk, the primary Islamic financial instrument. In 2001, the CBB pioneered its issuance of sukuk and later that same year, began to develop a Liquidity Management Centre (LMC) to purchase and restructure sukuk into short-term debt. Today, CBB is one of the largest lead managers for sukuk and sukuk capitalization in 2009 exceeded $100 billion, having seen a sharp increase after 2007. Sukuk now dominate the Bahrain debt market with over a 90 per cent

---

[176] 'Bahrain: Financial Services Report', *The Economist* (22 June 2010).

[177] Oxford Business Group, The Report: Bahrain 2008 (n 175), 69.

[178] 'Bahrain: Financial Services Report' (n 176).

[179] Oxford Business Group, The Report: Bahrain 2008, 'First to market—Bahrain's diversified financial sector serves as a centre for the region', 49.

[180] Oxford Business Group, The Report: Bahrain 2008 (n 179), 49.

[181] Oxford Business Group, The Report: Bahrain 2008 (n 175), 71.

[182] Volume 6 of the Rulebook on Capital Markets was aligned with EU Directives regarding retail funds. In 2012, the economic crisis coupled with the growing popularity of mutual funds in Bahrain prompted the country to introduce a revised framework for collective investment schemes. See Oxford Business Group, The Report: Bahrain 2008 (n 179), 50; Oxford Business Group, The Report: Bahrain 2009, 'Tailor-made: highly regulated business environment with numerous incentives', 207.

[183] Oxford Business Group, The Report: Bahrain 2008 (n 175), 72.

share.[184] In 2010, the CBB issued its third international sukuk, valued at $1.25 billion, listed on the London Stock Exchange.[185]

Islamic finance is notoriously resistant to standardization, one of its primary drawbacks as a commercial matter. In promoting its position as an Islamic finance centre, Bahrain has made itself home to several institutions designed to instill greater standardization into Islamic financial products. The AAOIFI, with some 200 members, sets the accounting, auditing, governance, ethics, and Sharia interpretation standards for Islamic finance institutions. Bahrain was the first country to make compliance with AAOIFI mandatory and other Gulf states followed suit. Bahrain also plays host to the IIFM, which sets international standards for Islamic capital and money markets and the Islamic International Rating Agency (IIRA), which, among other things, carries out Sharia compliance assessments. Finally, the LMC continues to inject liquidity into the sukuk market.

9.84

In 2011, a new exchange opened in Bahrain, BFX, part of a chain of nine exchanges owned by Financial Technologies India; the Bahraini government initially participated in setting up BFX. The products traded, overlap with those of the BHB, stocks, sukuk, and other Islamic securities, although diversified into derivatives and commodities, the idea being to create a 'multi-asset' exchange in the region.[186] Within the BFX sits an Islamic finance division known as Bait Al Bursa, which exclusively offers electronic exchange-traded Islamic financial instruments, offering a diversified portfolio and a single venue for all exchange-traded business in the Islamic finance sector.[187] At least, that was the plan. BFX had a troubled start, experiencing serious delays, drastic downsizing and a generalized lack of interest. BFX may represent something else entirely though; the exchange as commodity. Given the tie up of NYSE and Qatar as well as Dubai and NASDAQ, BFX may have been established to be sold to a larger, international group. Certainly in the region, the trend is towards exchange consolidation.

9.85

It may seem anomalous that such a small place as Bahrain could support not one, not two, but three exchanges. In another effort to capture specialized international trading, in January 2013 Bahrain became home to the Joint Arab Bourse (JAB), expected to begin operations in 2014.[188] JAB will be the first common Arab stock market and a private sector oriented initiative, with a market estimated at $3 trillion. As with exchanges elsewhere, JAB is reaching into the lower tiers for business, targeting small and medium-sized enterprises. JAB is as much a political statement as a trading venue,[189] and its establishment in Bahrain is consistent with Bahrain's efforts to foster the institutions supporting Islamic finance as well as traditional market activity which appears difficult to generate.

9.86

---

[184] Sat Pal Parashar, 'Sukuk Industry Development in the Bahrain Capital Market' in Mohamed Ariff, Munawar Iqbal, and Shamsher Mohamad (eds), *The Islamic Debt Market for Sukuk Securities: The Theory and Practice of Profit Sharing Investment* (Edward Elgar Publishing, 2012), 157.

[185] Pakashar (n 184).

[186] Oxford Business Group, The Report: Bahrain 2012, 'An expanding market: new regulations and the introduction of a second Bourse have boosted the kingdom's appeal'.

[187] Abdul Rahman Al Baker, 'Creating strong foundations for the next phase of development of Islamic Investment Markets 2010', 6th Annual World Islamic Funds and Capital Markets Conference Opening Remarks (Bahrain: Manama, 24 May 2010).

[188] Maryam Aziz, 'Forum announces Arab Bourse project', *Nuqudy News* (14 January 2013).

[189] See Aziz (n 188): The Joint Arab Bourse will offer 'a safe haven for domestic and regional capital,' attract foreign and migratory capital and harness 'modern technology to facilitate the flow in investment... bringing Arab investment opportunities to [the] attention of the world's major financial centres'.

9.87 On the formal regulatory side, capital markets activity in Bahrain is overseen by the Capital Markets Supervision Directorate (CMSD) within the CBB. The CMSD acts as the listing authority for companies and financial instruments on the country's exchanges. The transition phase to new regulations for capital markets is still in process; the 'Rulebook' is still incomplete and only applies to the extent that the relevant sections are available. For example, at present, the Capital Markets Volume of the Rulebook does not include a segment on Offering Securities, Listing Requirements, and Disclosure Requirements, possibly representing a lack of demand. As such, these areas of the prior capital markets regulations are still applicable, pending completion of the CBB Rulebook.

9.88 Reputation is important to Bahrain, so it pays close attention to compliance with international standards as a signalling mechanism to the international marketplace. In 2005–06, a Financial Sector Assessment (FSAP) was conducted in Bahrain by the IMF and its capital markets regulation and supervision assessed against the IOSCO Objectives and Principles of Securities Regulation.[190] The resulting report acknowledged Bahrain's generally high standard for capital markets regulation and supervision, noting that the country was in compliance with most of IOSCO's core principles.[191] This assessment was carried out at a pivotal time: numerous regulatory reforms were underway, the CBB Law 2006 was introduced and the CBB was being established as the successor to the Bahrain Monetary Authority. Two years later, Bahrain became the first national market regulator in the GCC to be accepted as an IOSCO member.

9.89 As one CBB official put it, 'it is not a question of whether we are the financial centre in the Gulf, it is a question of whether we will continue to be the centre. We have to be vigilant'.[192] So, Bahrain continues to diversify its finance sector, partly in response to competitive threats from nearby Dubai and Qatar. It benefits from having a sizeable and experienced finance sector labour force and an adaptable regulatory attitude towards changing market conditions. What began three decades ago as an effort to diversify the Bahraini economy away from its reliance upon the energy sector has created a modest, but so far effective, niche market.

3.3.2 Dubai

9.90 Dubai has pursued a different strategy from Bahrain for its financial markets. Dubai's ambitions have gone beyond creating a regional niche market; for Dubai it has been the big gesture, cutting a dashing figure on the world stage.[193] Coming later to the world of international finance, Dubai has mirrored some of Bahrain's attractions,[194] but from there Dubai has gone its own way, embarking on a novel and ambitious experiment.[195] It is not obvious the experiment will succeed.

---

[190] International Monetary Fund, *Financial System Stability Assessment: Kingdom of Bahrain* (12 January 2006).

[191] IOSCO in 2010 introduced eight new IOSCO principles which the CBB indicated it would integrate into its Rulebook.

[192] Oxford Business Group, The Report: Bahrain 2008 (n 179), 50.

[193] Dubai's monumental ambitions are made possible by the very deep pockets of its government.

[194] Permitting 100% foreign ownership, no taxes on profits or income, a range of double taxation treaties to the extent any tax liability is triggered and a showy adherence to international standards.

[195] See, generally, Jawad I Ali, 'Dubai International Financial Centre—entrance to the global economy' (King & Spalding LLP, 20 January 2012).

Unlike Bahrain, Dubai did not just import British bankers, with their rulebooks tucked **9.91** in their valises. In 2004, Dubai set about dropping a new, improved, City of London into the desert, the Dubai International Financial Centre (DIFC). Like the City of London, the DIFC is a small, geographically defined area, 110 acres, within the heart of Dubai City. It is recognized as a distinct and independent jurisdiction within Dubai, which is itself one of seven emirates, or principalities, which form the UAE. As a federal financial free zone, the DIFC has the legislative power to create its own laws, regulations and institutions for all of private (civil) and commercial law.[196] From the outset, the strategy behind the DIFC was to create an international financial centre of world stature, connecting business and financial institutions in both emerging and established markets throughout the world.[197] The US dollar, the undisputed reserve currency of the world at the time, was adopted as the operating currency in the DIFC.

As a legal and regulatory experiment, the DIFC is an interesting case, one that has caught **9.92** the imagination of many. Like Bahrain, the UAE (of which Dubai is a part) demonstrates a complex, hybrid, legal system, a mixture of civil, common and Islamic law. Despite the UAE now characterizing itself as a predominately civil law jurisdiction, the common law was traditionally present due to the UAE's informal colonial ties with Britain. However, after UAE independence, the common law was rejected in favour of civil law codes. Unsurprisingly, Islamic law—Sharia—also operates within the UAE, enjoying constitutional support. In practice, however, Sharia is treated as a subsidiary source of law, to be applied when civil law codal provisions and other available sources fail in specificity.[198]

At its creation in 2004, however, the DIFC adopted the common law, even going so far as to **9.93** import a common law judiciary. So along with the British bankers, in came British judges[199] and a UK-style regulator. But it is not quite so simple (and the common law itself is never simple). For example, the capital markets in the DIFC are governed by the Markets Law 2012 (DIFC Law No 1 of 2012)[200] and the Markets Rules (MKT), which are collectively

---

[196] However, federal criminal laws apply within the DIFC.

[197] Ali (n 195). The Dubai version of the creation of the DIFC somewhat ignores the role of Bahrain. Prior to the inception of the DIFC, the GCC lacked a regulated financial centre with internationally known and accepted standards. Therefore, Federal Decree No 35 of 2004 established the DIFC to correct the regional inadequacies and created a financial free zone in Dubai, though one distinguished from other such zones in the UAE. The overall framework of the DIFC was designed to attract and ensure continued connectivity with global banks and financial institutions. It was designed to centralize regional wealth in an environment designed for wholesale banking, capital markets, asset management, reinsurance, Islamic finance, and companies whose services are ancillary to these sectors.

[198] Nasser Saidi, 'The Success of the DIFC as an International Financial Centre', Working Paper (2009), <http://nassersaidi.com/2009/09/01/the-successes-of-difc-as-an-international-financial-centre-sept-2009/> accessed 16 January 2014.

[199] The DIFC Courts were established by Dubai Law No 12 of 2004. They are an independent, English-language common law judiciary within the autonomous DIFC exercising jursidiction over national and international civil and commercial law. Unless parties have selected otherwise, the Courts' substantive law is developed by the DIFCA and DFSA, with its procedure imported from the rules of the Commercial Court in London. They work alongside and in cooperation with the Dubai courts, where the language is Arabic and procedure stems from the continental civil tradition. The DIFC Courts' independence from executive policy in Dubai is one of the factors lending credence to its aspirations as a sound financial centre. See Anthony Evans, 'The facts about the DIFC Courts', *Financial Times* (11 November 2011) and Ludmila Yamolova, 'DIFC Courts: Redefining the judicial process' (HPL Yamalova and Plewka Legal Consultancy, February 2010) <http://www.lyhplaw.com/publications/02-10%20Ludmila%27s%20Article%20re%20DIFC%20Court.pdf> accessed 16 January 2014.

[200] Note the civil law formulation of the legislation.

referred to as the 'Markets Regime 2012'. However, Islamic finance also operates within the DIFC and must be supported by Islamic law. So there is also the Law Regulating Islamic Finance Business 2004 (DIFC Law No 13 of 2004) and the Islamic Finance Rules (IFR), known collectively as the Islamic Markets Regime.[201]

9.94 Not surprisingly, the regulator created for the DIFC in 2004 emulated the United Kingdom's FSA, then the leading model.[202] The DFSA is a unitary regulator within the DIFC and has complete jurisdiction over all the participants in the capital markets, banking and credit services, asset management, securities, collective investment funds, custody, trusts and services, commodities future trading, Islamic finance, insurance, and exchanges. Moreover, the DFSA authorizes, licenses, and registers markets participants operating within the DIFC. Again along FSA lines, the now somewhat tarnished risk-based regulatory approach was formally adopted.[203] A Financial Sector Assessment (FSAP) conducted by the IMF and The World Bank in 2007 against the IOSCO Objectives and Principles of Securities Regulation found the DFSA to have 'fully implemented' 27 out of the 29 principles assessed. The remaining two principles, dealing with collective investment schemes, were 'broadly implemented'.[204]

9.95 The FSAP results merit closer scrutiny. As a point of comparison, the FSAP conducted in the United States and published in May 2010 found the SEC/CFTC to have fully implemented only 16 out of 29 IOSCO principles, albeit being held to a higher standard. But the DIFC ratings must bring into question the utility of the FSAP exercises, when a capital market as dysfunctional as Dubai's rates so highly. The ratings demonstrate a phenonemon present in other developing economies, chasing the ratings. Developing economies comply blindly in creating regulatory structures which will 'check the boxes' in international standards, while failing to make real progress towards viable capital markets. The DFSA's continuous effort to meet global standards led to the new Markets Regime 2012,[205] which followed a new international model, the EU Prospectus Directive, as well as picking up more UK refinements such as the revised Corporate Governance Code.[206]

---

[201] The Islamic Markets Regime attaches special rules for Institutions Conducting Islamic Financial Business (ICIFB). Such an institution is defined as those 'carrying on,' or holds itself out as carrying on, a financial service in or from the DIFC as 'in accordance with Shari'a'. See the Law Regulating Islamic Finance Business 2004 (DIFC Law No 13 of 2004) s 10. There are two types of institutions that fall within this ambit: Islamic Financial Institutions (IFI) and Conventional Financial Institutions (CFI) whereby parts of their dealings are with Islamic securities, the so-called 'Islamic window' also found elsewhere in the world. It is worth noting that the regulator in the DIFC, the Dubai Financial Services Authority (DFSA), does not hold itself out as a Sharia regulator, but rather a Sharia systems regulator. Sharia compliance is not its concern; rather it requires ICIFB to implement a system of governance that oversees Sharia compliance.

[202] Dubai Law No 9 of 2004 established the DFSA as the single supervisory and regulatory authority of the DIFC. DIFC Law No 12 of 2004 (Regulatory Law) provides for the constitution of the DFSA and vests it with the necessary rule-making authority. The main responsibilities of the DFSA centre around administering the core financial services related laws, which include six laws created over the past decade that are aimed at regulating markets, trusts, investments, and Islamic financial business: Oxford Business Group, Bahrain Report 2008 (n 177).

[203] Saidi (n 198).

[204] IMF/World Bank, 'Dubai International Financial Centre: IOSCO Objectives and Principles of Securities Regulation' (FSAP, IMF Country Report No 07/365, Washington DC, November 2007).

[205] The Markets Regime 2012 repealed and replaced Markets Law 2004 the Offered Securities Rule (OSR) (Markets Regime 2004). The DFSA proposed the changes in 2011 in order to align itself with leading jurisdictions, while accommodating the capital markets of the GCC region. DFSA, 'Proposed Changes to the Market Law Regime Part 1', Consultation Paper No 75 (11 April 2011).

[206] DFSA, 'Proposed Changes to the Market Law Regime Part 2—Recognition and Auditing', Consultation Paper No 76 (15 June 2011).

The DIFC is not the only financial market in Dubai, and neither is the DFSA the only regu-   **9.96**
lator. Outside the geographic confines of the DIFC exists a parallel system. The Government
of Dubai incorporated the Dubai Financial Market in 2000, operating as one of two local
stock exchanges within the UAE, the second one being the Abu Dhabi Securities Exchange
(ADX). The Emirates Securities and Commodities Authority (ESCA) is the regulator for the
DFM. Again, in keeping up with international fashion, the DFM became a public joint stock
company in 2006, through an initial public offering of 20 per cent of its shares, the remaining 80 per cent being sold to Borse Dubai (BD) a government-owned holding company.[207]

Nasdaq, OMX, and Borse Dubai   In 2007 the NASDAQ, the US stock market operator   **9.97**
and Borse Dubai, the government-owned holding company, put an end to a protracted
battle over their bids for OMX, the Nordic exchange group, by deciding to work together
in a deal that has had wide-reaching implications for international capital markets. The
complex agreement involved Borse Dubai advancing its $4 billion cash bid for OMX,
only to have those shares acquired by NASDAQ in a cash-and-shares transaction that
left Borse Dubai with approximately 20 per cent of NASDAQ (but with voting rights
restricted to 5 per cent). Meanwhile, Borse Dubai acquired NADAQ's 27 per cent stake
in the London Stock Exchange for $1.6 billion. In addition, NASDAQ became the key
shareholder in the original DIFX, which became rebranded as NASDAQ Dubai under a
licencing agreement.[208]

Having fought over OMX for quite some time, NASDAQ and Borse Dubai realized that   **9.98**
their interests were compatible. NASDAQ was reportedly interested in using OMX to
expand into Scandanavia while Dubai was keen on using the technology it would acquire
to further its interests in emerging markets. The arrangement provided NASDAQ with
an entry into the Middle East. As for Dubai, though it had successfully developed into a
Middle Eastern financial hub, the DIFX had found it difficult to attract listings and a tie-up
with NASDAQ in the United States offered increased possibilities.[209] Other Gulf states—
including Qatar and Saudi Arabia—had also sought financial hub status; the NASDAQ
connection was perceived to be valuable in this regard. The NASDAQ-OMX-Borse Dubai
arrangement sat against a backdrop of the Dubai government's decision to combine DIFX
and its more successful domestic counterpart, the Dubai Financial Market (DFM), under
Borse Dubai. This was intended to offer investors a single platform across which to trade
a diverse set of asset classes.[210] The arrangement that led to the newly branded NASDAQ
Dubai was hoped to further this effort to compete by consolidating trading technology and
providing a platform to further diversification of asset classes.[211]

Nasdaq Dubai today   The 2008–09 global financial crisis added to Dubai's teething   **9.99**
problems, leading to a protracted period of depressed values and generally poor exchange
performance. Then, in 2009, Dubai faced an unprecedented crisis when Dubai World, a
state-owned enterprise, decided it would not make repayments to its creditors of $26 billion
of debt. Having opened up its housing market to foreign ownership in 2002, Dubai saw 20

[207] Oxford Business Group, The Report: Dubai 2007, 76
[208] Stanley Reed, 'Nasdaq, Dubai, OMX in Global Tieup', *Bloomberg Businessweek* (20 September 2007).
[209] Reed (n 208).
[210] Babu Das Augustine, 'Nasdaq DIFX will play key role in Mideast', *Gulf News* (21 November 2007).
[211] Augustine (n 210).

to 30 per cent annual growth in some areas between 2006–08. The bubble finally burst in 2009.[212] In 2011, Dubai's stock indices dropped due to poor performance in the construction and real estate sectors, as well as uncertainty stemming from the banking sector and the so-called Arab Spring, not to mention the Eurozone debt crisis which was in full swing at the time.[213]

9.100 Today, the prospects for Dubai's status as a financial hub are less clear than ever, and champions on both sides have ample evidence to cite. NASDAQ Dubai has only seven listed companies and 12 Islamic bonds. In 2012 and in the first half of 2013 there was a dramatic turnaround in Dubai's stock markets, making them some of the best performers in the world.[214] Also, after failing to secure emerging-market status from Morgan Stanley Capital International (MSCI) for four consecutive years, the UAE finally achieved this status in May 2013. This is expected to attract portfolio investments from an increasing number of global asset managers.[215]

9.101 Earlier in 2013, a few relatively small companies launched their plans for initial public offerings on NASDAQ Dubai. These are the first initial public offerings on the exchange since 2008, suggesting that the effects of the global financial crisis and Dubai's 2009 real estate crisis may be fading. Certainly, real estate prices have recovered strongly and Dubai's main stock index has risen 74 per cent in one year. Although it is still 55 per cent below its peak in 2008, Dubai looks ready to absorb new supplies of equity.[216] Yet both of Dubai's stock exchanges—the DFM and NASDAQ Dubai—need much more liquidity and this will not be easily addressed by small initial public offerings and trading will be low given their size. Much larger listings, perhaps including those of Dubai's large state-backed companies, are necessary if Dubai's capital markets are to get any real boost.[217] At present, a handful of large stocks comprise the majority of trading. Meanwhile, the DFM is represented largely by financial institutions which comprise more than two-thirds of the market and though it has enjoyed healthy liquidity levels over the past year, volatility and uncertainty remain.[218] This is partly because Dubai's success is very much dependent upon only two sectors—finance and property—and such concentration of risk discourages financial flows.

9.102 The largest recent listing to be announced is that of The Bank of London and The Middle East (BLME), the UK's largest Islamic bank, which has indicated that it will list $503 million worth of shares on NASDAQ Dubai in its hopes of encouraging Dubai's prospects as a centre for Islamic finance. It is estimated that Dubai's Islamic finance sector will have assets of up to $2 trillion by 2015.[219] Whether or not Dubai is able to attract more such listings—and larger ones—will determine its viability as an international financial hub. Dubai hosts a unique infrastructure in the form of the DIFC's internationally recognized legal and regulatory framework, a business environment which includes a wide variety of financial

[212] Lindo Xulu, 'Dubai Financial Market: a fresh look east', *Financial Mail* (1 March 2013).
[213] Economist Intelligence Unit, 'UAE: Financial Services Report' (26 July 2013).
[214] Economist Intelligence Unit (n 213).
[215] Economist Intelligence Unit (n 213).
[216] 'Dubai IPOs signal recovery but market wants bigger listings', *Asharq Al-Awsat* (3 October 2013).
[217] 'Dubai IPOs signal recovery but market wants bigger listings' (n 216).
[218] Xulu (n 212).
[219] Simeon Kerr, 'UK Islamic bank plans Dubai's first IPO in five years', *Financial Times* (16 September 2013).

services companies, and world-class infrastructure.[220] The question is whether, if you build it, will they come?

The DIFC is less than ten years old, but its history has been marked by constant change and repositioning in terms of finding its footing. Its international exchange, NASDAQ Dubai (the former DIFX), has gone through numerous restructurings and is largely considered a failure. With its deliberate exposure to international capital markets, the DIFC was also buffeted by the global financial crisis, bubbles and near collapses, all perhaps constituting a rite of passage along the way to its status as player in the international financial world. Yet the Dubai government definitely appears to be in the stock exchange business, with its majority state owned enterprise, Borse Dubai, holding 79.63 per cent stake in DFM, 33.3 per cent of NASDAQ Dubai, 20.64 per cent of the London Stock Exchange Group, and 16 per cent in the NASDAQ OMX Group itself.[221] Like a trophy wife, NASDAQ Dubai may be for show, with the real business taking place elsewhere.

9.103

4. Conclusion

It is a hard business being a niche market, operating in a competitive and often unforgiving environment, engaging in constant repositioning and facing inherent limitations on growth. Surprisingly, perhaps, there are lots of niche markets and a very diverse grouping they are, deploying a variety of survival strategies. In all cases, state capitalism, in various guises, supports these markets. In earlier times, reputation, a friendly regulator, and good business practices might have sufficed. Now, there is a new dynamic. The rise of large, new, Asian markets bent on establishing themselves in their own right, is eroding opportunities in the hinterland for jurisdictions like Singapore. Flash may be dethroning quiet discretion in establishing reputation; in theory, Dubai has one of the very best capital markets regulatory frameworks anywhere, as measured against international standards, and trumpets this fact to the world. As elsewhere, but more so in niche markets, technology is the gamechanger; small as well as large markets can be at the cutting edge. Technology is also providing the means for the creation of large interconnected networks of markets, which may continue to appear distinct on the surface, but which are deeply intertwined through integration of trading platforms as well as formal and informal alliances.

9.104

---

[220] 'What does the future hold for Dubai's global hub status?', *Albawaba Business* (18 September 2013).
[221] Oxford Business Group, The Report: Dubai 2013, 70.

Part IV

MARKET INSTITUTIONS AND INTERNATIONAL CAPITAL MARKETS

10

STOCK EXCHANGES—AN
ENDANGERED SPECIES[*]

1. Introduction

Among capital market institutions, exchanges are the most visible and vocal.[1] Only in the **10.01** aftermath of the global financial crisis has the spotlight of public (and possibly regulatory) interest turned in a critical fashion to the workings of other market systems and participants. Essential as they are, they were masked from view. Depositaries, custodians, clearing and settlement systems, credit rating agencies, were out of sight, relegated to the back office. The community of professional market intermediaries, the merchant and investment bankers, the broker-dealers, a clannish group wherever they are found,[2] operated behind the high walls of professional associations and self-regulation.[3]

Despite the waves of demutualization[4] and consolidation, exchanges remain idiosyncratic **10.02** institutions. Even where similar structural reorganizations have occurred, the underlying factors prompting such moves, and potentially the on-going operations of the exchanges, are often quite different. Some exchanges, such as Luxembourg and Switzerland, proudly assert their independence, bucking the trend towards consolidation (or demutualization). Nor is there convergence to an optimal model going on here. As IOSCO concluded in its 2006 study on the evolution of exchanges, 'steps taken have tended to be customized and pragmatic, based on an assessment of the particular circumstances in a jurisdiction'.[5]

Nor do market forces alone determine the nature of exchanges and their regulation. As **10.03** capital markets grew in importance, the role of exchanges extended beyond that of a trading venue. The modern exchange also serves political masters, acting as a national symbol in

---

[*] The author would like to thank Marco Garofalo and John Zelenbaba (Faculty of Law, McGill University), and Brendan Donohue and Sahil Sondhi (Melbourne Law School), for their able assistance in the preparation of this chapter.

[1] See Cally Jordan and Pamela Hughes, 'Which Way for Market Institutions? The Fundamental Question of Self-Regulation' (2007) 4 *Berkeley Business Law Journal* 205.

[2] Professor Gower complained about the 'veil of secrecy', which he encountered in the City of London when conducting his study on investor protection in 1984.

[3] In its strongest forms, self-regulation was found in the City of London prior to 2000, and continues in the United States together with a long history of regulatory oversight. Industry associations, such as International Swaps and Derivatives Association (ISDA) and the International Capital Markets Association (ICMA), are particularly important for their role in international capital markets.

[4] See definition of 'demutualization'.

[5] IOSCO Technical Committee, 'Consultation Report, Regulatory Issues Arising from Exchange Evolution' (2006), 28 <http://www.iosco.org/library/pubdocs/pdf/IOSCOPD212.pdf> accessed 27 September 2013.

some cases, and thus eliciting regulatory responses not based on market considerations alone. More importantly, exchanges are imbued, implicitly or explicitly, with a 'public interest' due to their impact on the related issues of economic growth, systemic financial stability and investor protection.

10.04 But herein lies a conundrum. The traditional exchange, even in its modern form, is a vulnerable species. Anyone with a computer can create an exchange; what is more, they can have global reach. Trading is migrating away from formal exchanges to alternative trading platforms.[6] Despite consolidation at the exchange level, multiple electronic trading venues are splintering the market. High frequency trading is driving institutional investors, who tend to hold large positions and relatively long term views, off the exchanges and into the 'dark pools'.[7] As the exchange has been the foundation stone of market institutions, the regulatory consequences of this shift are profound and still unappreciated. Even regulatory changes as recent as 2008, designed to adapt regulation to the electronic age, are now out-dated because of their assumptions about exchange trading.[8]

10.05 In addition to undermining the price discovery mechanism of exchanges,[9] the alternative trading platforms and other electronic markets may have little concern for the public interest. The notion of public interest justifies the application of regulation to exchanges. Yet, what is considered in the public interest, and how best to promote it, varies considerably from place to place.

10.06 Notions of public interest may also be highly culturally or politically specific and notoriously difficult to define with precision. The operation of public interest is more circumscribed in the United States than, say, in Singapore. In a fashion similar to German and Canadian law,[10] Hong Kong and Singapore both explicitly posited a public interest function in the legislation authorizing the demutualization of their exchanges.[11]

---

[6] In Europe, this trend is pronounced, with an estimated 36 per cent of trading in UK markets, and 14 per cent in Germany and France, respectively, taking place off exchange. See Philip Stafford, 'European dark pool equity trading jumps 45%', *Financial Times* (17 October 2013) <http://www.ft.com/intl/cms/s/0/fe837cec-3 6ad-11e3-8ae3-00144feab7de.html#axzz2qrQOruxS> accessed 19 January 2014. This may be a reaction to the historically high trading costs associated with the multiplicity of exchanges in Europe and the structural impediments to cross-border trading.

[7] In 2010, NASDAQ OMX, itself a transatlantic consolidated exchange, created a new platform, PBX, in an attempt to regain trading volume by institutional investors placing large orders in the dark pools.

[8] US 1934 Act, Rule 12g3-2(b) (US), applicable to non-US issuers, was updated 2008 to substitute public information made available on company websites for paper filings with the SEC, but made conditional on listing on an overseas exchange. With European trading shifting markedly off-exchange, many issuers may now fall outside Rule 12g3-2(b).

[9] See also the Efficient Market Hypothesis. For a good survey article, see Burton G Malkiel and Eugene F Fama, 'Efficient Capital Markets: A Review of Theory and Empirical work' (1970) 25 *Journal of Finance* 383.

[10] National Instrument 21-101 (CAN) states that the rules and policies of an exchange must not be contrary to the 'public interest' and must be designed to prevent fraudulent practices and promote 'just and equitable' principles of trade. Additionally, NI 21-101 introduces rules that prohibit an exchange from using its position to limit competition from other exchanges or ATSs, or unreasonably deny access to its services.

[11] Andreas M Fleckner, 'Stock Exchanges at the Crossroads' (2006) 74 *Fordham Law Review* 2541. See also John W Carson, 'Conflicts of Interests in Self-Regulation: Can Demutualized Exchanges Successfully Manage Them?', World Bank Policy Research Working Paper Series No 3183 (2003) <http://econpapers.repec.org/ paper/wbkwbrwps/3183.htm> accessed 3 October 2013; Technical Committee of the IOSCO, 'Responses to the IOSCO Consultation Report Entitled Regulatory Issues Arising from Exchange Evolution' (2006), 20–5, <http://www.iosco.org/library/pubdocs/pdf/IOSCOPD221.pdf> accessed 3 October 2013 (Deutsche Börse notes the requirements of German law with respect to the public interest function of exchanges); IOSCO, 'Consultation Report, Regulatory Issues Arising From Exchange Evolution' (n 5), 33 (the French Association

Among exchanges, there is also a definite, and dynamic, hierarchy. A few major exchanges **10.07** dominate (NYSE Euronext, LSE, NASDAQ OMX, Deutsche Börse, the Tokyo Stock Exchange). In just a handful of years though, newcomers have joined the upper echelons: the HKEx in Hong Kong, for example, the CME Group, the Chicago-based commodities and derivatives exchange and IntercontinentalExchange Group (ICE).

These exchanges share in the headlines, but differ greatly among themselves. The LSE is the **10.08** most internationalized equities exchange. The NYSE component of NYSE Euronext, especially after the takeover by Atlanta based upstart Intercontinental Exchange (ICE), is the largest in the United States, which in turn is the world's largest domestic market. Deutsche Börse is the largest in Europe. NASDAQ OMX is the major alternative to the NYSE in the United States, favoured by technology firms, and engaged in numerous international dalliances. The Tokyo Stock Exchange has long been (but perhaps not for long) the largest in Asia, yet is still primarily a domestic market. HKEx is the gateway to China. The rise of the CME reflects the increasing importance of non-equity based financial instruments. Euronext, after several marriages of convenience, surged (at least temporarily) to prominence due to its troubled merger with the NYSE. These exchanges can afford tailor-made regulatory regimes to suit the complex business and legal environments in which they operate.

In the second tier are smaller exchanges; some regional, others national, and some serving **10.09** specialized market segments such as the various commodities and futures exchanges. Among the second tier, for example, are found the Toronto Stock Exchange (TSX) in Canada, the OMX[12] in the Nordic/Baltic region (now part of NASDAQ OMX), the ASX in Australia, and the KSX in Korea. Again, although roughly similar in size (that is to say, smaller than the big exchanges), each is very different in its own way. Nevertheless, these exchanges appear to punch above their weight. They have significance and play a role greater than their size might otherwise warrant, especially over the last decade or two. These second tier exchanges have been innovators, open to technology, quick to change and adept at seizing opportunities. Of course, not all experiments have been successful, as the demise of the Neuer Markt[13] demonstrates, and not all marriages are made in heaven, as the failed merger between the TSX and the LSE or between the ASX and Singapore attest. But these exchanges have been learning from each other, as well as innovating for themselves, creating models responsive to their particular circumstances.

Exchanges with British roots, such as the ASX, TSX, and HKEx, have a long history of **10.10** self-regulation. However, in different ways and in response to different pressures, each has moved sharply away from a self-regulatory model. The TSX, buoyed by a strong Canadian economy and national primacy, which resulted from the sudden consolidation of most of Canadian equity markets, happily shed much of its regulatory role to focus on product innovation and serving as a national marketplace. Its decisions were pragmatic, determined by competitive pressures from its large southern neighbour and, ironically, the lack of a federal

---

of Investment Firms discusses the public interest implications of exchanges and they note it is a 'situation that demands appropriate governance arrangements and close regulatory scrutiny').

[12] OMX was formed by a progressive consolidation over time of a Swedish futures exchange with the Stockholm Exchange, the Copenhagen Exchange, and exchanges in Lithuania, Estonia, Latvia, Finland, and Armenia.

[13] The Neuer Markt was the technology segment of the Deutsche Börse, which enjoyed success between 1997 and 2000. It imploded when the dot com bubble burst, and was eventually shut down in 2003.

securities regulator in Canada (which places more pressures on the exchange to integrate market regulation on a nationwide basis).

10.11   Hong Kong's predecessor to HKEx relinquished most of its regulatory authority more reluctantly, only after years of skirmishes with a young regulator.[14] The resistance to realignment of regulatory authority in Hong Kong, however, could not withstand the combined pressures of the Asian financial crisis of 1997,[15] the dramatic shift in regulatory authority in the UK from the LSE to the FSA in 2000,[16] and the upsurge in mainland Chinese listings.[17] The longstanding potential for conflicts of interest, endemic in small financial communities such as Hong Kong, had not been sufficient, in and of itself, to prompt a major realignment of regulatory authority.

10.12   Australia's ASX, one of the first exchanges to demutualize,[18] has trodden a more tortuous path in trying to delineate the boundaries of regulatory authority between exchange and government regulator. For many years after the demutualization of 1998, the mechanisms designed to separate commercial and regulatory affairs within the exchange structure, as well as the relationship of exchange to regulator, were subject to constant rebalancing. This process of shedding self-regulatory authority by the exchange continues to evolve;[19] the longstanding tentativeness of the situation in Australia, in part at least, appears to be a legacy of path dependency and political ideology as much as anything else. A merger with the Singapore Exchange would have vaulted ASX into the top of the Asia league tables,[20] but that political joker, the national interest, as well as concerns over the dilution of government regulatory authority, derailed the transaction.

10.13   And then there are the rest, the small players and the sometimes not-so-small emerging, transitional or frontier markets, ranging from Johannesburg to Shanghai, from Jakarta to São Paulo, and from Bratislava to Bermuda. Some, like Johannesburg, have been around for a long time; others are brand new (or recently resurrected from the ashes). Some, like Bermuda, are sophisticated, niche market players that hardly fit the profile of exchanges found in emerging economies. And others, like Jakarta, serve large, resource-based economies, where considerable pools of domestic capital vie with significant levels of political risk in shaping the markets.

10.14   That said, dramatic changes in modern capital markets are upsetting the established hierarchies among exchanges. In a remarkable resurgence, Sao Paulo soared from near oblivion to international prominence in scarcely a decade. China is a story unto itself; its domestic markets are unlike any others in the world, as are its regulatory approaches.

10.15   Traditional self-regulatory models are fading away (or were never embraced), a demutualized form is the new norm, consolidations appear more successful on a domestic or regional level

---

[14] The Securities and Futures Commission (SFC) in Hong Kong was created in 1989, in response to the 1987 market crash, which shut the SEHK for several days.

[15] Which gave government regulators the upper hand.

[16] The UK market had long provided inspiration and technical expertise for Hong Kong.

[17] Which prompted heightened regulatory concerns.

[18] Number five, after Stockholm, Helsinki, Copenhagen, and Amsterdam.

[19] For further details, see Australian Stock Exchange, 'Media Release, ASX Markets Supervision: New Structure to Operate from 1 July' (29 June 2006) <http://www.asxgroup.com.au/media/PDFs/mr20060629_asx_markets_supervision.pdf> accessed 3 October 2013.

[20] See Ch 9 in this book .

and technological change is driving all. Everywhere, exchanges are under siege, rethinking their strategies and business model.

2. Foundations of the Modern Exchange

2.1 Early beginnings: Amsterdam, Paris, and Frankfurt

The modern stock exchange has its roots in the age of discovery and the rise in mercantilism **10.16** during the seventeenth century.[21] While the concept of 'exchange' is simple and timeless, the formal institution of the 'exchange', as a trading venue for various financial products, arose to fund colonial endeavours. The story of where money flowed therefore loosely tracked the geopolitical dynamics of the day.

Famously, the *Vereenigde Oost-Indische Compagnie* (VOC),[22] founded in 1602, became the **10.17** world's first truly multinational corporation, spearheading colonial development in Asia. While short distance trade could be financed by small groups of merchants pooling their capital, long distance trade to Asia required bigger ships capable of carrying greater cargo and crossing larger oceans. To raise capital, the VOC offered shares in a nascent, open air Amsterdam exchange.[23] Over 1,000 investors subscribed.[24] The modern stock exchange was born.

Amsterdam quickly established itself as the world centre of finance through its innovations **10.18** in trading equity and derivatives. As early as the 1550s, merchants in Amsterdam made agreement for future delivery of grain before it had been harvested.[25] By 1583, a *prix courant*, a listing price of quotations, emerged and by 1613 it was published in Amsterdam on a regular, bi-weekly basis.[26] Growth in European trade and banking created a greater demand for flexible investments represented by transferable securities.[27] Dutch merchants called one early form of futures trading the *windhandel*, or 'selling in the wind'.[28] Demand for this type

---

[21] Ranald Michie, *The Global Securities Market: A History* (Oxford University Press, 2006), 23.

[22] Commonly known as the Dutch East India Trading Company.

[23] Geoffrey Poitras, 'From the Renaissance exchanges to cyberspace: a history of stock market globalization', in Geoffrey Poitras (ed), *Handbook of Research on Stock Market Globalization* (Edward Elgar Publishing, 2012), 68, 79–84.

[24] Michie (n 21), 25–7.

[25] Jan De Vries and Ad Van Der Woude, *The First Modern Economy: Success, Failure and Perseverance of the Dutch Economy, 1500–1815* (Cambridge University Press, 1997), 150. Future contracts were written for a large range of contracts in the seventeenth century. Purchasers of these contracts increasingly had no intention of taking delivery (and sellers did not possess and did not intend to acquire the promised goods). This form of speculative trading found its most notorious expression in the tulip mania of 1636–37. See De Vries (n 25).

[26] De Vries (n 25), 147.

[27] Michie (n 21), 23.

[28] De Vries (n 25), 151. This early form of futures trading also led to the first form of state regulation. In 1609, Isaac Le Maire tried to manipulate prices in VOC shares. VOC lodged a protest with the government which issued the Dutch edict of 1610 banning short sales where, at the time of the short sale, the seller does not actually possess the shares being sold. Share transfers had to be made within one month of the sale date. Despite opposition, the ban on 'selling in the wind', or *windhandel* trade, was repeated in 1624, 1630, 1636, and 1677. See Poitras (n 23), 68, 79–84. See also Neil De Marchi and Paul Harrison, 'Trading "in the wind" and with guile: the troublesome matter of the short selling of shares in seventeenth-century Holland' in N Neil De Marchi and M Morgan (eds), *Higgling: Transactors and their Markets in the History of Economics, Annual Supplement to History of Political Economy* (Duke University Press, 1994), 26.

of trading stemmed from merchants' reluctance to allow too great a build up of idle funds at any one time.[29]

10.19 Ranald Michie identifies several factors that turned Amsterdam into a financial centre: Amsterdam was the only place where merchants and bankers could obtain the bills of exchange they required to settle transactions; merchants held credit balances in Amsterdam because they received or made payment there; and the *Wisselbank*, the Bank of Amsterdam, founded in 1609, provided the facility for bankers and merchants to transfer money between each other simply through debits and credits.[30] Amsterdam thus became a centre for equity and futures trading.

10.20 France, on the other hand, developed a bond market. The Paris Bourse started trading *rentes*, French government securities, in 1563.[31] While the French East India Company was formed in 1604, its securities did not generate much activity.[32] After the French Revolution, the *Caisse des Depots et Consignations*, the national savings bank, was established. The result was a massive expansion in the issue of French *rentes*, and Paris became a centre for sovereign bonds.[33]

10.21 Modern Europe's other notable exchange, located in Frankfurt, was limited. Traders have been recorded in Frankfurt as early as 1150, when they would gather for the autumn fair. In 1330, Emperor Ludwig the Bavarian positioned Frankfurt as a national commercial centre by adding a spring fair.[34] In the early sixteenth century, German commerce was limited to its European trading partners, owing to a lack of German unification and no colonial empire. However, Frankfurt welcomed the French and Dutch Protestants who fled persecution at home. The influx of immigrants added to Frankfurt's international status, and soon merchants from across Europe began attending the trade fairs.[35] In 1779, the German Emperor in Vienna issued Germany's first government bond offering using the *Bankhaus Bethmann*, or Bethmann Bank. The offering was broken down into fractions that anyone with ready funds could purchase.

10.22 The effect was that Frankfurt created a precedent for large bond issuances, which traders in the city were able to re-trade in the future.[36] By the 1820s, the demand for capital driven by the industrial revolution led to the first issuances of shares. Frankfurt saw an explosion of companies reorganizing as stock corporations and the Frankfurt exchange adapted with the times.

---

[29] Michie (n 21), 23.

[30] Michie (n 21), 23–4.

[31] Michie (n 21), 23.

[32] Mark Potter, *Corps and Clienteles: Public Finance and Political Change in France, 1688–1715* (Ashgate Publishing, 2003), 138–40, 161, 179–83.

[33] Michie (n 21), 63.

[34] Boerse Frankfurt, '11th to 17th Century' <http://www.boerse-frankfurt.de/en/basics+overview/history/11th+to+17th+century> accessed 3 October 2013.

[35] Boerse Frankfurt (n 34).

[36] Boerse Frankfurt, '18th to 19th Century' <http://www.boerse-frankfurt.de/en/basics+overview/history/18th-to-19th-century> accessed 3 October 2013.

The story of Amsterdam, Paris and Frankfurt illustrates the extent to which markets follow **10.23** the money. Capital and liquidity were needed in Amsterdam for the VOC: equity trading developed. The French government wanted to raise cash: Paris became a bond market. Germany had no colonial empire: Frankfurt took in persecuted religious groups with capital. If history drove the rise of these markets, it would also be their fall.

World War I was devastatingly disruptive on the continent. By the end of the war, all foreign **10.24** securities had disappeared from German exchange lists and Frankfurt lost its international reach.[37] While Amsterdam hosted a relatively large amount of foreign business prior to the war and served as an interface between the Entente and the Central Powers, the number of foreign securities quoted on the Amsterdam Stock Exchange fell from 840 in 1914 to 746 in 1918. In the same time, issues of Dutch government debt and domestic industrials expanded rapidly.[38] German banks setting up in Amsterdam after the war were refused admittance to trade in 1922, although they were later admitted.[39] Amsterdam never regained its international status.

Paris, too, fell into protectionism during World War I. The government controlled the activi- **10.25** ties of the Paris Bourse before and during the war, suspending transactions between July and December 1914.[40] Even once the Bourse reopened, government *rentes* could not be traded and the government introduced floor prices to control the market.[41] After the war, the government stifled the return of Paris to international finance by imposing various taxes and laws discriminating among French nationals and non-French.

World War II turned securities exchanges into a recognizable form. Amsterdam was reduced **10.26** to a domestic exchange populated only by blue-chip Dutch companies such as Royal Dutch Shell, Unilever, and Philips.[42] In France, the government banned dual listing in an effort to help preserve business on regional exchanges outside of Paris.[43] Exchange trading stagnated and by 1963, 60 per cent of bond issues in Paris were on behalf of the government or major state-owned enterprises.[44]

As Amsterdam and Paris lost international importance, Frankfurt, London and New York **10.27** rose to prominence. Frankfurt was well positioned to serve the financial needs of reconstructing post-war Germany. New York benefitted greatly from the role of the United States in reconstructing Europe. London increased in prominence, too. For example, when Paris refused to list shares of the German Commerzbank in 1962, London happily opened its doors.[45]

---

[37] Boerse Frankfurt, '20th Century' <http://www.boerse-frankfurt.de/en/basics+overview/history/20th+century> accessed 3 October 2013.

[38] Mitchie (n 21), 162.

[39] Youssef Cassis, *Capitals of Capital: The Rise and Fall of International Financial Centres 1780–2009* (Cambridge University Press, 2010), 177.

[40] Michie (n 21), 157–9.

[41] Michie (n 21), 157–9.

[42] Marjolein 't Hart, Joost Jonker, and Jan Luiten van Zanden, *A Financial History of the Netherlands* (Cambridge University Press, 1997), 169.

[43] Cassis (n 39), 213.

[44] Cassis (n 39), 284.

[45] Michie (n 21), 250.

10.28 Indeed, the 1980s saw London become the undisputed centre for European (and world) finance in a time period known as the 'Big Bang'. A number of deregulatory initiatives turned the London Stock Exchange (LSE) into a highly desirable trading venue.[46] For example, foreign or outside ownership of LSE member firms was permitted. Additionally, as part of a consolidation of a myriad of specialized market participants dating back to the medieval guilds, all firms became broker/dealers able to operate in a dual capacity. Minimum scales of commission were abolished, individual members ceased to have voting rights and trading moved from face-to-face on a market floor to computer and telephone operations.[47] Finally, the LSE became a private limited company under the Companies Act 1985. And so the nickname 'Big Bang' stuck, as trading on the LSE exploded and new vistas in world finance opened up.

10.29 At this point, demutualizations[48] and consolidations came into fashion. The Stockholm Stock Exchange was the first to break ground in 1993. A wave of securities exchange demutualizations followed: Helsinki, Copenhagen, Amsterdam, the *Borsa Italiana*, the Australian Stock Exchange, Iceland, Athens, Singapore, the Singapore International Monetary Exchange (SIMEX) and the London International Financial Futures and Options Exchange (LIFFE), all demutualized before 2000.[49] After the deluge of demutualizations, exchanges transformed themselves again through consolidation, in a process of 'creative destruction.'[50]

10.30 The first major consolidation was Euronext. On 22 September 2000, the Paris, Brussels and Amsterdam exchanges came together in a new entity called Euronext.[51] Since then, there

---

[46] London Stock Exchange, 'Our History' <http://www.londonstockexchange.com/about-the-exchange/company-overview/our-history/our-history.htm> accessed 3 October 2013.

[47] See, generally, Ch 6 of this book.

[48] Prior to exchange demutualization, exchanges were held as 'mutual' associations—essentially non-profit and member-owned. With demutualization, exchanges became shareholder held corporations and profit-maximizing business organizations. Thus, all exchange decisions were made by its members prior to demutualization, including whom to admit as members. Post-demutualization, shareholders influenced these decisions whether or not they were members.

[49] Benn Steil and André Meyer, 'Why do exchanges demutualize', *Mondovisione* (25 June 2002) <http://www.mondovisione.com/exchanges/handbook-articles/why-do-exchanges-demutualize/> accessed 3 October 2013. Not coincidentally, this wave of demutualizations coincided with a 'bull market' for equity securities and internationalization of the markets, resulting in tidy profits for the exchange participants benefiting from the change in structure. Timing is all.

[50] Shamshad Akhtar, 'Demutualization of Asian Stock Exchanges—Critical Issues and Challenges' in Shamshad Akhtar (ed), *Demutualization of Stock Exchanges: Problems, Solutions and Case Studies* (Asian Development Bank, 2002), 19. 'In order to remain competitive, exchanges need to continually restructure and upgrade themselves based on the latest technological advancements in trading and information dissemination technology. Members of mutual exchanges have been unable or unwilling to commit to such investments. A profit-making exchange with transferable (and listed) shares would be able to access a broader investor base for such funds.'

[51] Prior to its merger with the New York Stock Exchange, Euronext NV was a company domiciled in the Netherlands and was incorporated on 20 July 2000 by Société de Bourses Françaises SA (SBF), Amsterdam Exchanges NV (AEX) and Société de la Bourse de Valeurs Mobilères de Bruxelles SA (BXS). As at 22 September 2000, the three constituent companies merged into Euronext NV. With respect to Amsterdam, the merger was effected by means of a three-way legal merger between AEX, Euronext NV, and its wholly-owned subsidiary Euronext Amsterdam NV. In this merger, all assets and liabilities of AEX were transferred to Euronext Amsterdam NV and the shareholders and holders of profit-sharing certificates of AEX became shareholders of Euronext NV

On completion, all former shareholders of the Paris, Amsterdam, and Brussels exchanges became shareholders of the holding company, Euronext NV, which in turn had, as wholly owned subsidiaries, the former three exchanges. Under the exchange ratio that was deployed, the former shareholders of SBF, AEX, and BXS held, on completion, 60 per cent, 32 per cent and 8 per cent of the share capital of Euronext NV respectively.

have been a number of consolidations: for example, the NYSE and Euronext merged in 2006 and the LSE and the *Borsa Italiana* merged in 2007. In the global waves of demutualizations, exchanges mimicked each other's organizational structures. Demutualization also created a new dynamic among these exchanges.

2.2 Basics of an exchange

The exchange is a market place. Modern exchanges have usually combined three main func- **10.31**
tions: a trading system, a regulatory mechanism, and operational systems,[52] all to a greater
or lesser degree, depending on the exchange. The complexity of exchange structure and
the ancillary functions they performed increased over time. Concentric circles of intermediaries and supporting service providers spun out from the exchange, intersecting with
other existing private or public institutions.[53] Exchange members,[54] brokers and jobbers,[55]
broker-dealers,[56] market makers, investment bankers, promoters, introducers,[57] advisers, credit institutions, depositaries, clearing houses, payment systems, identification systems,[58]—all of these proliferated. Internal and external regulatory mechanisms developed.

The forces of technology, competition and demutualization[59] decoupled and realigned the **10.32**
traditional exchange functions of trading, regulating, and operating. Exchanges are struggling to redefine themselves now and still make money through fee generation. Some
exchanges have divested themselves or been relieved of their regulatory function; others have
bulked up on a broader array of operational systems; even the trading function of exchanges
is under threat from alternative trading systems. But exchanges continue to provide a nexus
of market expertise, systems, and information that can be put to new uses.[60]

As a market, exchanges used to be physical places. Most long-established exchanges are still **10.33**
known by their place names (London, New York, Chicago, Frankfurt, Tokyo, Toronto),
although place has now become more or less irrelevant. As the financial products traded on
exchanges dematerialized and diversified, electronic trading and virtual markets increasingly

---

[52] Jennifer Elliott, 'Demutualization of Securities Exchanges: A Regulatory Perspective', IMF Working Paper WP/02/119 (2002), 5–6.

[53] See also Jonathan R Macey and Maureen O'Hara, 'Globalization, Exchange Governance, and the Future of Exchanges' in Robert E Litan and Anthony M Santomero (eds), *Brookings-Wharton Papers on Financial Services* (Brookings Institution, 1999), 3. Five economic functions of exchanges have been identified: (1) liquidity, (2) monitoring of exchange trading against insider trading and manipulation, (3) standard-form, off-the-rack rules to reduce transaction costs for investors, (4) a signalling function to inform investors that the issuing company's stock is of high quality, and (5) a clearing function to ensure that secondary market participants receive cash for securities sold and timely delivery for securities purchased.

[54] Prior to demutualization.

[55] Before the 'Big Bang' in London; see Ch 6 of this book.

[56] The US terminology for the major form of exchange intermediary.

[57] Various forms of intermediary 'introduced' and monitored companies listing on an exchange, for example, the NOMAD of the London Stock Exchange. A NOMAD (nominated adviser) is a firm or company that the LSE licenses to manage new issuances to the AIM listing segment. It also acts as a *de facto* regulator.

[58] For example, CUSIP Numbers (Committee on Uniform Securities Identification Procedures): a CUSIP Number can be used to identify most securities for the purposes of clearing services.

[59] See following discussion of demutualization.

[60] For example, NYSE Euronext may assume responsibility for the management of the LIBOR rate setting system, which fell into disrepute under the aegis of the British Bankers Association. See NYSE Euronext, 'Press Release: NYSE Euronext subsidiary to become new administrator of LIBOR' (9 July 2013) <http://www.nyse.com/press/1373365567815.html> accessed 3 October 2013.

supplanted the physical exchange.[61] New exchanges, such as ICE (Intercontinental Exchange), which is taking over NYSE-Euronext, and Euronext itself, make no reference to their nominal country or place of origin. Older exchanges, such as the Chicago Mercantile Exchange, are rebranding themselves.[62]

An Example of Modern Exchange Structure: The Bolsa Mexicana

10.34 As markets have changed, so has institutional structure. The Bolsa Mexicana (BMV),[63] for example, illustrates one modern take on the traditional exchange. This particular model is noted for both vertical and horizontal integration of functions. The vertical integration refers to functions associated with core trading activities, often segmented by issuer identity or product, and closely related functions like clearing and settlement systems. Stacked one upon the other, these functions operate within the same organization, thus giving rise to the moniker of 'silos'.[64] Defenders of the silo structure for exchanges cite the efficiencies, in terms of time and cost, in integrating related trading functions. Detractors of the silo structure note the barriers it erects to new entrants, its monopolistic tendencies and potential to convey systemic risk. Detractors argue that cost efficiencies may be realized by the exchange but at the expense of investors and companies.

10.35 The horizontal aspect of exchange structure, on the other hand, refers to ancillary business lines associated with the exchange, usually in the interests of profit generation in the face of the declining revenues from traditional listing and trading activity.

10.36 The BMV runs a number of different trading systems or platforms: the Exchange itself (domestic equities or stocks); Global BMV Market (foreign companies' debt and equity); MexDer (derivatives[65]); and SIF ICAP (fixed income instruments and over-the-counter (OTC) products[66]). Associated trading services are provided by Indeval (BMV's central depositary, clearing and settlement agent) and Asigna (which provides counterparty services for trades executed on MexDer).

10.37 More controversially, the BMV regulates and supervises market activity in its own shares for compliance with its own rules and Mexican law. The potential efficiencies of the institution closest to the market regulating the market are obvious, especially in economies where governmental supervisory resources may be in short supply. The exchange as primary market regulator also reflects the persistent legacy of self-regulation in market institutions. The controversial element, however, arises with the new demutualized structure of exchanges operating as for-profit organizations, and often, as in the case of BMV, listing on

---

[61] The physical trading floor of the London Stock Exchange, eliminated in 1986, is now represented by a spectacular hanging light sculpture in the atrium of its new premises in Canary Wharf.

[62] Now usually referred to by its holding company name, CME Group Inc.

[63] The subject of a case study, discussed later on.

[64] The Deutsche Börse is the model for the silo.

[65] 'A derivative is a financial contract whose value is derived from the performance of underlying market factors, such as interest rates, currency exchange rates, and commodity, credit, and equity prices. Derivative transactions include an assortment of financial contracts, including structured debt obligations and deposits, swaps, futures, options, caps, floors, collars, forwards, and various combinations thereof.' Office of the Comptroller of the Currency, 'Derivatives' <http://www.occ.gov/topics/capital-markets/financial-markets/trading/derivatives/index-derivatives.html > accessed 3 October 2013.

[66] There is a crucial difference between on-exchange and off-exchange trading. On-exchange means that the sale of that property is concluded in accordance with the rules of the exchange: price is generally known, the standard rules apply, etc. Off-exchange (over-the-counter, or OTC) is a term used to describe sale of financial instruments that occurs off of the exchange (hence the creative name, *off-exchange*). The sale occurs as a bilateral contract between two parties, much like many types of non-financial property.

themselves. The potential for abuse, conflict of interest, and exclusionary anti-competitive practices is also obvious.

The BMV also offers 'other operational functions' as part of its horizontal integra- **10.38**
tion: Valmer provides investors with pricing, valuation and risk management products and services; Bursatech provides technology to streamline the BMV's business; and SIF ICAP Services and Corporativo provide personnel and management services.

3. Formative Forces and the Modern Exchange

3.1 Demutualization

The phenomenon of demutualization, the change in form of exchanges from member based **10.39**
associations (the exclusive country clubs of finance) to shareholder based commercial enti-ties, began over 20 years ago. It marked the beginning of a new era for exchanges, one that continues to unfold.

Exchanges are old institutions, the major ones predating the appearance of statutory busi- **10.40**
ness organizations, the corporation or registered companies. As a matter of practicality, they had assumed what over time became an increasingly archaic form of internal organization. It is somewhat ironic that one great motor of modern capitalism, the NYSE, would have been constituted for over a century[67] as a not-for-profit organization under New York law. The exclusivity and privacy of the mutual association form appealed to the clubbish proclivities of the market intermediaries associated with exchanges, until outweighed by the opportu-nity, presented by demutualization, to make a financial killing.[68]

3.1.1 The exchange as corporation

By demutualizing, an exchange changes organizational form to become a modern for-profit **10.41**
business organization, a corporation or shareholding company.[69] A mutually held and member-owned exchange may choose to become a privately held corporation, thereby

---

[67] Until demutualization in 2006.
[68] Pamela S Hughes, 'Background Information on Demutualization', in S Akhtar (ed), *Demutualization of Stock Exchanges: Problems, Solutions and Case Studies* (n 50), 33–4.
[69] See Reena Aggarwal, 'Demutualization and Corporate Governance of Stock Exchanges' [2002] *Journal of Applied Corporate Finance* 105 at 105–13: 'Traditionally, stock exchanges have been mutual associations owned by their members. Generally, they have been operated on a not-for-profit basis so that any profits are returned to members in the form of lower trading costs or access fees, but this has not always been the case. There are differences in the manner in which stock exchanges are operated and regulated. They differ in terms of the role of the board and the staff of the exchange, the powers of the chief executive and chairman and the composition and powers of exchange committees. Exchanges have a variety of voting structures and the balance of power between different users varies among them as well. Perhaps the most distinguishing feature of the traditional stock exchange structure is its cooperative governance model; the close identity between ownership of the organization and the direct use of its trading services. The owners of the mutual enterprise are also its custom-ers. Owner/customers may share in the net gains of the enterprise in proportion to their ownership interest. Decisions are usually made democratically, on a one member, one vote basis and often are made by committees of representatives of member firms. The ability to influence the decisions of the exchange is thereby separated from the level of economic interest a member has in the exchange. Ownership rights may not be freely tradable or exchangeable and on cessation of membership, those rights are forfeited. Because the organization's consti-tuting documents may expressly (or impliedly) adopt a non-profit objective and prohibit the distribution of surpluses, mutually owned exchanges are seldom able to raise capital from anyone other than their members.'

creating a share capital structure, but remaining member owned and controlled for all practical purposes.[70]

10.42 Further private offerings can expand the shareholder base of an exchange, while retaining the benefits of private company ownership.[71] A variation on demutualization makes shares publicly available although not listed, with caps or restrictions on voting so as to preserve original member control.[72] Finally, a demutualized exchange that lifts the trading restrictions on its shares can become fully publicly traded and list its shares to trade on exchange like any over corporation

10.43 The twist here is whether the exchange lists its shares on its own listing platform, thereby creating potential conflicts of interest.[73] With the exception of this last twist, the choices and organizational permutations available to a demutualized exchange are not very different from those open to any other business entity with a share capital structure. As with any other corporation, there is no inevitability about this linear trajectory from mutual association to publicly listed corporation. Some exchanges demutualize immediately into fully-fledged publicly listed corporations (such as the Bolsa Mexicana).[74] And, like any other corporation, profit maximization to the benefit of shareholders becomes their reason for being.

10.44 Interestingly, very little attention has been paid to the implications of use of the corporate form itself by an exchange.[75] In the United States, the corporate form does mean that a listing will trip numerous triggers designed to increase transparency and reduce conflicts of interest: insider trading regulations, extensive disclosure, and other issuer regulation. The debate surrounding demutualization of the NYSE in 2006, for example, noted that demutualization would address the opaqueness of the member association form and perceived internal governance abuses. Adoption of the corporate form potentially extends the reach of external regulation applicable to the exchange.

10.45 Compared to the United States, corporation law in continental Europe is prescriptive and quite regulatory to begin with. There are still minimum capital requirements for commercial corporations, as well as more structured and mandatory internal corporate governance mechanisms. Corporate law in Europe demonstrates a greater degree of public interest (workers councils or workers representation in dual board structures, for example). There is little of the balancing of external regulation against self-regulatory functions. In Europe, the regulators regulate.

---

[70] For example, the London Stock Exchange in 1986. London Stock Exchange, 'Our History' <http://www.londonstockexchange.com/about-the-exchange/company-overview/our-history/our-history.htm> accessed 3 October 2013.

[71] Aggarwal (n 69), 107.

[72] A typical restriction is to limit ownership or voting rights for any one shareholder to 5 per cent. See Aggarwal (n 69), 107.

[73] The conflict of interest arises due to the dual capacities in which the exchange is operating; as an exchange it is engaging in decision-making as to its operations which may affect its listed companies. The danger lies in the potential for self-interested decision-making favouring the exchange itself in its capacity as a listed company.

[74] See case study.

[75] Euronext, Inc, Registration Statement (Form S-4) (21 September 2006) <http://www.sec.gov/Archives/edgar/data/1368007/000104746906011989/a2173235zf1_s-4.pdf> accessed 3 October 2013. The merger of NYSE and Euronext focused attention on the significance of the use of the corporate form. Each of the NYSE and Euronext proposed the creation of non-corporate entities (in the case of Euronext, a Dutch foundation, and NYSE, a Delaware trust) to which shares of the ultimate holding company would be transferred in the event of untoward regulatory actions that might otherwise catch the holding company and result in 'regulatory creep'.

The concept of the independent, privately-funded, self-regulatory organization is somewhat **10.46** alien in continental Europe. Regulators may not be as close to the market, but many believe there is vigorous regulatory oversight. For an exchange to adopt corporate form is seen as a fairly non-contentious move, with little internal resistance from self-interested parties chary of losing autonomy. It also means that the exchange becomes subject to the real strictures of corporate law. Euronext, for example, was formed as a Dutch limited liability company with a two-tier board structure (arguably providing a superior form of internal governance than the Anglo-American single board structure). In addition, Euronext triggered oversight by multiple regulators, the Dutch Ministry of Finance, the French *Autorité des marchés financiers*, various interagency memoranda of understanding and EU directives (to name a few sources of external regulatory pressure and oversight).

Share ownership restrictions, implemented to deter self-interested behaviour on the part of **10.47** a dominant shareholder, also appear in demutualized exchanges.[76] Such restrictions already exist in some European corporate laws and some Commonwealth banking laws. The more cynical might see such restrictions as a form of protectionism, deterring foreign control of a national symbol.

The substantial differences in national corporate laws may result in persistent differences in **10.48** internal and external governance of demutualized exchanges and the extent of government regulatory intervention. There are other intriguing implications for exchange structures. Because United States corporate law is enabling and non-regulatory in nature, the NYSE found itself creating compensatory internal governance measures when demutualizing. Some of these compensatory mechanisms, such as the dual board structure and a chief regulatory officer reporting to a regulatory committee rather than the CEO,[77] were directly or indirectly inspired by European corporate law. In a further twist, the NYSE and Euronext, in their merger, employed associated non-corporate law vehicles (a Delaware trust and a Dutch foundation) as an escape hatch if unwelcome regulatory triggers were tripped in the future.

3.1.2 Benefits of demutualization

Demutualization brings benefits, at least in theory: better corporate governance mecha- **10.49** nisms, the possibility of raising capital without admitting new operational members to the exchange itself and more flexible structuring of exchange alliances.[78] In a mutual exchange, members are owner operators. Members, usually brokers, tended to close ranks and in the absence of open corporate governance practices designed to promote accountability and organizational renewal, became attached to their old ways. 'Brokers inadvertently resisted changes if these entailed additional costs, loss of revenue or competitive threat. This resistance eventually impeded the ability of the company to react quickly to a rapidly changing market environment.'[79] Demutualization resulted, to a greater or lesser degree, in a formal separation of ownership and management.

---

[76] See the for-profit private company stage, and following stages, in Aggarwal's five stage demutualization process, Aggarwal (n 69), 107.

[77] Roberta Karmel, 'Government Regulatory Intervention in the Governance of Market Infrastructure Institutions', Working Paper in the author's possession (2006).

[78] For a more comprehensive discussion of the benefits of demutualization, see Richard A Grasso (Chairman, NYSE), Testimony before Committee on Banking, Housing and Urban Affairs, US Senate regarding Public Ownership of the US Stock Markets (28 September 1999).

[79] Akhtar (n 50), 12.

10.50   Exchanges are also subject to external oversight in most cases, given their public interest function. Other governance mechanisms may overlay the usual ones associated with corporate form, such as public 'fit-and-proper' screenings and regulatory reports by the board and management.[80]

10.51   Demutualization can also lead to the admission of a greater number of traders. When the country club of existing members decides to grant trading rights to a new party under a mutually held organization, they effectively must give that party equity in the exchange (to be consistent with the mutual form).[81] Members may attempt to protect their territory and be disinclined to admit many (or any) new partners. The demutualized corporate form solves that problem. Exchanges become much more likely to extend trading rights to new participants, as that can lead to beneficial effect on profits and exchange value.[82]

10.52   Demutualization makes structuring alliances with other exchanges easier. The same competitive forces that push exchanges to demutualize and reinvent themselves demand that exchanges form alliances with other exchanges. The incentives built into mutually held organizations are woefully inadequate in this respect.

10.53   Factionalization is always a risk in mutual exchanges, fracturing the exchange along lines of interest. Fearing the disproportionate impact of a merger on trading activity, smaller members of an exchange may oppose it. In contrast, a demutualized exchange with a board and management accountable to shareholders will seek profit-generating alliances.

10.54   Demutualization facilitates friendly mergers and alliances through share exchanges and issuances. But some demutualized exchanges became the targets in hostile takeover bids. The City of London expressed its indignation when the London Stock Exchange found itself, several times, assailed by unwelcome suitors, such as the upstart OMX or later by NASDAQ.

3.1.3 Problems with demutualization

10.55   Demutualization also brings problems, primarily conflicts of interest created or intensified by the profit motive, as well as with respect to rule-making and self-listing arrangements. The concern is 'whether the commercial pressures (or governance structure) of a for-profit entity will undermine the commitment of resources and capabilities of the exchange to effectively fulfil its regulatory and public interest responsibilities to an appropriate standard'.[83]

10.56   Demutualization intensifies the conflicts of interest inherent in self-regulation to the extent exchanges retain such powers. A demutualized exchange must balance profit generation and the promotion of business opportunities against its role in supporting the 'integrity and efficiency of capital markets by setting and enforcing appropriate rules to regulate its market'.[84] A traditional exchange assumes a number of different responsibilities, including devising rules for trading and ensuring that they are observed, determining qualifications for listing or admission to trading, and conducting surveillance of the market and its participants,

---

[80]   Akhtar (n 50), 13.

[81]   Akhtar (n 50), 14.

[82]   Akhtar (n 50), 14.

[83]   AUS HR, Deb 27 November 1997, 11541 (from the speech presenting legislation authorizing demutualization of Australian Stock Exchange).

[84]   Frank Donnan, 'Self-regulation and the Demutualisation of the Australian Stock Exchange' (1999) 10 *Australian Journal of Corporate Law* 1.

investigating violations, and disciplining violators.[85] Demutualized exchanges may be reluctant to spend adequate resources on regulation and may not be willing to enforce rules against themselves or participants who bring in large volumes of trading or liquidity.

The quandary created by exchanges listing their own shares on themselves is obvious enough. **10.57** However, such an arrangement presents a novel conflict of interest. IOSCO expressed the concern that 'the market disciplines on proper behaviour may not be strong enough where the exchange is being asked to regulate its own listing'.[86] Generally though, even if an exchange's securities are only admitted to trading on its own market, some of the potential conflicts may be lessened if a third party regulates the trading of that exchange's securities.

Case Study in Demutualization: The Bolsa Mexicana de Valores

On 18 June 2008 the Bolsa Mexicana de Valores, SAB de CV (the BMV) raised 4.6 billion **10.58** pesos (US$443.5 million) in a domestic Mexican public offering and a separate international offering (which included the United States) on an exempt basis.[87] Its shares are now traded on itself under the ticker 'BOLSAA'. The structure of this offering indicates the level both of maturity reached by an emerging market and interest by international institutional investors. Fifteen years earlier, the privatization of Telmex[88] had required a public offering of shares (in the form of ADRs) in the United States, with listing on the NYSE.[89] By 2008, the Mexican domestic market was considered sufficiently developed to be the sole public market for BMV shares and international institutions had sufficient confidence in BMV, both as an investment and a trading venue,[90] to take positions on a private placement basis outside Mexico.

The reinvigorated Mexican economy inspired confidence in the BMV's members that **10.59** they could expand its operations.[91] In 2008, Mexico was still very much an emerging market economy, but one which increasingly had attained macroeconomic stability. In the years leading up to the demutualization of the BMV, Mexico experienced relatively strong growth[92] and an optimistic future.

The BMV, confident that the Mexican economy would maintain macroeconomic stabil- **10.60** ity, saw opportunities in the underdeveloped state of the Mexican securities market: 'when compared with other economies in Latin America, Mexico's capital markets still present opportunities for expansion at a pace that exceeds economic growth. The ratio of the

---

[85] Donnan (n 84), 1.

[86] IOSCO Technical Committee, 'Issues Paper on Exchange Demutualization' (2011), 9 <http://www.iosco.org/library/pubdocs/pdf/IOSCOPD119.pdf> accessed 3 October 2013.

[87] Milbank, Tweed, Hadley, and McCloy LLP, 'News Release: Milbank Advises on Mexican Stock Exchange IPO' (1 July 2008) <http://www.milbank.com/news/milbank-advises-on-mexican-stock-exchange-ipo.html> accessed 3 October 2013.

[88] The Mexican telecommunications company.

[89] Which promptly became the primary trading market, draining liquidity from the Mexican domestic market. See also Coffee (n 95) for a discussion of this phenomenon.

[90] By taking positions on a private placement basis outside Mexico, institutional investors would potentially be looking to offload their shares in the public Mexican market, ie over the BMV itself.

[91] And make substantial sums of money in the process. Members sell their interests in the demutualization process.

[92] Bolsa Mexicana de Valores, SAB de CV, 'Offering circular' (12 June 2008), 5 <http://www.bmv.com.mx/wb3/work/sites/BMV/resources/LocalContent/1378/1/Listing_Prospectus.pdf> accessed 3 October 2013 Reuben Lee, 'Changing Market Structures, Demutualization and the Future of Securities Trading. Growth was 2.8% (2005), 4.8% (2006) and 3.3% (2007).

average market capitalization of listed companies to GDP in Mexico reached 44.5% in 2007 while the same ratio is 123.8% for Chile and 95.2% for Brazil, the two most developed capital markets in Latin America'.[93] For every $1 of value held in the stock of a company, less of that value was publicly listed in Mexico than elsewhere in the big Latin American markets as compared to each country's individual GDP.[94] There was room to grow the public market in Mexico.

10.61 In the five years immediately prior to the initial public offering in 2008, the BMV's business model changed dramatically. Since its inception, BMV had been, unsurprisingly, a US-style institution, focused almost exclusively on domestic equity markets, listing shares of Mexican companies. Similar to other exchanges, this business model was failing, but the problem was more acute in Latin American exchanges than elsewhere. US exchanges had been draining liquidity from Latin American markets as Latin American issuers were enticed to list and trade in the United States using ADRs.[95] Diversification out of equity markets was the first response. BMV, as had other exchanges, looked to fixed-income instruments, over-the-counter (OTC) products trading in the secondary market, foreign debt and equities, derivatives and market data products. [96]

10.62 Increasing internationalization and competition among exchanges (the Brazilian exchange had just demutualized, for example[97]) as well as maturing markets in developing economies also prompted serious efforts at reform to invigorate domestic markets.

10.63 Demutualization was supported by concurrent tax and legal reforms, starting in the early 1990s and leading up to 2008.[98] Amendments to the Mexican Securities Market Law had facilitated the issuance of new types of fixed-income instruments and structured products, together with measures to increase investor confidence in the Mexican capital markets. Pension fund reforms, as elsewhere, played an important role, permitting greater diversification and stoking demand for more sophisticated products listed on the BMV. Tax reforms created a friendlier environment for both domestic and non-domestic investors in Mexican markets. Financial markets were opened up to non-Mexican financial groups and financial intermediaries.

10.64 The BMV itself is a poster child for the current trends in exchange structure. See Figure 10.1. It exhibits both vertical and horizontal integration of trading and ancillary services so as to promote fee generation. There are multiple, specialized listing boards, including one for non-domestic issuers. The goal is to become a regional trading hub for Spanish-speaking Latin America.[99] Demutualization prompts 'global electronic

---

[93] Bolsa Mexicana (n 92), 5.

[94] The problem may have been one of large monopolies and large family holdings such as those held by Carlos Slim, by some accounts the world's richest man. 'Samba v Ranchero: As stockmarkets go public, Mexico struggles to keep up with Brazil', *The Economist* (29 May 2008) <http://www.economist.com/node/11460053> accessed 3 October 2013.

[95] See John C Coffee Jr, 'Competition among Securities Markets: A Path Dependent Perspective', Columbia University Law School, The Center for Law and Economic Studies, Working Paper No 192 (25 March 2002) <http://papers.ssrn.com/sol3/papers.cfm?abstract_id=283822> accessed 10 October 2013.

[96] Bolsa Mexicana (n 92), 1.

[97] In 2007 the Bovespa, Brazil's main exchange, and the BM&F, Brazil's commodities and futures exchange, demutualized with much success. In 2008 the two exchanges merged and created an alliance with the Chicago Mercantile Exchange. The result was an increase in trading of Brazilian securities by those abroad and of securities abroad by Brazilian traders. The Brazilian experience demonstrated the potential benefits of demutualization.

[98] See generally Bolsa Mexicana (n 92).

[99] Michael Fitzgerald of Milbank, Tweed, Hadley & McCloy, a firm that advised the BMV, noted that '[t]his IPO represents a significant landmark for the Mexican securities markets and should bring about improved trading efficiency and increased trading volume. The Mexican stock exchange is also increasingly being viewed

markets supporting one-stop shopping for securities and derivatives, financials and commodities'.[100]

The BMV is positioning itself to take advantage of these developments. The funding raised through the demutualization was intended to further the development of information systems and technology,[101] so as to expand electronic trading platforms accommodating increased volumes generated by algorithmic trading.[102] Additionally, the company wanted to integrate their 'equity and derivatives trading platforms in order to make it possible for [their] clients to execute trades on both the Exchange and MexDer simultaneously'.[103]

10.65

Now, BMV itself runs the Exchange, on which domestic equities continue to trade. The BMV's natural starting point for international expansion is its Global BMV Exchange, originally established in 2003, permitting foreign companies to list both equities and fixed-income instruments.[104] The BMV structures its other business units as subsidiaries. MexDer handles derivatives trading and SIF ICAP handles the trading of fixed income instruments and OTC products. The Contraparte Central de Valores de México (the CCV) is a central counterparty service for trades executed on the BMV, the central counterparty ensuring trades do not fail. Asigna provides the same counterparty services for MexDer. Indeval is the BMV's central depositary, clearing, and settlement agent. Valmer provides pricing, valuation and risk management products and services, an example of the creation of new business from existing expertise and information pools. Bursatech provides integration technology to streamline all of the BMV's business units. Finally, management and personnel services are provided by SIF ICAP Services and Corporativo.

10.66

Since its offerings in 2008, the BMV has expanded significantly.

10.67

The market capitalization of the Exchange increased from 3,220,900.19 million Pesos to 5,634,401.14 million Pesos—an increase of 75 per cent in the context of a global financial crisis.[105] At the same time, the Exchange's trading volume increased from 53,317 million shares to 74,539 million shares—an increase of 39 per cent.[106] In 2012, Banco Santander's Mexico unit raised US$4 billion on the BMV.[107] This sale sparked serious interest in listing on the BMV: as of January 2013, an additional five issuers were lined up to offer stocks on the exchange.[108]

10.68

---

as the most viable exchange for companies to list on in Spanish speaking Latin America. [Brazil is a Portuguese speaking country.] This offering should further reinforce that position of regional prominence'. Taisa Markus of the same firm commented that 'international securities exchanges have become increasingly competitive in recent years. This IPO allows the [BMV] the currency it needs to maintain its competitive edge on the international stage as the second largest securities exchange in Latin America': Milbank (n 87).

[100] André Cappon and Stephan Mignot, 'Exchange Consolidation: Scenarios for Eastern Europe' (CMB Group, 2012), 2 <http://www.thecbmgroup.com/publications.asp#capitalmarkets> accessed 3 October 2013.

[101] Cappon and Mignot (n 100), 2.

[102] Higher volume of trades means more revenue for the BMV.

[103] Bolsa Mexicana (n 92), 97.

[104] Bolsa Mexicana (n 92), 96. However, the BMV noted that the fixed-income trading on the Global BMV is not very active.

[105] Bolsa Mexicana de Valores SAB de CV, 'Informe Anual 2011 de la Bolsa Mexicana de Valores, S.A.B. de C. V' (2011), 12 <http://www.bmv.com.mx/wb3/wb/BMV/BMV_informacion_financiera_consolidada> accessed 3 October 2013.

[106] Bolsa Mexicana (n 105).

[107] Jonathan J Levin, 'Bolsa Soars to Record High Amid IPO Optimism: Mexico City Mover', *Bloomberg* (3 January 2013) <http://www.bloomberg.com/news/2013-01-02/bolsa-surges-most-since-09-amid-ipo-optimism-mexico-city-mover.html> accessed 3 October 2013.

[108] Levin (n 107).

10.69 | The BMV has also used its capital to develop the technologies that it seeks. In September 2012, the BMV installed a new trading engine that can accommodate high frequency (and therefore algorithm-based) traders.[109]

10.70 | Additionally, BMV made a strategic alliance with the Chicago Mercantile Exchange (CME) in March 2010, following in the footsteps of the Brazilian BM&F-Bovespa.[110] The alliance focused on derivatives trading and allowed traders access to assets on both exchanges, as well as administrative efficiency when dealing between exchanges.[111]

10.71 | The BMV's demutualization has so far been a success story. The convergence of Mexico's macroeconomic conditions, the legal and tax reforms and the example set by Brazil's BM&F-Bovespa provided the right conditions for such a move. One of the primary advantages of demutualization, the ease of effecting-mergers, reorganizations and affiliations, was quickly apparent in the arrangement with the CME, which utilized a stock-swap.

3.2 Technology and globalization

10.72 The twin forces of technology and globalization are commonly credited with revolutionizing securities trading and the exchanges.[112] Floor trading involved traders shouting out bids 'in

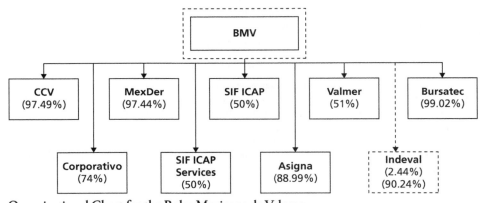

Organizational Chart for the Bolsa Mexicana de Valores
Figure 10.1 Bolsa Mexicana de Valores, SAB de CV, 'Offering circular' (12 June 2008), 9 9<http://www.bmv.com.mx/ wb3/work/sites/BMV/resources/LocalContent/1378/1/ Listing_Prospectus.pdf> accessed 3 October 2013.

---

[109] Levin (n 107).
[110] Brazil's alliance with the Chicago Mercantile Exchange had a positive effect on the BM&F-Bovespa's trading volume. In that alliance, the BM&F-Bovespa took 1.7% equity in Chicago's exchange and Chicago took 5% equity in the Brazilian exchange. See Chicago Mercantile Exchange Group, 'News Release CME-G BVMF3 CME Group, BM&FBOVESPA Announce February 9 Start Date for Order Routing CME Group Products on BM&FBOVESPA's GTS Platform' (6 February 2010) <http://cmegroup.mediaroom.com/index.php?s=43&item=2799> accessed 3 October 2013.
[111] Bolsa Mexicana de Valores SAB de CV, 'Informe Anual 2012 de la Bolsa Mexicana de Valores, S.A.B. de C. V' 22' (2012) <http://www.bmv.com.mx/wb3/wb/BMV/BMV_informacion_financiera_consolidada> accessed 3 October 2013.
[112] See Ruben Lee, 'Changing Market Structures, Demutualization and the Future of Securities Trading', Paper delivered at the 5th Annual Brookings/IMF/World Bank Financial Markets and Development Conference (15 April 2003) [unpublished]: 'It is widely recognized that the pressures of competition, globalization, and technological change, are threatening the development, and in some instances the very survival, of many developing capital markets.' See also Ruben Lee, *Running the World's Markets: The Governance of Financial Infrastructure* (Princeton University Press, 2011); Elliott (n 52); Akhtar (n 50) 3; Aggarwal (n 69), 107; and Hughes (n 68), 33. There are, however, many more sources in the literature affirming this principle.

the pits', aided by arcane hand signals. Despite the 'fear and loathing' with which electronic trading was greeted by some old-timers, it has rendered floor trading virtually obsolete.[113]

Trading has now become divorced from geographic place, and possibly regulatory reach, which **10.73** remains territorially based; trading is in the cloud. Trades take place at lightning speed, exponentially increasing potential trading volume, liquidity, and volatility, as well as the potential for disastrous error.[114] In addition to the 'fat finger' effect attributed to human error, the robustness of the systems themselves to handle the new trading patterns is a serious and growing concern, the consequences of which may be seriously underestimated.[115]

On the other hand, technology requires new skills and breeds new industries and players. New **10.74** forms of organization, together with alliances that might not have been imaginable in even the recent past, have transformed exchanges, sometimes in unexpected ways. For example, the Amsterdam Exchange, seeking flexibility and competitive advantage demutualized then merged with Paris and Brussels to form a new regional exchange, Euronext. The NYSE then rolled Euronext into the gargantuan transatlantic exchange, NYSE-Euronext, which Atlanta-based ICE is now swallowing.[116] Euronext may be spat out in the process[117] and the Amsterdam Exchange, its best laid plans having gone awry, appears to have sunk into oblivion, with its best talent moving away to high frequency trading centres scattered around Amsterdam.[118]

Others, financial centres to be reckoned with, have multiplied, in a process dubbed 'multipo- **10.75** larity';[119] Hong Kong, Singapore, Kuala Lumpur, for example.[120] These rising regional centres place competitive pressures on the established exchanges. The closed cells of finance, and the cosy clubs, have burst open. 'The traditional exchange governed by its members is seen to be unable to adequately respond to competitive pressures—a governance structure that relies on member decision making is slow and encumbered by the many, and often conflicting, interests of the individual members.'[121] Demutualization was an early, but perhaps ultimately inadequate, response.

---

[113] Jack Farchy, 'End of an era as LME is sold for £1.4bn', *Financial Times* (25 July 2012) <http://www.ft.com/intl/cms/s/0/1db65672-d668-11e1-bd9c-00144feabdc0.html?siteedition=intl&siteedition=intl#axzz2gCk5Phsy> accessed 3 October 2013.

[114] The so-called 'fat finger' mistakes, where a slip of a finger on a keyboard can throw markets into freefall.

[115] For example, the SEC has recently fined NASDAQ OMX for system failures associated with the debacle of the highly publicized Facebook initial public offering. See Arash Massoudi, 'Nasdaq prepares for $10m SEC fine over botched Facebook IPO', *Financial Times* (24 April 2013) <http://www.ft.com/intl/cms/s/0/a39fb2ee-acd5-11e2-b27f-00144feabdc0.html#axzz2gCk5Phsy> accessed 3 October 2013.

[116] Jacob Bunge, 'SEC approves ICE-NYSE Deal', *Wall Street Journal* (16 August 2013) <http://online.wsj.com/article/SB10001424127887323639704579016521606693810.html>.

[117] Bunge (n 116).

[118] 'Dutch Fleet: The home of the world's first stock exchange is now a high-frequency heartland', *The Economist* (20 April 2013) <http://www.economist.com/news/finance-and-economics/21576423-home-worlds-first-stock-exchange-now-high-frequency-heartland-dutch> accessed 3 October 2013.

[119] See Nicholas Véron, Guntram B Wolff, and Jacob Funk Kirkegaard (eds), *Transatlantic Economic Challenges in an Era of Growing Multipolarity* (Bruegel Institute, 2012).

[120] See also the case study on the Bolsa Mexicana in this chapter. The Bolsa Mexicana demutualized to raise capital, which it committed to consolidating its businesses and improving the technology of the trading platform it runs. The Bolsa's demutualization, IPO and subsequent performance illustrates a securities exchange that is competing to remain technologically up to date, trying to find a niche (through its derivatives alliance with the Chicago Mercantile Exchange), and which is trying to remain regionally relevant (exploring the possibility of a pan-Latin American alliance, MILA). For more on MILA, see Philippe Carré, 'Comment: Pan-Latin American exchange in sight?', *Financial Times* (10 January 2010) <http://www.ft.com/intl/cms/s/0/72a33da4-3b71-11e1-a09a-00144feabdc0.html#axzz2X6TTymy5> accessed 3 October 2013.

[121] Elliott (n 52), 8.

10.76 Technology and globalization have eaten away at the traditional business model of established exchanges. 'Trading has become global as the role of the exchange has become less relational.'[122] No more long lunches needed. Additionally, the cost of information, once to the advantage of a domestic exchange, has plummeted.[123] The swing away from autonomous, self-regulatory, exchanges has also played into the 'commoditization of exchange trading'. Regulators, from the SEC and the CFTC in the United States to the European Commission[124] and the new European regulator, ESMA, are shaping the exchanges.

10.77 The market has also found a way to separate clearing from the listing and trading functions. According to O'Hara and Macey, of the five economic functions usually associated with exchanges,[125] only liquidity remains. So the fight is over liquidity. Exchanges need the capital to keep up with changing technology to promote trading volume and the flexibility to create global alliances, to the same end. These alliances invariably gravitate to the epicentre of economic growth. In sum, globalization giveth whereas technology and regulation taketh.[126]

3.2.1 Alternative Trading Systems and their regulation

10.78 Hollowing out the heart of the traditional exchange are alternative trading systems (ATSs), technology's gift to modern trading. ATS is a slippery concept, a generic term for an exchange which is not an exchange. Different jurisdictions use different terminology, and the same terminology can lead to different interpretations.[127] These systems take several forms, among them automated trading systems, proprietary trading systems (broker run platforms), and dark pools. According to ESMA, the European securities regulator, an 'ATS is an entity which, without being regulated as an exchange, operates an automated system that brings together buying and selling interests—in the system and according to rules set by the system's operator—in a way that forms, or results in, an irrevocable contract'.[128] The first characteristic, *without being regulated as an exchange*, is the characteristic that (naturally) causes the most concern from a regulatory perspective.

10.79 Because alternative trading systems are not regulated as an exchange, they break down barriers to entry and thereby challenge the monopoly of the exchange. Anyone with a computer can create an online trading platform. More often, however, already established exchanges or investment providers such as banks create ATSs, primarily because they have the level of financial sophistication to attract liquidity. These platforms perform the same function as a formal exchange: they facilitate the purchase and sale of securities. However, they fall outside the scope of traditional securities exchange regulation.

---

[122] Macey and O'Hara (n 53), 2–3.

[123] Macey and O'Hara (n 53), 2–3.

[124] Which is currently developing the MiFID 2 regime.

[125] Macey (n 53).

[126] '[E]xchange births are positively correlated with economic growth and commodity booms, while closures are associated with advances in communications technology, such as telephone and the Internet, and heightened regulation, such as the 1934 Securities Exchange Act and state-level blue sky laws in the United States and the 1963 Stock Transfer Act in the United Kingdom.' See Bjorn N Jorgensen, Kenneth A Kavajecz, and Scott N Swisher, 'The Historical Evolution of Financial Exchanges' (4 September 2011) <http://ssrn.com/abstract=1922250> accessed 3 October 2013.

[127] ESMA, 'The Regulation of Alternative Trading Systems in Europe: A paper for the EU Commission', The Forum of European Securities Commissions FESCO/00-064c (September 2000), 4 <http://www.esma.europa.eu/system/files/00_064c.pdf> accessed 3 October 2013.

[128] ESMA (n 127), 4–5.

ATSs fragment the market and drain liquidity from formal exchanges[129] by attracting order **10.80** flow that would otherwise go to an exchange. Exchanges work best when they have high amounts of liquidity, and if providing liquidity is now the only remaining economic function of the exchange, according to O'Hara and Macey, then exchanges are not facing a rosy future. Fragmentation of the markets raises other concerns; price differences across markets can fuel unwelcome varieties of arbitrage, to the detriment of the hapless retail investor in particular. Institutional investors, on the other hand, may find it more difficult or expensive to place large orders.[130]

The regulatory responses to ATSs have been unsatisfactory. The menu of options, perhaps **10.81** somewhat unimaginatively, have included developing a new regulatory category for ATS, incrementally changing the regulatory status of investment firms also operating ATSs, and replacing a 'regulated market' regime with a 'trading system regime', effectively lumping all trading platforms in the same regulatory category.[131] The United States acted early,[132] but in the interests of disrupting the status quo as little as possible, simply tweaked the broker-dealer category of registered intermediary. The SEC gave ATSs the option of registering as a national exchange or as a broker-dealer.[133] The SEC then cast its net widely, expanding its definition of exchange to capture ATSs:

> Any organization, association, or group of persons that: (1) brings together the orders of multiple buyers and sellers; and (2) uses established, non-discretionary methods (whether by providing a trading facility or by setting rules) under which such orders interact with each other, and the buyers and sellers entering such orders agree to the terms of a trade.[134]

Once caught by the definition of exchange, however, an organization can wriggle free by choosing to be classified as a broker-dealer, provided it meets the criteria in Regulation ATS.[135]

The Europeans, on the other hand, have expanded on the pre-existing 'regulated market' **10.82** concept and created a residual category called, 'Mutual Trading Facility' (MTF), which captures all trading facilities operated by an investment firm or market operator. While a regulated market trips regulatory triggers in MiFID, the Prospectus Directive and the Transparency Directive, MTFs do not.

---

[129] Trading on ATSs is said to regularly comprise 10–15% of US equity trading volume. Laura Tuttle, 'Alternative Trading Systems: Description of ATS Trading in National Market System Stocks', SEC DERA White Paper (October 2013), 2 <http://www.sec.gov/marketstructure/research/ats_data_paper_october_2013.pdf> accessed 19 January 2014. Research by Tabb Group puts Europe's share at 11%. See Matthew Philips, 'European Investors Are Diving Into Dark Pools', *Bloomberg Businessweek* (13 November 2013) <http://www.businessweek.com/articles/2013-11-14/european-investors-are-diving-into-dark-pools#r=rss> accessed 19 January 2014.
[130] For a description of the creation of PBX by NASDAQ OMX, see (n 7).
[131] ESMA (n 127), 16.
[132] In 1998.
[133] For a fuller discussion of the history of ATS in the United States, see Ian Domowitz and R Lee, 'On the Road to Reg ATS: A Critical History of the Regulation of Automated Trading Systems', eBusiness Research Center Working Paper 10-2001 (June 2001) <http://www.smeal.psu.edu/cdt/ebrcpubs/res_papers/2001_10.pdf> accessed 5 October 2013.
[134] 17 Code of Federal Regulations 240, § 3b-16(a) (US).
[135] SEC Release No 34-40760 (12/8/98), 'What is the exemption in Reg ATS, ie the criteria to escape the exchange definition' (US).

10.83   The difference between the US and European approaches is that the former forces ATSs into one of two stringently regulated categories, while the latter allows some exchanges to opt in to the more stringent requirements, such as trade and market data reporting associated with a regulated market. Consequently, markets, such as proprietary trading in dark pools,[136] can ignore regulatory reporting requirements with impunity.

10.84   ATSs, and other forms of electronic trading, are sounding the death knell of the formal exchange. They also undermine the bedrock of the assumptions surrounding exchange trading, price discovery, and the efficient market hypothesis. Information remains trapped in the dark pool or trading fragments to the point where price discovery ceases to operate.

3.2.2 Dark pools

10.85   Regulators currently regard dark pools[137] as both a threat and a complement to securities exchange integrity. Dark pools solve a very simple problem: how do investors, invariably institutions or professionals, trade large blocks of securities without moving the market. They do so off the exchange, out of the glare of public scrutiny. In effect, dark pools are alternative markets for savvy professionals and institutions only, facilitated by electronic trading facilities and proprietary trading platforms. Market access is restricted, as many dark pool operators are banking institutions.[138] The pools are dark, because they are designed to prevent information concerning trades seeping back into the daylight of the public marketplace, at least not until after the trading has taken place.

10.86   This feature of dark pools is the source of the gravest concerns about them. The operation of modern capital markets, and their regulation, has been premised on the availability of information.[139] Economists worry about the price discovery mechanism. 'If enough orders are not transparent to participants, or there is unequal or incomplete information about transparent orders, there may be insufficient information about prices for market participants to identify trading opportunities.'[140]

10.87   Regulators worry about market manipulation. Algorithmic electronic trading has led to some traders attempting to go on fishing expeditions, trading in dark pools to discover who is trying to sell what. Algorithms are able to detect the identity of these trades based on the size and frequency of particular offers.[141]

10.88   Dark pools are also indicative of another pronounced trend that bodes ill for exchanges, the growth in off exchange trading which siphons off exchange liquidity.[142] Dark pools are also challenging the fundamentals of exchange trading rules, such as who is a buyer and who is a seller. Some dark pools use a step process: first they will list a security, but not whether the offer is to buy or sell or the quantity. Trading will proceed from there.

---

[136]   Discussed later on.

[137]   Previously also known as 'upstairs trading'. In formal exchanges, public trading was done 'downstairs'. When traders wanted to execute trades off-exchange, they would go 'upstairs'.

[138]   For an example of an institutional investor operating a dark pool, see 'Off-exchange trading: some like it not', *The Economist* (20 August 2010) <http://www.economist.com/node/21526387> accessed 5 October 2013.

[139]   Going back to that famous maxim, 'sunlight is the best disinfectant'.

[140]   IOSCO Technical Committee, 'FR 06/11 Principles for Dark Liquidity' (2011), 20 <http://www.iosco.org/library/pubdocs/pdf/IOSCOPD353.pdf> accessed 5 October 2013.

[141]   For a comprehensive discussion on dark pools and the regulation thereof, see IOSCO (n 140).

[142]   Which according to Macey and O'Hara is all that exchanges have left to sell (n 53).

Obviously, the ability to assess actual trading volume in dark pools is impaired. Because no **10.89** one really knows how much of what is being traded in dark pools, regulators worry about price distortion and exacerbated volatility.[143] However, dark pools are a market driven initiative, serving the needs of the professional market; regulators have been loath to intervene.

3.2.3 High frequency trading: speed demons hit the exchanges

Technology driven electronic trading, as manifested in high frequency trading (HFT), has **10.90** transformed capital markets and exchanges. This is the age of the automaton in the exchange; humans need not apply. HFT uses algorithms to predict the market or to take advantage of discrepancies in price in different marketplaces. How frequent is frequent? Second by second, sometimes with untoward results.[144] How fast is fast? Milliseconds.

The price discrepancies driving HFT are very small and profit per trade miniscule. Making **10.91** money requires thousands of trades a day. But speed is key, as traders exploit differences before either their competitors or the market gets to them. The computers are so fast that traders—competing for microsecond advantages—even try to physically position themselves closer to the exchange servers.[145]

HFT has the potential to make markets both more efficient and more volatile. In its benign **10.92** form, HFT can correct across markets. For example, if the price of a security is different on the NASDAQ OMX and the LSE, the algorithms will produce selling on one exchange and buying on the other until the price convergences. A more malevolent manifestation amounts to market manipulation, by artificially creating price differences between exchanges and dark pools. [146]

Exchanges enjoy an ambivalent relationship with HFT. On the one hand, beleaguered **10.93** exchanges looking for fee generation, welcome increased trading volume, irrespective of origin. But exchanges have gone even further, in terms of cutting deals with HFT so as to increase volume by concentrating it on one exchange to the detriment of another. HFT, however, can undermine exchanges. Has the Amsterdam Exchange sunk with the rise of a Dutch HFT industry? Do the volatility and propensity for 'accidents' associated with HFT outweigh easy trading profits for the exchange.

The blame for the current increased volatility of public markets has been laid at the door of **10.94** HFT. During the 'Flash Crash' of 6 May 2010, the Dow Jones Industrial lost and regained 9 per cent market capitalization within minutes.[147] Markets, investors, intermediaries,

---

[143] Schumpeter Blog, 'Off-exchange share trading: shining a light on dark pools', *The Economist* (18 August 2011) <http://www.economist.com/blogs/schumpeter/2011/08/exchange-share-trading> accessed 5 October 2013.

[144] Matthew Phillips, 'How the robots lost: high-frequency trading's rise and fall' *Businessweek* (6 June 2013) <http://www.businessweek.com/articles/2013-06-06/how-the-robots-lost-high-frequency-trading s-rise-and-fall> accessed 5 October 2013: 'Over about 45 minutes that morning, Knight accidentally bought and sold $7 billion worth of shares—about $2.6 million a second'.

[145] Stephen Foley, 'High-frequency traders face speed limits', *Financial Times* (28 April 2013) <http://www.ft.com/intl/cms/s/0/d5b42402-aea3-11e2-8316-00144feabdc0.html> accessed 5 October 2013.

[146] For example, 'causing a temporary fall in the exchange-price of a share by selling a small quantity, and then placing a large buy order on a dark pool to purchase the share at the reduced price'. Schumpeter Blog (n 143).

[147] For a full timeline, see Matthew Phillips, 'Nasdaq: Here's Our Timeline of the Flash Crash', *The Wall Street Journal* (11 May 2010) <http://blogs.wsj.com/marketbeat/2010/05/11/nasdaq-heres-our-timeline-of-the-flash-crash/> accessed 5 October 2013.

regulators, all were understandably shaken. There was no immediately apparent cause, although ultimately a faulty algorithm appeared as the culprit.[148]

10.95 Speed bumps and circuit breakers have been put in place to slow the market down, a somewhat anomalous response to technological innovation. Circuit breakers date back to the Wall Street 'crash' of 1987, which in retrospect appears like a blip on the screen. Circuit breakers shut down trading for a defined period of time once the market drops out of a predetermined range,[149] preventing algorithms from cascading the market into greater volatility. Markets demonstrate much greater correlation than previously assumed, and circuit breakers also prevent volatility in one market infecting other markets, either domestically or internationally.

10.96 The European response to HFT has been to issue guidelines for systems of control that various market actors such as trading platforms and investment firms can implement.[150] ESMA's approach is to require testing and monitoring of algorithms used by high frequency traders with a view to improving risk management procedures. Reintroducing old-fashioned 'stamp taxes', taxing transactions trade by trade is a more controversial, and again somewhat anomalous, proposition.

10.97 Technology has been racing ahead of markets and regulators alike, blithely ignoring national boundaries and concepts of jurisdiction. The implications are profound. Until the new normal emerges to provide some modicum of stability and predictability to market developments, regulators and exchanges are engaging in unprecedented market interventions, scrambling to apply quick fixes.

3.3 The courting game: exchange consolidations

10.98 Freed by technology from the imperatives of geography and facilitated by demutualization, exchanges set about hunting for liquidity and competitive advantage through regional and international alliances, partnerships, joint ventures, and formal mergers. Survival was at stake, and to survive they had to make a profit. 'No matter how often stock exchanges say they are capital-raising venues, and futures exchanges say they are risk-management venues, the bottom line in a profit-driven model is: anything that generates more trading and speculative activity is going to generate more commercial activity for them.'[151]

10.99 As technology and competition drove down trading costs, resulting in diminished fee generation, and capital raising shifted from public to private markets, exchanges have looked to

---

[148] The true cause: a trader decided to sell 75,000 futures contracts to hedge an existing position. To sell such a large block of shares, it used an algorithm. However, the algorithm was not programmed to consider price or time. Consequently, the automated sale of futures contracts caused a crisis of liquidity when not enough buyers were found, sending the price tumbling and the market into disarray. For the SEC/CFTC's report on the event, see CFTC and SEC, 'Findings Regarding the Market Events of May 6, 2010: Report of the Staffs of the CFTC and SEC to the Joint Advisory Committee on Emerging Regulatory Issues' (30 September 2010) <http://www.sec.gov/news/studies/2010/marketevents-report.pdf> accessed 5 October 2013.

[149] For a fuller discussion of regulatory responses to HFT induced volatility, see IOSCO Technical Committee, 'FR 09/11 Regulatory Issues Raised by the Impact of Technological Changes on Market Integrity and Efficiency' (2011) <http://www.iosco.org/library/pubdocs/pdf/IOSCOPD354.pdf> accessed 5 October 2013.

[150] See ESMA Guidelines 2012/122, 'Systems and controls in an automated trading environment for trading platforms, investment firms and competent authorities' (2012).

[151] Jeremy Grant, 'A market to capture', *Financial Times* (17 February 2011) <http://www.ft.com/cms/s/0/11c61144-3aca-11e0-9c1a-00144feabdc0.html#ixzz2VxuCEkza> accessed 5 October 2013.

diversify across product lines and services. Jurisdictional restraints, especially regulation in the United States, made international alliances and partnerships attractive. Small exchanges, seeking to avoid irrelevancy, overcame longstanding historical and political rivalries, to join forces.[152] To remain competitive, exchanges began reorganizing themselves in response to economic conditions, the size of other exchanges, and their particular niche. And, profit-maximizing entities tend to seek growth.

The phenomenon of cross-listing, whereby companies expanding operations internationally list their securities on several exchanges, tempts exchanges to consolidate so as to increase efficiency of trading and profit.[153] If providing liquidity is now the primary economic function of an exchange, then the market that can provide the most liquidity will be the most competitive. That market will also be the largest.   **10.100**

It is an on-going game of courtship and conquest, as exchanges realign, reconfigure, and sometimes retrench. See Table 10.1. Several basic categories of consolidation have been helpfully identified, although some have spent their force and newer variations continue to appear.   **10.101**

Most domestic mergers have run their course.[154] By achieving economies of scale and perhaps attracting foreign investors due to their critical mass, they produced cost-saving benefits for the exchange. However, domestic mergers inevitably raised issues of reduced competition leading to monopolistic behaviour[155] which persists until routed by either a new domestic trading venue (exchange or not) or foreign rivals poaching domestic listings.   **10.102**

Regional or global mergers quickly followed domestic consolidations. These supra-national exchanges can become very large, achieving economies of scale. Since the trading infrastructure is the biggest fixed cost of an exchange, the cost to the exchange per trade decreases as more trades are executed on its platform. NYSE-Euronext executes 7 million derivatives contracts per day.[156] It can therefore compete much more effectively in terms of the commission   **10.103**

Table 10.1 Types of exchange consolidation[157]

Type	Summary
Domestic merger	Two or more domestic exchanges merge into a single national exchange, which could attract foreign investors.
Regional/global merger	Two or more domestic or regional exchanges (trading the same securities) merge into a regional exchange.
Vertical integration	A single exchange takes ownership of clearing, settlement and depositary institutions.
Niche integration	Exchanges trading in specific securities, such as derivatives, merge into a niche regional or global exchange for that particular security.

---

[152] Euronext, for example. Another example would be the Baltic and Nordic exchanges, which have come together under the NASDAQ OMX Group, including Copenhagen Stock Exchange, Riga Stock Exchange, Icelandic Stock Exchange, and Armenian Stock Exchange.

[153] Susan Wolburgh Jenah, 'Commentary on: A Blueprint for Cross-Border Access to U.S. Investors: A New International Framework' (2007) 48 *Harvard International Law Journal* 69.

[154] Although the current ICE-NYSE-Euronext merger proves the exception to the rule.

[155] Akhtar (n 50), 18.

[156] NYSE-Euronext News Release, 'NYSE Euronext Announces Trading Volumes for April 2013' (7 May 2013) <http://www.nyse.com/press/1367834502271.html> accessed 5 October 2013.

[157] Akhtar (n 50), 16–18.

it charges traders per trade. Such low trading fees require sustained high volumes of trading, which only mega-exchanges can really guarantee.

10.104   The benefits of regional and global mergers on an exchange's profits are so great that some even foresee that the future will be populated by a few global exchanges.[158] The proposed ICE-NYSE-Euronext, the proposed MILA exchange in Latin America, and the NASDAQ-OMX merger suggest the future is now. However, the inability of any exchange to merge with the LSE[159] suggests that geopolitical, historical and other economic obstacles persist.

10.105   Consolidation can take other forms than mergers across exchanges. An exchange can consolidate activities through vertical and horizontal integration of services and products. An excellent example of vertical integration is the BMV initial public offering. Prior to the offering, the BMV held equity in several ancillary service providers. By consolidating these services and bringing everything in-house, the BMV has been able to streamline its business, lowering costs. Additionally, the consolidation provides the BMV with alternative sources of revenue, which offset unexpected drops in trading volume.

10.106   However, vertical integration can become a source of conflict in other merger contexts. For example, during the failed LSE-Deutsche Börse merger, the issue of choice of clearing and settlement system arose. The Deutsche Börse owned Clearstream, a clearinghouse, as part of its vertical 'silo'; the LSE had arrangements in place with London Clearing House, which was owned by a third party.[160] In theory, where trades are cleared and settled should be a clerical matter of little significance. However, the tight integration of clearing and settlement within the Deutsche Börse structure left the LSE vulnerable in case of disagreement with its future partner. While the issue was not pivotal in that case, it demonstrates non-economic factors that can affect the success or failure of a merger.

10.107   Finally, niche integration has the benefit of attracting investors interested in a specific financial product. Identification of an exchange with that product will lead to concentration of the market, greater trading volumes and, again in theory, cost efficiencies and better price discovery. Consequently, some exchanges specialize in certain types of securities. For example, the Toronto Stock Exchange (TSX) attempts to attract equities in specific sectors: mining, energy, and clean technology.[161] Creating an index for energy companies listed on the TSX, such as the S&P/TSX Capped Energy Index, signals the expertise and specialization to investors.

10.108   Another good example of niche integration is the CME-BMV alliance. Prior to its demutualization and initial public offering, the BMV held a monopoly on Mexican derivatives trading, through its MexDer platform. After demutualizing, it sought a way to expand its

---

[158]   See 'Battle of the bourses', *The Economist* (25 May 2006) <http://www.economist.com/node/6978712> accessed 5 October 2013. See also Cappon and Mignot (n 100), 2.

[159]   For a chronology of the many attempts to merge with the LSE, see 'London Stock Exchange's tumultuous history of bids', *The Telegraph* (2 September 2011) <http://www.telegraph.co.uk/finance/newsbysector/banksandfinance/8311679/London-Stock-Exchanges-tumultuous-history-of-bids.html> accessed 5 October 2013.

[160]   Jane Martinson, 'We won't sell Clearstream to win LSE', *The Guardian* (2 September 2011) <http://www.guardian.co.uk/business/2005/jan/04/1> accessed 5 October 2013.

[161]   'Sector Profiles—Energy' (Toronto Stock Exchange) <http://www.tmx.com/en/listings/sector_profiles/energy.html> accessed 5 October 2013.

derivatives business. By linking up with the CME the largest futures exchange in the United States, MexDer was able to extend its global reach. Jorge Alegría, MexDer's CEO, stated: 'This is very important for us because it is essentially an alliance with the biggest exchange in the world. It will enable us to connect our derivatives market with that exchange, and that will allow us to achieve much more liquidity and increase our capacity to distribute our products globally.'[162] The alliance allowed BMV and CME investors to trade in the other's securities without opening two accounts. The CME already had a similar arrangement with Brazil's BM&F Bovespa, meaning that BMV investors tapped into a pan-Americas derivatives market through their own exchange.

4. Changing Roles for Exchanges

4.1 The waning importance of exchanges as market regulators

The earliest exchanges in Amsterdam, Paris, Frankfurt, and London regulated both them- **10.109** selves and the markets more generally. In modern times, state regulation overlaid or displaced entirely the role of exchange as market regulator. In some cases, the public utility function of the exchange dominated. Demutualization of exchanges put the viability of the self-regulatory model squarely into question. Although some market participants may continue to insist on the virtues of self-regulation and the powerful incentive of their 'brand' to produce appropriate regulatory outcomes, such authority is slipping away. Critics, on the other hand, have little trouble pointing to the scandals and failures of self-regulation,[163] and the 'brand' argument now appears less compelling.[164]

In Hong Kong and London, where self-regulation and exchanges as market regulators **10.110** found a strong form of expression, self-regulation has been shoved to the margin. At other exchanges, such as Toronto, pragmatism prevailed, separating regulatory and commercial aspects of exchange function. With few regrets, the TSX itself quickly shuffled off market regulatory authority to another entity.[165]

The creation of the consolidated regulator, the FSA, in 2000 in the United Kingdom ousted **10.111** self-regulation in the City of London. However, the 'light touch,' risk based, regulation of the FSA, much vaunted as a major competitive advantage for the London markets, represented a continuation of self-regulatory concepts being played out through the regulator, rather than the exchange and market participants. More recently, 'light touch' regulation, and along with it, much of self-regulation, has gone by the by, collateral victims of the global financial crisis.[166]

---

[162] Jeremy Grant and Adam Thomson, 'CME agrees to Bolsa Mexicana alliance', *Financial Times* (8 March 2010)   <http://www.ft.com/intl/cms/s/0/db13e39c-2adf-11df-886b-00144feabdc0.html#axzz2XIYtEcTc> accessed 5 October 2013.

[163] Karmel (n 77). Karmel notes the Report Pursuant to § 21(a) of the Securities Exchange Act of 1934 regarding the NASD and the Nasdaq Market, Exchange Act Release No 37542 (8 August 1996). See also SEC Press Release, 'SEC Charges the New York Stock Exchange with Failing to Police Specialists' (12 April 2005) <http://www.sec.gov/news/press/2005-53.htm> accessed 5 October 2013.

[164] See IOSCO (n 5), 9.

[165] The market regulatory authority of the TSX was transferred to Market Regulation Services Inc. However, the corporate governance of an issuer is regulated by the securities regulators pursuant to National Instrument 58–101—*Disclosure of Corporate Governance Practices*.

[166] See <http://webarchive.nationalarchives.gov.uk/+/http://www.hm-treasury.gov.uk/2277.htm> accessed 5 October 2013; see also Norma Cohen, 'IOSCO to Push for Regulatory Consistency', *Financial Times* (15

10.112 The United States market witnessed a more gradual shift in influence from self-regulatory bodies to greater government oversight and direct intervention. Tensions and compromise between self-regulation and government intervention continue in the United States.[167] Attempts are being made to maintain the façade of self-regulation (for example, a market-neutral SRO with governmental members, a third party SRO supplying regulatory services, or constituency representation dominating SRO boards). Overlapping oversight and shared responsibilities are now characteristic of US market regulation, a function of market evolution, technology and international pressures.[168] Self-regulation will persist in the United States, although perhaps not in as vigorous and unchallenged a form as in the past. The industry, which prefers to mind its own shop, is sophisticated, politically savvy and well financed.

10.113 There are several obvious advantages to self-regulation for exchanges; self-regulation creates a virtuous circle, enhancing regulatory knowledge, experience, and expertise, resulting in better self-regulation. Exchanges are at the coalface.

> Trading is a fluid activity and rule books need to deal with matters and concepts which do not lend themselves to statutory language and formal principles of statutory interpretation. Furthermore, self-regulatory rules can be more effective because of the self-regulatory organization's (SRO) intimate knowledge of the trading environment and market practices compared to government officials and the judiciary. Exchange management and regulatory staff are closer to the market activity and likely to be better placed to understand what may be going on.[169]

Securities regulation is not nimble or subtle enough to catch the essence of what must be regulated.

10.114 However, in light of the new realities of today's evolving exchanges, the justifications for self-regulatory powers, in their traditional guise, ring somewhat hollow.[170] Self-regulation has demonstrated numerous weaknesses, exacerbated by the move to demutualization: lack of adequate statutory enforcement powers; conflicts of interest; duplicative (and possibly contradictory) regulation; the race to the bottom problem; ineffectiveness or inappropriateness in certain legal environments (as is found in many civil code countries). In the international arena, the enforcement problem is particularly acute. Self-regulatory organizations may be devoid of enforcement powers or not recognized as an acceptable counterparty in cross-border cooperative efforts by regulators.[171]

10.115 Separating regulatory from operational functions in a demutualized exchange has been the most common mechanism for addressing inherent conflicts of interest. Outsourcing

---

November 2006) <http://www.ft.com/cms/s/7f4cd74a-744d-11db-8dd7-0000779e2340.html> accessed 5 October 2013.

[167] Karmel (n 77).

[168] Karmel (n 77).

[169] William Pearson, 'Demutualization of Exchanges—The Conflicts of Interest (Hong Kong)' in Akhtar (n 50), 88.

[170] See generally Jordan and Hughes (n 1).

[171] For example, the London Stock Exchange, the primary market regulator prior to the appearance of the FSA in 2000, was not recognized as 'competent authority' for purposes of EU legislative instruments; that task had to be assumed by the Bank of England, in the absence of any other formal regulatory body.

regulatory functions, variously to a separate company within the exchange group, an outside SRO, or a statutory regulator, is the favoured approach.[172]

The crisis of identity over exchanges as market regulators though may be drawing to a close. **10.116** As revenues slip away with the migration of trading to alternative venues, exchanges are reinventing their business model, bolting on more purely commercial activities, such as data collection or depository functions, which do not trip regulatory triggers. In the regulatory lag associated with the rise of alternative trading systems, self-regulation may also be finding a new expression, outside the exchanges.

4.2 Exchanges as market reformers

Exchanges can transform a market. For example, the *Novo Mercado*, a listing segment created **10.117** by the Sao Paulo exchange, then known as the Bovespa,[173] helped bring Brazilian markets back to life by promoting, and signalling, better corporate governance for Brazilian companies. Through the creation of new listing segments, echoing internationally recognized standards but tailored to Brazilian circumstances, the Bovespa enlisted the forces of peer pressure to encourage better corporate governance and improved investor protection.

Reform had been overdue in Brazil. At the end of the 1990s 'Brazil's capital markets were **10.118** less developed and representative of the country's economy, and it was facing devastating times'.[174] Very few companies sought to list on the Bovespa and liquidity had drained away to the United States. Companies and investors alike believed a US listing enhanced credibility.[175] Brazilian markets were moribund due to corporate governance abuses, real and perceived, reaching back decades to an era when intense financial speculation had threatened the existence of the Rio de Janeiro Stock Exchange.[176]

The Bovespa decided to act unilaterally to increase standards of corporate governance in **10.119** Brazil, without waiting for the legislative changes then being contemplated.[177] An intense international debate about the relationship between levels of corporate governance and capital markets development, particularly the 'bonding hypothesis',[178] bolstered the initiatives.

---

[172] Pearson (n 169), 97–8. See also Securities Industry Association, 'Reinventing Self-Regulation', White Paper for the Securities Industry Association's Ad Hoc Committee on Regulatory Implications of Demutualization (4 January 2000).

[173] Since 2008, a consolidated commodities, futures and equities exchange, the BM&F Bovespa.

[174] Maria Helena Santana, 'The Novo Mercado' in Maria Helena Santana et al (eds), *Novo Mercado and Its Followers: Case Studies in Corporate Governance Reform* (Global Corporate Governance Forum, Focus 5, 2008), 2. See also Cally Jordan and Michael Lubrano, 'Corporate Governance and Emerging Markets: Lessons from the Field', International Labour Organization, Legal Studies Research Paper No 356 (2007), 14.

[175] Helena Santana (n 174), 5.

[176] Helena Santana (n 174), 7.

[177] Subsequently, some of the Bovespa initiatives were mirrored in revisions to the corporations legislation.

[178] 'A newer interpretation is today emerging that cross-listing may also be a bonding mechanism by which firms incorporated in a jurisdiction with weak protection of minority rights or poor enforcement mechanisms can voluntarily subject themselves to higher disclosure standards and stricter enforcement in order to attract investors who would otherwise be reluctant to invest (or who would discount such stocks to reflect the risk of minority expropriation)': John C Coffee, 'Competition Among Securities Markets: A Path Dependent Perspective', Columbia Law and Economics Working Paper 192 (2002), See also Cally Jordan, 'The Chameleon Effect: Beyond the Bonding Hypothesis for Cross-Listed Securities' (2006) 3 *New York University Journal of Law & Business* 37.

10.120 The Bovespa created different levels of 'good practices of corporate governance', each indicating measures taken by the companies above and beyond the requirements of Brazilian law.[179] For example the first level, *Nivel 1*, or Level 1, requires listing companies to implement better disclosure policies and increase the public float (ie the number of shares held by non-controlling public investors). Level 1 listing catered to the status quo, established Brazilian companies with a dual class share structure that permitted founders and families to retain voting control of listed companies by offering non-voting or disparate voting shares to the public.

10.121 The *Novo Mercado*[180] looked to new market entrants, requiring them to issue only voting shares.[181] Companies listing on the *Novo Mercado* were also required, in their constitutional documents, to provide minority investor protections, in particular 'tag along rights'. Originally a Canadian approach created in a corporate landscape dominated by majority controlled, publicly traded companies, tag along rights permit minority shareholders to share in the economic benefits associated with the sale of a controlling block, benefits from which they might otherwise be excluded.[182] Rather than taking the easy route of copying the voluntary, and largely ineffective, corporate governance codes in fashion at the time, the Bovespa knew its markets, its issuers and the potential pool of investors. It identified the

---

[179] 'Corporate Governance' (BM&F Bovespa) <http://www.bmfbovespa.com.br/en-us/markets/equities/companies/corporate-governance.aspx?idioma=en-us> accessed 5 October 2013.

[180] The conditions associated with admission to the Novo Mercado included:

- Public share offerings have to use mechanisms to favour capital dispersion and broader retail access.
- Maintenance of a minimum free float, equivalent to 25% of the capital.
- Same conditions provided to majority shareholders in the disposal of the Company's Control will have to be extended to all shareholders (Tag Along).
- Establishment of a two-year unified mandate for the entire Board of Directors, which must have five members at least, of which at least 20% shall be Independent Members.
- Disclosure of annual balance sheet, according to standards of the US GAAP or IFRS.
- Improvements in quarterly reports, such as the requirement of consolidated financial statements and special audit revision.
- Obligation to hold a tender offer by the economic value criteria, in case of delisting or cancellation of registration as publicly-held company.
- Compliance with disclosure rules in trades involving securities issued by the company in the name of controlling shareholders.

Some of these obligations must be approved at the General Shareholders Meetings and included in the corporate bylaws. See (n 179).

[181] The 'one share, one vote' debate between the NYSE and the US regulator, the SEC, had festered for years.

[182] 'One key problem in Brazil, as pointed out by domestic and international investors, was the predominance of non-voting stock known as "preferred shares" ("ações preferenciais nominativas" in Portuguese, or simply PN). Brazil's Corporation Law authorized publicly held companies to issue up to two-thirds of their capital in the form of such preferred shares. This enabled holders of voting shares to control companies by owning as little as 17 percent of the company's total equity or stock. In some cases, control structures took the form of pyramids that made it possible for control to be wielded by someone who owned an even smaller portion of the company. This arrangement produced a fundamental misalignment of interests between those who held preferred shares and those who controlled the companies. In addition to the fundamental differences between the two groups of shareholders, the structural changes taking place within the companies clearly showed that shareholders didn't have equitable treatment. For instance, in the process of delisting, the mandatory tender offer to purchase the stock of minority shareholders did not have to assure them of a price that was determined by the company's economic value. More than that, regulations allowed "the squeeze out" of minority shareholders at unfair prices, by permitting the controlling shareholder to purchase outstanding shares, reducing the free float and the liquidity. They could do so even when they were not able to obtain a sufficient quorum to delist the company' (Santana (n 174), 9).

sticking points and effected structural changes, not dependent on legislation or engaging the gears of political process.

Despite a slow start, the *Novo Mercado* has been a resounding success; investors returned to **10.122** Brazil in droves. By 2008, the *Novo Mercado* had listed 100 companies,[183] their shares trading at nearly twice the price of companies listed on other segments of the exchange.[184] Success breeds success, and peer pressures work wonders. 'Today, any company that does not list on the . . . *Novo Mercado* needs a good excuse.'[185]

The *Novo Mercado* is not the only story at the BM&F Bovespa, as its new acronym indicates. **10.123** Unrestricted by the regulatory restraints present in the United States, it diversified away from its NYSE equities exchange model to trade commodities and futures as well. Riding the wave of a commodities boom in resource rich economies, it entered into an alliance in 2010 with the Chicago-based CME group, now the second largest exchange group in the world.[186] In a little more than a decade, the BM&F Bovespa transformed Brazilian markets in meteoric fashion as well as creating a new, indigenous, Latin American model for exchanges.

5. Will Exchanges Survive?

Exchanges are changing, rapidly, as they search for a business model that will promote their **10.124** survival. The jurisdictional apartheid model found in the United States, where segregated exchanges are restricted to trading along product lines,[187] has collapsed elsewhere. Exchanges are eager to increase the range of products traded. Exchanges are stratifying, developing multiple listing segments or boards to accommodate different kinds of issuers, financial products and trading markets. To this extent, the global financial crisis has been an unexpected boon to the traditional exchange, given the call for moving off exchange products, particularly derivatives, to exchange trading in the interests of greater transparency. Traders are a wily, scrappy bunch, quick to adapt, so it is too soon to predict the demise of the traditional exchange.

---

[183] Mondovisione Press Release, 'BM&F Bovespa Celebrates 100 Companies Listed on the Novo Mercado— Exchange Announces New projects—BDRs And BM&FBOVESPA in the Countryside' (29 July 2008) <http://www.mondovisione.com/media-and-resources/news/bmandfbovespa-celebrates-100-companies-listed-on-the-novo-mercado-exchange-annou/> accessed 5 October 2013.

[184] Mondovisione Press Release (n 183).

[185] 'Brazilian IPOs: New wave for the Novo Mercado', *The Economist* (23 February 2006) <http://www.economist.com/node/5563405> accessed 5 October 2013. From the same article: 'Today, any company that does not list on the ON-only Novo Mercado needs a good excuse. One such is Gol, Latin America's first publicly traded low-cost airline, which is not allowed to sell control to foreigners. It listed on Bovespa's "level 2," which requires "tag-along rights" in takeovers for PN investors and refers disputes to arbitrators rather than to Brazil's slow courts. Few would dare offer less.'

[186] '. . . macroeconomic stability, falling income inequality and the global commodity boom ensured Brazil's steady, politically harmonious growth. Strong banks and domestic demand made for a speedy rebound from the 2008 credit crunch. In 2010 Brazil's economy grew by 7.5% to become the world's seventh-largest.' See 'Brazil's economy: A bull diminished', *The Economist* (19 May 2012) <http://www.economist.com/node/21555588> accessed 5 October 2013. The CME Group owns the Chicago Mercantile Exchange, which trades commodities, futures and derivatives.

[187] Even in the United States, the compartmentalization of exchanges along product line is more or less a formality. It is said that the interest of the NYSE in merging with Euronext was to participate in trading various products, especially derivatives, which the NYSE was precluded from trading at home. That the NYSE, an equities exchange, is in the process of being acquired by ICE, an independent open access electronic exchange for trading wholesale energy and metals commodities, is a sign of the times.

11

INTERMEDIARIES—FROM HANDMAIDEN TO NEW MARKET[*]

1. The Triple I—Intermediary, Issuer, Investor

11.01 As exchanges developed in Western Europe and the colonies, they spun out a widening web of intermediaries participating in the process of trading financial products: exchange members, market makers, brokers, dealers, jobbers, underwriters, agents, custodians, depositories, clearing and settlement facilities, asset managers, advisers, arrangers. Financial markets grew and changed; the intermediaries were instrumental in providing the infrastructure for both growth and change. However, the market infrastructure erected by intermediaries could also be monopolistic, driving up user costs and acting as a barrier to entry by competitors. Intermediaries also pushed the poles of buyer and seller further and further apart, inserting themselves in roles of all stripes and colours, serving an expanding universe of investors.

11.02 The essence of intermediation has been fee for services, and services proliferated. New financial products, complex derivatives and credit default swaps, are fee-generating machines, often serving little purpose other than enriching the numerous intermediaries greasing their wheels.[1] However, the roles assumed by intermediaries, and their sources of revenue, mutated over time. Intermediaries became issuers and capital raisers in their own right.

11.03 Exchanges became issuers, demutualizing and listing, sometimes on themselves. On Wall Street, investment banks, formerly partnership vehicles, became publicly traded corporations, like any other commercial operation. Regulatory capital requirements kicked in, increasing pressures to raise capital.

11.04 Intermediaries, ever hungry for new sources of revenue, also became investors, engaging in proprietary trading and playing with 'house' money. In North America, bonds migrated off exchanges to dealer inventories where investors bought directly from the dealers; fees were easily concealed and hefty profits made. Other intermediaries, collective investment vehicles (in the very widest sense), were providers of capital, investors, by their very nature, acting on behalf of others. Constellations of intermediaries began to form, operating outside or in parallel to the formal, public markets; these were not galactic black holes, but rather dark pools of capital accessible only to the intermediaries. Originally handmaidens to the exchanges, intermediaries have created a new, free floating, trading world.

---

[*] The author would like to thank John Zelenbaba (Faculty of Law, McGill University), in particular, for his assistance with this chapter.

[1] At least until the gears seized in the global financial crisis.

In this new trading world, the potential conflicts of interest inherent in agency relationships **11.05**
have been exacerbated by the multiple roles intermediaries have assumed. Further intensifying the stresses on market relationships have been the rapid changes in trading practices now
permitted by technology and the internationalization of the capital markets.

2. The New World of Intermediaries

2.1 Information as Commodity and New Roles for Old Systems

In the modern world of electronic transactions, price signals and other information pro- **11.06**
liferate, and though sunlight may be the best disinfectant, too much of it can blind the
individual investor. Where investors are met with a dizzying array of questionable information, profit opportunities for intermediaries holding more 'perfect' information emerge.[2]
Seen in this light, many non-bank intermediaries primarily deal in superior information
derived from their professed expertise.[3] These intermediaries, the various broker-dealers,
voice brokers, advisers, managers of mutual funds, private equity firms, hedge funds—even
'funds-of-funds', stand between issuer and investor,[4] mining and profiting from the bewil-
dering increase in information. Indeed, one 2008 estimate suggests that in the United States,
the cost of investment advice (for both retail and institutional investors) was at least 10 per
cent of the entire market capitalization.[5]

Depositories and clearing and settlement systems, rather than professing expertise, deal **11.07**
principally in risk, the latter taking contracts onto their own books for a time and guarding
against default among counterparties. Clearing and settlement platforms, in particular, are
proliferating across borders and expanding services for an increasing number of products.[6]
But there is a new function, trade information repository, now associated with derivatives
trading, with light shining on a once dark corner.

---

[2] See generally Franklin Allen, 'The Market for Information and the Origin of Financial Intermediation'
(1990) 1(1) *Journal of Financial Intermediation* 3. Former SEC General Counsel Brian Cartwright notes that
the increasing deference to advisers, funds, and other intermediaries is a rational reaction by the amateur retail
investor confronting a world with a more sophisticated and mathematical understanding of financial markets.
See Brian G Cartwright, *Speech by SEC Staff: The Future of Securities Regulation* (University of Pennsylvania Law
School Institute for Law and Economics, 2007). Another rationale for their emergence is that they reduce transaction costs by more cheaply matching buyers and sellers of securities, among other things. On this, see George
J Benston and Clifford W Smith, 'A Transactions Cost Approach to the Theory of Financial Intermediation'
(1976) 31(2) *The Journal of Finance* 215. They may also take on risk as a counter-party (eg clearing system).
Economist John Kay adds that a principal driver of 'intermediation has been the decline of trust and confidence
in the investment chain. The role of custodian came into being because the asset manager could not be trusted
to hold shares on behalf of the ultimate shareholder. . . . The question of who guards the guards is inevitably followed by the question of who guards the guards who guard the guards . . .': John Kay, 'The Kay Review of UK
Equity Markets and Long-Term Decision Making: Final Report' (UK: Report Commissioned by the Secretary
of State for Business, Innovation and Skills, 2012), 30.
[3] Danny Busch and Deborah DeMott, 'Introduction', in Danny Busch and Deborah DeMott (eds), *Liability
of Asset Managers* (Oxford University Press, 2012), 3.
[4] Kay gives an alternative sampling: 'Between the company and the saver are now interposed registrars,
nominees, custodians, asset managers, managers who allocate funds to specialist asset managers, trustees,
investment consultants, agents who "wrap" products, retail platforms, distributors and independent financial
advisers.' Kay (n 2), 30.
[5] Kenneth R French, 'Presidential Address: The Cost of Active Investing' (2008) 63(4) *The Journal of
Finance* 1537.
[6] Jeremy Grant, 'A market to capture', *Financial Times* (17 February 2011) <http://www.ft.com/intl/cms/
s/0/11c61144-3aca-11e0-9c1a-00144feabdc0.html#axzz2VvfMxXty> accessed 24 December 2013.

11.08 The regulatory push following the global financial crisis has been a bonanza for clearing and settlement systems as well as trade repositories. The European Market Infrastructure Regulation (EMIR) entered into force in August 2012, mandating central clearing of all 'standardised OTC derivatives contracts determined to be subject to the clearing obligation', margin requirements, reporting of all derivatives contracts to trade repositories, and prudential requirements for central clearing parties.[7] Since March 2013, EMIR has also imposed risk mitigation rules for derivatives transactions.[8] The finalized clearing requirements are to be submitted to the European Commission for approval in September 2014, after which they will be enforceable.[9] These developments are in line with the trend of ESMA extending its supra-national regulatory purview over the whole of Europe's capital markets.

11.09 In the United States, the CFTC and SEC have finalized the rules regarding the scope of products subject to Title VII of Dodd-Frank[10] and central clearing and reporting requirements, as well as having delineated their respective authority over them. The International Swaps and Derivatives Association (ISDA)—which has since 1993 prominently published the industry standard framework governing all future OTC transactions between two counterparties— has been playing a supporting role in the process. In addition to collaborating with global supervisors since the regulatory wave launched by the crisis, ISDA has published protocols enabling market participants to amend existing derivatives relationship documentation to facilitate compliance with the new regulations and reporting requirements.[11]

2.2 Retail and professional markets

11.10 Within this sampling, a stark contrast has emerged between retail and professional or institutional markets. In the United States, a retail market, once deemed worthy of emulation, has over the last 30 years substantially shifted towards institutionalization.[12] More bluntly, the 'American retail investor is dying'.[13] In 1950, ' retail investors owned 90% of the stock of US corporations';[14] today, the figure stands at less than 30 per cent. In the United Kingdom, as

---

[7] Financial Stability Board, 'OTC Derivatives Market Reforms: Fourth Progress Report on Implementation' (31 October 2012), 42–3 <http://www.financialstabilityboard.org/publications/r_121031a.pdf> accessed 24 December 2013.

[8] Including rules requiring that parties confirm the terms of their transactions within certain time frames. Since September 2013, more extensive risk mitigation requirements obligate parties to create procedures to '(i) conduct portfolio reconciliation exercises, and (ii) to resolve disputes with counterparties. Although less likely, counterparties may also be required to consider engaging in portfolio compression exercises.' Cleary Gottlieb, EMIR (European Regulation (EU) No 648/2012 on OTC Derivatives, Central Counterparties and Trade Repositories) (2013).

[9] Rachel Morison, 'Regulator Delays Start of EMIR Derivatives Reporting to February', *Bloomberg* (13 September 2013) <http://www.bloomberg.com/news/2013-09-13/regulator-delays-start-of-emir-derivatives-r eporting-to-february.html> accessed 24 December 2013.

[10] Title VII deals with regulation of over-the-counter 'swaps markets' and grants authority to the CFTC and SEC to oversee these derivatives markets. The CFTC and SEC have clarified that 'swaps markets' includes the following swaps: 'interest rate swaps; basis swaps, currency swaps; foreign exchange swaps, total return swaps; equity swaps and equity index swaps, debt and debt index swaps, credit default swaps, energy swaps, metal swaps, agricultural swaps, and other commodity swaps.' See Financial Stability Board, 'OTC Derivatives Market Reforms: Fourth Progress Report on Implementation', (31 October 2012), 47 <http://www.financial-stabilityboard.org/publications/r_121031a.pdf> accessed 24 December 2013.

[11] See, for example, among others, *ISDA August 2012 Dodd-Frank Protocol, ISDA 2013 EMIR Portfolio Reconciliation,* or *Dispute Resolution and Disclosure Protocol, ISDA 2013 Reporting Protocol.*

[12] Donald C Langevoort, 'The SEC, Retail Investors, and the Institutionalization of the Securities Markets' (2009) 95 *Virginia Law Review* 1025. See also Cartwright (n 2).

[13] Alicia Davis Evans, 'A Requiem for the Retail Investor?' (2009) 95 *Virginia Law Review* 1105.

[14] Evans (n 13).

of end-2010, retail assets accounted for approximately 22 per cent of assets under management; institutions accounted for the other 72 per cent. The figures for Europe are similar, standing at 31 and 69 per cent, respectively.[15]

Despite the dominance of institutional investors (intermediaries in one shape or another) on both sides of the Atlantic, it is worth noting that neither the United Kingdom nor Europe was ever permeated by an ethos of the retail investor as existed in the United States.[16] Instead, both the United Kingdom and Europe have historically been institutional arenas, and both undertook policy reforms to stimulate a retail investment culture.[17] Despite the degree of institutionalization across jurisdictions, at the end of the intermediation chain, one still often finds the retail investor holding the ultimate economic interest (and potentially all of the risk) in a security.[18] **11.11**

Many institutional markets are both relatively closed and, to a large extent, incomprehensible to the retail investor. 'Dark pools' of liquidity are one example of the closure.[19] With algorithmic trading on the rise (which often works against traditional institutional investors), these pools have given institutional investors a venue to execute large block orders through broker-dealers acting as OTC market makers. Due to concealed quoting and *ex-post* price reporting, these trades minimize market impact and insulate their principals from rapid market shifts induced by high-frequency traders.[20] In the United States, dark trading has increased by about 50 per cent over the last three years, now accounting for approximately 13 per cent of total volume.[21] In Europe, trading in dark pools has more than doubled in the last two years.[22] **11.12**

Institutions-only trading markets are not new. The operative regulatory assumption here is the relative acumen of institutions as investors. Famously, offerings to those that can 'fend for themselves', in the words of the US Supreme Court, do not trigger a level of protection equivalent with that of a public offering.[23] Those that can 'fend for themselves', following the SEC's promulgation of Regulation D, which provides oft-used exemptions for non-public offerings, are 'accredited investors' including 'banks, broker-dealers, insurance companies, registered investment companies' and high net worth or high income individuals.[24] **11.13**

---

[15] European Fund and Asset Management Association, *Asset Management in Europe: Facts and Figures* (2012).

[16] Langevoort (n 12), 1025.

[17] On the United Kingdom, see Ch 6 of this book. Regarding Europe, see Niamh Moloney, 'Building a Retail Investment Culture through Law: The 2004 Markets in Financial Instruments Directive' (2005) 6 *European Business Organization* 341.

[18] Luis A Aguilar, 'Market Upheaval and Investor Harm Should Not be the New Normal' US Securities and Exchange Commission Compliance Week 2010 (Washington, DC 24 May 2010) <http://www.sec.gov/news/speech/2010/spch052410laa-1.htm> accessed 17 January 2014, 'After all, a single sophisticated institutional investor, whether it is a bank, pension fund, mutual fund, or other entity, often represents investments from many individual retail investors. And these small investors ultimately bear the cost.'

[19] Cartwright (n 2). But see Preece (n 20), 'Internalisation can provide savings to retail investors in the form of price improvement...'.

[20] Rhodri Preece, 'The pros and cons of dark pools of liquidity', *Financial Times* (6 January 2013), <http://www.ft.com/intl/cms/s/0/b594f978-54dd-11e2-a628-00144feab49a.html#axzz2Wh7EAPfx> accessed 24 December 2013.

[21] Preece (n 20).

[22] Preece (n 20).

[23] *SEC v Ralston Purina Co* 346 US 119 (1953).

[24] Cary Martin, 'Private Investment Companies in the Wake of the Financial Crisis: Rethinking the Effectiveness of the Sophisticated Investor Exemption' (2012) 37 *Delaware Journal of Corporate Law* 67–8 <http://papers.ssrn.com/abstract=2028768> accessed 24 December 2013.

11.14 Rule 144A[25] provides an even more exclusive private market in the United States, restricting eligible participants to 'qualified institutional buyers'—generally institutions with over $100 million invested in securities—and allowing them to trade immediately in their own bespoke secondary market.[26] By reducing regulatory impediments, the Rule 144A market dominates institutional trading.[27] That many institutional investors were victims of Bernard Madoff,[28] and that the obscure derivatives cast as culprits of the global financial crisis were largely held in the institutional world,[29] however, does raise questions as to some of the assumptions underlying institutional exemptions. For example, the insurance industry has historically formed the largest investor group in the Rule 144A market.[30] With its archaic, fragmented, state-level regulatory framework and stable of obscure, untransparent products,[31] the insurance industry in the United States may be a financial disaster in waiting.

11.15 On the other hand, by designating institutions as the sole players in certain marketplaces, regulators in effect limit the profit opportunities available to retail investors,[32] or so the argument goes. Also, institutional only markets promote the development of more intermediaries, funds capable of pooling retail investments and providing retail investors with access to these markets otherwise closed to them, for a fee.[33] The parallel market-driven development of institutions-only asset classes has a similar effect. High minimal investment requirements exclude retail investors from direct ownership of classes such as venture capital, private equity and hedge funds.[34] Pity the poor retail investor.[35]

11.16 Another element in the profit equation is risk; depending on the nature of the institution, it may be able to take on more risk and deal in more exotic financial products than a retail counterpart. In the lead up to the global financial crisis, demand among retail investors for more 'risk' was evidenced by mutual fund managers advertizing access to hedge fund managers or, where possible, adopting similar trading strategies in lieu of their traditional 'buy long' passive management.[36]

---

[25] See BMV IPO in Ch 10 of this book.

[26] Langevoort (n 12), 1059.

[27] Leslie N Silverman, 'Case Study on Rule 144A and Regulation S: The IPO of the Mexican Stock Exchange', Cleary Gottlieb Steen and Hamilton LLP (2010), 5, in the author's possession. This preference and side-stepping of general US 1933 Act provisions is among the factors that has led one commentator to declare that 'The increased proportion of institutional private placements has substantially reduced the scope of the Securities Act . . . in effect representing the most significant erosion of the federal securities laws' mandatory disclosure system since the New Deal period.' Joel Seligman, cited in Martin (n 24), 65.

[28] Amy Or, 'Funds of Hedge Funds Try Smaller, Niche Funds', *Wall Street Journal* (22 April 2011) <http://online.wsj.com/article/SB10001424052748703387904576279270504296608.html> accessed 24 December 2013. See also Langevoort (n 12), 1058.

[29] Anita I Anand, 'Is Systemic Risk Relevant to Securities Regulation' (2010) 60 *The University of Toronto Law Journal* 941, 949; Langevoort (n 12), 1026.

[30] A 1991 SEC report showed that 54.89% of Rule 144A placements were purchased by insurance companies, with investment companies forming the next largest industry category of purchaser at 27.37%. Securities and Exchange Commission, 'SEC Staff Report on Rule 144A' (1991).

[31] Many of which, such as annuities, are designed for an aging population.

[32] So-Yeon Lee, 'Why the Accredited Investor Standard Fails the Average Investor' (2012) 31 *Review of Banking and Financial Law* 987.

[33] For a description of this phenomenon, see Jeff D Opdyke, 'Funds Tout Access to Top Managers', *Wall Street Journal* (15 June 2005) <http://online.wsj.com/article/0,,SB111879333358959746,00.html> accessed 24 December 2013.

[34] Cartwright (n 2).

[35] The importance of the retail investor, especially the retail equity investor, is characteristic of US markets and does not necessarily play out in the same fashion elsewhere.

[36] Opdyke (n 33); Vikas Agarwal, Nicole M Boyson, and Narayan Y Naik, 'Hedge Funds for Retail Investors? An Examination of Hedged Mutual Funds' (2009) 44(2) *Journal of Financial and Quantitative Analysis* 273.

Investors in the now infamous mortgage-backed securities market were 'overwhelming insti-   **11.17**
tutional'.[37] There are countless stories of pension funds, mutual funds, and other institutional
investors suffering colossal losses from over-exposure to products derived from sub-prime
mortgages.[38] Relaxed protection and exemptions for sophisticated parties may encourage
this phenomenon. In the United Kingdom, the professionals in the market saw little need
to 'protect fools from their own folly' and argued that regulatory intervention in a market
dominated by professionals was unnecessary.[39] Professionals thus benefited from a number
of exemptions to which the public were not privy.[40] The Markets in Financial Instruments
Directive (MiFID), now implemented in the United Kingdom and almost all of Europe,
distinguishes between retail clients, professional clients, and eligible counterparties. The
latter two categories are subject to weaker levels of protection.[41] Again, the fact that these
institutions, sophisticated as they are, often had to defer to their own agency relationships
(with credit rating agencies) to evaluate complex products leading up to the last crisis,[42] and
the fact they often implicated retail investors (whether through the intermediation chain
or from the negative externalities they eventually emitted),[43] raises international regulatory
red flags.

The global financial crisis has drawn regulatory attention to 'systemically important financial   **11.18**
institutions', the Systemically Important Financial Institutions (SIFIs) of the world, and a
risk taking culture bordering on sheer recklessness. Scandals and enormous losses, such as
those at UBS[44] and JP Morgan Chase,[45] have resulted in huge fines and regulatory castigation
on both sides of the Atlantic. Regulators are poking their noses under the hood, so to speak,
chastising intermediaries for inadequate internal controls and risk management systems,
matters once considered beyond the regulatory pale.[46]

---

[37] Steven L Schwarcz, 'Protecting Financial Markets: Lessons from the Subprime Mortgage Meltdown'
(2008) 93 *Minnesota Law Review* 348.

[38] See, for example, David Evans, 'Banks Sell "Toxic Waste" CDOs to Calpers, Texas Teachers Fund',
Bloomberg (1 June 2007), <http://www.bloomberg.com/apps/news?pid=newsarchive&sid=aW5vEJn3LpVw>
accessed 24 December 2013. The notorious collapse and subsequent sale of Bear Stearns was brought about by
its exposure to credit derivatives chiefly through two hedge funds. See Gillian Tett, *Fool's Gold: The Inside Story
of J.P. Morgan and How Wall St. Greed Corrupted Its Bold Dream and Created a Financial Catastrophe* (Reprint
edn, Free Press, 2010), 220–4.

[39] See Ch 6 of this book.

[40] See Ch 6 of this book.

[41] Christel Grundmann-van de Krol, 'The Markets in Financial Instruments Directive and Asset
Management' in Danny Busch and Deborah DeMott (eds), *Liability of Asset Managers* (Oxford University
Press, 2012), 43–4.

[42] Anand (n 29), 949. It is said that even a computer programme can take days to value certain collateralized debt obligations. See Martin (n 24), 83. The typical prospectus and prospectus supplement of many of the
securities in question were about 400 pages long—a long read for even a sophisticated investor. See Schwarcz
(n 37), 383.

[43] Aguilar (n 18).

[44] Where a rogue trader lost US$2 billion in September 2011.

[45] Where the 'London Whale' lost up to US$7 billion in a series of derivatives transactions in April and May
2012. See Jessica Silver-Greenberg, 'New Fraud Inquiry as JPMorgan's Loss Mounts', *New York Times* (13 July
2012) <http://dealbook.nytimes.com/2012/07/13/jpmorgan-says-traders-obscured-losses-in-first-quarter/>
accessed 24 December 2013.

[46] In a notable case, in response to the 'London Whale' losses, UK and US authorities levied $920 million
in fines against JPMorgan for, among other things, inadequate risk management systems. See Tom Braithwaite,
Kara Scannell in New York and Daniel Schäfer in London, 'JPMorgan hit with $920m in fines over "whale"
trade', *Financial Times* (19 September 2013) <http://www.ft.com/intl/cms/s/0/11ea2dc4-2125-11e3-a92a-
00144feab7de.html#axzz2ffp59LpA> accessed 24 December 2013.

11.19 Incurring an enormous fine on top of a huge loss might seem to be adding public insult to private injury. In theory, losses of these proportions should carry their own lessons and constitute their own punishment. However, the investment services industry has entered the era of careless driving; these institutions can kill everyone on the road, including hapless retail pedestrians.

2.3 Proprietary trading

11.20 Wearing their investor hat, intermediaries engage in trading on their own behalf and, theoretically, with their own funds. This proprietary trading, as it is called, is an area fraught with difficulties, primarily due to concerns over the conflicts of interest it generates and its implications for systemic risk. The growth in size and capitalization of market intermediaries has permitted them to become large institutional investors in their own right, trading for themselves, while continuing to execute trades on the behalf of clients. Proprietary trading can occur on or off exchange, but where on exchange, proprietary trading is particularly problematic.

11.21 Two incidents in particular have drawn attention and stirred controversy in the past few years. The first was during the financial crisis of 2008, when it became apparent that Goldman Sachs traded mortgage-backed securities to its clients while shorting the same security on its own behalf.[47] The second is the 'London Whale', where a trader at JP Morgan Chase lost nearly $6 billion in proprietary trading.[48]

11.22 Proprietary trading creates conflicts of interest; banks compete with their clients. Given the serious dilution of fiduciary obligations imposed on intermediaries in modern finance, especially in the United States, intermediaries stand to profit at the expense of their clients.[49] Endemic conflicts of interest also erode client-intermediary relations, effecting a cultural change where intermediaries feel little sense of responsibility towards their clients.

11.23 The second danger is that proprietary trading exacerbates risk taking. A UK Parliamentary report has labelled it '*casino banking*, where traders are speculating on markets using the bank's capital and borrowed money, for no purpose other than to make a profit and without any connection to trading on behalf of customers' (emphasis added).[50] Because banks foster a high-intensity, hothouse environment, pushing for greater and greater profits, internal controls and risk management systems can be overwhelmed. More London Whales may be cruising close beneath the surface of the Thames.

---

[47] Graeme Wearden, 'Goldman Sachs denies betting against clients', *The Guardian* (7 April 2010) <http://www.guardian.co.uk/business/2010/apr/07/goldman-sachs-letter-shareholders> accessed 24 December 2013.

[48] Parliamentary Commission on Banking Standards, Third Report of Session 2012–13, First Report, HC 1034/HL 138, para 19.

[49] '[I]f a bank is allowed to do proprietary trading, or proprietary investments, you will not have a culture that you like, because de facto, you are then competing with the client, and it is a heck of a lot easier to do proprietary work than it is to do client service. The best and the brightest within the institution will gravitate to the proprietary activity and we will end up where we have ended up, which is with bankers who sometimes do not understand right from wrong, or at least a pool of them.' Oral evidence taken before the Parliamentary Commission on Banking Standards Panel on Regulatory Approach on 11 December 2012, HC (2012–13) 821-i, Q 25.

[50] Parliamentary Commission (n 48), para 10.

The Volcker rule, named after Paul Volcker, the former US Federal Reserve Chairman, has **11.24** been one response, and a controversial one, much delayed in its appearance.[51] Proprietary trading, according to Volcker, is 'at odds with the basic objectives of financial reforms: to reduce excessive risk, to reinforce prudential supervision, and to assure the continuity of essential services'.[52] The Volcker Rule prohibits proprietary trading:

> In essence, proprietary trading activity, hedge funds, and equity holdings should stand on their own feet in the market place, not protected by access to bank capital, to the official safety nets, and to any presumption of public assistance as failure threatens. That, in essence, was the de facto distinction maintained until the last decade or two. Today, thousands of hedge funds operating with relatively little leverage and dependent on the equity capital of partners, represent much more limited risk to the financial system in the event of failure.[53]

The Volcker rule has drawn predictable criticism from Wall Street institutions,[54] where pro- **11.25** prietary trading is firmly entrenched, but other critics too, in more unexpected places.[55] European reaction is hostile across the board, in part due to differences in the structure of its industry and the potential for cross-border consequences.[56]

3. The Business Model and Its Hazards

3.1 Mounting fees and a lack of transparency

Financial intermediaries deal in information, risk, or a combination of both. Each participant **11.26** in the chain of intermediation takes a slice, and given the multiplication of intermediaries,

---

[51] A final rule implementing the Volker rule was adopted on 10 December 2013. It becomes effective on 1 April 2014, though the conformance period for all banking entities extends until 21 July 2015. See Skadden, Arps, Slate, Meagher, and Flom LLP, 'The Volcker Rule: A First Look at Key Changes' (12 December 2013) <http://www.skadden.com/insights/volcker-rule-first-look-key-changes> accessed 18 January 2014. A parallel US development is an August 2013 proposal suggesting that sponsors of asset-backed securitizations retain a portion of the risk of the assets securitized on their balance sheets, thereby realigning to some extent the securitizers' incentives with those of the security's purchaser. See Cleary Gottlieb, 'Credit Risk Retention: The New Proposal and its Implications for Securitization Markets' (19 September 2013), <https://clients.clearygottlieb.com/rs/vm.ashx?ct=24F76F15D4E10AE0C5DD83A5D42D981ED8FB55B2DF8E0BD15EE56360 69FFCB1CDB7A3A9C5> accessed 24 December 2013.

[52] Paul Volcker, 'Commentary on the Restrictions on Proprietary Trading by Insured Depositary Institutions', *Wall Street Journal* (13 February 2012), 1, <http://online.wsj.com/public/resources/documents/Volcker_Rule_Essay_2-13-12.pdf> accessed 24 December 2013.

[53] Volcker (n 52), 4.

[54] See also Ben Protress 'The Volcker Rule's Unusual Critics', *New York Times* (13 January 2012) <http://dealbook.nytimes.com/2012/02/15/the-volcker-rules-unusual-critics/> accessed 24 December 2013.

[55] Arguing it could make it more difficult for the Japanese to raise capital on the sovereign bond market. 'Japan Joins the Chorus of Volcker Critics', *Wall Street Journal* (13 January 2012) <http://online.wsj.com/article/SB10001424052970203721704577157131852089296.html> accessed 24 December 2013.

[56] European banks, in particular, are worried that the rule (which originated outside of the internationally coordinated regulatory agenda) will catch them as well. The prevalence of the universal banking business model in Europe could make it quite costly for European banks. Interlinkages between various parts of a European bank may be hard to untangle. For instance, 'structured finance may involve deposit funding coupled with derivatives structured internally..., which in turn is "manufactured" and hedged by trading desks... The hedging of these derivatives may be done with an external counterparty... which makes it difficult to "unbundle" the complicated relationships'. See Julian TS Chow and Jay Surti, 'Making Banks Safer: Can Volcker and Vickers Do It?' (2011) IMF Working Paper, 10 <http://www.imf.org/external/pubs/ft/wp/2011/wp11236.pdf> accessed 24 December 2013.

charges of imposing exorbitant costs on investors are not surprising.[57] Much of the growth in the US financial services industry from 1980 to 2007, for example, can be attributed to rising asset management fees.[58]

11.27   At the most basic level, transactions on an exchange require a broker acting as agent for the principal's trading account, for which the broker charges a commission, before transmitting the order to an exchange to which the broker is customer.[59] At a second degree of separation, funds are often channelled to brokers by advisers or asset managers (who perhaps have received funds from other managers).

11.28   Asset managers have generally changed their business models from transactional or commission-based to 'assets-under-management' or fee-based models, taking a percentage value of the client's portfolio, come rain or shine.[60] Often, those advisers or managers are required to safeguard the client's assets against the risk of misappropriation by maintaining them with a qualified custodian. Custodians therefore pass on 'safe-keeping' fees through to the ultimate investor. Typically, then, there are multiple players mediating between the investor and the exchange, but depending on the transaction, independent financial advisers, investment consultants (hired by funds), clearing platforms, trustees, underwriters (in primary transactions) and other agents who 'wrap' products can all generate fees along the chain.[61]

3.2 Complexity pays

11.29   The more complex distribution channels and products become, the more fees are generated. Collateral debt obligations (CDOs) of mortgage-backed securities, for example, generated revenue for the realtor, mortgage broker, lending bank, asset-backed paper manager, CDO manager not to mention credit rating agencies, guarantors, other arrangers, swap counterparties, the list goes on. A mutual fund or hedge fund that invests in other funds may pass on fees from the secondary manager, 'plus brokers, custodians, lenders (where the funds use leverage)' and so forth.[62] The continued trend of paying ballooning fees along the investment chain is somewhat difficult to reconcile with the well-known observation that professional

---

[57] Phil Davis, 'Industry defends soaring fees: Investors "have not questioned costs" in spite of underperformance', *Financial Times* (20 September 2004); Matthew Vincent, 'Poll reveals fund fees anger', *Financial Times* (20 January 2012), <http://www.ft.com/intl/cms/s/0/4743e1e8-436b-11e1-9f28-00144feab49a.html#axzz2X4tqSI3o> accessed 24 December 2013.

[58] Robin Greenwood and David Scharfstein, 'The Growth of Modern Finance' Harvard Business School Working Paper (2012) <http://www.people.hbs.edu/dscharfstein/Growth_of_Modern_Finance.pdf> accessed 24 December 2013. According to Evans, 'advisory fees, sales loads, and commissions pad to brokers on portfolio transactions...consumed approximately 45% of the real returns earned on managed portfolios over the last 20 years' Evans (n 13).

[59] David L Ratner and Thomas Lee Hazen, *Securities Regulation in a Nutshell* (Westgroup, 2002), 4–5. Alternatively, the broker can exchange with a third party market maker, an electronic network, or in the case of a broker running an internalized business model, fill out the order from its own inventory in order to profit from the spread. US Securities and Exchange Commission, 'Investor Tips: Trade Execution', <http://www.sec.gov/investor/pubs/tradexec.htm> accessed 24 December 2013.

[60] Josh Brown, 'Business Model Darwinism', *Wall Street Journal* (29 November 2011) <http://blogs.wsj.com/wealth-manager/2011/11/29/business-model-darwinism/> accessed 24 December 2013. Other fee models exist, including hourly, flat fees, commissions on the product they sell the client, salary structures, and combinations of fees and commissions.

[61] Kay (n 2), 30.

[62] 'Complexity pays', *The Economist* <http://www.economist.com/blogs/buttonwood/2009/11/complexity_pays> accessed 24 December 2013.

money managers tend to underperform passive investment strategies (or broad index-based investment) net of fees.[63] Adding to the difficulty is that the proliferation of costs along the chain also 'creates the potential for misalignment of incentives' and conflicts of interest at each one of its links.[64]

Hedge funds are notorious when it comes to fee structure. They have also been resistant to precise definition, and until recently referred to as 'unregulated investment funds'.[65] Essentially, they are mutual funds, 'with one important caveat: [their] mandate is typically much broader in terms of the techniques employed to generate profit'.[66] They also traditionally cater to investors who pass 'high net worth' or high income tests[67] so as to benefit from the exemptive provisions of securities regulation. Like a typical adviser, hedge fund managers usually receive a fixed fee based on aggregate assets in the 1–2 per cent range.[68] Unlike the registered adviser, however, unregistered hedge fund advisers receive incentive fees too—the industry standard is 20 per cent of profits.[69] Compounding the potential for misaligned incentives created by these performance arrangements[70] is that the funds do not follow any standard performance fee methodology, and often invest in securities that are 'relatively illiquid and difficult to value'.[71] Given this lack of transparency and complex fee structures, the oft-cited cost of due diligence for an investor seeking to invest in a hedge fund is said to be US$50,000.[72]

11.30

When, in July 2007, two Bear Stearns hedge funds that had invested heavily in mortgage-based CDOs collapsed, it signalled not only the deteriorating US mortgage market,[73] but the likely end of their status as largely 'unregulated investment funds'. The response since has been palpable. In December 2012, the European Commission adopted implementing measures in relation to the Directive on Alternative Investment Fund Managers (AIFMD), putting it into effect as regulation without the need for national implementing legislation within Europe.[74] Hedge funds, presumably caught by the instrument,[75] will now be subject to a

11.31

---

[63] Nicola Gennaioli, Andrei Shleifer, and Robert W Vishny, 'Money Doctors', NBER Working Paper No 18174 (June 2012), <http://www.nber.org/papers/w18174> accessed 24 March 2014. See also 'Quest for test of investment skill persists', *Financial Times* (11 January 2013), <http://www.ft.com/intl/cms/s/0/8d f368a4-5bd7-11e2-bef7-00144feab49a.html#axzz2Wh7EAPfx> accessed 24 December 2013.

[64] Kay (n 2), 30.

[65] Howard Davies, *The Financial Crisis: Who is to Blame?* (Polity, 2010), 164.

[66] Anand (n 29), 955.

[67] Anand (n 29), 955.

[68] US Securities and Exchange Commission, *Investor Bulletin: Hedge Funds* (SEC Office of Investor Education and Advocacy).

[69] US Securities and Exchange Commission (n 68); Martin (n 24), 81.

[70] These performance arrangements can lead to misaligned incentives by encouraging the fund manager to maximize short-term performance with little regard for the client's long term returns. 'Losses flow through to the investor and the use of high water marks allows managers to receive incentive fees once losses are made up': Martin (n 24), 81.

[71] US Securities and Exchange Commission (n 68).

[72] Rene M Stulz, 'Hedge Funds: Past, Present and Future' (2007) 21(2) *Journal of Economic Perspectives* 175, 179.

[73] Luther R Ashworth, 'Is Hedge Fund Adviser Registration Necessary to Accomplish the Goals of the Dodd-Frank Act's Title IV' (2013) 70 *Washington and Lee Law Review* 651, 653.

[74] Peter McGowan and Kimberly Everitt, 'New Requirements Imposed on the European Alternative Investment Funds Industry' (2013) 14(2) *Business Law International* 105.

[75] The Commission has not explicitly clarified which funds and mangers are covered by the Directive, though the Directive sets out general parameters based on certain assets-under-management thresholds (€100 million where funds are leveraged or €500 million where funds are unleveraged and meet other conditions): McGowan and Everitt (n 74), 106.

number ofequirements, including those concerning leverage and capital levels, conflicts of interest, risk management, liquidity, evaluation, and new transparency and disclosure rules.

11.32 The rules will be equally applicable in the United Kingdom, where most European hedge fund activity occurs (though, of course, they are not physically based there for fear of both corporate income and capital gains taxation). Eschewing the oxymoron, the FSA never regulated these unregulated entities under the Financial Services and Markets Act 2000, but did peer into the hedge fund managers themselves, who engage in 'regulated activities', and therefore had to register to do so.[76]

11.33 Until July 2011, many hedge fund managers in the United States relied on an exemption from registration in the Advisers Act. This 'private adviser exemption' has since been eliminated by Title IV of Dodd-Frank, and generally, any adviser with more than US$100 million under management must now register with the SEC.[77] Despite the regulatory response, it may be the failures in the business model itself that weed out the industry.[78]

3.3 Grey and not so grey areas

11.34 Conflicts between principal and agent emerging from compensation schemes are not limited to hedge funds. Commission-based pay by third parties[79] and even assets-under-management schemes[80] can give rise to them. The infamous 'Friends of Frank' abuses,[81] the near-*de facto* pump and dumps of the tech bubble,[82] and the traditional churning and scalping schemes populating law school casebooks are other examples.

---

[76] John Horsfield-Bradbury, 'Hedge Fund Self Regulation in the US and the UK', Harvard Corporate Governance Working Paper (2008), 39.

[77] Deborah DeMott and Arthur Laby, 'United States' in Danny Busch and Deborah DeMott (eds), *Liability of Asset Managers* (Oxford University Press, 2012), 418. Title IV does, however, feature new exemptions, see Ashworth (n 73), 685. Some fund managers have already converted their funds to 'family office' funds so as to benefit from the exemption. See Madison Marriage, 'Hedge funds copy Soros's regulatory sidestep', *Financial Times* (4 August 2013), <http://www.ft.com/intl/cms/s/0/3106417e-fb60-11e2-8650-00144feabdc0. html#axzz2fqhXJqhf> accessed 24 December 2013.

[78] See, among others, Dan McCrum, 'Hedge funds gripped by crisis of performance', *Financial Times* (28 July 2013), <http://www.ft.com/intl/cms/s/0/33defe3a-f3d7-11e2-942f-00144feabdc0.html#axzz2fqhXJqhf> accessed 24 December 2013, 'Since the turn of the decade, Wall Street's master stock pickers have spectacularly failed to beat the market'; Gregory Zuckerman, Juliet Chung, and Michael Corkery, 'Hedge Funds Cut Back on Fees', *Wall Street Journal* (9 September 2013) <http://online.wsj.com/article/SB10001424127887323893930 04579054952807556352.html> accessed 24 December 2013; 'Investors Exit Hedge Funds After Another Bad Month', *CNBC.com* <http://www.cnbc.com/id/48929720> accessed 24 December 2013.

[79] Some jurisdictions, like the United Kingdom and Australia, have banned these pay structures. See Patrick Collinson, 'FSA ban on commission-based selling sparks "death of salesman" fears', *The Guardian* (30 December 2012), <http://www.guardian.co.uk/business/2012/dec/30/fsa-ban-commission-selling-death> accessed 24 December 2013.

[80] As in the case where the adviser suggests that that the client not pay off a mortgage and thereby diminish her managed asset base, even when the cost of its high interest rate exceeds the opportunity cost of earnings from the managed investment. See Bert Whitehead, 'There are conflicts inherent in assets-under-management pricing' (27 November 2011) <http://www.investmentnews.com/article/20111127/REG/311279984> accessed 24 December 2013.

[81] As inducement for selecting his firm as their bank of choice, Quattrone's team gave technology company executives access to a 'Friends of Frank' account that would give them allocations of newly issued shares in 'hot IPOs', shares typically only available to large investing institutions. After a day or two of trading and a soaring share price, Credit Swiss First Boston brokers would 'flip' or 'spin' the shares to a less fortunate buyer at a huge profit to Frank's friends.

[82] Investment bank analysts regularly issued buy ratings only to see the stock plummet almost immediately after, often to the chagrin of investors following the analysis and caught up in market euphoria. Analysts were

Many of these practices are not unlawful per se but depend on case-by-case enforcement and **11.35** other factors, though jurisdictions of course differ as to their requirements. In the United States, for example, in its disclosure based regulatory regime, agents are often considered to have discharged their duties and mitigated many of the above conflicts if they have given adequate disclosure.[83] Securities lending and bilateral and tri-partite[84] repurchase agreements, or 'repos', are also considered generally acceptable practices,[85] but can subject client assets to significant risk with little to no transparency. A repurchase agreement is a 'sale of securities [for cash] coupled with an agreement to repurchase the securities at a specified price on a later date'. Economically, a repurchase agreement resembles a secured loan.[86] Some broker-dealers or fund managers lend out portfolio securities they hold (but do not own) to earn incremental returns for their clients. Borrowers, such as hedge funds, may do it to cover short positions.[87] In these transactions, firms regularly 're-hypothecate (i.e., use for its own account) customer assets. . . . Once the assets have been re-hypothecated, title transfers to the . . . broker-dealer, and the client's proprietary interest in the securities is replaced with a contractual claim to redelivery of equivalent securities'.[88]

That these transactions have been characterized as part of the 'shadow sector' is telling. Some of **11.36** them are reported on the intermediary's balance sheet, but in other cases repos can be off-balance sheet, 'depending on the accounting standards used'.[89] In addition to this, since many participants do not hold adequate cash to settle the many transactions on a day-to-day basis, third party clearers extend intraday and day-to-day credit, leaving billions of dollars of value at risk should liquidity spirals materialize or computer systems go down. Reporting these activities to clients—even sophisticated ones—has been questionable. According to the Financial Stability Board, prior to the global financial crisis, many brokers 'did not provide sufficient disclosure on re-hypothecation activities to their hedge fund clients. For example, following the collapse of Lehman . . . , many hedge funds unexpectedly became unsecured general creditors because they had not realised the extent to which . . . securities'[90] had been rehypothecated.

There are, of course, less 'grey' areas too. Instances of outright fraud can be devastating to **11.37** investors of all kinds—the Madoff fraud, for example.[91] The temptation to misappropriate

---

compensated on the basis of bringing in business, not on the quality of their analysis, thus fostering cosiness between the analyst and the company serving as the object of analysis.

[83] Deborah DeMott and Arthur Laby, 'United States', in Danny Busch and Deborah DeMott (eds), *Liability of Asset Managers* (Oxford University Press, 2012), 423.

[84] The third party acts as a clearing agent. See 'Current Practices and Infrastructure', in Federal Reserve Bank of New York, 'Tri-Party Repo Infrastructure Reform', Federal Reserve White Paper (2010) <http://www.newyorkfed.org/banking/nyfrb_triparty_whitepaper.pdf> accessed 24 December 2013.

[85] In the United States, various SEC 'no-action' letters authorize it, though participants are subject to 're-hypothecation' caps and may have to seek exemptions from the Investment Company Act (1940). US Securities and Exchange Commission, 'Securities Lending by US Open-End and Closed-End Investment Companies', <http://www.sec.gov/divisions/investment/securities-lending-open-closed-end-investment-companies.htm#P11_3185> accessed 24 December 2013. In Australia and the United Kingdom, re-hypothecation is permitted with no cap. Financial Stability Board, *Securities Lending and Repos: Market Overview and Financial Stability Issues: Interim Report of the FSB Workstream on Securities Lending and Repos* (2012).

[86] Federal Reserve Bank of New York (n 84), 5.

[87] The Investment Company Institute, *Re: Comments on Interim Report on Securities Lending and Repos* (25 May 2012).

[88] Financial Stability Board (n 85), 10.

[89] Financial Stability Board (n 85), 14.

[90] Financial Stability Board (n 85), 14–15.

[91] The most notorious 'Ponzi' scheme in recent Wall Street history.

client assets may be particularly strong for those having custody or discretionary authority given the rewards that can be reaped, and apparently, the length of time a fraudster can operate with impunity.[92] Indeed, it is hard to understand why clever criminals devote time to other endeavours when the opportunity cost of criminal opportunism in financial markets would be so great.[93]

3.4 Lack of regulation, fiduciary duties, or redress

11.38 Regulatory responses providing adequate deterrence and remedies for these and other conflicts are problematic. Some intermediaries, until very recently, have not had to consider many rules at all, operating in spheres characterized by an absence of regulation. Some have had to consider fiduciary duties owed to their clients; many have not. A lack of redress plagues individual investors. Asset management or brokerage contracts, even for supposedly sophisticated investors, may be one-sided, standard forms, drafted in favour of the intermediary[94] and requiring arbitration of claims before industry panels. Indeed, arbitration before industry constituted panels has become the 'customary method of resolving disputes between individual investors and brokerage firms' in the United States.[95] Some US jurisdictions invoke principles of freedom of contract to permit mandatory arbitration clauses to effectively preclude large-scale class actions, thereby marginalizing the deterrence effect of any individual claim. Further limiting redress for individual investors in the United States has been the hostility demonstrated by the US Supreme Court to investor class actions.[96]

11.39 In light of this sorry litany of grievances about professional intermediaries, it is not surprising that there have been calls for 'heads on stakes',[97] at least in the City of London (where the practice, historically, is not unknown). Regulation of intermediaries though is no easy task, especially where cross-border consequences arise in the interconnected world of finance. There are no easy regulatory answers here.

4. Regulation of Intermediaries

4.1 'Blue sky' and licensing

11.40 Securities abuses are no new phenomenon. While the speculative issues of the twenty-first century are often in high technology fields like biological engineering or derivatives products, those of the early twentieth century were in mining and petroleum companies, land

---

[92] 'Incredibly, Madoff's Ponzi scheme was only discovered by regulators after he confessed.' Cheryl Nichols, 'Addressing Inept SEC Enforcement Efforts: Lessons from Madoff, the Hedge Fund Industry, and Title IV of the Dodd-Frank Act for U.S. and Global Financial Systems' (2011) 31 *Northwestern Journal of International Law and Business* 637.

[93] A similar point is made by Romer in Paul M Romer, 'Process, Responsibility and Myron's Law', in Olivier Jean Blanchard et al (eds), *In the Wake of the Crisis: Leading Economists Reassess Economic Policy* (MIT Press, 2012), 123.

[94] In the United States, standard form contracts may contain clauses permitting unilateral modification in favour of the intermediary.

[95] Barbara Black, 'Arbitration of Investors' Claims against Issuers: An Idea Whose Time Has Come' (2012) 75 *Law and Contemporary Problems* 107.

[96] See eg *Morrison v National Australia Bank* 130 S Ct 2869 (2010).

[97] Jeremy Warner, 'Cutting the City of London down to size will shrink Britain too', *The Telegraph* (3 July 2012), <http://www.telegraph.co.uk/finance/rate-swap-scandal/9373103/Cutting-the-City-of-London-down-to-size-will-shrink-Britain-too.html> accessed 24 December 2013.

development and patent development promotions.[98] In the United States, a high appetite for such ventures coupled with a propensity for fraudulent activity often produced calamitous results for investors.[99] One regulatory entrepreneur took particular exception. In 1910, a Banking Commissioner from Kansas named JN Dolley famously complained about 'the enormous amount of money the Kansas people are being swindled out of by these fakers and "blue-sky merchants"'.[100] In the United Kingdom, nearly 75 years later, Professor Gower warned that the City of London risked becoming known as a 'haven for crooks'.[101]

Arguably, Dolley was more successful than Professor Gower in prompting a regulatory **11.41** response. In 1911, Dolley convinced the state legislature to pass a remedial statute. At its core was the requirement that firms selling securities in Kansas 'obtain a license from the bank commissioner and file regular reports of financial condition'.[102]

Dolley quickly received requests for copies of the new law from nearly every state in the **11.42** country. Other countries, including England, Germany, and Canada made the same request.[103] Many American states adopted similar requirements mandating the licensing and registration of dealers. Other states adopted more stringent regulations, requiring that an administrative agency inquire as to the intrinsic worth or 'merit' of new issues.[104] This last approach was deliberately discarded in favour of a disclosure-based model in the drafting of US federal securities legislation in the 1930s.[105] For more than 20 years, until the passage of the US 1933 Act, securities sales in the United States were regulated by the states' 'blue sky' laws, as they had come to be known. Still today, US states retain authority over licensing, registration, and qualification of 'an adviser's supervised persons' located within their bounds.[106] Non-exempt investment advisers are also required to register federally with the SEC.[107]

More broadly, almost all national or sub-national jurisdictions operating within the two **11.43** Western legal traditions of civil and common law today—with the notable exception of Switzerland—require intermediaries such as asset managers to comply with licensing or registration requirements.[108] Across jurisdictions, these requirements may vary. In European jurisdictions that have adopted MiFID, authorization is required to perform investment services as an occupation or profession. Membership in an investor compensation scheme is a prerequisite to receiving authorization.[109] In Ireland, a meeting with the Central Bank

---

[98] Jonathan R Macey and Geoffrey Miller, 'Origin of the Blue Sky Laws' (1991) 70 *Texas Law Review* 347, 353.

[99] The conventional wisdom tends to emphasize the abuses while downplaying the fact that many supposed abuses were really just risky investments. Macey and Miller (n 98), 348–9.

[100] Macey and Miller (n 98), 360. The etymology of the term 'blue-sky' is a matter of contention. Its birth is often attributed to the press release containing the aforementioned quotation, but it appears to have been readily used in Kansas prior to Dolley's statement. For a discussion, see Macey and Miller (n 98), 360 at fn 59.

[101] See Ch 6 in this book.

[102] Macey and Miller (n 98), 361.

[103] Macey and Miller (n 98), 364.

[104] Macey and Miller (n 98), 349.

[105] James M Landis, 'Legislative History of the Securities Act of 1933' (1959) 28 *George Washington Law Review* 29.

[106] DeMott and Laby (n 83), 415.

[107] Busch and DeMott (n 3), 12.

[108] Busch and DeMott (n 3), 11.

[109] Busch and DeMott (n 3), 11.

is required. In Canada (unlike the United States), licensing requires demonstrating a certain level of proficiency along with industry experience, unless the regulator grants an exemption.[110]

4.2 Self-regulation lingers on

11.44 Licensing with a state authority contrasts with and often overlaps with self-regulation based in the industry in question, traditionally a prominent feature of common law regulatory landscapes.[111] Organizations exercising monopoly power over membership fees and normative authority floating free of regulatory oversight are somewhat anachronistic in modern markets; exchanges have largely lost their self-regulatory powers, but for other intermediaries it is a more complex story.

11.45 After centuries of dominance, in Britain the self-regulatory organization per se succumbed in the troubled regulatory experiment of the Securities Investment Board, which had attempted to corral and rationalize the self regulatory organizations in the City of London without doing away with them. The Financial Services and Markets Act 2000, by creating a formal regulator, the FSA, put the self-regulatory organizations out of their misery. The European Union played its part too, since the concept was more or less incompatible with EU regulatory principles and impeded the operation of mutual recognition for EU purposes.[112]

11.46 Rather, given Britain's historical reliance on private law, self-regulation seems now to smooth the inefficiencies or improve the protection of already-existing private law vehicles. For example, where the power of the common law, including its emphasis on freedom of contract, remains strong, those with sufficient bargaining power (read, institutional clients) accept heavy transaction costs in drawn-out asset management contract negotiations. The UK-based Asset Management Association therefore developed model standard form agreements 'for use by asset managers with institutional customers', balancing customer and manager interests.[113] Additionally, the Investment Management Association publishes guidelines and standard form samples assisting its membership in meeting state-promulgated regulation. Recent publications, for example, are designed to facilitate compliance with enhanced fee-disclosure rules for funds, and include model 'Key Investor Information Documents' required under UCITS rules.[114]

11.47 In contrast, in the United States, despite the heavy regulatory apparatus in place, self-regulatory organizations play a more prominent regulatory and enforcement role with respect to professional intermediaries, a testament to their lobbying prowess and clout on Capitol Hill. The National Association of Securities Dealers (NASD) was rolled into the Financial Industry Regulatory Authority (FINRA) in July 2007. Although ultimately subject to the oversight of the SEC, FINRA is charged with regulating broker-dealers, and has administrative-like rule-making authority. For example, both the suitability doctrine—the

---

[110] Busch and DeMott (n 3), 11–12.

[111] Switzerland, though a smaller jurisdiction, serves as an example of SRO rule-making par excellence. Busch and DeMott (n 3), 16.

[112] See Ch 6 of this book.

[113] Lodewijk Van Setten and Tim Plews, 'England and Wales' in Danny Busch and Deborah DeMott (eds), *Liability of Asset Managers* (Oxford University Press, 2012), 351.

[114] Investment Management Association, 'Fund charges and costs' <http://www.investmentfunds.org.uk/current-topics-of-interest/charges/> accessed 24 December 2013.

requirement that before executing a trade a broker must take reasonable effort to ascertain a customer's characteristics and objectives—and the similar 'know-your-client' rule are codified in FINRA rules.[115] FINRA also has enforcement authority, and can take the traditional disciplinary actions of fining or expelling non-abiding members.[116] In January 2011, the SEC also recommended to Congress that FINRA (or another SRO) be authorized to oversee investment advisers, but the matter remains undetermined.[117]

Given that self-regulation has fallen into disrepute, it may be surprising that it remains a **11.48** conspicuous feature of the Canadian regulatory landscape too. Most Canadian professional intermediaries, dealers, advisers, asset managers, participate in the Investment Industry Regulatory Organization of Canada (IIROC);[118] some informal forces of harmonization along industry lines as between the United States and Canada may be operating in this regard. However, even the oligopolistic 'Big Six' chartered banks in Canada, with the option to provide investment services within their federally-regulated entities, choose to provide them through investment-arm subsidiaries regulated by IIROC.[119] IIROC is overseen by Canadian Securities Administrators—an informal grouping of the chairs of the provincial securities regulators—and having 'quasi-judicial powers', is responsible for creating and enforcing its own rules.[120] Given that securities law in Canada is partitioned along provincial and territorial boundaries, IIROC serves another, important role, promoting nationwide harmonization,[121] in the absence of a federal regulator comparable to the SEC.

4.3 Industry associations

Industry associations too act as compensatory, *de facto*, albeit self-interested, regulators **11.49** across jurisdictional boundaries.[122] Although not recognized as formal self-regulatory bodies, industry associations may operate in tandem with them, supporting regulatory requirements.[123] In addition to their lobbying activities, industry associations do tend to mitigate the propensity for detrimental behaviour by their members; participating in a 'club' may promote adherence to rules and standards viewed as 'their own'.[124]

While most jurisdictions do not impose *ex ante* industry association membership require- **11.50** ments on professional intermediaries, Canada's lead jurisdiction does. In order to register as an adviser[125] under the Ontario Securities Act, registrants must possess a Chartered Financial

---

[115] DeMott and Laby (n 83), 429.

[116] But see Steven Irwin et al, 'Self-Regulation of the American Retail Securities Markets—An Oxymoron for What Is Best for Investors' (2011) 14 *University of Pennsylvania Journal of Business Law* 1055, 1072 regarding the revealed impotence of said authority in *Fiero Brothers*, 550 F.3d 569 (2d Cir 2011).

[117] DeMott and Laby (n 83), 420. Caitlin Nish, 'Finra CEO Still Seems Eager to Oversee Advisers', *Wall Street Journal* (14 March 2013), <http://online.wsj.com/article/SB10001424127887324077704578360502816221548.html> accessed 24 December 2013.

[118] Cally Jordan and Pamela Hughes, 'Canada' in Danny Busch and Deborah DeMott (eds), *Liability of Asset Managers* (Oxford University Press, 2012), 462.

[119] Jordan and Hughes (n 118), 462.

[120] Jordan and Hughes (n 118), 482.

[121] Jordan and Hughes (n 118), 482.

[122] Industry associations play this role internationally as well; see Cally Jordan and Pamela Hughes, 'Which Way for Market Institutions: The Fundamental Question of Self-Regulation' (2007) 4 *Berkeley Business Law Journal* 205.

[123] The relevant distinction is that industry associations, as used here, lack power 'to impose statutory or regulatory requirements' See Busch and DeMott (n 3), 12.

[124] Busch and DeMott (n 3), 15.

[125] A broad category capturing a wide range of intermediation activities in the market.

Analyst (CFA) designation.[126] The CFA designation and membership in the CFA Institute are used as a proxy for competence and understanding of ethical conduct. Taking as example the fact that the CFA Institute's membership is spread across 137 countries, associations can serve to propagate normativity and best practices internationally in a very effective manner. Moreover, in Ontario, CFA membership as a condition precedent to registration has no doubt contributed to Toronto being second only to New York City in the number of residents holding the designation.[127]

4.4 Fiduciary duties...sometimes

11.51 Fiduciary standards, in theory, are the investor's good friend. The application of fiduciary standards to intermediaries though varies significantly across jurisdictions and categories of intermediary. Fiduciary relationships are, of course, creatures of the common law, not native to the civilian codal tradition. Civilian codal systems have, however, historically developed doctrines and standards, such as good faith in contract, with similar protections. Some mechanisms look back to Roman law institutions like the *fiducia* and *fideicommissum*; others have been imported together with common law vehicles such as the trust.[128]

11.52 The central axiom of English fiduciary responsibility is that 'a person who assumes responsibility to serve the interests of another, to the exclusion of his own interest, shall owe a duty of loyalty as a fiduciary, as far as that other person is entitled to expect this'.[129] Under English law, agency relationships, in addition to their contractual obligations, also trigger implied fiduciary duties.[130] Grounding this implication is the fact that the principal may be at the mercy of an agent's discretion. Intermediaries often wield considerable or total discretion over client assets, resulting in fiduciary duties. Generally, under English law and in much of the Commonwealth, fiduciary obligations are divided into four categories. Fiduciaries must avoid conflicts of interest; they must make no secret profits from their agency relationship; they must not put themselves into a position where duty to one beneficiary conflicts with duty to another; and they must not use information obtained from a beneficiary for purposes other than the benefit of that beneficiary.[131] As there is a 'linear correlation between the scope of applicable fiduciary duties and the scope of the designated fiduciary's discretion', the extent of an intermediary's duties will be subject to the realities of the relationship with the client.

11.53 Although the law surrounding agency relationships in the United States grew from many of the same English principles, they are no longer an adequate descriptor. Fiduciary principles have been supplanted by statute in some instances and may operate, on their own, in a much less vigorous way than they do in the United Kingdom. For example, even if advisers in the United States are not acting as agents or trustees, they generally owe a statutory fiduciary duty under the Advisers Act, unless an exemption applies.[132] Fiduciary standards for advisers, however, do not incorporate the entire body of fiduciary law but are generally informed by federal court cases

---

[126] Jordan and Hughes (n 118), 471.
[127] Jordan and Hughes (n 118), 12.
[128] See eg the Civil Code of Quebec rules on the administration of the property of others: Jordan and Hughes (n 118), 467.
[129] Van Setten and Plews (n 113), 346.
[130] Van Setten and Plews (n 113), 346.
[131] Van Setten and Plews (n 113), 347.
[132] DeMott and Laby (n 83), 438.

and SEC enforcement actions.[133] The familiar duty of loyalty resulting in the requirement that the agent act in the beneficiary's best interest nevertheless remains central to the relationship.[134]

Brokers, on the other hand are excluded from the Advisers Act, and so not subject to its **11.54** statutory fiduciary duties. Nevertheless, by the operation of private law, if a broker assumes significant discretionary authority and gains the trust of an investor, 'a court may subject the broker to a fiduciary standard'.[135] But this is an open issue, subject to the particular facts and circumstances surrounding the relationship and the transactions involved. In 2010, the Dodd-Frank legislation authorized the SEC to 'impose on broker-dealers a fiduciary standard of conduct generally applicable to investment advisers when the broker provides personalized advice . . . to a retail customer'.[136] The SEC has since reiterated the need to impose fiduciary duties on brokers, but action has not ensued.[137]

4.5 Cross-border implications: the transatlantic dialogue

Leading up to the global financial crisis, the regulatory stances of the United States and **11.55** Europe were far from coordinated. On the contrary, the two 'waged a smouldering battle' over cross-border regulations applicable to intermediaries.[138] Regulation of European trading screens in the United States was perhaps at its apogee. Such terminals allow US broker-dealers to become members of, and trade directly on, European exchanges, freeing up the flow of capital to Europe.[139] Europe repeatedly pressed for authority to locate trading screens in the United States without having to comply with SEC rules applicable to American exchanges.[140] The SEC, concerned primarily with protecting investors (and perhaps by the fact that the Sarbanes-Oxley Act had already 'substantially slowed' the rate of new European listings on US exchanges[141]), repeatedly said no. The Europeans, who naturally were not keen to hear that their jurisdiction offered insufficient investor protection—even after several EU directives offering new protections[142]—are, of course, also free traders par excellence. They viewed the denial as protectionist.[143] The claim was not an entirely unfounded one.

In 2007, a system of 'substituted compliance' as an alternative was proposed by an SEC **11.56** official, albeit not in an official SEC capacity.[144] Under the approach, foreign exchanges and broker-dealers could apply for exemption from SEC registration. If their home-country regulations were deemed substantially in compliance with US laws, they could continue

---

[133] DeMott and Laby (n 83), 421.

[134] DeMott and Laby (n 83), 421.

[135] DeMott and Laby (n 83), 414.

[136] DeMott and Laby (n 83), 414.

[137] DeMott and Laby (n 83), 414.

[138] Howell E Jackson, Andreas Fleckner, and Mark Gurevich, 'Foreign Trading Screens in the United States' (2006) 549 Harvard John M Olin Discussion Paper Series, 3 <http://www.law.harvard.edu/programs/olin_center/papers/pdf/Jackson_et%20al_549.pdf> accessed 24 December 2013.

[139] Jackson, Fleckner, and Gurevich (n 138), 3.

[140] Jackson, Fleckner, and Gurevich (n 138), 3.

[141] Jackson, Fleckner, and Gurevich (n 138), 20.

[142] Jackson, Fleckner, and Gurevich (n 138), 21.

[143] See eg the US rules regarding EU trading screens being characterized as an 'external trade barrier' impeding market integration in 'Final Report of the Committee of Wise Men on the Regulation of European Securities Markets' (Brussels, 2001), 10–11.

[144] Ethiopis Tafara and Robert J Peterson, 'A Blueprint for Cross-Border Access to U.S. Investors: A New International Framework' (2007) 48 *Harvard International Law Journal* 31.

to operate under their domestic rules. An exchange in a complying European jurisdiction could then place trading screens on the NYSE to access US investors directly. Given the size of the US market, such schemes would also incentivize regulatory convergence by putting pressure on nonparticipants.[145] Despite some early momentum, the proposal eventually fizzled, though it did serve as the impetus for a pilot mutual recognition arrangement with the Australian Securities and Investments Commission.[146] Substituted compliance remains relevant, though its objects as of late have been the derivative rules and clearing obligations drafted since the global financial crisis. Most of these are within the purview of the CFTC, which has historically been more open to the operation of recognition principles.[147]

11.57 Much of the substance of this dialogue will no doubt be shaped by the final rules contained in the revision to MiFID started in 2010. MiFID II, as it has come to be known, is in its final legislative stage: the 'trilogue' wherein the European Commission, European Parliament and Council of the European Union come together to produce a single text, expected sometime in 2015. The anticipated scope of MiFID II is vast and takes on much of the subject matter that is proving internationally contentious, including regulating derivatives, clearing houses and imposing limits on high-frequency and dark pool trading. Much of its subject matter therefore aligns with that of the September 2013 passage of the Market Abuse Regulation, which although originally spurred by the LIBOR scandal,[148] also addresses abuses in high frequency and derivatives markets.[149] MiFID II also contains strict equivalence conditions applying to third country firms: only after a declaration of equivalence regarding their home state's regulatory and tax regimes will they be granted EU market access.[150] The revised directive's form is yet unknown and it has already come under frequent attack for its alleged overreach.[151]

---

[145] Chris Brummer, 'Stock Exchanges and the New Markets for Securities Laws' (2008) 75 *University of Chicago Law Review* 1435, 1484.

[146] Securities and Exchange Commission, 'Press Release: Director of International Affairs Ethiopis Tafara to Leave SEC' (15 February 2014) <http://www.sec.gov/News/PressRelease/Detail/PressRelease/1365171512798#.UkW6pj8cvTo> accessed 24 December 2013.

[147] Shahien Nasiripour in Washington and Stephen Foley in New York, 'CFTC to delay some swaps rules', *Financial Times* (21 December 2012) <http://www.ft.com/intl/cms/s/0/001fef32-4b03-11e2-929d-00144feab49a.html#axzz2g7HXchIV> accessed 24 December 2013. Gregory Meyer in New York, 'Talks on US derivatives rules run to the wire', *Financial Times* (8 July 2013), <http://www.ft.com/intl/cms/s/0/68818ce2-e7da-11e2-babb-00144feabdc0.html#axzz2g7HXchIV> accessed 24 December 2013.

[148] Libor is a collection of interest rates providing a measure of the cost of borrowing between banks. In July 2012, regulators revealed that the rate had been manipulated by banks, allowing them to pass on higher borrowing costs and welfare losses onto customers and the real economy. See James O'Toole, 'Explaining the Libor interest rate mess', *CNN* (3 July 2012) <http://money.cnn.com/2012/07/03/investing/libor-interest-rate-faq/index.htm> accessed 24 December 2013.

[149] European Commission, 'Press release—Statement by Commissioner Michel Barnier on the endorsement by the European Parliament of the political agreement on new European rules for market abuse' (10 September 2013) <http://europa.eu/rapid/press-release_MEMO-13-773_en.htm?locale=en> accessed 24 December 2013.

[150] Shearman and Sterling LLP, *A Changing Landscape: The MiFID II Legislative Proposal* (2011), 12.

[151] Tim Cave, 'LSE, lobbyists and fund managers unite in last-ditch Mifid II plea' *Financial News* (26 September 2013) <http://www.efinancialnews.com/story/2013-09-26/lse-lobbyists-and-fund-managers-make-last-ditch-plea-on-mifid?mod=sectionheadlines-PE-TTmod=sectionheadlines-PE-TT&ea9c8a2de0ee111045601ab04d673622> accessed 24 December 2013.

5. Future Prospects for the World of Intermediaries

The regulation of intermediaries is a particularly thorny area, with no obvious or easy **11.58** ways forward. Domestically, in the United Kingdom, the major Commonwealth countries and the United States, it can be an area of complex, overlapping, underlapping and potentially duplicative forms of regulation, larded with ticking political bombs. The issues involved in regulating intermediaries are straining the limits of transatlantic cooperation and coordination; formal convergence and harmonization are not the operative concepts.

The European Union, bravely, is making a stab at systematization at least on a European-wide **11.59** basis, with a suite of new legislative initiatives including MiFID II, the proposed Market Abuse Regulation (replacing the much less robust and largely ineffectual Market Abuse Directive), the Alternative Investment Fund Managers Directive, and caps on investment bankers' compensation. However, each of these initiatives presents its own difficulties and, as a general matter, leaves the European Union open to the usual criticisms of engaging in an unhelpful form of overregulation.

Cross-border issues involving the regulation of financial intermediaries are even more fraught **11.60** and resistant to resolution. Even the identification of 'systemically important financial institutions' is a sensitive and highly charged process, much less what to do about them. The Financial Stability Board sees itself playing a role here. The financial crisis eclipsed previous, lower-level regulatory stabs at various forms of mutual or unilateral recognition of licensing and regulatory oversight.[152] Concepts of comity and regulatory deference, more acceptable in other areas, are at war with the 'level playing field' arguments, which often amount to industry protectionism in another guise.

There are also several jokers in the pack. Technology is transforming trading and market **11.61** practices, but can cut both ways as far as intermediaries are concerned. New kinds of intermediaries and associated market infrastructure are popping up, such as Swap Execution Facilities (SEFs), with the traditional closed categories of intermediary becoming blurred.[153] Institutions like SEFs can be operated by different kinds of intermediaries, and are operating in the professional markets, offering the sort of certainty (and transparency) usually reserved for the public retail markets, all in the name of addressing systemic risk.

New forms of institutional investors, with unpredictable appetites and proclivities, are also **11.62** entering the international markets, the sovereign wealth funds. To date, the discourse about intermediaries and their regulation has been very much a transatlantic one. But what of Asia and its burgeoning retail investor culture? A former Hong Kong regulator has recently warned of the disaster in waiting in China, where product starved investors are massively shifting to wealth management schemes with no set of uniform standards governing their investment vehicles, only an 'implicit understanding... that if something goes wrong, the

---

[152] For example, the rather clunky 'substituted compliance' mechanism for recognition of intermediaries, floated in 2007 in the United States. See Tafara and Peterson (n 144).

[153] See 'Not with a bang', *The Economist* (5 October 2013), 7: 'The past few weeks have seen a flurry of applications for SEF [Swap Execution Facilities] status. There are almost 20 platforms in this newly competitive market, including established operators of electronic markets such as Bloomberg, futures exchanges like IntercontinentalExchange, brokers (GFI Group) and new start-ups like Javelin Capital Markets'.

government will come in and protect them'.[154] So much for the international effort to reduce moral hazard.[155]

11.63 At the least, the global financial crisis and the intensified regulatory vigilance which followed have cast light on the dark corners of the new world of the intermediaries. However, in such a complex, multifaceted industry (and one so adept at darting and dodging), it is hard to imagine radical industry-wide structural changes in the short term. The Volcker Rule in the United States limiting proprietary trading, and various regulatory interventions in the European Union, are certainly attempting to make a difference. Internally, the big investment banks in the glare of unwanted publicity are purportedly attempting cultural change. As memories of crisis subside and economic activity accelerates though, these efforts may dissipate, at least until the next time.

---

[154] 'China Stock Market Dysfunctional Amid IPO Halt, Neoh Says', *Bloomberg* (1 August 2013) <http://www.bloomberg.com/news/2013-08-01/china-s-stock-market-dysfunctional-amid-ipo-freeze-neoh-says.html> accessed 24 December 2013.

[155] See eg Financial Stability Board, 'Reducing the moral hazard posed by systemically important financial institutions' (20 October 2010) <http://www.financialstabilityboard.org/publications/r_101111a.pdf> accessed 24 December 2013.

12

CONCLUSION

1. New Markets, Old Rules

Capital markets are changing, dramatically so. The massive innovation in investment products over the last 25 years is giving way to shifting trading patterns, changing investor profiles and new forms of capitalism and finance. The dynamics of international markets have changed, even since the Asian financial crisis, when 'contagion' entered the financial lexicon. Now, information, investments, and capital can be transmitted instantaneously. So can risk.

12.01

The new markets defy the old rules. Information technology has exploded the assumptions of a disclosure based regulatory regime, such as in the United States. Demographics and economic development are transforming investing patterns and investor profile. In Western Europe and Japan (and North America, to a lesser degree), an aging population produces risk-averse investors. The financial intermediaries servicing this population's needs, the pension funds and insurance companies, lulled by steady incoming investment, now face the turning tide, as payment streams reverse direction. On the other hand, in Asia (ex-Japan), Latin America,and perhaps soon Africa, a rising middle class is increasingly seeking investment opportunities, sometimes oblivious to risk. In the cash rich Gulf region, wealthy individuals have the sophistication and wherewithal to invest anywhere they choose; keeping their money and investments in their home markets is still not a compelling proposition for them.

12.02

High frequency traders, swarming markets at lightning speed, are harrying the more lumbering institutional investors, long used to dominating the market, driving them off the exchanges and into the dark pools. The traditional stock exchanges are in crisis; the waves of cross-border consolidations may have spent their energy. Upstarts, alternative trading platforms, designed for new products and new opportunities, are fragmenting the marketplace. The activities of intermediaries are under intense scrutiny. The world of finance has been a fine and private place, but now the once hidden practices, the collusion and the corruption in the interests of personal gain, are being exposed. Technology is a double edged sword, fostering collusive activity, but also facilitating its detection. Obscure practices, long accepted in the specialized corners of finance, interest rate and currency setting, are now attracting regulatory attention.

12.03

Capitalism is also undergoing a metamorphosis. With the evolution of state capitalism, everyone is an investor, willing or not. Despite the shock therapy of the post-Soviet era, the state-owned enterprise has not sunk into oblivion. Much to the contrary; it is a staple of the new capitalism, with even the United States indulging in state ownership on occasion. Chinese capital markets are the story of this century. Sovereign wealth funds, of various hues

12.04

and colours, are also seeking international portfolio diversification, raising political issues associated with capital inflows. Market infrastructure, both domestically and internationally, is being shaped by sovereign wealth funds; exchanges, are a favourite form of investment for them.

12.05   Islamic finance, inherently international and with a potential market of well over a billion investors, is also changing the face of traditional finance. That the Islamic population is not concentrated in the transatlantic corridor, but in Asia, the Gulf, Africa, means capital and regulatory initiatives are moving away from the traditional international financial centres, reinforcing the phenomenon dubbed 'the rise of the rest'. The structure and costs associated with Islamic financial products, as well as their resistance to standardization, are limiting factors for Islamic finance. Nevertheless, increasingly Islamic finance operates side by side with conventional finance, drawing inspiration from its institutions and structures.

2. Topography of the New Regulatory Landscape

12.06   The topography of the new regulatory landscape is just beginning to unfold in front of us. The big economies, and their regulatory approaches, will continue to impact strongly international markets. But there are more and more big economies with resurgent capital markets, so the international dynamics will change.

12.07   For example, domestic regulators have long cooperated informally, coordinating their efforts to combat international financial fraud. Early efforts at formalizing international cooperation among regulators focused on enforcement and information sharing in the interests of curtailing cross-border criminal activity. If anything, informal coordination and cooperation has intensified, facilitated by the ease of communication and the heightened awareness of the interconnectedness of finance. But there are differences now from the old days of cross-border regulatory coordination. A broader range of market activity and practices is triggering coordinated efforts, and among a larger number of key regulators. Inevitably, however, a widening 'perimeter of regulation', a proliferation of new centres of gravity in the capital markets and greater institutional interconnectedness, will also increase the potential for regulatory conflict.

12.08   The global financial crisis has led to the recharacterization of acceptable activity and practices in the capital markets. Concern spread and with it the 'perimeter of regulation'. The extent and importance of the 'unregulated' markets was a shock to policy makers and the public alike, although no secret to market participants. The result has been a rethinking and recharacterization of concepts such as market manipulation and systemic risk, with potential regulatory encroachment into hitherto unregulated corners of the financial markets: swaps, derivatives, interest rate setting, now currency markets. It is no accident that these products and practices are creatures of the international markets, first and foremost. Even risk taking, the lifeblood of capital markets, if considered excessive, will attract regulatory attention.

12.09   Market failure has prompted the creation of new regulators, the most significant of which are the Financial Conduct Authority (FCA) in the United Kingdom and the European Securities and Markets Authority (ESMA) in Paris.

12.10   The FCA is a national regulator, of course, but with authority over one of the world's most diverse and internationalized marketplaces. In keeping with its origins in the City of London and its Guildhall, focus of the FCA is squarely on the participants in the markets, the intermediaries. Much debate, and handwringing, went into its creation, but on the whole, and in the interests of continuity and stability of oversight, the FCA constitutes a re-expression of its predecessor, the Financial Services Authority (FSA). This is good news for the myriad of regulatory authorities around the world which emulated the FSA form of consolidated financial services regulator.

Structurally and institutionally, little may have changed in the transition from the FSA to **12.11** the FCA, except for the underlying regulatory philosophy. Gone are the days of 'light touch' regulation. One further factor may also be influencing the expression of formal financial regulation in the United Kingdom, and that is the diminishing importance of the City itself as an autonomous centre of finance. Place matters, and now there are two centres of finance in London, the old geographically bound Corporation of the City of London, and the new Docklands (Canary Wharf) some five kilometres down the river, home to the FCA.

In one sense, ESMA too represents a continuation of its predecessor institution, the **12.12** Committee for European Securities Regulators or CESR. However, ESMA is a bold new initiative, the first truly supra-national capital markets regulator. ESMA is unique. It operates within a complex, formal, institutional structure created by treaty; it is a 'quasi-regulator', to the extent that its direct regulatory authority is limited to certain areas; it acts, as did CESR, as a coordinator of national authorities which remain the front line regulators. At this point, it is unclear whether ESMA will remain constrained by the confines of its original remit, or whether in the evolutionary way characteristic of EU institutions, it will grow into a larger, more developed role.

Sui generis institutions, like ESMA, are difficult to emulate so ESMA may not provide a **12.13** model for institutional change elsewhere. Nevertheless, ESMA will be closely watched. The European Union generally, given its supra-national nature, has been a testing ground for regulatory techniques, like mutual recognition or councils of supervisors, later deployed elsewhere in the world. The open question, and a keenly debated one, is the extent to which ESMA will encroach on London's market and regulatory hegemony.

Intuitively, the internationalization of capital markets would seem to call for regulatory **12.14** responses at the international level. There are new international institutions, and new roles for existing ones, but as of yet, no international regulator. Intuitive as that response may be, the likelihood of an international capital markets authority appears remote. Capital markets, and the regulatory approaches to them, remain too diverse, too complex, and ultimately, too close to the heart of political and economic sensitivities.

The Financial Stability Board (FSB), a successor institution to the failed Financial Stability **12.15** Forum, is one international initiative to emerge from the wreckage of international financial disaster. A regulator it is not, nor an international standard setter, nor an assessor. Rather, the FSB exercises broad oversight and coordination functions. Neither does it specialize in capital markets. Taking the consolidated financial regulator as its institutional model, capital markets is only one branch of finance to which it attends. The International Organization of Securities Commissions (IOSCO), an organization dating back several decades, now plays handmaiden to the FSB. IOSCO, unlike the FSB, is a standard setter as well as gathering place for securities regulators and institutions which possess the market insights as well as the applied skills and technical expertise which may be lacking at the FSB. And, financial sector assessment exercises, the FSAPs, conducted by the IMF, and The World Bank roll on relentlessly, benchmarking economies against international standards.

12.16 Some international financial standards, and there are dozens of them, have disappointed, mesmerized as they were by the chimeras of the past. The IOSCO Objectives and Principles of Securities Regulation (the IOSCO Objectives) fall within this category; they drew their inspiration from the past, markets, regulatory principles and institutions which have been radically transformed. In looking at the regulated markets of a certain time and place (the United States of the booming 1990s), the IOSCO Objectives are a fly caught in amber.

12.17 Yet, this is an exciting time, and one full of possibility and potential. The old ways and the old rules have not quite exhausted themselves, but are certainly being challenged by new markets, new practices, and new regulatory struggles. Little remains that can be characterized as purely domestic or of local interest only. The future of capital markets law and institutions is necessarily the story of the international markets.

INDEX